Internal Control Procedures

Segregation of Duties
Authorization Procedures
Documented Transaction Trails
Physical Controls That Limit Access to Assets
Independent Reconciliations

Internal Control Tests

Inquiries of Employees
Inspection of Documents, Records, and Computer Files
Observation of the Application of the Control
Reperformance of the Control

Substantive Audit Tests

Analytical Procedures
Inspection of Records, Documents, or Tangible Assets
Observation
Inquiry
Confirmation
Recalculation
Reperformance

Auditing and Assurance Services

An Applied Approach

Auditing and Assurance Services

An Applied Approach

Iris C. Stuart
The Norwegian School of Economics
and Business Administration

AUDITING AND ASSURANCE SERVICES: AN APPLIED APPROACH

Published by McGraw-Hill, a business unit of The McGraw-Hill Companies, Inc., 1221 Avenue of the Americas, New York, NY 10020.

Some ancillaries, including electronic and print components, may not be available to customers outside the United States.

This book is printed on acid-free paper.

1 2 3 4 5 6 7 8 9 0 QDB/QDB 1 0 9 8 7 6 5 4 3 2 1

ISBN 978-0-07-340400-4
MHID 0-07-340400-4

Vice President & Editor-in-Chief: *Brent Gordon*
Vice President EDP/Central Publishing Services: *Kimberly Meriwether David*
Editorial Director: *Stewart Mattson*
Publisher: *Tim Vertovec*
Sponsoring Editor: *Donna Dillon*
Marketing Manager: *Michelle Heaster*
Developmental Editor: *Katie Jones*
Project Manager: *Robin A. Reed*
Design Coordinator: *Brenda A. Rolwes*
Cover Designer: *Studio Montage, St. Louis, Missouri*
Cover Image: © *Royalty-Free/Corbis*
Buyer: *Nicole Baumgartner*
Media Project Manager: *Balaji Sundararaman*
Compositor: *Laserwords Private Limited*
Typeface: *10/12 Times New Roman*
Printer: *Quad/Graphics*

Library of Congress Cataloging-in-Publication Data

Stuart, Iris, 1950-
    Auditing and assurance services : an applied approach / Iris Stuart.
        p. cm.
    ISBN 978-0-07-340400-4 (alk. paper)
    1. Auditing. I. Title.
    HF5667.S854 2012
    657'.45—dc22

                                                            2010044756

To my family: My husband, Bruce, for his friendship and patient, professional support, and my sons, Christopher and Scott, with love that crosses international borders and thousands of miles.

—Iris Stuart

Brief Contents

Preface   xix

Acknowledgments   xxi

1   What Is Auditing?   1

2   The Audit Planning Process: Understanding the Risk of Material Misstatement   21

3   Internal Controls   50

4   Auditing the Revenue Business Process   87

5   Audit Evidence and the Auditor's Responsibility for Fraud Detection   138

6   Auditing the Acquisition and Expenditure Business Process   168

7   Auditing the Inventory Business Process   206

8   Audit Sampling: Tests of Controls   233

9   Audit Sampling: Substantive Tests of Details   260

10   Cash and Investment Business Processes   285

11   Long-Term Debt and Owners' Equity Business Process   310

12   Completing the Audit   338

13   Audit Reports   364

14   The Auditing Profession   393

GLOSSARY   418

INDEX   424

Contents

Preface   xix

Acknowledgments   xxi

Chapter 1
What Is Auditing?   1

Description of Auditing and Its Importance   1
Unique Characteristics of the Auditing Profession   3
Management's Incentive to Misstate Financial Statements   4
The Role of the Auditor in the Corporate Governance Process   5
Auditing Standards   6
  Auditing Standards Board   6
  The Public Company Accounting Oversight Board   7
  International Auditing and Assurance Standards Board   11
Evidence Requirements of Auditing Standards   11
The Auditing of Business Processes, Classes of Transactions, and Account Balances   13
Management's Assertions   13
Audit Reports   14
Accounting Regulatory Bodies   16
  Regulatory Bodies and the Accounting Profession   16
Chapter Takeaways   19
Review Questions   19
Real-World Auditing Problem   20
Internet Assignments   20

Chapter 2
The Audit Planning Process: Understanding the Risk of Material Misstatement   21

Describe the Audit Process   22
Step 1: Consider the Preconditions for an Audit   23
  Preconditions for an Audit   23
  Initial Audits   24
Step 2: Audit Engagement Planning Phase: Assess Risk   27
  Step 2a. Understanding the Entity and Its Environment   27
  Step 2b. Determining Materiality   29
  Step 2c. Designing Procedures to Assess the Risk of Material Misstatement   32
  How Does the Auditor Use the Information from the Risk Assessment Procedures?   33
Step 3: Audit Engagement Planning Phase: Develop an Audit Strategy and Audit Plan   35
Reduction of Audit Risk to an Acceptably Low Level   36
  Applying the Audit Risk Model   39
  Controlling Audit Risk   39
Quality Control Measures That Accounting Firms Use   41
  Quality Control Elements of the Accounting Firm   41
Chapter Takeaways   43
Review Questions   43
Multiple Choice Questions from CPA Examinations   43
Discussion Questions and Research Problems   45
Real-World Auditing Problems   46
Internet Assignments   49

Chapter 3
Internal Controls   50

The Impact of Internal Controls on Financial Statements   51
Auditor's Responsibility for Internal Control   54
Auditor's Responsibility for Testing Internal Controls in Financial Statement Audits   55
  For Public and Private Companies   55
Sufficient Appropriate Evidence for a Client Using a Service Organization   55
Methods Used to Test Internal Controls   56
  For Public and Private Companies   56
  Use of the Work of Internal Auditors   58
Dual-Purpose Tests   58
  A Word of Caution about Internal Control Tests   59
Auditor's Reporting Requirements for Internal Control Deficiencies in a Financial Statement Audit   60
  For Public and Private Companies   60
Internal Controls Over the Financial Reporting Process   61
  For Public Companies in the United States Only   61
  Management's Assessment of Internal Controls over Financial Reporting   62
  Auditor's Assessment of Internal Controls over Financial Reporting   64
  Mystery Bookstore Example: Identification of Controls to Test   66
  Testing Internal Control over Financial Reporting   69
  Management's Written Representations Regarding Internal Control over Financial Reporting   69
Auditor's Reporting Requirements for an Audit of Internal Controls over Financial Reporting   70
  Control Deficiencies and Material Weaknesses   70
  Auditor's Opinion on the Effectiveness of Internal Control over Financial Reporting   70
Role of Internal Controls in the Corporate Governance Process   75
Chapter Takeaways   76
Appendix A
Information Systems Auditing   77
    Clients' Use of Computer Systems to Record Transactions   77
    Auditor's Use of Computer Systems to Review the Audit Client's Recorded Transactions   79
Review Questions   80
Multiple Choice Questions from CPA Examinations   81
Discussion Questions and Research Problems   82
Real-World Auditing Problems   84
Internet Assignment   86

Chapter 4
Auditing the Revenue Business Process   87

Overview of the Revenue Business Process   88
Transactions Recorded in the Revenue Process   91
  Documents in the Business Process   91
GAAP Rules for Accounts in the Revenue Business Process   92
Misstatements That Could Occur in the Revenue Process   94
  Auditor's Responsibility for Detecting Fraud   96
Management Assertions for the Revenue Business Process   98
Identification of Relevant Assertions for the Revenue Business Process   98
Internal Control Testing   99
Substantive Tests for the Revenue Process   103
  Analytical Procedures   103
  Substantive Tests of Transactions   105
  Substantive Tests of Balances   106
  Accounts Receivable Confirmations   107

Evaluation of the Allowance for Uncollectible Accounts   109
Auditor's Understanding at This Point in the Audit   112
Disclosure Requirements for the Revenue Business Process   112
Presentation and Disclosure for the Revenue Process   112
Chapter Takeaways   115
Appendix A   116
Appendix B   123
Review Questions   124
Multiple Choice Questions from CPA Examinations   125
Discussion Questions and Research Problems   127
Real-World Auditing Problems   132
Internet Assignments   137

Chapter 5
Audit Evidence and the Auditor's Responsibility for Fraud Detection   138

Chapter Overview   139

Part I
Audit Evidence   140
Audit Evidence and Its Role in the Audit Process   140
Analytical Procedures   140
Inspection   141
Observation   141
Inquiry   141
External Confirmation   142
Recalculation   142
Reperformance   142
The Auditor's Use of Management's Assertions to Organize Audit Evidence   142
Evaluation of the Sufficiency and Appropriateness of Evidence   143
How Do the Accounting Standards Define Relevant and Reliable Information?   144
The Auditor's Response to Risk   145
Documentation Requirements for Evidence   146

Part II
Fraud Detection   149
The Auditor's Responsibility for Fraud Detection   149
What Is Fraud?   149
The Fraud Triangle   150
How the Auditor Identifies Fraud   150
Methods Used to Prepare Fraudulent Financial Statements   152
The Role of Professional Skepticism   152
The Audit Team's Fraud Discussion   154
An Example of Fraudulent Financial Reporting   154
Example of Misappropriation of Assets   157
Assessing the Risk of Material Misstatement Due to Fraud   158
Use of Evidence to Control the Risk of Material Misstatement Due to Fraud   160
The Reporting of Fraud to Management and the Audit Committee   160
Auditor Documentation Regarding the Consideration of Fraud   161
Chapter Takeaways   161
Review Questions   162
Multiple Choice Questions from CPA Examinations   162
Discussion Questions and Research Problems   164
Real-World Auditing Problems   165
Internet Assignments   167

Chapter 6
Auditing the Acquisition and Expenditure Business Process   168

Chapter Overview   169
The Acquisition and Expenditure Business Process   169
Transactions Recorded in the Acquisition and Expenditure Process   172
    Documents in the Business Process   172
Accounting Standards for Recording Transactions in the Acquisition and Expenditure Business Process   174
Possible Misstatements in the Acquisition and Expenditure Business Process   175
Management's Assertions for the Acquisition and Expenditure Business Process   178
Internal Control Testing   179
Substantive Tests for the Acquisition and Expenditure Process   184
    Analytical Procedures   184
    Substantive Tests of Transactions   186
    Substantive Tests of Balances   187
    Search for Unrecorded Liabilities   188
    What the Auditor Knows at This Point in the Audit   188
Auditing Changes in Land, Building, Equipment, and Intangible Assets Accounts   189
Auditing Accrued Liabilities   190
    Accrued Liabilities   190
Disclosure Requirements for the Acquisition and Expenditure Business Process   194
Chapter Takeaways   199
Review Questions   199
Multiple Choice Questions from CPA Examinations   200
Discussion Questions and Research Problems   201
Real-World Auditing Problems   204
Internet Assignments   205

Chapter 7
Auditing the Inventory Business Process   206

Chapter Overview   207
Overview of the Inventory Process   207
Procedures for Recording Transactions in the Inventory Process   208
    Documents in the Business Process   209
Accounting Rules for Recording Transactions in the Inventory Business   210
    Accounting Rules Applicable to the Inventory Process   210
Possible Misstatements in the Inventory Process   211
Management's Assertions for the Inventory Business Process   212
Relevant Assertions for the Inventory Business Process   213
Internal Control Testing   213
Substantive Tests for the Inventory Process   214
    Analytical Procedures   214
    Substantive Tests of Balances   216
Physical Inventory Counting   217
FIFO and LIFO Inventory Pricing and Inventory Reserves   219
    Inventory Pricing and the LIFO Inventory Reserve   219
    Lower-of-Cost-or-Market Adjustment for Inventory   220
    The Auditor's Knowledge at This Point in the Audit   221
    Presentation and Disclosure Requirements for the Inventory Business Process   222
Chapter Takeaways   226
Review Questions   227
Multiple Choice Questions from CPA Examinations   227
Discussion Questions and Research Problems   229
Real-World Auditing Problems   231
Internet Assignment   232

Chapter 8
Audit Sampling: Tests of Controls   233

Chapter Overview   233
Audit Sampling for Tests of Internal Controls   234
Sampling and Nonsampling Risks   236
Statistical and Nonstatistical Sampling   237
The Use of Sampling to Determine the Effectiveness of Internal Controls   238
   Step 1. Describe the Internal Control Being Tested   239
   Step 2. Determine the Control Objective   239
   Step 3. Define the Population and the Sampling Unit for Test of Controls over Financial Statements   *239*
   Step 3a. Define the Population for Test of Controls over the Financial Reporting *Process   240*
   Step 4. Define the Deviation Condition   240
   Step 5. Determine the Sample's Tolerable Rate of Deviation, Expected Rate of Deviation,
      and Desired Level of Assurance   240
   Step 6. Determine the Method of Sample Size Determination   241
   Step 7. Determine the Method of Selecting the Sample   241
   Step 8. List the Selected Sample Items   242
   Step 9. Describe How the Audit Procedure Was Performed   242
   Step 9a. Describe the Performance of Audit Procedures with a Dual-Purpose Test   243
   Step 10. Evaluate the Sample Results and Reach Conclusions   243
Audit Sampling Plan to Perform a Test of Controls   245
Audit Sampling Using Sequential Sampling   248
Using a Statistical Sampling Table for Nonstatistical Sampling   249
Determining Sample Sizes Based on the Frequency of the Control   252
Chapter Takeaways   253
Review Questions   253
Multiple Choice Questions from CPA Examinations   254
Discussion Questions and Research Problems   255
Real-World Auditing Problems   258

Chapter 9
Audit Sampling: Substantive Tests of Details   260

Chapter Overview   261
The Use of Variables Sampling in Substantive Testing   261
Sampling and Nonsampling Risk   261
Statistical and Nonstatistical Sampling   263
A Sampling Plan for Substantive Tests of Details   264
   Step 1. Describe the Objectives of the Test, the Accounts, and the Assertions Affected   264
   Step 2. Define the Population and the Sampling Unit   264
   Step 3. Define Misstatement   265
   Step 4. Determine the Desired Level of Assurance, the Estimated Misstatement, and the Tolerable Misstatement   265
   Step 5. Determine the Audit Sampling Technique Used   266
   Step 6. Select the Method for Determining Sample Size   267
   Step 7. Determine the Method of Selecting the Sample   268
   Step 8. List the Sample Items   269
   Step 9. Describe How the Sampling Procedure Was Performed and List Any Misstatements
      Identified in the Sample   269
   Step 10. Evaluate the Sample Results and Reach a Conclusion   270
The Use of Nonstatistical Sampling for Substantive Tests of Balances   272
   Sampling Plan 1   272
The Use of Nonstatistical Sampling for Substantive Tests of Transactions   276
   Sampling Plan 2   276
Chapter Takeaways   277
Review Questions   278

Multiple Choice Questions from CPA Examinations   278
Discussion Questions and Research Problems   279
Real-World Auditing Problems   283

Chapter 10
Cash and Investment Business Processes   285

Chapter Overview   286
Describe the Cash and Investment Business Processes   287
Transactions in the Cash and Investment Business Processes   289
   Documents in the Business Processes   289
Applicable Financial Reporting Frameworks for the Investment Process   290
Possible Misstatements in the Cash and Investment Processes   291
Management's Assertions for the Cash and Investment Business Processes   293
Relevant Assertions for Significant Accounts in the Business Processes   293
Internal Control Testing   294
   Cash   295
   Investments   295
Substantive Tests for the Cash and Investment Business Processes   296
   Analytical Procedures   296
   Substantive Tests of Transactions   298
   Substantive Tests of Balances   299
   Fair Value of Investment Securities   300
   Standard Bank Confirmation   300
   Bank Reconciliation and Cutoff Statement   302
   What the Auditors Know at This Point in the Audit   303
Disclosure Requirements for Accounts in the Cash and Investment Business Processes   304
Chapter Takeaways   305
Review Questions   305
Multiple Choice Questions from CPA Examinations   306
Discussion Questions and Research Problems   307
Real-World Auditing Problems   309
Internet Assignment   309

Chapter 11
Long-Term Debt and Owners' Equity Business Process   310

Chapter Overview   311
The Long-Term Debt and Owners' Equity Business Process   312
Transactions in the Long-Term Debt and Owners' Equity Business Process   314
   Documents in the Business Process   314
Applicable Financial Reporting Frameworks for the Long-Term Debt and Owners' Equity Process   314
Possible Misstatements in the Long-Term Debt and Owners' Equity Business Process   316
Management's Assertions for the Long-Term Debt and Owners' Equity Business Process   318
Relevant Assertions for Significant Accounts in the Business Process   318
Internal Control Testing   319
Substantive Tests for the Long-Term Debt and Owners' Equity Business Process   321
   Analytical Procedures   322
   Substantive Tests of Transactions   323
   Substantive Tests of Balances   324
   What the Auditor Knows at This Point in the Audit   326
Disclosure Requirements for the Long-Term Debt and Owners' Equity Business Process   326
Chapter Takeaways   331
Review Questions   332
Multiple Choice Questions from CPA Examinations   332
Discussion Questions and Research Problems   334

Real-World Auditing Problems   336
Internet Assignment   337

Chapter 12
Completing the Audit   338

Chapter Overview   339
Audit Procedures for Contingent Liabilities   341
Audit Procedures for Subsequent Events and Subsequently Discovered Facts   344
Audit Procedures for Related Party Transactions   346
Auditors' Responsibility for Client Compliance with Laws and Regulations   347
Audit Procedures for Going Concern Assessments   347
Use of a Management Representation Letter as Evidence   349
Audit Documentation Requirements   349
    Audit Documentation for Public and Private Companies   351
Use of Audit Evidence to Determine Whether the Financial Statements are Materially Misstated   352
Evaluation of the Consistency of Financial Statements   355
Review of Footnotes and Other Financial Statement–Associated Information   356
End of Field Work   357
Chapter Takeaways   358
Review Questions   358
Multiple Choice Questions from CPA Examinations   359
Discussion Questions and Research Problems   360
Real-World Auditing Problems   362
Internet Assignment   363

Chapter 13
Audit Reports   364

Chapter Overview   365
Auditing Standards for Reporting   366
Formation of an Opinion and Reporting on Financial Statements   367
Emphasis of Matter and Other Matter Paragraphs in the Independent Audit Report   370
Report Modifications: Qualified Opinion, Disclaimer of Opinion, and Adverse Opinion   371
    A Qualified Audit Opinion   371
    An Adverse Audit Opinion   371
    A Disclaimer of Opinion   371
The Auditor's Reporting Responsibilities   374
    Use of a Component Auditor's Work for a Group Audit Report   374
    Audit Responsibility for Quarterly Information in the Annual Report   379
    Restriction of the Use of the Auditor's Report   379
    Communication with Those Charged with Governance   379
Reporting on Financial Reporting Frameworks Generally Accepted in Another Country   380
    Accepting the Audit Engagement   380
    Planning and Performing the Audit Engagement   380
    Reporting—More Than Limited Use in the United States or Use Only Outside of the United States   380
The Auditor's Report on Internal Controls over Financial Reporting   381
Modifications to the Auditor's Report on Internal Control over Financial Reporting   384
    Management's Assessment of Internal Control Incomplete or Improperly Presented   384
    Scope Limitations   384
    Auditors' Decision to Refer to the Report of Other Auditors in the Auditor's Report   386
    Occurrence of a Significant Subsequent since Year-End   386
    Other Information Provided in Management's Report on Internal Control over Financial Reporting   386
    Management's Certification Pursuant to Section 302 of the Sarbanes-Oxley Act   387
Chapter Takeaways   388
Review Questions   388

Multiple Choice Questions from CPA Examinations   389
Discussion Questions and Research Problems   390
Real-World Auditing Problems   391
Internet Assignment   392

Chapter 14
The Auditing Profession   393

Chapter Overview   393
Certification Procedures for the Accounting Profession   394
Limitations of Current Audit Methodology   395
Pressure on Management and Auditors   397
Auditor Responsibility for Different Service Levels   397
Audit   397
Attest Services   397
Compilations and Reviews   398
AICPA Code of Professional Conduct   398
The Principles   399
The Rules   399
Additional Independence Requirements Imposed by the Sarbanes-Oxley Act for Public Companies   403
IESBA Code of Ethics for Professional Accountants   405
Legal Liability Associated with an Audit Engagement   406
Legal Liability from Audit Clients   407
Third-Party Liability under Common Law   407
Civil Liability under the Federal Securities Laws   407
Criminal Liability   409
Legal Liability for Management under the Sarbanes-Oxley Act   410
Chapter Takeaways   411
Review Questions   411
Multiple Choice Questions from CPA Examinations   411
Discussion Questions and Research Problems   413
Real-World Auditing Problems   415
Internet Assignments   417

Glossary   418
Index   424

About the Author

Dr. Iris Stuart is currently Professor of Accounting at the Norwegian School of Economics and Business Administration (NHH), Bergen, Norway, teaching auditing and accounting ethics. She also has an appointment to the Norwegian Institute of Public Accountants where she is involved in continuing education for Norwegian accountants.

Dr. Stuart earned her MBA in Business Administration at the University of Minnesota and her PhD in Business Administration at the University of Iowa.

She has worked as an auditor for KPMG and as a consultant for small business. She also has worked in internal auditing for Cargill Corporation in Asia. Dr. Stuart has had appointments at the liberal arts colleges Luther College (Iowa) and Concordia College (Moorhead, Minnesota) and the research universities Nanyang Technological University (Singapore) and California State University–Fullerton. She also has taught at Ramkhamhaeng University in Bangkok, Thailand.

Dr. Stuart's research areas include behavioral auditing topics and accounting ethics.

Preface

"It is an exciting time to be an accountant." This is the way I've started my auditing classes for the last five years. With all of the changes that have occurred in the audit environment, it is an exciting time to study accounting and to be an auditing teacher.

This book recognizes the changes that have occurred in the profession in the past 10 years: new regulatory boards, ever-changing auditing and accounting standards, and a move in the profession to merge U.S. standards with international standards. All of these changes make this an exciting time to work as an auditor.

Why a new auditing textbook? This textbook was written to combine the teaching of theory and practice. Accounting students usually do not like theory; they are happier solving problems and focusing on "practical" issues. Contemporary texts weigh in heavily on theory, many of them devoting most of the first half of the text to theory and waiting until the second half to address the issues and the problem solving of auditing. In my teaching experience, I have found that students often thought the theory sections to be boring, causing them to become discouraged and stifling their interest in the business process rules that came later in the course. Obviously, students need a theoretical basis so they can understand the logic of audit practice, but current textbook approaches need to be modified.

Introducing the revenue business process early in the text allows instructors to talk about audit theory with the revenue process providing concrete examples and challenging problems for resolution. This approach promises to help students see that theory is important to grasp because it supports problem solving and can be learned in relation to practical issues encountered in business environments. Such linkage, I think, supports student learning. Students' experience of connecting theory to practice through specific problem-solving exercises shows them the importance of theory and that it is useful because it shapes how the professional addresses practical issues as they arise. Having used this approach, I find that an early mix of practice and theory works well.

The book begins with a discussion of the audit process and audit risk. It moves smoothly into the treatment of internal controls and the revenue business process. It then introduces some theoretical concerns and covers the acquisition and expenditure and inventory business processes. Following two chapters of sampling, the text discusses the remaining business processes. The book concludes with chapters on procedures performed at the end of the audit and audit reports and on the audit profession.

When I talk to former students now working in the audit profession, they tell me that they use what they learned in the auditing class in their jobs. (They even remark that they "return to that theory stuff.") Such conversations brighten my day, for the goal of this text and the courses that I lead is to teach students what they need to work as auditors.

Change makes it difficult for a teacher to keep up with the current rules and regulations. Students do not fully appreciate how much things have changed because they don't have a long history with the profession. This book is designed to educate the teacher as well as the student. Auditing standards from three sources are listed at the beginning of each chapter: the PCAOB, the Auditing Standards Board, and the International Auditing and Assurance Standards Board. Changes to these standards will be posted to the book's website as soon as they are passed—and there will be changes. The Auditing Standards Board will soon reissue all auditing standards after they have been converged with international auditing standards. This will result in a complete renumbering of auditing standards. The PCAOB will continue to issue new standards, and the interim standards it adopted in 2003 will be revised. Companies can now file financial statements with the SEC using U.S. or international accounting standards. This will mean that students must become familiar with international accounting rules. For this reason, I have included the accounting rules for both U.S. and IFRS international accounting standards when I discuss the applicable financial reporting frameworks the auditor uses to evaluate whether the audit client complies with the financial reporting framework. The website for the book provides a good resource for teachers that will allow them to keep up with the changes.

Please visit the book's Online Learning Center at **www.mhhe.com/stuart1e** for access to the:

- Instructor Solutions Manual
- Instructor Teaching Manual
- Instructor Test Bank/Student Online Quizzes
- Instructor PowerPoint Presentations
- Instructor/Student Text Updates/Errata

I have taught in four countries (the United States, Singapore, Thailand, and Norway) and have learned a great deal about teaching and auditing from my international colleagues. All of my education occurred in the United States. I am a licensed CPA in Minnesota. My international teaching experience and my professional experience as an internal auditor in Asia give me a unique perspective on today's business world. I find the international business world to be an interesting place to work and expect that our students will fully appreciate what it means to work in a global economy. This book is intended to prepare today's students for the business world they will face tomorrow.

Acknowledgments

I would like to thank my international colleagues for the opportunity to work with them: Hun Tong Tan and Joanne Tay from Nanyang Technological University in Singapore; Trond Bjørnenak, Aasmund Eilifsen, and Frøystein Gjesdal from the Norwegian School of Economics and Business Administration in Norway. Special thanks go to the talented people who prepared the supplements: Karl Dahlberg of Rutgers University for the Test Bank and online Quizzes and Heidi Meier of Cleveland State University for the instructor PowerPoints and Instructor's Manual. Also, thank you to Patricia Wellmeyer of University of California Riverside for accuracy checking the Solutions Manual and Test Bank. Additionally, I am sincerely grateful to the following individuals for their participation in the manuscript review process:

Jeffrey Archambault
Marshall University

MaryAnne Atkinson
Central Washington University

Pervaiz Alam
Kent State University

Walter Baggett
Manhattan College

Constance Crawford
Ramapo College of New Jersey

Karl Dahlberg
Rutgers University

Kevin Den Adel
University of Iowa

William Dilla
Iowa State University

Timothy Dimond
Northern Illinois University

Esther Feller
Brooklyn College

Gary Frank
University of Akron

Dana Garner
College of Charleston

Michele Henney
University of Oregon

John R. Kuhn, Jr.
University of Louisville

Ralph Licastro
The Pennsylvania State University

Josephine Mathias
Mercer County Community College

Heidi Meier
Cleveland State University

Duane Ponko
Indiana University of Pennsylvania

William Quilliam
University of South Florida St. Petersburg

Raymond Reisig
Pace University

Ira Solomon
University of Illinois

Nate Stephens
Utah State University

Robert Susich
Diablo Valley College

Marilyn Vito
Richard Stockton College of New Jersey

Bruce Walter
University of Massachusetts—Dartmouth

Satina Williams
Marist College

Jia Wu
University of Massachusetts—Dartmouth

Douglas Ziegenfuss
Old Dominion University

Much credit is also due to the development and production team: Donna Dillon, Sponsoring Editor; Katie Jones, Developmental Editor; Robin Reed, Project Manager; Michelle Heaster, Marketing Manager; and Brenda Rowles, Design Coordinator.

Iris Stuart

Chapter

1

What Is Auditing?

Learning Objectives

After studying this chapter, you should be able to:

1. Describe auditing and explain why it is important.
2. Explain the unique characteristics of the auditing profession.
3. Understand management's incentive to misstate financial statements.
4. Explain the role of the auditor in the corporate governance process.
5. Describe auditing standards.
6. Explain the evidence requirements of the auditing standards.
7. Understand how the auditor uses business processes to structure the collection of evidence.
8. Explain how management's assertions about the financial statements are used in the audit process.
9. Describe the audit report.
10. Identify accounting regulatory bodies and describe their functions.

Auditing standards relevant to this topic

For private companies

- Auditing standards issued by the American Institute of Certified Public Accountants' Auditing Standards Board

For public companies

- Auditing standards issued by the Public Company Accounting Oversight Board
- Auditing standards issued by the American Institute of Certified Public Accountants' Auditing Standards Board that have not been superseded or amended by the Public Company Accounting Oversight Board

International standards

- Auditing standards issued by the International Federation of Accountants' International Auditing and Assurance Standards Board

Description of Auditing and Its Importance

LO1

Describe auditing and explain why it is important

What is the auditing process? For society, what purpose does it serve? What role does auditing play in corporate governance? Why is the process so important? As we begin the study of auditing, these are key questions to answer. Unless we understand the unique role that auditing performs in our society for contemporary business and the public, we will not appreciate the significance of the various auditing standards as we discuss principles, rules, and professional practice.

Auditing is the process of reviewing the financial information prepared by the management of a company (the financial statements and the footnotes) to determine that it conforms to a particular standard (the applicable financial reporting framework). The person who conducts the assessment follows a set of standards (generally accepted auditing standards). The person completing the assessment is not an employee of the company but works for an accounting firm that is associated with the company only by being hired to perform an audit (a firm that is independent from the company). The individual doing the assessment is hired to verify the fairness and completeness of the decisions recorded by the firm so that outsiders have accurate information to make decisions. The outsiders may be bankers, current or potential stockholders, or regulatory bodies (outsiders to company management). The accountants making the assessment provide a valuable, indeed, a crucial, service. Without such an assessment, outsiders would be forced to rely solely on the information the firm provided. Even without deliberately misleading outsiders, the firm's executives are likely to be more optimistic about the firm's status than an outsider might be. Would you lend money to a company or buy its stock based solely on management's optimistic picture of the firm's performance? Would you trust financial reports that use an "optimistic viewpoint" to report all information without any independent checks or review?

The relationship of the audit firm to the client can be described in the framework of a principal-agent relationship. The principals in this relationship are the shareholders of the company. The agent is management. A principal-agent relationship exists because the owners of the company (the principals) are not involved in the daily management of the company. They hire an agent (management) to run the company for them and to make daily decisions for the company. This means that the owners of the company (the principals) are removed from its daily operations and that management has more knowledge about the daily operations than the owners. The owners (the principals) would like management (the agent) to report correctly what its members know, so the principal hires an auditor to increase the likelihood of correct reporting. Knowing that an auditor will assess the financial statements, management is more likely to prepare them in accordance with the accounting standards because it is the auditor's job to determine that management has complied with this requirement. Outsiders benefit when the owners hire an auditor to protect their interests in the company because the information available to outsiders is more likely to correspond to financial accounting standards.

The corporate governance process should protect outsiders from misstated financial statements. Auditors perform an important job in corporate governance because their role as trained professionals who are independent from the firm is unique in the corporate governance process. Because auditors are independent, they are in a perfect position to provide an opinion on whether the financial statements that management presents have been prepared according to an applicable financial reporting framework. Outsiders might reasonably trust such an opinion from an independent professional but would not trust such an opinion from a person who was not independent. The review of the independent auditor is not necessarily a pessimistic assessment, but it will likely be a less optimistic assessment than that of management because an outsider without any relationship (ownership, financial, employment) to the company issued it. The auditor will present a relatively unbiased picture of the firm's compliance or noncompliance with the applicable financial reporting framework.

The capital markets system in the United States and the rest of the world rely on accurate information. If auditors fail to perform their job, outsiders are hurt because they make decisions about the companies based on information disclosed, and if the information is wrong, the decision is likely to be wrong. For example, bankers may lend money when they shouldn't or may lend at a lower interest rate than appropriate if they had known the correct information. Investors may fail to sell stock or buy stock in companies that they wouldn't if they had information that fairly presented the firm's financial position.

If the auditors fail to do their job, no one else does it. The financial statements for public companies are filed with the Public Company Accounting Oversight Board (PCAOB) and the Securities and Exchange Commission (SEC), but neither organization conducts audits of the information (unless to review the statements). The financial statements for private companies are simply given to the owners and are not reviewed by any outside source. For all practical purposes, "the buck stops" with the auditors, so if they fail to do their job, their failure has serious implications for the decisions made by outsiders.

Unique Characteristics of the Auditing Profession

LO2

Explain the unique characteristics of the auditing profession

The auditing profession offers a wide range of employment opportunities for new accountants. Most accounting firms offer client services in three areas: auditing, tax, and consulting. A new accountant might be hired to work in any of these areas. This book describes the job of an accountant working in the audit area. Even in the audit area, the accountant may work for a variety of clients including private or public companies, clients in banking, insurance, manufacturing, technology, retail, health care, or government. Individuals working in the audit area may also spend most of their time providing internal audit services to clients rather than working as an external auditor. Working in any of the areas in an accounting firm may be one of the most demanding jobs you will ever have, but it is also one of the most interesting, exciting experiences and a great way to prepare yourself to work in the corporate business world. Working as a certified public accountant (CPA) will greatly expand your career opportunities if you choose to leave public accounting for other fields.

Accounting firms are structured as partnerships or limited liability corporations. This means that someone in the accounting firm has *personal* liability for the firm's decisions (this differs from the corporate form of organization in which no one has personal liability for the firm's decisions). There are four large accounting firms (the "big four") in the world—KPMG, Ernst & Young, Deloitte & Touche, and PricewaterhouseCoopers. They have offices in most U.S. states and in many foreign countries. The big four audit most of the public companies listed on the U.S. stock exchanges. There are regional accounting firms with offices in several cities and many smaller accounting firms that may have only one office. The United States is often referred to as the most litigious country in the world. That means that the auditor is more likely to be sued in the United States than in any other country when outsiders believe that they have been harmed by the information disclosed in the financial statements (that later turn out to be misstated).

Auditors work in many places in addition to accounting firms. There are government auditors, tax auditors (for both federal and state tax authorities), and internal auditors working in corporations. As an auditor, you have a wide range of places in which you might work. You can also choose large or small companies in each of these categories as your employer. You might work for a large public accounting firm or a small local accounting firm. You might work for the city of Fargo, North Dakota, or the city of New York. Your job will be very different in each of these situations, but the skills that you learn in one job will help you get your next one. This means that the job skills that you learn in one place will give you skills that transfer to another job. This is a very nice aspect of the accounting profession.

We often speak of auditors providing *audit and assurance services.* This means that auditors provide several services. They provide the *audit function,* which involves having the auditor assess whether the financial statements are presented in accordance with the applicable financial reporting framework. This book focuses on the audit function of auditors. Auditors also provide services that do not involve the review of a complete set of financial statements or the issue of an opinion on the financial statements. For example, each year PricewaterhouseCoopers certifies the winners of the Academy

Awards. In this case, an auditor provides an assurance service, not an audit service. The nominees for the various awards have more confidence in the process that determines the winners when an outside, independent source is involved in preparing the information. The other services provided by an auditing firm (that are not tax or consulting) are referred to as *attest services.* For these services, the auditor typically *attests* or authenticates the accuracy of some type of information. The attestation standards provide the auditor guidance for such services. Some of the services that fall under attestation standards are reports on (1) descriptions of systems of internal controls, (2) compliance with statutory, regulatory, and contractual requirements, and (3) investment performance statistics. An opinion is not issued as a result of attestation services. Instead, the auditor issues a signed report containing the information requested by the outside party.

What would your life be like working in a public accounting firm? Exciting certainly, occasionally tedious, and sometimes stressful because of deadlines and the constant pressure to finish an audit, a tax return, or a consulting engagement by the deadline and within the hours allowed for the job. A unique aspect of this profession is its promotion policy. Accountants are typically promoted every year to assume new and increased responsibilities. The profession relies on the constant influx of new employees (staff accountants) at the lower levels to perform many of the daily auditing tasks. Fewer managers and partners are needed at the upper levels to review the work of the lower level staff. You will seldom be bored, and you will constantly be challenged. If these factors sound appealing to you, then by all means consider joining this group of professionals who are responsible to outsiders for information used in the business world to make important decisions about companies.

Management's Incentive to Misstate Financial Statements

LO3

Understand management's incentive to misstate financial statements

To be a good auditor, it is important that you understand management's incentive to misstate financial statements. If you understand how management gains by misstating certain transactions, it is easier to plan your audit to devote an increased amount of time to transactions that are more likely to be wrong than other transactions. The areas in which management is more likely to misstate transactions are riskier for the auditor because failing to correct the misstatements may lead to issuing a clean audit opinion on financial statements that are materially misstated. This would give outsiders the view that the financial statements are presented fairly in accordance with the applicable financial reporting framework when they are not.

Management of public companies typically prefers higher net income to lower net income. Net income can be increased by either *reducing expense* or *increasing revenue.* Various methods, for example, recording fictitious revenue will increase net income, allowing the company to report higher net income; failing to record expenses at the end of the year will also increase net income. *Growth* in revenue is also an important factor for many companies. In this situation, managers try to show that revenue has increased from the previous year even if net income has not. The desired outcome in many businesses is for revenue and possibly net income to increase at a rate at least equal to the prior year's increase, and if possible, more than the previous year's rate. Outsiders, particularly stockholders, expect this level of growth, and if companies fail to meet these targets, their stock price may drop as investors sell their stock and invest in other companies that can meet the growth level desired.

The principal reason to misstate financial statements is to keep the company's stock price from falling. Investors react unfavorably when companies report lower revenue or net income numbers from the previous year. Stock analysts from investment firms provide advice on company stocks. These analysts generate expectations for quarterly earnings per share for the companies they follow. If a company fails to meet these earnings targets, even by $0.01, their stock price is likely to fall. A falling stock price is generally bad for a company and often for the management of a company because managers frequently have stock options in the firm in their compensation packages or own shares of their company's stock in their investment portfolios. A falling stock price hurts the firm and often its management. If at all possible, it is to be avoided.

How can a company avoid a falling stock price? If revenue has not increased and net income is lower this year than the prior year, one way to prevent a drop in the stock price is to misstate the financial statements. It is the auditor's job to gather sufficient appropriate evidence and to assess with professional skepticism the decisions that management made in preparing the financial statements. Before issuing a clean opinion on the client's financial statements, the auditor should be sure that the evidence gathered during the audit supports the assessment that the financial statements are prepared using an applicable financial reporting framework.

The incentives for misstatement in the financial statements for private companies may completely differ from the incentives in a public company. Private companies' management may prefer lower net income to higher net income because it reduces their tax burden, so it improves their cash flow. Or they may prefer higher net income because they need to show growth in earnings to gain a bank loan. Understanding the incentives of the company to misstate the financial statements is an important part of the audit process. It is crucial for the auditor to identify the financial statement accounts with the most potential for misstatement and to design audit procedures to determine that the accounts are fairly presented according to the applicable financial reporting framework.

The Role of the Auditor in the Corporate Governance Process

LO4

Explain the role of the auditor in the corporate governance process

Today's auditors play a crucial role in business and society. A consequence of recent audit failures includes the loss of public reputation for the accounting profession. Along with the awareness of recent business scandals, you should realize that the accounting profession is reforming itself. This is good news. Public scrutiny of the profession prompts auditors to become more careful and efficient in their fundamental tasks in their daily work. The value of clear and accurate financial disclosure and the auditor's responsibility to outside users of financial statements to provide financial information consistent with accounting regulations have never been more important than in today's business environment.

Auditors exercise a strong bargaining position with management. The high financial and social costs of failed audits reflect both public interest and business necessity. Recognition of the crucial place of the audit for users of financial statements serves notice that accounting firms cannot merely use the audit process as "a loss leader" marketing device to gain lucrative management consulting fees from their clients. The public value of the audit cannot be too highly emphasized. The negative impact of failed audits—loss of public confidence and investors' trust—is apparent to observers of the profession.

Recent scandals have demonstrated the vulnerability of firms and the high cost of audit failures. In 2002, Arthur Andersen's audit failure, its legal battles, and the loss of public reputation forced it out of business. This may not have been in the public's best interest or fair to the firm's many partners, but Arthur Andersen's damaged reputation and a felony conviction related to its Enron audit led inevitably to the firm's undoing.

Accounting firms do not sell a product; they produce a service. They have nothing to offer except the quality of the service they provide and their image of integrity. Once a firm's reputation is destroyed, its professionals have little to offer clients. In 2002, in the aftermath of the Enron scandal, would you have wanted to issue stock with Arthur Andersen's name on your financial statements?

With the many changes in the profession, you will face the challenge of learning new rules and performing new internal control tests. Federal and state regulators and interested outsiders will watch auditors as they perform their professional duties. Attention will be focused on the auditors' responsibility to determine whether the financial statements present fairly the financial position of the firm and the results of its operations. The auditors are expected to approach an audit with an independent mind and to recognize that they are hired to protect the interests of outsiders. As an auditing student, you must understand the importance of presenting unbiased information to these outsiders, and you must avoid conflicts of interest and even the appearance of such conflicts as you perform your job. This is an exciting and challenging time to enter the profession.

Auditing Standards

Three standard-setting organizations are involved in establishing auditing standards:

- The Auditing Standards Board (ASB) of the American Institute of Certified Public Accountants (AICPA)
- The Public Company Accounting Oversight Board (PCAOB)
- The International Auditing and Assurance Standards Board (IAASB) of the International Federation of Accountants (IFAC)

Auditing Standards Board

The ASB, formed in 1978 as a committee of the AICPA, is a committee of nineteen members composed of five members from local, regional, and non-big four firms, five members appointed by the National Association of State Boards of Accountancy (NASBA), four members from the big four accounting firms, and five members from user groups and the public. The ASB is authorized to issue auditing standards related to the performance of the audit and the issuance of audit reports for *private* companies, also referred to as *nonissuers* of stock.

Rule 202 of the AICPA Code of Professional Conduct authorizes the ASB to write auditing regulations. This rule requires members of the AICPA who perform professional services to comply with the ASB's standards. Auditors follow the ASB's established rules because the failure to do so violates the Professional Code of Conduct. Failure to follow these rules means that members can lose their license to practice as certified public accountants.

The Preface to the Auditing Standards describes the fundamental principles that govern an audit.[1] According to these principles, the purpose of an audit is to increase the level of confidence that outsiders place in the financial statements. The auditor increases confidence in the financial statements by issuing an opinion on them. This opinion states whether the financial statements have been prepared in accordance with an applicable financial reporting framework. In other words, the opinion states whether the company has followed the accounting standards (the applicable financial reporting framework) in preparing the financial statements. The audit itself is conducted using generally accepted auditing standards. The auditing standards recognize that management is required to prepare the financial statements and to maintain a system of internal controls relevant to the preparation of the financial statements. Management also provides the auditor all information relevant to the preparation of them and unrestricted access to those in the company from whom the auditor may need additional evidence. The fundamental principles are listed in three general categories: (1) responsibilities, (2) performance, and (3) reporting. See Exhibit 1-1 for a description of the specific principles for each of these categories.

The Auditing Standards Board issues new auditing standards as Statements on Auditing Standards, most commonly referred to as *SASs*. They are numbered consecutively (more than 100 "statements on auditing standards" have been issued). The auditing standards are *compiled* each year and *organized by topic* in the Codification of Statements

---

[1] The Preface to the Codification of Statements on Auditing Standards, *Principles Governing an Audit Conducted in Accordance with Generally Accepted Auditing Standards,* replaces the 10 Generally Accepted Auditing Standards. Auditors following the standards of the PCAOB instead of the ASB will still use the 10 Generally Accepted Auditing Standards. They are listed in Exhibit 1-2.

| **Principles Governing an Audit Conducted in Accordance with Generally Accepted Auditing Standards** | **Exhibit 1-1** |

RESPONSIBILITIES

Auditors are responsible for having appropriate competence and capabilities to perform the audit, complying with relevant ethical requirements, including those pertaining to independence and due care; and maintaining professional skepticism and exercising professional judgment, throughout the planning and performance of the audit.

PERFORMANCE

To express an opinion, the auditor obtains reasonable assurance about whether the financial statements as a whole are free from material misstatement, whether due to fraud or error.

To obtain reasonable assurance, which is a high, but not absolute level of assurance, the auditor

- Plans the work and properly supervises any assistants.
- Determines appropriate materiality level or levels.
- Identifies and assesses risks of material misstatement, whether due to fraud or error, based on an understanding of the entity and its environment, including the entity's internal control.

- Obtains sufficient appropriate audit evidence about whether material misstatements exist, through designing and implementing appropriate responses to the assessed risks.

The auditor is unable to obtain absolute assurance that the financial statements are free from material misstatement because of inherent limitations, which arise from

- The nature of financial reporting,
- The nature of audit procedures, and
- The need for the audit to be conducted within a reasonable period of time and at a reasonable cost.

REPORTING

The auditor expresses an opinion in accordance with the auditor's findings, or states that an opinion cannot be expressed, in the form of a written report. The opinion states whether the financial statements are prepared, in all material respects, in accordance with the applicable financial reporting framework.

of Auditing Standards. The AICPA issues a new codification each year. When the sections are codified, they are listed with Auditing (AU) paragraph numbers. The codification section numbers used by the ASB follow. These standards constitute what is known as *generally accepted auditing standards* (GAAS).

- AU § 100—Introduction
- AU § 200—The General Standards
- AU § 300—The Standards of Field Work
- AU § 400—The First, Second, and Third Standards of Reporting
- AU § 500—The Fourth Standard of Reporting
- AU § 600—Other Types of Reports
- AU § 700—Special Topics
- AU § 800—Compliance Auditing
- AU § 900—Special Reports of the Committee on Auditing Procedures

Within each section are many subsections. For example, subsection AU § 316 describes one of the auditor's responsibilities during field work: the responsibility to consider fraud in a financial statement audit. Auditing standards issued by the ASB relevant to each chapter will be listed at its beginning. You can go to the codification of auditing standards book and read the referenced material. A practicing auditor uses the material contained in the auditing standards issued by the ASB to determine the procedures performed, the evidence gathered, and the audit report issued for an audit of a private (nonissuer) company.

The Public Company Accounting Oversight Board

The Public Company Accounting Oversight Board (PCAOB) is a five-member board created with the passage of the Sarbanes-Oxley Act in 2002. The PCAOB is a private sector, nonprofit organization created to oversee auditors of public companies in order to "protect the interests of investors and further the public interest in the preparation of informative, fair and independent audit reports." The SEC appoints the members of the

PCAOB. Two of the five members must be or have been CPAs. The SEC has oversight authority over the PCAOB, including the approval of its rules, standards, and budget. The vision of the PCAOB is to "improve audit quality, reduce the risks of auditing failures in the U.S. public securities market and promote public trust in both the financial reporting process and auditing profession" (http://pcaobus.org/about/history/pages/default.aspx).

The Sarbanes-Oxley Act (SOX) requires accountants who audit *public* companies in the United States to follow the PCAOB's auditing standards. Before the PCAOB's creation, the ASB's auditing standards were used to audit all companies, both private and public. In 2003, the PCAOB adopted certain auditing standards of the ASB as interim standards to allow the PCAOB time to develop new auditing standards. The interim standards remain in effect to the extent not superseded or amended by the Board. The interim standards are revised by the PCAOB when they issue auditing standards that change the requirements of the interim standards. However, the PCAOB does not adopt the revisions made by the ASB as they revise the standards adopted by the PCAOB as interim standards. This means that an auditor must use the text of the interim standard from the PCAOB web site when auditing a public company, rather than the text from the ASB standards, because the two standards, even with the same number, may be different. The fifteen new auditing standards that it has issued and the current standards adopted as interim standards follow:

PCAOB Standards

- **Auditing Standard No. 1:** References in Auditors' Reports to the Standards of the Public Company Accounting Oversight Board
- **Auditing Standards No. 2:** An Audit of Internal Control Over Financial Reporting Performed in Conjunction With an Audit of Financial Statements (Superseded)
- **Auditing Standard No. 3:** Audit Documentation
- **Auditing Standard No. 4:** Reporting on Whether a Previously Reported Material Weakness Continues to Exist
- **Auditing Standard No. 5:** An Audit of Internal Control Over Financial Reporting That Is Integrated with an Audit of Financial Statements
- **Auditing Standard No. 6:** Evaluating Consistency of Financial Statements
- **Auditing Standard No. 7:** Engagement Quality Review
- **Auditing Standard No. 8:** Audit Risk
- **Auditing Standard No. 9:** Audit Planning
- **Auditing Standard No. 10:** Supervision of the Audit Engagement
- **Auditing Standard No. 11:** Consideration of Materiality in Planning and Performing an Audit
- **Auditing Standard No. 12:** Identifying and Assessing Risks of Material Misstatement
- **Auditing Standard No. 13:** The Auditor's Responses to the Risks of Material Misstatement
- **Auditing Standard No. 14:** Evaluating Audit Results
- **Auditing Standard No. 15:** Audit Evidence

Interim Standards from the AICPA Auditing Standards Board

- AU 110 Responsibilities and Functions of the Independent Auditor
- AU 150 Generally Accepted Auditing Standards
- AU 161 The Relationship of Generally Accepted Auditing Standards to Quality Control Standards
- AU 201 Nature of the General Standards
- AU 210 Training and Proficiency of the Independent Auditor
- AU 220 Independence
- AU 230 Due Professional Care in the Performance of Work

- AU 310 Appointment of the Independent Auditor
- AU 311 Planning and Supervision
- AU 313 Substantive Tests Prior to the Balance Sheet Date
- AU 315 Communications Between Predecessor and Successor Auditors
- AU 316 Consideration of Fraud in a Financial Statement Audit
- AU 317 Illegal Acts by Clients
- AU 319 Consideration of Internal Control in a Financial Statement Audit
- AU 322 The Auditor's Consideration of the Internal Audit Function in an Audit of Financial Statements
- AU 324 Service Organizations
- AU 325 Communications About Control Deficiencies in an Audit of Financial Statements
- AU 328 Auditing Fair Value Measurements and Disclosures
- AU 329 Analytical Procedures
- AU 330 The Confirmation Process
- AU 331 Inventories
- AU 332 Auditing Derivative Instruments, Hedging Activities, and Investments in Securities
- AU 333 Management Representations
- AU 334 Related Parties
- AU 336 Using the Work of a Specialist
- AU 337 Inquiry of a Client's Lawyer Concerning Litigation, Claims, and Assessments
- AU 341 The Auditor's Consideration of an Entity's Ability to Continue as a Going Concern
- AU 342 Auditing Accounting Estimates
- AU 350 Audit Sampling
- AU 380 Communication With Audit Committees
- AU 390 Consideration of Omitted Procedures After the Report Date
- AU 410 Adherence to Generally Accepted Accounting Principles
- AU 411 The Meaning of Present Fairly in Conformity with Generally Accepted Accounting Principles
- AU 435 Segment Information
- AU 504 Association With Financial Statements
- AU 508 Reports on Audited Financial Statements
- AU 530 Dating of the Independent Auditor's Report
- AU 532 Restricting the Use of an Auditor's Report
- AU 534 Reporting on Financial Statements Prepared for Use in Other Countries
- AU 543 Part of Audit Performed by Other Independent Auditors
- AU 544 Lack of Conformity With Generally Accepted Accounting Principles
- AU 550 Other Information in Documents Containing Audited Financial Statements
- AU 551 Reporting on Information Accompanying the Basic Financial Statements in Auditor-Submitted Documents
- AU 552 Reporting on Condensed Financial Statements and Selected Financial Data
- AU 558 Required Supplementary Information
- AU 560 Subsequent Events
- AU 561 Subsequent Discovery of Facts Existing at the Date of the Auditor's Report
- AU 622 Engagements to Apply Agreed-Upon Procedures to Specified Elements, Accounts, or Items of a Financial Statement
- AU 623 Special Reports

Generally Accepted Auditing Standards PCAOB

Exhibit 1-2

GENERAL STANDARDS

1. The audit is to be performed by a person having adequate technical training and proficiency as an auditor.
2. In all matters relating to the assignment, an independence in mental attitude is to be maintained by the auditor.
3. Due professional care is to be exercised in the performance of the audit and the preparation of the report.

STANDARDS OF FIELD WORK

1. The work is to be adequately planned and assistants, if any, are to be properly supervised.
2. A sufficient understanding of internal control is to be obtained to plan the audit and to determine the nature, timing, and extent of tests to be performed.
3. Sufficient competent evidential matter is to be obtained through inspection, observation, inquiries, and confirmations to afford a reasonable basis for an opinion regarding the financial statements under audit.

STANDARDS OF REPORTING

1. The report shall state whether the financial statements are presented in accordance with generally accepted accounting principles (GAAP).
2. The report shall identify those circumstances in which such principles have not been consistently observed in the current period in relation to the preceding period.
3. Informative disclosures in the financial statements are to be regarded as reasonably adequate unless otherwise stated in the report.
4. The report shall contain either an expression of opinion regarding the financial statements, taken as a whole, or an assertion to the effect that an opinion cannot be expressed, the reasons therefor should be stated. In all cases where the auditor's name is associated with financial statements, the report should contain a clear-cut indication of the character of the auditor's work, if any, and the degree of responsibility the audit is taking.

- AU 625 Reports on the Application of Accounting Principles
- AU 634 Letters for Underwriters and Certain Other Requesting Parties
- AU 711 Filings Under Federal Securities Statutes
- AU 722 Interim Financial Information
- AU 801 Compliance Auditing Considerations in Audits of Governmental Entities and Recipients of Governmental Financial Assistance
- AU 901 Public Warehouses—Controls and Auditing Procedure for Goods Held

The PCAOB receives its authority from U.S. federal law. The SEC must approve auditing standards issued by the PCAOB. Anyone who wants to list a stock on a U.S. stock exchange must follow SEC rules. One of these rules includes the requirement for an integrated audit (a financial statement audit and an audit of the internal controls over the financial reporting process) by an auditor registered with the PCAOB. All audit firms performing audits of public companies are registered with the PCAOB and agree to comply with its established auditing standards. The SEC is discussed in more detail later in the chapter. Auditors follow the rules established by the PCAOB because they are required by law to do so.

According to AU 150, *Generally Accepted Auditing Standards,* an independent auditor plans, conducts, and reports the results of an audit in accordance with generally accepted auditing standards. Auditing standards provide a way to measure audit quality and the objectives achieved in the audit. The general, field work, and reporting standards provide a framework for the auditing standards. They are listed in Exhibit 1-2.

An important aspect of the PCAOB is its ability to enforce the rules it develops. It is required to conduct continuing inspections of public accounting firms registered with it. The PCAOB inspects firms with more than 100 public clients on an annual basis. Firms with fewer than 100 public clients are inspected at least every three years. The inspection reports are posted on the PCAOB's website and are available to the public. In the development of new auditing standards, the members of the PCAOB consider whether the rule can be "inspected to" and enforced. While peer review procedures are in place for audits performed under the rules of the ASB, these review procedures were believed to be inadequate in enforcing compliance with the auditing standards for companies issuing stock on U.S. exchanges.

References related to the PCAOB standards are listed at the beginning of each chapter so you can refer to these standards as you read the chapter material. They may be downloaded from the PCAOB website (http://www.pcaobus.org).

International Auditing and Assurance Standards Board

The International Auditing and Assurance Standards Board (IAASB) was formed in 1978 as an independent standard-setting board of the International Federation of Accountants (IFAC). The IAASB has eighteen members nominated by the IFAC; the members serve in a part-time capacity for three years. IFAC's headquarters is in New York City (both the ASB and the PCAOB are also headquartered in the United States).

The IAASB has issued thirty-two International Standards of Auditing (ISAs). It develops and issues auditing standards *under its own authority* for use around the world. Individual countries are free to adopt or incorporate the ISAs into their national auditing standards. ISAs are intended for use in all types of audits: private or public companies, small or large companies, government or for-profit businesses. More than 100 countries have adopted the ISAs issued by the IAASB. The ISAs are also codified and presented by topic area to make it easier for an auditor to find all auditing regulations about a topic (for example, fraud) in one place.

The ISAs are often considered the most up-to-date and comprehensive of the three sets of standards. They are global in nature—an important fact for those of you preparing for a forty-year career in accounting. Public accounting firms start with the ISAs when developing audit programs and adjust their programs for changes imposed by the ASB and the PCAOB. The auditing standards among the three groups are becoming increasingly similar. The ASB and the IAASB have agreed to a convergence project for the auditing and assurance standards issued by the two groups. The convergence is expected to be completed by 2013 or 2014. Because ISAs are more comprehensive than the auditing standards issued by the ASB, the auditing standards in the United States are being revised to correspond with the ISAs. Differences in wording between the international standards and U.S. standards may occur because each standard-setting body applies terms that can be understood in the environment where the standards are used, but the differences are viewed as minor. The ASB auditing standards should correspond with the ISAs by 2014.

This book has been written using the current auditing standards in the United States at the time of its publication. International auditing standard references will also be listed at the beginning of each chapter as reference material. The ISAs may be downloaded from the IFAC website (http://www.ifac.org).

Evidence Requirements of Auditing Standards

LO6

Explain the evidence requirements of the auditing standards

An important requirement of the auditing standards is that the auditor gather sufficient appropriate evidence to determine whether the financial statements have been prepared in a manner consistent with the applicable financial reporting framework used by the company.

Audit evidence, which is crucial to the audit process, is the information used by the auditor to determine which audit opinion to issue. Audit evidence includes the information in the accounting records, which contains the records of initial entries; supporting documents such as checks, invoices, and contracts; and the company's general and subsidiary ledgers. Management is responsible for preparing the financial statements. The auditor is responsible for gathering sufficient (enough), appropriate (relevant and reliable) *evidence* to determine that management has prepared the financial statements in accordance with the applicable financial reporting framework.

The evidence gathered by the auditor can be described as one of three types:

- *Substantive evidence* that describes whether the transactions and balances listed in the financial statements are presented fairly according to the applicable financial reporting framework

- *Internal control evidence* that determines whether internal controls can be relied on to detect or prevent misstatements in the financial statements
- *Analytical procedure evidence* that identifies changes from prior year financial statements

Each type of evidence is discussed in more detail in the following discussion.

Substantive tests conducted by the auditor to determine whether the financial statements are prepared in accordance with the applicable financial reporting framework are either **substantive tests of transactions** or **substantive tests of balances.** Substantive tests of *transactions* are conducted to gather evidence on income statement accounts (revenue and expense accounts). Substantive tests of *balances* are performed to gather evidence on balance sheet accounts (assets, liabilities, and owners' equity). Both types of substantive tests answer the question regarding whether the financial statement accounts present fairly the financial condition of the firm in accordance with the applicable financial reporting framework. If the financial statements do not fairly present the firm's financial condition in accordance with the applicable financial reporting framework, the auditor should gather sufficient evidence to arrive at the correct financial statement number.

Tests performed by the auditor to determine whether the company's internal controls prevent or detect misstatements in the financial statements are referred to as **internal control tests.** These tests answer the question of whether the control is working (at the level expected) to prevent or detect misstatements in the financial statements. If controls are not working, the auditor performs more substantive tests.

Analytical procedures are a third form of evidence gathered by the auditor. They are calculations of financial ratios, comparisons of nonfinancial information with financial information, and comparisons of the prior year's audited financial statements with the current year's unaudited statements. These analytical procedures are a form of substantive audit procedure and may be used to obtain evidence regarding income statement accounts or account balances on the balance sheet.

Substantive tests of *transactions* and internal control tests are typically conducted on transactions for the entire year for a financial statement audit. An exception to this rule occurs when the auditor tests internal controls related to the effectiveness of controls over the financial reporting process (according to the requirements of SOX). Internal controls for the financial reporting process, not for the financial statement audit, are required to be effective only at the year-end, so the entire year is not tested in this case. Substantive tests of *balances* are made on the year-end balance only.

Several evidence-gathering concepts are important. At the beginning of the audit, the auditor presents her or his credentials to the client as an individual with training and knowledge in accounting and auditing, someone who has the ability to conduct the audit. To perform the job, the auditor must be **independent** from the client. This independence takes two forms. The auditor must be "intellectually honest" to be independent (this is referred to as *independence in fact*), **and** she or he must be recognized by outsiders as being independent (this is referred to as *independence in appearance*). He or she must be free from any interest in or obligation to the client.

The auditor must gather evidence guided by the standard of **due professional care,** which requires the auditor to perform audit duties with the skill comparable to that of any other auditor and to gather evidence and interpret evidence in a manner that any other professional would have done. The auditor should know the accounting and auditing standards and be knowledgeable about the client.

Professional skepticism is closely linked to due professional care. To gather evidence with due professional care, an auditor must perform the audit with an attitude of professional skepticism that is present when the auditor maintains a questioning mind and makes a critical assessment of the evidence gathered. Professional skepticism is used throughout the audit to determine the evidence to be gathered and the interpretation of the evidence.

If the auditor applies the concept of professional skepticism in the audit, he or she should be able to obtain **reasonable assurance** that the financial statements are free from material misstatements. Reasonable assurance is not absolute assurance, however, so an audit may fail to detect material misstatements in the financial statements. The standard of reasonable assurance is sufficient for issuing an audit opinion. The subsequent discovery of a material misstatement in the financial statements does not indicate that the auditor failed to obtain reasonable assurance or that the audit was performed without due professional care.

The Auditing of Business Processes, Classes of Transactions, and Account Balances

LO7

Understand how the auditor uses business processes to structure the collection of evidence

Over the years, the methods used by auditors to gather evidence have changed. In the past, auditors gathered evidence by performing an audit of the balance sheet. It was assumed that if the auditor knew that the balances reported on the balance sheet were prepared in accordance with the applicable financial reporting framework, the income statement would also be prepared in accordance with the applicable financial reporting framework. In the next stage of audit procedures, the auditor gathered evidence for an accounting cycle rather than a balance sheet account.

An accounting cycle involves both balance sheet and income statement accounts and follows a transaction through a process from its beginning to its conclusion (usually at the point of cash flow). For example, in an audit of the revenue cycle, auditors would include accounts receivable and the allowance for doubtful accounts on the balance sheet and revenue and bad debt expense on the income statement. This cycle would include the procedures for initiating a sale, shipping the goods or providing a service, invoicing the customer, and collecting payment for the sale. When obtaining evidence for the revenue cycle, the auditor will gather evidence relating to all accounts in the cycle.

Today the auditor uses an even broader term to organize the gathering of evidence. He or she considers the firm's **business processes.** For the business process of selling a product, for example, the auditor considers evidence related to the transactions involving revenue and accounts receivable including the allowance for doubtful accounts and bad debt expense. A business process audit might consider, for example, the business processes of selling a product and collecting cash, borrowing money to operate, paying short-term liabilities, producing inventory to sell, or buying fixed assets to use. The auditor identifies the client's business processes at the beginning of the audit and structures the evidence collection process to gather sufficient appropriate evidence to determine that the financial statement accounts in the business process are fairly stated according to the applicable financial reporting framework. Because the auditor's time during an audit is limited, structuring the audit according to business processes is an efficient way to conduct it. The auditor considers related accounts at the same time and identifies the processes that are important to the audit client.

In the business process model, the auditor identifies classes of transactions and account balances in the business process. The *classes of transactions* are the income statement accounts, and the *account balances* are the balance sheet accounts. After the auditor has completed gathering evidence for the business process, he or she should be able to determine whether the classes of transactions and account balances in the business process are presented in accordance with the applicable financial reporting framework.

Management's Assertions

LO8

Explain how management's assertions about the financial statements are used in the audit process

The auditor structures the evidence process by considering the assertions made by management in preparing the company's financial statements. At the beginning of an audit, management gives the auditor a set of financial statements that it has prepared and asks her or him to gather sufficient evidence to issue an opinion stating whether the financial statements are presented in accordance with the applicable financial reporting framework. When management presents the financial statements to the auditor, it makes several assertions about the financial statements. These assertions are listed in the table below.[2]

Management's Assertions
***

Existence or occurrence—for both classes of transactions and account balances
Completeness—for both classes of transactions and account balances
Valuation and allocation—for account balances
Rights and obligations—for account balances
Accuracy—for classes of transactions
Cutoff—for classes of transactions
Classification—for classes of transactions
***

The auditor gathers evidence during the audit process to determine whether the financial statements are prepared in accordance with the applicable financial reporting framework, organizing the evidence collection according to management's assertions regarding the financial statements.

The first two assertions apply to both balance sheet and income statement accounts. Assertions about **existence** and **occurrence** address whether assets and liabilities are valid (whether they exist) at year-end and whether transactions recorded in the income statement have occurred (occurrence) during the year. Assertions regarding **completeness** address whether all transactions that *should* have been recorded in the year according to the applicable financial reporting framework *were* actually recorded.

The assertions for (1) valuation and allocation and (2) rights and obligations apply only to balance sheet accounts. Assertions relating to **valuation** or **allocation** deal with whether the asset, liability, or owners' equity account has been included in the financial statements at the correct amount based on the applicable financial reporting framework (GAAP). The **rights and obligations** assertion states that the company has the right to the asset or the obligation to pay the liability at year-end.

Three assertions apply only to income statement accounts. The **accuracy** assertion specifies that the amounts of the transactions have been recorded appropriately. The **cutoff** assertion states that all transactions have been recorded in the correct accounting period according to the applicable financial reporting framework. The **classification** assertion states that all transactions have been recorded in the proper accounts.

Assertions relating to **presentation and disclosure** determine whether assets, liabilities, revenues, and expenses are properly presented in the financial statements and whether the financial statement disclosures are complete and in accordance with the applicable financial reporting framework. These assertions are discussed in more detail later in the book.

The auditor gathers evidence to determine whether management's assertions are true. The chapters in this textbook that cover the audit of business processes use the assertion approach for organizing evidence to illustrate how the auditor gathers it to determine that the financial statements are prepared in accordance with the applicable financial reporting framework.

Audit Reports

LO9

Describe the audit report

At the conclusion of the audit, the auditor issues an audit opinion to the client based on the evidence gathered and reflecting the auditor's assessment of whether the financial statements are prepared in accordance with the applicable financial reporting framework.

***

[2] The PCAOB uses five assertions in their auditing standards: existence, completeness, valuation, rights and obligations, and presentation and disclosure. The ASB and the IAASB use 11 assertions. The PCAOB allows auditors to use either set of assertions in the audit process. In this text, the assertions adopted by the ASB and the IAASB will be used because the auditing firms use the international auditing standards to develop their audit programs.

Report of Independent Registered Public Accounting Firm *Hewlett-Packard Company October 31, 2008*

Exhibit 1-3

To the Board of Directors and Stockholders of Hewlett-Packard Company

We have audited the accompanying consolidated balance sheets of Hewlett-Packard Company and subsidiaries as of October 31, 2008 and 2007, and the related consolidated statements of earnings, stockholders' equity and cash flows for each of the three years in the period ended October 31, 2008. Our audits also included the financial statement schedule listed in the Index at Item 15(a)(2). These financial statements and schedule are the responsibility of the Company's management. Our responsibility is to express an opinion on these financial statements and schedule based on our audits.

We conducted our audits in accordance with the standards of the Public Company Accounting Oversight Board (United States). Those standards require that we plan and perform the audit to obtain reasonable assurance about whether the financial statements are free of material misstatement. An audit includes examining, on a test basis, evidence supporting the amounts and disclosures in the financial statements. An audit also includes assessing the accounting principles used and significant estimates made by management, as well as evaluating the overall financial statement presentation. We believe that our audits provide a reasonable basis for our opinion.

In our opinion, the financial statements referred to above present fairly, in all material respects, the consolidated financial position of Hewlett-Packard Company and subsidiaries at October 31, 2008 and 2007, and the consolidated results of their operations and their cash flows for each of the three years in the period ended October 31, 2008, in conformity with U.S. applicable financial reporting framework. Also, in our opinion, the related financial statement schedule, when considered in relation to the basic financial statements taken as a whole, presents fairly in all material respects the information set forth therein.

We also have audited, in accordance with the standards of the Public Company Accounting Oversight Board (United States), the effectiveness of Hewlett-Packard Company's internal control over financial reporting as of October 31, 2008, based on criteria established in Internal Control—Integrated Framework issued by the Committee of Sponsoring Organizations of the Treadway Commission and our report dated December 15, 2008 expressed an unqualified opinion thereon.

As discussed in Note 1 to the consolidated financial statements, in fiscal year 2008, Hewlett-Packard Company changed its method of accounting for income taxes in accordance with the guidance provided in Financial Accounting Standards Board (FASB) Interpretation No. 48, "Accounting for Uncertainty in Income Taxes, an interpretation of FASB Statement No. 109" and, in fiscal year 2007 Hewlett-Packard Company changed its method of accounting for defined benefit postretirement plans in accordance with the guidance provided in Statement of Financial Accounting Standards No. 158, "Employers' Accounting for Defined Benefit Pension and Other Postretirement Plans—An Amendment of FASB No. 87, 88, 106 and 132(R)."

/s/ ERNST & YOUNG LLP
San Jose, California
December 15, 2008

An example of the opinion issued by Ernst & Young for Hewlett-Packard is provided in Exhibit 1-3.

Before you begin the study of auditing, it is helpful to understand the outcome of the audit. If the auditor determines that the financial statements present fairly the financial position of the firm and the results of their operations and cash flows are in conformity with the applicable financial reporting framework, a "clean opinion" will be issued to the client. This standard clean opinion (also known as an *unqualified opinion*) always includes at least three paragraphs: an introductory paragraph, a scope paragraph, and an opinion paragraph. The Hewlett-Packard report also contains two additional explanatory paragraphs (the fourth paragraph in the report refers the reader to the audit opinion for the effectiveness of internal controls, and the fifth paragraph explains a change in accounting principles).

You can see that the opinion is addressed to the stockholders and the board of directors, who hired the independent registered public accounting firm to perform the audit and to protect the interests of outsiders. The auditors do not work for the firm's management. In the United States, auditors usually issue an audit opinion on two years of balance sheet and three years of income statement, statement of stockholders' equity, and statement of cash flows. The responsibilities of management and the auditor are clearly expressed in the first paragraph of the audit report. Management is responsible for preparing the financial statements. The auditor is responsible only for expressing an opinion of the financial statements based on her or his assessment.

The second paragraph of the audit report explains how the auditor has conducted the audit. This audit was conducted in accordance with the standards of the PCAOB because Hewlett-Packard is a public company subject to the PCAOB's reporting rules.

The opinion paragraph of the audit report states that the financial statements **present fairly, in all material respects,** the financial position of the firm (the balance sheet), the results of the firm's operations (the income statement), and its cash flows (the statement of cash flows) for the years under audit in conformity with the applicable financial reporting framework in the United States. Present fairly, in all material respects, is the highest evaluation for an audit opinion. This is the audit opinion that companies hope to receive. This opinion does not mean that the financial statements contain no misstatements. It means only that the financial statements present fairly, in all *material* respects, the firm's financial condition. This means that any misstatements in the financial statements are not large enough to change the decision of an outside user of the financial statements. Opinions issued for financial statements that do not present fairly the firm's financial condition will be covered in the audit report chapter.

Accounting Regulatory Bodies

Regulatory Bodies and the Accounting Profession

In addition to the three audit standard-setting bodies already discussed, several regulatory bodies are involved in the audit process: the Securities and Exchange Commission (SEC), the Financial Accounting Standards Board (FASB), the International Accounting Standards Board (IASB), the American Institute of Certified Public Accountants (AICPA), and state accounting societies. These bodies exert influence over the accounting profession, and it is important for a new auditor to understand these groups' potential influence in terms of the regulations they impose on the auditor.

The Securities and Exchange Commission (SEC)

Following World War I (1914–1918), many businesspeople began to invest in the securities market. At that time, there were no regulations related to financial disclosure or to the prevention of the fraudulent sale of stock. When the stock market crashed in October 1929, public confidence in the securities market declined. As a result of this crash, investors lost large sums of money, and there was a consensus that for the economy to recover, the public's faith in the capital markets must be restored. The U.S. Congress held hearings to identify the problems that caused the 1929 crash and to search for solutions. Based on the hearings, Congress passed the Securities Act of 1933. This law, together with the Securities Exchange Act of 1934, was designed to restore investor confidence in the capital markets. These acts restored confidence by providing more reliable information and clear rules of honest trading to investors. The SEC was given the power to require independent audits of public companies, which had to register with the SEC before selling their securities to the public. The main purpose of these two laws can be described in the following way:

- Companies that sell securities to the public must tell the public the truth about their businesses, the securities they are selling, and the risks involved in investing.
- People who sell and trade securities (brokers, dealers, and exchanges) must treat investors fairly and honestly, putting the investors' interests first.

The SEC consists of five commissioners appointed by the President of the United States. Its responsibilities are organized into five divisions and sixteen offices with approximately 3,500 staff. The headquarters for the divisions is Washington, D.C. The SEC's responsibility is to:

- Interpret federal securities laws
- Issue new rules and amend existing rules
- Oversee the inspection of securities firms, brokers, investment advisers, and ratings agencies

- Oversee private regulatory organizations in the securities, accounting, and auditing fields
- Coordinate U.S. securities regulation with federal, state, and foreign authorities.

The SEC's mission is "to protect investors, maintain fair, orderly, and efficient markets, and facilitate capital formation." The SEC has the authority to write financial accounting and reporting standards (to establish the applicable financial reporting framework) for public companies under the authority of the Securities Exchange Act of 1934. Throughout its history, the SEC's policy has been to rely on the private sector for this function to the extent that the private sector demonstrates its ability to fulfill the responsibility in the public interest.

The SEC has the authority to regulate the sale of securities for all firms listed on the public stock exchanges in the United States. Its authority extends to international companies that list their stock on a U.S. exchange. The SEC requires an annual filing with it within 60 days of the company's year-end. This annual filing includes the financial statements, footnotes, auditor's report, and additional information requested by the SEC. The annual filing is a 10-K report. Until 2008, all companies filing with the SEC were required to use U.S. accounting standards in their 10-K reports. At that time, the SEC agreed to accept international accounting standards for the 10-K reports of foreign companies. These firms can now file their 10-K reports using one of two applicable financial reporting frameworks, either U.S. or international GAAP. The decision reflects the international nature of the business world and is an indication of the importance of international accounting standards in the business world. But the decision may complicate the use of some financial statements. Using different accounting standards to prepare financial statements could make it difficult for financial statement readers to compare performance between and across companies.

The SEC requires quarterly and annual reporting from companies selling stock on the U.S. stock exchanges. The quarterly reports are *reviewed* by an independent accounting firm, and the annual reports are *audited* by the same CPA firm. Quarterly and annual information for public companies is available on the SEC website (www.sec .gov). Individual companies often include financial information on their company's website. One of the hallmarks of the U.S. capital markets system is this availability of information. In 2008, the SEC approved a proposal to allow all companies (U.S. based and international) selling stock on the U.S. exchanges to use international accounting principles in the preparation of their financial statements. This proposal does not have an effective date, but it has important implications for the potential use of international accounting standards by U.S. companies. At some point, will auditors have to learn both the international and U.S. financial reporting frameworks, or will U.S. and international accounting principles converge into one set of standards? These are not questions that we can answer today but are issues to be resolved by regulatory bodies in the future.

Once the auditor has issued an opinion on the yearly financial statements, the statements become public information, available to anyone requesting the information. Outsiders have free access to financial information, so when they make decisions about the company, those decisions should be based on accurate information. The U.S. capital markets system is often referred to as a *transparent reporting system.* Auditors play an important role in making the U.S. capital markets system one of the best systems in the world for raising capital whenever companies need money to finance expansion or investment decisions.

Financial Accounting Standards Board (FASB)

The FASB's mission established in 1973 is "to establish and improve standards of financial accounting and reporting for the guidance and education of the public, including issuers, auditors, and users of financial information." The FASB, which develops broad accounting concepts as well as standards for financial reporting in the United States, is part of a structure that is independent of all other business and professional organizations. Before the FASB was created in 1973, accounting standards were established by the Committee on Accounting Procedures of the AICPA from 1936–1959, and then by the Accounting Principles Board, also a part of the AICPA, from 1959–1973. The FASB receives its authority from the accountants who follow the standards it sets.

The FASB is made up of five members who serve full-time and are required to sever all ties with the institutions or firms they served before joining the board. The FASB has an extensive list of people who serve in an advisory capacity. The FASB issues exposure drafts when new accounting principles are proposed, and then, after reviewing the comments regarding the exposure draft, it writes a final standard for a new accounting principle. The accounting standards are codified on a yearly basis by topic to allow accountants to easily find those applicable to a particular topic. At times, the business community has criticized the FASB for acting too slowly or for being too rule based, but it has been in existence since 1973, and this method of developing GAAP has generally been satisfactory to all the parties interested in the process. The board is important to the auditing profession. The auditor's job is to determine whether the financial statements are prepared according to the applicable financial reporting framework written by the FASB, so the auditor must understand the accounting principles it writes.

International Accounting Standards Board (IASB)

The IASB is the standard-setting board of the International Financial Reporting Standards (IFRS) Foundation. The objective of the IFRS Foundation is to "develop a single set of high quality, understandable, enforceable and globally accepted international financial reporting standards" (www.ifrs.org). This board has the responsibility for writing standards that form the applicable financial reporting framework required or permitted by more than 100 countries. The standards issued by the IASB have been referred to as IRFS standards since 2001. This independent standard-setting board, with 15 full-time members, develops and publishes IRFSs. Accounting standards issued by the predecessor accounting standards board are referred to as international accounting standards (IASs). The international accounting and reporting standards currently comprise eight IFRSs issued from 2001–2010 and forty-one ISAs issued from 1973 to 2000.

The American Institute of Certified Public Accountants (AICPA)

The AICPA was established in the 1880s when the American Association of Public Accountants was formed. The organization went through several name changes. In 1916, it was renamed the Institute of Public Accountants and had 1,150 members. The name was changed to the American Institute of Accountants in 1917 and finally to its current name in 1957. The AICPA is a private organization for all certified public accountants. It gains its authority from the accountants who are its members. After the passage of the Securities Acts in 1933 and 1934, the accounting profession persuaded the SEC to rely on the American Institute of Accountants, the AICPA's predecessor, to set accounting and auditing standards for the purpose of filing financial reports with the SEC. In 1973, the AICPA gave the FASB the right to prepare accounting standards. In 2002, the right to set auditing standards for public companies was granted to the PCAOB. The Auditing Standards Board committee of the AICPA retains the right to issue auditing standards for companies in the private sector.

The AICPA has three main responsibilities today. They are to:

- Prepare and grade the CPA exam
- Establish the Professional Code of Conduct, the ethics code for licensed CPAs
- Write auditing standards for private companies

State Boards of Accountancy

The state board of accountancy for each state regulates who can take the CPA examination and the experience and continuing education requirements for licensing those individuals who have passed the exam. The rules vary from state to state, so it is important to check for current information with the state board of accountancy in the state where you expect to be licensed. Normally, CPA licenses are reciprocal. Many states have passed the 150-hour education requirement to take the CPA exam, although a few states allow individuals to take the exam with fewer than 150 hours. A license earned in a state accepting fewer than 150 hours is not usually transferable to a state with a 150-hour requirement.

Chapter Takeaways

Learning about auditing is similar to learning a new language. By the end of the course, you will be conversant in this new language. Each chapter will add to your knowledge of the accounting profession and the specialized area of auditing. Eventually, all of the pieces that you learn will fit together into the coherent body of knowledge that is necessary for you to become a staff auditor. At the end of each chapter, you will find a list of statements summarizing the pieces of the puzzle that have been discussed in the chapter. Review these lists as you go through the text to determine whether you understand the concepts important to the particular chapter. Many concepts will be repeated from chapter to chapter. You won't understand the story until you have all the pieces, so it is important that you master the concepts in each chapter before you go on to the next chapter. Each chapter builds on the knowledge in the previous chapters.

This text is designed to mix theory and practical applications of auditing procedures, so some chapters will emphasize concepts related to theory and other chapters will emphasize practical applications. At the end of the course, you should have a good idea of how to conduct an audit (what procedures to perform). You should also understand the "why's" of auditing (why perform them, why outsiders rely on its information, why an independent CPA firm should perform the audit instead of an accountant in the company, why the auditor should use sampling in the audit process). As you understand the theory behind auditing and the steps associated with it, you should develop an increased appreciation for the professional responsibilities of the accountant and an understanding of the importance of performing these responsibilities using professional skepticism and the standard of due care.

This chapter presented these important facts:

- The importance of auditing in the corporate governance process. The unique role that auditors perform serves to protect the interests of outsiders.
- Some of the unique features of the auditing profession.
- The role of management's incentives to misstate the financial statements in the audit.
- The use of generally accepted auditing standards (GAAS) to perform an audit.
- The important concepts of *due professional care, professional skepticism,* and *reasonable assurance* in the audit process.
- The role of evidence in the audit process, including *substantive tests of transactions, substantive tests of balances, analytical procedures,* and *internal control tests.*
- The importance of auditing using business processes.
- The assertions made by management regarding the financial statements and the role of the assertions in gathering evidence.
- The information contained in an audit opinion.
- The importance of the accounting regulatory bodies.

Be sure that you understand these concepts before you go on to the next chapter.

Review Questions

LO4	1.	Explain the role of the auditor in the corporate governance process. Is this role more important or less important today than twenty years ago?
LO1	2.	What is involved in the auditing process?
LO1	3.	How does the principal–agent relationship apply to the audit process?
LO5	4.	Describe the three standard-setting organizations involved in writing auditing standards and the roles of each in establishing guidelines for auditors.
LO6	5.	What is evidence? How does the auditor use it in the audit process?
LO6	6.	How does the auditor gather evidence using internal control testing?

LO6   7. How does the auditor gather evidence using substantive testing? Describe three types of substantive tests.

LO7   8. What are classes of transactions? What other terms might be used to describe them? How does the auditor use the concept of transaction classes in the audit process?

LO6   9. What are tests of account balances? How are they used in the audit process?

LO8   10. Describe management's assertions regarding the financial statements.

LO9   11. Explain how the audit report is used to describe the responsibilities of the auditor and management, the work done by the auditor during the audit, and the conclusions reached by the auditor regarding the financial statements being audited.

LO10   12. What are the various regulatory bodies that regulate the accounting profession? Describe the functions of each.

LO1   13. How would you describe the auditing profession to a friend? Describe at least one element of the profession that is appealing to you. Describe another element that is less appealing, and explain why.

LO3   14. Describe management's incentive to misstate financial statements. What challenge do auditors face as they review such misstatements?

Real-World Auditing Problem

LO2   15. After it was convicted of a felony in connection with the failed Enron audit, Arthur Andersen went out of business in August 2002 because it could no longer file audit opinions with the SEC. In 2005, the conviction was overturned due to procedural errors in the instructions the judge gave to the jury. Do you believe it was fair that Arthur Andersen firms around the world were forced to close as a result of a failed audit in Dallas, Texas? Explain your answer.

Internet Assignments

LO1   16. Go to the websites for the SEC, PCAOB, AICPA, and your state CPA society. Review the information that it provides, and describe the individuals who might be interested in the information.

LO2   17. Go to the website for one of your favorite companies. Describe the information on the website related to financial information. Is there any information on corporate governance? Who is the company's auditor? Did the company receive a clean opinion on the financial statements?

LO4   18. Review the websites for one of the big four accounting firms (Deloitte & Touche, KPMG, PricewaterhouseCoopers, or Ernst & Young). Describe the information available on the website related to careers in public accounting.

2

The Audit Planning Process: Understanding the Risk of Material Misstatement

Learning Objectives

After studying this chapter, you should be able to:

1. Describe the audit process including its planning, testing, and decision phases.
2. Understand the preconditions for an audit.
3. Explain how the auditor gains an understanding of the entity and its environment, determines materiality, and assesses the risk of material misstatement.
4. Describe how the auditor develops an audit strategy and an audit plan to respond to the assessed risk of material misstatement.
5. Understand how the auditor reduces audit risk to an acceptably low level.[1]
6. Explain the systems of quality control for accounting firms.

Auditing standards relevant to this topic

For private companies[2]

- **AU 311,** Planning an Audit
- **AU 312,** Materiality in Planning and Performing an Audit

---

[1] Auditing standards of the PCAOB use the term "acceptably low level" to explain the reduction in audit risk (AS No. 8). Auditing standards written by the Auditing Standards Board and the International Auditing and Assurance Board use the term "appropriately low level."

[2] The Auditing Standards Board (ASB) is involved in redrafting the auditing standards for the purpose of converging its standards with those of the International Auditing and Assurance Standards Board (IAASB). As part of this project, the ASB will issue the redrafted standards in one Statement on Auditing Standards (SAS) that will be codified in "AU section" format. When this process is finished, the auditing standards will be renumbered. The renumbering will follow the structure of the preface to the codification of statements on auditing standards, Principles Governing an Audit Conducted in Accordance with Generally Accepted Auditing Standards. This structure addresses the following areas: the purpose of an audit, personal responsibilities of the auditor, auditor actions in performing the audit, and reporting. The section numbers listed in the textbook may change when the redrafted standards are issued. The titles of the sections should remain the same.

- **AU 314,** Understanding the Entity and Its Environment and Assessing the Risks of Material Misstatements
- **AU 316,** Consideration of Fraud in a Financial Statement Audit
- **AU 318,** Performing Audit Procedures in Response to Assessed Risks and Evaluating the Audit Evidence Obtained
- **AU 333,** Written Representations and Terms of Engagement
- **QC 10,** A Firm's System of Quality Control
- **Preface to the Codification of Statements on Auditing Standards,** Overall Objectives of the Independent Auditor and the Conduct of an Audit in Accordance with Generally Accepted Auditing Standards

For public companies

- **PCAOB Auditing Standard No. 8,** Audit Risk
- **PCAOB Auditing Standard No. 9,** Audit Planning
- **PCAOB Auditing Standard No. 10,** Supervision of the Audit Engagement
- **PCAOB Auditing Standard No. 12,** Identifying and Assessing Risks of Material Misstatement
- **PCAOB Auditing Standard No. 13,** The Auditor's Responses to the Risks of Material Misstatement
- **PCAOB Auditing Standard No. 15,** Audit Evidence
- **AU 311,** Planning and Supervision
- **AU 316,** Consideration of Fraud in a Financial Statement Audit (interim standard adopted by PCAOB)
- **AU 333,** Written Representations and Terms of Engagement (interim standard adopted by PCAOB)
- **QC 10,** A Firm's System of Quality Control

International standards

- **ISA 210,** Agreeing the Terms of Audit Engagements
- **ISA 220,** Quality Control for an Audit of Financial Statements
- **ISA 240,** The Auditor's Responsibilities Relating to Fraud in an Audit of Financial Statements
- **ISA 315,** Understanding the Entity and Its Environment and Assessing the Risks of Material Misstatement
- **ISA 320,** Audit Materiality
- **ISA 330,** The Auditor's Procedures in Response to Assessed Risks

Describe the Audit Process

LO1

Describe the audit process including its planning, testing, and decision phases

The purpose of an audit is to increase the level of confidence that users of the financial statements can place in them. The level of confidence increases when an auditor, independent of the client company, expresses an opinion on whether the financial statements are prepared in accordance with the applicable financial reporting framework (generally accepted accounting principles—GAAP). An audit conducted in accordance with generally accepted auditing standards and relevant ethical requirements allows the auditor to form that opinion.

Generally accepted auditing standards require that, as an objective of the audit process, the auditor obtain *reasonable assurance* about whether the financial statements are free from *material misstatements*. The auditor obtains reasonable assurance by collecting *sufficient appropriate* audit evidence to reduce *audit risk* to an acceptably low level. **Reasonable assurance** is a high level of assurance but not absolute. A **material misstatement** is an error or fraud in the financial statements that might cause a user of them to change his or her decision about the company. **Sufficient appropriate audit**

The Audit Process	Exhibit 2-1

PLANNING PHASE

Consider the Preconditions for an Audit and Accept or Reject the Audit Engagement

Understand the Entity and Its Environment, Determine Materiality, and Assess the Risks of Material Misstatements

Develop an Audit Strategy and an Audit Plan to Respond to the Assessed Risks

TESTING PHASE

Test Internal Controls? Yes No

Perform Tests of Controls if "Yes"

Perform Substantive Tests of Transactions

Perform Substantive Tests of Balances

Assess the Likelihood of Material Misstatement

DECISION PHASE

Review the Presentation and Disclosure Assertions

Evaluate the Evidence to Determine Whether the Financial Statements Are Prepared in Accordance with the Applicable Financial Reporting Framework

Issue Audit Report

Communicate with the Audit Committee[3]

evidence refers to the quantity and quality of the evidence gathered. **Audit risk** is the risk that the auditor will fail to issue an opinion saying that the financial statements are materially misstated when they actually are. These concepts will be discussed in more detail in the chapter. The auditor bases the assessment of both "audit risk" and "sufficient appropriate evidence" on his or her professional judgment.

The audit process has three main parts: (1) planning, (2) testing, and (3) decision. This chapter discusses the planning process. Later chapters will discuss the testing process and the decision process. Exhibit 2-1 summarizes the main steps in the audit process.

Step 1: Consider the Preconditions for an Audit

LO2

Understand the preconditions for an audit

Preconditions for an Audit

To accept an audit engagement for a new or current client, the auditor must assess whether the *preconditions* for an audit are present. Auditing standards describe how an auditor determines whether the preconditions for an audit are present. The auditor (1) decides whether the financial reporting framework (the set of accounting standards) the client used to prepare the financial statements is acceptable and (2) obtains its management's agreement that it

- Acknowledges and understands its responsibility for preparing the financial statements in accordance with the financial reporting framework
- Understands its responsibility to establish internal controls so that financial statements can be prepared free of misstatement
- Agrees to provide the auditor all information that managers are aware of that might be relevant to the preparation of the financial statements and any other information the auditor may request

If the preconditions for an audit are not present, the auditor should not accept the proposed audit engagement. The auditor assesses whether the circumstances of recurring audits require the terms of the audit to be revised and whether she or he needs to remind the client of the engagement terms.

Generally accepted auditing standards require the auditor to obtain sufficient appropriate audit evidence to reduce audit risk to an acceptably low level. If the auditor

---

[3] The auditor may communicate with the audit committee at any point in the audit process when significant difficulties are encountered.

determines that he or she cannot comply with this standard due to the client's risk level before the engagement, he or she will reject the audit engagement.

Did You Know?

WPT is a U.S. company offering online poker through its website. In July 2005, Deloitte & Touche, LLP, dropped WPT Enterprises as an audit client saying that the Internet gambling client's audit risk was too high.

The U.S. Federal Wire Act passed in 1961 prohibits its citizens from placing bets over the telephone or by the Internet. Because Internet gambling is illegal in the United States, most Internet gambling companies are incorporated outside the country. WBT must follow U.S. law as a company registered in the United States on the NASDAQ stock exchange. WBT's auditor must make sure that the company does not take bets from U.S. citizens.

Source: Seren Ng, "For Audit Firms, All Bets Are Off," *The Wall Street Journal,* July 21, 2005.

The decision by Deloitte & Touche reflects an assessment that the firm would not be able to gather sufficient appropriate evidence to reduce audit risk to an acceptably low level.

When an auditor agrees to perform an audit because the preconditions for it have been met and believes that she or he can gather sufficient appropriate audit evidence to reduce audit risk to an acceptably low level, her or his firm prepares an engagement letter that includes the following:

- The objective and scope of the audit (to express an opinion on particular financial statements)
- Management's responsibilities (to prepare the financial statements, select accounting policies, establish effective internal controls, design programs to prevent and detect fraud, provide written representations, inform the auditor of subsequent events that may affect the financial statements, and make all financial records and information available to the auditor)
- The auditor's responsibilities (to conduct the audit in accordance with generally accepted auditing standards and obtain an understanding of the client's internal control)
- The inherent limitations of an audit engagement (material misstatements may not be detected)
- The basis on which fees are computed and any billing arrangements
- Arrangements regarding the planning and performance of the audit including the composition of the audit team (the partner, manager, and staff accountants assigned to the engagement)
- Arrangements concerning the involvement of other auditors and specialists in the audit
- Arrangements concerning the involvement of internal auditors and other staff of the company
- Arrangements to be made with the predecessor auditor (discussed later) in the case of an initial audit
- A request for management to acknowledge receipt of the audit engagement letter and to agree to its terms

An example of an engagement letter is found in Exhibit 2-2.

Initial Audits

There is an additional precondition for accepting an audit engagement for a new client. Before accepting a new client, the auditor should request information from the previous auditor. Because client information is confidential (according to the rules of the Code of Professional Conduct), the predecessor auditor will not respond to the request

Engagement Letter   Exhibit 2-2

May 1, 2011

Mr. Matt Hensrud, President
Music Productions
511 Burnsville Avenue
Minneapolis, MN 55411

Dear Mr. Hensrud,

[*The objective and scope of the audit*]

You have requested that we audit the financial statements of Music Productions, which comprise the balance sheet as at December 31, 2011, and the related statements of income, retained earnings, and cash flows for the year then ended. We are pleased to confirm our acceptance and our understanding of this audit engagement by means of this letter. Our audit will be conducted with the objective of our expressing an opinion on the financial statements.

[*The responsibilities of the auditor*]

We will conduct our audit in accordance with the auditing standards of The Public Company's Accounting Oversight Board [*or the Auditing Standards Board for private companies*]. Those standards require that we plan and perform the audit to obtain reasonable assurance about whether the financial statements are free of material misstatement. An audit involves performing procedures to obtain audit evidence about the amounts and disclosures in the financial statements. The procedures selected depend on the auditor's judgment, including the assessment of the risks of material misstatement of the financial statements, whether due to fraud or error. An audit also includes evaluating the appropriateness of accounting policies used and the reasonableness of accounting estimates made by management, as well as evaluating the overall presentation of the financial statements.

Because of the inherent limitations of an audit, together with those of internal control, there is an unavoidable risk that some material misstatements may not be detected, even though the audit is properly planned and performed in accordance with the auditing standards.

In making our risk assessments, we consider internal control relevant to the entity's preparation of the financial statements in order to design audit procedures that are appropriate in the circumstances but not for the purpose of expressing an opinion on the effectiveness of the entity's internal control. [*In the case of an audit for a public company, this paragraph would be modified to include the auditor's responsibility to obtain sufficient evidence to support the auditor's opinion on internal control over financial reporting.*] However, we will communicate to you in writing concerning any significant deficiencies and material weaknesses in internal control relevant to the audit of the financial statements that we have identified during the audit.

[*The responsibilities of management and identification of the applicable financial reporting framework*]

Management is responsible for the preparation and fair presentation of these financial statements in accordance with accounting principles generally accepted in the United States of America; this includes the design, implementation, and maintenance of internal control relevant to the preparation and fair presentation of consolidated financial statements that are free from material misstatement, whether due to fraud or error.

Our audit will be conducted on the basis that you acknowledge and understand that you have responsibility:

(a) For the preparation and fair presentation of the financial statements in accordance with the accounting standards of the Financial Accounting Standards Board (FASB) [*or the International Financial Reporting Standards if international accounting standards are used*]

(b) For the design, implementation, and maintenance of internal control relevant to the preparation of fair presentation of financial statements that are free from material misstatement, whether due to fraud or error

(c) To provide us with:

    i. Access to all information of which you are aware that is relevant to the preparation of the financial statements such as records, documentation, and other matters

    ii. Additional information that we may request from you for the purpose of the audit

    iii. Unrestricted access to persons within the entity from whom we determine it necessary to obtain audit evidence

As part of our audit process, we will request from you written confirmation concerning representations made to us in connection with the audit.

continued

Engagement Letter   *concluded*

[Insert other information, such as fee arrangements, billings, and other specific terms as appropriate.]

We will issue a written report upon completion of our audit of Music Productions' financial statements. Our report will be addressed to the board of directors of Music Productions. We cannot provide assurance that an unqualified opinion will be expressed. Circumstances may arise in which it is necessary for us to modify our opinion, add an emphasis of matter or other matter paragraph, or withdraw from the engagement.

We will also issue a written report on [*insert appropriate reference to other auditor's reports expected to be issued*].

Please sign and return the attached copy of this letter to indicate your acknowledgement of, and agreement with, the arrangements for our audit of the financial statements including our respective responsibilities.

Stuart and Cram, LLP

Acknowledged and agreed on behalf of Music Productions by

(signed)

_____

Name and Title
Date

---

without the client's written permission. If the client refuses to allow the new auditor to contact the predecessor auditor, the auditor should consider the implications of this refusal in deciding whether to accept the engagement. When receiving the request from the new auditor, the predecessor auditor should respond to the auditor's inquiries promptly and fully. If the response is limited due to unusual circumstances (pending litigation, disciplinary procedures), the predecessor auditor should indicate that he or she has limited the response in the reply. In the request for information from the predecessor auditor, the new auditor may ask for information about the following items:

- Management's integrity
- Disagreements with management about accounting policies or auditing procedures
- Communications to those charged with governance regarding fraud, illegal acts by clients, and internal-control-related matters
- The predecessor auditor's understanding regarding the reasons for the change of auditors

The decisions made by the auditor to accept a new audit client or to perform a recurring audit for a current audit client are summarized in Exhibit 2-3.

With a signed audit engagement letter, the auditor has a contract to perform the audit and then enters the next stage in the planning process.

The Planning Phase of The Audit Process: Step 1

Planning Phase	Completed
Step 1. Consider the preconditions for an audit and accept or reject the audit engagement	√
Step 2. Understand the entity and its environment, determine materiality, and assess the risks of material misstatements	
Step 3. Develop an audit strategy and an audit plan to respond to the assessed risks	

Precondition Decisions	Exhibit 2-3

HAVE THE PRECONDITIONS FOR AN AUDIT BEEN MET?

- Is the financial reporting framework acceptable?
- Does management acknowledge its responsibility to:
  - Prepare the financial statements according to the financial reporting framework?
  - Assume responsibility for internal controls so the financial statements are free of misstatement?
  - Provide the auditors with all information that they need and all information that they request?

- Can the auditors obtain sufficient appropriate evidence to reduce audit risk to an acceptably low level?
- For an initial audit, have the auditors contacted the predecessor auditor?

If the answer to each of these questions is "yes," the auditor can accept the audit engagement. If the answer to *any* of these questions is "no," the auditor should not accept the audit engagement. If the auditor accepts the engagement, the next step is to prepare an audit engagement letter outlining the terms of the agreement.

Step 2: Audit Engagement Planning Phase: Assess Risk

LO3

Explain how the auditor gains an understanding of the entity and its environment, determines materiality, and assesses the risk of material misstatement

Step 2 of the planning process is the risk assessment stage during which the auditor develops an understanding of the entity and the environment in which it operates, determines materiality, and assesses the risks of material misstatements. At this stage of the planning process, the auditor's objective is to *identify* and *assess* the risk of material misstatement by:

1. Gaining an understanding of the company and its environment, including its internal controls
2. Determining materiality
3. Performing procedures to assess the risk of material misstatement at the financial statement and assertion levels.

Let's discuss each of these components of the risk assessment process in more detail.

Step 2a. Understanding the Entity and Its Environment

The auditor obtains an understanding of the entity and its environment by asking the client questions about the business and becoming familiar with the industry and economic conditions by reading public information about the company (press releases or reports by analysts, for example), reading transcripts of earnings calls (**teleconferences** in which a **public company** discusses the financial results of a reporting period), obtaining an understanding of compensation arrangements with senior management, and obtaining information about trading activity in the company's securities and holdings in the company's securities by majority holders. The auditing standards require the auditor to understand:

- The entity's industry and relevant regulatory and other external factors
- The entity's nature including its operations, ownership and governance structures, types of investments made, and the way it is structured and financed
- The entity's selection and use of accounting policies, including any changes in them
- The entity's objectives and strategies and the related business risks that could lead to the risk of material misstatement
- The methods the entity uses to measure and review its financial performance

Let's consider this process to gain an understanding of a company such as General Mills, which manufactures food products and sells them to grocery stores. Some of the products it sells are breakfast cereal, flour, cake mix, and frosting. To understand a company and its environment, the auditor might determine the following, for example, about General Mills:

Industry, regulatory and other external factors relevant to the entity	General Mills is a public company, so it is subject to the regulations of the SEC and the PCAOB. Its stock is traded on the New York Stock Exchange under the trading symbol GIS. Because it is in the food industry, it is subject to laws related to the production of food. General Mills alone produces the particular brand names (Cheerios, Betty Crocker Cake Mix and Frosting, Yoplait Yogurt, Hamburger Helper, and Häagen-Dazs ice cream), but several other companies produce product brands (cornflakes and other brands of yogurt and ice cream) that compete with it. General Mills does business in the United States and in 130 markets around the worldwide.
The nature of the entity, including its operations, ownership and governance structures, types of investments made, and the way it is structured and financed	The company's worldwide headquarters is in Minneapolis, Minnesota. The transfer agent and registrar for stock is the Wells Fargo Bank in St. Paul, Minnesota. General Mills is a public company owned by its stock shareholders. The company has an audit committee. It acquired several new companies during the year and sold several others. General Mills also has several joint ventures, some of whose financial statements are consolidated with its own and some joint ventures that it records as equity investments. General Mills finances its expansion with net income generated by the company and through debt. The company is structured in operating divisions including Small Planet Foods, Baking Products, Yoplait, Pillsbury USA, Big G Cereals, International Segment, Meals, Snacks, Bakeries and Food Service. Net sales from all divisions increased in the current year.
The entity's selection and use of accounting policies, including any changes in these policies	Significant accounting policies of the company include inventory valuation in the United States at the lower of cost or market using the last in, first out (LIFO) inventory method to determine cost and inventory valuation outside the United States at the lower of cost or market using the first in, first out (FIFO) inventory method to determine cost. Land, buildings, and equipment are recorded at cost. Buildings and equipment are depreciated over their estimated useful lives using straight-line depreciation. Goodwill is tested for impairment yearly. Sales revenue is recognized when the customer accepts the shipment. Research and development expenditures are expensed in the year incurred. The local currency is used as the functional currency for foreign operations. Foreign currency is translated at year-end for all foreign operations. Assets and liabilities are translated at the year-end exchange rate. Income statement accounts are translated using an average exchange rate for the year. In the current year, the company adopted two new accounting standards, one related to recording pension costs and the other to fair value measurements.
The entity's objectives, strategies, and related business risks that could lead to the risk of material misstatement	General Mills seeks to increase its market positions in the food categories in which it competes. Its strategy in terms of product pricing is to keep its gross margin steady at 35.6% of net sales. This means that it increases a product's price when the cost to produce it increases. The company faces pressure from lower priced store brands and is concerned about losing market share because of those brands.
The methods the entity uses to measure and review its financial performance	Management of each division, which reviews that division's performance weekly, reports to upper management. Each division is expected to show growth annually. If it does not, it may be sold. Management receives performance-based compensation in the form of stock options when earnings targets are met.

Source: General Mills Annual Report, 2009.

Internal controls are part of the "environment of the client." To understand the client's environment, the auditor must understand the entity's internal controls by gaining this knowledge in conversations with the client and reviewing any client documentation that might relate to internal controls. A financial statement audit does not require the auditor to understand all of the company's control activities; however, the auditor should understand control activities required to assess the risk of material misstatement and to design audit procedures to respond to those risks. This requirement to understand internal controls relevant to the audit typically means that the auditor must understand the internal controls for the *relevant assertions* related to the *significant* or *material accounts* under audit. **Relevant assertions** are those that management makes about the company's financial statements that have a reasonable possibility of containing a material misstatement. For the internal controls identified as relevant to the audit, the auditor should understand the *design* of the controls and its *implementation.* Understanding the entity's internal controls is discussed more fully in the following chapter.

At the end of this stage of the planning process, the auditor has knowledge about the company, its internal controls, and the industry in which the company operates. The next step is to determine materiality for the company, which enables the auditor to determine the level of misstatement necessary for it to be considered material. In other words, how much can the financial statements vary from the "true" amount without causing outsiders to change their decisions about the company?

Step 2b. Determining Materiality

The determination of materiality is based on the auditor's professional judgment. Generally accepted auditing standards require him or her to "obtain *reasonable assurance* about whether the financial statements are free from *material misstatements.*" The auditing standards of the PCAOB require the auditor to determine a materiality level that is appropriate after taking into account the particular circumstances of the client, including the consideration of the company's earnings and other relevant factors. Remember that a **material misstatement** is an error or fraud in the financial statements that could cause the users of the financial statements to change their decision about the company. Auditing standards specify that misstatements are considered to be material, *individually* or in the *aggregate,* if they would cause decisions to be changed. Judgments about materiality must be made in light of the circumstances surrounding the misstatement and can be affected by the *size* or *nature* of the misstatement. After calculating materiality, the auditor uses the concept in (1) planning and performing the audit and (2) evaluating the effect of uncorrected misstatements on the financial statements in forming an opinion on the financial statements. In this chapter, we discuss the use of materiality to plan and perform the audit. A later chapter discusses the use of materiality to evaluate the effect of uncorrected misstatements on the financial statements.

In the audit planning stage, the auditor makes decisions about the size of misstatements that will be considered material. These decisions allow the auditor to determine the nature, timing, and extent of *risk assessment procedures,* to identify and assess the risk of material misstatement, and to determine the nature, timing, and extent of *audit procedures.* The materiality level determined when planning an audit does not establish an amount below which misstatements will always be evaluated as immaterial. The circumstances related to the misstatement may cause the auditor to evaluate an immaterial misstatement as material solely because of its nature. This issue is discussed in a later chapter when materiality is used to evaluate uncorrected misstatements identified during an audit to determine the audit report type to issue.

What are these misstatements that have to be judged as material or immaterial? The auditing standards list the source of several misstatements. In the planning process, the auditor assesses the *risk* that these misstatements have occurred in the financial statements. The source of misstatements includes:

- Inaccuracies in gathering or processing data used to prepare the financial statements
- Differences between the amount or classification of a financial statement item and what should have been reported under generally accepted accounting principles

Worksheet for Calculating Materiality	Exhibit 2-4

Base amount (the greater of total assets or total revenue) _____

CALCULATING MATERIALITY

Planning Materiality + Excess × Factor = Preliminary Materiality Level

Use the following table to determine the percentage and additional amount to be used to calculate materiality.

MATERIALITY TABLE

	Larger of Total Revenues or Total Assets Is				
Over	But not More Than	Planning Materiality	Factor	×	Excess More Than
$0	$30 thousand	0	+ 0.0593	×	0
30 thousand	100 thousand	1,780	+ .0312	×	30 thousand
100 thousand	300 thousand	3,960	+ .0215	×	100 thousand
300 thousand	1 million	8,260	+ .0145	×	300 thousand
1 million	3 million	18,400	+ .00995	×	1 million
3 million	10 million	38,300	+ .00674	×	3 million
10 million	30 million	85,500	+ .00461	×	10 million
30 million	100 million	178,000	+ .00312	×	30 million
100 million	300 million	396,000	+ .00215	×	100 million
300 million	1 billion	826,000	+ .00145	×	300 million
1 billion	3 billion	1,840,000	+ .000995	×	1 billion
3 billion	10 billion	3,830,000	+ .000674	×	3 billion
10 billion	30 billion	8,550,000	+ .000461	×	10 billion
30 billion	100 billion	17,800,000	+ .000312	×	30 billion
100 billion	300 billion	39,600,000	+ .000215	×	100 billion
300 billion	—	82,600,000	+ .000148	×	300 billion

Source: AICPA Audit Guide, *Audit Sampling* (New York: AICPA, 2001).

- Omissions of financial statements items
- Financial statement disclosures that are not in accordance with generally accepted accounting principles
- An incorrect accounting estimate
- The use of an accounting principle that the auditor may consider unreasonable or inappropriate.

How does the auditor determine materiality if it is a matter of professional judgment? One method the auditor might use to determine it is to calculate materiality following the guidance in the AICPA's Audit Guide, *Audit Sampling* (see Exhibit 2-4 for the worksheet included in it). Another method that an auditor might use is based on a decision rule that is a percentage of pretax income (for example, 1%) or income from operations.

Let's consider an example to see how we might use (1) the *Audit Sampling* worksheet and (2) a percentage of pretax income to calculate materiality for General Mills Inc. It reported pretax income of $1,806.1 million, net income of $1,295 million, and revenue of $13,652 million in 2008. Total assets were $19,042 million. Because total assets are higher than total revenues, we will use total assets as the base amount.

Materiality Based on the Worksheet

Base amount	$19,042 million
Calculating materiality	$12,718,362 or
8,550,000 + (.000461 × 9,042,000,000)	$12.718 million

Materiality Based on a Percentage of Pretax Income

Materiality based on 1% of pretax income	$18.061 million

Auditor Choice

The auditor must use professional judgment to choose the number that represents the level below which outsiders will not change their decisions about the company. Let's assume that the auditor believes that $12.718 million is an appropriate measure of materiality.

How Does the Auditor Use Materiality?

The auditor is responsible for planning the audit to obtain reasonable assurance that misstatements in the financial statements of more than $12.718 million **individually** or in **aggregate** will be found. After the audit, when the financial statements are released, the "true" net income for General Mills should be $1,295 million plus or minus $12.718 million (a net income between $1,308 million and $1,282 million). If the reported income of $1,295 million is *materially correct,* financial statement users who know that net income was between $1,308 million and $1,282 million would not change their decisions about the company. The process just discussed is often referred to as *determining materiality for the financial statements as a whole.*

The auditor can also determine materiality for individual accounts in the financial statements if she or he believes that *misstatements of particular items* on the financial statements in lower amounts than the materiality level could influence the decision of financial statement users. This is referred to as *determining materiality for particular items on the financial statements.* When the auditor assigns a portion of the materiality to individual accounts, we refer to this amount as the *tolerable misstatement* (according to the PCAOB auditing standards) or *performance materiality* (according to the ASB and IAASB auditing standards) for the account, which is defined as the maximum misstatement in the account that the auditor is willing to accept. Accounting firms often use 50–75% of materiality as the tolerable misstatement for the individual accounts in the financial statements. Assuming that they use 75%, the tolerable misstatement for accounts receivable would be determined to be 75% of the materiality amount. This method of assigning materiality is useful because it would be possible for the overall financial statements to be materially correct but one account to contain 100% of the misstatement. This one account could be important to a certain group of outsiders, and if they rely on the information in the account, they could make decisions about the financial statements that would differ from the ones they would make had they known the amount of the account's misstatement.

The accounts receivable balance for General Mills was $1,081.6 million in 2008. If the auditor used 75% of materiality as the tolerable misstatement, then $9.539 million (75% × 12.718) is the tolerable misstatement for accounts receivable. If the reported accounts receivable balance of $1,081.6 million is *materially correct,* financial statement users would not change their decisions if they knew that the accounts receivable balance was $1,072.1 million or $1,091.1 million.

Did You Know?

Enron reported income of $88 million in 1997. During the audit, it declined to make certain audit adjustments proposed by its auditor Arthur Andersen. Arthur Andersen had determined that the audit adjustments were immaterial and did not force Enron to record the adjustments to receive an unqualified opinion. In 1997, these audit adjustments added up to nearly half of Enron's net income.

An outside reader of the financial statements might ask whether Arthur Andersen made the correct decision about the "materiality" of the audit adjustments. If outside readers of the financial statements had known that net income was really $44 million rather than $88 million, would they have changed their decisions regarding the company? Do outside readers really not care if net income is recorded at twice the correct amount?

Source: "A Chronology of Enron's Woes," *The Wall Street Journal,* October 3, 2002.

> *How did the auditor use professional judgment to determine that misstatements equal to 50% of net income were not material?*

Step 2c. Designing Procedures to Assess the Risk of Material Misstatement

How does the auditor gather the information needed to assess the risk of material misstatements for a company? The auditor designs a risk assessment process that he or she believes will be effective in assessing the risk of material misstatement for the entity. According to auditing standards, this process should include:

- Making inquiries of management about the risk of material misstatement due to errors or fraud
- Performing analytical procedures
- Observing and inspecting

The audit engagement team is required during the planning phase of the audit to *discuss* the susceptibility of the entity's financial statements to material misstatement. The purpose is to allow members of the team to gain a better understanding of the potential for material misstatement in the audit areas assigned to them. This discussion must be documented in the audit work papers. *Work papers* or *working papers* are the written record of the evidence gathered by the auditor. For public companies, the discussion among engagement team members must include a discussion of the risk of fraud. The specific fraud procedures required during an engagement are discussed in a later chapter. The three steps that are required to be included in the risk assessment process are discussed in more detail next.

The Risk Assessment Process: Inquiries of Management and Other Company Employees

Much of the information regarding the risk of material misstatement in the company is obtained from management. However, the auditor may find it useful to talk to employees at different levels of authority to make this assessment and to plan the audit. For example, the auditor may make inquiries of individuals charged with corporate governance in the company (the audit committee). Internal audit personnel may be useful in identifying the company's material misstatement risks because these employees are typically testing internal controls in financial statement areas with high risk. The in-house legal counsel may be able to provide the auditor evidence regarding the risk of litigation, compliance with laws and regulations, arrangements with business partners, and knowledge of fraud in the company. Employees involved in initiating, processing, or authorizing complex or unusual transactions may be helpful in determining the appropriateness of accounting policies. Marketing and sales personnel may provide useful information on changes in marketing strategies or sales trends.

The Risk Assessment Process: Analytical Procedures

The auditor performs analytical procedures during the audit planning stage to increase his or her understanding of the business. Calculating financial ratios and comparing the financial statement numbers for the current year with those of the prior year will help to identify any unexpected changes. The auditor is required to gather evidence to corroborate management's explanations regarding unexpected changes. Analytical procedures are part of the planning process because they allow the auditor to identify areas of concern in which the risk of material misstatement might be present.

An auditor has limited time to perform an audit. For this reason, identifying financial statement accounts that have a high risk of being materially misstated as quickly as possible is important to allow the auditor to gather evidence more efficiently during the audit process. Therefore, performing analytical procedures is an important part of the planning process. When beginning the audit with some expectation as to client performance, the auditor may believe that sales revenue should have increased because the client expanded into new markets or that collections on accounts receivable should have been slower because of general economic conditions. Performing analytical procedures during the planning process allows the auditor to identify areas where client performance is inconsistent with the auditor's expectations. These expectations allow the auditor to develop an audit program to gather evidence regarding financial statement areas that are most likely to be materially misstated.

The Risk Assessment Process: Observation and Inspection

Observation and inspection may provide the auditor useful information to support the data obtained from management and other employees related to the risk of material misstatement. The auditor might observe or inspect the entity's operations, documents, records and internal control manuals, reports prepared by management, and plant and office facilities.

How Does the Auditor Use the Information from the Risk Assessment Procedures?

The auditor is not expected only to determine the risk of material misstatement during an audit but also to design audit procedures to reduce this risk to an acceptably low level. This risk assessment process requires two steps: an assessment and then a response.

Step 1	Step 2
The auditor performs risk assessment procedures.	The auditor modifies the audit procedures to control the risk of material misstatement to an acceptably low level.

We know what the word *material* means in the audit context, but what is a misstatement? A *misstatement* is either an error (an unintentional mistake) or fraud (an intentional mistake) in the financial statements. The word is used to refer to both. Some misstatements are material and some are too small to be material. When a misstatement is *material,* knowing about it would cause an outsider to change her or his decision regarding the company.

To identify the risk of a material misstatement, the auditor considers material misstatements at **both** (1) the financial statement level and (2) the relevant assertion level. A *material misstatement at the financial statement level* has the potential to affect many assertions or many accounts in the financial statements. Management that is incompetent could cause a misstatement at the financial statement level that could be material. A *material misstatement at the relevant assertion level* involves a declaration (for example, existence or completeness) for a class of transactions or account balances that has the potential to affect whether the financial statements are materially misstated. For example, existence is often a relevant assertion for revenue. If the revenue recorded by the company does not exist, the financial statements are likely to be materially misstated.

When handing the financial statements to the auditor, the audit client makes assertions about the financial statements including the following:

Management's Assertions

Existence or **occurrence**—for both classes of transactions (e.g., income statement accounts) and account balances (e.g., balance sheet accounts)

Completeness—for both classes of transactions and account balances

Valuation and allocation—for account balances

Rights and obligations—for account balances

Accuracy—for classes of transactions

Cutoff—for classes of transactions

As an example, consider management's assertions related to sales revenue and accounts receivable:

- Transactions recorded as sales revenue are valid transactions (they occurred).
- The accounts receivable amount at year-end is valid (it exists).
- All transactions related to sales revenue and accounts receivable have been recorded (completeness).
- Accounts receivable is valued correctly at year-end (according to the applicable financial reporting framework).
- The company has the right to collect the accounts receivable (rights).
- Sales revenue has been accurately recorded (accuracy).
- Cutoff for sales revenue is correct (cutoff).

The relevant assertions for these accounts are those related to the income statement or balance sheet accounts where management's declarations must be materially correct if the auditor is to say that the financial statements are materially correct. For example, existence is often a relevant assertion for sales revenue. Existence and valuation are often relevant assertions for accounts receivable. If sales are not valid (they do not exist), the financial statements will be materially misstated. Completeness could be a relevant assertion for an audit client that had trouble recording sales revenue. However, clients with such problems do not stay in business for very long, so completeness is usually not a relevant assertion for sale revenue and accounts receivable.

The information gathered from step 2 of the planning process allows the auditor to develop an audit strategy and an audit plan in step 3 to respond to the risks of material misstatement.

Did You Know?

OfficeMax, the third largest office supply store in the United States, restated its earnings for the first three quarters of 2004 because of problems related to its employees' fabrication of vendor payments. The retail world uses vendor payments extensively as a marketing tool. Companies pay a fee and receive better shelf space or advertisements showing their products. OfficeMax employees had generated false supporting documents for several million dollars billed to a vendor. OfficeMax estimated that income had been overstated by $4 to $6 million for the three quarters.

The nature of vendor payments makes them susceptible to fraud. When companies need to make quarterly revenue targets set by management or Wall Street analysts, they ask a supplier to give them a vendor allowance at that time for something they will buy in the future, allowing the company to meet its target revenue for the quarter. The vendor allowances are recorded as revenue at the end of the quarter, even though the inventory purchase will not be made until the following quarter, thus allowing the company to meet revenue targets for the quarter.

With a client in an industry that uses vendor payments, an auditor might increase the amount of evidence gathered for the existence assertion of the revenue cycle indicating an increased level of risk associated with these payments.

Source: David Armstrong, "OfficeMax CEO Resigns; Results to be Restated," *The Wall Street Journal,* February 15, 2005.

Why would a company recognize a reduction in cost of goods sold as sales revenue?

Planning Phase of the Audit Process: Step 2

Planning Phase	Completed
Step 1. Consider the preconditions for an audit and accept or reject the audit engagement	√
Step 2. Understand the entity and its environment, determine materiality, and assess the risks of material misstatements	√
Step 3. Develop an audit strategy and an audit plan to respond to the assessed risks	

Step 3: Audit Engagement Planning Phase: Develop an Audit Strategy and Audit Plan

The auditor determines the overall audit strategy for the audit during the planning process, which establishes its scope, timing, and direction and guides the auditor when preparing the plan. After determining the audit strategy for the engagement, the auditor can decide how many staff to appoint to it and how to use specific staff members by identifying specific audit areas to which to assign more experienced team members or specialists. The auditor also can determine whether to assign the staff at an interim stage of the audit (before year-end) or at year-end. See the following for some factors the auditor may consider in developing the overall audit strategy.

Factors to consider when establishing audit strategy follow:

- **Characteristics of the audit engagement,** such as the financial reporting framework, industry-specific reporting requirements, the number and locations of the components of the business to be audited, the need for statutory or regulatory audit requirements, the availability of internal auditors' work, whether the entity uses a service organization to process transactions, the effect of information technology on audit procedures, and the availability of client personnel and data.

- **Reporting objectives, timing of the audit, and nature of communications,** such as identifying the entity's timetable for reporting, including interim period reports; scheduling meetings with management to discuss the nature, timing, and extent of audit work and the expected type and due dates of reports to be issued and other communications including management letters and communications to those charged with governance; and determining whether any communications with third parties including statutory or contractual reporting responsibilities are needed.

- **Preliminary engagement activities, knowledge gained on other engagements, and other significant factors,** such as determining materiality for planning purposes; identifying areas that might have a high risk of material misstatement; identifying the impact of the assessed risk of material misstatement at the overall financial statement level on direction, supervision, and review; choosing the way the auditor will stress the need to maintain a questioning mind and exercise professional skepticism in gathering and evaluating evidence; reviewing the results of previous audits involving the effectiveness of internal controls and identified weaknesses; obtaining evidence of management's commitment to maintaining sound internal controls; determining the volume of transactions in the company; and identifying significant business developments (including changes to information technology; to the business processes; in key management positions; in acquisitions, mergers, and divestments involving the company; in industry regulations or reporting requirements; in the financial reporting framework including accounting standards; and in the legal environment affecting the entity).

- **Nature, timing, and extent of resources,** such as the selection of the engagement team and the assignment of work to members, determining the appropriate amount of supervision for the members, designing elements of unpredictability when selecting auditing procedures, and budgeting time to use for areas with high risks of material misstatement.

The auditor should document in the form of a memorandum the audit strategy containing the key decisions about its scope, timing, and conduct. This documentation includes a list of the key decisions necessary to plan the audit and to communicate the planning process to engagement team members. The documentation is a required part of the work papers.

The next task facing the auditor is to develop an audit plan that responds to the possible risks of material misstatement identified during steps 1 and 2 of the audit process. Auditing standards require the auditor to develop an audit plan that includes the following elements:

- The nature, timing, and extent of *planned* risk assessment procedures for identifying the risk of material misstatement at the financial statement and assertion level
- The nature, timing, and extent of audit *procedures* for responding to the assessed risks of material misstatement at the relevant assertion level
- Other necessary audit procedures to allow the auditor to comply with generally accepted auditing standards

The auditor is expected to revise the audit plan as needed during the audit. During the planning process, the auditor also considers the nature, timing, and extent of supervision needed for audit team members and plans for reviewing their work. The engagement partner is responsible for proper supervision of the work of the engagement team. While supervising the engagement team, the partner should: (1) inform the engagement team members of their responsibilities, (2) tell team members to bring significant accounting and auditing issues to the attention of the engagement partner, and (3) review the work of engagement team members to evaluate whether the work was performed and documented and to determine whether the results of the evidence support the conclusions reached.

A plan can be developed to address the important issues identified in the audit strategy after it has been completed. The audit plan, which is more detailed than the audit strategy, lists specific procedures that depend on the outcome of the risk assessment procedures. The audit plan's documentation is a record of the nature, timing, and extent of risk assessment procedures and additional audit procedures at the relevant assertion level in response to the assessed risks. For this documentation, which must be a part of the working papers, the auditor may use standard audit programs or audit completion checklists.

Changes to either the audit strategy or the audit plan that occur during the audit must also be documented in the work papers. This documentation should explain why the change was made.

See Exhibit 2-5 for an example of an audit program for the accounts receivable balance in the revenue business process. Some audit programs used for an engagement include standard audit procedures performed on all engagements and others that are tailored to the specific risks identified during the planning process. Additional examples of audit programs are presented in the business process chapters. The audit program documentation, which describes the evidence to be gathered during the audit process, demonstrates to an outside reviewer that the audit was planned and that the audit program is consistent with the risks of material misstatement identified during the planning stage. From a review of this program and the evidence gathered while following the program, an outsider can determine the audit process the auditor used to gather evidence to support the report issued.

Reduction of Audit Risk to an Acceptably Low Level

LO5

Understand how the auditor reduces audit risk to an acceptably low level

At the end of the audit planning stage, the auditor has identified an audit strategy and prepared an audit plan to respond to the risks of material misstatement that were identified during the process. The audit plan will be followed for gathering sufficient appropriate evidence to reduce audit risk to an acceptable level. Let's consider audit risk now and what might be an "acceptably low" level of it.

The auditing standards define *audit risk* as the possibility that the auditor will express an inappropriate audit opinion when the financial statements are materially misstated. An inappropriate audit opinion issued when the financial statements are materially misstated would be an *unqualified audit opinion*. Therefore, audit risk is the risk that the auditor will issue an unqualified opinion when the financial statements are materially misstated. Audit risk does not include the possibility that the auditor will issue a qualified opinion when the financial statements are not materially misstated. It is assumed that the auditor who issues a qualified audit opinion does so only when it is appropriate and after gathering additional audit evidence.

Audit Program for Substantive Testing of Accounts Receivable

Exhibit 2-5

Audit Procedures	Working Paper Reference	Completed by	Date

1. Compare accounts receivable balances with expected amounts and investigate any significant deviations.

2. Obtain the year-end aged accounts receivable trial balance and
   a. Foot the trial balance and check that the total agrees with the general ledger.
   b. Randomly select 36 accounts from the aged trial balance that alphabetically lists accounts receivable with outstanding balances and displays one balance for every account by age. Check whether the information from the aged trial balance agrees with the original sales invoice and the shipping document. Determine that the sales invoice was properly aged and that the quantity billed for equals the quantity shipped.

3. Select a sample of 24 accounts receivable from the aged trial balance for external confirmation. Send positive confirmations to the customer accounts.
   a. For all customer account responses with exceptions, follow up on the cause of the error.
   b. For all nonresponses, examine subsequent cash receipts or supporting documents.
   c. Summarize the results of the confirmation process.

4. Test sales cutoff by identifying the last shipping document for the year. Trace entries in the (1) sales journal and (2) the shipping reports for 5 days before and 5 days after year-end to determine that they were recorded in the correct time period.

5. Review accounts written off during the period and determine that significant ones have been properly authorized.

6. Test the reasonableness of the allowance for uncollectible accounts by doing the following:
   a. Review the percentage of debts actually written off in the last 2 years to evaluate whether the current year's allowance is reasonable.
   b. For any large account that is more than 90 days past due, test for subsequent cash receipts.
   c. Compare the current year financial ratios to those of the prior year, specifically:
      • Number of days outstanding in receivables
      • Accounts receivable turnover ratio
      • Write-offs as a percentage of sales
      • Bad debt expense as a percentage of sales.

7. Document the conclusions as to whether the accounts are prepared in accordance with the applicable financial reporting framework

Did You Know?

The SEC fined Gemstar-TV Guide International $10 million for overstating its revenue by $250 million from 1999 through 2002. Gemstar improperly recorded revenue for expired, disputed, or nonexistent contracts, accelerated the recognition of revenue under long-term agreements, used swap transactions to generate revenue by which Gemstar paid money to a third party who used the funds to buy advertising from Gemstar, and improperly reported advertising revenue based on nonmonetary and barter transactions.

KPMG LLP, auditor for Gemstar, was censured for engaging in "improper professional conduct" in connection with its audit work for Gemstar. The SEC stated that KPMG allowed Gemstar to record revenue in the absence of customer agreements. According to the SEC, KPMG relied on statements made by company executives about Gemstar's sales rather than gathering evidence to support the company statements.

KPMG failed to gather sufficient appropriate evidence to keep audit risk to an acceptably low level. This failure led to the issuance of a clean opinion when the financial statements were materially misstated.

Source: Jonathan Weil, "KPMG Is Censured in Gemstar Matter," *The Wall Street Journal,* October 21, 2004; U.S. Securities and Exchange Commission, Press Release 2004–86, June 23, 2004.

Why did the auditor fail to control audit risk for this audit?

Audit risk is a function of two types of risk: (1) material misstatement and (2) detection; the latter is the risk that substantive audit procedures will fail to detect misstatements in the financial statements. Material misstatement risk of is a function of two risks, inherent risk and control risk, although some auditors consider them to be separate risks. *Inherent risk* is the susceptibility of management assertions to a material misstatement assuming no internal controls, and *control risk* is the possibility that internal controls will fail to prevent or detect misstatements in the financial statements. Based on professional judgment, auditors will assess the two risks together as the risk of material misstatement. The risk of material misstatement is combined with detection risk to determine audit risk, the risk of issuing a clean opinion when the financial statements are materially misstated.

The Audit Risk Model:

$$\text{Audit Risk} = \text{Risk of Material Misstatement} \times \text{Detection Risk}$$
$$\text{Audit Risk} = \text{Inherent Risk} \times \text{Control Risk} \times \text{Detection Risk}$$

The only risks that the auditor controls are audit risk and detection risk. In the planning process, she or he must correctly *assess* the risk of material misstatement (inherent risk and control risk) and then *determine* the amount of detection risk needed to keep audit risk to an acceptably low level. The auditor controls detection risk by determining the amount of substantive testing to perform.

The risk of material misstatement must be considered at two levels: the overall financial statement level and the individual assertion level for classes of transactions, account balances, and disclosures.

Auditing standards require the auditor to obtain sufficient appropriate audit evidence to reduce audit risk to an acceptably low level. This enables him or her to determine the audit opinion to be issued. Auditing standards do not define "acceptably low level," so the auditor sets this level based on professional judgment. Business writers believe that audit risk typically is set at about 5%.

Did You Know?

The firm of Deloitte and Touche, LLP, was censured in April 2005 for the failed audit of Just for Feet, a Birmingham, Alabama, shoe store. Just for Feet issued fraudulent financial statements by recognizing fictitious revenue from its vendors and by failing to write off worthless inventory. The SEC noted that Deloitte's National Risk Management Program had identified Just for Feet as a high-risk client, but the firm failed to perform audit procedures suggested by this designation.

Source: U. S. Securities and Exchange Commission 2005–66, "SEC Charges Deloitte & Touche and Two of its Personnel for Failure in the Audit of Just for Feet," April 26, 2005.

Why did Deloitte & Touche fail to gather evidence in accordance with its risk assessment for the client?

Auditing firms use similar levels of audit risk for comparable clients. Audit risk determines the amount of evidence to be gathered, and this amount determines the audit fees. If auditing firms use different levels of audit risk, the fees they would charge would not be comparable to other firm' fees. The audit firm with the highest level of audit risk (for example, 15% rather than 5%) would charge the lowest fee and gain all the business.

At an audit risk of 5%, the auditor issues the correct opinion 95 times out of 100. With a correct opinion, the auditor says the financial statements have been prepared in accordance with the applicable financial reporting framework and is correct in that assessment. Five times out of 100, the auditor says the financial statements have been prepared in accordance with the applicable financial reporting framework and is incorrect in the assessment. Auditors are willing to live with being wrong 5 times out of 100 because reducing audit risk to less than 5% would require more substantive testing and higher audit fees. Unless the public decides to pay to lower audit risk, it is not likely to happen.

Applying the Audit Risk Model

The auditor uses the audit risk model to control the level of risk assumed in issuing an audit opinion by controlling the amount of substantive testing (to determine detection risk) performed in the audit. The amount of audit risk is determined by three factors: inherent risk, control risk, and detection risk, which are discussed next.

In an accounting business process, *inherent risk* refers to the susceptibility of management assertions to a material misstatement assuming no internal controls. The auditor *assesses* inherent risk for relevant assertions for each account and disclosure based on professional judgment. The auditor does not gather evidence to support her or his assessment of inherent risk but bases it on her or his knowledge about the client's industry and business operations.

Control risk is the possibility that internal controls will fail to prevent or detect misstatements in the financial statements. During a financial statement audit, auditors make a preliminary assessment of control risk for relevant assertions for significant accounts in a business process based on their understanding of the internal control system. If control risk is less than 100%, this *assessment must be supported by evidence* (tests of internal controls). Auditors may assess control risk as maximum, high, medium, or low, and if it is maximum, they will not test controls. When the control risk is maximum (1.0), the auditors gather evidence using substantive tests. Some control risk will always exist because of the limitations of internal controls.

Detection risk is the risk that substantive audit procedures will fail to detect misstatements in the financial statements. Gathering substantive audit evidence to determine whether there are misstatements in the financial statements controls for this risk. It is calculated for relevant assertions for each business process and should be related to the risk of material misstatements. The higher the risk of material misstatement for the relevant assertion in the business process, the lower is the level of detection risk that the auditor will accept.

Detection risk is related to the auditor's procedures and can be changed at his or her discretion. Control risk and inherent risk exist independently of the audit. The auditor *assesses* the risk of material misstatement (control risk and inherent risk) and then *changes* detection risk to keep audit risk to an acceptable level.

Controlling Audit Risk

The audit risk model can be stated in two forms. The first form describes the relationship between audit risk, material misstatement risk (control risk and inherent risk), and detection risk. In this model, audit risk is equal to the risk of material misstatement (control risk times inherent risk) multiplied by the detection risk. According to the model, the risk of issuing a clean opinion when the financial statements are materially misstated is equal to the risk that the account balances or class of transactions include a misstatement multiplied by the risk that substantive audit procedures fail to detect misstatements in the financial statements.

$$AR = MMR \times DR \qquad or \qquad AR = CR \times IR \times DR$$

where
   DR = detection risk
   AR = audit risk
   CR = control risk
   IR = inherent risk
MMR = material misstatement risk

The terms of the audit risk model are rearranged to calculate detection risk. Because it is the only risk the auditor controls, this form of the model is useful because it allows the auditor to determine the level of detection risk needed to keep audit risk at an acceptably low level. Using the previous terms,

$$DR = AR/MMR \qquad or \qquad DR = AR/(CR \times IR)$$

This second form of the model says that the risk that substantive audit procedures will fail to detect misstatements in the financial statements is equal to the risk of issuing a clean opinion when the financial statements are materially misstated divided by the risk of a material misstatement.

Audit risk should be considered at both the overall financial statement level and the individual account balance, class of transactions, or disclosure levels. It is controlled for by gathering sufficient appropriate evidence to keep audit risk to an acceptably low level.

The audit risk model is a *theoretical* model designed to guide the auditor's decision processes to control the risk of issuing the wrong opinion. It could be used as an equation to calculate detection risk, but it is probably more useful to think of the model as expressing *relationships* among the risks included in the model.

Some of these relationships include:

- A *higher risk of material misstatement* will result in a *lower* detection risk. A lower detection risk means that the auditor will gather *more substantive* evidence.

- A *lower risk of material misstatement* will result in a *higher* detection risk; the auditor will gather *less substantive* evidence.

- Substantive testing is always performed for relevant assertions for each significant account balance, class of transaction or disclosure because the risk of material misstatement will never be zero. Detection risk determines how much substantive testing is to be done.

- A *lower* detection risk means that more substantive testing will be done.

- A *higher* detection risk means that less substantive testing will be done.

- In the model, audit risk is a constant number for the level of audit risk that should remain at the audit's end, usually 5%. When the auditor uses this theoretical model, the goal is to gather sufficient appropriate evidence to keep audit risk at an acceptably low level.

Did You Know?

In April 2005, Deloitte & Touche, LLP, agreed to pay $50 million to settle SEC charges that it had failed to find fraud at Adelphia, the fifth largest cable company in the United States. The fine is the largest the SEC has levied against a public accounting firm. In its settlement statement, the SEC indicated that the audit firm had engaged in unprofessional conduct because it failed to implement audit procedures to allow it to detect illegal acts at Adelphia. Deloitte & Touche had identified Adelphia as one of its riskiest clients but had failed to design audit procedures to appropriately address the company's level of risk. Deloitte issued an unqualified opinion for Adelphia for fiscal 2000 when it should have known that Adelphia had failed to record or disclose $1.6 billion of debt on its balance sheet, failed to disclose significant related-party transactions, and overstated stockholders' equity by $375 million.

Sources: U.S. Securities and Exchange Commission, Press Release 2005–65, April 26, 2005; Deborah Solomon, "Deloitte Statement about Adelphia Raises SEC's Ire," *The Wall Street Journal,* April 27, 2005.

Why did the auditor fail to design audit procedures consistent with the level of Adelphia's risk?

Quality Control Measures That Accounting Firms Use

LO6

Explain the systems of quality control for accounting firms

To ensure that audits are done in accordance with generally accepted auditing standards, accounting firms often establish quality control measures that must be in place during the planning phase.

When an accounting firm establishes a system of quality control, its objective is to obtain reasonable assurance that (1) the firm complies with professional standards and applicable legal and regulatory requirements and (2) the reports it issues are appropriate in the circumstances.

Quality Control Elements of the Accounting Firm

The system of quality control an accounting firm establishes should address the following elements:

- Leadership responsibilities for quality within the firm
- Relevant ethical requirements
- Acceptance and continuance of client relationships and specific engagements
- Human resources
- Engagement performance
- Monitoring process and procedures
- Documentation

The accounting firm is expected to document its policies and procedures and communicate them to the firm's personnel. Each of these factors is discussed next in more detail.

Leadership Responsibilities for Quality

The policies and procedures established by the audit firm should be designed to promote an internal culture based on the recognition that quality is essential in performing audit engagements. The firm's leadership (the managing partner or the chief executive officer) should assume responsibility for the firm's quality control system.

Relevant Ethical Requirements

The audit firm should establish policies and procedures designed to provide reasonable assurance that it complies with relevant ethical requirements for an audit. These procedures include the fundamental principles of the professional ethics codes and the independence requirements described in the auditing standards. At least yearly, the firm should obtain written confirmation of compliance with its policies and procedures on independence from all firm members required to be independent.

Acceptance and Continuance of Client Relationships and Specific Engagements

The audit firm should establish policies and procedures for the acceptance and continuance of client relationships that are designed to provide the firm the assurance that it will undertake engagements only when it (1) is competent to perform the engagement and has the time and resources to do so, (2) can comply with legal and ethical requirements for the audit, and (3) has considered the client's integrity and does not have information that would lead the firm to believe that the client lacks integrity.

Human Resources

The audit firm should establish policies and procedures designed to ensure that it has sufficient personnel with the competence, capabilities, and commitment to ethical principles necessary to perform engagements in accordance with professional standards and legal and regulatory requirements and to enable the firm to issue reports that are appropriate in the circumstances. The firm's policies should also require that individuals selected for promotion have the qualifications necessary to fulfill the responsibilities of the new job.

Engagement Performance

The audit firm should establish policies and procedures designed to ensure that engagements are performed in accordance with professional standards and legal and regulatory requirements and that the firm issues reports that are appropriate for specific circumstances. These policies should include matters relevant to promoting consistency in the quality of engagement performance as well as supervision and review responsibilities. The firm should establish policies to ensure that consultation regarding difficult or contentious issues occurs.

Monitoring Process and Procedures

The audit firm should establish a monitoring process and procedures to ensure that the policies relating to the quality control system are relevant, adequate, and operating effectively. The monitoring process should include a review of engagement documentation, reports, and selected clients' financial statements to determine the quality control system's effectiveness, and any deficiencies in it should be identified and appropriately remedied.

Documentation

The firm should establish policies and procedures requiring appropriate documentation to provide evidence that each element of the quality control system is performing as intended.

Planning Phase of the Audit Process: Step 3

Planning Phase	Completed
Step 1. Consider the preconditions for an audit and accept or reject the audit engagement	√
Step 2. Understand the entity and its environment, determine materiality, and assess the risks of material misstatements	√
Step 3. Develop an audit strategy and an audit plan to respond to the assessed risks	√

At this stage of the audit, the planning process is complete. The next chapter focuses on internal controls.

Chapter Takeaways

This chapter has discussed how the auditor should plan the audit in order to gather sufficient appropriate evidence to reduce audit risk to an acceptably low level. To do this, the auditor must understand the client and the environment in which it operates. The auditor also must correctly assess the risk of material misstatement at both the financial statement and assertion levels and then design an audit plan that is consistent with those risks.

This chapter presented these important facts:

- The process the auditor uses to plan an audit
- The definitions of *audit risk, control risk, inherent risk,* and *detection risk* and how these terms are used in the *audit process* to control the risk of issuing the wrong opinion
- The definition of *materiality* and how the auditor uses it to plan the audit.

Be sure that you understand these concepts before you go on to the next chapter.

Review Questions

LO1   1. What is the purpose of an audit?

LO1   2. Describe the phases in the audit process including the steps in each phase.

LO2   3. What is the purpose of the engagement letter? How does it benefit both the auditor and the client's management?

LO6   4. Describe the quality control measures the audit firm uses to ensure that the audit process corresponds to professional standards.

LO3   5. How does the auditor gain an understanding of the audit client and its environment?

LO3   6. The auditing standards require the auditor to determine materiality. How does the auditor do this?

LO3   7. What is the risk of material misstatement in the financial statements? How should the auditor respond to this risk?

LO4   8. How do *audit strategy* and *audit plan* differ? How are both related to the assessed risk of material misstatement?

LO5   9. What is *audit risk?* Explain how the auditor reduces it to an "acceptably low level."

Multiple Choice Questions from CPA Examinations

LO1   10. During the initial planning phase of an audit, a CPA most likely would
   a. Identify specific internal control activities that are likely to prevent fraud.
   b. Evaluate the reasonableness of the client's accounting estimates.
   c. Discuss the timing of the audit procedures with the client's management.
   d. Inquire of the client's attorney as to whether any unrecorded claims are probably of assertion.

LO4   11. When planning an audit, an auditor should
   a. Consider whether substantive tests may be reduced based on the results of the internal control documentation.
   b. Make preliminary judgments about materiality levels for audit purposes.
   c. Conclude whether changes in compliance with prescribed controls require a change in the assessed level of control risk.
   d. Prepare a preliminary draft of the management representation letter.

LO3   12. An auditor obtains knowledge about a new client's business and its industry to
   a. Make constructive suggestions concerning improvements to the client's internal control.
   b. Develop an attitude of professional skepticism concerning management's financial statement assertions.
   c. Evaluate whether the aggregation of known misstatements causes the financial statements taken as a whole to be materially misstated.
   d. Understand the events and transactions that may have an effect on the client's financial statements.

LO5   13. The existence of audit risk is recognized by the statement in the auditor's standard report that the
   a. Auditor is responsible for expressing an opinion on the financial statements, which are the responsibility of management.
   b. Financial statements are presented fairly, in all material respects, in accordance with the financial reporting framework.
   c. Audit includes examining, on a test basis, evidence supporting the amounts and disclosures in the financial statements.
   d. Auditor obtains reasonable assurance about whether the financial statements are free of material misstatement.

LO5   14. The risk that an auditor's procedures will lead to the conclusion that a material misstatement does not exist in an account balance or class of transactions when, in fact, such misstatement does exist is
   a. Audit risk.
   b. Inherent risk.
   c. Control risk.
   d. Detection risk.

LO5   15. Inherent risk and control risk differ from detection risk in that they
   a. Arise from the misapplication of auditing procedures.
   b. May be assessed in either quantitative or nonquantitative terms.
   c. Exist independently of the financial statement audit.
   d. Can be changed at the auditor's discretion.

LO5   16. As the acceptable level of detection risk decreases, an auditor may
   a. Reduce substantive testing by relying on the assessments of inherent risk and control risk.
   b. Postpone the planned timing of substantive tests from interim dates to the year-end.
   c. Eliminate the assessed level of inherent risk from consideration as a planning factor.
   d. Lower the assessed level of control risk from the maximum level to below the maximum.

LO5   17. As the acceptable level of detection risk decreases, an auditor may change the
   a. Timing of substantive tests by performing them at an interim date rather than at year-end.
   b. Nature of substantive tests from a less effective to a more effective procedure.
   c. Timing of tests of controls by performing them at several dates rather than at one time.
   d. Assessed level of inherent risk to a higher amount.

LO5   18. Which of the following audit risk components may be assessed in nonquantitative terms?

	Control Risk	Detection Risk	Inherent Risk
a.	Yes	Yes	Yes
b.	No	Yes	Yes
c.	Yes	Yes	No
d.	Yes	No	Yes

Discussion Questions and Research Problems

LO4   19. **Using the audit risk model to plan the audit.** You are in charge of planning the audit for BCS, Inc., and will use the audit risk model to plan the internal control testing and the substantive testing for the client.
  a. If inherent risk is assessed at 0.5 for the purchase cycle and internal control risk is assessed at 0.3, what is detection risk? Assume that audit risk = 0.05.
  b. What evidence would you gather to support the assessment of inherent risk and control risk?
  c. Assume that you determine that control risk is 0.5 instead of 0.3 after your internal control testing.
    (1) Calculate the new detection risk.
    (2) In this situation, will you perform more or less substantive test work than when the control risk was assessed at 0.3? Explain your answer using the audit risk model.
    (3) In general, will you perform more or less internal control test work when control risk is 0.3 than when control risk is 0.50
  d. If you decrease control risk from 0.7 to 0.5, will you do more or less internal control testing? More or less substantive testing? Explain your answer using the audit risk model.
  e. Does the auditor control inherent risk, control risk, detection risk, or audit risk? Explain your answer.
  f. What is audit risk? Does it differ from one client to another client? Explain your answer.
  g. How does the auditor control audit risk? Explain why it is important to keep audit risk to an acceptably low level? What is an acceptably low level?

LO3   20. **Materiality and audit opinions.** Describe how materiality is used in (1) planning and performing the audit and (2) evaluating evidence gathered during the audit process.
  a. Provide an example describing how materiality might be used in planning and performing the audit.
  b. Provide an example describing how materiality might be used in evaluating the results of test work in the audit of the revenue business process.
  c. Should an auditor issue an unqualified opinion if the evidence gathered during the audit indicates that the dollar amount of misstatement in the financial statements is material? Explain your answer. What should the auditor do in this situation?
  d. Can an auditor issue an unqualified opinion gathering only internal control evidence for some business processes? Explain your answer.
  e. Can an auditor issue an unqualified opinion after gathering only substantive evidence for some business processes? Explain your answer.
  f. Can an auditor issue an unqualified opinion based on a combination of internal control and substantive testing? How does the auditor combine the results from internal control testing and substantive testing to keep audit risk to an acceptably low level?

LO3   21. **Calculating materiality.** Dell Computers reported total revenue of $49,205,000,000 and total assets of $23,215,000,000 in 2005.
  a. Calculate materiality for the company using the worksheet in this chapter.
  b. How will the auditor use this materiality level in planning the audit?
  c. Describe how the materiality level might be used in evaluating audit evidence.
  d. How does the materiality level impact the audit opinion?

LO4   22. **Using the audit process to plan and perform the audit.** You are in charge of planning the audit for a large bookstore selling CDs, DVDs, and books. Follow the steps discussed in the chapter. Assume that you have agreed to perform the audit and an engagement letter has been signed. The client has a December 31 year-end.

You are planning the audit in September. The company expects revenue to be $1,675,000,000 and total assets to be $1,235,000,000 at year-end. Use these numbers to calculate materiality.

a. Describe an audit strategy appropriate for planning the audit.

b. Calculate the bookstore's materiality. Describe how you will use it in the audit.

c. Identify significant accounts and relevant assertions for them. How will you assess inherent risk and control risk for the significant accounts? Assume that the bookstore leases its retail site and has no long-term debt.

d. Describe at least two analytical procedures you would perform during the planning process. What will you do with the results?

e. Assume that control risk for inventory has been assessed at 0.50. How will you support this assessment? What will happen if the results of the tests do not support an assessment of control risk at 0.50?

f. What impact does the control testing have on substantive testing?

g. Assume that during substantive testing, you found misstatements in net income equal to $2,837,000. What decision would you make regarding the financial statements? What action would you take?

h. Describe how you would determine the appropriate audit opinion for the client.

LO4   23. **Identifying significant accounts and calculating materiality.** Anaheim Enterprises, which operates in California, sells patio furniture imported from China; the merchandise is marketable twelve months of the year in California. Shipments from China come by sea and take two months to arrive unless a strike idles the shipping ports. The firm does not have a retail store but rents warehouse space with a small office. Anaheim sells on the Internet and through phone orders from customers and retail shops. The firm stocks fifty different sets of tables and chairs and a variety of benches, lounge chairs, and table umbrellas. It places all orders four months before delivery, and its payment is expected when it places the order. Anaheim accepts credit cards and extends thirty days of credit to retail stores. Its balance sheet shows cash, accounts receivable, inventory, and office equipment. On the liability side of the balance sheet are a few accounts payable and a short-term bank loan to cover the payment for goods before they arrive. The income statement shows revenue from both Internet and phone sales, cost of goods sold (averaging about 60% of revenue), and a few operating expenses (mainly rent and utilities). At any one time, the firm has on hand a three-month supply of inventory, which turns over about four times a year. The inventory does not tend to become obsolete. Anaheim is not a public company, but its books are audited to allow it to obtain bank financing. The company's two owners have no employees. The firm's total revenue is $2,800,000 for the current year; it had total assets of $700,000 at year-end. You are working on the year-end audit.

a. Calculate the company's materiality, and describe how you used it in the audit.

b. Identify significant accounts and disclosures for the company as well as any relevant assertions associated with the significant accounts. Explain how you determined the significant accounts and disclosures.

c. Did you test internal controls at this company? Explain your answer.

d. How did you gather evidence regarding the significant accounts and disclosures?

e. Assume that during substantive testing, you found misstatements in net income equal to $32,206. What decision would you make regarding the financial statements? What action would you take?

Real-World Auditing Problems

LO5   24. **Xerox**

The Securities and Exchange Commission sued KPMG, LLP, and four KPMG partners in 2004 in connection with the Xerox Corporation audits from 1997–2000. According to the SEC, KPMG allowed Xerox to manipulate its earnings by making "top-side" adjustments to its financial statements at year-end to meet earnings targets. KPMG auditors in Europe, Brazil, Canada, and Japan warned KPMG auditors in Rochester, New York, the main Xerox office, that its executives were preparing entries to improve revenue and that the entries distorted true income. The partners charged in the lawsuit worked in KPMG's New York headquarters or in its Stamford, Connecticut, office near the Xerox headquarters. The partners ignored the warnings from those working on the audit in KPMG offices around the world and failed to investigate the practices Xerox used to manipulate income. According to the SEC, the auditors failed in their professional duty as auditors because they did not want to risk a "lucrative financial relationship with a premier client."

To manipulate earnings, Xerox accelerated the recognition of revenue from its sales type leases. According to the financial reporting framework (U.S. GAAP), revenue related to a product's value should be recognized immediately, but revenue related to financing, servicing, and supply services should be recognized over the life of the lease. Beginning in 1997, Xerox recognized financing and service revenue as part of the value of the equipment, allowing it to recognize revenue immediately. Either executives in Stamford or local managers gave instructions for the calculations to use to accelerate revenue recognition. Xerox told KPMG that it needed to make these changes because the method previously used to calculate revenue was outdated.

When the accelerated revenue policies became known to KPMG auditors in Europe, Brazil, Canada, and Japan, they expressed reservations about the change. Some of their comments included these: the new method was "not supportable" and it presented an "unnecessary control risk with regard to accounting methods." KPMG auditors in the United Kingdom (U.K.) repeatedly objected to the new revenue calculations, stating that they carried a "high risk of significant misstatement" and were "potentially arbitrary." In 2000, the U.K. auditor told Michael Conway, the partner in charge of the audit in the United States at that time, that the method for accelerating revenue did not produce earnings results that reflected economic reality.

Ronald Safran, KPMG engagement partner for Xerox in 1998 and 1999, expressed misgivings to Conway, the managing partner of KPMG's Department of Professional Practice, in 1999. Safran expressed concern about the risk of fraudulent financial reporting at Xerox. He worried about its tendency to adjust its methods to accelerate revenue recognition late in the year so the auditors would not have enough time to review the proposed change. Safran believed that company executives made adjusting entries at the end of the quarter as needed to meet earnings targets. He also believed that KPMG had an obligation to report these concerns to the Xerox Audit Committee but did not do so and ultimately signed off on the 1999 financial statements.

After the investigation, Xerox restated its earnings for $6.1 billion for 1997–2000. The company also paid a $10 million civil penalty for the earnings fraud.[4]

a. Describe how the audit risk model might have helped the auditor perform the Xerox audit.
b. Did the auditors assess control risk too low? Explain your answer.
c. Did the auditors assess inherent risk too low? Explain your answer.
d. How should an auditor use materiality to plan the audit work related to revenue?
e. Why did the auditors fail to give Xerox a qualified opinion or to ask the company to stop its accelerated revenue recognition program?

LO5

25. **Parmalat**
Parmalat, one of Italy's largest companies, is best known for its shelf stable milk products. The company filed for bankruptcy protection in December 2003 after a

---

[4] U.S. Securities and Exchange Commission, "SEC Charges KPMG and Four KPMG Partners with Fraud in Connection with Audits of Xerox," January 29, 2003.

ten-year fraud that removed at least $17.4 billion from the company. The fraud was referred to as a Ponzi scheme in which company executives borrowed billions of dollars from investors around the world to cover up the company's losses. As a result of the fraud, U.S. investors suffered one of their largest losses in foreign securities when the debt securities became worthless.

Deloitte & Touche SpA, the Italian arm of the international accounting firm Deloitte & Touche, was hired as the Parmalat audit firm in 1999. At the end of the audit engagement in 2001, Parmalat's audit committee requested Deloitte to reexamine its audit fee. The Deloitte office in Italy referred to the Parmalat audit as a "crown jewel for our organization worldwide." To keep the prized audit client happy, Deloitte agreed to lower its audit fees. Auditors in Deloitte's office in New Jersey, where the U.S. Parmalat office was located, found their audit fee reduced from $165 per hour rate to about $90 per hour.

Many Deloitte offices were involved in the audit because Parmalat had business operations in at least thirty countries. The Deloitte working papers indicate that auditors outside of Italy frequently gave in to the wishes of the Italian auditor because they feared being fired by such an important client. Deloitte auditors of Bonlat Financing Corporation, located in the Cayman Islands, a unit of Parmalat, expressed concern about the financial transactions recorded in Bonlat. Despite the warnings given by several Deloitte offices involved in the audit, the office in Italy continued to issue clean audit reports. Its Italian office warned auditors in the other Deloitte offices to avoid asking questions regarding the business operations at Bonlat to prevent Parmalat from being annoyed and ending its multimillion-dollar audit engagement with Deloitte.

Parmalat officials later acknowledged that they had created Bonlat to hide fraudulent business transactions, referring to it as a "virtual garbage can." Auditors at Deloitte in Italy missed an opportunity to expose one of Europe's largest accounting frauds and to prevent shareholder loss when stock price declined.[5]

a. Describe how the audit risk model might have helped the auditor perform the Parmalat audit.
b. Did the auditor control audit risk to an acceptably low level? Explain your answer.
c. What role would the risk of material misstatement have played in the audit decisions Deloitte made?
d. Did the auditor fail to ask Parmalat to correct the financial statements because the audit adjustments were quantitatively immaterial? Explain your answer.
e. What do you think of the request to keep audit fees low to please a multinational client?
f. What do you think of a request to avoid asking the client difficult questions because it might fire the auditor?

LO5   26. **BJ Services**

BJ Services, a U.S. company, sells products and services to petroleum companies worldwide. BJ Services, S.A., a wholly owned subsidiary of BJ that operates in Argentina, made illegal payments of $72,000 in 2001 to Argentine customs officials so they would allow the company to import equipment. If the payments had not been made, the equipment would not have cleared customs and would have been returned to Venezuela (the source of the shipment). From 1998 to 2002, other improper payments of $151,000 were made to custom agents to facilitate custom

[5] Galloni, Alessandra, and David Reilly, "Auditor Raised Parmalat Red Flag," *The Wall Street Journal,* March 29, 2004; Reilly, David, and Alessandra Galloni, "Facing Lawsuits, Parmalat Auditor Stresses Its Disunity," *The Wall Street Journal,* April 28, 2005; Galloni, Alessandra, David Reilly, and Carrick Mollenkamp, "Skimmed Off: Parmalat Inquiry Find Basic Ruses at Heart of Scandal," *The Wall Street Journal,* December 31, 2003.

clearance of equipment in Argentina. Once an internal investigation discovered the payments, the board of directors ordered a full investigation into potential foreign corrupt practices violations.

The Foreign Corrupt Practices Act makes bribing foreign officials illegal. The investigation found no indication that anyone in management had approved the payments. The SEC issued a cease-and-desist order against the company, which agreed to improve its internal controls to prevent future illegal payments.[6]

a. In 2001, BJ Services had revenue of $2,233,520,000 and total assets of $1,985,367,000. Calculate the company's materiality.
b. Are the illegal payments quantitatively material? Explain your answer.
c. Are the illegal payments material for other reasons? Explain your answer.
d. What impact would the illegal payments have on your risk assessment for the company?
e. What audit procedures would you perform to control the risk arising from the illegal payments?

Internet Assignments

LO5   27. Select a company that you believe is in a risky business. Review its annual report to determine how it handles risk. Is it mentioned in the opinion or in the footnotes? Discuss the auditor's disclosure of risk in the financial statement.

LO5   28. Using a database that contains audit opinions, search for qualified opinions (adverse, disclaimer, except for) and review some of the opinions to determine the factor that risk played in the qualification. Describe several opinions related to risk.

[6] Accounting and Auditing Enforcement, Release No. 1972 (Washington, DC: Securities and Exchange Commission, March 10, 2004).

3

Internal Controls

Learning Objectives

After studying this chapter, you should be able to:

1. Understand management's use of internal controls to achieve financial statements prepared in accordance with an applicable financial reporting framework.
2. Describe the auditor's responsibility for internal controls in audits of financial statements and audits of internal controls over financial reporting.
3. Explain the auditor's requirement for performing tests of controls in an audit of financial statements.
4. Understand how the auditor gathers sufficient appropriate evidence when the client uses a service organization.
5. Describe how the auditor tests internal controls.
6. Discuss dual-purpose tests.
7. Describe the auditor's reporting requirements for internal control deficiencies in a financial statement audit.
8. Explain internal controls over financial reporting.
9. Describe the auditor's reporting requirements for internal control deficiencies and material weaknesses in an audit of internal controls over financial reporting.
10. Understand the role of internal controls in the corporate governance process.

Appendix A—Information Systems Auditing

Learning Objectives

11. Understand the role of information systems in an audit of the financial statements and an audit of the financial reporting process.
12. Describe how the auditor uses computer applications as part of the audit process.

Auditing standards relevant to this topic

For private companies

- **AU 314,** Understanding the Entity and Its Environment and Assessing the Risks of Material Misstatements
- **AU 322,** The Auditor's Consideration of the Internal Audit Function in a Audit of Financial Statements
- **AU 324,** Audit Considerations Relating to an Entity Using a Service Organization
- **AU 325,** Communicating Internal Control Related Matters Identified in an Audit

For public companies

- **PCAOB Auditing Standard No. 4,** Reporting on Whether a Previously Reported Material Weakness Continues to Exist

- **PCAOB Auditing Standard No. 5,** An Audit of Internal Control over Financial Reporting That Is Integrated with an Audit of Financial Statements
- **AU 322,** The Auditor's Consideration of the Internal Audit Function in an Audit of Financial Statements (Interim Standard Adopted by PCAOB)
- **AU 324,** Audit Considerations Relating to an Entity Using a Service Organization (Interim Standard Adopted by PCAOB)
- **AU 325,** Communicating Internal Control Related Matters Identified in an Audit (Interim Standard Adopted by PCAOB)

International standards

- **ISA 315,** Understanding the Entity and Its Environment and Assessing the Risks of Material Misstatement

The Impact of Internal Controls on Financial Statements

LO1

Understand management's use of internal controls to achieve financial statements prepared in accordance with an applicable financial reporting framework

Chapter 1 described management's responsibility to prepare financial statements in accordance with an applicable financial reporting framework. One of the principal methods used by the management of the company to do this is by using an internal control function. The internal control function in a company is a *process* designed by management and others charged with governance to provide *reasonable* assurance that the financial statements are prepared in accordance with the applicable financial reporting framework. Management develops internal controls to prevent or detect misstatements in the financial statements. The auditor reviews the internal controls developed by management to assess whether they are effective in preventing or detecting misstatements.

The auditing standards define *internal controls over financial statements* as **processes designed by management and others charged with governance** to provide reasonable assurance that company's responsibilities in three areas are met: (1) the reliability of financial reporting, (2) the effectiveness and efficiency of operations, and (3) compliance with laws and regulations. The auditor is primarily interested in assessing management's performance in the first area—the reliability of its financial reporting. Testing internal controls is the first step in the testing phase of the audit. Exhibit 3-1 summarizes the main steps in the audit process.

Management designs the **processes** to provide reasonable assurance that the financial statements are prepared in accordance with the applicable financial reporting framework. Management might develop controls related to: (1) segregation of duties between members involved in initiating, approving, implementing, and recording transactions, (2) procedures to authorize transactions, and (3) requirements for documented transaction trails before transactions can be processed, (4) physical controls that limit access to assets, and (5) independent reconciliations. These controls may be manual or computerized (also referred to as *IT*). The client company may have information systems that use automated procedures to initiate, record, process, and report transactions. Controls in information systems often use a combination of automated ones built into the computer programs (to check for mathematical accuracy or transaction approval) and manual ones (for example, to resolve exception reports for transactions not processed).

A company using enterprise risk management would first consider risk at the overall company (enterprise) level and then at the business process level for relevant assertions for significant accounts or balances.

Sometimes companies decide that implementing particular control procedures is not cost effective. For example, small companies may not have enough employees to establish adequate segregation of duties. In these situations, companies might design compensating controls for their systems. Management uses **compensating controls** to offset the risk in another procedure. For example, some companies allow employees to file expense reports for travel and entertainment without supervisory approval (a control that might prevent misstatements). After the expense is paid, the employee's supervisor receives a monthly report of the expenses charged to her or his budget. The

The Audit Process   Exhibit 3-1

Steps in the Audit Process	Discussed in this Section
Planning Phase	
Consider the Preconditions for an Audit and Accept or Reject the Audit Engagement	√
Understand the Entity and Its Environment, Determine Materiality, and Assess the Risks of Material Misstatements	
Develop an Audit Strategy and an Audit Plan to Respond to the Assessed Risks	
Testing Phase	
Test Internal Controls? Yes No	√
Perform Tests of Controls if "Yes"	√
Perform Substantive Tests of Transactions	
Perform Substantive Tests of Balances	
Assess the Likelihood of Material Misstatement	
Decision Phase	
Review the Presentation and Disclosure Assertions	
Evaluate the Evidence to Determine Whether the Financial Statements Are Prepared in Accordance with the Applicable Financial Reporting Framework	
Issue Audit Report	
Communicate with the Audit Committee	

supervisor's review of the report for improper charges serves as a compensating control. The control occurs after the transaction is complete (the expense has been paid), but misstatements in travel and entertainment expense will likely be detected in a timely fashion (before year-end).

Client management is responsible for *designing* the controls, and the auditor is responsible for *testing* them only if he or she chooses to rely on them to prevent or detect misstatements in the financial statements. The auditor has a variety of techniques to use to gather evidence about the control's effectiveness. These include (1) making inquiries of company employees, (2) inspecting documents, reports, or computer files, (3) observing the application of the control, and (4) reperforming the control (for example, performing the reconciliation required by the control procedure). These specific tests are covered in a later section of the chapter.

Management designs specific internal controls in the context of an overall control framework to provide reasonable assurance that the company's internal control objectives are met. The Committee of Sponsoring Organizations of the Treadway Commission (COSO) developed the most widely used internal control framework in the United States, COSO's *Enterprise Risk Management—Integrated Framework*. It lists five components of the internal control function. The five components are listed next.

1. The **control environment** sets the organization's tone, which might be aggressive or conservative. A company might be risk adverse or risk seeking. The remaining components of the internal control system function within the firm's overall control environment.

2. A company develops a **risk assessment** process to identify risks to its ability to achieve its objectives. For example, a university might consider a lack of students, a shortage of parking, or a lack of qualified faculty to be a risk. An airline might consider the high cost of jet fuel to be one.

Five Components of Internal Control and Subdivisions of Control Components (if applicable)				Exhibit 3-2

1. Control Environment
- Integrity and ethical values
- Commitment to competence
- Board of director and audit committee participation
- Management's philosophy and operating style
- Organizational structure
- Human resource policies and practices

2. Risk Assessment	3. Control Activities (Five Procedures)	4. Information and Communication	5. Monitoring
• Identify factors that could affect risks • Assess the significance of risk and likelihood of its occurrence • Determine actions necessary to manage risks	• Segregation (Separation) of duties • Authorization of transactions and procedures • Documented transaction trails from adequate documents and records • Physical control over assets and records • Independent checks on performance	(Not applicable)	(Not applicable)

3. A company's **control activities** are the procedures it uses to help achieve its objectives. To guard against the unauthorized use of the company's cash, management may require monthly bank reconciliations by an individual who doesn't issue checks or deposit cash.

4. A company uses **information** and **communication** systems to exchange the data needed to make decisions. For example, company executives may review monthly expense reports to determine whether their information is consistent with actual budgets.

5. A company **monitors** its internal controls to determine whether they effectively prevent or detect misstatements in the financial statements. A company may test monthly bank reconciliations to determine whether financial statement errors have been made.

Refer to Exhibit 3-2 for a summary of the five components of internal control and their subdivisions (if applicable).

See Exhibit 3-3 for additional information about the components of an internal control function.

Did You Know?

Citigroup, the world's largest financial services firm, announced its renewed commitment to ethical values in 2004. Charles Prince, CEO of the company, stated, "We need to have the right moral compass that steers us down the middle of the road." Prince took steps to improve Citigroup's codes of conduct and internal control functions for monitoring compliance. He expects employees to internalize a strong code of ethics, to understand the rules and regulations that govern their tasks within the business, and to make decisions consistent with the ethical values advocated by the company.

Source: Mitchell Pacelle, "Citigroup CEO Makes 'Values' a Key Focus," *The Wall Street Journal,* October 1, 2004.

What does this statement by the CEO tell you about the control environment in this company?

Five Components of Internal Control   Exhibit 3-3

CONTROL ENVIRONMENT

The control environment sets the tone of the organization. This component is referred to as the "tone at the top." An organization's tone is critical to its overall control environment. If management fails to emphasize the importance of internal control, employees may assume that it is appropriate to ignore internal control procedures. Specific factors evaluated under the control environment include integrity and ethical values of the organization; the organization's commitment to competence; participation of the board of directors or audit committee members; management's philosophy and operating style; the organizational structure; the assignment of authority and responsibility and human resource policies and practices.

RISK ASSESSMENT

The company assesses risks that could affect its ability to initiate, record, process, or report financial data consistent with management's assertions. The purpose of management's risk assessment is to identify and control risks that could prevent the company from meeting its objectives. Risks can be associated with changes in the operating environment, new personnel and new or revamped information systems; rapid growth; new technology; new business models, products, or activities; corporate restructuring; expansion of foreign operations; or new accounting pronouncements.

INFORMATION AND COMMUNICATION

A company's information system consists of the procedures and records established to initiate, record, process, and report the entity's transactions and to maintain accountability for the asset, liability, and equity accounts. The auditor should gather data regarding the information system to understand significant transactions that this system processes; the procedures used to initiate, record, process, and report transactions in the financial statements, the accounting records, supporting documentation, and specific accounts in the financial statements used for initiating, recording, processing, and reporting transactions; how the information system captures events and conditions significant to the financial statements; and the reporting process used to prepare the financial statements, including significant estimates and disclosures.

CONTROL ACTIVITIES

A company's control activities are the policies and procedures it has developed to ensure that management's directives are followed.

What Are Internal Control Procedures?

1. Segregation of duties
2. Authorization procedures
3. Documented transaction trails
4. Physical controls that limit access to assets
5. Independent reconciliations

MONITORING

Management is responsible for monitoring internal controls to ensure that they are operating as intended. Internal auditors or other employees may be involved in the monitoring process. The external auditor should obtain an understanding of the monitoring procedures the entity uses.

Auditor's Responsibility for Internal Control

LO2

Describe the auditor's responsibility for internal controls in audits of financial statements and audits of internal controls over financial reporting

The passage of the Sarbanes-Oxley Act (SOX) in 2002 dramatically expanded the auditor's responsibility for internal control evaluation for *public* companies. SOX was a logical follow-up to the Foreign Corrupt Practices Act (1977), which made management responsible for designing a system of internal controls. SOX makes management responsible for assessing the system of internal controls to measure its effectiveness.

Before the passage of SOX, auditors were permitted to document their understanding of the internal control function and to choose whether to test specific internal controls described during the documentation process. After SOX, the responsibility for internal controls became sharply different for public companies (also referred to as *stock issuers*) and private companies (referred to as *nonissuers*).

SOX *requires* auditors to perform *integrated* audits for public companies. During an integrated audit, the auditor must test internal controls and provide an **opinion** on their effectiveness over financial reporting. The auditor also must provide an opinion on the financial statements in an integrated audit. The auditing procedures related to testing internal controls over financial statements in an integrated audit are referred to as **testing controls in an audit of internal controls over *financial statements*.** The auditing procedures related to testing internal controls over financial reporting in an integrated audit are referred to as **testing controls in an audit of internal controls over *financial reporting*.**

We will discuss testing internal controls in an audit of the financial statements first. These procedures apply to the audit of public *and* private companies.

Auditor's Responsibility for Testing Internal Controls in Financial Statement Audits

LO3

Explain the auditor's requirement for performing tests of controls in an audit of financial statements

For Public and Private Companies

Auditing standards describe the auditor's responsibility for testing internal control in an **audit of financial statements.** According to the standards, "the auditor should obtain an understanding of internal control relevant to the audit" (AU 314). In a financial statement audit, the auditor is *required to understand* the *relevant* internal controls of the company but is *not* required to test them. This understanding of internal controls includes assessing the design of the controls and whether they have been implemented correctly. To understand the company's relevant internal controls, the auditor should understand the company's: (1) control environment, (2) risk assessment process, (3) (a) information system including the business processes relevant for financial reporting and (b) communication of financial reporting roles and responsibilities, (4) response to risks arising from IT, and (5) monitoring of internal control over financial reporting.

In a financial statement audit, the auditor decides either (1) to rely on the company's internal controls to prevent or detect misstatements or (2) not to rely on them. An auditor who decides to rely on internal controls believes that controls are effective in preventing or detecting misstatements in the financial statements and must test *internal controls that will be relied on.* The auditor therefore prepares additional documentation of the internal control function identifying *specific* controls to test. The auditor typically documents specific information on the control system's effectiveness in internal control questionnaires, flowcharts, walk-throughs, and memos that document discussions held with the client. Some examples of this documentation will be given in the business process chapters.

An auditor who decides *not* to rely on internal controls documents her or his understanding of the company's relevant internal controls. The documentation required to obtain an understanding of the internal control function will likely be less than that required to test controls. If internal controls will not be relied on, they need not be tested. In this case, the auditor increases the amount of substantive testing because no evidence related to internal control testing will be gathered.

At the end of the audit but before issuing the audit opinion, the auditor should have *sufficient appropriate evidence to reduce audit risk to an acceptably low level. Sufficiency* is a measure of the quantity of the evidence. *Appropriateness* is measured by the quality of the evidence, in particular its relevance and reliability. The auditor uses professional judgment to determine whether sufficient appropriate audit evidence has been obtained to reduce audit risk to an acceptably low level. This evidence might come from a combination of internal control evidence and substantive evidence or only from substantive evidence. How the auditor determines the necessary amount of evidence using either (1) internal control and substantive testing or (2) substantive testing alone is discussed in a later chapter.

Sufficient Appropriate Evidence for a Client Using a Service Organization

LO4

Understand how the auditor gathers sufficient appropriate evidence when the client uses a service organization

Many companies outsource parts of their operations to other businesses. Auditing standards refer to the businesses that provide specific services to the companies as *service organizations.* Some examples include trust departments of banks and insurance companies, transfer agents and custodians for investment companies, mortgage companies that service loans for others, Internet service providers and Web hosting service providers, and payroll processors. *When an audit client uses a service organization, the auditor is required to obtain an understanding of the nature and significance of the services the organization provides and of the design and operation of the service organization's relevant controls. The auditor uses this understanding to assess the risk of material misstatement related to the relevant controls the service organization performs.*

During the planning process, the auditor obtains an understanding of the audit client and an understanding of how the audit client uses the service organization. An auditor who identifies controls performed *only* at the service organization that are relevant to his or her expectation that controls operate effectively for certain assertions must obtain audit evidence about the service organization's operational effectiveness of controls. The auditor obtains this evidence by doing one or more of the following: (1) obtaining a report prepared by the service organization's auditor that describes its system, evaluates the appropriateness of the design of internal controls, and tests the operating effectiveness of the controls, (2) requesting the service organization's auditor to perform specific tests of controls, (3) performing tests of controls at the service organization himself or herself, or (4) performing tests of the client's controls over the activities the service organization performs.

Service organizations often hire auditors to document and test their internal controls and to report on their findings. Auditors for companies that employ the service organization often use these reports. A service organization's auditors can prepare two types of reports. Type 1 describes the service organization's controls and evaluates whether they are appropriate to achieve specific control objectives. Type 2 contains the information in the type 1 report and the results of internal control tests the service's auditors conducted to determine whether the controls provide reasonable assurance that the control objectives were achieved. An auditor of a company that uses a service organization can use only a type 2 report to reduce control risk below the maximum value. Users of the service's reports should be satisfied by the professional reputation, competence, and independence of its auditors.

Auditors who use the service organization's report do not refer to it in an unqualified opinion audit report. If reference to the work of the service auditors is necessary for outsiders to understand a modification in the audit report, the audit report must state that the auditor of the company using the service organization is responsible for the audit opinion (and must not indicate that the responsibility is shared with the service organization auditor).

Methods Used to Test Internal Controls

LO5

Describe how the auditor tests internal controls

For Public and Private Companies

Internal control tests that the auditor uses to gather evidence about the effectiveness of internal controls to prevent or detect misstatements in the financial statements include (1) making inquiries of employees (asking them questions about the procedures they use to process transactions), (2) inspecting documents, reports, and computer files, (3) observing the application of the control, and (4) reperforming it. These procedures are a subset of the seven audit procedures used to gather evidence. Audit procedures that are not used for testing internal controls are external confirmation, recalculation, and analytical procedures. Internal control tests used are listed from least effective to most effective. For example, invoices related to the purchase of inventory are often paid after a review of the quantities, prices, and product description on the invoice and the receiving report. The accounting clerk indicates his or her performance of the control by initialing the invoice. The least effective internal control test is to *ask* the accounting clerk if he or she reviewed the items on the invoice and the receiving report before initialing the invoice. The most effective internal control test is for the auditor to *reperform* the control, comparing the information on the invoice with the information on the receiving report to see if the two agree.

Internal Control Tests

Inquiries of employees
Inspection of documents, records, and computer files
Observation of the application of the control
Reperformance of the control

Internal Control Function: Cash

Let's consider an example of internal controls in a cash system to see how the *auditor could test the controls designed by management* to determine whether they are effective.

1. Isobel receives cash and checks for BCS Company and records the payments in the cash receipts journal. She immediately stamps the checks with a restrictive endorsement limiting the check's deposit to the company's bank account. She writes the amount of the payment on the payment voucher returned by the customer with the cash payment. She totals the cash or check payment on the daily cash report and sends the cash and checks to Jorgen to count. He sends the payment vouchers to Abhu to record. A copy of the cash receipts journal is sent to Scott.

2. Jorgen counts the cash. He then prepares and signs the bank deposit ticket. This signature indicates that he has reviewed the payments and determined that they should be recorded in BCS's bank account. He sends the cash and the bank deposit ticket with his signature to Scott.

3. Scott receives a listing from the cash receipts journal from Isobel and compares it to the cash recorded by Jorgen on the bank deposit ticket. Scott *initials* the bank deposit ticket indicating that he has agreed (checked them for agreement) the cash on the cash receipts journal and the bank deposit ticket with the cash he receives. He investigates and resolves any discrepancies. Scott stores the cash in a locked safe until it is ready for deposit and is deposited daily.

4. Abhu prepares the journal entries to debit cash and credit accounts receivable based on the payment vouchers. He compares the debits to the cash account and the credits to accounts receivable with the bank deposit ticket on a daily basis and *initials* the daily reconciliation report indicating that they agree. He investigates and resolves discrepancies.

Identify the internal controls that are in place:

- *Segregation of duties.* We have identified four employees involved in processing cash in the internal control function. Each individual performs a part of the job of recording cash and posting it to cash and accounts receivable. The auditor determined the controls that are in place by making *inquiries of employees* or by performing a walk-through of the cash process.

  - The auditor evaluates segregation of duties by *observing* and *inspecting* the documents. The auditor watches the work performed by Isobel, Jorgen, Scott, and Abhu to determine whether the employees are following the company's procedures for the segregation of duties. The auditor also reviews the initials and signatures on the documents. Often significant differences exist between what employees are supposed to do and what they actually do. This is why the auditor observes the process firsthand.

- *Authorization procedures.* When Jorgen signs the bank deposit ticket, he authorizes the receipt of cash as something the company is entitled to and approves the deposit of cash in the company's bank account.

  - The auditor could test the authorization by selecting a sample of daily bank deposit tickets and *inspecting* them to determine whether Jorgen's signature is on the bank deposit ticket. If it is missing, a control to prevent misstatements is not in place.

- *Documented transaction trails.* This accounting system has several documented transaction trails. The *daily cash reports* document the amount of cash the company initially received. The *bank deposit ticket* documents the amount of cash sent to the bank. The *payment vouchers* document the amount of cash received as payment on each customer account. These three reports are internally generated. Either the accounting system or an outside source also generates several reports. The *cash receipts journal* and the *accounts receivable subsidiary ledger* document the transaction trails for cash receipts and payments on accounts receivable. The accounting system produces these reports. The monthly *bank statement* reports the bank transaction information. The bank, an outside source, generates this statement.

- The auditor could *inspect* the *documents, reports,* and *computer files* to determine whether the initialed documents indicate that the individual has applied the control procedures. For example, the auditor might inspect the bank deposit ticket to see whether Scott's initials are on it. When he initials the deposit ticket, he is indicating that he has compared the cash amount in the cash receipts journal with the amount on the deposit ticket and that it agrees with the actual amount of cash received.
- Does a missing initial mean that Scott failed to compare the cash on the cash receipts journal and the deposit ticket or that he forgot to initial the deposit ticket? Are both errors equally serious? Failing to make the comparison (to perform the control) is more serious than making the comparison but failing to initial the deposit ticket. The auditor has no idea which error has occurred and must assume the employee failed to make the comparison.
- Does the presence of the initials mean that Scott compared the amount of cash on the cash receipts journal and the amount on the deposit ticket? The only way the auditor could determine whether the two amounts agree is to *reperform* the control.
- *Physical controls that limit access to assets.* The restrictive endorsement on the checks is a physical control that limits access to them. Because cash is susceptible to theft, it should be locked in a safe as quickly as possible.
  - To determine whether the checks are restrictively endorsed as soon as Isobel opens the envelopes, the auditor could *observe* the process she used. To evaluate the security of cash as it is processed, the auditor could also *observe* the process the accounting clerks use as they handle cash.
- *Independent reconciliations.* Both Scott and Abhu perform independent reconciliations. Scott reconciles the amount of cash from the cash receipts journal to the amount deposited in the bank account. Abhu reconciles the credits to the accounts receivable account with the amount of cash deposited in the bank.
  - The auditor could *inspect* the bank deposit ticket and the daily reconciliation report to determine whether Scott and Abhu have recorded their initials on the report indicating they have performed the control. The auditor could also *reperform* the control, for example, by inspecting the daily reconciliation report to see whether Abhu's initials are on the report and then comparing the credits to accounts receivable with the daily cash deposit to determine that they are equal.

Use of the Work of Internal Auditors

Auditing standards allow the auditor to use the work of the *internal auditors,* who work for the audit client, to gather evidence about the effectiveness of internal controls. The internal auditors may have tested some of the internal controls that the auditor determines are relevant to the audit. To use the evidence of work done by the internal auditors, the auditor must evaluate both the internal auditors' competence and objectivity as well as supervise, review, evaluate, and test the internal auditors' work performed. The internal auditors' competence relates to their education level and professional certification. Their objectivity depends on to whom in the organization they report; this should be an individual at a level in the organization who will give adequate consideration to the internal auditors' findings.

Dual-Purpose Tests

LO6

Discuss dual-purpose tests

At times, the only way to determine whether a control is effectively preventing or detecting misstatements in the financial statements is to reperform the control. To reperform the control, the auditor gathers evidence about whether the control is *working* and evidence about whether the account balance or class of transactions is *correct.* When the auditor *reperforms* a control procedure, she or he conducts a **dual-purpose test** that meets two objectives: to provide evidence to evaluate whether a control is operating effectively and to efficiently gather evidence to detect misstatements in the financial statements. Dual-purpose tests function as tests of controls as well as substantive tests of transactions.

In the internal control function documented for BCS Company, Scott initials the deposit ticket, indicating that he has compared the cash amount in the cash receipts journal to the cash amount on the bank deposit ticket and the actual cash he received. When testing this control to determine whether it is working, the auditor *inspects* the bank deposit ticket to determine that Scott's initials are on the deposit ticket. This evidence gives the auditor information about whether the control operated effectively. When *reperforming* the controls by verifying that the cash listed in the cash receipts journal equals the cash listed on the bank deposit ticket, the auditor's action provides an opportunity to gather evidence to detect misstatements in the financial statements. In the reperformance of the control, the auditor uses a dual-purpose test to gather evidence about both the effectiveness of internal controls and the accuracy of the financial statements.

A Word of Caution about Internal Control Tests

Internal controls performed by employees rather than by computers are subject to several types of errors. If Scott's job—to compare the amount of cash on the cash receipts journal and on the bank deposit ticket and then to recount the cash to make sure that all the totals agree—is performed 100 or more times daily, might he sometimes fail to initial one or several deposit tickets?

If the initials are missing on the bank deposit ticket, the auditor might assume that the control—the comparison—was not performed. But perhaps Scott just forgot to initial a deposit ticket, even though he did perform the comparison. In such a case, a missing control does not necessarily indicate that controls were ineffective.

If the initials are present on the bank deposit ticket, the auditor could assume that the control, the comparison, was performed. But maybe Scott initialed the deposit ticket but did not perform the control. In this case, the presence of a control does not necessarily indicate that it was effective.

In both situations, the only way the auditor can verify that the control was effective would be to reperform the control to determine whether the cash amount listed in the cash receipts journal is equal to the cash amount on the deposit ticket.

The only information the auditors obtain from an internal control test is whether the control is present. Yes or No is the only answer possible. In a test of controls, the answer is likely to be a combination of them, however. For example, 70% of the time, the control is present, and 30% of the time it is missing.

There are other inherent limitations to internal controls. Any control performed by a person is subject to fatigue factors. During a given year, people may quit and new employees are hired, but they may not be trained to perform the control or may not understand the reasons for performing the control. The company may experience IT problems during the year. The company may change from one accounting software package to another. Controls that should be in place may not have been installed in the new package.

Remember the following:

- It is possible to have perfect (materially correct) financial statements and no internal controls.

- It is possible to have perfect internal controls (low control risk) and materially incorrect financial statements.

- Testing internal controls does *not* determine whether the financial statements are correct but only whether the controls are working to prevent or detect misstatements in the financial statements.

- Substantive tests determine whether the account balances or classes of transactions are correct.

- What companies say they do is often quite different from what they actually do. The documented internal control procedures may require an employee to perform a control, but that individual may seldom, never, or always perform the control. Individuals who do not perform the control may have no idea why it is important. Employees who do not understand the control's purpose will likely do a poor job of performing the control.

To the Board of Directors of BCS Company:

Management of BCS Company is responsible for establishing and maintaining adequate internal controls over financial statements. The Company's internal control over financial statements is a process designed to provide reasonable assurance regarding the reliability of financial reporting and preparation of financial statements in accordance with an applicable financial reporting framework. Because of its inherent limitations, internal controls may not prevent or detect misstatements. Also, projections of any evaluation of effectiveness to future periods are subject to the risk that controls may become inadequate because of changes in conditions, or that the degree of compliance with the policies or procedures may deteriorate.

The objective of our audit was to report on the financial statements, not to provide assurance on internal controls. Significant deficiencies or material weaknesses discovered during the course of an audit must be reported to the board of directors.

A significant deficiency is a control deficiency or a combination of control deficiencies that adversely affects the company's ability to initiate, authorize, record, process, or report external financial data reliably in accordance with an applicable financial reporting framework so that there is more than a remote likelihood that a misstatement of the company's annual financial statements that is more than inconsequential will not be prevented or detected. A material weakness is a significant deficiency or combination of significant deficiencies that results in more than a remote likelihood that a material misstatement of the annual financial statements will not be prevented or detected.

We believe that the oversight of the company's external financial reporting and internal control over financial reporting by the company's audit committee is ineffective and represents a material weakness.

This report is intended solely for the information and use of the board of directors, audit committee, management, and others within the organization.

Stuart and Steigler, LLP
February 16, 2012

Auditor's Reporting Requirements for Internal Control Deficiencies in a Financial Statement Audit

For Public and Private Companies

During an audit, the auditor may become aware of deficiencies in a client's internal control functions that could be of interest to the company's audit committee. The deficiencies identified in a financial statement audit may be reported in one of two ways. Internal control deficiencies that fail to reach the level of *significant* deficiencies or *material* weaknesses are reported in a letter to management. Control deficiencies that reach the level of significant deficiencies or material weaknesses are reported in a letter to **both** management and the audit committee. A *significant deficiency* is one or a combination of control inadequacies that adversely affect the company's ability to initiate, authorize, record, process, or report external financial data reliably in accordance with an applicable financial reporting framework (GAAP). A *material weakness* is a significant deficiency or a combination of significant deficiencies that results in more than a remote likelihood that a material misstatement in the financial statements would not be prevented or detected. The auditor must communicate in writing *all* significant deficiencies and material weaknesses to management and the audit committee. The reports to management and the audit committee are not available outside the company. The auditor's communication should clearly distinguish significant deficiencies from material weaknesses (the most serious deficiencies). The written communication from the auditor should include (1) the definitions of significant deficiency and material weakness, (2) a statement that the audit's objective is to report on the financial statements, not to provide assurance on internal controls, and (3) a statement that the communication is intended solely for the use of the board of directors, the audit committee, and management. See Exhibit 3-4 for a sample report on significant deficiencies and material weaknesses for BCS Company.

If the control deficiencies are less severe and fail to reach the level of significant deficiencies or material weaknesses, the auditor communicates internal control deficiencies

---

Management Letter *BCS Company December 31, 2011*   **Exhibit 3-5**

Management of BCS Company, is responsible for establishing and maintaining adequate internal controls over financial statements. The auditor is responsible for issuing an opinion on the financial statements.

We noted the following inefficiencies in internal controls during our audit.

Physical control over assets. Management has failed to provide adequate physical control over inventory in the retail store. Cash registers are located in the middle of the salesroom, and customers can easily put additional items in their shopping bag as they leave the store. We recommend that the cashiers be moved to a location

close to the three doors. Although the loss from theft is currently immaterial, improving the physical control over inventory could reduce the loss of inventory in the future.

Timely reconciliations. Bank reconciliations for the payroll account were not performed on a timely basis. They should be completed within 30 days of month-end so recording errors are corrected on a timely basis.

The objective of our audit was to report on the financial statements, not to provide assurance on internal controls. This report is intended solely for the information and use of the board of directors, audit committee, and management, and others within the organization.

---

in a management letter. This letter is a service to the client but is not required by auditing standards. The internal control comments of the management letter suggest improvements to the efficiency or effectiveness of the accounting system. Clients are free to follow or ignore the suggestions in the management letter. The comments in the management letter are not related to the opinion given on the financial statements. Despite the weaknesses described in the management letter, the auditor gathers sufficient evidence to support the audit opinion (see Exhibit 3-5 for a sample management letter for BCS Company).

Internal Controls Over the Financial Reporting Process

LO8

Explain internal controls over financial reporting

For Public Companies in the United States Only

Management is responsible for developing internal controls over the financial reporting process. These controls designed to ensure that a company's financial reporting process is effective as of year-end as mandated by the Sarbanes-Oxley Act (SOX) for all public companies. Effective financial reporting provides reasonable assurance regarding the reliability of financial reporting and the preparation of financial statements for external purposes.

Auditors and management are involved in testing internal controls over financial reporting. Management is required to *identify* controls related to the financial reporting process and to *test* them to determine whether they are effective at *year-end*. Then the auditor reviews management's assessment of internal controls and expresses an opinion on the company's internal controls' effectiveness over financial reporting. The accounting firm performing the financial statement audit must also audit internal controls over financial reporting. An audit in which an accounting firm issues an audit report on the financial statements and provides an opinion on the effectiveness of the company's internal controls over financial reporting is referred to as an **integrated audit.** SOX requires integrated audits for all public companies.

The auditor's *objective* in an audit of internal controls over the financial reporting process is *to express an opinion on the effectiveness* of the company's internal control over financial reporting. **If one or more material weaknesses exist, the company's internal control over financial reporting will not be considered effective.** To meet this objective, the auditor must plan and perform the audit to obtain competent evidence that provides reasonable assurance about whether material weaknesses in the internal control function exist as of the end of the reporting period.

Auditing standards define internal control *over financial reporting* as

A process designed by, or under the supervision of, the company's principal executive and principal financial officers, or persons performing similar functions, and effected by the company's board of directors, management, and other personnel, to provide reasonable assurance regarding the reliability of financial reporting and the preparation of financial statements for external purposes in accordance with GAAP and includes those policies and procedures that (1) pertain to the maintenance of records that, in reasonable detail, accurately and fairly reflect the transactions and dispositions of the assets of the company; (2) provide reasonable assurance that transactions are recorded as necessary to permit preparation of financial statements in accordance with an applicable financial reporting framework, and that receipts and expenditures of the company are being made only in accordance with authorizations of management and directors of the company; and (3) provide reasonable assurance regarding prevention or timely detection of unauthorized acquisition, use, or disposition of the company's assets that could have a material effect on the financial statements. (AS5.A5)

Management develops the internal control process associated with financial reporting, which is designed to ensure that the company maintains records in sufficient detail to record its transactions to permit the preparation of financial statements in accordance with the applicable financial reporting framework (GAAP) and to demonstrate that the company spends its money and acquires and disposes of its assets in ways consistent with management's wishes.

Did You Know?

In defending himself against charges that he stole millions of dollars from the company, Dennis Kozlowski, former chief executive of Tyco International, said that he did not notice when a $25 million bonus was omitted from his W-2. Kozlowski indicated that a board member who had later died had approved the bonus. Prosecutors alleged that the $25 million was part of the more than $150 million that Kozlowski stole from Tyco. In June 2005, he was convicted of the theft charge and sentenced to ten years in prison. In convicting Kozlowski, the jury determined that the Tyco board had not authorized the $25 million expenditure.

Source: Kara Scannell and Chad Bray, "Kozlowski Says He Didn't Notice $25 Million Missing From W-2," *The Wall Street Journal,* April 29, 2005.

How did this transaction slip through the authorization process?

Management's Assessment of Internal Controls over Financial Reporting

Management assesses its internal controls and issues a report on their effectiveness in connection with the audit of its financial statements. This report includes statements (1) of management's responsibility for establishing and maintaining adequate internal controls over financial reporting, (2) of management's assessment of the effectiveness of internal controls over financial reporting, (3) of the identification of the framework management used to evaluate the effectiveness of internal controls over financial reporting and (4) that the registered public accounting firm that audited the company's financial statements has issued an attestation report on (2). Refer to Exhibit 3-6 for the management report on internal control over financial reporting for Hewlett-Packard.

In the past, companies considered internal controls from the perspective of the effect of the controls on the financial statement accounts. Today companies find it useful to consider internal controls from the perspective of the company (the enterprise), a process of controlling risk from an enterprise perspective referred to as *enterprise risk management.* It takes a broader perspective on risk management by considering risk management across the entire enterprise. Management bases its assessment on the effectiveness of internal controls over financial reporting using a *recognized framework for documenting control systems.* The auditor must use the same framework to assess the effectiveness of the controls.

One internal control framework often used by management is COSO developed by the Committee of Sponsoring Organizations of the Treadway Commission (COSO), a voluntary organization dedicated to improving the quality of financial reporting through business ethics, effective internal control, and corporate governance. COSO's members are the American Institute of Certified Public Accountants, the American Accounting Association, Financial Executives International, the Institute of Management Accountants,

Hewlett-Packard   *Management's Report on Internal Control over Financial Reporting*   Exhibit 3-6

HP's management is responsible for establishing and maintaining adequate internal control over financial reporting for HP. HP's internal control over financial reporting is a process designed to provide reasonable assurance regarding the reliability of financial reporting and the preparation of financial statements for external purposes in accordance with U.S. generally accepted accounting principles. HP's internal control over financial reporting includes those policies and procedures that (i) pertain to the maintenance of records that, in reasonable detail, accurately and fairly reflect the transactions and dispositions of the assets of HP; (ii) provide reasonable assurance that transactions are recorded as necessary to permit preparation of financial statements in accordance with generally accepted accounting principles, and that receipts and expenditures of HP are being made only in accordance with authorizations of management and directors of HP; and (iii) provide reasonable assurance regarding prevention or timely detection of unauthorized acquisition, use, or disposition of HP's assets that could have a material effect on the financial statements.

Because of its inherent limitations, internal control over financial reporting may not prevent or detect misstatements. Also, projections of any evaluation of effectiveness to future periods are subject to the risk that controls may become inadequate because of changes in conditions, or that the degree of compliance with the policies or procedures may deteriorate.

HP's management assessed the effectiveness of HP's internal control over financial reporting as of October 31, 2008,

utilizing the criteria set forth by the Committee of Sponsoring Organizations of the Treadway Commission (COSO) in Internal Control-Integrated Framework. As discussed in Note 6 to the Consolidated Financial Statements, HP completed its acquisition of Electronic Data Systems Corporation ("EDS") in August 2008. HP has excluded EDS from its assessment of the effectiveness of its internal control over financial reporting as of October 31, 2008. Revenue from the business operations acquired from EDS represented approximately 3 percent of HP's total net revenue for the fiscal year ended October 31, 2008, and the fair value assigned to tangible assets for purposes of applying the purchase method of accounting as of the date of the acquisition accounted for approximately 11 percent of HP's total assets as of October 31, 2008. Based on the assessment by HP's management, we determined that HP's internal control over financial reporting was effective as of October 31, 2008. The effectiveness of HP's internal control over financial reporting as of October 31, 2008, has been audited by Ernst & Young LLP, HP's independent registered public accounting firm, as stated in its report which appears on page 78 of this Annual Report on Form 10-K.

/s/ MARK V. HURD
Mark V. Hurd

Chairman, Chief Executive Officer and President

December 15, 2008

/s/ CATHERINE A. LESJAK
Catherine A. Lesjak

Executive Vice President and Chief Financial Officer

December 15, 2008

and The Institute of Internal Auditors. The organization was formed in 1985 to study factors that could lead to fraudulent financial reporting and to develop recommendations to prevent it. In 1992, the committee published *Internal Control—Integrated Framework*. PricewaterhouseCoopers (PWC), working under the guidance of the committee, developed the COSO framework, which in 2004 was updated when the committee published *Enterprise Risk Management—Integrated Framework*.

The COSO framework identifies three objectives of internal control: (1) efficiency and effectiveness of operations, (2) reliability of financial reporting, and (3) compliance with laws and regulations. Managers can use this framework to document controls when performing their assessment of their internal controls' effectiveness.

Did You Know?

In November 2004, MedQuist a U.S. medical transcription company, announced that its 2002 annual report and its 2002 and 2003 quarterly reports "should no longer be relied upon." The 2003 annual report was delayed because KPMG was unable to complete its review of the 2003 financial results due to problems with the financial reporting system. KPMG found that the company's billing practices were improper; it had used ratios and formulas to calculate bills rather than counting the number of transcription lines completed, as called for in its contracts with medical facilities. The financial reporting in 2002 and 2003 was not reliable because controls had failed to detect or prevent revenue misstatements in the financial statements.

Source: Cassell Bryan-Low, "Philips's MedQuist Will Restate Some Past Financial Statements," *The Wall Street Journal*, November 3, 2004.

What internal control procedure might have detected this problem?

Auditor's Assessment of Internal Controls over Financial Reporting

The auditing standards require the auditor to use a *top-down approach* to audit internal controls over the financial reporting process. Using this approach, the auditor (1) identifies entity-level controls, (2) considers whether the company maintains controls to address the risk of fraud including the risk of management override of controls, and (3) identifies relevant assertions associated with significant accounts and disclosures. In assessing the effectiveness of internal controls over financial reporting, the auditor considers both entity-level controls (items 1 and 2) and transaction level controls (item 3). If the auditor identifies risks at the enterprise level he or she should consider how the identified risks could affect risks of material misstatement at the transaction level.

Entity-Level Controls

Entity controls listed in auditing standards issued by the PCAOB include the following:

- Controls related to the control environment;
- Controls over management override;
- The company's risk assessment process;
- Centralized processing and controls, including shared service environments;
- Controls to monitor results of operations;
- Controls to monitor other controls, including activities of the internal audit function, the audit committee, and self-assessment programs;
- Controls over the period-end financial reporting process; and
- Policies that address significant business control and risk management practices. (AS5.24)

The auditor tests *entity*-level controls that are important to the auditor's assessment of whether the company maintains effective internal control over financial reporting.

Questions the auditor could address in assessing controls related to the *control environment* include these: What is management's philosophy and operating style? Does that style promote effective internal control over financial reporting? Are integrity and ethical values of top management seen as important? Does the board or the audit committee understand and use its oversight responsibility concerning financial reporting and internal control?

To investigate the likelihood of *management override,* the auditor might consider the company's procedures to approve transactions. Does management have the authority to authorize transactions without an approval process? Are controls in place to prevent or detect the override of internal controls?

The *risk assessment* process used by the firm is very important to the auditor. If the firm does a good job assessing its risk(s) and installs controls to mitigate the risk(s), the auditor's job will be easier. The auditor should understand the risk assessment process the firm uses and consider the adequacy of management's controls to identify and correct risk in the firm.

The auditor's evaluation of a firm that has *centralized processing* and controls is easier than evaluating a decentralized system with many sets in various locations or countries. A centralized processing system probably has less control risk than a decentralized one (unless controls for the centralized system do not exist).

An auditor hopes that management monitors the *results of operations*. One auditor concern is about controls that require management to meet earnings targets each quarter. Controls that emphasize such targets are invitations for management to misstate the results of operations to meet these targets. The existence of such controls in a company should prompt the auditor to increase its risk. Public companies are required to maintain an anonymous tip line as a result of SOX. The auditor is required to ask management and the audit committee about tips or complaints received from the tip line related to the company's financial reporting and review management's resolution of the complaints received from this source.

Companies with *internal auditors,* an active *audit committee,* or *self-assessment programs* are more likely to have effective internal controls over financial reporting than companies without them.

Controls over the period-end financial reporting process are important because of the goal of preparing financial statements that are consistent with the applicable financial reporting framework. Factors in the period-end reporting process include the procedures (1) to enter transaction totals into the general ledger, (2) to select and apply accounting policies, (3) to initiate, authorize, record, and process journal entries in the general ledger, (4) to record recurring and nonrecurring adjustments to the annual and quarterly financial statements, and (5) to prepare annual and quarterly financial statements and related disclosures (AS5.26). Auditors are required to evaluate whether significant changes in the company from prior periods, including changes in internal controls over financial reporting, affect the risks of material misstatement. Auditors should also consider whether information obtained during a review of quarterly financial information is relevant to identifying risks of material misstatement at year-end.

Entity-Level Controls Related to the Risk of Fraud

The auditor is required to consider the risk of fraud when performing an audit of internal control over financial reporting and should reflect on whether the company has controls that sufficiently address its risk of material misstatement due to fraud (intentional misstatement in the financial statements) and of management override of controls (one way that fraud might occur).

The following could address the risk of fraud:

- Controls over significant, unusual transactions, particularly those that result in late or unusual journal entries
- Controls over journal entries and adjustments made in the period-end financial reporting process
- Controls over related-party transactions
- Controls related to significant management estimates
- Controls that mitigate the incentive for, and pressures on, management to falsify or inappropriately manage financial results. (AS5.14)

An auditor who identifies deficiencies in these controls designed to prevent or detect fraud in the audit of internal control over financial reporting should investigate these deficiencies during the financial statement audit. The auditor should gather sufficient evidence to evaluate the risk of material misstatement in the financial statements as a result of fraud.

Relevant Assertions for Significant Accounts and Disclosures

As part of the audit of internal controls over the financial reporting process, the auditor should identify relevant assertions associated with significant accounts and disclosures. The relevant assertions include the existence or occurrence, completeness, valuation or allocation, rights and obligations, and presentation and disclosure.[1] To identify an account or disclosure as significant, the auditor should consider the qualitative and quantitative risk factors associated with it. The risk factors considered for an audit of internal control over financial reporting are the same as those considered for an audit of the financial statements, so the significant accounts and disclosure and their relevant assertions are the same for both audits. The following factors should be considered in determining whether an account or a disclosure is significant.

- Size and composition of the account
- Susceptibility to misstatement due to errors or fraud

---

[1] The PCAOB uses five assertions in the auditing standards issued by the PCAOB. Auditing standards issued by the Auditing Standards Board use different assertions for account balances, transactions, and disclosure. Several of the auditing standards (issued by either board) allow the auditor to choose the set of assertions to use in the audit process.

- Volume of activity, complexity, and homogeneity of transactions in the account or reflected in the disclosure
- Nature of the account or disclosure
- Accounting and reporting complexities associated with the account or disclosure
- Exposure to losses in the account
- Possibility of significant contingent liabilities arising from the activities reflected in the account or disclosure
- Existence of related-party transactions in the account
- Changes from the prior period in account or disclosure characteristics (AS5.29)

In identifying significant accounts and disclosures, the auditor should consider the likely source of the misstatement by considering what could go wrong in each significant account or disclosure. To determine this, the auditor must (1) understand the flow of transactions related to the relevant assertions, including how these transactions are initiated, authorized, processed, and recorded, (2) verify that he or she has identified the points within the company's processes where a material misstatement could arise, (3) identify the controls implemented by management to address a potential misstatement, and (4) identify the controls that management has implemented over the unauthorized acquisition, use, or disposition of the company's assets that could result in a material misstatement (AS5.34).

The best way to gather evidence about a likely source of misstatement in a significant account or disclosure is to perform a walk-through. In doing so, the auditor follows a transaction from its origination, through the company's processes, including information systems, until it is reflected in the financial records. In the walk-through, the auditor uses the same documents and information technology that an employee uses when processing the transaction and inquiry as well as observation, inspection of documentation, and reperformance of controls to gather evidence. Following a transaction from origination to recording in the financial records allows the auditor to gain a sufficient understanding of the process to be able to identify places that are missing an important control as well as controls that are important to her or his conclusion about whether the company's controls address the risk of misstatement for the relevant assertion.

Mystery Bookstore Example: Identification of Controls to Test

Consider how the auditor identifies controls to test in the following situation.

1. Auditors for Stuart and Steigler, LLP, are conducting an audit for Mystery Bookstore, which sells books to customers in the store and on the Internet. Customers pay by cash or credit card. Store sensors on the doors go off when customers leave without paying for a book. The company owns the store furniture but leases the building. Mystery Bookstore has five employees.
2. In the annual report, the company discloses the following accounting policies:
   a. FIFO is used to determine the cost of its inventories.
   b. Lower of cost or market is used to value inventory at year-end.
   c. Equipment is depreciated on a straight-line basis over a five-year useful life.
3. Footnotes in the annual report include information on the operating leases for the buildings and on a contingent liability related to a lawsuit involving a salary dispute.

Identify Significant Accounts and Relevant Assertions

- The auditors have identified revenue and inventory as Mystery Bookstore's significant accounts. The contingent liability is a significant disclosure.
  - Revenue is a significant account because of its size and volume of activity.
  - Inventory is a significant account because of the accounting complexities associated with it, its susceptibility to misstatement due to errors or fraud, and the volume of its activity.

- The contingent liability is a significant disclosure because of its susceptibility to misstatement and the accounting and reporting complexities associated with its disclosure.

- The auditors have identified existence as a relevant assertion for the revenue account and existence and valuation as relevant assertions for the inventory account. Completeness and valuation have been identified as relevant assertions for the contingent liability disclosure.

  - Existence of revenue because the likely source of revenue misstatement is an overstatement of this account. If revenue is not valid (does not exist), revenue is overstated.

  - Existence and valuation of inventory because it is the major asset on the company's balance sheet, and if its balance is not valid (does not exist), it is overstated. The valuation rules for inventory are complex, and if it is not presented in accordance with the applicable financial reporting framework, the financial statements will be materially misstated because the inventory account's balance is material to the financial statements.

  - Completeness and valuation are relevant assertions for the disclosure of any and all contingent liabilities. To disclose a contingent liability in accordance with GAAP, it must be valued according to the applicable financial reporting framework.

- The auditors have identified several sources of likely misstatement: (1) daily reconciliations between the sales recorded on the cash registers and cash received for the day, (2) daily reconciliations between the number of goods shipped based on Internet sales and items invoiced for the sales, (3) the year-end physical count of inventory, (4) the year-end pricing of inventory according to FIFO, (5) the lower of cost or market valuation at year-end, (6) the process of identifying contingent liabilities, and (7) the process of recording year-end adjustments to the financial statements.

Perform a Walk-Through for Each Process Associated with a Significant Account or Disclosure

- The auditors have performed a walk-through for each process listed as a likely misstatement. During the walk-through, they document the processes followed from the initiation of the transaction to its recording in the financial records or in the preparation of its disclosure for the financial statements.

Identify Controls to Test Based on the Walk-Through

- The auditors have reviewed the walk-through documentation and determined whether the controls are in place to prevent or detect misstatements in revenue or inventory or in disclosure. The auditors have tested the identified controls to determine whether they are operating effectively at year-end.

Let's use one of these processes to consider a walk-through for daily reconciliations between goods shipped from Internet sales and items invoiced for the sale. The purpose of the walk-through is to identify controls that are in place and to determine where a control might be missing. This reconciliation process involves both of the significant accounts—revenue and inventory—and should include controls for management's assertion of existence for both accounts. The point of the reconciliation is to determine whether everything recognized as revenue for Internet sales is valid (inventory was shipped), and everything shipped was billed (invoices were prepared for inventory shipped). Reconciliation between goods shipped and goods invoiced provides *evidence* about management's assertion that revenue exists because the process includes controls to prevent or detect revenue from being recorded unless inventory is shipped. The reconciliation also determines whether everything shipped has been billed (evidence about management's assertion of completeness, that is, that all revenue and inventory transactions have been recorded).

The Shipping Process and Related Controls

- In a walk-through, the auditor follows a transaction from its origination until it is reflected in the financial records.

- Because there are Internet sales, these transactions originate when someone logs onto the company's website and places an order, and controls are built into the website to accept orders only after the credit card has been verified. This control prevents shipping goods when the cash will not be collected.
- The order generates a shipping document that is sent electronically to the warehouse so personnel there can gather the books for shipping.
- Personnel in the shipping department print the shipping document and collect the books, noting on the shipping document in the computer file whether any books are out of stock so that the invoice generated includes only the books shipped and shows any that are out of stock. The company knows that it should not recognize revenue for goods until they are shipped.
- As a book is removed from the shelves, its International Standard Book Number (ISBN) code is scanned to remove this inventory item from the general ledger inventory file. The accounting software generates a daily report listing items removed from inventory based on this scanning.
- A printout of the shipping document (listing the books ready to ship and those out of stock) and the corresponding books are placed in a tray and sent on a conveyer belt to the shipping department.
- Before packing the books in a box, accounting personnel in the shipping department verify that the books shipped are the same as those ordered by checking off the book titles on the shipping document. The specific person verifying the information initials the bottom of the shipping document. This copy of the shipping document is filed in the shipping department (daily) and is input into the computer to indicate that the inventory has been shipped. The accounting system can generate the invoice as soon as the shipping department approves the inventory for shipping by entering a code in the file to indicate that the items shipped agree with those listed on the shipping document.
- The accounting department receives a daily report listing the shipments that have been approved and invoiced. It uses the totals on this report to adjust the revenue and cash account in the general ledger. An entry for inventory and cost of goods sold is also made at this time.
- The report of items shipped is reconciled daily with the warehouse report of items removed from inventory. The accounting software reconciles the two reports by matching ISBNs and comparing the items removed from inventory with the items invoiced. Any differences between the two reports are listed as exceptions.
- The accounting department reviews the exception report daily. All exceptions are resolved, and the resolution is noted on the exception report. The accountant resolving the exceptions signs the reconciliation each day. If books were shipped and not invoiced, revenue and cash are corrected (upward). If out-of-stock books were invoiced, revenue and cash are adjusted (downward).
- The daily reconciliations and exception reports are filed by day and available for the auditor to review at year-end.

Controls to Test

- Of the controls, the most important is the resolution of daily exception reports. The auditors should select a sample of those reports to review to verify that they were signed (the signature is the control) and that the exceptions have been resolved in a reasonable manner. The auditors should look for patterns in the exceptions to see whether a control is missing in this system and allows exceptions to occur. If the exception report is not resolved, the business could have a control deficiency that fails to prevent or detect misstatements in the financial statements. The misstatement that is most likely to occur is early revenue recognition (before goods are shipped).
- IT control verifies credit cards before a sales order can be processed. The auditors should determine whether the IT control works, that only authorized sales generate a sales order, and that a sales order cannot be generated in other ways.

- Daily shipping documents filed in the shipping department with inventory items checked off and initials on the bottom of the documents provide another control. Auditors should determine whether the shipping documents have been filed, inventory items have been checked off, and the document has been initialed.
- An IT control determines that the accounting system generates an invoice only when the shipping department has approved the order for shipping. Auditors would check for this.
- Auditors check that the accounting software compares on a daily basis the ISBNs for items shipped and items invoiced.

Testing Internal Control over Financial Reporting

The auditors should perform tests of controls over a period of time so they can determine whether the controls are working "as of" the report date. Auditors could obtain evidence about the effectiveness of a control at an interim date and not test its operation at year-end, which is referred to as a *roll-forward procedure.* To perform it, the auditor must consider the risk associated with the control and its nature, the results of the previous test, the length of the remaining period, and whether any changes to the control have been made since the interim date. In some cases, the auditors could use inquiry alone as a roll-forward procedure.

Auditors must evaluate the operating effectiveness of controls involving all relevant assertions for all significant accounts and disclosures each year except for controls that have been replaced with more effective ones. The auditors also are expected to vary the internal control testing from year to year to introduce unpredictability into the testing.

Auditors can use the work of others including internal auditors and other company personnel to evaluate internal control. Auditors should assess the competence and objectivity of the persons whose work they plan to use (the higher the degree of competence and objectivity, the more use the auditor may make of the work). As the risk associated with a particular control increases, the need for the auditor to increase the level of testing also increases.

Management's Written Representations Regarding Internal Control over Financial Reporting

Auditors should obtain a written statement from management regarding internal control that should:

- Acknowledge management's responsibility for establishing and maintaining effective internal control over financial reporting
- State that management has assessed the effectiveness of internal control over financial reporting and specify the control criteria used
- State that management did not use the auditors' procedures for the financial statement audit or the audit of internal controls over financial reporting as the basis for management's assessment of the effectiveness of internal control over financial reporting
- State management's conclusion about the effectiveness of internal control over financial reporting based on the control criteria as of a specific date
- State that management has disclosed to the auditors all deficiencies in the design or operation of internal control over financial reporting identified as part of management's assessment, including the disclosure of significant deficiencies or material weaknesses in internal control over financial reporting
- Describe any fraud resulting in material misstatements to the company's financial statements and any other fraud that does not result in a material misstatement but involves senior management or other employees who have a significant role in the company's internal control over financial reporting
- State whether control deficiencies identified and communicated to the audit committee during previous engagements have been resolved and specifically identifying any that have not

- State whether there were, subsequent to the date reporting on, any changes in internal control over financial reporting or other factors that may significantly affect internal control over financial reporting, including corrective action taken by management with regard to significant deficiencies and material weaknesses (AS5.77).

Management's refusal to furnish a written representation regarding internal control over financial reporting constitutes a limitation on the audit scope. In this case, the auditor either withdraws from the audit or issues a disclaimer of opinion.

Did You Know?

Kmart announced that it was tightening its financial controls over recording vendor allowances after the SEC sued the company's executives regarding a $24 million accounting fraud. The fraud involved recording vendor allowances, which suppliers pay to Kmart for advertising costs and markdown allowances. While investigating the fraud, Kmart determined that vendor allowances had been recorded early, allowing Kmart executives to meet their divisional profit targets. Kmart fired the executives, who agreed to pay civil penalties ranging from $25,000 to $55,000 to settle the suit.

Source: Amy Merrick, "Former Employees of Kmart, Vendors are Sued by SEC," *The Wall Street Journal,* December 3, 2004.

What internal control would have prevented or detected this misstatement?

Auditor's Reporting Requirements for an Audit of Internal Controls over Financial Reporting

LO9

Describe the auditor's reporting requirements for internal control deficiencies and material weaknesses in an audit of internal controls over financial reporting

Control Deficiencies and Material Weaknesses

In assessing the effectiveness of internal controls, management must identify any control deficiencies. A control deficiency exists when the control does not allow management or employees to prevent or detect misstatements. Deficiencies can be of two types: deficiencies in design or deficiencies in operation. A **deficiency in design** exists when a control is either missing or does not operate as designed. A **deficiency in operation** exists when a control does not operate as it should or when the person performing the control does not have the authority to do so or the knowledge to perform it effectively.

A *material weakness* is a deficiency or a combination of deficiencies that indicates a reasonable possibility that a material misstatement of the company's annual or interim financial statements will not be prevented or detected on a timely basis (AS5.A7). If the internal controls over financial reporting for the company have any material weaknesses, the auditor must express an *adverse* opinion on the effectiveness of internal control over financial reporting. The auditor can issue a clean opinion on the financial statements even when he or she issues an adverse opinion on the effectiveness of internal controls over financial reporting *if* the auditor determines that the financial statements are fairly presented in accordance with the applicable financial reporting framework.

A *significant deficiency* is a weakness or a combination of weaknesses that is less severe than a material deficiency yet important enough to warrant attention by those responsible for the oversight of the company's financial reporting (AS5.A11). Auditors consider whether significant deficiencies are material weaknesses by examining their severity. This determination depends on (1) whether a reasonable possibility exists that the company's controls will fail to prevent or detect misstatements in an account balance or disclosure *and* (2) the magnitude of the potential misstatement (AS5.63). A deficiency's severity is not related to whether a misstatement has actually occurred but whether a reasonable possibility exists that the company's internal controls will fail to prevent or detect the misstatement.

Auditor's Opinion on the Effectiveness of Internal Control over Financial Reporting

Auditors issue an unqualified opinion when no material weaknesses exist in the internal control and when the scope of their work has not been limited. In determining whether

Management's Report on Internal Control over Financial Reporting *Goodyear Tire & Rubber Co. December 31, 2004*	Exhibit 3-7

Management of the Company is responsible for establishing and maintaining adequate internal control over financial reporting as such term is defined under Rule 13a-5 (1) promulgated under the Securities Exchange Act of 1934, as amended. The Company's internal control over financial reporting is a process designed to provide reasonable assurance regarding the reliability of financial reporting and preparation of financial statements for external purposes in accordance with an applicable financial reporting framework. Because of its inherent limitations, internal control over financial reporting may not prevent or detect misstatements. Also, projections of any evaluation of effectiveness to future periods are subject to the risk that controls may become inadequate because of changes in conditions, or that the degree or compliance with the policies or procedures may deteriorate.

In order to evaluate the effectiveness of the Company's internal control over financial reporting as required by Section 404 of the Sarbanes-Oxley Act, management conducted an assessment, including testing, using the criteria in the *Internal Control–Integrated Framework,* issued by the Committee of Sponsoring Organizations of the Treadway Commission.

A material weakness is a control deficiency or combination of control deficiencies that result in more than a remote likelihood that a material misstatement of the annual or interim consolidated financial statements will not be prevented or detected. As of December 31, 2004, the Company did not maintain effective controls over certain account reconciliations and did not maintain adequate segregation of duties at the application control level in certain information technology environments. A description of the material weaknesses that existed as of December 3l, 2004, as well as their actual and potential effect on the presentation of the Company's consolidated financial statements issued during their existence, is discussed below.

Account reconciliations. At December 3l, 2004, the Company did not maintain effective control over the preparation and review of account reconciliations of certain general ledger accounts. This control deficiency primarily related to account reconciliations of goodwill, deferred charges, fixed assets, compensation and benefits, accounts payable-trade and the accounts of a retail subsidiary in France. This control deficiency resulted in misstatements that were part of the restatement of the Company's consolidated financial statements for 2003, 2002 and 2001, for each of the quarters for the year ended December 31, 2003, and for the first, second, and third quarters for the year ended December 31, 2004. Additionally, this control deficiency could result in a material misstatement to annual or interim consolidated financial statements that would not be prevented or detected. Accordingly, management has determined that this control deficiency constitutes a material weakness.

Segregation of duties. At December 3l, 2004, the Company did not maintain effective controls over the segregation of duties at the application control level in certain information technology environments as a result of not restricting the access of certain individuals in both information technology and finance. These deficiencies existed in varying degrees in certain business segments within the revenue and purchasing processes. This control deficiency did not result in any adjustments to the annual or interim consolidated financial statements; however, this control deficiency could result in a material misstatement to annual or interim consolidated financial statements that would not be prevented or detected. Accordingly, management has determined that this control deficiency constitutes a material weakness.

Because of the material weaknesses just described, management has concluded that, as of December 3l, 2004, the Company did not maintain effective internal controls over financial reporting, based on criteria established in *Internal Control—Integrated Framework.*

Management's assessment of the effectiveness of the Company's internal control over financial reporting as of December 3l, 2004, has been audited by Pricewaterhouse-Coopers LLP, an independent registered public accounting firm, as stated in their report which is included herein.

2004 Annual Report, Goodyear Tire & Rubber Co.

a control deficiency or a combination of control deficiencies reaches the level of a material weakness, auditors must consider the effect of *compensating* controls and whether they prevent or detect a material misstatement in the financial statements (AS5.68). If a material weakness exists in internal control, the auditor expresses an adverse opinion on the effectiveness of internal control over financial reporting. See management's report on internal controls over financial reporting for Goodyear Tire & Rubber Co. and the auditors' adverse opinion on internal controls over financial reporting (Exhibits 3-7 and 3-8). The Goodyear opinion was adverse because of a material weakness in internal controls over financial reporting.

Goodyear Tire & Rubber Company *Opinion Paragraph, Internal Control*	Exhibit 3-8

over Financial Reporting, Report of Independent Registered Public Accounting Firm, December 31, 2004

To the Board of Directors and Shareholders of The Goodyear Tire & Rubber Company:

We have completed an integrated audit of The Goodyear Tire & Rubber Company's 2004 consolidated financial statements and of its internal control over financial reporting as of December 31, 2004, and audits of its 2003 and 2002 consolidated financial statements in accordance with the standards of the Public Company Accounting Oversight Board (United States). Our opinions, based on our audits, are presented below.

INTERNAL CONTROL OVER FINANCIAL REPORTING

In our opinion, management's assessment that The Goodyear Tire & Rubber Company did not maintain effective internal control over financial reporting as of December 31, 2004, is fairly stated, in all material respects, based on criteria established in Internal Control—Integrated Framework issued by the COSO. Also, in our opinion, because of the effects of the material weaknesses described above on the achievement of the objectives of the control criteria, The Goodyear Tire & Rubber Company has not maintained effective internal control over financial reporting as of December 31, 2004, based on criteria established in Internal control—Integrated Framework issued by the COSO.

PricewaterhouseCoopers LLP
Cleveland, Ohio
March 16, 2005

Excerpt from 2004 Annual Report, Goodyear Tire & Rubber Co.

Refer to Exhibit 3-9 for an example of Ernst & Young's unqualified opinion on the effectiveness of Hewlett-Packard's internal control over financial reporting.

Management's failure to provide a written representation constitutes a scope limitation. An unqualified opinion on internal control over financial reporting would not be issued without the management representation letter. A *scope limitation* results in either a qualified opinion or a disclaimer of opinion, depending on the significance of the scope limitation. See Exhibit 3-10 for an example of a disclaimer of opinion issued by BDO Seidman for Hecla Mining Company. BDO Seidman issued a disclaimer of opinion because "management was unable to complete all of its testing of internal controls" (Hecla Mining Annual Report, 2004).

The opinion issued on internal controls over financial reporting does not have to be the same as the opinion issued on the financial statements. For example, the auditor can issue a disclaimer of opinion on internal controls over financial reporting and a clean opinion on the financial statements (see Exhibit 3-11 for the auditor's opinion on the financial statements of Hecla Mining). The auditors issued an unqualified opinion on the financial statements and a disclaimer of opinion on internal controls over financial reporting.

Tests of controls performed by the auditor for an audit of internal controls over financial reporting allow her or him to express an opinion on the effectiveness of the company's internal control over financial reporting as of a **point in time** (at year-end or quarter-end). The auditor may choose to issue a combined report giving an opinion on the client's financial statements and an opinion on internal control over financial reporting or to issue separate reports on the company's financial statements and on internal control over financial reporting. If separate reports are issued, the reports should have the same date.

A new auditing standard issued in 2006 allows the auditor to conduct a voluntary audit to report on whether a material weakness previously reported during an annual audit still exists. When a company reports a material weakness in internal controls over financial reporting, outsiders may wonder about the reliability of its financial reporting. In this situation, the company could correct the material weakness and then ask the auditor to conduct an engagement to report on whether the material weakness reported in the previous audit report still exists. This report provides outsiders information about the reliability of reporting in the company without the necessity of waiting for next

Report of Independent Registered Public Accounting Firm *Hewlett-Packard*

Exhibit 3-9

To the Board of Directors and Stockholders of Hewlett-Packard Company

We have audited Hewlett-Packard Company's internal control over financial reporting as of October 31, 2008, based on criteria established in Internal Control—Integrated Framework issued by the Committee of Sponsoring Organizations of the Treadway Commission (the COSO criteria). Hewlett-Packard Company's management is responsible for maintaining effective internal control over financial reporting and for its assessment of the effectiveness of internal control over financial reporting included in the accompanying Management's Report on Internal Control over Financial Reporting. Our responsibility is to express an opinion on the effectiveness of the Company's internal control over financial reporting based on our audit.

We conducted our audit in accordance with the standards of the Public Company Accounting Oversight Board (United States). Those standards require that we plan and perform the audit to obtain reasonable assurance about whether effective internal control over financial reporting was maintained in all material respects. Our audit included obtaining an understanding of internal control over financial reporting, assessing the risk that a material weakness exists, testing and evaluating the design and operating effectiveness of internal control based on the assessed risk, and performing such other procedures as we considered necessary in the circumstances. We believe that our audit provides a reasonable basis for our opinion.

A company's internal control over financial reporting is a process designed to provide reasonable assurance regarding the reliability of financial reporting and the preparation of financial statements for external purposes in accordance with an applicable financial reporting framework. A company's internal control over financial reporting includes those policies and procedures that (1) pertain to the maintenance of records that, in reasonable detail, accurately and fairly reflect the transactions and dispositions of the assets of the company; (2) provide reasonable assurance that transactions are recorded as necessary to permit preparation of financial statements in accordance with generally accepted accounting principles, and that receipts and expenditures of the company are being made only in accordance with authorizations of management and directors of the company; and (3) provide reasonable assurance regarding prevention or timely detection of unauthorized acquisition, use, or disposition of the company's assets that could have a material effect on the financial statements.

Because of its inherent limitations, internal control over financial reporting may not prevent or detect misstatements. Also, projections of any evaluation of effectiveness to future periods are subject to the risk that controls may become inadequate because of changes in conditions, or that the degree of compliance with the policies or procedures may deteriorate.

As indicated in the accompanying Management's Report on Internal Control over Financial Reporting, management's assessment of and conclusion on the effectiveness of internal control over financial reporting did not include the internal controls of Electronic Data Systems Corporation, which is included in the 2008 consolidated financial statements of Hewlett-Packard Company. For the fiscal year ended October 31, 2008, Electronic Data Systems Corporation constituted 3 percent of Hewlett-Packard Company's total net revenue, and the fair value assigned to tangible assets for purposes of applying the purchase method of accounting as of the acquisition date accounted for approximately 11 percent of Hewlett-Packard Company's total assets as of October 31, 2008. Our audit of internal control over financial reporting of Hewlett-Packard Company also did not include evaluation of the internal control over financial reporting of Electronic Data Systems Corporation.

In our opinion, Hewlett-Packard Company maintained, in all material respects, effective internal control over financial reporting as of October 31, 2008, based on the COSO criteria.

We also have audited, in accordance with the standards of the Public Company Accounting Oversight Board (United States), the accompanying consolidated balance sheets of Hewlett-Packard Company and subsidiaries as of October 31, 2008 and 2007, and the related consolidated statements of earnings, stockholders' equity and cash flows for each of the three years in the period ended October 31, 2008 and our report dated December 15, 2008 expressed an unqualified opinion thereon.

/s/ ERNST & YOUNG LLP
San Jose, California
December 15, 2008

year's audit report. This type of engagement is voluntary. The PCAOB standards do not require the auditor to undertake an engagement to report on whether a material weakness continues to exist.

Did You Know?

Nortel Networks Corp. restated its financial statements in 2004 after announcing, "Our auditors have informed our audit committee of the existence of material weaknesses in internal control." Deloitte & Touche LLP, auditors for the telecommunications equipment company, advised Nortel that they had found a lack of compliance with company procedures for monitoring balances related to accruals and provisions, including restructuring

Report of Independent Registered Public Accounting Firm *Hecla Mining Company*

Exhibit 3-10

The Board of Directors and Shareholders of Hecla Mining Company Coeur d'Alene, Idaho

We were engaged to audit management's assessment, included in the accompanying Management's Report on Internal Control over Financial Reporting appearing under item 9A, that Hecla Mining Company did not maintain effective internal control over financial reporting as of December 31, 2004 because of the material weaknesses noted below, and based on the criteria established in Internal Control—Integrated Framework issued by the Committee of Sponsoring Organizations of the Treadway Commission (COSO). Hecla Mining Company's management is responsible for maintaining effective internal control over financial reporting and for its assessment of the effectiveness of internal control over financial reporting.

The Company's financial statements include Greens Creek Joint Venture, a 29.73 percent owned subsidiary that is proportionately consolidated in accordance with Emerging Issues Task Force No. 00-1. Management has been unable to assess the effectiveness of internal control at this subsidiary due to the fact that the Company does not have the ability to dictate or modify the controls of the subsidiary and also does not have the ability to assess those controls.

The Company's employees at the Velardena Mill in Mexico initiated a strike in October, 2004. As a result of this strike, the Velardena Mill has been temporarily idled. Additionally, the terms of the strike are such that access to the facility is limited.

As this strike occurred before management was able to complete all of its testing of the internal controls for the Velardena Mill operations, we are unable to evaluate the effectiveness of the Company's internal controls over the Velardena Mill operations.

A material weakness is a control deficiency, or combination of control deficiencies, that results in more than a remote likelihood that a material misstatement of the annual or interim financial statements will not be prevented or detected. The following material weaknesses have been identified and included in management's assessment. The Company's accounts payable process in Mexico has an insufficient level of monitoring, training and oversight, which restricts the Company's ability to analyze, reconcile and accurately report information relative to the accounts payable. In addition, inventory that was in process at the date of the strike at the Velardena Mill in Mexico was disposed of into the tailings pond by operations, but this event did not get communicated to accounting, and was therefore not properly expensed until the matter was discovered by us during the financial statement audit procedures. As a result, the Company recorded an adjustment as of December 31, 2004 to decrease the year end inventory balance and to increase the net loss by $421,000. We believe these conditions represent a material weakness under the standards of the Public Company Accounting Oversight Board (United States), in the design and operation of the internal control of Hecla Mining Company in effect as of, and for the year ended, December 31, 2004.

A company's internal control over financial reporting is a process designed to provide reasonable assurance regarding the reliability of financial reporting and the preparation of financial statements for external purposes in accordance with an applicable financial reporting framework. A company's internal control over financial reporting includes those policies and procedures that (1) pertain to the maintenance of records that, in reasonable detail accurately and fairly reject the transactions and dispositions of the assets of the company, (2) provide reasonable assurance that transactions are recorded as necessary to permit preparation of financial statements in accordance with an applicable financial reporting framework, and that receipts and expenditures of the company are being made only in accordance with authorizations of management and directors of the company, and (3) provide reasonable assurance regarding prevention or timely detection of unauthorized acquisition, use, or disposition of the company's assets that could have a material effect on the financial statements.

Because of its inherent limitations, internal control over financial reporting may not prevent or detect misstatements. Also, projections of any evaluation of effectiveness to future periods are subject to the risk that controls may become inadequate because of changes in conditions, or that the degree of compliance with the policies or procedures may deteriorate.

Since management was unable to complete all of its testing of internal control related to the Velardena Mill operations, the scope of our work was not sufficient to enable us to express, and we do not express, an opinion either on management's assessment or on the effectiveness of the company's internal control over financial reporting.

We have also audited, in accordance with the standards of the Public Company Accounting Oversight Board (United States), the consolidated financial statements of Hecla Mining Company as of December 31, 2004 and 2003 and our report dated March 10, 2005 expressed an unqualified opinion on these consolidated financial statements.

/s/ BDO Seidman, LLP
March 10, 2005
Spokane, Washington

2004 Annual Report, Hecla Mining

Audit Opinion on the Financial Statements   *Hecla Mining*   Exhibit 3-11

REPORT OF INDEPENDENT REGISTERED PUBLIC ACCOUNTING FIRM

The Board of Directors and Shareholders of Hecla Mining Company Coeur d'Alene, Idaho

We have audited the accompanying consolidated balance sheets of Hecla Mining Company as of December 31, 2004 and 2003, and the related consolidated statements of operations and comprehensive income (loss), cash flows and changes in shareholders' equity for each of the three years in the period ended December 31, 2004. These financial statements are the responsibility of the Company's management. Our responsibility is to express an opinion on these financial statements based on our audits.

We did not audit the financial statements of the Greens Creek Joint Venture, a 29.73 percent owned subsidiary, which statements reflect total assets constituting 24.2 percent and 19.4 percent of the consolidated total assets as of December 31, 2004 and 2003, respectively, and 26.1 percent, 26.9 percent and 24.0 percent, respectively, of the consolidated revenues for the years ended December 31, 2004, 2003 and 2002, respectively. Those statements were audited by other auditors whose reports have been furnished to us, and our opinion, insofar as it relates to the amounts included for the Greens Creek Joint Venture, is based solely on the reports of the other auditors.

We conducted our audits in accordance with the standards of the Public Company Accounting Oversight Board (United States). Those standards require that we plan and perform the audit to obtain reasonable assurance about whether the financial statements are free of material misstatement. An audit includes examining, on a test basis, evidence supporting the amounts and disclosures in the financial statements. An audit also includes assessing the accounting principles used and significant estimates made by management, as well as evaluating the overall financial statement presentation. We believe that our audits and the reports of the other auditors provide a reasonable basis for our opinion.

In our opinion, based on our audits and the reports of other auditors, the consolidated financial statements referred to above present fairly, in all material respects, the financial position of Hecla Mining Company at December 31, 2004 and 2003, and the results of its operations and its cash flows for each of the three years in the period ended December 31, 2004, in conformity with accounting principles generally accepted in the United States of America.

As discussed in Note 1 to the consolidated financial statements, the Company changed its method of accounting for asset retirement obligations in 2003.

We also have audited, in accordance with the standards of the Public Company Accounting Oversight Board (United States), the effectiveness of Hecla Mining Company's internal control over financial reporting as of December 31, 2004, based on criteria established in Internal Control—Integrated Framework issued by the Committee of Sponsoring Organizations of the Treadway Commission and issued our report dated March 10, 2005, which disclaimed an opinion on the Hecla Mining Company's internal controls over financial reporting.

/s/ BDO Seidman, LLP
March 10, 2005
Spokane, Washington

2004 Annual Report, Hecla Mining

---

charges and a lack of understanding of an applicable financial reporting framework regarding the recording of liabilities.

Source: Mark Heinzl, "Nortel Executives Put on Leave Are Finance Chiefs of 4 Divisions," *The Wall Street Journal,* May 7, 2004.

> ***What is the effect of issuing a report indicating that the company has a material weakness?***

For a summary of the various opinions that can be issued by an auditor in an audit of internal controls over the financial reporting process, see Exhibit 3-12.

Role of Internal Controls in the Corporate Governance Process

LO10

Understand the role of internal controls in the corporate governance process

The corporate governance process in the United States and in countries around the world is designed to provide outsiders information they need to make decisions about a company. The benefit to society is an efficient distribution of capital, which occurs when outsiders make decisions about a company based on accurate information. Accurate information also helps potential investors make correct investment decisions and

Audit Opinions   *Internal Controls over the Financial Reporting Process*   Exhibit 3-12

| | Circumstance | | | |
Opinion Issued	Internal controls over Financial Reporting Are Effective	Limitation on the Scope of the Audit	Material Weakness	Management Fails to Provide Written Representation
Unqualified opinion	√			
Disclaimer of opinion		√		√
Adverse opinion			√	

allows banks to loan money at the correct interest rates. Because outsiders have no information about the company other than what it provides, the accuracy of the information given to outsiders is extremely important.

Internal controls are part of the corporate governance process. They work best when management takes the responsibility to establish and test internal controls for significant accounts and disclosures in the financial statements. If internal controls fail, what happens? The auditor gathers evidence about the significant accounts and disclosures in the financial statements using substantive audit procedures. The internal control documentation and testing process improve the company's efficiencies—perhaps not at first glance because internal controls are cumbersome and quite inefficient; yet in the long run, if they prevent or detect misstatements in the financial statements, they will improve efficiency. The role that internal controls play in the corporate governance process is to make management responsible for the procedures used in financial reporting. Unfortunately, having effective internal controls does not mean that the financial statements are fairly stated; they mean that documentation of the control occurred.

Chapter Takeaways

Chapter 3 has discussed the auditor's responsibility for internal controls in an audit of both the financial statements and the controls over the financial reporting process. The auditor's responsibility in the internal control area is more involved today than it has been at any point in the past. When you begin your work as an auditor, you will be required to understand the internal control process.

This chapter presented these important facts:

- The auditor's responsibility for internal control testing in audits of financial statements and of internal controls over financial reporting
- The specific internal control procedures management used to design controls to prevent or detect misstatements
- The specific auditing techniques the auditor used to test internal controls.
- The use of compensating controls in the internal control function.
- The importance of dual-purpose tests in the evidence collection process.
- Management's and the auditors' reporting responsibilities for internal control deficiencies.
- The process the auditor used to identify significant accounts and disclosure during the audit of internal controls over financial reporting.
- The importance of internal controls in the corporate governance process.

Information Systems Auditing
Clients' Use of Computer Systems to Record Transactions

LO11

Understand the role of information systems in an audit of the financial statements and the financial reporting process

Today computers play an important role in the audit process. Companies use computers, both mainframe and personal, to process accounting transactions. Auditors use computers to audit the client's accounting systems. Computer operations perform many internal control procedures (segregation of duties, authorization procedures, documented transaction trails, and independent reconciliations). Computerized internal controls are reliable because computers perform tasks consistently. A computerized control will always be performed; the computer will not forget to do it or be too tired to do it. Once a computer correctly performs a control, it will always perform the control in the same fashion. The auditor's goal in working with computerized internal controls is to verify that the computer does indeed perform the control of interest to the auditor. In other words, the auditor must determine whether the computer has been correctly programmed to perform the control operation and does so without exception.

According to the auditing standards, the auditor's responsibility for computerized internal controls during an audit is to understand the audit client's internal control systems to understand the client's *environment.* Whether the internal control system is computerized or not, the auditor must develop an understanding of the internal control system that is sufficient for planning the audit to reduce the risk of material misstatement to an acceptably low level.

The auditor determines whether the internal controls that the computer system should perform actually occur when it processes a transaction. This will happen only when the auditor understands the internal control system including the parts that the computers perform. Understanding the system must come before the testing phase of an audit.

A computerized information system typically includes six different elements: (1) hardware, (2) software, (3) documentation, (4) personnel, (5) data, and (6) information processing controls related to (a) input, (b) processing, and (c) output of data. Let's look at each of these elements in a little more detail.

Computer *hardware,* which is the physical equipment that makes up the computer, is quite reliable today. The auditor should understand the hardware controls that are part of the computer equipment. He or she may review operating reports for the hardware to determine that regular maintenance is being performed on it and to review the downtime logs to see how often the computer is not operational.

Computer *software* includes both the system operating software and the application software. The operating system software (Windows, Unix, or Linux, for example) controls the operation of the hardware, and the application software (such as Excel or Oracle's JD Edwards Enterprise) performs the information processing tasks. For example, JD Edwards Enterprise software sells application programs for accounts payable, account receivable, cost accounting, asset management, expense management, fixed asset accounting, and general ledger accounting.

Some audit clients may use enterprise resource planning programs (ERPs) such as SAP and PeopleSoft that are designed to be *integrated* processing programs. This means that the software integrates processing over accounting areas, such as purchasing, shipping, and sales revenue. ERP programs are costly to implement and when systems are integrated, a problem with processing transactions in one area can cause problems in all integrated areas.

Documentation of the computer software programs is crucial to both the audit client and the auditor. The documentation of a software program includes the system and the controls for (1) input of information, (2) information processing, (3) output of information, (4) report processing, (5) logic of the software program, and (6) operator instructions. The auditor reviews the documentation of computer software programs for an audit client as part of developing an understanding of the internal control system.

The *employees* of the information technology (IT) department— systems analysts, programmers, computer operators, data conversion operators, librarians, and a group that controls the flow of input and output in the department are important to the operation of the controls. Segregation of duties between the systems analyst, the programmers, and the operators is crucial. The goal of segregation of duties in the IT department is to ensure that the people who design the systems do not program them and that neither the designer nor the programmer should operate the system when data are processed. A lack of segregation of duties among these three positions would be viewed as a weakness in internal controls.

Computer systems are designed to process *data*. The transaction data enter the computer system, is processed by it, and it produces and distributes a report regarding the transaction data. For example, a sales report for a car showroom might function as follows: sales data enter the computer system, which processes the data as a cash sale or a credit sale and could produce a report showing daily sales information for each car salesperson. The report is distributed to each salesperson and his or her supervisor.

Information technology application controls are important for monitoring how the information is processed once it enters the IT system. The *application* controls are specific to each accounting application (for example, the sales revenue business process). They regulate the information's input, processing, and output. Input controls can include commands to determine that the input was authorized and approved, to count how many transactions were submitted for processing, total of batches (the total dollar amount of the transactions submitted), and to perform valid character tests (fields should contain numbers, not letters), missing data tests (all fields are completed that are needed), and limit or reasonableness tests (pay for this salary grade should not be more than . . .). Many of the processing controls are the same as the application controls and are used during the processing of the transaction. In addition, the processing controls can include a control total report (from the items processed), file and operator controls (to determine that the correct files are used in processing the applications), and limit and reasonableness tests. Output controls determine that only authorized people receive the output or have access to the files where the transactions were recorded. Output controls include totals, changes in the master file, and lists for distribution of output.

Let's consider how misstatements can occur in a computerized information processing system. They can enter the data file when:

- Fictitious transactions or unauthorized transactions enter the system.
- The source data are converted into machine-readable form.
- The wrong input file is used for processing transactions.
- Information is transferred from one software system to another (the accounts receivable system provides data to the general ledger).
- Output files are created that do not reflect the transactions that the system processed.
- Master files are changed in error.

Because information is processed by computer software, it is transferred from one file or one accounting system program to another. Anytime information is transferred, it could be lost or altered. The auditor prefers to see internal controls in place to avoid the loss or misapplication of transaction data.

Auditor's Use of Computer Systems to Review the Audit Client's Recorded Transactions

LO12

Describe how the auditor uses computer applications as part of the audit process

Auditors purchase audit software or develop proprietary software to use in the audit process. One software package that auditors frequently use is Audit Command Language (ACL).

Audit software can do many things including:

- Perform mathematical operations (compute averages, verify totals)
- Identify outliers in data
- Perform analytical procedures by computing ratios and comparing balances from one year to the next
- Select randomized samples
- Prepare trial balances and post adjusting entries to the trial balance
- Generate audit programs and reports
- Prepare consolidated financial statements
- Provide access to audit and accounting standards
- Access client files to perform statistical analysis on the data in the file

Consider some techniques that an auditor could use to perform statistical analysis on the client's files: (1) live data, (2) simulated data, and (3) historical data to gather evidence from the client data files.

When using *live* data, the auditor tags transactions processed by the data programs the client uses as the accounting software processes them. The data can then be saved for the auditor to review at a later date. The auditor could, for example, choose to review ten sales transactions per month and tag them as they are processed to review at year-end during the audit engagement. To do this, the auditor installs software in the client's computer programs that will identify client data for audit as they are processed during the year, not just at an interim time period or year-end. This process could allow the auditor to perform *continuous auditing.*

An auditor could use two types of *simulated* data to evaluate the IT system's operation: (1) test data or (2) an integrated test facility to examine the client's computerized information system. The auditor uses test data to evaluate the information system's operating process. The auditor develops a number of test transactions, some with errors and some that are error free, for the system to process. This is one way to test whether the controls described in the system's documentation operate as they should. The integrated test facility approach also uses simulated data to test the system's operation, but in this case, the facility is a dummy company or branch. Fictitious data developed for the test facility allows the auditor to determine how the client's IT system processes the data. Both internal and external auditors may use these two methods to review the controls of the computerized computer system.

Auditors could test the processing of the client's computer systems by reprocessing its data. This is referred to as using *historical* client data to evaluate the IT system's operation. When using this technique, the auditor writes a computer program to determine whether the controls in the client's IT system operate as planned, then runs the program on the client's historical data, and compares the results obtained with results reported by the client, referred to as *parallel simulation.* Parallel simulation requires the auditor to have programming expertise.

Computerized audit procedures that gather and document evidence are used in most audits. These computer-assisted audit tools and techniques are often referred to as *CAATTs.* Their use during an audit provides one way to standardize audit procedures performed for each audit. CAATTs can also provide standardized audit documentation that is useful for demonstrating that the auditor gathered sufficient appropriate audit evidence as the basis for the audit opinion to issue. The auditing firm provides training on the CAATT when it hires a new auditor.

Be sure that you understand these concepts before you go on to the next chapter.

Review Questions

LO1	1. Describe the five components of an internal control system. As an auditor, how will you document the five parts of the internal control system?
LO3	2. Explain how the auditor tests internal controls in a financial statement audit.
LO2	3. According to auditing standards, what is the auditor's requirement regarding internal controls in a financial statement audit? Is this requirement different in an integrated audit? Explain.
LO2	4. Must the auditor test internal controls in a financial statement audit? Explain your answer.
LO3	5. The auditing standards require the auditor to gather "sufficient appropriate evidence." What does this mean?
LO3	6. Define *control risk*. When does the auditor perform control tests to test his or her assessment of control risk? Is it assessed for the audit as a whole or for each business process?
LO5	7. Why would an auditor gather evidence using a combination of internal control testing and substantive testing?
LO5	8. Describe compensating controls, and provide one example.
LO5	9. Describe five procedures a company might use as internal control procedures.
LO6	10. What are dual-purpose tests? How does the auditor use them?
LO3	11. What information does the evidence the auditor gathers using internal control tests provide? What information does the evidence the auditor gathers using substantive testing provide? Which type of evidence is better?
LO7	12. How does the auditor communicate internal control deficiencies to management and the audit committee in a financial statement audit?
LO8	13. What is an integrated audit? Which companies use it?
LO8	14. What is management's requirement relating to internal controls over financial reporting?
LO8	15. What is the COSO internal control framework? How is it used?
LO1	16. What is reasonable assurance? Is it good?
LO2	17. What are internal control deficiencies in design and in operation?
LO5	18. Describe how internal controls can prevent or detect misstatements.
LO9	19. Describe management's report on internal controls over financial reporting. Where is it reported and how often?
LO9	20. What does it mean for an audit client if the auditor discloses a material weakness in internal controls over financial reporting?
LO8	21. What are significant accounts and disclosures? How do management and the auditor identify them?
LO8	22. Describe a walk-through. How does the auditor use this auditing technique?
LO5	23. How does the auditor identify controls to test?
LO8	24. Explain how the auditor tests internal controls over financial reporting.
LO5	25. Can the auditor use the work of others in the internal control testing process? If so, explain the process.
LO9	26. Regarding the effectiveness of internal controls over financial reporting, when does the auditor issue an unqualified opinion? Under what circumstances does the auditor issue an adverse opinion and a disclaimer of opinion?
LO10	27. What role do internal controls play in the corporate governance process?

Multiple Choice Questions from CPA Examinations

LO2 28. As part of understanding internal control, an auditor is not required to
  a. Consider factors that affect the risk of material misstatement.
  b. Ascertain whether internal control policies and procedures have been placed in operation.
  c. Identify the types of potential misstatements that can occur.
  d. Obtain knowledge about the operating effectiveness of internal control.

LO2 29. The primary objective of procedures performed to obtain an understanding of internal control is to provide an auditor with
  a. Evidence to use in reducing detection risk.
  b. Knowledge necessary to plan the audit.
  c. A basis for modifying tests of controls.
  d. Information necessary to prepare flowcharts.

LO3 30. The ultimate purpose of assessing control risk is to contribute to the auditor's evaluation of the risk that
  a. Tests of controls may fail to identify controls relevant to assertions.
  b. Material misstatements may exist in the financial statements.
  c. Specified controls requiring segregation of duties may be circumvented by collusion.
  d. Entity policies may be overridden by senior management.

LO3 31. Audit evidence concerning segregation of duties ordinarily is best obtained by
  a. Performing tests of transactions that corroborate management's financial statement assertions.
  b. Observing the employees as they apply specific controls.
  c. Obtaining a flowchart of activities performed by available personnel.
  d. Developing audit objectives that reduce control risk.

LO5 32. Regardless of the assessed level of control risk, an auditor would perform some
  a. Tests of controls to determine their effectiveness.
  b. Analytical procedures to verify the design of controls.
  c. Substantive tests to restrict detection risk for significant transaction classes.
  d. Dual-purpose tests to evaluate both the risk of monetary misstatement and preliminary control risk.

LO5 33. Which of the following is a step in an auditor's decision to assess control risk below the maximum?
  a. Apply analytical procedures to both financial data and nonfinancial information to detect conditions that may indicate weak controls.
  b. Perform tests of details of transactions and account balances to identify potential errors and fraud.
  c. Identify specific controls that are likely to detect or prevent material misstatements.
  d. Document that the additional audit effort to perform tests of controls exceeds the potential reduction in substantive testing.

LO5 34. In an audit of financial statements, an auditor's primary consideration regarding a control is whether it
  a. Reflects management's philosophy and operating style.
  b. Affects management's financial statement assertions.
  c. Provides adequate safeguards over access to assets.
  d. Enhances management's decision-making processes.

LO5 35. After gaining an understanding of internal control, the auditor may attempt to assess control risk at less than the maximum. For this purpose, the auditor should (1) identify specific controls that are likely to prevent or detect material misstatements in the relevant financial statement assertions, (2) perform procedures directed at the effectiveness of the design of the controls, and (3) perform tests of controls. The purpose of tests of controls is to

a. Assure that the auditor has an adequate understanding of internal control.
b. Evaluate the effectiveness of such controls.
c. Provide recommendations to management to improve internal control.
d. Evaluate inherent risk.

LO5   36. Tests of control are least likely to be omitted with regard to
a. Accounts believed to be subject to ineffective controls.
b. Accounts representing few transactions.
c. Accounts representing many transactions.
d. Subsequent events.

LO5   37. When obtaining an understanding of an entity's internal control, an auditor should concentrate on the substance of controls rather than their form because
a. The controls may be operating effectively but may not be documented.
b. Management may establish appropriate controls but not act on them.
c. The controls may be so inappropriate that no reliance is contemplated by the auditor.
d. Management may implement controls with costs in excess of benefits.

Discussion Questions and Research Problems

LO7   38. **Management letter suggestions.** The chapter described a cash internal control system for BCS, Inc. Can you suggest some improvements to the current system?

LO5   39. **Evaluation of internal control system.** Explain the statement, "It is possible to have perfect financial statements and no internal controls."

LO5   40. **Evaluation of internal control system.** What does it mean to say that it is possible to have perfect internal controls and materially incorrect financial statements?

LO5   41. **Design of control tests for significant accounts and disclosures.** The chapter described an audit by Stuart and Steigler for Mystery Bookstore. Refer to this example.
a. Describe how you might test the controls identified in the chapter. Think about the relevant assertions as you consider the controls to test. If testing controls is not possible, consider alternative procedures the auditor might use to gather evidence needed to determine if misstatements have occurred.
(1) The daily reconciliation between sales recorded in the cash registers and cash received for the day.
(2) The daily reconciliation between goods shipped for Internet sales and goods invoiced.
(3) The year-end physical count of inventory.
(4) The lower of cost or market inventory valuation at year-end.
(5) The process of identifying contingent liabilities.
(6) The year-end adjusting process for the financial statements.
b. What is true about the procedures where internal control testing is possible? When does the auditor use substantive testing in place of control testing?

LO5   42. **Identification of internal controls.** Go to the campus bookstore and buy something. Pay for your purchase and keep the receipt to bring to class.
a. Consider the assets of value in the bookstore. Identify these assets and describe the risk of misstatement associated with the asset.
b. If misstatements occur in the transactions recorded in the bookstore, what are the misstatements likely to be?
c. Note everything that the cashier does during the payment process. Explain why you think these procedures are done. Can you identify the controls the bookstore used in recording the purchase?
d. Examine the information on your receipt and explain what it represents and why it is useful to the bookstore.

    e. Note the store's physical layout and the way in which the items for sale are arranged. Explain how this facilitates the safeguarding of the store's assets.

    f. Describe the procedures that you believe are in place to reconcile the daily sales with the cash counts. What is the purpose of these procedures?

    g. Do you believe that sales clerks are assigned to a register? Do you think the cash box is changed as clerks are replaced? Is it likely that a clerk works for a full eight-hour day in a campus bookstore?

    h. Suggest improvements that might be made to the physical layout of the store or the internal controls of the store to reduce the risk of material misstatement in the bookstore.

    i. Can you identify a control the bookstore used to make sure that all sales are recorded (completeness)?

    j. What are the relevant assertions for the sales revenue and inventory account for the bookstore?

    k. How will the bookstore decide whether recommendations made by the auditor to improve controls in the bookstore are worth implementing?

LO5 43. **Identification of internal controls.** Stan Stuart from Stuart and Steigler LLP has been assigned to audit the local college bookstore. One of the first things he does to plan the evaluation of the company's internal control is to tour the bookstore. The store has three main areas with items available for sale: one for clothing and one for office supplies and computer accessories on the first floor, and one on the second floor for textbooks and reference books. Customers can enter the bookstore through three doors, two on the first floor and one on the second floor. Students can pay for their purchases on either floor. The first floor has two places to pay for purchases, one in the middle of the clothing area and the other in the office supply area. The third place to pay for purchases is on the second floor in the book section. All cash registers are conveniently located in the middle of the sales area.

    After completing the tour, Stan asked Jean Harris, the bookstore manager, several questions. Explain why he asks each.

    a. What is the dollar amount of inventory lost to theft each year? How does the bookstore attempt to control this loss? Are the items stolen books, supplies, or clothing?

    b. How do you stop customers from leaving the store without paying?

    c. Do you use sensor codes on the inventory items that beep if someone leaves the store without paying?

    d. How do you prevent the salesclerks from stealing cash?

    e. How do you prevent the salesclerks from recording only a portion of a purchase for their friends?

    f. Stan made a purchase in the bookstore the week before the tour and paid for it at the cash register in the back of the first floor. He waited for the receipt, but the salesclerk had thrown it in the trash. When he asked for the receipt (because he planned to exit at the front door and wanted proof that he had paid), the salesclerk refused to give it to him, indicating that he wouldn't need it. This practice disturbed Stan, and he wondered if it was common practice for the clerks to refuse to provide purchase receipts to customers.

LO8 44. **Management's report on internal controls.** Refer to Management's Report on Internal Control over Financial Reporting in Exhibit 3-7 for Goodyear Tire & Rubber Co.

    a. Describe the steps taken by management to assess the company's internal controls.

    b. Can you tell what framework management used to assess internal controls? Explain.

    c. Management has listed two material weaknesses in its report. Are these weaknesses "deficiencies in design" or "deficiencies in operation" of internal controls? Do the internal control deficiencies involve preventive or detective controls?

    d. Management has identified segregation of duties as a material weakness. What are the two departments where segregation of duties was important?

e. Explain the evidence the auditor gathered to review management's assessment of internal controls over financial reporting.

f. Review the opinion issued by the auditor regarding management's assessment in Exhibit 3-8, "Excerpt from the Auditor's Report" for Goodyear Tire & Rubber Company. What type of report did the auditor issue on management's assessment of internal controls? Explain why.

LO9   45. **Auditor's report in an integrated audit.** Refer to Exhibit 3-9 for the Report of Independent Registered Public Accounting Firm for Hewlett Packard Company.

a. What type of opinion did the auditor issue regarding management's assessment of internal controls?

b. What type of opinion did the auditor issue regarding Hewlett Packard's financial statements?

c. Explain the third paragraph of the auditor's opinion, "Because of its inherent limitations, internal control over financial reporting may not prevent or detect misstatements. Also, projections of any evaluation of effectiveness to future periods are subject to the risk that controls may become inadequate because of changes in conditions, or that the degree of compliance with the policies or procedures may deteriorate."

LO9   46. **Auditor's report on internal control.** Refer to Exhibit 3-10 for the Report of Independent Registered Public Accounting Firm for Hecla Mining Company.

a. What type of opinion did the auditor give Hecla Mining for its internal controls over financial reporting? Explain why.

b. Refer to Exhibit 3-11 for the auditor's opinion on the financial statements. Did the company receive a qualified opinion or a disclaimer of opinion?

c. What information have outsiders received about the company from these two reports from the auditors? How should outsiders evaluate the company?

Real-World Auditing Problems

LO2   47. **Tyco International Ltd.**

In June 2005, Dennis Kozlowski, former CEO of Tyco, was convicted of charges involving grand larceny, conspiracy, securities fraud, and falsifying business records. He was sentenced to ten years in prison for his crimes against the company. Prosecutors stated that Kozlowski stole more than $150 million from the company by increasing his salary for performance bonuses without board approval and by borrowing money from the company and then forgiving the loans. Kozlowski claimed the bonuses had been approved verbally by a board member, but the member had died, so it was impossible to verify this statement.[2] Reports from *The Wall Street Journal* described Kozlowski's actions as an attempt "to transfer massive sums of wealth to himself at the expense of shareholders."[3]

Tyco hired Kozlowski in 1976 and named him CEO in 1992, when Tyco had $3 billion in annual sales from sprinklers and packaging materials. Twelve years later, Tyco was a manufacturing and service company selling electrical components, circuit boards, undersea cable systems, fire detection systems, electronic security systems, special valves, and medical supplies[4] with sales of $40.1 billion. Kozlowski became one of the highest paid corporate executives in the country for his efforts to expand the business by acquiring new businesses and extending the reach of its current products by building a worldwide distribution system.

Richard Scalzo, a PricewaterhouseCoopers auditor, testified during the trial. According to him, the auditors were aware of the bonuses. He believed that it was

[2] Mark Maremont, "Kozlowski, Swartz Are Found Guilty in Tyco Retrial," *The Wall Street Journal,* June 17, 2005.

[3] Mark Maremont and Laurie P. Cohen, "Tyco Spent Millions for Benefit of Kozlowski, Its Former CEO," *The Wall Street Journal,* August 8, 2002.

[4] "Key Facts for Tyco International Ltd.," *The Wall Street Journal,* September 19, 2002.

the auditor's job to determine whether the compensation had been recorded correctly on the financial statements but not to determine whether the compensation had been authorized.[5] Tyco admitted overstating income from 1998 to 2001 by $1.15 billion.[6]

a. According to the auditing standards, internal control policies should include controls necessary to provide assurance that transactions are recorded so company expenditures are made in accordance with management and board authorizations and to provide assurance that unauthorized use of company assets has not occurred. Explain how Kozlowski's policies violated internal control standards.

b. Was Kozlowski entitled to live well because under his direction the company was doing very well? If so, did he have the right to use company funds in the manner he did? Give your reasons.

c. What type of oversight should the auditors and the board of directors have exercised with regard to these expenditures? Do you agree with the Scalzo auditor's statement that it was not the auditor's responsibility to determine whether the compensation was authorized?

LO2   48. **General Electric, Inc.**

In September 2002, the SEC opened an informal investigation into the retirement packages General Electric had offered to former CEO Jack Welch, who retired in 2001.[7] The compensation package, negotiated in 1996, became public information as a result of divorce proceedings between Welch and his wife, Jane. Her divorce filings reported an "extraordinary" lifestyle, largely paid for by GE funds, even after Jack's retirement in 2001.[8]

The divorce filing reported that GE had paid for country club memberships; family phones and computers in five homes; flowers; wine and maid service; sports tickets to the Red Sox, Yankees, and Knicks games; Wimbledon tickets; and opera tickets in addition to expenses for autos, many of the costs of a GE-owned apartment in New York City (valued at $80,000 per month), and the use of GE-owned jets valued at $291,865 per month.

SEC regulations require companies to disclose such benefit contracts but do not specify the nature of the disclosure. SEC regulations require companies to disclose the compensation to the five highest paid executives but do not require companies to disclose the amount paid to retired executives. GE said that the board had approved Welch's retirement package in 1996. The company included a copy of the agreement in its 1996 proxy filing. The contract, according to the GE report, stated that Welch would have access for the remainder of his life to company services provided to him prior to retirement, "including access to company aircraft, cars, office, apartments and financial-planning services" plus reimbursement for "reasonable" travel and living expenses.[9]

The SEC requested information from GE regarding the disclosure to shareholders and the public for the executive perks given to Welch. He insisted that all benefits had been disclosed but also said that he would give up most of the perks and begin paying GE $2 to $2.5 million per year for the use of the company's apartment and planes. Welch said he would give up the perks, even though he thought they were reasonable at the time of negotiation, to avoid misperception in the current environment of corporate scandal.

a. Management and the auditors are required to identify the company's significant accounts and disclosures. Would you identify the disclosure of the

[5] Chad Bray, "Tyco Ex-Auditor Testifies on Bonuses," *The Wall Street Journal,* April 1, 2005.

[6] "Executives on Trial," *The Wall Street Journal,* June 17, 2005.

[7] "SEC Investigates Package That GE Offered to Welch," *The Wall Street Journal,* September 16, 2002.

[8] Matt Murray, JoAnn Lublin, and Rachel Emma Silverman, "Welch's Lavish Retirement Package Angers General Electric Investors," *The Wall Street Journal,* September 9, 2002.

[9] Ibid.

retirement package to be a significant disclosure for the company? What internal controls would you expect to be in place regarding the disclosure?

b. Is it the auditor's job regarding the CEO's benefits package to determine whether the compensation package is reasonable? Is it the auditor's job to determine how the compensation package should be disclosed?

LO2

49. **Adelphia Communications Corporation**

In July 2004, John Rigas, the founder and former CEO of Adelphia and his son Timothy Rigas, former chief financial officer of the company, were convicted of fraud and conspiracy for looting more than $100 million from the company, for hiding more than $2 billion in debt from the public, and for lying about the company's financial condition the to the public.[10] In June 2005, John Rigas was sentenced to fifteen years in prison for his crimes; his son Timothy was sentenced to twenty years for his role in the fraud scheme.[11]

According to the SEC report, between 1999 and 2001, company executives engaged in a series of transactions to improve the company's financial position including (1) the exclusion of $2.3 billion in debt on the Adelphia financial statements by recording Adelphia debt on the books of unconsolidated subsidiaries, (2) the issuance of false statements about the company in press releases, earnings reports, and filings with the SEC, and (3) the concealment of the use of Adelphia funds for personal use by the Rigas family including the purchase of stock and timber rights, the use of funds to construct a golf course for the family, the payment of personal debt using company funds, and the purchase of luxury condominiums in Colorado, Mexico, and New York City for the family.[12] According to the complaint, the Rigases used company jets for private vacations, including an African safari, and borrowed billions of dollars from Adelphia for their private use. John Rigas began withdrawing so much money from the company to cover his personal debts that finally his son had to limit him to $1 million per month.[13]

In April 2005, Adelphia agreed to pay a $715 million fine to the SEC to settle claims relating to the corporate looting charges. The settlement is the second largest fine paid by a company to the SEC after its $750 million settlement with WorldCom.[14]

a. According to the auditing standards, internal control policies should include controls necessary to provide assurance that transactions are recorded so that company expenditures are made in accordance with management and board authorizations and to provide assurance that unauthorized use of company assets has not occurred. Explain how the Rigas family's policies violated internal control standards.

b. Did the auditor correctly assess the risk associated with this audit? How should the auditor have used the audit risk model to gather evidence for this company?

Internet Assignment

LO9

50. Select a company, and go to its website. Review management's report on its assessment of internal controls and the auditor's report on the integrated audit. What type of opinion did the auditor give on the internal controls over financial reporting and the financial statements?

[10] Peter Grant and Christine Nuzum, "Adelphia Founder and One Son Are Found Guilty," *The Wall Street Journal,* July 9, 2004.

[11] Dionne Searcey and Li Yuan, "Adelphia's John Rigas Gets 15 Years," *The Wall Street Journal,* June 21, 2005.

[12] U.S. Securities and Exchange Commission, Litigation Release No. 17627, July 24, 2002.

[13] Dinah Wisenberg Brin, "Adelphia Decides not to Pay Rigas $4.2 Million Severance," *The Wall Street Journal,* September 11, 2002.

[14] Peter Grant and Deborah Solomon, "Adelphia to Pay $715 Million in 3-Way Settlement," *The Wall Street Journal,* April 26, 2005.

Auditing the Revenue Business Process

Learning Objectives

After studying this chapter, you should be able to:

1. Describe the revenue business process.
2. Explain the transactions in the revenue process.
3. Understand an applicable financial reporting framework (GAAP) for recording and valuing the accounts in the revenue process.
4. Describe misstatements (errors and fraud) that could be expected in the revenue process.
5. Explain financial statement assertions for accounts in the revenue process.
6. Understand the relevant assertions for the revenue process.
7. Describe the methods the auditor uses to gather evidence for internal controls in the revenue process.
8. Understand the methods the auditor uses to gather evidence regarding the transactions in the revenue process including sales transactions recorded during the year and the accounts receivable balance at year-end.
9. Explain the disclosure requirements for accounts in the revenue business process.

Accounting and auditing standards relevant to this topic

For private companies

- **FASB Statement of Financial Accounting Concepts No. 5,** Recognition and Measurements in Financial Statements of Business Enterprises
- **AU Section 316,** Consideration of Fraud in a Financial Statement Audit
- **AU Section 326,** Audit Evidence
- **AU Section 330,** External Confirmations
- **AU Section 342,** Auditing Accounting Estimates, Including Fair Value Accounting Estimates and Related Disclosures
- **Preface to the Codification of Statements on Auditing Standards,** Overall Objectives of the Independent Auditor and the Conduct of an Audit in Accordance with Generally Accepted Auditing Standards

For public companies

- **FASB Statement of Financial Accounting Concepts No. 5,** Recognition and Measurements in Financial Statements of Business Enterprises
- **SEC Staff Sections Bulletin No. 101,** Revenue Recognition in Financial Statements

- **AU Section 316,** Consideration of Fraud in a Financial Statement Audit (Interim Standard Adopted by PCAOB)
- **AU Section 330,** External Confirmations (Interim Standard Adopted by PCAOB)
- **AU Section 342,** Auditing Accounting Estimates, Including Fair Value Accounting Estimates and Related Disclosures (Interim Standard Adopted by PCAOB)
- **PCAOB Auditing Standard No. 3,** Audit Documentation
- **PCAOB Auditing Standard No. 15,** Audit Evidence

International standards

- **ISA 230,** Audit Documentation
- **ISA 240,** The Auditor's Responsibility to Consider Fraud in an Audit of Financial Statements
- **ISA 320,** Audit Materiality
- **ISA 330,** The Auditor's Procedures in Response to Assessed Risks
- **ISA 500,** Audit Evidence
- **ISA 505,** External Confirmations
- **ISA 520,** Analytical Procedures
- **ISA 540,** Audit of Accounting Estimates
- **IAS 18,** Revenue

Overview of the Revenue Business Process

LO1

Describe the revenue business process

This chapter is the first of five that describes specific auditing procedures used to gather evidence to determine whether the accounts in a specific business process are prepared in accordance with the applicable financial reporting framework. In the revenue business process, the auditor gathers evidence relating to the following: (1) transactions recorded when a sale is made, (2) transactions when cash is collected on an accounts receivable balance, (3) transactions to record sales returns or allowances, and (4) transactions to value the accounts receivable balance at year-end and to match the expense of not collecting an accounts receivable (bad debt expense) with sales revenue recognized during the year. The transactions in the revenue process are tested as part of the testing phase of the audit process. Exhibit 4-1 summarizes the main steps in the audit process.

The revenue business process is a good place to begin. Reporting sales revenue in accordance with an applicable financial reporting framework is critical to the overall process of preparing financial statements without material misstatements. This is so because of the significance of revenue to the net income the company reported. The majority of misstatements in the financial statements investigated by the SEC involve the revenue process. Overstating revenue increases net income, which provides a positive result for company management. Bonuses to management often depend on growth in net income. Increases in net income often lead to growth in earnings per share, which in turn tend to increase the price of the company's stock.

Did You Know?

From 1999 to 2001, Bristol-Myers fraudulently overstated its sales by $2.5 billion to meet earnings forecasts established by management and Wall Street analysts. The company accomplished the overstatement by engaging in channel stuffing (selling more inventory items to the suppliers than they can sell to the consumer) at the end of each quarter to meet earnings targets and by improperly recognizing $1.5 billion in consignment sales. When these methods failed to meet earnings targets, the company used "cookie jar reserves" (recording excess liability accruals in one year that can be reversed to increase revenue or decrease expense in future years) to further inflate earnings. At no time did the company disclose that it was artificially inflating earnings by channel stuffing or using cookie jar reserves to build up earnings. In March 2003, the company restated its 2000 and 2001 financial statements and disclosed its channel stuffing and improper accounting.

| The Audit Process | Exhibit 4-1 |

Steps in the Audit Process	Discussed in this Section
Planning Phase	
Consider the Preconditions for an Audit and Accept or Reject the Audit Engagement	
Understand the Entity and Its Environment, Determine Materiality, and Assess the Risks of Material Misstatements	
Develop an Audit Strategy and an Audit Plan to Respond to the Assessed Risks	
Testing Phase	
Test Internal Controls? Yes No	
Perform Tests of Controls if "Yes"	√
Perform Substantive Tests of Transactions	√
Perform Substantive Tests of Balances	√
Assess the Likelihood of Material Misstatement	√
Decision Phase	
Review the Presentation and Disclosure Assertions	√
Evaluate the Evidence to Determine Whether the Financial Statements Are Prepared in Accordance with the Applicable Financial Reporting Framework	
Issue Audit Report	
Communicate with the Audit Committee	

In August 2004, the company settled a class action lawsuit by paying a $300 million fine and an additional $150 million to the SEC in settlement of a civil investigation. In June 2005, Bristol-Myers paid $89 million to settle a lawsuit with shareholders who had opted out of the class action suit. In June 2005, the company agreed to pay an additional $300 million to settle a criminal lawsuit with the U.S. Attorney in New Jersey. As part of the settlement, the company agreed to improve its corporate governance procedures.

Sources: U.S. Securities and Exchange Commission, Litigation Release No. 18820, August 4, 2004; Barbara Martinez and Heather Won Tesoriero, "Former Bristol-Myers Executives Are Indicted in Accounting Case," *The Wall Street Journal,* June 15, 2005.

Where were the auditors in this fraud? What role did the use of earnings targets by upper management play in the fraud?

The revenue business process involves income statement and balance sheet accounts. On the income statement, the revenue process includes sales revenue, sales returns and allowances and bad debt expense. On the balance sheet, the revenue process includes accounts receivable, allowance for doubtful accounts, and increases to the cash account. The revenue process may include millions of transactions each year (consider the revenue transactions in a company such as Walmart). As with all business processes, the auditor is concerned with determining that the income statement and balance sheet accounts in the business process are recorded in accordance with the applicable financial reporting framework and that disclosure in the accounts associated with the business process is consistent with GAAP. Refer to Exhibit 4-2 for an example of activity in the accounts in the business process.

As with all *income statement* accounts, the Sales Revenue, Sales Returns and Allowances, and the Bad Debt Expense accounts begin the year with a zero balance. During the year, daily transactions are recorded in the accounts. Normally, no debit entries are made to revenue accounts or credit entries made to expense accounts. The year-end totals

Accounts in Revenue Process	Exhibit 4-2

− Sales +	
	Cash sales
	Credit sales
	Ending Balance

+ Accounts Receivable −	
Beginning Balance	
	Cash payments on credit sales
Credit sales	Sales returns and allowance
	Accounts written off
Ending Balance	

+ Allow for Doubtful Accounts −	
	Beginning Balance
Accounts written off during year	Estimate of bad debt expense
	Ending Balance

+ Bad Debt Expense −	
Estimate of bad debt expense	
Ending Balance	

− Sales Returns & Allowances +	
Sales returned or allowance given on sale	
Ending Balance	

in the revenue and expense accounts reflect *all* the transactions recorded during the year, and it is *this total* that the auditor is responsible for gathering evidence to support. The auditor must determine whether the transactions recorded in these accounts during the year are recorded in accordance with the applicable financial reporting framework.

The totals in the *balance sheet* accounts reflect only the amounts in the accounts on the last day of the year, not all transactions recorded during the year; they reflect the *net* amount of the transactions recorded during the year. The balance sheet accounts have a beginning balance on the first day of the year, which reflects the ending (audited) balance from the previous year. During the year, *increases and decreases* in the balance sheet accounts are recorded in the appropriate accounts. Balance sheet accounts typically have both debit and credit entries (increases and decreases). The year-end balance in the balance sheet accounts reflects only the balance in the account as of the last day of the year. The auditor is responsible for determining only whether the *ending balance* in the balance sheet accounts are prepared in accordance with the applicable financial reporting framework. The auditor is not responsible for reviewing all transactions recorded on the balance sheet during the year.

The auditor gathers evidence to support the transactions recorded in the *income statement* accounts for 12 months. The auditor gathers evidence to determine whether the account balances on the *balance sheet* on one day of the year, the year-end, are correct. The tests that the auditor performs to gather evidence relating to income statement transactions are called *substantive tests of transactions* and those to gather evidence relating to balance sheet transactions are called *substantive tests of balances.* These tests provide evidence about whether the accounts in the revenue business process are prepared in accordance with the applicable financial reporting framework. After gathering evidence using internal controls tests, substantive tests of transactions, substantive tests of balances, and analytical procedures, the auditor will conclude whether the accounts in this business process are prepared in accordance with the applicable financial reporting framework. If they are not, the auditor will prepare adjusting journal entries to correct the accounts.

| Journal Entries and Related Documents for the Revenue Process | Exhibit 4-3 |

Journal Entries	Documents

Accounts Receivable
Cost of Goods Sold
    Revenue
    Inventory
(To record credit sale.)
	Sales order, credit approval form, sales invoice, shipping document

Cash
Cost of Goods Sold
    Revenue
    Inventory
(To record cash sale.)
	Sales invoice, shipping document

Cash Accounts Receivable *(To record the collection of cash on a credit sale.)*	Remittance advice
Sales Return and Allowances Accounts Receivable or Cash *(To record a sales return or a sales allowance given as an adjustment on a sale.)*	Credit memo
Bad Debt Expense Allowance for Uncollectible Accounts *(To estimate at year-end the amount of accounts receivable and sales revenue recognized in the current year that will not be collected the following year.)*	Aged trial balance for accounts receivable, Adjusting journal entry report
Allowance for Uncollectible Accounts Accounts Receivable *(To write off an account when it has been determined to be uncollectible.)*	Write-off authorization Adjusting journal entry report

Transactions Recorded in the Revenue Process

LO2

Explain the transactions in the revenue process

The journal entries used to record transactions in the accounts in the revenue business process are listed in Exhibit 4-3.

Documents in the Business Process

The auditor may find several documents useful for gathering evidence in the business process. They are discussed next.

> *Sales order.* This document contains the details of the inventory items or services ordered by the customer, including number and type of goods or services ordered. The credit approval may be noted on this form or the credit approval form.

> *Credit approval form.* This form documents the extension of credit to the customer by the client's credit department.

> *Shipping document.* A form the client prepared to indicate the number and type of goods shipped to the customer (but usually not the price). It instructs the shipping department to send the goods and to include a copy in the shipment to the customer. The shipping document generates the sale invoice and usually determines the date when revenue should be recognized according to the financial reporting framework.

> *Sales invoice.* A form prepared by the client including a description of the goods or services provided, the number of goods sold, the total amount owed including taxes

and shipping costs, and the due date for the payment. A copy of the sales invoice is sent to the customer, usually after the goods have been shipped. The journal entry is often made based on the sales invoice date, not that of the shipping document, resulting in the need for a year-end adjustment in accounts receivable and sales revenue if the dates on the shipping document and the sales invoice are not the same.

Sales journal. A report containing entries of daily sales transactions.

Accounts receivable subsidiary ledger. A report containing a detailed list of account receivable balances by customer. This account's total should agree with the accounts receivable balance in the general ledger (and on the balance sheet).

Aged trial balance for accounts receivable. A detailed list of accounts receivable balances outstanding at a specific point in time. Customer balances are reported in categories indicating their age relative to their due date according to the credit terms (current, over 30 days, over 60 days, over 90 days, over 120 days). This listing is used to evaluate the allowance for doubtful accounts at year-end.

Remittance advice. A document sent to the customer to use when mailing the payment to the client. When the client receives the cash, he or she can separate it and the remittance advice, deposit the cash immediately, and use the remittance advice to prepare the journal entry to record the customer payment and the reduction in accounts receivable.

Prelisting of cash receipts. A list prepared by the client when cash payments are received by someone not involved in recording sales, accounts receivable, or cash; it is used to verify that cash deposits in the bank agree with cash received according to the accounting records to ensure that all cash received was deposited.

Credit memo. A form used to record credits given to the client based on returned goods or adjustments in the sales price of the items sold.

Write-off authorization. A document the client prepares to indicate that an account receivable balance is uncollectible and will be written off. The approval to write off an account should be noted on this form.

Adjusting journal entry report. This report is a record of all adjusting journal entries made during a specific time period, organized by month-end, quarter-end, and year-end. It is supported by documentation for the adjusting journal entries with the signature of the person initiating the entry.

GAAP Rules for Accounts in the Revenue Business Process

LO3

Understand an applicable financial reporting framework (GAAP) for recording and valuing the accounts in the revenue process

Because the auditor is responsible for determining that the accounts in the revenue business process are prepared according to the applicable financial reporting framework, he or she must review the accounting (GAAP) rules the client used for recording *transactions* in the revenue process and *balances* in the revenue process at year-end.

Two financial reporting frameworks might be used by a company for preparing financial statements: (1) accounting standards for U.S. companies and (2) international accounting standards. We refer to the first set of standards as U.S. GAAP and the second set as International Financial Reporting Standards (IFRS). The international accounting standards are written by the International Accounting Standards Board (IASB). The revenue recognition rules for each set of standards will be discussed next.

FASB Concept Statement No. 5, *Recognition and Measurements in Financial Statements of Business Enterprises,* provides the basic rule for recording transactions in the revenue process according to U.S. GAAP. According to this standard, revenue is recognized when it is earned (the service has been provided or the goods have been shipped) and when the revenue is realized or realizable (the cash related to the sale has been collected or is expected to be collected). The amount of revenue recognized equals the amount of cash the seller will receive.

SEC Staff Accounting Bulletin: No. 1—*Revenue Recognition in Financial Statements* also provides guidance on revenue recognition for public companies in the United States. According to it, a company should recognize revenue when *it is realized or realizable and earned,* which occurs when all of the following criteria have been met:

- Persuasive evidence of an arrangement exists.
- Delivery has occurred or services have been rendered.
- The seller's price to the buyer is fixed or determinable.
- Collectivity is reasonably assured.

According to IFRS, revenue is recognized when all of the following conditions are met:

- The company has transferred to the buyer the risks and rewards of ownership.
- The company retains neither continuing managerial involvement nor effective control over the goods sold.
- The amount of revenue can be measured reliably.
- It is probable that the economic benefits associated with the transactions will go to the company.
- The costs incurred related to the transaction can be measured reliably (IAS 18).

The amount of revenue recognized according to IFRS is also equal to the amount of cash the seller expects to receive in the transaction.

At year-end, the accounts receivable must be *valued.* This is an accounting term used to describe adjustments made *at the end of the year* because an accounting principle states that a balance currently in the account is not in compliance with the applicable financial reporting framework. According to both the U.S. and international framework, the company has recognized revenue assuming that all the accounts receivable will be collected, so a journal entry must be made to value or correct the balance in accounts receivable and to match the expense of not collecting revenue (bad debt expense) with the revenue recognized. This entry records "bad debt expense" and adjusts the "allowance for uncollectible accounts," (a contra-account to accounts receivable), so both revenue and accounts receivable reflect the amount of cash that the company expects to collect related to sales revenue in the following year.

Did You Know?

Suprema Specialties, Inc., a public company engaged in manufacturing and distributing cheese, was involved in a scheme to falsify sales revenue, accounts receivable, and inventory from 1998 to 2002. Management perpetrated the fraud with the assistance of Suprema's employees, vendors, and customers. The company falsified financial statements when it engaged in round-trip transactions generating $700 million in fictitious sales revenue, approximately 60% of the company's total reported revenue. The company also relabeled imitation cheese and noncheese products as premium cheeses to inflate its reported inventory and adulterated certain cheese products with imitation cheese and noncheese ingredients to reduce costs.

The round-trip transactions were executed by a circle of entities, including Suprema, a customer, and a vendor. The customer and the vendor had the same owner. Fictitious paperwork, including purchase orders, invoices, and bills of lading were created to represent sales of Suprema products to the customer and then from the customer to the vendor, and finally from the vendor back to Suprema. Checks were generated to support the transactions, although no goods were actually exchanged in the transactions.

The SEC filed suit against the company, the customer, and vendor indicating it is taking action against the executives of both Suprema and those who did business with it. The defendants agreed to settle the SEC's charges including judgments ordering permanent injunctive relief against future violations of federal securities laws, permanent officer and director bars against the individual defendants, and payment of fines.

Sources: U.S. Securities and Exchange Commission, Litigation Release No. 18534, January 7, 2004; U.S. Securities and Exchange Commission, "Civil Complaint" for Litigation Release No. 18534, January 6, 2004.

***Would this fraud have been difficult for the auditor to detect?*[1]**

---

[1] This fraud would have been difficult for the auditor to find because the company created fictitious documents. The sales also resulted in cash payments, so it would have been difficult for the auditor to identify these sales as fictitious. The only way the auditor could have discovered the fraud is if she or he had known about the shared ownership of the vendor and the customer.

The accounting standards for revenue recognition are some of the simplest rules we have. Many have said that the rules need to be revised to account for contemporary business practices. For example, the standards are unclear concerning how to recognize revenue from swap transactions, in which one company agrees to exchange a good, say capacity on a phone line, with another company, **buying the same thing** that it just sold. Both parties provide the service that was agreed upon and pay for it. This transaction would appear to meet the requirements for revenue recognition, but the SEC has ruled that swap transactions should not be recognized as revenue. The rationale for failing to recognize these transactions as revenue is that neither company has given up anything or received anything new in the transaction, so revenue is not involved.

Misstatements That Could Occur in the Revenue Process

LO4

Describe misstatements (errors and fraud) that could be expected in the revenue process

The auditor's role in an audit of a business process is to determine whether the accounts in it are prepared in accordance with the applicable financial reporting framework. The most efficient manner to do this is for the auditor to consider misstatements that could occur in the business process and then to gather evidence to see whether they have occurred. It is important for the auditor to understand what is likely to go wrong in a process and then to *plan* the audit and determine the *nature* of the evidence (whether to use internal control testing or substantive testing), the *timing* of the evidence collection (before or at year-end), and the *extent* of the evidence to be gathered (the amount of testing needed). The higher the likelihood of misstatement in a business process, the more likely the auditor is to do more substantive testing at year-end than if the likelihood is lower.

An auditor who considers misstatements in a business process looks for intentional *(fraud)* and unintentional misstatements *(errors)* in the financial statements. The accounts in the revenue business process are susceptible to both errors and fraud.

A misstatement in the revenue process can involve overstating or understating an account. Clients may understate revenue and accounts receivable due to cutoff problems (recognizing revenue at the end of the year based on the invoice date rather than the shipping date, which understates revenue and accounts receivable), but misstatements that overstate revenue and accounts receivable amounts are more likely to occur in the revenue business process. When overstatements occur, outsiders receive incorrect information (the amount of the future cash flow generated by the company is less than outsiders were led to expect) and can be harmed by it. Thinking that they will have the cash to repay a loan or to pay for a purchase based on the cash flow suggested by the accounts receivable reported on the financial statements, outsiders could make business decisions about the company. If the cash flow is less than outsiders expect, they could make the wrong decision because the company could not have the cash to pay for the transaction. (An understatement has the opposite effect; understating revenue or accounts receivable results in higher future cash flow than expected based on the financial statements. Outsiders are not harmed when a company has more cash than expected except by the fact that the information was wrong.)

Fraudulent actions (intentional misstatement) by the client often cause overstatements in revenue and accounts receivable. The SEC has identified improper revenue recognition as the most common problem it encounters in reviewing financial statement filings. A client may use a variety of methods to overstate revenue and receivables:

- Recording fictitious sales, recognizing revenue on shipments that were not made.
- Early recognition of sales: recognizing revenue in the current year even though shipment of goods or providing the service occurs in the following year.
- Early shipment of goods: recognizing revenue before the customer requests delivery.
- Shipment of more goods than the customer ordered.
- Recognition of revenue based on swap (exchange) transactions by which the customer and the client exchanged products or services and both recognize revenue based on the exchange.

| Examples of Revenue or Accounts Receivable Fraud | Exhibit 4-4 |

Qwest inflated revenue by $2.5 billion in 2000 and 2001 by early recognition of revenue and recognition of revenue based on swap transactions.

Computer Associates admitted that it had wrongly booked more than $2.2 billion in 2000 and 2001 by backdating contracts in order to meet financial projections.

Xerox overstated revenue by $6.4 billion from 1997 to 2000 by accelerating revenue recognition to meet or exceed analysts' expectations.

HealthSouth understated its allowance for uncollectible accounts by $2.7 billion to deceive auditors and investment bankers.

Bristol-Myers Squibb overstated revenue by $2.5 billion from 1999 to 2001. It provided sales incentives to wholesalers to encourage them to purchase more drugs than needed so that Bristol-Myers managers could show favorable financial results.

Time Warner overstated revenue in 2000 and 2001 during merger negotiations by converting nonoperating revenue into operating revenue and by recognizing revenue earlier than it was earned. Restatements for this time period totaled $190 million and $500 million.

Ahold overstated revenue by $41 billion for fiscal years 2000 through 2002 by ordering large amounts of inventory and recording the rebates on the inventory purchases as revenue rather than a reduction in the purchase price of the inventory.

Lucent improperly recognized $1.148 billion in revenue in 2000 by entering into hidden side agreements, falsifying documents, and using poor internal controls.

Sources respectively: Young, S., D. Solomon, and D. Berman, "Qwest Engaged in Fraud, SEC Says," *The Wall Street Journal,* October 22, 2004; Martinez, B. and H. Won Tesoriero, "Former Bristol-Myers Executives Are Indicted in Accounting Case," *The Wall Street Journal,* June 15, 2005; Forelle, C., "Computer Associates Strikes Deal," *The Wall Street Journal,* September 22, 2004; "SEC v. Time Warner Inc.," *U.S. Securities and Exchange Commission Litigation Release No. 19147,* March 21, 2005; "Xerox Settles SEC Enforcement Action Charging Company with Fraud," *U.S. Securities and Exchange Commission Enforcement Action 2002-52,* April 11, 2002; Raghavan, A. and D. Ball, "Ahold and SEC Settle with No fine," *The Wall Street Journal,* October 14, 2004; Mollenkamp, C. and A. Davis, "HealthSouth Ex-CFO Helps Suit," *The Wall Street Journal,* July 26, 2004; and Young, S. and D. Berman, "SEC Unveils Details of Lucent Pact," *The Wall Street Journal,* May 18, 2004.

AU 316, *Consideration of Fraud in a Financial Statement Audit,* requires the auditor to *presume* a risk of material misstatement exists due to fraud relating to revenue recognition. The auditor should use this presumption in planning the revenue process audit and gather evidence to address this potential misstatement. See Exhibit 4-4 for examples of fraud involving the revenue process reported by the SEC.

As you can see, several companies including Qwest, Computer Associates, Xerox, and Time Warner recognized revenue early. Their revenue recognition policies failed to correspond to the applicable financial reporting framework (the companies had not provided the service or shipped the products when the revenue was recognized). The auditors for all of these companies failed to notice that revenue was not recognized in accordance with GAAP, so the financial statements were released when revenue and accounts receivable were not in accordance with the applicable financial reporting framework. Bristol-Myers Squibb recognized revenue based on aggressive sales promotions by which customers purchased more drugs than they actually needed. This resulted in large amounts of inventory being returned the following year and a mismatch between when sales revenue was recognized and when sales returns were recognized (in such situation, the company should establish a reserve for sales returns to reduce revenue in the year of sale). Lucent recognized fictitious revenue by creating false sales documents. Qwest engaged in swap transactions, inflating revenue by an exchange of phone line capacity with another company in the industry. HealthSouth and Ahold engaged in even more creative frauds. HealthSouth understated its allowance for uncollectible accounts, which overstated revenue and accounts receivable, and Ahold recorded the rebates on inventory that it purchased as revenue rather than reductions in the purchase price of inventory, again inflating sales revenue. These revenue frauds represent a range of *creative* activity employed in the past by companies. Auditors missed all of these frauds; in each situation, the company's financial statements were misstated, often for several years. The information that outsiders received about the company was not in accordance with the applicable financial reporting framework.

Did You Know?

KPMG LLP agreed to pay $22.5 million in 2005 to settle charges made by the SEC related to the 1997 to 2000 audits of Xerox Corporation. At the time of the settlement, the payment was the largest SEC fine for an audit firm and included a return of audit fees made during the period as well as penalties.

In the settlement agreement, the SEC emphasized the importance of auditors as gate-keepers to ensure the integrity of the financial reporting process. The SEC said that senior KPMG executives approved many of the accounting procedures used by Xerox and ignored many warnings from KPMG affiliates around the world. According to the SEC, "instead of being gatekeepers, KPMG held the gate open for the company to drive through a truckload of accounting irregularities." According to the SEC complaint, KPMG auditors occasionally "meekly challenged" Xerox's aggressive accounting practices but were easily satisfied by management explanations.

The SEC said that Xerox had overstated its revenue by $3 billion during the four-year period in an effort to maintain its stock price. According to the SEC, Xerox used a number of measures to improve the quality of its earnings and to "create the illusion that its operating results were substantially better than they really were." The methods used to narrow the gap between market expectations and company results included accelerating revenue recognition and using cookie jar reserve accounts to improve earnings as needed to meet market expectations.

Xerox recognizes revenue from its customers from three sources: equipment sold to the customer (according to GAAP, revenue is recognized at point of sale), lease payments received for servicing the equipment (revenue is recognized over the life of the lease), and financing revenue earned on loans to the lessees (revenue is recognized as time passes). Xerox shifted revenue from the lease payments to equipment so it could recognize revenue earlier.

Xerox paid KPMG $26 million for audit work from 1997 to 2001 and $56 million for nonaudit services during the same time period. Xerox paid a $10 million penalty in 2002 related to the revenue fraud. Senior Xerox executives paid penalties totaling $22 million.

Sources: James Bandler and Mark Maremont, "SEC Files Civil-Fraud Charges Against KPMG for Xerox Audit," *The Wall Street Journal,* January 30, 2003; U.S. Securities and Exchange Commission, "Xerox Settles SEC Enforcement Action Charging Company with Fraud," April 11, 2002; and William M. Bulkeley, "KPMG to Settle SEC Charges," *The Wall Street Journal,* April 20, 2005.

Why did the auditors fail to correct the misstatements in the financial statements?*[2]

Auditor's Responsibility for Detecting Fraud

According to the auditing standards, the auditor has the *responsibility to plan the audit to obtain reasonable assurance about whether the financial statements are free of material misstatement* (misstatements that would cause outsiders to change their decision about the company), *whether the misstatements are caused by **errors** or **fraud** (emphasis added by author)* (AU316).

A company's management is in a good position to perpetrate fraud if it chooses to do so. A manager can either tell employees to carry out the fraud or because of his or her unique position in the company may be in a position to carry out the fraud. Management that commits fraud will take steps to conceal it from the auditors by misrepresenting information, withholding evidence, or falsifying documentation. Fraud may also be concealed by collusion among management or among or between management and third parties. If collusion occurs, the auditor may rely on false evidence. Even a properly planned audit may not detect a material misstatement due to fraud if management conceals it, withholds evidence, colludes, or prepares false documentation.

Did You Know?

Time Warner agreed to pay a $300 million fine in March 2005 for materially overstating its online advertising revenue and the number of its Internet subscribers in its America Online (AOL) division. Time Warner agreed to restate its financial statements to reduce its advertising revenues by approximately $500 million for the fourth quarter of 2000 through 2002. This reduction in revenue is in addition to a $190 million revenue restatement that occurred in 2002.

[2] One can only speculate about the reasons, but this seems to be an example of a situation in which the auditors believed that they worked for management and therefore should support its interests rather than the interests of the shareholders.

From 2000 to 2002, the AOL division of Time Warner engaged in fraudulent round-trip transactions to increase advertising revenue when it was declining in the industry. These transactions were structured in several ways including (1) those for which AOL agreed to pay inflated prices for goods or services purchased from customers in exchange for the customers' purchase of online advertising in the same dollar amount, (2) those that converted nonoperating revenue from lawsuit settlements into online advertising revenue, (3) transactions involving business acquisitions in which AOL increased the purchase price paid for the acquisition in exchange for online advertising revenue in the same amount, and (4) transactions in which AOL and its customers falsely created and reported revenue. In each of these transactions, which were concealed by creating two separate and seemingly independent exchanges, AOL funded advertising revenue by giving its customers the money to pay for advertising that they otherwise would not have purchased.

AOL's recognition of advertising revenue related to these transactions did not conform to an applicable financial reporting framework (GAAP), which requires the company to report the substance rather than the form of a transaction. According to this concept, revenue should not be recorded in a round-trip transaction because it is merely a circular flow of cash when the customer does not want or need the goods or services provided or would not normally have purchased the goods or services at that time. AOL's recognition of revenue in these transactions was based on their form rather than their substance.

Sources: U.S. Securities and Exchange Commission, Litigation Release No. 19147, March 21, 2005; SEC Complaint, *Securities and Exchange Commission v. Time Warner Inc.,* March 21, 2005.

Why is it important to recognize revenue based on the substance rather than the form of the transaction?

To find misstatements in the revenue business process. the auditor should conduct the audit with an attitude of **professional skepticism.** This means gathering evidence and planning the audit with a questioning mind and a critical assessment of audit evidence (*Overall Objectives of the Independent Auditor and the Conduct of an Audit in Accordance with Generally Accepted Auditing Standards*). The auditor should plan the audit of the business process with the *presumption* that a risk of material misstatement exists because of fraud relating to revenue recognition. This risk is present regardless of the auditor's past experience with the client or belief in the honesty of management. During the planning, audit team members should discuss the potential for misstatement due to fraud in the revenue process, including the pressure on management to commit fraud, the opportunity for fraud to be perpetrated in the company, and the general environment or tone in the company that could allow management to rationalize committing fraud.

Did You Know?

In October 2004, Qwest Communications, one of the largest telecommunications companies in the United States, agreed to pay a $250 million fine to the SEC for overstating revenue between 1999 and 2002. According to the SEC, the scheme to overstate revenue by $3.8 billion was driven by Qwest's need to meet optimistic revenue projections generated by company management. The SEC report characterized the company as so desperate to satisfy Wall Street analysts that it engaged in various means to meet their outrageously optimistic revenue projections, including a prediction that Qwest would achieve double-digit revenue growth. Top-level executives directed the fraud and executed it by generating sham transactions, turning nonoperating income into operating income, backdating contracts, and understating sales commission and vacation-related expenses.

The $250 million penalty imposed on the company is the second largest SEC fine after the $750 million penalty on WorldCom. The revenue misstatements described by the SEC represent a striking example of the desperation that pervaded the telecommunications industry in 2000 and 2001 when the market for its services declined and revenue from services provided failed to meet company executives' optimistic projections.

Sources: U.S. Securities and Exchange Commission, Litigation Release No. 18936, October 21, 2004; Shawn Young, Deborah Solomon, and Dennis K. Berman, "Qwest Engaged in Fraud, SEC Says—Regulator Claims Misdeeds Were Led by Top Officials; Firm to Pay $250 million," *The Wall Street Journal,* October 22, 2004.

What role did economic conditions play in this fraud?

Management Assertions for the Revenue Business Process

LO5

Explain financial statement assertions for accounts in the revenue process

Auditors gather evidence related to the revenue business process to evaluate management's assertions about the accounts in the revenue process.

Management's Assertions

Existence or occurrence—for both classes of transactions and account balances
Completeness—for both classes of transactions and account balances
Valuation and allocation—for account balances
Rights and obligations—for account balances
Accuracy—for classes of transactions
Cutoff—for classes of transactions
Classification—for classes of transactions (AU 314 and ISA 315)

Regarding the revenue business process, management asserts that accounts receivable exist at the balance sheet date and that the sales transactions recorded in the revenue process occurred during the year (existence and occurrence). Management asserts that all sales transactions and accounts receivable that should be recorded in the financial statements based on the applicable financial reporting framework are included (completeness). Management also asserts that accounts receivable are valued correctly according to GAAP rules at year-end (valuation) and that the company has the right to collect the accounts receivable balance (rights). Finally, management asserts that sales revenue is accurate, that cutoff for sales revenue was in accordance with GAAP, and that sales revenue is properly classified on the financial statements.

The auditor will gather *evidence* to evaluate relevant assertions for significant accounts in the revenue process and will decide at the end of the audit whether the accounts in the revenue business process are presented in accordance with the applicable financial reporting framework. If they are not, the auditor will propose audit adjustments to correct the accounts.

Identification of Relevant Assertions for the Revenue Business Process

LO6

Understand the relevant assertions for the revenue process

The auditor is required to gather audit evidence to support *relevant* assertions for *significant* accounts for each business process. The relevant assertions are related to the **risk** in the business process and the likelihood of misstatement in the process. Because the most likely misstatement in the revenue process is an overstatement, existence and valuation are the two most important assertions for this process in many companies. Auditors will gather *evidence* to support the *existence* and *valuation* of the accounts in this business process (sales revenue, accounts receivable, bad debt expense, and the allowance for uncollectible accounts).

Did You Know?

Computer Associates, one of the world's largest software companies, routinely kept its books open after the end of a quarter to record revenue from contracts that were not signed until after the quarter ended. This practice allowed the company to meet analysts' earnings forecasts; it recorded $2.2 billion in revenue incorrectly in 2000 and 2001 and more than $1.1 billion in revenue in previous quarters.

When Computer Associates discontinued this practice in 2001, the company's stock price dropped 43% in one day when it failed to meet analysts' forecasts for earnings.

The company agreed to settlements with the SEC and the Justice Department and will pay a $225 million fine. It also agreed to improve its corporate governance process.

Source: U.S. Securities and Exchange Commission, Litigation Release No. 18891, September 22, 2004.

What role did the analysts' forecasts play in this fraud?

The auditor gathers evidence to evaluate management's assertions using either (1) internal control tests or (2) substantive tests of transactions or balances and often uses a combination of both. Let's consider internal control testing for the revenue business process first.

Internal Control Testing

LO7

Describe the methods the auditor uses to gather evidence for internal controls in the revenue process

Management could have designed internal controls in the revenue process to prevent or detect misstatements in financial statements and often uses these controls because of the large volume of transactions in the process (it is important for management to design controls to prevent or detect misstatements when many transactions are processed). The auditor can choose to test these internal controls if she or he believes that they are effective in preventing or detecting misstatements in the financial statements. The decision to test internal controls for a financial statement audit is always based on whether it is an efficient way to gather evidence for the business process. This means that sometimes management has designed internal controls but the auditor chooses not to test them because he or she believes that it is more efficient to use substantive testing to gather evidence for the business process.

Although we focus primarily on manual controls in this book and leave the discussion of IT controls to an information systems course, let's consider a few of the IT controls that we could expect in this process.

- Goods are shipped only to customers with approved credit.
- Goods are shipped only to customers with valid sales orders.
- The accounting system matches the information on the sales order and the shipping document with the sales invoice before revenue is recognized.
- Sales revenue is recognized based on the date on the shipping document.
- The IT system prepares reports listing sales orders that have not been shipped and shipments that have not been billed.
- The IT system restricts access to individuals who are authorized to input sales orders, shipping documents, and sales invoices.

Whether choosing to test internal controls or not, the auditor is required to obtain an understanding of internal control relevant to the audit.

Every control system developed by management is different. An auditor who decides to rely on internal control evidence will first document the internal control system using flowcharts and questionnaires. See Exhibit 4-5 for standard documentation using an internal control questionnaire. In this questionnaire, questions that are answered "no" indicate control weaknesses; those answered "yes" indicate controls that could be tested.

An auditor may **test** internal controls for *relevant assertions* for *significant accounts*. The significant revenue process accounts may be (1) sales revenue or (2) sales revenue and accounts receivable. Sales returns and the allowance for uncollectible accounts may be significant for some businesses (depending on the size of the account, the complexity of the transactions recorded in the accounts, or the amount of estimation needed to determine the balance in the account). Auditors often determine that the relevant assertion is existence for both sales revenue and accounts receivable and valuation for accounts receivable. Depending on the industry or economic conditions, other accounts may be identified as significant, and the auditor may consider other assertions to be relevant. Internal controls that management often uses for the revenue business process to prevent or detect misstatements in the financial statements are listed in the following according to internal control procedures. The key control procedures for this business process are discussed next.

What Are Internal Control Procedures?

Segregation of duties
Authorization procedures
Documented transaction trails
Independent reconciliations
Physical controls that limit access to assets

Internal Control Questionnaire—Revenue Process · Exhibit 4-5

ENVIRONMENT

1. Are customers' subsidiary records maintained by someone who has no access to cash?
2. Is the cashier denied access to the customers' records and monthly statements?
3. Are delinquent accounts listed periodically for review by someone other than the credit manager?
4. Are written-off accounts kept in a memo ledger or a credit report file for periodic access?
5. Is the credit department separate from the sales department?
6. Are notes receivable in the custody of someone other than the cashier or accounts receivable record keeper?
7. Is custody of negotiable collateral in the hands of someone not responsible for handling cash or keeping records?
8. Is there undue pressure to maximize revenues?

EXISTENCE OR OCCURRENCE

9. Is access to sales invoice blanks restricted?
10. Are prenumbered bills of lading or other shipping documents prepared or completed in the shipping department?
11. Are customers' statements mailed monthly by the accounts receivable department?
12. Does the internal auditor periodically obtain direct confirmations of accounts and notes?
13. Are reports of discrepancies in accounts receivable billing routed to someone outside the accounts receivable department for investigation?
14. Are returned goods checked against receiving reports?
15. Are returned sales credits and other credits supported by documentation (receipt, condition, and amount) and approved by an appropriate, responsible officer?
16. Are write-offs, returns, and discounts allowed after the discount date subject to approval by an appropriate, responsible officer?
17. Are large loans or advances to related parties approved by the directors?

COMPLETENESS

18. Are sales invoice forms prenumbered?
19. Is the invoice number sequence checked for missing invoices?
20. Is the shipping document's numerical sequence checked for missing bills of lading numbers?
21. Are credit memo documents prenumbered and the sequence checked for missing documents?

RIGHTS AND OBLIGATIONS

22. Does a responsible officer authorize factoring or pledging of receivables?

VALUATION OR ALLOCATION

23. Is customer credit approved before orders are shipped?
24. Are sales prices and terms based on approved standards?
25. Are shipped amounts compared to invoice amounts?
26. Are sales invoices checked against customers' orders for errors in amount, price, extension and footing, and freight allowance?
27. Do the internal auditors confirm customer accounts periodically to determine accuracy?
28. Does the accounting manual contain instructions to date sales invoices on the shipment date?

PRESENTATION AND DISCLOSURE

29. Is there an overall check on arithmetic accuracy of period sales data by a statistical or product-line analysis?
30. Are periodic sales data reported directly to general ledger accounting independent of accounts receivable accounting?
31. Does the accounting manual contain instructions for classifying sales?
32. Are summary journal entries approved before posting them?
33. Are sales to employees, COD sales, disposals of property, cash sales, and scrap sales controlled by the same procedures as sales to outsiders?
34. Are receivables from officers, directors, and affiliates identified separately in the accounts receivable records?
35. Does someone reconcile the accounts receivable subsidiary ledger to the control account regularly?

The key control procedures for the revenue business process are as follows:

- Segregation of duties
  - Various departments process revenue transactions, and no individual performs more than one activity in the business process. Different employees (1) initiate the sales transaction (the sales orders), (2) approve credit, (3) ship goods, (4) prepare sales invoices, (5) collect cash payments on accounts receivable, and (6) write off uncollectible accounts.
- Authorization procedures
  - Sales contracts are approved by management.
  - Credit sales are approved by the credit department.

- Goods are shipped after credit approval.
- Prices used to prepare sales invoices come from an authorized price list.
- Uncollectible accounts are written off on a timely basis by authorized personnel.
- Sales returns and allowances are properly authorized and classified.
- Documented transaction trails
  - Bills of lading or shipping documents exist for all sales invoices for products sold.
  - Approved customer sales orders support each sales invoice when appropriate.
  - Sales recorded as revenue are supported by a sales invoice.
  - Invoices, shipping documents, and sales orders are prenumbered and accounted for on a timely basis.
  - The allowance for uncollectible accounts is reviewed on a timely basis and adjusted to reflect the expected amount to be collected on the receivables.
- Independent reconciliations
  - Invoice amounts are compared to shipping and sales order amounts.
  - Sales data are periodically compared to budgeted or expected sales.
  - Prices are checked, mathematical accuracy of sales invoices is verified, and the date of the shipping document is compared with the invoice date.
  - The accounts receivable subsidiary ledger is reconciled to the general ledger on a timely basis.
  - The sales journal is properly posted from the subsidiary ledger to the general ledger.
- Physical controls that limit access to assets
  - Specific controls should exist to protect the assets of value (sales invoices, shipping documents, cash payments, credit approval forms) from theft.

The only controls the auditor can test are those that are documented. Audit procedures to test these controls follow.

Internal Control Tests
Make inquiries of employees
Inspect relevant documentation
Observe the application of the control
Reperform the control

For example, to test the authorization controls, the employee must have initialed or signed the form when she or he performed the control. Auditors perform tests of controls to determine whether the internal control procedures developed by management are **designed** effectively and whether the controls are **operating.** The auditor selects from a variety of **audit procedures** such as those listed in the table. If the controls are not designed appropriately or are not operating properly, the auditor needs to design substantive tests to determine whether the missing internal controls have led to misstatements in the financial statements.

Consider an internal control test that an auditor could perform in the revenue business process. The auditor has documented the internal control system and has found several controls relevant to the existence assertion for sales revenue.

- First the auditor considers the segregation of duties in the control system documented. If one person performs all of the duties, testing internal controls would not be useful. In this case, different people perform the six duties described earlier: (1) initiating the sales order, (2) granting credit, (3) shipping goods, (4) preparing sales invoices, (5) collecting cash payments on accounts receivable, and (6) writing off accounts when they are uncollectible. Because this is a large company, we appear to have a good segregation of duties.

- The auditor tests segregation of duties by using inquiry and observation.
- The auditor asks the client about the processing of transactions and performs a walk-through to gather information about the process used to record sales transactions.
- The next step is for the auditor to observe how employees actually process sales transactions. This could be done on one day or several days. At the end of the observation, the auditor should be able to determine whether the individuals perform the job assigned to them or whether they share the work with other employees.

- Next, we select a sample of sales transactions to review. The sample is taken from all twelve months (because internal controls must be effective for the entire year). Half of the sample is selected from the monthly sales registers and half from the monthly shipping reports. The audit firm's policy determines the exact number of sales transactions for review. The auditor reviews all documents related to the sale (sales orders, sales invoices, credit approval forms, and shipping documents), which are filed by date in the client files (either computer files or paper files).

  - The sample is selected from two sources to allow the auditor to gather evidence related to two assertions: occurrence and completeness. Items selected from the monthly sales registers provide the auditor with evidence about occurrence (the fact that the goods were shipped verifies the sale's validity). Items selected from the monthly shipping reports provide evidence about completeness (all items shipped were invoiced). The first step is an inspection procedure called *vouching,* and the second is an inspection procedure called *tracing,* which differ according to the direction of the testing. The auditor cannot obtain evidence about completeness from vouching; if the sample comes from the sales register, it will represent only the items that were recorded. In this situation, obtaining evidence about any items not recorded would be impossible.

  - The auditor *inspects the documentation* (this is the internal control test performed) for the items selected to determine whether the control is present. The control is either the initial or signature of the person who performed the control. A second control is the presence of all the required evidence in the customer file (sales order, sales invoice, credit approval, and shipping document). The auditor looks for the following in the transactions selected:

    - Shipping documentation for all sales selected from the sales register. Any documentation missing is a control deviation.

    - Sales invoices for all shipments selected from the shipping records. Any shipment without a sales invoice would be a control deviation.

    - A comparison of the amount of goods sold noted on the invoice with the amount of goods shipped to determine that the company recognized revenue consistent with the amount shipped. The amount of goods on the sales order may also be compared with the amount on the sales invoice and the shipment document if the company processes sales transactions through the use of sales orders. An employee *initials* one of the forms to indicate that the comparison has been made. Any sales transaction lacking the initials would be a control deviation.

  - For the items selected, the auditor could also perform a substantive test of transactions (a dual-purpose test) that involves an internal control test in which the auditor *reperforms the control.* This would involve the following:

    - Compare the invoice amount to the amount on the shipping document and the amount on the sales order form to see whether they agree. Compare the invoice price to the sales order price to determine whether the company recognized revenue in accordance with the original agreement (the shipping report does not contain a sales price).

After performing this internal control test, the auditor decides whether internal control is effective based on the number of deviations found in the internal controls. At the end of internal control testing, the auditor may conclude that (1) internal controls are effective in preventing or detecting misstatements for the assertions tested for the significant accounts in the business process or (2) that internal controls were not effective. If the determination is that the controls were effective, the auditor reduces the amount of substantive testing for the relevant assertion for the significant account. If the determination is that the internal controls were not effective, the auditor gathers evidence about whether the accounts in the business process are prepared in accordance with the applicable financial reporting framework using only substantive testing.

Substantive Tests for the Revenue Process

LO8

Understand the methods the auditor uses to gather evidence regarding the transactions in the revenue process including sales transactions recorded during the year and the accounts receivable balance at year-end

Auditing standards describe several procedures the auditor could use to gather evidence to evaluate whether the financial statements are prepared according to the applicable financial reporting framework; see the following table. Analytical procedures will be discussed after it because they are usually performed as part of the planning process. The other audit procedures are part of key substantive tests.

Substantive Audit Procedures
Analytical procedures
Inspection of records, documents, or tangible assets
Observation
Inquiry
Confirmation
Recalculation
Reperformance

Analytical Procedures

An auditor often uses analytical procedures as evidence as to whether the financial statement accounts have been prepared in accordance with the applicable financial reporting framework. Two main types of analytical procedures are used. In the first, the auditor compares the financial statement numbers for the current year with those of the previous year and calculates the dollar amount and the percentage of any change. In the second analytical procedure, the auditor calculates financial ratios for the current financial statements and compares them with ratios for the previous year's financial statements. The auditor may also compare the client's financial statement numbers or ratios with industry data if they are available. When using analytical procedures for this business process, the auditor often considers nonfinancial measures to evaluate changes from one year to the next, for example, the number of customer accounts in the current year and the previous year.

In the revenue business process, the auditor could perform the following analytical procedures:

1. Investigate unreasonable deviations in the account balance for the current year compared to the previous year.
2. Calculate the accounts receivable turnover ratio and the number of days outstanding in accounts receivable for the current and previous years. Investigate a change from the auditor's expectations if it appears to be unreasonable.
3. Consider the number of customer accounts for the current year and the previous year and the new accounts added and lost in each year.

Companies do not dramatically change from year to year *without a reason* (planned expansion, poor economic conditions), so large increases or decreases in the accounts

Selected Financial Information for BCS — Exhibit 4-6

	Year 3	Percentage Change	Year 2	Percentage Change	Year 1
Sales Revenue	$12,000,000	20%↑	$10,000,000	5%↑	$9,500,000
Accounts Receivable	1,100,000	38%↑	800,000	60%↑	500,000
Allowance for Uncollectible Accounts	100,000	17%↓	120,000	140%↑	50,000
Sales Returns and Allowances	50,000	19%↑	42,000	62%↑	26,000
Bad Debt Expense	120,000	8%↓	130,000	30%↑	100,000
Accounts receivable turnover ratio	12.63 times		15.38 times		16.25 times
Days accounts receivable outstanding	29 days		24 days		22 days
Number of customer accounts	3,600		3,200		3,000
Number of new customer accounts added	460		220		100
Number of customer accounts lost during the year	60		20		5

can be unreasonable. To decide whether a change is unreasonable, an auditor needs to (1) know the client's industry, (2) current economic conditions, and (3) have an understanding of the business under audit.

Let's consider an example for the revenue process for BCS (see Exhibit 4-6 for selected financial information for the company for three years).

Year 3 is the current year, the year under audit. Sales revenue increased by $500,000, a 5% increase from year 1 to year 2. Sales revenue increased by $2,000,000, a 20% increase from year 2 to year 3 ([12,000,000 − 10,000,000] / 10,000,000). The auditor could ask the client why sales revenue increased so much from year 2 to year 3. There may be many good explanations: The client expanded the business in the United States or marketed its product outside the United States. This dramatic increase may also indicate fraud (for example, the company could have recorded fictitious revenue or recognized revenue early on shipments to be made the following year). The auditor would calculate the change for all accounts in the revenue process to determine whether the change from one year to the next appeared reasonable. The changes in the Allowance for Uncollectible Accounts, Sales Returns and Allowances, and Bad Debt Expense accounts represent small dollar amounts. However, the change in the Accounts Receivable balance and the accounts receivable turnover ratio could be inconsistent with the auditor's expectations.

To determine whether the change in the Accounts Receivable balance and in the number of days accounts receivable have been outstanding is unreasonable, the auditor considers possible explanations for the changes. The accounts receivable turnover ratio is 12.63 (12,000,000 / ([1,100,000 + 800,000] / 2) for year 3 and 15.38 for year 2. This corresponds to 29 days of outstanding accounts receivable for year 3 and 24 days for year 2. This means that the company's collection of its accounts receivable was slower in year 3 than in year 2. Faster collection is usually better than slower collection because fast turnover provides the company the cash to reinvest in it more quickly. Therefore, the auditor would ask the client why the accounts receivable collection was slower in year 3 than in year 2 and would gather *evidence* to evaluate the client's response. The reason customers are paying the accounts more slowly could be something as simple as poor economic conditions in year 3 compared with year 2. If economic conditions have not changed between the two years, the company could be extending more credit to customers, meaning that the allowance for uncollectible accounts should be increased. According to data in Exhibit 4-6, sales revenue increased by 20% from year 2 to year 3, but accounts receivable increased by 38%. Accounts receivable are normally expected to grow at about the same rate as sales revenue, so these two numbers also indicate that collections were not made as quickly in year 3 as in year 2.

The number of customer accounts increased from 3,200 in year 2 to 3,600 in year 3. The increase in the Accounts Receivable balance may reflect this change. The decrease in accounts receivable turnover ratio from approximately 15 times in year 2 to about 13 times in year 3 could suggest that the new customers pay more slowly than the previous customers. One way a company could increase sales revenue is to extend credit to customers that are greater credit risks. This may have been what BCS Company did in year 3 because the number of customer accounts increased by 400 and the customer accounts are being paid on average five days later than in year 2. If this is so, it is another indication that the allowance for uncollectible accounts is too low. Inquiries with the audit client will allow the auditor to confirm the reasons for the changes between year 2 and year 3 suggested by the analytical procedures and to identify areas where the risk of material misstatement may be high. In this case, it appears that the allowance for uncollectible accounts may be understated.

Other audit procedures (inspection, observation, external confirmation, recalculation, reperformance, and inquiry) may be used for the substantive tests of transactions and substantive tests of balances. See the later list of the key substantive tests for the revenue process.

Substantive Tests of Transactions

The auditor uses substantive tests of transactions to gather evidence regarding income statement accounts in the revenue business process: Revenue, Sales Returns and Allowances, and Bad Debt Expense. These substantive tests of transactions for revenue may be performed as part of the audit of internal controls. To gather this evidence, the auditor performs dual-purpose tests by selecting one sample of transactions and performing internal control and substantive tests of transactions on it.

In the following list of the key substantive tests of transactions for the revenue business process, the audit *procedure* used to perform the test is listed before the test (identified in boldface, italic print) and the **assertion** that the procedure tests is identified in blue print. Depending on the amount of evidence gathered using internal control tests, the auditor may perform *some or all* of the audit procedures listed.

The key substantive tests of transactions for the revenue business process are as follows:

1. *Inspection.* Select a sample of sales recorded in the sales journals and determine that the sales recorded in the sales accounts are supported by sales invoices and shipping documents—**existence, accuracy.**

2. *Inspection.* Select a sample of shipping documents for the year. Trace the shipping document to the sales invoice and the sales journal to determine that all shipping documents have been recorded as sales—**completeness, accuracy.**

3. *Inspection.* Perform sales cutoff tests. Trace *entries in the sales journal* for five to ten days before and after year-end to determine that sales were recorded in the proper time period by reviewing the sales invoice and the shipping document—**cutoff, existence.**

4. *Inspection.* Perform sales cutoff tests. Trace *shipping documents* for five to ten days before and after year-end to determine that sales were recorded in the proper time period—**cutoff, completeness.**

5. *Inspection.* Select a sample of sales recorded in the sales journals. Determine that the sales prices on the invoices agree with the prices on an approved price list. Determine that the cash collected on the sale was equal to the invoice total for sales that have been collected—**accuracy.**

6. ***Inquiry, inspection.*** Determine that bad debt expense is recorded on a timely basis permitting the proper matching of expense and revenue. The expense associated with not collecting an accounts receivable should be recognized in the same time period as the revenue is recognized—**completeness, accuracy.**

Tests 1 and 2 are the dual-purpose tests from the internal control example. Tests 3 and 4 are sales cutoff tests by which the auditor uses the inspection procedure of vouching and tracing to gather evidence about two assertions: (1) existence and occurrence and (2) completeness. Test 5 is to evaluate whether sales revenue is recorded at the correct amount and whether the cash collected on the sale is equal to the invoice amount. Test 6 evaluates whether the company has recognized "bad debt expense" in accordance with an applicable financial reporting framework.

After completing the substantive tests of transactions, the auditor determines whether the income statement accounts in the revenue process have been prepared in accordance with the applicable financial reporting framework. If the auditor has evidence that they have not been, he or she will propose an audit adjustment to the accounts.

Substantive Tests of Balances

The auditor uses substantive tests of balances to gather evidence for balance sheet accounts in the revenue process. These tests are typically done at year-end but can be performed earlier and the balances "rolled forward" to the balance sheet date. Early testing is done only when the client has a good system of internal controls relating to the account balances. The balance sheet accounts in this business process are Accounts Receivable and Allowance for Uncollectible Accounts. In the following list of key substantive tests of balances for the revenue business process, the audit ***procedure*** used to perform the test is listed before the test (identified in boldface, italic print) and the **assertion** that the procedure tests is identified in blue print. Depending on the amount of evidence gathered using internal control tests and substantive tests of transactions, the auditor may perform *some or all* of the audit procedures listed.

The key substantive tests of balances for the revenue business process are as follows:

1. ***External confirmation.*** Select a sample of accounts receivable from the year-end Accounts Receivable balance.
   a. Send confirmation letters to the customers and resolve all discrepancies—**existence, rights.**
   b. Perform alternative procedures if the confirmation reply is not received—**existence, rights.**
2. ***Inspection.*** Perform sales cutoff tests. Trace *entries in the sales journal* for five to ten days before and after year-end to sales documents (sales invoice, shipping document, sales order, and credit approval form) to determine that the sale was recorded in the proper time period—**cutoff, existence, rights.**
3. ***Inspection.*** Perform sales cutoff tests. Trace *shipping documents* for five to ten days before and after year-end to sales documents (sales invoice, sales order, and credit approval form) to determine that the sale was recorded in the proper time period—**cutoff, rights, completeness.**
4. ***Inquiry.*** Review the client's procedures for evaluating the Allowance for Doubtful Accounts to determine that it is properly valued based on (1) the accounts written off during the year, (2) the accounts receivable balance at the end of the current year, (3) economic conditions, and (4) the economic status of customers—**valuation.**
5. ***Inquiry.*** Determine that uncollectible accounts are written off on a timely basis—**valuation.**

The first test is an audit procedure referred to as *confirmation.* When gathering evidence by using confirmations, the auditor sends a letter to someone outside the company (for example, a customer, the bank, a vendor) asking the outside party to confirm some information about the company under audit. When gathering evidence by using accounts receivable confirmations, the auditor asks some of the client's customers to confirm in writing the amount the customer owes the client at year-end. Tests 2 and 3 are cutoff tests. Cutoff procedures in the revenue process are used to determine whether revenue has been recognized in accordance with the applicable financial reporting framework. These are the same as the cutoff tests listed in the substantive tests of transactions section. The auditor performs cutoff tests for the revenue process if he or she believes that the accounts in this business process are misstated because the company has not recorded revenue in accordance with the applicable financial reporting framework. Tests 4 and 5 evaluate the adequacy of the allowance for doubtful accounts. Accounts receivable confirmations and tests used to evaluate the allowance for uncollectible accounts are discussed in more detail next.

Accounts Receivable Confirmations

The auditing standards presume that the auditor requests confirmation of accounts receivable balances unless (1) the balance in accounts receivable is immaterial, (2) the use of confirmations would be ineffective, or (3) the auditor can reduce the risk of issuing the wrong audit opinion to an acceptably low level without confirming accounts receivable. An Accounts Receivable balance is immaterial when knowing the correct one would not change the decision of an outside user of the financial statements. The use of confirmations could be ineffective if the auditor knows from past experience that the audit client's customers do not return confirmations. The issue of risk was discussed in more detail in Chapter 3.

The auditor gathers evidence using the confirmation procedures by selecting a sample of customer balances from the year-end accounts receivable subsidiary ledger. Each customer selected for confirmation is sent a letter asking it to confirm the balance that it owes the audit client at year-end. The auditor can choose to send either *positive* or *negative* confirmations. Positive confirmations request the customer to return the confirmation directly to the auditor if the balance is correct *or* incorrect. Negative confirmations request the customer to return the confirmation directly to the auditor only if the balance is incorrect. Unfortunately, the response rate for confirmations is often less than 50%, so an auditor who uses negative confirmations is unable to determine whether the confirmation was not returned because it was correct or because the customer threw it away. See Exhibits 4-7 and 4-8 for examples of positive and negative confirmations.

The client prepares confirmation letters on its letterhead, and the auditor controls their mailing shortly after year-end. The auditor provides an envelope so the customer can return the confirmation directly to the audit firm. The client must not mail the confirmation letters or have them returned to it because the auditor wants the response from the customer but does not want the client to have the opportunity to falsify it. Second and third requests of confirmation letters may be sent.

The auditor performs alternative procedures for all customer balances selected for confirmation if the customer does not return the confirmation letter. Two alternative tests are often used (1) to determine whether the account has been paid in the following year (this is referred to as *reviewing subsequent cash receipts;* customers that do not owe money will not pay the bill) or (2) to examine the invoices and shipping documents associated with the accounts receivable. If the goods were shipped or the service provided, a valid receivable exists. If the auditor uses positive confirmations *and* has determined that a response to a request for one is *necessary* to obtain sufficient appropriate evidence, alternative audit procedures will not provide that evidence. In this case, the auditor must determine the implications of being unable to obtain the confirmation request evidence for the audit and the audit report. This situation would be unusual for accounts receivable confirmations but could occur if the accounts receivable balance was for only one customer or for services the audit client provided but were impossible for the auditor to verify.

Positive Accounts Receivable Confirmation   Exhibit 4-7

BCS, Inc
400 Central Avenue
Bloomington, MN 55431

January 4, 2011

Tennant Company
812 Nutwood Avenue
Fullerton, CA 92831

Dear Customer:

In connection with an examination of our financial statements, please confirm the correctness of the balance of your account with us as of December 31, 2010, directly with our auditors:

Scott & Morrison, LLP
412 8th Street
Minneapolis, MN 55404

This is not a request for payment; please do not send your remittance to our auditors.

Your prompt attention to this request is much appreciated. A stamped self-addressed envelope is enclosed for your convenience.

Yours Truly,

Sandy Huston

Sandy Huston
Controller

The balance receivable from us of $3,474.70 as of December 31, 2010, is correctly stated except as noted below:

Date: _____   Confirmed by: _____

Many customer replies to the confirmation letters require follow-up with the audit client because of timing differences in payments and billings to determine when the payments on the accounts were received and when the goods were actually shipped. For example, an audit client believes that it owes $500 if the goods have been shipped, but if the customer does not receive the bill or the goods until the first week of the following year, the customer does not think it owes the amount. The same thing happens with customer payments. A customer mails the check and reduces the amount of the account receivable owed to the audit client. The audit client does not receive the check until after year-end, so on its books, the account is outstanding at year-end. See Exhibit 4-9 for an example of a confirmation response that requires a follow-up to determine whether the client balance or the balance on the confirmation response is correct. The auditor resolves this issue by asking the client when the payment was received and verifying the client's response with the bank records. If the payment was received before year-end, then the balance on the confirmation letter is the correct amount. If the payment was received after year-end, the client balance is correct.

Negative Accounts Receivable Confirmation — Exhibit 4-8

BCS, Inc
400 Central Avenue
Bloomington, MN 55431

January 4, 2011

Tennant Company
812 Nutwood Avenue
Fullerton, CA 92831

Dear Customer:

In connection with an examination of our financial statements, please return this confirmation if the balance of your accounts receivable is incorrect. Please return the confirmation directly to our auditors:

Scott & Morrison, LLP
412 8th Street
Minneapolis, MN 55404

This is not a request for payment; please do not send your remittance to our auditors.

Your prompt attention to this request is much appreciated. A stamped self-addressed envelope is enclosed for your convenience.

Yours Truly,

Sandy Huston

Sandy Huston
Controller

_____

The balance receivable from us of $3,474.70 as of December 31, 2010, is incorrect. The correct balance is noted below:

Date: _____   Confirmed by: _____

Evaluation of the Allowance for Uncollectible Accounts

Management estimates the allowance for uncollectible accounts for the following year by considering the accounts receivable on the books at year-end that it does not expect to collect. The applicable financial reporting framework in the U.S. allows the audit client to calculate the balance in the Allowance for Uncollectible Accounts in one of two ways: using (1) the percentage of sales method or (2) the aging of accounts receivable method. If the allowance balance is calculated using the first method, the client determines the year-end adjusting entry based on the amount needed to cover estimated write-offs for the following year. This method ignores the unadjusted balance in the allowance account. Using the aging of accounts receivable method, the client calculates the ending balance required in the allowance account to cover the estimated write-offs for the following year. The unadjusted balance in the allowance account is used with this method to determine the adjusting entry.

It is the auditor's job to review this estimate to evaluate whether it has been determined in accordance with the applicable financial reporting framework. To do this, the auditor considers whether the allowance for doubtful accounts is properly valued based

Confirmation Reply	Exhibit 4-9

BCS, Inc.
400 Central Avenue
Bloomington, MN 55431

January 4, 2011

Tennant Company
812 Nutwood Avenue
Fullerton, CA 92831

Dear Client:

In connection with an examination of our financial statements, please confirm the correctness of the balance of your account with us as of December 31, 2010, directly with our auditors:

Scott & Morrison, LLP
412 8th Street
Minneapolis, MN 55404

This is not a request for payment; please do not send your remittance to our auditors.

Your prompt attention to this request is much appreciated. A stamped self-addressed envelope is enclosed for your convenience.

Yours Truly,

Sandy Huston

Sandy Huston
Controller

The balance receivable from us of $3,474.70 as of December 31, 2010, is correctly stated except as noted below:

We made a payment of $ 1,859.60 to you on December 30, 2010. The balance should be $1,615.10.

Date: Jan 12, 2011   Confirmed by: Rachel Lunde

on (1) the accounts written off during the previous year, (2) the accounts receivable balance at the end of the current year, (3) economic conditions, and (4) the economic status of customers. The net receivable balance (accounts receivable minus the allowance for uncollectible accounts) should represent the amount of cash the company expects to collect in the following year on the accounts receivable balances outstanding at the end of the year under audit.

Consider the following financial information from Exhibit 4-6 for the allowance for uncollectible accounts and bad debt expense.

	Year 3	Year 2	Year 1
Allowance for Uncollectible Accounts	$100,000	$120,000	$ 50,000
Bad Debt Expense	120,000	130,000	100,000

The year 3 numbers are the estimates management made for the balance needed in the Allowance for Uncollectible Accounts (and Bad Debt Expense). The auditor must evaluate these estimates to determine whether they are reasonable based on the applicable financial reporting framework. Posting all of these numbers to the Allowance for Uncollectible Accounts and to Bad Debt Expense gives the following information:

+ Allow for Doubtful Accounts −		+ Bad Debt Expense −	
	50,000 *Beginning balance year 2*	**0** *Beginning balance year 2*	
60,000 *Accounts written off during year 2*	**130,000** *Estimate of bad debt expense year 2*	**130,000** *Estimate of bad debt expense year 2*	
	120,000 *Ending balance year 2*	**130,000** *Ending balance year 2*	
140,000 *Accounts written off during year 3*	**120,000** *Estimate of bad debt expense year 3*	**120,000** *Estimate of bad debt expense year 3*	
	100,000 *Ending balance year 3*	**120,000** *Ending balance year 3*	

Journal entries for years 2 and 3 follow. The write-offs are shown in one summary entry:

Year 2

Bad Debt Expense		130,000
Allowance for Uncollectible Accounts		130,000
Allowance for Uncollectible Accounts.	60,000	
Accounts Receivable		60,000

Year 3

Bad Debt Expense		120,000
Allowance for Uncollectible Accounts		120,000
Allowance for Uncollectible Accounts.	140,000	
Accounts Receivable		140,000

Let's now look at the numbers. Accounts receivable written off (determined to be uncollectible) totaled $60,000 in year 2 and $140,000 in year 3. Bad debt expense totaled $130,000 in year 2 and $120,000 in year 3. The balance in the allowance for uncollectible accounts was $120,000 in year 2 and $100,000 in year 3. What do these numbers mean? Is there anything unusual about year 3, the year under audit?

At the end of year 2, the client estimated that in year 3, it would write off $120,000 in accounts receivable that were on the books at the end of year 2. It actually wrote off $140,000. This estimate of accounts receivable to be written off in year 3 was too low.

At the end of year 3, the client estimated that in year 4, it would write off $100,000 in accounts receivable on the books at the end of year 3. This estimate is the one that the auditor must evaluate. Why does the client think that write-offs will decline in the following year, particularly given that sales increased by $2,000,000 in year 3? The client may have estimated the allowance account too low in an attempt to keep net income above a certain level. The auditor must decide whether the estimate of allowance of uncollectible accounts made by the client is reasonable. In this case, it appears to be too low. The auditor makes his or her decision based on whether this estimate of uncollectible accounts reduces the accounts receivable balance to a level representing the amount of cash the company expects to collect in the following year on the accounts receivable outstanding at the end of the year.

Auditor's Understanding at This Point in the Audit

The auditor should at this time have *sufficient appropriate* evidence to determine whether the accounts in the revenue process—Sales Revenue, Sales Returns And Allowances, Bad Debt Expense, Accounts Receivable, and the Allowance For Uncollectible Accounts—are presented on the financial statements in accordance with the applicable financial reporting framework. If not, the auditor gathers more evidence. If the accounts in the business process are prepared in accordance with the applicable financial reporting framework, the auditor concludes that the accounts are prepared in accordance with the applicable financial reporting framework:

Based on the results of the audit work performed, the accounts in the revenue process are prepared in accordance with the applicable financial reporting framework.

An auditor who has proposed audit adjustments would modify the above statement to read:

Based on the results of the audit work performed, **except for the adjustments noted,** *the accounts in the revenue process are prepared in accordance with the applicable financial reporting framework.*

All of the evidence the auditor has reviewed to make this decision is kept in the audit working papers (discussed in more detail in a later chapter) on which the auditor has recorded the evidence gathered from internal control tests, analytical procedures, substantive tests of transactions, and substantive tests of balances including the particular items tested and the conclusions derived from all the evidence reviewed.

Disclosure Requirements for the Revenue Business Process

LO9

Explain the disclosure requirements for accounts in the revenue business process

Presentation and Disclosure for the Revenue Process

The auditor gathers evidence concerning the revenue business process to evaluate management's assertions about the presentation and disclosure of the accounts in the revenue process. These assertions are:

- Occurrence and rights and obligation: Disclosed events and transactions have occurred and pertain to the company.
- Completeness: All disclosures that should have been made have been made.
- Classification and understandability: Financial information is appropriately presented and described, and disclosures are clearly expressed
- Accuracy and valuation: Financial information and all other information are disclosed fairly and at appropriate amounts (AU 314 and ISA 315).

Management prepares the financial statements and the footnotes to them. When management hands the financial statements to the auditor, it is asserting that the accounts in the revenue process are presented in the financial statements according to the applicable financial reporting framework and that all required disclosures regarding the accounts have been made. The disclosures related to the financial statements are usually made in one of two places: (1) the footnotes to the financial statements or (2) in the Management's Discussion and Analysis (MD&A) section of the annual report.

Did You Know?

In April 2005, Coca-Cola Co. reached an agreement with the SEC to settle allegations of accounting and marketing fraud. The SEC concluded that Coca-Cola had engaged in the practice of channel stuffing with its Coke bottler in Japan. The SEC stated that Coca-Cola had inflated sales and misled investors by shipping $1.2 billion of extra beverage concentrate to bottlers in Japan during the period 1997 to 1999. During this time, Coke was facing increasing competition, making it difficult for the company to meet its earnings targets. The channel stuffing allowed Coke to meet analysts' earnings expectations in eight of the twelve quarters from 1997 to 1999. Although sales were recorded correctly (the product was shipped and payment was collected), Coke failed to disclose the existence of the practice or to suggest that revenue would not continue to grow at the level of that period.

At the end of each quarter between 1997 and 1999, Coca-Cola implemented its channel stuffing practice. The Japanese bottlers agreed to buy concentrate in excess of their demand to maintain their relationship with Coca-Cola. At the same time that the bottlers increased their purchases, their sales of Coke were decreasing. The Japanese market was Coca-Cola's most profitable division throughout the world, so it was the most efficient location to engage in pushing additional inventory purchases for the purpose of managing earnings for the company.

Coca-Cola knew that quarter-end channel stuffing could not continue and likely would cause a reduction in sales in future time periods. However, the company did not disclose to shareholders the channel stuffing impact on current or future income although it should have done so. According to the SEC, the 10-K and 10-Q statements filed with the SEC from 1997 to 1999 were misleading because they failed to disclose in the MD&A section or anywhere else the likely impact of the practice on future earnings. According to the SEC, an investor would want to know the existence and purpose of channel stuffing as a sales practice used by the company at the end of each quarter.

Regulation S-K Item 303 requires companies registered to disclose in the MD&A section "any known trends or uncertainties that have had or that the registrant reasonably expects will have a material. . .unfavorable impact on net sales or income from continuing operations."

Coca-Cola agreed to remedial efforts to avoid future reporting violations.

Source: Chad Terhune and Betsy McKay, "Coca-Cola Settles Regulatory Probe," *The Wall Street Journal,* April 19, 2005; U.S. Securities and Exchange Commission, Accounting and Auditing Enforcement Release No. 2232, April 18, 2005.

Why would disclosure of this practice be important to outsiders? Why did the auditors fail to require its disclosure?

To evaluate management's presentation and disclosure assertions, the auditor should review the financial statements, the footnote disclosures, and the disclosures made in the MD&A section to determine that they are presented in accordance with the applicable financial reporting framework. See the financial statement accounts and footnotes related to the revenue process for General Mills in Exhibit 4-10. In the financial statements, the accounts related to the revenue process are boldface.

General Mills, Inc. has reported sales revenue of $13,652.1 million for the year ending May 25, 2008. The sales revenue reported by General Mills is classified as operating revenue on the income statement (it is not listed as nonoperating revenue). Operating revenue is revenue earned from the normal business activities of the company. General Mills has reported accounts receivable of $1,081.6 million at May 25, 2008. The number is net of the allowance for doubtful accounts of $16.4 million. If the $1,081.6 million is the correct amount, it will reflect the amount of cash that will be collected the following year related to the accounts receivable balance at May 25, 2008.

Activities relating to the revenue process are reflected in the cash flow from operations section of the Statement of Cash Flows. Net earnings (sales revenue minus expenses) provides positive cash flow from operations (cash flow would be negative if the company had a net loss). Changes in accounts receivable are reflected as increases or decreases in cash from operations, depending on the direction of the change. For General Mills, Inc., cash flow decreased by $129 million because the accounts receivable balance increased by $129 million from 2007 to 2008.

Disclosure for the revenue process will typically include an explanation of the revenue recognition policy for the company. This General Mills disclosure comes in Footnote 2, "Summary of Significant Accounting Policies." The auditor should review this statement to determine that it is consistent with the way the company recognizes revenue and that it is in accordance with the applicable financial reporting framework. The auditor would also review "Management's Discussion and Analysis" section of the financial statements. You can find this section on the website for General Mills if you are interested in reviewing it (www.generalmills.com).

| Revenue Business Process Accounts and Disclosures for General Mills | Exhibit 4-10 |

CONSOLIDATED STATEMENTS OF INCOME
GENERAL MILLS, INC. AND SUBSIDIARIES

| | Fiscal Year | | |
In Millions	2008	2007	2006
Net Sales	$13,652.1	$12,441.5	$11,711.3
Cost of sales	8,778.3	7,955.1	7,544.8
Selling, general, and administrative costs	2,625.0	2,389.3	2,177.7
Restructuring, impairment, and other exit costs	21.0	39.3	29.8
Operating Profit	$ 2,227.8	$ 2,057.8	$ 1,959.0

CONSOLIDATED BALANCE SHEETS
GENERAL MILLS, INC. AND SUBSIDIARIES

In Millions	May 25, 2008	May 28, 2007
Current assets:		
Cash and cash equivalents	$ 661.0	$ 417.1
Receivables	1,081.6	952.9
Inventories	1,366.8	1,173.4
Prepaid expenses and other current assets	510.6	443.1
Deferred income taxes	—	67.2
Total current assets	$3,620.0	$3,053.7

CONSOLIDATED STATEMENTS OF CASH FLOWS
GENERAL MILLS, INC. AND SUBSIDIARIES

| | Fiscal Year | | |
In Millions	2008	2007	2006
Cash Flows—Operating Activities			
Net earnings	$1,294.7	$1,143.9	$1,090.3
Adjustments to reconcile earnings to cash			
Depreciation and amortization	459.2	417.8	423.9
After-tax earnings from joint ventures	(110.8)	(72.7)	(69.2)
Stock-based compensation	133.2	127.1	44.6
Deferred income taxes	98.1	26.0	25.9
Distributions of earnings from joint ventures	108.7	45.2	77.4
Tax benefit on exercises options	(55.7)	(73.1)	40.9
Pension and other benefits costs	(24.8)	(53.6)	(74.2)
Restructuring, impairment, and other exit costs	(1.7)	39.1	29.8
Changes in current assets, liabilities (except accounts receivable)	2.3	190.1	225.9
Change in accounts receivable	(129.0)	(41.0)	(42.0)
Other, net	(44.3)	2.4	70.2
Net cash provided by operating activities	$1,729.9	$1,751.2	$1,843.5

NOTES TO CONSOLIDATED FINANCIAL STATEMENTS
GENERAL MILLS, INC. AND SUBSIDIARIES

Note 2. Summary of Significant Accounting Policies

Revenue Recognition.   We recognize sales revenue when the shipment is accepted by our customer. Sales revenue includes shipping and handling charges that are billed to the customer and reported net of consumer coupon redemption, trade promotion and other costs, including estimated allowances for returns, unsalable product, and prompt pay discounts. Sales, use, value-added, and other excise taxes are not recognized in revenue. Coupons are recorded when distributed, based on estimated redemption rates. Trade promotions are recorded based on estimated participation and performance levels for offered programs at the time of sale. We generally do not allow a right of return. However, on a limited case-by-case basis with previous approval, we may allow customers to return product. In limited circumstances, product returned in salable condition is resold to other customers or outlets. Receivables from customers generally do not bear interest. Terms and collection patterns vary around the world and by channel. The allowance for doubtful accounts represents our estimate of probable non-payments and credit losses in our existing receivables, as determined based on a review of past due balances and other specific account data. Account balances are written off against the allowance when we deem the account is uncollectible.

Note 17. Supplemental Information
The components of certain Consolidated Balance Sheet accounts are as follows:

In Millions	May 25, 2008	May 27, 2007
Receivables:		
From customers	$1,098.0	$969.3
Less allowance for doubtful accounts	(16.4)	(16.4)
Total	$1,081.6	$952.9

Chapter Takeaways

The revenue process is one of the most important business processes for the auditor to investigate. An auditor's failure to identify misstatements in the revenue process can lead to lawsuits against her or him because outsiders rely on the cash flow projections from sales revenue. Incentives to misstate revenue are strong because the payoff is high in terms of the impact on net income. The audit procedures for this business process include testing internal controls and performing substantive tests with professional skepticism. The auditor should presume that misstatements may occur in the recording of revenue and therefore gather sufficient appropriate evidence to determine that the accounts in the process are presented in accordance with the applicable financial reporting framework.

This chapter presented these important facts:

- The transactions recorded in the revenue process, the applicable financial reporting framework that applies to these transactions, and the importance of the revenue process to the financial statements
- The susceptibility of the revenue process to fraud and the auditor's responsibility to detect it
- The way the auditor gathers evidence to support management's assertions of existence or occurrence, completeness, valuation and allocation, rights and obligations, accuracy, cutoff, and classification using internal control tests and substantive tests
- How the auditor evaluates the relevant assertions for the significant accounts in the business process, especially the two most important assertions in the revenue process, existence and valuation and how revenue and accounts receivable tend to be overstated in a number of ways including recording fictitious revenues, recording revenue early, and understating the allowance for uncollectible accounts
- The importance of internal controls in the revenue process due to the volume of transactions typically recorded in the process, and the importance of revenue to the overall financial statements

- How to audit the *presentation* and *disclosures* made by the client related to the transactions recorded in the process

Before you go to the next chapter, make sure you can explain all of the statements described in this chapter.

Appendix A

BCS
Private Limited

01-32 People's Park Complex
Singapore 059888

5 January 2011

Ba Choo San
#04-02 People's Park Complex
Singapore

Dear Sir/ Madam:

In connection with an examination of our financial statements, please confirm the correctness of the balance of your account with us as of December 31, 2010, directly with our auditors:

Stuart & Cram
Chinatown Point P.O. Box 888
Singapore

This is not a request for payment; please do not send your remittance to our auditors.

Your prompt attention to this request is much appreciated. A stamped self-addressed envelope is enclosed for your convenience.

Yours Truly,

Tay Seah
General Manager (Administration & Finance)

Stuart & Cram
Chinatown Point P.O. Box 888
Singapore

The balance receivable from us of $3,474.70 as of December 31, 2010, is correctly stated except as noted below:

My boss is disputing Invoice 11417 dated June 30, 2010. Poor-quality goods supplied. Also a credit note of $500 is yet to be given for goods returned by us in Nov 2010. Balance as per our books @ December 31, 2010 = $2,924.70

Date: Jan. 7, 2011   Confirmed by: Tan Lee Heng Accountant
                                         (Name, designation and company stamp)

BCS
Private Limited

01-32 People's Park Complex
Singapore 059888

5 January 2011

Sure Cure Clinic
Block 92 #02-03
Circuit Road
Singapore

Dear Sir/ Madam:

In connection with an examination of our financial statements, please confirm the correctness of the balance of your account with us as of December 31, 2010, directly with our auditors:

Stuart & Cram
Chinatown Point P.O. Box 888
Singapore

This is not a request for payment; please do not send your remittance to our auditors.

Your prompt attention to this request is much appreciated. A stamped self-addressed envelope is enclosed for your convenience.

Yours Truly,

Tay Seah
General Manager (Administration & Finance)

Stuart & Cram
Chinatown Point P.O. Box 888
Singapore

The balance receivable from us of $7,937.45 as of December 31, 2010, is correctly stated except as noted below:

Check payment of $1,984.30 has not been recorded

Date: Jan. 10, 2011   Confirmed by: Koh Ling Ling, Accounts Clerk
                          (Name, designation and company stamp)

BCS
Private Limited

01-32 People's Park Complex
Singapore 059888

5 January 2011

Serangoon Medical Store
Block 465 #01-18
Serangoon Central
Singapore

Dear Sir/ Madam:

In connection with an examination of our financial statements, please confirm the correctness of the balance of your account with us as of December 31, 2010, directly with our auditors:

Stuart & Cram
Chinatown Point P.O. Box 888
Singapore

This is not a request for payment; please do not send your remittance to our auditors.

Your prompt attention to this request is much appreciated. A stamped self-addressed envelope is enclosed for your convenience.

Yours Truly,

Tay Seah
General Manager (Administration & Finance)

_____

Stuart & Cram
Chinatown Point P.O. Box 888
Singapore

The balance receivable from us of $5,488.80 as of December 31, 2010, is correctly stated except as noted below:

We sent a payment check of $ 1,829.60 to you on December 30, 2010. The balance should be $3,659.20

_____

Date: Jan. 12, 2011   Confirmed by: Rachel Teo, Accountant
                                          (Name, designation and company stamp)

BCS
Private Limited

01-32 People's Park Complex
Singapore 059888

5 January 2011

Oh So Soon Clinic
70 Old Airport Road
Singapore

Dear Sir/ Madam:

In connection with an examination of our financial statements, please confirm the correctness of the balance of your account with us as of December 31, 2010, directly with our auditors:

Stuart & Cram
Chinatown Point P.O. Box 888
Singapore

This is not a request for payment; please do not send your remittance to our auditors.

Your prompt attention to this request is much appreciated. A stamped self-addressed envelope is enclosed for your convenience.

Yours Truly,

Tay Seah
General Manager (Administration & Finance)

_____

Stuart & Cram
Chinatown Point P.O. Box 888
Singapore

The balance receivable from us of $7,912.25 as of December 31, 2010, is correctly stated except as noted below:

My account shows $ 6,912.25 but I received Invoice 11715 dated December 31, 2010 on January 5, 2011 for an amount of $1,000.

_____

_____

Date: Jan. 12, 2010   Confirmed by: Eric Goh, General Clerk
                                        (Name, designation and company stamp)

BCS
Private Limited

01-32 People's Park Complex
Singapore 059888

5 January 2011

Eastern Acupuncture
685 North Bridge Road
Singapore

Dear Sir/ Madam:

In connection with an examination of our financial statements, please confirm the correctness of the balance of your account with us as of December 31, 2010, directly with our auditors:

Stuart & Cram
Chinatown Point P.O. Box 888
Singapore

This is not a request for payment; please do not send your remittance to our auditors.

Your prompt attention to this request is much appreciated. A stamped self-addressed envelope is enclosed for your convenience.

Yours Truly,

Tay Seah
General Manager (Administration & Finance)

Stuart & Cram
Chinatown Point P.O. Box 888
Singapore

The balance receivable from us of $6,243.10 as of December 31, 2010, is correctly stated except as noted below:

My book shows only $5,833.10. Please check.

Date: Jan. 10, 2011   Confirmed by: Edward Liu, Accounts Clerk
                                       (Name, designation and company stamp)

BCS
Private Limited

01-32 People's Park Complex
Singapore 059888

5 January 2011

Rimei Clinic & Health Food
Blk 12 #01-434   **DUPLICATE**
Upper Thomson Road   **2nd request sent 17 January 2011**
Singapore

Dear Sir/ Madam:

In connection with an examination of our financial statements, please confirm the correctness of the balance of your account with us as of December 31, 2010, directly with our auditors:

Stuart & Cram
Chinatown Point P.O. Box 888
Singapore

This is not a request for payment; please do not send your remittance to our auditors.

Your prompt attention to this request is much appreciated. A stamped self-addressed envelope is enclosed for your convenience.

Yours Truly,

Tay Seah
General Manager (Administration & Finance)

_____

Stuart & Cram
Chinatown Point P.O. Box 888
Singapore

The balance receivable from us of $3,708.50 as of December 31, 2010, is correctly stated except as noted below:

_____
_____

Date: _____   Confirmed by: _____
                                      (Name, designation and company stamp)

BCS
Private Limited

01-32 People's Park Complex
Singapore 059888

5 January 2011

Lok Meng Free Clinic
Block 107 #01-1895
Bukit Batok St 31
Singapore

DUPLICATE
2nd request sent 15 January 2011

Dear Sir/ Madam:

In connection with an examination of our financial statements, please confirm the correctness of the balance of your account with us as of December 31, 2010, directly with our auditors:

Stuart & Cram
Chinatown Point P.O. Box 888
Singapore

This is not a request for payment; please do not send your remittance to our auditors.

Your prompt attention to this request is much appreciated. A stamped self-addressed envelope is enclosed for your convenience.

Yours Truly,

Tay Seah
General Manager (Administration & Finance)

_____

Stuart & Cram
Chinatown Point P.O. Box 888
Singapore

The balance receivable from us of $4,841.20 as of December 31, 2010, is correctly stated except as noted below:

_____
_____

Date: _____   Confirmed by: _____

Appendix B

BCS Private Ltd.

Accounts Receivable Listing as of December 31, 2010

Customer	Year-End Balance (in dollars)	Amount in Dollars ($)				
		Current	>30 days	> 60 days	>90 days	Subsequent Receipts
Ang Siew Min	421.25				421.25	
Beng Kok Med Hall	1108.00	277.00	277.00	277.00	277.00	277.00
Ba Choo San	3474.70	2474.70	500.00		500.00	
Chan Chin Chai Med Hall	4306.20		2002.00		2306.20	
Chang's Female Clinic	125.40	125.40				125.40
Chia Ho Soon	244.15					244.15
Chin Sook Fan	1212.75	1212.75				1212.75
Choy Ear Clinic	561.30	561.30				561.30
Eastern Acupuncture	6243.10	6243.10				
Eng Siang Ear, Nose & Throat Clinic	450.00		450.00			450.00
Foo King Chu Med Hall	1259.05				1259.05	
Ghim Moh Med Specialists	1448.75	474.10	474.15	500.50		500.50
Hui Min Chinese Physician	276.00		276.00			276.00
Jie Ying Clinic	788.90				788.90	
King Kong Kong Med Store	350.00	175.00	175.00			175.00
Koh Thiam Siew	8187.25	954.10	1395.40	2711.50	3126.25	3126.25
Lai Kah Shing Clinic	4312.60	1078.15	1078.15	1078.15	1078.15	
Lim Siong Tye	847.50				847.50	
Lim Seah Clinic	2747.00		2747.00			2747.00
Loh Chong Yick	783.65	783.65				
Lok Meng Free Clinic	4841.20	2420.60	2420.60			
Mee Na Tan Clinic	598.75	300.00	298.75			298.75
Min Hin Med Hall	3874.00	968.50	968.50	968.50	968.50	968.50
Moo Moo Kow	1908.45	1908.45				
Nan Hwa Med Hall	5178.15	3178.15			2002.00	2002.00
New Man & Woman Acupuncture	139.60	139.60				
New World Herbalist Store	463.40	231.70	231.70			231.70
Oh No Lah Med Hall	219.50				219.50	
Oh So Soon Clinic	7912.25	3756.05	4156.20			
Oh Seok Tin Clinic	1409.75			1409.75		1409.75
Ong Thean Tin & Co	2753.00	2753.00				
Pao Pao Med Hall	804.80		804.80			804.80
Poh Heng Clinic	250.00		250.00			250.00
Ren Her Med Store	1415.65	353.90	360.00	325.70	376.05	376.05

continued

auditors had completed the field work. The returned merchandise was included in the physical inventory. What control should have prevented the misstatement?

a. Aged trial balance of accounts receivable is prepared.

b. Credit memoranda are prenumbered and all numbers are accounted for.

c. A reconciliation of the trial balance of customer's accounts with the general ledger control is prepared periodically.

d. Receiving reports are prepared for all materials received and such reports are accounted for on a regular basis.

LO7   35. The sales manager credited a salesperson, Jack Smith, with sales that were actually "house account" sales. Later Smith divided his excess sales commissions with the sales manager. What control should have prevented the misstatement?

a. The summary sales entries are checked periodically by persons independent of sales functions.

b. Sales orders are reviewed and approved by persons independent of the sales department.

c. The internal auditor compares the sales commission statements with the cash disbursements records.

d. Sales orders are prenumbered, and all are accounted for.

LO7   36. A sales invoice for $5,200 was computed correctly, but, by mistake, was entered as $2,500 to the sales journal and to the accounts receivable master file. The customer remitted only $2,500, the amount on his monthly statement. What control should have prevented the misstatement?

a. Prelisting and predetermined totals are used to control posting.

b. Sales invoice numbers, prices, discounts, extensions, and footing are independently checked.

c. The customer's monthly statements are verified and mailed by a responsible person other than the bookkeeper who prepared them.

d. Unauthorized remittance deductions made by customers or other matters in dispute are investigated promptly by a person independent of the accounts receivable function.

LO7   37. Copies of sales invoices show different unit prices for apparently identical items. What control should have prevented the misstatement?

a. All sales invoices are checked as to all details after their preparation.

b. Differences reported by customers are satisfactorily investigated.

c. Statistical sales data are compiled and reconciled with recorded sales.

d. All sales invoices are compared with the customer's purchase orders.

The following sales procedures were encountered during the annual audit of Marvel Wholesale Distributing Company. Use this information to answer questions 38, 39, and 40.

Customer orders are received by the sales order department. A clerk computes the approximate dollar amount of the order and sends it to the credit department for approval. Credit approval is stamped on the order and sent to the accounting department. A computer is then used to generate two copies of a sales invoice. The order is filed in the customer order file.

The customer copy of the sales invoice is routed through the warehouse, and the shipping department has authority for the respective departments to release and ship the merchandise. Shipping department personnel pack the order and manually prepare a three-copy bill of lading: the original copy is mailed to the customer, the second copy is sent with shipment, and then the other is filed in sequence in the bill of lading file. The sales invoice shipping copy is sent to the accounting department with any changes resulting from lack of available merchandise.

A clerk in accounting matches the received sales invoice shipping copy with the sales invoice customer copy from the pending file. Quantities on the two invoices are compared and prices are compared to an approved price list. The customer copy is then mailed to the customer, and the shipping copy is sent to the data processing department.

The data processing clerk in accounting enters the sales invoice data into the computer, which is used to prepare the sales journal and update the accounts receivable master file. She files the shipping copy in the sales invoice file in numerical sequence.

LO7   38. To determine whether the internal controls operate effectively to minimize instance of failure to post invoices to customers' accounts receivable master file, the auditor would select a sample of transactions from the population represented by the:
a. Customer order file.
b. Bill of lading file.
c. Customer's accounts receivable master file.
d. Sales invoice file.

LO7   39. To determine whether the internal controls operated effectively to minimize instances of failure to invoice shipment, the auditor would select a sample of transactions from the population represented by the:
a. Customer order file.
b. Bill of lading file.
c. Customers' accounts receivable master file.
d. Sales invoice file.

LO8   40. To gather audit evidence that uncollected items in customers' accounts represented existing trade receivables, the auditor would select a sample of items from the population represented by the:
a. Customer order file.
b. Bill of lading file.
c. Customers' accounts receivable master file.
d. Sales invoice file.

Discussion Questions and Research Problems

LO7   41. **Performing tests of controls for the revenue process.** Review the list of controls that could be present in the revenue process and determine the audit procedures that could be performed to test the control. For each procedure, indicate the management assertion that the auditor gathers evidence to evaluate while performing the test.
a. Prenumbered shipping documents are completed in the shipping department.
b. Sales invoices are prenumbered.
c. Customer credit is approved before orders are shipped.
d. Credit memos are prenumbered and the sequence is checked for missing documents.
e. Customer statements are mailed monthly by the accounts receivable department.

LO8   42. **Analyzing the results from analytical procedures.** The auditor performs preliminary analytical procedures to plan the audit. Results from the analytical procedures for the revenue process follow. In addition to the below questions, for each result, indicate how the auditor adjusts the audit program to gather evidence regarding the potential misstatements in the financial statements that could be suggested by the results from the analytical procedures.
a. The auditor compares the accounts receivable balance with the previous year's balance and finds that it has decreased. What questions should the auditor ask? What misstatement could the auditor anticipate in the financial statements?
b. The auditor calculates the accounts receivable turnover for the current year and the previous year and finds that it decreased for the current year. What questions should the auditor ask? What misstatement could the auditor anticipate in the financial statements?

c. The auditor compares the balance in the Allowance for Doubtful Accounts for the current year and the previous year and finds that it has declined in the current year. What questions should the auditor ask? What misstatement could the auditor anticipate in the financial statements?

d. The auditor compares the balance in the Sales Returns account for the current and previous year and finds that it has increased. What questions should the auditor ask? What misstatement could the auditor anticipate in the financial statements?

LO8   43. **Performing substantive tests of transactions.** The auditor performs substantive tests of transactions for sales revenue to determine that the sales revenue reported on the income statements is not materially misstated. For each procedure performed in the audit of the revenue process in the following list, indicate the management assertion that is tested during the audit procedure.

a. The auditor selects a sample of shipping documents and traces the documents to the sales invoices.

b. The auditor selects a sample of sales invoices and traces the documents to the shipping notices.

c. The auditor selects a sample of recorded sales from the sales journal and determines whether credit was approved for the sale.

d. The auditor selects a sample of recorded sales from the sales journal and vouches the prices on the sales invoices to an approved price list.

e. The auditor selects a sample of recorded sales from the sales journal and determines whether the amount billed equals the amount shipped.

LO7   44. **Internal control procedures.** The auditor has documented the following internal control procedures used by the client. For each procedure, explain the test you would perform to determine whether the control was working and the assertion that you would be testing.

a. The warehouse clerk is required to have an approved sales order before goods are released from the warehouse to be sent to the shipping department.

b. Shipping clerks compare goods received from the warehouse with approved sales orders and initial the sales order indicating their agreement.

c. The accounting department compares the sales invoice price with the master price file and initials the sales invoice indicating agreement.

d. Control amounts posted to the accounts receivable ledger are compared with control totals of invoices. A daily reconciliation report is prepared by the accounting clerk and initialed at the end of each day.

e. Sales invoices are compared with shipping documents and approved customer orders before invoices are mailed. The accounts receivable clerk initials the shipping document indicating the agreement.

f. Goods returned for credit are approved by the supervisor of the sales department. The credit memo is initialed by the supervisor indicating approval.

g. The total cash payments posted to the accounts receivable ledger from remittance advices is compared to the bank deposit slip by the treasury department. The clerk in the treasury department indicates that the two agree by initialing the reconciliation report.

LO8   45. **Performing substantive tests of transactions.** The following audit steps are part of the audit program for the revenue process. Indicate the assertion supported by the evidence gathered in performing each procedure.

a. Select a sample of sales invoices from the sales journal.

(1) Vouch to the supporting shipping document.

(2) Determine whether credit was approved.

(3) Vouch prices on the invoice to the approved price list.

(4) Compare the amount billed to the amount shipped.

(5) Recalculate the invoice.

   (6) Compare the shipping date with the invoice date.
   (7) Trace the invoice to the posting in the control account for accounts receivable and the general ledger control account.
   b. Select a sample of shipping documents from the shipping department file and trace the shipments to the recorded sales invoices.
   c. Scan the sales invoices and the shipping documents for missing numbers in sequence.

LO8   46. **Performing substantive tests of balances.** The following audit steps are part of the revenue process audit program. Indicate the assertion supported by the evidence gathered in performing each procedure.
   a. Select a sample of customers' accounts.
   (1) Vouch debits in the accounts to sales invoices.
   (2) Vouch credits in the accounts to cash receipts documentation and approved credit memos.
   b. Select a sample of credit memos.
   (1) Review for proper approval.
   (2) Trace to posting in customers' accounts.
   c. Scan the accounts receivable control account for postings from sources other than the sales and cash receipts journals. Vouch a sample of such entries to supporting documents.

LO7   47. **Testing internal control procedures in computerized and manual accounting systems.** Accounting systems typically implement controls to prevent misstatements in processing transactions. For each of the following controls described, (1) indicate the misstatement that could occur if the control is not implemented and (2) identify an audit procedure to test the control's effectiveness.
   a. Sales transactions less than $25,000 are approved by the accounting system automatically (without involvement of the credit manager). Sales transactions higher than $25,000 require written approval by the credit manager.
   b. All sales invoices are priced according to an authorized price list. Any exceptions to this pricing must be approved by the sales manager.
   c. All shipping document are prenumbered and accounted for. Shipping document numbers are noted on all sales invoices.
   d. A report of exceptions noting the failure of the invoice amount and the shipping amount to match is sent to the sales manager.

LO8   48. **Substantive tests of transactions.** Two auditors are discussing the audit procedures for sales revenue. Stacy Mendoza believes that the best way to test sales revenue is to select a random sample of recorded sales and to trace these sales back through the system to the supporting documents, noting that all items billed were shipped and that the sales were invoiced at the correct prices. Takai Wong disagrees. He believes that it is better to gather evidence for the sales process by starting with the prenumbered shipping documents and then tracing them forward through the system to the invoice, noting the existence of control procedures and the correctness of the invoice processing.
   a. If you follow Stacy's audit approach, identify the assertion supported by your evidence.
   b. If you follow Takai's audit approach, identify the assertion supported by your evidence.
   c. Which auditor is correct?

LO8   49. **Cutoff tests.** While performing a sales cutoff test for your audit client, you review all shipping documents for five days before and five days after year-end. All sales are on credit and are sent FOB shipping point. Cost of goods sold is 75% of sales revenue. You are using the shipping log for the ten-day time period of the test. Test results follow.

Shipping Number	Sales Price	Date Shipped	Date Billed	Date Cash Collected
450783	$ 10,249	Dec 26, 2010	Dec 30, 2010	Jan 28, 2011
450784	24,990	Dec 27, 2010	Dec 31, 2010	Dec 15, 2010
450785	2,156	Dec 28, 2010	Jan 2, 2011	Jan 31, 2011
450786	1,937	Dec 29, 2010	Dec 31, 2010	Feb 3, 2011
450787	110,895	Dec 31, 2010	Jan 3, 2011	Feb 8, 2011
450789	45,761	Jan 2, 2011	Jan 5, 2011	Feb 4, 2011
450790	240,441	Jan 3, 2011	Jan 6, 2011	Jan 25, 2011
450791	235,000	Jan 4, 2011	Jan 10, 2011	Dec 25, 2010
450792	1,250,000	Jan 5, 2011	Jan 8, 2011	Feb 25, 2011

a. Identify by shipping number the sales that the company has recorded as sales revenue at December 31, 2010.

b. Identify by shipping number the sales that should have been recorded as sales revenue at December 31, 2010.

c. Prepare the adjusting entry needed to correct the sales revenue and inventory at December 31, 2010.

d. Prepare the journal entries needed to record the sale represented by shipping document 450784, including the cash collection and the revenue recognition.

e. What accounting rule should the company use to recognize revenue?

f. How is the company currently recognizing revenue?

g. What questions should you ask the client to clarify the evidence you have gathered during this audit test?

LO8   50. **Analytical procedures.** You have been asked to audit the revenue from membership fees for the Orange County Master Gardeners Club. Your spouse is a member of the club.

a. What questions would you ask the club treasurer to verify the revenue?

b. Let's assume that we have the following information: the club had approximately 200 members at the end of last year. Each year the club loses 15% of its members and gains 20% in new members. The dues are $50 per year, but members over 65 have a life-time membership where they do not pay dues. Approximately 20% of our membership is over 65 at any time. Describe some analytical procedures that you might use to determine that the membership revenue reported on the club's financial statements is not materially misstated.

c. Assume that membership revenue reported by the treasurer is $6,000. What would you conclude about the revenue?

LO8   51. **Sales cutoff tests.** Sales cutoff tests are performed to determine that sales are recorded in the correct time period according to the revenue recognition rules of the applicable financial reporting framework.

a. What is the revenue recognition rule for recording revenue when your audit client sells a product that it ships to the customer?

b. What is the accounting rule for recognizing revenue when your client performs a service such as one a dentist could perform?

c. How would you perform cutoff tests for a product that is shipped to the customer if your primary audit concern is gathering evidence to support the existence of the sales? What conditions could be present in an audit client resulting in a risk that sales recorded at year-end do not exist?

d. How would you perform cutoff tests for a service that your client performs (for example, a dentist's office) if your primary audit concern is completeness of sales?

e. What conditions could be present in an audit client leading to a risk that sales recorded at year-end are incomplete?

LO8   52. **Substantive test of balances.** Refer to Appendix A for five replies from customers of BCS Inc. in response to the receivables confirmation conducted by Stuart & Cram, the BCS auditor and a copy of two letters for which replies have not yet been received.

a. For each reply, explain what you think has happened, how you would verify your explanation, and whether the reply represents a misstatement in the BCS accounts. If so, prepare the adjusting entry.

b. For the two nonreplies, explain what other method the auditor could use to obtain some assurance on the balances involved.

LO8   53. **Evaluating the allowance for doubtful accounts.** See Appendix B for the aged receivables trial balance for BCS. Review it and explain what the information in each column represents.

a. Use this information to calculate a bad debt provision for BCS at December 31, 2010? Last year BCS used the following percentages to calculate the bad debt provision: current accounts, −.05%; > 30 day accounts, −2%; >60 day accounts, −10%; > 90 day accounts, 40%. First calculate the allowance using the percentages applicable in the previous year. Then, if you determine that actual write-offs last year were $20,000 more than the provision and that the economic conditions for BCS customers has worsened in the current year, explain how you could adjust the allowance.

b. Why is it necessary for BCS to estimate bad debt expense at year-end? What accounting principle does BCS violate if it does not estimate bad debt?

LO7   54. **Evaluating management's assertions.** An auditor could use the procedures listed after the following lettered items to evaluate management's assertions for the revenue process.

a. Identify the procedure as a test of controls or substantive test of transactions or balances and indicate the assertion it tests.

b. Describe how you would design a test to determine whether the control is effective or the account balance or transaction has been recorded correctly.

c. What misstatement is the client trying to prevent by using the control? What misstatement does the auditor attempt to prevent by using the substantive test?

Audit Procedures

(1) Trace a sample of shipping documents to sales invoices and sales journals to make sure that the shipment was billed.

(2) Examine a sample of sales invoices to determine whether each one has a shipping document attached.

(3) Trace a sample of debit entries in the accounts receivable subsidiary ledger to the sales journal to determine whether the date, customer name, and amount are the same.

(4) Perform cutoff tests by reviewing the shipping documents for five days before and five days after year-end to determine that the sales revenue was recorded in the correct time period.

(5) Review the allowance for doubtful accounts at year-end to determine that it is correctly stated.

(6) Confirm accounts receivable at year-end.

LO8   55. **Evaluating misstatements found during an audit.** The misstatements that you found during your audit of the year-end accounts receivable balance are listed after the following lettered items.

a. For each item, indicate the audit procedures that could evaluate the potential misstatement in the financial statements and the management assertion addressed by the audit procedure.

b. How would you determine whether the misstatements were caused by errors on the part of the audit client or fraud? Does it matter?

Misstatements

(1) Sales totaling $1,254,721 were shipped on January 3, 2012, and recorded on December 31, 2011.

(2) Balances in individual customer accounts do not agree with the supporting documents (invoices, shipping documents, cash receipts).

(3) Some sales transactions were not recorded.

(4) A customer account in the > 0–30 days category in the aged trial balance is actually more than 120 days old.

(5) Actual accounts receivable written off in 2011 were higher than the December 31, 2010, allowance for uncollectible accounts balance.

LO5 56. **Audit assertions.** Auditing has been defined as a process of determining the degree to which assertions correspond to the rules. Explain this statement by discussing the assertions and the rules for the revenue process.

Real-World Auditing Problems

LO8 57. **Qwest Communications International, Inc.**

In July 2002, Qwest, a telecommunications company based in Denver, Colorado, acknowledged that it had improperly recorded revenue for 2000, 2001, and 2002. The company restated its financial results for 2000 and 2001 and reduced its estimate of earnings for 2002.[3] With 61,000 employees and yearly sales revenue of $19.7 billion in 2001, Qwest provides telecommunication services to residential, business, and government customers. Its revenue misstatements originated from its handling of revenue from transactions in which it sold long-term capacity on its network and bought similar capacity from its trading partners (referred to as *swap transactions* or *round-trip trades*).

Arthur Andersen, LLP, advised several telecommunications clients how to structure swap transactions in a 48-page document referred to as the "white paper."[4] According to the document, swap transactions are not barter arrangements, which would prevent the two firms from recognizing revenue. The document suggests that two given companies structure their transactions so the capacity sold is an operating asset and the capacity bought is a capital asset. This practice allows the seller to recognize revenue and to record the cost of providing the capacity as a capitalized cost rather than an expense, moving the cost off the income statement and putting it in a capital asset account on the balance sheet. From Andersen's point of view, because the risks and rewards of buying capital leases were different than those of operating leases, the companies involved in the swaps were no longer exchanging similar assets. If the assets exchanged were not similar, it was possible to recognize revenue on the capacity swapped in the transaction.

Companies in the telecommunications industry relied heavily on the use of swap transaction accounting to inflate revenue, which was commonly believed to be the most reliable measure of a company's health. These companies included Qwest, Global Crossing, and WorldCom. Arthur Andersen was the auditor for many telecommunications firms. Officials of the Securities and Exchange Commission (SEC) were concerned that such revenue-increasing tactics were widely used by these companies to "give the appearance of economic activity and growth when there was none."[5] These companies, in effect, were following advice similar

---

[3] Sharon Young, "Qwest Says It Plans to Restate Financial Results for 2000, 2001," *The Wall Street Journal,* July 29, 2002.

[4] Dennis Berman, "Regulators Are Taking a Look at Andersen's "Swaps' Method," *The Wall Street Journal,* March 19, 2002.

[5] Susan Pulliam and Rebecca Blumenstein, "SEC Broadens Investigation into Revenue-Boosting Tricks—Agency Finds New Focus as 'Round Trip' Deals Appear to Be Widespread," *The Wall Street Journal,* May 15, 2002.

to that given in the Andersen "white paper." SEC officials believed that telecommunications companies' swap transactions had no business purpose other than to increase revenue.

In August 2002, the SEC formally concluded that the telecommunications companies improperly booked revenue from capacity swaps with other companies. This SEC decision officially put an end to the widely used industry practice that had inflated revenue for many telecommunications companies.[6] The ruling resulted in earnings restatements by several companies and prompted shareholder lawsuits alleging accounting fraud.

Joseph Nacchio, the chief executive officer of Qwest, resigned under pressure in June 2002. He and other top Qwest executives had sold Qwest stock during the years the swap accounting was used. His stock sales alone netted $130 million in profit. Qwest insiders sold stock worth $530 million between January 2000 and July 2001, raising questions about their interest in keeping the stock price as high as possible by reporting growth in sales revenue.[7]

a. Evaluate the revenue recognition principle used by Qwest to record revenue based on swap transactions.
b. What is the role of the auditor in evaluating the audit client's revenue recognition policy? Would you have approved it? What is wrong with the policy?
c. Do you believe that company executives engaged in fraudulent activity by their use of swap transactions to increase revenue? Do you think the executives should be shielded from liability for swap transactions that occurred before the SEC issued a formal statement prohibiting these companies from recognizing revenue using these transactions?
d. If company executives received stock options based on performance, how could this have influenced their choice of accounting method for revenue recognition? How should the auditor evaluate the audit client's use of stock options for executives? How would you include stock options in the audit risk model?

LO7, LO8   58. **Bristol-Myers Squibb**

Bristol-Myers produces and distributes medicines and health care products. In 2002, the company experienced one of its worst years in its 100-year history. Three of its top-selling drugs lost patent protection, and sales dramatically declined due to their generic substitutes produced by other companies. The share price of Bristol-Myers stock declined by nearly two-thirds, from about $75 in September 1999 to $25 in September 2002.

In April 2002, the company disclosed that it had used sales incentives to encourage wholesalers to buy more drugs and health care products than necessary. In July 2002, Bristol-Myers was notified that the SEC was opening a formal inquiry to determine whether the company had inflated revenue by as much as $1 billion in 2001 through the use of sales incentives.[8] The company restated its earnings to remove the amount of excessive sales.

a. Evaluate Bristol-Myers Squibb's revenue recognition policy. Why did the SEC object to it?
b. If you had been Bristol-Myers Squibb's auditor, what questions would you have asked the client about the sales incentives? How would you modify the audit risk model to account for them?
c. Identify an internal control procedure that could have prevented the revenue misstatement that occurred.

[6] Henry Sender, "SEC Deals Blow to Telecom by Rejecting Capacity Swaps," *The Wall Street Journal,* August 21, 2002.

[7] Deborah Solomon and Susan Pulliam, "SEC Adopts Tougher Position on Qwest Accounting Methods," *The Wall Street Journal,* June 26, 2002.

[8] Gardiner Harris, "SEC Is Probing Bristol-Myers over Sales-Incentive Accounting," *The Wall Street Journal,* July 12, 2002.

LO8

59. **Time Warner**

In July 2002, the SEC reviewed revenue transactions by the America Online (AOL) unit of Time Warner to determine whether the company used "unconventional" ad deals to increase revenue to meet expectations of Wall Street analysts. An article appearing in *The Washington Post* on July 18, 2002, alleged that AOL had manipulated its ad revenue when it was waiting for approval of its merger with Time Warner, which owns CNN cable news, HBO, Warner Brothers, and *Time* magazine. The new company known as AOL Time Warner was created on January 11, 2001. As a result of the merger, American Online and Time Warner each became a wholly owned subsidiary of AOL Time Warner. In 2003, the name of the company was changed to Time Warner.[9,10,11]

A *Washington Post* reporter reviewed a number of AOL's revenue transactions from July 2000 to March 2002. Without the unconventional deals described in the article, quarterly earnings per share would not have met analysts' forecasts for two quarters in 2000. According to the *Post,* during this time, "Investors punished companies whose earnings were off by even a cent."[12] AOL employees interviewed for the article said that the company was under tremendous pressure to meet its revenue targets due to the $112 billion merger pending with Time Warner. Ad revenue became very important to the Internet division as competition from other Internet service providers hurt AOL's monthly subscriber fees. Unfortunately, the contracts for the advertising services were with dot-com companies, which also were suffering from declining sales and many of which did not have the cash to pay for the ads they had agreed to buy from AOL.

The unconventional deals include a variety of methods to increase revenue. AOL's business affairs department contacted companies that were unable to pay for their long-term ad contracts and renegotiated the terms, requiring the companies to make one-time payments to renegotiate or get out of the contracts. AOL recognized all revenue for the renegotiated contracts immediately as ad revenue. Earlier, in September 2000, AOL had used another unconventional ad deal to generate revenue. It recorded ad revenue based on a lawsuit settlement. AOL purchased Movie Fone in 1999, which had won a $26.8 million settlement from Wembley PLC, a British entertainment company, but had not yet collected the claim. Instead of collecting the settlement, AOL offered Wembley the opportunity to buy $23.8 million in online ads (a good deal for Wembley because it saved $3 million). Because AOL was short of advertising revenue for the quarter ending on September 30, 2000, it had to create the Wembley ads and air them before the end of the quarter. Wembley considered the proposal for some time, but AOL could not wait for its decision because this revenue had to be booked in September 2000. Without Wembley's knowledge, AOL took artwork from Wembley's British website (24 Dogs.com, an online greyhound racing website) and created banner and button ads using the artwork and started running them on various AOL sites. Within an hour of posting the greyhound ads, the Wembley website crashed, due to the traffic generated by the AOL ads.

Despite AOL's action, Wembley reached an ad agreement with it that generated $16.4 million in ad revenue for the September 30, 2000, quarter, effectively taking

---

[9] Securities and Exchange Commission, Form 10-K, "AOL Time Warner Inc.," For the Fiscal Year Ended December 31, 2001; Securities and Exchange Commission, Form 10-Q, "Time Warner Inc." For the quarter ended September 30, 2003.

[10] Securities and Exchange Commission, Form 10-K, "AOL Time Warner Inc.," For the Fiscal Year Ended December 31, 2001; Securities and Exchange Commission, Form 10-Q, "Time Warner Inc." For the quarter ended September 30, 2003.

[11] Key facts for AOL Time Warner, Inc., (http://www.wsj.com), September 18, 2002.

[12] Alec Klein, "Unconventional Transactions Boosted Sales; Amid Big Merger, Company Resisted Dot-Com. Collapse," *The Washington Post,* July 18, 2002; Jonathan Weil, "AOL Could Soon Need to Take Another Gargantuan Write-Off," *The Wall Street Journal,* August 23, 2002.

a nonoperating gain on a lawsuit settlement and converting it to a more valuable operating revenue number.[13]

a. Evaluate the revenue recognition policies used by AOL. Are the policies consistent with the applicable financial reporting framework?

b. How would the auditor discover the misstatements in the financial statements?

c. Describe how the audit risk model could be used in the AOL audit to consider the pending acquisition and the decline in sales revenue.

LO8   60. **Xerox Corporation**

Xerox Corporation, a company based in Stamford, Connecticut, is involved in the production and management of documents in the form of copy machines, fax machines, and commercial printing equipment. In the late 1990s, competition had a negative impact on Xerox sales (among others things, computer printers were replacing copiers to generate print copies). A poorly organized business restructuring also caused administrative problems and billing and sales slowdowns for Xerox. The accounting department at Xerox began being pressured to compensate for the poor sales results with accounting measures. Xerox "assigned accountants numerical goals to produce profits through accounting actions. It just became standard operating procedure that, you know, you look to the accountants to find income."[14]

In April 2002, Xerox settled a case with the SEC, agreeing to pay a $10 million fine and restating its results back to 1997. The restatement showed that it had recorded $6.4 billion of revenue early and had overstated its pretax income by $1.41 billion over the five years, a 36% overstatement. Paul R. Berger, Associate Director of Enforcement at the SEC, described the actions of Xerox executives in the SEC enforcement notice: "Xerox's senior management orchestrated a four-year scheme to disguise the company's true operating performance. Such conduct calls for stiff sanctions, including in this case, the imposition of the largest fine ever obtained by the SEC against a public company in a financial fraud case. The penalty also reflects, in part, a sanction for the company's lack of full cooperation in the investigation."[15]

The SEC enforcement notice reported that the company had recorded long-term leasing agreements for copiers over shorter periods than the leases ran in order to record more revenue during the early years of the leases. The company also had made a one-time sale of accounts receivable to increase operating results but failed to disclose this fact to outsiders. Xerox established a "cookie jar" reserve account that was set up to cover merger costs but instead was used to meet analysts' quarterly earnings forecasts. From 1997 to 2000, the SEC alleged that senior managers at Xerox were paid more than $5 million on performance-based compensation and made more than $30 million from the sale of company stock.

In a related SEC inquiry, notices of possible civil action for fraud were sent to KPMG, Xerox's former auditor (that had been fired in 2001), and a number of Xerox executives (both current and former). KPMG responded that it did nothing wrong in its work for Xerox and had, in fact, been fired for forcing Xerox to conduct an independent accounting exam that resulted in an earlier Xerox restatement. The restatement in 2001 prompted the SEC investigation in 2002. Xerox executives argued that they had relied on the accounting guidance provided by KPMG.

---

[13] "AOL Time Warner Reports First Quarter 2003 Results," *The Wall Street Journal,* April 23, 2003; Alec Klein, "Unconventional Transactions Boosted Sales; Amid Big Merger, Company Resisted Dot-com. Collapse," *The Washington Post,* July 18, 2002; Jonathan Weil, "AOL Could Soon Need To Take Another Gargantuan Write-off," *The Wall Street Journal,* August 23, 2002.

[14] James Bandler and Mark Maremont, "How Ex-Accountant Added Up to Trouble for Humbled Xerox," *The Wall Street Journal,* June 28, 2001.

[15] U.S. Securities and Exchange Commission, "Xerox settles SEC enforcement action charging company with fraud," http://www.sec.gov/news.

a. Evaluate the revenue recognition policies used by Xerox. As an auditor, would you have approved them?

b. Describe how the audit risk model could have been used in the Xerox audit to consider the performance-based compensation and the decline in sales revenue.

c. How would the auditor evaluate management in this company? Would the auditor be aware of management's position to "look to the accountants to find income"?

LO8, LO9   61. **Gemstar-TV Guide International, Inc.**

KPMG and Gemstar, publisher of *TV Guide* magazine, agreed to pay the SEC a $10 million fine as a penalty for overstating revenue from 1999 to 2002. The overstatements involved improperly reporting licensing and advertising revenue. The SEC said that the auditors should have known that the company improperly recognized revenue.[16] The SEC stated that KPMG auditors substituted "management representations for competent evidence."[17]

The revenue recognition problems were described in an accounting and auditing enforcement notice disclosing the earnings misstatement. According to the report, the revenue recognition problems were in two areas of revenue: licensing and advertising.

Licensing Revenue and Disclosure in the Footnotes

Gemstar recognized $23.5 million in licensing revenue from AOL in 2000. This revenue represented an upfront fee that should have been recognized over the eight-year time period in which the services were to be provided. Gemstar recognized $113.5 million in licensing revenue from Scientific-Atlanta for 2000–2002 and $18.1 million in licensing revenue from Time Warner Cable (TWC) for 2001–2002. According to the report, the KPMG auditors should have known that the Scientific-Atlanta and TWC revenue recognition did not conform to a financial reporting framework because the contract terms did not meet the requirements. The company did not have a contract with Scientific-Atlanta or TWC, Gemstar had not received any of the revenue, the companies disputed the revenue recognized by Gemstar, and the revenue payments were contingent on then-current contract negotiations.

According to the enforcement notice, KPMG auditors should have known that Gemstar's revenue recognition disclosure in the footnotes did not comply with disclosure requirements consistent with the financial reporting framework. Accounting Principles Board (APB) Opinion No. 22 requires disclosure of all significant accounting policies. Under generally accepted auditing procedures, auditors should read the company's annual report. The disclosure related to the AOL revenue was inadequate because the company disclosed that it recognized revenue over the life of the contract and described the AOL contract as long term but failed to recognize revenue in accordance with the disclosure (it recognized all revenue in the first year of the eight-year contract).

The disclosure for the Scientific-Atlanta and TWC revenue indicated that Gemstar had recognized revenue when it received notification that a manufacturer had shipped units using Gemstar technology. According to the SEC, the auditors should have known that Gemstar's disclosure regarding revenue recognition based on licensing revenue was inadequate to describe the actual revenue recognition for this contingent revenue.[18]

Advertising Revenue and Disclosure in the Footnotes

Gemstar recognized $60.1 million of advertising revenue in 2001 and 2002 from Motorola, (Chicago) Tribune Company, Fantasy Sports, and various print advertisers

---

[16] "KPMG Settles Gemstar Audit Case," *Los Angeles Times,* October 21, 2004.

[17] Securities and Exchange Commission, Accounting and Auditing Enforcement Release No. 2125, October 20, 2004.

[18] U.S. Securities and Exchange Commission, Accounting & Auditing Enforcement Release No. 2125, October 20, 2004.

that did not conform to the financial reporting framework. The revenue came from noncash arrangements with customers as part of various business transactions. For example, the Motorola revenue originated with an arrangement by which it paid $188 million to use Genstar's IPG technology, to settle a litigation award, and to purchase $17.5 million of prepaid advertising. The Tribune revenue originated with an arrangement between it and Gemstar in which the Tribune agreed to purchase the WGN distribution business from Gemstar in exchange for $106 million in cash and $100 million in advertising. According to the SEC, KPMG auditors should have known that the Motorola and Tribune revenue were not recognized in accordance with the financial reporting framework. According to the SEC, Gemstar could not "reliably, verifiably, and objectively"[19] determine the fair value of the advertising portion of the arrangement because it had not sold IPG advertising that was not part of a related-party or nonmonetary transaction.

The SEC also determined that the auditors should have known that Gemstar's disclosure in its 10-K was inconsistent with the company's method of accounting for the transaction. For example, the company described its substantial growth in the Interactive Sector revenue and attributed the growth to the "successful launch of IPG advertising."[20] However, the company did not disclose that the revenue came from the Motorola and Tribune transactions. The auditor also should have known that the company disclosed the sale of WGN but not the $100 million of advertising revenue associated with the sale.

The SEC censured KPMG, which paid a fine of $10 million to settle the charges of improper conduct. KPMG partners involved in the audit were prohibited from working for public companies for a period of one to three years. At the time, the KPMG fine was the largest ever obtained by the SEC from an accounting firm. Cash from the settlement went to the Gemstar shareholders.

a. Evaluate Gemstar's revenue recognition decisions related to the licensing and advertising revenue. Explain why the SEC disagreed with the decisions made by management.

b. Why did the SEC determine that the disclosure made by Gemstar was not consistent with the financial reporting framework? Explain the proper disclosure relating to the licensing and advertising revenue.

c. What does the SEC mean that the auditors substituted "management representations for evidence"? What should the auditors have done to verify the revenue?

Internet Assignments

LO9   62. Go to the website for a company of your choice and determine how it recognizes revenue, estimates sales returns, and determines the amount of uncollectible accounts. List the revenue reported for the last two years as well as the balance in Accounts Receivable and the Allowance for Doubtful Accounts for each year. Does the change in the allowance account appear reasonable? Explain your answer.

LO8   63. Go to the SEC website (www.sec.gov) and identify a company that it has cited for revenue recognition problems. Describe the problem and identify the accounting principle that the company violated.

[19] Securities and Exchange Commission, Accounting and Auditing Enforcement Release No. 2125, October 20, 2004.

[20] Securities and Exchange Commission, Accounting and Auditing Enforcement Release No. 2125, October 20, 2004.

5

Audit Evidence and the Auditor's Responsibility for Fraud Detection

Learning Objectives

Part I: Audit Evidence

After studying Part I of this chapter, you should be able to:

1. Describe audit evidence and explain its role in the audit process.
2. Explain how the auditor uses management's assertions to organize audit evidence.
3. Understand how an auditor evaluates the sufficiency and appropriateness of audit evidence.
4. Describe changes to the nature, timing, and extent of evidence related to risk assessments.
5. Explain the documentation requirements for evidence.

Part II: Fraud Detection

After studying Part II of this chapter, you should be able to:

6. Describe the auditor's responsibility for fraud detection in a financial statement audit.
7. Understand the fraud triangle and how the auditor could use it to identify the risk of material misstatement because of fraud.
8. Explain how the auditor gathers evidence to assess the risk of material misstatement because of fraud.
9. Explain how the auditor gathers evidence to control the risk of material misstatement because of fraud.
10. Describe the reporting requirements for fraud.

Accounting and auditing standards relevant to these topics

For private companies

- **FASB Statement of Financial Accounting Concepts No. 1,** Objectives of Financial Reporting by Business Enterprises

- **FASB Statement of Financial Accounting Concepts No. 2,** Qualitative Characteristics of Accounting Information
- **Preface to Codification of Statements on Auditing Standards,** Principles Governing an Audit Conducted in Accordance with Generally Accepted Auditing Standards
- **Preface to Codification of Statements on Auditing Standards,** Overall Objectives of the Independent Auditor and the Conduct of an Audit in Accordance with Generally Accepted Auditing Standards
- **AU 110,** Responsibilities and Functions of the Independent Auditor
- **AU 150,** Generally Accepted Auditing Standards
- **AU 312,** Audit Risk and Materiality in Conducting an Audit
- **AU 314,** Understanding the Entity and Its Environment and Assessing the Risk of Material Misstatements
- **AU 316,** Consideration of Fraud in a Financial Statement Audit
- **AU 318,** Performing Audit Procedures in Response to Assessed Risks and Evaluating the Audit Evidence Obtained
- **AU 326,** Audit Evidence
- **AU 339,** Audit Documentation

For public companies

- **FASB Statement of Financial Accounting Concepts No. 1,** Objectives of Financial Reporting by Business Enterprises
- **FASB Statement of Financial Accounting Concepts No. 2,** Qualitative Characteristics of Accounting Information
- **AU 110,** Responsibilities and Functions of the Independent Auditor (Interim Standard Adopted by PCAOB)
- **AU 150,** Generally Accepted Auditing Standards (Interim Standard Adopted by PCAOB)
- **AU 312,** Audit Risk and Materiality in Conducting an Audit (Interim Standard Adopted by PCAOB)
- **AU 316,** Consideration of Fraud in a Financial Statement Audit (Interim Standard Adopted by PCAOB)
- **PCAOB Auditing Standard No. 3,** Audit Documentation
- **PCAOB Auditing Standard No. 15,** Audit Evidence

International standards

- **ISA 230,** Audit Documentation
- **ISA 240,** The Auditor's Responsibility to Consider Fraud in an Audit of Financial Statements
- **ISA 500,** Audit Evidence

Chapter Overview

This chapter is divided into two parts. The first part discusses audit evidence and the auditor's responsibility for documenting the evidence collected during an audit. The second part discusses the auditor's responsibility for fraud detection in an audit. The auditor is responsible for planning the audit to gather evidence to be able determine whether the financial statements are materially misstated from fraud.

Why *does* the auditor gather evidence during an audit? The auditing standards (Overall Objectives of the Independent Auditor and the Conduct of an Audit in Accordance with Generally Accepted Auditing Standards and AU 150, PCAOB Interim Standard) require the auditor to obtain sufficient appropriate evidence to allow him or her to reach a conclusion about whether the financial statements have been prepared in accordance with the applicable financial reporting framework. This evidence will be the basis for the audit opinion issued. To meet the requirements of this standard, the auditor must be familiar with the documentation requirements of the auditing standards. These standards describe the collection, evaluation, and documentation of evidence and are important to the auditor because evidence provides the basis for her or his opinion. If the auditor's decision is questioned, outsiders will review the evidence to determine whether the auditor gathered sufficient appropriate evidence consistent with what any other auditor would have gathered and whether the auditor evaluated the evidence in a manner consistent with another auditor's evaluation.

Why **does** the auditor gather evidence related to fraud during an audit? The auditor gathers evidence related to fraud because the auditing standards require him or her to determine whether the financial statements are materially misstated due to errors or fraud. The standards that describe the auditor's responsibilities to consider the risk of fraud in the various business processes are important to the auditor. Frauds missed by the auditor and are made public later cause a loss of reputation for the audit firm. There is also the problem of issuing a clean report on financial statements that were materially misstated. When frauds become public, outsiders often ask where the auditors were during the fraud. To suggest that the auditors did not do their job during an audit does harm to the accounting firm's reputation.

Part I: Audit Evidence

Audit Evidence and Its Role in the Audit Process

LO1

Describe audit evidence and explain the role of evidence in the audit process

The auditing standards (AU #326 and AS #15) describe audit evidence as the "information used by the auditor in arriving at the conclusions on which the auditor's opinion is based." Audit evidence includes information from the accounting records and from other sources both inside and outside the company. The auditor uses audit procedures to obtain evidence including (1) analytical procedures, (2) inspection, (3) observation, (4) inquiry, (5) external confirmation, (6) recalculation, and (7) reperformance. Evidence is important to the audit because the only way the auditor can obtain reasonable assurance that the financial statements are prepared in accordance with the applicable financial reporting framework is when the auditor has *sufficient appropriate evidence* to reduce audit risk to an acceptably low level. Each audit procedure is described next.

Substantive Audit Procedures

Analytical procedures
Inspection
Observation
Inquiry
External confirmation
Recalculation
Reperformance

Analytical Procedures

When performing **analytical procedures,** the auditor evaluates the financial statements in the current year by analyzing relationships between financial and nonfinancial data. For example, the auditor could know that general economic conditions are worse in the current year than in the prior year. Based on this knowledge, the auditor expects the allowance for doubtful accounts to be higher in the current year than in the previous year because customers are more likely to default on their accounts receivable when economic conditions worsen. If the allowance for doubtful accounts is not higher this year, the auditor would ask the client to explain the lower estimate.

The auditing standards require the auditor to perform analytical procedures during the audit's planning stage and the final stage. PCAOB standards also require the auditor to perform analytical procedures for revenue at all stages of the audit. The auditor performs **analytical procedures** to identify changes in the current year's financial statements compared to those in the prior year that are inconsistent with other information known to the auditor or that represent larger fluctuations than the auditor might expect. To identify changes in the financial statements in the current year, the auditor can calculate financial ratios or compare the balances in the financial statement accounts from the current year to the balances in the prior year to see how they have changed.

The auditor often uses *scanning,* a type of analytical procedure often electronically performed to identify significant—for instance, large items—or unusual items in the accounting data and then to examine those items. For example, the auditor could scan weekly payroll reports to identify large payments (such as those made for more than the maximum salary amount) or salary payments made to the same bank account or to the same employee name. The auditor could also use scanning to review all debit entries in revenue accounts or credit entries in expense accounts because they are unusual items or to examine adjusting journal entries or entries made to temporary suspense accounts (holding accounts for transactions used by the accountant when he or she is in the processing of determining where the transaction should be recorded) for signs that misstatement can have occurred.

Inspection

The auditor uses the **inspection** procedure when examining records or documents, either external or internal to the company, on paper and in electronic or other media format, or when physically examining an asset. Inspection provides evidence of varying degrees of reliability, depending on the nature and source of the records or documents and on the effectiveness of the internal controls over the preparation of the records or documents.

Inspection provides evidence about the *existence* of the asset. Inspecting stock certificates provides evidence of the asset's existence but does not necessarily provide evidence about the rights of the stock certificate or its value (relating to the assertions of "rights and obligations" and "valuation"). The auditor uses comparable caution with regard to inventory, often *observing* it being counted and opening some of the cartons containing inventory to *inspect* the individual inventory items. This allows the auditor to verify the existence of the inventory, but it does not provide evidence of the valuation of the inventory or the audit client's right to the inventory (related to the assertions of "valuation" and "rights and obligations").

Observation

The auditor uses the audit procedure of **observation** by watching the audit client perform a process or procedure—for example, the inventory count or an internal control process. Observation evidence is, of course, limited to the point in time that the auditor observes. The fact that the auditor is observing a process can also affect how it is performed.

Inquiry

Inquiry is the process of acquiring information from knowledgeable people both within and outside the company. It could be the most frequent audit procedure the auditor uses to gather evidence. Evaluating the responses to inquiries is an important part of the process related to evidence. The response to an inquiry could provide information to corroborate other audit evidence or could indicate that it differs from the information the auditor has obtained. The auditor often tries to corroborate the information gained during an inquiry with other evidence to verify the accuracy of the inquiry response. The auditor turns an inquiry into evidence by preparing a memo documenting the conversation. Sometimes the auditor could consider obtaining written representations from the client (signed statements) to be necessary rather than relying on verbal inquiry evidence.

External Confirmation

The auditor uses **external confirmation** as evidence when obtaining a written response directly from a third party. This response can be in paper, electronic, or another medium form. The auditor frequently uses external confirmations to obtain evidence about account balances: accounts receivable, accounts payable, cash balances, and long-term debt balances. External confirmations are often considered to be a reliable source of evidence because the information comes from a third party that is independent from the client. External confirmations will not provide reliable information if the auditor has had experience with this client in the past to suggest that the confirmation replies are not reliable, perhaps because the third party is careless in gathering the information or has strong economic ties to the client (if, for example, the client is the only supplier for a product the customer needs).

Recalculation

The auditor uses **recalculation** to check the mathematical accuracy of documents and records. This can be done either manually or electronically. The audit client prepares many schedules for the auditor (for example, schedules of prepaid insurance and assets in the building and equipment account). The auditor recalculates the totals on these schedules to verify the detailed schedule's mathematical accuracy. The auditor could also recalculate items such as depreciation expense and interest expense to verify the accuracy of the client's calculations.

Reperformance

The auditor uses the audit procedure of **reperformance** by executing the procedures or controls that the client originally performed as part of the company's internal controls. When the auditor reperforms a procedure, he or she gathers substantive evidence. The quality of evidence gathered from any of these procedures reflects the *relevance* and *reliability* of the information on which it is based.

The Auditor's Use of Management's Assertions to Organize Audit Evidence

LO2

Explain how the auditor uses management's assertions to organize audit evidence

The auditor gathers evidence using analytical procedures, inspection, observation, inquiry, external confirmation, recalculation, or reperformance to evaluate management's assertions regarding the financial statements. Without evidence, the auditor would be unable to determine whether the financial statements were prepared in accordance with the applicable financial reporting framework.

Management's Assertions for the Financial Statements

Existence or occurrence—for both classes of transactions and account balances
Completeness—for both classes of transactions and account balances
Valuation and allocation—for account balances
Rights and obligations—for account balances
Accuracy—for classes of transactions
Cutoff— for classes of transactions
Classification—for classes of transactions

Management's Assertions for Presentation and Disclosure

Occurrence and rights and obligation
Completeness
Classification and understandability
Accuracy and valuation (AU 314 and ISA 315)

The auditor's job during an audit is to gather "sufficient appropriate" evidence to determine whether the assertions are true. The auditor uses them to structure both internal control testing and substantive testing. The auditor gathers evidence to determine whether the evidence supports *relevant assertions* for *significant accounts and disclosures.* An auditor whose evidence fails to support an assertion then proposes an adjusting entry or modifies the financial statement disclosure so the financial statements are consistent with the assertion.

Although there is no one-to-one correspondence between audit procedures and management assertions, standard procedures are performed during the audit of each business process to gather evidence regarding management's assertions. It is also possible to identify relevant assertions for accounts in a business process.

Sometimes an audit procedure (for example, confirmation, inspection, inquiry) provides evidence for more than one assertion. For example, confirming accounts receivable can provide evidence of **existence** and **rights.** Sometimes the auditor performs several audit procedures to gather sufficient evidence about one assertion. For example, the auditor can perform cutoff tests for the accounts receivable process and test sales transactions recorded for all twelve months to evaluate the **completeness** of the sales transactions.

Evaluation of the Sufficiency and Appropriateness of Evidence

LO3

Understand how an auditor evaluates the sufficiency and appropriateness of audit evidence

The **sufficiency** of audit evidence is a measure of the *quantity* of evidence needed. **Appropriateness** is a measure of the *quality* of audit evidence needed. We measure the quality of evidence by its **relevance** and its **reliability.** Both the quantity and the quality of audit evidence needed for an audit are affected by the risk of material misstatement for the relevant assertion in a significant account or disclosure. The greater the risk of material misstatement is, the more audit evidence is likely to be required. If the quality of audit evidence is high, the auditor could need less evidence. Regardless of the risk assessment, the auditor should design and perform substantive audit procedures for all relevant assertions for each significant class of transaction, account balance, or disclosure to obtain sufficient appropriate audit evidence.

What is *relevant* and *reliable* evidence? The *relevance* of information is related to the **connection** between the audit procedure's purpose and the evidence it gathers. Evidence relevance is often related to the assertion being tested. For example, evidence that is relevant for testing the existence assertion would not be relevant for testing the completeness assertion. The *reliability* of evidence is related to its **source** and **nature** and the **circumstances** under which it is obtained. For example, evidence from a source outside the company is generally more reliable than evidence from a source inside the company. However, evidence from an external source that is not knowledgeable could be unreliable.

Consider the relevance of the information provided by inspecting documents using vouching or tracing. Vouching is not a *relevant* procedure for obtaining evidence about the completeness assertion because when gathering evidence by vouching, the auditor begins with the sales journal and goes back to the shipping records. The auditor would never find sales transactions that have not been recorded when selecting the sample from the source in which the sales transactions are recorded. Vouching therefore will not provide relevant evidence for the completeness assertion. Vouching does, however, provide relevant evidence for existence because with vouching, the auditor examines the sale **from** the sales register **to** the shipping document. This gives the auditor *relevant* evidence that the sale is valid (it exists) because the client recorded the sale and shipped the goods for the sale.

The source and nature of the audit evidence influence its *reliability.* Auditing standards have established some general guidelines so the auditor can judge the reliability of evidence.

- Audit evidence is more reliable when it comes from *knowledgeable* outside sources.
- Audit evidence from the audit client is more reliable when the company's related internal controls are effective.
- Audit evidence obtained directly by the auditor (observation of the application of a control) is more reliable than that obtained indirectly (for example, by inquiry from the client).
- Audit evidence is more reliable when it exists in documentary form.
- Audit evidence provided by original documents is more reliable than audit evidence provided by photocopies, fax, film, digital, or other electronic documents. The reliability of this evidence must include a consideration of controls over the preparation and retention of the documents.

How Do the Accounting Standards Define Relevant and Reliable Information?

The accounting standards (in Concept Statement No. 2, *Qualitative Characteristics of Accounting Information*) also provide guidance to help management and the auditor evaluate the quality of information disclosed in the financial statements. According to the accounting standards, *relevant* financial information reduces uncertainties in the decision process. Relevant information reflects the financial reality of the situation; it improves the user's ability to make a decision because it provides data useful to the decision process. Relevant information provides a clear view of the past that can be used to predict the future; it is presented in a *timely* fashion. The information is available in time to influence users' decisions.

Did You Know?

eToys, an Internet toy retailer, issued pro forma earnings in its press releases. During the second quarter of 1999, it reported a loss per share of $-0.27. The company indicated that the loss excluded nonrecurring items. This loss beat the analyst's forecasts of $-0.28 per share. The actual loss reported to the SEC for the second quarter of 1999 was $-0.38 per share.

Sources: Karen Kaplan, "eToys Posts Huge Gain in Sales, Along with Big Loss," *The Los Angeles Times,* July 28, 1999; and 8-K report eToys, SEC, www.sec.gov, July 1999.

How did the auditor evaluate the relevance of this information?

According to **accounting standards,** the *reliability* of information is also important; it should *faithfully represent* what it claims to stand for. For example, a transaction recorded as operating revenue should be revenue earned from the firm's normal business practice, not as revenue from a one-time transaction. Reliable information is *verifiable:* another individual measuring the transaction would arrive at a similar valuation. Reliable information is also *neutral* and is *free from bias* regarding a particular result. For example, the information is not presented in a manner to guarantee that management receives a performance-based bonus. Accounting information that is reliable reports economic events in a manner that faithfully represents the transaction without influencing behavior in a particular direction.

Did You Know?

The WorldCom fraud is the largest accounting fraud in U.S. history. In 2005, Bernard Ebbers, the former chief executive of WorldCom, was convicted of conspiracy and securities fraud and sentenced to 25 years in prison for his role in directing it.

The fraud, which overstated revenue and understated expenses, eventually totaled $11 billion. It involved recording operating expenses as capitalized assets. In effect, WorldCom removed expenses from its income statement and recorded them as assets on the balance sheet. Rather than deducting expenses from revenue each quarter, WorldCom recorded expenses as capital assets to be deducted from earnings over a long period of time. During the trial, Scott Sullivan, the former chief financial officer, testified that the company was "tampering with the books solely to meet earnings and revenue targets."

The telecommunications company filed for bankruptcy in 2002. During the bankruptcy proceedings, the company was renamed MCI Inc. In 2005, Verizon Communications Inc. acquired the company.

Sources: A. LaTour, S. Young, and L. Yuan, "Ebbers Is Convicted in Massive Fraud," *The Wall Street Journal,* March 16, 2005; and S. Young, D. Searcey, and K. Scannell, "Ebbers Is Sentenced to 25 years," *The Wall Street Journal,* July 13, 2005.

> ***How did the WorldCom auditors determine that the information presented in the financial statements was reliable? Did the information faithfully represent what it claimed to represent? Was it neutral and free from bias?***

In forming the audit opinion, the auditor is expected to rely on evidence that is *persuasive,* not conclusive, to obtain reasonable assurance that the financial statements are prepared in accordance with the applicable financial reporting framework. The auditor uses *professional judgment* to evaluate the sufficiency and the appropriateness of evidence needed to support an audit opinion. **Professional judgment** is the application of relevant training, knowledge, and experience within the context provided by auditing, accounting, and ethical standards to make informed decisions about the courses of action that are appropriate in the circumstances of the audit engagement (Overall Objectives of the Independent Auditor and the Conduct of an Audit in Accordance with Generally Accepted Auditing Standards).

The Auditor's Response to Risk

LO4

Describe changes to the nature, timing, and extent of evidence related to risk assessments

How does the auditor alter the evidence gathered during the audit in response to the risk assessments performed during an audit? The auditor can change (1) the nature of the evidence, (2) the timing of the evidence, or (3) the extent of evidence gathered in response to the risk assessment.

The **nature** of the evidence refers to its purpose (internal control test or substantive test) and the specific audit procedure used to gather the evidence (inspection, observation, inquiry, external confirmation, recalculation, reperformance, and analytical procedure). The relationship between risk and the *nature* of testing can be summarized as follows:

- The higher is the risk of material misstatement, the more relevant and reliable is the evidence that the auditor must gather from substantive audit procedures.
- In determining the audit procedures to perform, the auditor should consider the reason for the risk. Is it related to the nature of the account or to the control risk for the account? If it is related to the level of control risk, the auditor should perform tests of controls to evaluate their effectiveness. If it is related to the nature of the account that has a low risk of material misstatement, using analytical procedures could be appropriate.
- If the auditor has identified a significant risk for a relevant assertion and performs only substantive procedures, the substantive procedures must include tests of details (they cannot be limited to analytical procedure tests).

The **timing** of evidence collection is related to whether the evidence is gathered at an interim basis or at year-end. The relationship between the risk and the *timing* of audit evidence can be summarized as follows:

- The higher the risk of material misstatement, the more likely the auditor is to perform substantive procedures at or near year-end.
- When performing internal control tests or substantive tests at an interim period, the auditor must consider whether additional evidence is needed for the remaining period. The higher the risk of material misstatement, the more likely additional evidence is needed for the remaining period.

- Some audit procedures can be done only at year-end, for example, agreeing the financial statements to the accounting records or examining year-end adjustments.
- The auditor should also consider the company's control environment when relevant information is available, the nature of the risk, and the date or time period to which the audit evidence relates in determining the timing of audit procedures.

The **extent** of audit evidence is related to the amount of audit evidence gathered during internal control testing or the sample size necessary for substantive tests of balances and transactions. The sample size needed is determined by materiality, the assessed risk, and the degree of assurance the auditor plans for the audit procedure. The relationship between risk and the *extent* of testing can be summarized as follows:

- As the risk of material misstatement increases, the auditor increases the extent of an audit procedure (for example, uses a larger sample size for an audit procedure).
- As the risk of material misstatement increases, the auditor can use computer-assisted audit techniques (CAATs) to test an entire population rather than take only a sample.

In summary, the higher the risk of material misstatement, the more likely the auditor is to (1) gather more relevant and reliable evidence, (2) perform substantive tests at or near year-end and gather additional evidence for the remaining period for the internal control and substantive tests performed on a interim basis, and (3) increase the extent of substantive testing. These changes are made so the auditor can keep the risk of material misstatement to an acceptably low level. These changes are made so the auditor is more likely to find evidence of material misstatements in the financial statements if they are there.

Did You Know?

Between 1999 and 2001, Merck-Medco recorded $12.4 billion of revenue that it will never collect. During this time, Merck included as part of revenue the copayments collected by pharmacies from patients even though Merck did not receive these funds. These copayments accounted for nearly 10 percent of Merck's total revenue during this time period.

The $12.4 billion represents the copayment paid directly to the pharmacies by customers using a prescription drug card from an insurance company. The copayment is typically $10–$25 per prescription.

Merck reported expenses equal to $12.4 billion to offset the copayment revenue on the income statement so that the net income it reported was correct. Recording the copayments as revenue allowed the company to report growth in sales revenue.

Sources: Barbara Martinez, *"Merck Books Co-payments to Pharmacies as Revenue," The Wall Street Journal,* June 21, 2002; and Barbara Martinez, "Merck Recorded $12.4 Billion in Revenue It Never Collected," *The Wall Street Journal,* July 8, 2002.

Why did the auditor permit Merck-Medco to recognize revenue that it would not collect? Why is growth in sales revenue so important to a company?

Documentation Requirements for Evidence

LO5

Explain the documentation requirements for evidence

Audit documentation, referred to as *working papers* or *work papers,* includes a record of the audit procedures performed, the audit evidence obtained, and the conclusions the auditor reached from reviewing the evidence. The audit documentation can be recorded on paper or in electronic form.

An auditor should prepare audit documentation that will enable an experienced auditor with no previous connection to the audit to understand:

- The nature, timing, and extent of auditing procedures performed
- The results of the audit procedures performed and the audit evidence obtained
- The conclusions reached by the auditor on significant matters
- That the accounting records agree to the audited financial statements (AU 339 and AS 3).

The auditor is to document significant findings including the actions taken to address them and the basis for the final resolution reached. Findings that could be significant include the (1) accounting for complex or unusual transactions, accounting estimates, or uncertainties, (2) results of audit procedures indicating that the financial statements or disclosure could be materially misstated or the need for an auditor to revise her or his previous assessment of the risk of material misstatement, (3) circumstances that made it difficult for the auditor to apply auditing procedures (for example, lack of response to confirmations), (4) findings that could result in modifications to the auditor's report, and (5) adjustments to the financial statements that the auditor has proposed.

In documenting the nature, timing, and extent of audit procedures, the auditor should indicate who performed the audit work, the date it was completed, who reviewed it, and the date of the review. The audit documentation for internal control tests and substantive tests should include documentation of the specific items tested. The auditor should complete the assembly of the final audit file within 45 days of the report release date (60 days for private companies). After the 45/60 day time period, the auditor should not delete or discard any information from the client's file. New information can be added if necessary but only if accompanied by an explanation for the addition, the name of the person adding the information, and its effect on the auditor's conclusions.

Audit documentation, which is the auditor's property, should be retained for at least seven years from the report release date (five years for private companies). The auditor has an ethical and, in some cases, a legal obligation to treat the client information as confidential (cannot be disclosed to an outsider without the client's permission). Audit documentation can, however, be subpoenaed.

Refer to Exhibit 5-1 for an example of a work paper that would be included in the audit of the revenue process. This work paper illustrates some of the requirements for documentation just discussed, including who performed the audit procedures, when they were done, who reviewed them, when the review was performed, the specific accounts sampled, and the conclusions reached based on the evidence gathered from the auditing procedures.

The tick marks used in the working paper identify the auditor's specific audit procedures. Auditors use external confirmations to gather evidence related to the assertions of existence and rights and obligations. This work paper shows that the auditor mailed positive confirmations to ten customers of the audit client BCS Company. Eight of the ten external confirmations indicate the customer agreed with the balance of the audit client (as described by the tick mark P). Two confirmation replies indicate that the customer disagreed with the balance reported by the audit client. After reviewing the files, the audit client agreed that the customers' balances were correct, so the accounts receivable balance was misstated. The confirmation returned by Vila Cini indicates that the audit client failed to record a credit memo (indicated by tick mark E). The confirmation returned by Lin Jewelers indicates that a payment made at the end of the year was not correctly posted to the customer's account (indicated by tick mark S). The auditor has also performed the audit procedure of reperformance by agreeing the confirmation balance to the accounts receivable subsidiary ledger (indicated by tick mark √). This is done to assure that the detail tested by the auditor agrees with the client's balance in the accounts receivable subsidiary ledger.

Based on the audit procedure of external confirmation, accounts receivable is overstated by $50,500. To correct the misstatement, the auditor proposes the following audit adjustment:

Sales Revenue	50,500	
Accounts Receivable		50,500

The external confirmation procedure likely was performed on a portion (referred to as a *sample*) of the accounts receivable outstanding at year-end. If that is the true, the

| Accounts Receivable Confirmations | Exhibit 5-1 |

Reference:	C-3
Prepared by:	ICS
Date:	January 24, 2012
Reviewed by:	BRT
Date:	January 30, 2012

BCS Company
Accounts Receivable Confirmations
For the Year Ended December 31, 2011

Customer Name	Account Balance per Balance Sheet		Confirmed Balance	
Mengrai Kilns	$200,450	√	$200,450	P
2 Design	350,200	√	350,200	P
Pelage	180,000	√	180,000	P
Vila Cini	200,500	√	180,000	E
Pasaya	300,600	√	300,600	P
Green Cotton	500,700	√	500,700	P
Worldstock.com	300,500	√	300,500	P
Lin Jewelers	200,400	√	170,400	S
Tang Heng Lee Silver	150,000	√	150,000	P
Amari	300,800	√	300,800	P

Tickmark symbols	Provide an explanation of the audit procedures performed
P	Response to positive confirmation received from customer (that is, customer agrees with amount confirmed)
E	Customer confirmation indicates a credit memo that was not issued. Client agrees with customer response. Accounts receivable overstated by $20,500.
S	Customer confirmation indicates that it made payment on December 23 that was not properly posted to the customer account. Client agrees with customer. Accounts receivable overstated by $30,000.
√	Agreed confirmation balance to accounts receivable subsidiary ledger

| Conclusion: | Based on the results of test work performed, accounts receivable appear to be prepared in accordance with the applicable financial reporting framework at December 31, 2011, except for the adjustments noted. *ICS* auditor's conclusion |

proposed audit adjustment based on the sample is extended to the entire population of accounts receivable. The audit adjustment based on the population is referred to as the *likely misstatement.*

The auditor reviews the audit adjustment schedule at the end of the year. At that time, the auditor makes the decision about whether the financial statements are materially misstated based on the proposed audit adjustments on the schedule. If the decision is that the financial statements are materially misstated, the auditor asks the audit client to record some or all of the proposed audit adjustments.

Did You Know?

On August 31, 2002, Arthur Andersen surrendered its license to practice accounting in all fifty states as a result of its June 2002 felony conviction for **obstruction of justice** during the Enron investigation. The jury found that at least one member of the firm, Nancy Temple, an Arthur Andersen attorney, had attempted to alter work papers to protect the firm from SEC scrutiny.

Nancy Temple had advised David Duncan, the Andersen audit partner for Enron, to alter work papers to protect the firm because investors could misunderstand the quarterly earnings information stated in the Enron press release. Duncan had advised Enron against the disclosure. Temple wanted this information removed from the audit work papers because Enron had disregarded Andersen's advice and had issued the misleading earnings release.

The felony conviction came from a charge filed against Arthur Andersen in federal court in Houston alleging that the firm "knowingly, intentionally, and corruptly" (Wigfield, M. "Indictment Claims 'Wholesale Destruction' of Enron Files," *Dow Jones International News,* Match 14, 2002) persuaded Andersen employees to "alter, destroy, mutilate and conceal" audit-related documents. During the trial, Andersen admitted to destroying thousands of electronic and paper documents in September, October, and November 2001. Andersen said the staff destroyed documents before receiving a subpoena from the SEC in November 2001. At the time of the document destruction, however, Andersen partners were aware that the SEC had initiated a probe into Enron's aggressive accounting practices. Andersen managers ordered employees to work overtime, if necessary, to complete the destruction before the work papers had to be turned over.

The collapse of Enron and Arthur Andersen's conviction put 85,000 employees worldwide out of work and left 2,300 companies without an auditor.

Sources: R. Smith and J. Emshwiller, *24 Days* (New York: Harper Business, 2003); E. Sanders and J. Leeds, "US Indicts Enron Auditor over Shredding Inquiry," *Los Angeles Times,* March 1, 2002; K. Brown, M. Pacelle, C. Bryan-Low, J. Weil, R. Frank, and S. Craig, "Andersen Indictment in Shredding Case Puts Its Future in Doubt as Clients Bolt," *The Wall Street Journal,* March 15, 2002.

Why did Arthur Andersen shred work papers?

Part II: Fraud Detection

The Auditor's Responsibility for Fraud Detection

LO6

Describe the auditor's responsibility for fraud detection in a financial statement audit

An auditor who conducts an audit in accordance with generally accepted auditing standards is responsible for "obtaining reasonable assurance that the financial statements as a whole are free from material misstatement, whether caused by fraud or error" (AU316). The primary responsibility for fraud prevention and detection rests with the company's managers, who are responsible for designing and implementing internal control programs to prevent and detect fraud. The auditor's responsibility is to plan the audit to gather sufficient appropriate evidence to determine whether the financial statements are free of material misstatement.

What Is Fraud?

A misstatement in the financial statements could be caused by unintentional acts of the company (**errors**) or intentional acts of the company (**fraud**). The auditor is responsible for gathering evidence to detect both *unintentional errors* and *intentional fraud* that would materially misstate the financial statements. We use the term **misstatements** to indicate both errors and fraud. In the past, an auditor was responsible for gathering evidence to determine that the financial statements had no material *errors,* but at the present time, the auditor is responsible for gathering evidence to determine whether the financial statements are free from misstatement because of errors *and* fraud.

Two types of fraud might occur in a company: (1) misstatements from *fraudulent financial reporting* and (2) misstatements regarding *assets that are misappropriated* from the business. Fraudulent financial reporting occurs when a company prepares financial statements that are materially misstated. Asset misappropriation occurs when employees in a company steal its assets (for example, cash or inventory) or cause the entity to pay for goods or services that it has not received. The auditor is expected to gather evidence to evaluate both types of fraud to determine that the financial statements are free of material misstatement.

Did You Know?

AOL Time Warner inflated its revenue in 2000 and 2001 by entering into "round-trip" transactions and various other unconventional revenue-generating methods with customers with which it had business relationships. For example, AOL provided its customers the funds to pay for online advertising. The customer entered into an agreement with AOL to purchase online advertising from it in an amount equal to the payment from AOL. AOL recognized revenue for the amounts received based on these "advertising agreements." The SEC determined that round-trip transactions were not appropriate revenue recognition methods but are barter transactions.

AOL executives committed fraud by engaging in **fraudulent financial reporting** from 2000–2002. Time Warner paid a $300 million fine to the SEC in 2005 to settle charges brought against the company for violating securities laws. At the time of the levy, this fine was the second largest levied against a company by the SEC.

Sources: Julia Angwin, "SEC Fines Time Warner $300 Million," *The Wall Street Journal,* March 22, 2005; and U.S. District Court for the District of Columbia, Case No. 1:05CV00578-GK, *SEC v. Time Warner,* www.sec.gov, March 21, 2005.

What was the auditor's responsibility in regard to this fraudulent financial reporting fraud?

Did You Know?

Former Tyco Chief Executive Dennis Kozlowski was sentenced to up to 25 years in prison for stealing hundreds of millions of dollars from the company. Kozlowski took advantage of the company's prosperity to misappropriate massive sums of money from it. Business writers referred to his spending spree as the "brazen use of a public company as his personal cash machine"(Maremont, M. and L. Cohen, "Tyco Spent Millions for Benefit of Kozlowski, Its Former CEO," *The Wall Street Journal,* August 7, 2002).

Kozlowski borrowed money from the company and then forgave his own loans. He granted stock options to himself and paid himself substantial bonuses. He spent company funds to purchase and decorate several personal residences, including an apartment in New York City with a $6,000 shower curtain. He purchased an art collection worth $13.1 million, donated millions of dollars of Tyco funds to charity in his own name, and spent $2 million on a fortieth birthday party in Italy for his wife.

Tyco is an example of fraud caused by **misappropriation of assets.** When questioned about his use of company funds during the trial, Kozlowski stated he did not receive anything from Tyco to which he wasn't entitled and furthermore did not try to hide the benefits he received from the board or from the auditors.

Sources: "Kozlowski, Swartz Sentenced to Up to 25 Years in Prison," *The Wall Street Journal,* September 19, 2005; M. Maremount and L. Cohen, "Tyco Spent Millions for Benefit of Kozlowski, Its Former CEO," *The Wall Street Journal,* August 7, 2002; and M. Maremont, "Kozlowski, Swartz Are Found Guilty in Tyco Retrial," *The Wall Street Journal,* June 17, 2005.

What was the auditor's responsibility in regard to this misappropriation of assets fraud?

The Fraud Triangle

LO7

Understand the fraud triangle and how the auditor could use it to identify the risk of material misstatement because of fraud

How the Auditor Identifies Fraud

Three conditions are present in a company when fraud occurs: (1) pressure, (2) opportunity, and (3) rationalization. When they are present in a company, fraud is more likely to occur; however, the elements do not have to be present at the same level. For example, a high level of pressure in a company could mean that an individual can more easily rationalize a fraudulent action. We typically refer to these factors as the *fraud triangle.* See Exhibit 5-2 for this scenario. Each factor is discussed in the following sections.

| Fraud Triangle | Exhibit 5-2 |

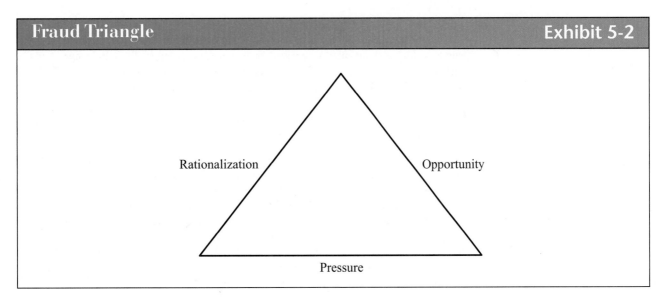

Pressure

A company's management can feel **pressure** from inside or outside to achieve an earnings target or maintain a certain level of growth. The consequences for failing to meet earnings targets can be severe (lack of bonus payment, decline in value of stock options, poor performance evaluation, loss of a job). Individuals can also feel pressure to misappropriate assets to solve personal financial problems such as addiction (gambling, alcohol, drugs), high medical expenses, credit card debt, and inability to pay monthly bills or for special expenses such as college tuition for children or special vacations for the family.

We often use the term *earnings management* to refer to management's efforts to make earnings look better. Some of these earnings management efforts can be considered to fall within the applicable financial reporting framework. However, many of such efforts are outside the financial reporting framework and result in fraudulent misstatements. Depending on the company, earnings can "look better" if management maintains a constant rate of growth each year (for example, 10%) or shows growth in revenue, net income, or earnings per share (EPS). In the contemporary business environment, management feels the pressure to "look better" to keep shareholders and financial analysts happy. Earnings management measures typically begin with small actions and continue to grow until managers have *manipulated* a large portion of net earnings. It can be difficult for auditors to evaluate the personal financial pressures on management, but the auditors can gain some understanding of the pressure to meet earnings targets. The higher the pressure is to meet earnings targets, the greater is the risk of fraud.

Opportunity

A second condition, the **opportunity** to commit fraud, is present when an individual believes that internal controls are weak or are not designed to prevent fraud and can be overridden. Fraudulent financial reporting often involves management override of controls, which can be done by (1) recording fictitious journal entries (particularly at year-end), (2) inappropriately changing assumptions and methods used to estimate account balances, (3) omitting, advancing, or delaying the recognition of events that occurred during the reporting period, (4) failing to disclose facts that could affect the amounts recorded in the financial statements, (5) engaging in complex transactions designed to misrepresent the financial condition of the company, and (6) altering the records relating to significant and unusual transactions.

Misappropriation of assets involves the theft of the company's assets in a variety of ways: (1) embezzling cash, (2) stealing physical assets (inventory, equipment) or intellectual property (disclosing technical data in return for cash from a competitor), (3) making payments for goods and services that were not received (payments to fictitious vendors, kickback payments received from vendors in return for purchasing items at inflated prices, payments to fictitious employees), and (4) drawing on the company's assets for personal use (for example, as collateral on a personal loan). Misappropriation of assets involves the creation of false or misleading documents to conceal the fact that the assets are missing. Misappropriation often leads to fraudulent financial reporting. When misappropriation occurs, the company could issue fraudulent financial statements.

Rationalization

An individual engaging in fraudulent activity can rationalize that the action is justifiable. Some individuals have a mind-set that allows them to commit fraud knowingly, and even normally honest individuals can commit fraud in an environment if sufficient pressure is present. Some examples of **rationalization** include these: It is okay to steal this money because the company has not treated me very well or we will hide the amount of debt we owe for a short time and then everything will be fine.

Did You Know?

In 2002 the U.S. Congress investigated the telecommunications industry about the practice of recognizing revenue by swapping fiber-optic capacity. Companies such as Qwest and Global Crossing exchanged equal amounts of line capacity. Each company recognized revenue for the exchange and recorded the cost of providing the capacity as a capital expense. Witnesses before the House Energy Panel described the business environment in the telecom industry as a pressure cooker. During this time, executives at the companies pushed their sales representatives to meet the companies' quarterly earnings targets.

According to Patrick Joggerst, former head of sales at Global Crossing, "Not meeting the number was absolutely unacceptable." To meet the revenue targets, representatives from one company called their counterparts at another company and worked out swap arrangements that helped both companies meet their sales targets. Robin Szwliga, Qwest's chief financial officer, testified that "there were well known consequences for not making the numbers but no clear consequences for cutting corners."

Source: D. Berman, "Three Telecom Companies Testify They Cut Side Deals with Qwest," *The Wall Street Journal,* September 25, 2002.

How did pressure play a role in the fraud committed at Qwest and Global Crossing?

Methods Used to Prepare Fraudulent Financial Statements

Management can prepare fraudulent financial statements in three ways: (1) manipulate, falsify, or alter accounting records used to prepare the statements, (2) misrepresent or intentionally omit events, transactions, or other significant information, and (3) intentionally misapply accounting principles. A company's management has a unique ability to perpetrate fraud because internal controls often apply only to transactions that occur frequently in a company. We call these **routine** transactions. For example, recording sales revenue or collecting cash on accounts receivable are usually routine transactions. Internal controls, however, rarely apply to management-initiated estimation transactions, which involve a management decision to estimate a future amount (for example, the amount of uncollectible accounts at year-end). Because estimation transactions are likely to be more susceptible to fraud, when assessing the risk of fraud, the auditor should be review these transactions especially carefully.

The Role of Professional Skepticism

The auditor is expected to conduct an audit with an attitude of **professional skepticism** when considering a company's risk of fraud. Professional skepticism is an attitude or a state of mind. It involves having a *questioning* mind and making a *critical* assessment of the evidence. Maintaining an attitude of professional skepticism requires a continuous questioning of the evidence gathered to determine whether it suggests that a misstatement because of fraud exists and considering the *reliability* of the evidence gathered and the *controls* over the company's preparation of statements. Because of the nature of fraud, it is important that the auditor maintain an attitude of professional skepticism when considering the risk of material misstatement because of fraud. A good auditor must question management's statement when it does not appear to be supported by the evidence.

People tell us all kinds of things. Television ads tell us to buy their product; friends tell us how much they study. Do we believe all the things that we are told? The auditor's job is to believe statements made by management only if the evidence supports them. The auditor must take a "show-me" approach to gathering evidence rather than an "anything-you-say" approach. For example, the company states that net income increased this year because operating expenses were reduced. If this statement is true, the auditor should see that operating expenses as a percentage of revenue is lower in the current year than in the year before. If, in fact, net income increased because of a one-time gain on the sale of a building, the evidence should indicate the real reason for the increase. Professional skepticism is crucial. The auditor must look for the evidence rather than believe every explanation given by management.

Did You Know?

Kevin Hall and Rosemary Meyer (KPMG partner and manager, respectively) were investigated by the SEC for improper professional conduct on the U.S. Foodservice (USF) audit.

Hall and Meyer found numerous examples in which USF recognized revenue that it should not have. Although Hall and Meyer obtained and reviewed evidence documenting these improper transactions, they failed to act on the evidence. In some cases, the transactions were identified as audit exceptions requiring adjustment in the working papers, but the exceptions were subsequently covered with liquid whiteout.

Hall and Meyer ignored red flags in the audit evidence. According to the SEC complaint, they "improperly and repeatedly relied on management representations to confirm previous management representations, even though these statements were contradicted by objective evidence." Hall and Meyer failed to comply with generally accepted auditing standards by "failing to exercise **due professional care;** failing to maintain an attitude of **professional skepticism;** failing to obtain **sufficient competent evidential matter;** substituting management representations for competent evidence. . ." (emphasis added by author).

USF is the nation's second largest distributor of food to restaurants, schools, hospitals, and hotels. For the years under investigation, a significant portion of its income was based on inflated manufacturer rebates. The company ordered huge quantities of food from major manufacturers including Sara Lee Corp., Kraft Food Inc., Georgia-Pacific Corp, and Nestle SA. These manufacturers agreed to pay USF rebates that ranged from 8.5% to 46% of the purchases.

According to accounting rules, rebates should be recorded as reductions in inventory cost when the inventory is paid for. USF recorded the rebate amounts before the inventory was paid for and greatly inflated the dollar amount of the rebates. This allowed executives to meet earnings targets and earn bonuses. The amount of inventory ordered was much more than the company could sell. In fact, it had to rent additional warehouse space and hire cold storage trucks to hold the inventory. Eventually, the company had to reduce the price on the inventory (in some cases, to less than its original cost) to get rid of it.

According to the SEC, USF inflated income by using the payments to reduce the cost of purchases when it received the allowance notice from the vendor rather than when it was earned. In many cases, the promotional allowances were completely fictitious. Several vendors have also been fined by the SEC for their role in perpetrating the fraud.

U.S. Foodservice is owned by Ahold NV, a Dutch supermarket chain. Ahold is the world's third largest supermarket chain behind Walmart Stores, Inc. and Carrefour SA of France.

The SEC alleged that Ahold's filings with the SEC for 2000–2002 were false because the company's U.S. foodservice unit fraudulently reported promotional allowances.

Sources: A. Raghavan and D. Ball, "Ahold and SEC Settle with No Fine," *The Wall Street Journal,* October 14, 2004; S. Stecklow, A. Raghavan, and D. Ball, "How a Quest for Rebates Sent Ahold on an Odd Buying Spree," *The Wall Street Journal,* March 6, 2003; and SEC Administration Proceeding File No. 3-12208, www.sec.gov, February 16, 2006.

The Audit Team's Fraud Discussion

The auditing standards require the *audit team* assigned to an audit to discuss the *susceptibility* of the financial statements to fraud. This discussion allows the more experienced members of the audit team to explain how they believe the financial statements could be susceptible to fraud and gives the team the opportunity to plan an appropriate response to the susceptibility. The fraud discussion (which must be documented in the work papers) can include the following elements:

- A discussion of management's involvement in supervising employees with access to cash or other assets susceptible to misappropriation
- A consideration of unusual or unexplained changes in the behavior or lifestyle of employees that have come to the auditor's attention
- A consideration of the types of circumstances that could indicate the possibility of fraud
- A discussion of how an element of unpredictability can be built into the nature, timing, and extent of audit procedures
- A consideration of the types of audit procedures that could be effective in responding to the susceptibility of the company's financial statements to material misstatement and whether some of the audit procedures can be more effective than others
- A discussion of any allegations of fraud that have come to the auditor's attention

Other factors can influence the extent of the fraud discussion among audit team members. If the audit involves more than one location, multiple fraud discussions can be needed. The auditor can also consider whether the specialists assigned to the audit team (for example, the IT auditors) should be included in the discussion.

In addition, auditors are required to audit the revenue process with the *presumption that improper revenue recognition is a fraud risk* and to evaluate the types of revenue, revenue transactions, or assertions that increase the risk of material misstatement for revenue.

Auditing standards have identified fraud risk factors that can be present in an audit. These factors are listed by type of fraud (fraudulent financial reporting or misappropriation of assets) and by the three conditions generally present when fraud occurs. Not all of these factors are relevant for all circumstances, and the list is not necessarily complete; the auditor could identify additional fraud risk factors for an audit client. Refer to Exhibits 5-3 and 5-4 for a list of the fraud risk factors for misstatements arising from fraudulent financial reporting and misstatements related to misappropriation of assets.

An Example of Fraudulent Financial Reporting

Consider the discussion of fraud by the audit team for AOL Time Warner to see how members could use the fraud triangle and the fraud risk factors from Exhibit 5-3 to identify fraud in this company.

- AOL and Time Warner agreed to merge into one company in January 2000. The U.S. regulatory authorities did not approve the merger until January 2001. The merger cost of $156.14 billion was the highest acquisition cost in history.
- Beginning in the late 1990s, AOL faced competition for its Internet services, a major source of revenue. Internet revenue could not be seen as a growth area for the future. To meet earnings targets, AOL tried to increase its advertising revenue, but many of its advertising contracts were with "dot.com companies" that were also suffering from sales declines, so they canceled their advertising contracts.
- AOL management believes that meeting analyst forecasts, maintaining its earnings per share, and showing strong growth in earnings each year are important. Two upper-level managers exercised stock options worth more than $200 million in 2000. Declines in stock price would have a major effect on the value of their stock options.
- Management created a special unit within the company to improve advertising revenue. This unit is known as the BA (business affairs) unit, and its revenue deals are referred to as "BA Specials." This unit has engaged in several unconventional advertising deals to generate revenue for the company this year.

Risk Factors Relating to Misstatements Arising from Fraudulent Financial Reporting	**Exhibit 5-3**

PRESSURE

1. The financial stability of the business is threatened by economic-, industry-, or company-specific conditions including

    - A high degree of competition in the industry or market saturation accompanied by declining margins
    - High vulnerability to rapid change in the industry
    - Significant declines in customer demand and increasing business failures in the industry or economy
    - Operating losses
    - Recurring negative cash flow from operations
    - Rapid growth
    - New accounting or regulatory requirements

2. Excessive pressure to meet third-party demands, which can include:

    - Expectations from investment analysts, institutional investors, significant creditors, or management's statements regarding expected profitability in press releases or unaudited material in the annual report
    - Need to obtain cash in form of debt or stock issue
    - The situation of being barely able to meet stock listing requirements on the exchanges or debt covenants
    - Possible negative effects on future transactions (business combinations or future contracts) of reporting poor financial results.

3. The possibility that the personal finances of management or the board of directors are affected by the company's financial performance. Some signs that this situation is present include:

    - Management or the board of directors has significant financial interest in the company.
    - A significant portion of compensation is linked to company performance.
    - A member of management or the board of directors has personally guaranteed the company's debt.

4. Pressure on management or employees to meet financial targets established by the board or management (AU 316).

OPPORTUNITIES

The opportunity to commit fraud can be present in the following situations.

1. The nature of the company's business or the operations provides opportunities for fraudulent financial reporting. These include:

    - Significant related-party transactions with entities not audited or audited by another firm
    - Strong financial presence or ability to dominate a certain industry
    - Assets, liabilities, revenues, or expenses based on significant estimates
    - Significant, unusual, or complex transactions
    - Significant foreign operations
    - Use of business intermediaries without a clear business justification
    - Significant bank accounts in tax haven countries.

2. Ineffective monitoring of management can include:

    - Management domination by a single person or a small group
    - Ineffective oversight over the financial reporting process and internal control by management or the board of directors

3. The company has a complex or unstable organizational structure. Some signs of this include:

    - Difficulty in determining who has controlling interest in the company
    - High turnover of senior management, legal counsel, or board members

4. Internal control components are deficient in some of the following ways:

    - Inadequate monitoring of controls
    - High turnover of accounting, internal audit, or IT staff
    - Ineffective accounting and IT systems.

RATIONALIZATION

An individual can rationalize that the action is justifiable for the following reasons:

1. Ineffective communication of the firm's ethical values or inappropriate ethical values

2. Nonfinancial management's participation in the selection of accounting principles or significant estimates

3. History of violating securities laws, claims against management or the board alleging fraud or violations of laws or regulations

4. Management's excessive interest in maintaining or increasing the company's stock price

5. Management commitments to analysts or creditors to achieve aggressive earnings forecasts

6. Management's failure to correct material deficiencies in internal control on a timely basis

7. Management's use of inappropriate means to minimize reported earnings for tax reasons

8. Low morale among senior management

9. No distinction between the owner's personal and business expenditures

10. Disputes between shareholders in a closely held company

11. Management's justification of inappropriate accounting on the basis of immateriality

12. A strained relationship between management and the current or predecessor auditor, which can include:

    - Frequent disputes with the auditor on accounting, auditing, or reporting issues
    - Unreasonable demands made on the auditor regarding the time to complete the audit or to issue the audit report
    - Restrictions on the auditors limiting their access to people or information
    - Domineering behavior in dealing with the auditor (AU 316)

Risk Factors Related to Misstatements Arising from Misappropriation of Assets	Exhibit 5-4

PRESSURE

1. The personal financial obligations of employees or management can create pressure on individuals to misappropriate company assets (cash or other items of value).

2. Adverse relationships between individuals with access to assets and the company can cause individuals to misappropriate company assets. Some of these adverse conditions include:
   - Employee layoffs
   - Changes to compensation or benefit plan
   - Promotions or compensation inconsistent with expectations.

OPPORTUNITIES

1. Sometimes assets are more susceptible to misappropriation. Circumstances in which this might be true include:
   - Processing large amounts of cash
   - Having inventory items that are small in size and of high value or demand
   - Having easily convertible assets (for example, bearer bonds, diamonds, or computer chips)
   - Having fixed assets that are small in size and readily marketable

2. Inadequate internal controls over assets can increase their susceptibility to misappropriation. Weaknesses in internal controls can occur under these situations:
   - Lack of segregation of duties
   - Inadequate oversight of senior management's expenditures
   - Inadequate oversight of employees responsible for assets
   - Inadequate screening of job applicants who would have access to assets
   - Inadequate record-keeping of assets
   - Inadequate system of authorization or approval of transactions in the purchase cycle
   - Inadequate physical safeguards over assets
   - Incomplete reconciliations of assets
   - Lack of timely documentation of transactions
   - Lack of mandatory employee vacations
   - Inadequate understanding of IT functions
   - Inadequate access control over computerized records

RATIONALIZATIONS

1. The company's disregard of the need to monitor risks related to misappropriation of assets

2. Disregard for internal controls over misappropriation of assets by overriding controls over failing to correct known deficiencies in controls

3. Employee behavior that indicates displeasure or dissatisfaction with the company

4. Changes in behavior by employees that can indicate assets have been misappropriated

5. Tolerance of petty theft (AU 316)

- AOL Time Warner reported a net loss of $1.37 billion for the first quarter of 2001, $734 million for the second quarter, $996 million for the third quarter, and $1.82 billion for the fourth quarter. The stock price fell from $49 at the end of the first quarter of 2001 to less than $20 by the end of the first quarter of 2002.

Based on the facts disclosed during the fraud discussion, the team could identify some of the risk factors related to fraudulent financial reporting in this company:

Pressure

- Market saturation for Internet services in the industry plus a high degree of competition in the industry for Internet services
- Decline in customer demand and understanding that Internet subscriptions will not grow and could dramatically decline because customers will no longer pay a monthly fee for Internet services when they can get the same service free or at a lower cost from other providers
- Operating losses beginning in 2001
- Expectations from analysts to maintain earnings growth
- The effect on management's personal finances by the company's financial performance because of the stock options awarded to management and their link to the company's stock price
- Pressure to appear to be good business partners so the regulators will approve the merger

Opportunity

- Management's creation of the special BA unit to create revenue indicates management's "ineffective monitoring"
- Deficient internal controls that would fail to prevent managers from "creating" revenue (in fact, they were encouraged to do so) by recognizing revenue based on unconventional, one-time arrangements to generate sales revenue to prop up earnings to meet targets

Rationalization

- AOL paid a penalty of $3.5 million to the SEC in 2000 for violating securities laws in 1995 and 1996.
- Company management exhibited "excessive interest" in maintaining or increasing the company's stock price.
- Management's commitment to achieving aggressive earnings forecasts set by analysts

AOL Time Warner appears to have many fraud risk factors, and all three elements of the fraud triangle are present. The pressure on management to meet expectations, appear to be a good merger partner, and maintain earnings growth in an industry where competition is taking away their revenue source was huge. The company's opportunity for fraud appears to be present in several ways. Management has created a special unit to find revenue, so controls will be ineffective in regulating this unit's actions. Management can rationalize their fraudulent actions by stating that these actions are necessary only for a short time: "until the merger is approved or until we find a new revenue source". Management can also believe that it is more important to maintain earnings growth than to report financial information according to the applicable financial reporting framework.

How will the auditor control the risks that seem to be present in this audit? The only way the auditor can control this risk is by gathering evidence to determine that the financial statements have been prepared in accordance with the applicable financial reporting framework. Because revenue is so important to this company, the auditor must consider the risk of material misstatement as high and gather sufficient appropriate evidence to reduce this risk to an acceptable level. This means that the auditor must gather a higher *quantity* of evidence for the revenue process and that the *quality* of evidence must also be higher. This is the only way the auditor can perform the audit to obtain reasonable assurance that the revenue process in AOL is free of material misstatement from fraud.

Example of Misappropriation of Assets

Consider how the audit team for Tyco could have used the fraud risk factors for misappropriation of assets in Exhibit 5-4.

- Several loans to Dennis Kozlowski, the CEO, have been forgiven this year.
- Management has granted bonuses and stock options to itself.
- Company funds have been used to purchase and decorate an apartment in New York City and two houses in Florida for Dennis Kozlowski's use.
- The company purchased an art collection worth $13.1 million to be displayed in Kozlowski's various residences.
- Donations to various charitable organizations were made during the year with company funds in the name of Kozlowski.
- The company had its winter sales meeting in Italy in connection with a fortieth birthday party for Kozlowski's wife.

Based on the facts disclosed during the fraud meeting, the auditors could identify some of the fraud risk factors related to the misappropriation of assets in this company. They include:

Pressure

- As the chief executive officer for a large, major company, Kozlowski felt pressure to live well because the company had grown under his direction.

Opportunity

- Internal controls over cash payments were not designed to prevent the chief executive officer from spending money.

Rationalization

- The board of directors disregarded the need to monitor controls for misappropriation of assets. In fact, several of the board members also received benefits from the company (loans forgiven, bonuses).
- As Dennis Kozlowski said, "Everyone knew what I was doing, including the board and the auditor, and no one stopped me, so my actions must have been fine."

Tyco has several of the fraud risk factors identified in the auditing standards. All three elements of the fraud triangle are present. The pressure on management to live well puts pressure on management to find the funds to accomplish this. The opportunity for fraud related to misappropriation of assets appears to be present when no one monitors or controls the actions of the "guy at the top." Kozlowski rationalized his fraudulent actions by stating that everyone knew what he was doing and no one stopped him.

How does the auditor control the risks that seem to be present in this audit? The only way the auditor can do this is by gathering evidence to determine whether misappropriation of assets has occurred at Tyco. The auditor might consider loans made to Kozlowski and their resolution, payments authorized by Kozlowski and the items purchased based on these authorizations, and bonuses given to upper management. The auditor would review the documents related to the loans and bonuses to verify that these were issued in accordance with the rules of the organization.

Assessing the Risk of Material Misstatement Due to Fraud

LO8

Explain how the auditor gathers evidence to assess the risk of material misstatement because of fraud

The auditor's assessment of fraud is part of the assessment of the risk of material misstatement and has an impact on the evidence gathered in the audit. The assessment of fraud determines the **nature, timing,** and **extent** of audit procedures. Based on the auditor's fraud assessment, he or she gathers enough evidence to keep audit risk to an acceptably low level (around 5% typically). If the risk of fraud is high, the auditor can obtain evidence that is more reliable or obtain evidence from independent sources (changing the nature of audit procedures). The auditor can alter the timing of audit tests to perform substantive tests near year-end to gather evidence related to a material misstatement because of fraud (changing the timing of audit procedures). The extent of the audit procedures performed during the audit reflects the auditor's assessment of the risk of fraud in the audit. A higher risk of fraud causes the auditor to gather more evidence (changing the extent of audit evidence gathered).

Did You Know?

In April 2005, Deloitte & Touche agreed to pay $50 million to the SEC to settle charges relating to the audit of Adelphia. The SEC issued an order finding that Deloitte & Touche had engaged in "improper professional conduct . . . because it failed to detect a massive fraud perpetrated by Adelphia and certain members of the Rigas family."

Deloitte & Touche identified Adelphia as a high-risk client but failed to design the audit to address the areas of risk that had been identified. Deloitte issued an unqualified audit opinion for the fiscal 2000 audit when it knew or should have known that Adelphia failed to record all debt on its balance sheet or failed to disclose that it had improperly excluded $1.6 billion in debt from its balance sheet, failed to disclose

Assessing the Risk of Material Misstatement Because of Fraud	Exhibit 5-5

The following conditions can indicate the presence of material misstatement because of fraud in the financial statements:

1. Discrepancies in the accounting records including:
   - Transactions in the company that are not recorded in a timely manner
   - Unsupported or unauthorized account balances or transactions
   - Significant last-minute adjustments
   - Employee access to systems or records beyond what they need to perform their duties
   - Tips or complaints about fraud

2. Information that is conflicting or missing including:
   - Documents
   - Altered documents
   - Photocopied documents
   - Significant unexplained items on reconciliations
   - Unusual balance sheet changes or changes in trends
   - Inconsistent, vague, or implausible responses from management or employees to questions related to analytical review procedures
   - Unusual discrepancies between confirmations and the company's records
   - Large numbers of credit entries and other adjustments made to accounts receivable records
   - Unexplained differences between the accounts receivable ledger and the control account or between customer statements and the accounts receivable ledger
   - Missing cancelled checks

- Significant missing inventory or assets
- Missing electronic evidence from the accounting information system
- Fewer responses to confirmations than expected
- Inability to produce evidence of systems development, program changes, and program testing.

3. Unusual relationships between the auditor and management including:
   - Lack of access to facilities, records, employee customers, or vendors
   - Undue time pressures imposed by management
   - Complaints by management about the audit or intimidation by management of audit team members
   - Delays by management in providing information
   - Unwillingness to allow auditor access to electronic files for testing by using computer-assisted audit techniques
   - Denial of access to key IT personnel
   - Management's unwillingness to revise or add financial statement disclosures requested by the auditor
   - Unwillingness to address identified weaknesses in internal control on a timely basis.

4. Other circumstances, including the following:
   - Unwillingness to let the auditor to meet privately with those charged with governance
   - Accounting policies that vary with industry norms
   - Frequent changes in accounting estimates for no apparent reason
   - Tolerance of violations of the company's code of conduct (AU 316)

significant related-party transactions, and overstated its stockholders' equity account by $375 million.

Deloitte agreed to revise its audit procedures for high-risk clients to include increased involvement of forensic accounting specialists and to increase the training of audit professionals in fraud detection.

Source: U.S. Securities and Exchange Commission, "SEC Charges Deloitte & Touche for Adelphia Audit," www.sec.gov/news/press/2005-65.htm.

Why did Deloitte & Touche fail to gather evidence consistent with its risk assessment?

The auditor's assessment of the risk of misstatement because of fraud is initially made at the beginning of the audit, but assessment continues throughout. Evidence gathered can support or refute the auditor's initial decision about the possibility of material misstatement because of fraud in the financial statements. See Exhibit 5-5 for examples of evidence that could support a decision about the possibility of fraud in the company. A lack of these conditions can refute the possibility of material fraud.

Use of Evidence to Control the Risk of Material Misstatement Due to Fraud

LO9

Explain how the auditor gathers evidence to control the risk of material misstatement because of fraud

The auditing standards require the auditor to control the risk of material misstatement because of fraud to an acceptably low level. How does the auditor do this? The auditor controls this risk by using the following procedures:

- Test the appropriateness of journal entries recorded in the general ledger and other adjustments made in the preparation of the financial statements. Adjusting entries are recorded in the financial statements during the year (recorded as adjustments to the general ledger) and at year-end (as adjustments made when the financial statements are prepared). Fraudulent journal entries often have unique characteristics such as (1) the use of an unrelated, unusual, or seldom-used account in the entry, (2) an entry made by an individual who does not normally make journal entries, (3) an entry recorded at the end of the time period or as a postclosing entry with little or no explanation of the reason for it, (4) no account numbers associated with the entry, and (5) the journal entry contains round numbers or numbers with consistent ending digits.
- Review the accounting estimates made by management for bias. Do managers meet earnings targets or receive a bonus based on the accounting estimates made by management?
- For significant transactions outside the normal course of business, determine whether the business reason for the transaction suggests that it has been made to engage in fraudulent financial reporting or to hide misappropriation of assets (AU 316).

In evaluating the audit evidence obtained, the auditor should consider whether it is consistent with his or her understanding of the company and its environment. When identifying a misstatement during the audit, the auditor should evaluate whether the misstatement indicates that fraud has occurred. If a fraudulent misstatement seems to be present, the auditor should consider its implications in relation to other aspects of the audit. Fraud is unlikely to be an isolated occurrence. When identifying one fraud incident, the auditor must ask what does this say about the integrity of management and the reliability of its representations.

Even when following all procedures in auditing standards to detect fraud, the auditor can still fail in this endeavor. Management's override of internal controls and collusion are the two main roadblocks to fraud detection. The authority of managers puts them in a position to ignore internal control procedures or to request the creation of fictitious documentation to support fraudulent journal entries. One owner of a company rented mailboxes all over the United States for his fictitious customers. When the auditors mailed the confirmation requests to the customers, the owner completed them indicating that the fictitious balances were correct. The same owner colluded with his employees to generate fictitious bank statements. Detecting fraud in situations in which management overrides controls or employees collude is very difficult for an auditor.

The Reporting of Fraud to Management and the Audit Committee

LO10

Describe the reporting requirements for fraud

An auditor who believes that misstatements in the financial statements can be the result of fraud must consider its impact on other aspects of the audit. The auditor can consider withdrawing from the engagement if there is a significant risk of material misstatement in the financial statements. In this case, the auditor communicates the reasons for withdrawal to those responsible for corporate governance in the company. The auditor's decision to withdraw is based on (1) the implications of the fraud regarding management's integrity and (2) the diligence and cooperation of management or the board of directors in investigating the fraud and in taking appropriate action in response to it. When fraud is likely, management and the auditor often consult legal counsel before making a decision.

When the auditor believes that fraud can exist in the company, this should be brought to the attention of the appropriate level of management as soon as possible (even if the fraud is inconsequential). Usually the appropriate level of management is one level above the level where the fraud occurred. Fraud that involves management and that materially misstates the financial statements should be reported to the audit committee.

When identifying risks of material misstatement related to the internal control system, the auditor should consider whether these items reach the level of material weaknesses (significant deficiencies in the design or operation of an internal control, which could result in the reporting of inaccurate financial information). If so, the risks should be reported to management and the audit committee even if fraudulent actions have not occurred. Even if they do not reach the level of reportable conditions, the auditor can choose to report other potential fraud risks to management or the audit committee.

The auditor is not required or permitted to disclose possible fraud to individuals other than management and the audit committee. The auditor's ethical obligation for confidentiality prevents her or him from disclosing any information to outsiders unless the issue is discussed in the auditor's report. The auditor can be required to report fraud to outsiders in response to a subpoena or to successor auditors when they inquire about the reason for a change in auditors.

Auditor Documentation Regarding the Consideration of Fraud

The auditor is required to document in the work papers her or his *understanding* of the company and its environment and her or his assessment of the risks of material misstatement. This documentation should include:

- Significant decisions made during the audit team's discussion regarding the susceptibility of the company's financial statements to material misstatement because of fraud
- How and when the discussion occurred and the audit team members who participated
- The identified and assessed risks of material misstatement because of fraud at both the financial statement level and the assertion level as well as the procedures performed to obtain the information (AU316)

The auditor's documentation of his or her *response* to the assessed risk of material misstatement should include:

- The overall response to the assessed risk of material misstatement because of fraud at the financial statement level; the nature, timing, and extent of audit procedures at the assertion level; and a linkage between the audit procedures and the assessed risk of material misstatement
- The results of the audit procedures including those designed to address the risk of management override of internal controls
- Other conditions and analytical procedures that cause the auditor to believe that additional auditing procedures were appropriate to address the risk of material misstatement because of fraud (AU316)

In the event of an outside review of the audit decision, this documentation is important and will be the primary method the auditor uses to support her or his decision.

Chapter Takeaways

The audit standards related to audit evidence and fraud are important for the auditor. If outsiders question the audit opinion, the auditor will "live and die" (stay in business or be subject to a heavy fine or prevented from performing audits) by the evidence reported in the financial statements. The working papers are also useful to the audit team as its members consider the evidence gathered to evaluate management's assertions for the financial statements under audit.

This chapter presented these important facts:

- A description of audit evidence and its role in the audit process
- How management's assertions are used to structure evidence collection
- What it means to refer to evidence as *appropriate* and *sufficient*
- Documentation requirements for audit evidence
- The auditor's responsibilities for fraud detection in a financial statement audit
- The implications of the elements of the fraud triangle to the audit process
- How the auditor gathers evidence relating to the risk of fraud and modifies the audit related to fraud risk factors
- The reporting requirements for fraud

Be sure you understand these concepts before you go to the next chapter.

Review Questions

LO1   1. What is audit evidence? How is it used in the audit process?

LO1   2. Describe the audit procedures the auditor uses to obtain evidence.

LO1   3. How does the auditor determine the amount of evidence that must be gathered?

LO2   4. Describe management's assertions. How does the auditor use these assertions in the evidence process?

LO3   5. How does the auditor evaluate the *sufficiency* and *appropriateness* of the evidence gathered?

LO4   6. How does the auditor's assessment of risk affect the evidence process?

LO5   7. Describe the Auditing Standards Board's documentation requirements.

LO5   8. Explain the PCAOB documentation policy. How long must the working papers for public company audits be retained?

LO6   9. Describe the auditor's responsibility for fraud detection in a financial statement audit.

LO6   10. What is fraud?

LO7   11. When fraud occurs, what factors could be present in a company?

LO7   12. Describe how management prepares fraudulent financial statements and misappropriates assets.

LO8   13. What is the purpose of the fraud discussion in an audit engagement?

LO8   14. Why should the auditor presume that revenue recognition is a fraud risk?

LO10   15. Is the auditor responsible for reporting fraud to outsiders? Explain your answer.

Multiple Choice Questions from CPA Examinations

LO1   16. Which of the following presumptions is correct about the reliability of evidential matter?

    a. Information obtained indirectly from outside sources is the most reliable evidential matter.

    b. To be reliable, evidential matter should be convincing rather than persuasive.

    c. Reliability of evidential matters refers to the amount of corroborative evidence obtained.

    d. Effective internal control provides the most assurance about the reliability of evidential matter.

LO3   17. Which of the following statements relating to the appropriateness of evidential matter is always true?
a. Evidential matter gathered by an auditor from outside an enterprise is reliable.
b. Accounting data developed under satisfactory conditions of internal control are more relevant than data developed under unsatisfactory internal control conditions.
c. Oral representations made by management are **not** valid evidence.
d. Evidence gathered by auditors must be both valid and relevant to be considered appropriate.

LO3   18. In evaluating the reasonableness of an accounting estimate, an auditor most likely would concentrate on key factors and assumptions that are
a. Consistent with prior periods.
b. Similar to industry guidelines.
c. Objective and not susceptible to bias.
d. Deviations from historical patterns.

LO5   19. Which of the following is least likely to be a factor in the auditor's decision about the extent of the documentation of a particular audit area?
a. The risk of material misstatement.
b. The extent of the judgment involved in performing the procedures.
c. The nature and extent of exceptions identified.
d. Whether or not the client has an internal audit function.

LO8   20. Which of the following is an example of fraudulent financial reporting?
a. Company management changes inventory count tags and overstates ending inventory, while understating cost of goods sold.
b. The treasurer diverts customer payments to his personal due, concealing his actions by debiting an expense account, thus overstating expenses.
c. An employee steals inventory and the "shrinkage" is recorded in cost of goods sold.
d. An employee steals small tools from the company and neglects to return them; the cost is reported as a miscellaneous operating expense.

LO8   21. Which of the following best describes what is meant by the term "fraud risk factor"?
a. Factors whose presence indicates that the risk of fraud is high.
b. Factors whose presence have often been observed in circumstances where frauds have occurred.
c. Factors whose presence requires modification of planned audit procedures.
d. Reportable conditions identified during an audit.

LO6   22. Audits of financial statements are designed to obtain assurance of detecting misstatement due to

	Errors	Fraudulent Financial Reporting	Misappropriation of Assets
a.	Yes	Yes	Yes
b.	Yes	Yes	No
c.	Yes	No	Yes
d.	No	Yes	No

LO8   23. Which of the following characteristics most likely would heighten an auditor's concern about the risk of intentional manipulation of financial statements?
a. Turnover of senior accounting personnel is low.
b. Insiders recently purchased additional shares of the entity's stock.
c. Management places substantial emphasis on meeting earnings projections.
d. The rate of change in the entity's industry is slow.

LO6   24. Which of the following statements reflects an auditor's responsibility for detecting misstatements due to errors and fraud?
a. An auditor is responsible for detecting employee errors and simple fraud, but **not** for discovering fraud involving employee collusion or management override.

    b. An auditor should plan the audit to detect misstatements due to errors and fraud that are caused by departures from the applicable financial reporting framework.

    c. An auditor is **not** responsible for detecting misstatements due to errors and fraud unless the application of GAAS would result in such detection.

    d. An auditor should design the audit to provide reasonable assurance of detecting misstatements due to errors and fraud that are material to the financial statements.

LO6 25. Under Statements on Auditing Standards, which of the following would be classified as an error?

    a. Misappropriation of assets for the benefit of management.

    b. Misinterpretation by management of facts that existed when the financial statements were prepared.

    c. Preparation of records by employees to cover a fraudulent scheme.

    d. Intentional omission of the recording of a transaction to benefit a third party.

Discussion Questions and Research Problems

LO8 26. **Audit procedures for fraud detection in the revenue process.** Assume that you have been assigned to the audit of Italian Home Stores, which sells Italian furniture and home furnishings in two retail shops and on a website for online sales. Italian Home Stores' main customers are interior design consultants, and the majority of their sales in the retail stores are on account. Accounts receivable are material to the overall financial statements.

    a. Describe the auditor's responsibility for fraud detection in the revenue process.

    b. Describe how you would design audit procedures with the presumption that fraud could occur in the revenue process.

    c. Use the assertions of existence, completeness, and valuation to describe how you would design audit procedures to determine whether the assertions were true for the revenue and accounts receivable process.

    d. How will you determine whether you have gathered sufficient evidence for this company's revenue process?

    e. How will you determine whether the evidence you have gathered is appropriate?

    f. If Italian Home Stores is a public company, describe the documentation requirements related to the revenue process.

LO8 27. **Audit procedures for fraud detection in the revenue process.** You are planning the audit for Sole Comfort, a high-end shoe store selling imported shoes to men and women.

    a. Describe how you will use evidence to evaluate the accounts associated with the revenue process on the financial statements.

    b. Use the assertions of existence, completeness, and valuation to describe how you would design audit procedures to determine whether the assertions were true for the revenue process.

    c. Describe two types of fraud that might occur in a shoe store. Explain how you would design audit procedures to detect the fraud.

    d. How do you know when to stop gathering evidence?

    e. How do you determine whether the evidence you have gathered supports your decision?

LO3 28. **Sufficient appropriate evidence and professional skepticism.** Assume that you are responsible for designing the audit procedures to detect fraud at Alberto's Grocery Store.

    a. Describe how you would identify risk factors for a small independent grocery store.

    b. How will you use the auditing standard concepts of "sufficient appropriate evidence" and "professional skepticism" in your planning process?

LO3   29. **Evidence requirement.** You have been assigned to supervise Jason, a new audit hire. He doesn't understand why auditors gather so much evidence and wants to know why they do not simply talk to the client and then make a decision. He is confident that he could gather good information in his conversations with the client. He wonders why he is being asked to doubt the client's word and is not sure that he is prepared to do this.

a. What would you say to him to explain the evidence requirements?

b. How would you *convince* him of the necessity of gathering sufficient documentation?

LO3   30. **Auditor responsibilities.** Your roommate, a history major, doesn't understand what auditors do or how they make their decisions.

a. Describe the audit process including a discussion of the role of evidence in this process.

b. Explain the audit standards of "sufficient appropriate evidence" and "professional skepticism."

c. The history major thinks that auditors guarantee the financial statements and are responsible for all fraud. Is she correct?

LO3   31. **Explaining the company's performance.** Your audit client wants to disclose in a press release that net income for the year increased because of management's efforts. You know that net income increased because the client's pension assets had an unusually high return, and the pension expense on the income statement turned into "pension income." Excluding the increase in net income from the positive pension expense, the firm's net income actually declined.

a. If management issues the press release, describe how you might evaluate the quality of the information the client disclosed.

b. List some criteria for evaluating the quality of this information according to the accounting standards.

c. Would you let the client make the intended disclosure? Explain your answer.

Real-World Auditing Problems

LO3   32. **Merck-Medco**

Refer to the description in the text of the revenue recognition procedures used by Merck-Medco. Merck recognized revenue for the prescription drug copayments paid to the pharmacy.

a. Why did Merck choose this method to recognize revenue? What impact did this choice have on the financial statements?

b. If shareholders or lenders reviewed the Merck financial statements, what conclusion would these outsiders reach about the company?

c. Evaluate the quality of information given to outsiders based on Merck's revenue recognition policy. Determine whether the information is:
   - Relevant
   - Reliable
   - Verifiable
   - Neutral
   - Free from bias

d. Did the revenue reported "faithfully represent what it claims to represent"? Explain your answer.

LO3   33. **eToys**

Many companies have used pro forma earnings disclosures to report favorable earnings in the newspapers. In 2001, the SEC issued a statement limiting the use of pro forma earnings. The SEC requested that companies disclosing pro forma earnings include a reconciliation between pro forma earnings and earnings according to the financial reporting framework.

Refer to the description in the text of eToys and its use of pro forma earnings. This disclosure was made before the SEC issued its recommendation to include earnings according to the financial reporting framework in the press release.

a. What did eToys gain by issuing a press release using only pro forma earnings?
b. Explain how the SEC's recommendation improves the quality of information available to outsiders.
c. When you are an auditor, would you (a) encourage, (b) discourage, or (c) be indifferent to your client's use of pro forma earnings in press releases?

LO3, LO8

34. WorldCom

The WorldCom fraud described in the text is one of the simplest frauds committed. Company executives simply took expenses and made them into assets. They did this with a simple adjusting entry: debit assets, credit expenses, and the expenses recorded on the income statement (lowering net income) became assets (having no effect on net income.) The chapter description of WorldCom posed several questions.

a. Did outsiders receive information that was relevant and reliable when they reviewed WorldCom's financial statements?
b. Was the information free from bias?
c. Did the capitalized assets recorded on WorldCom's books "faithfully represent what they claimed to represent"? Were they really assets?
d. Did shareholders have the information to make a good decision regarding WorldCom if they held its stock?
e. Could lenders make a good decision regarding WorldCom loans? Explain your answer.

LO8

35. Time Warner

Consider the "round-trip" transactions recorded by Time Warner described in the chapter.

a. Describe how the company committed fraud.
b. What type of fraud did it commit?
c. What was the auditor's responsibility regarding this fraud?
d. Evaluate the quality of information that outsiders received in 2000 and 2001 for Time Warner.

LO7

36. Tyco

The Tyco fraud described in the text has been referred to as one of the worst examples of executives who "feed at the corporate trough."

a. Describe the fraud committed at Tyco.
b. What type of fraud did it commit?
c. Consider the fraud conditions of pressure, opportunity, and rationalization. Which of these three elements seem to dominate in this fraud? Explain your answer.
d. Describe the auditor's responsibility regarding this fraud.
e. Why are outsiders dismayed when they learn about this type of fraud?
f. Is the description of executives "feeding at the corporate trough" an accurate description? Explain your answer.

LO8

37. Global Crossing and Qwest

Review the information presented in the chapter in the discussion of "swap" transactions between Global Crossing and Qwest.

a. What type of fraud did the companies commit?
b. Consider the fraud conditions of pressure, opportunity, and rationalization. Which of these elements seem to dominate in this fraud? Explain your answer.
c. Describe the auditor's responsibility regarding this fraud.

d. Evaluate the quality of information that outsiders received during the time period when these companies recorded swap transaction. Identify the specific concepts related to the quality of information that the company violated.

e. Did outsiders receive the information they needed to make good decisions about the company? Explain your answer.

LO3, LO8 38. **U.S. Foodservices**

Consider the information presented in the chapter regarding the audit of U.S. Foodservices (USF).

a. Describe how the auditors failed to gather "sufficient appropriate evidence" in the audit.

b. Did Hall and Meyer exercise "professional skepticism" in the audit? Explain your answer.

c. What type of fraud did the company commit?

d. What were the auditors' responsibilities regarding the fraud committed at USF? Did they meet these responsibilities?

e. Consider the fraud conditions of pressure, opportunity, and rationalization. Which of the elements seems to dominate in this fraud? Explain your answer.

LO9 39. **Adelphia**

The chapter describes a fraud at Adelphia Communications and the failure of Deloitte & Touche to detect the fraud.

a. What does it mean to identify a client as being "high risk"? How did the auditor make this determination? How does the audit of a high-risk client differ from that for a low-risk client?

b. When the SEC holds the auditor responsible for detecting the fraud, what is it implying about the standards of "sufficient appropriate evidence" and "professional skepticism" for the audit? Was the auditor's performance consistent with these standards?

c. Describe how the assessment of Adelphia as a "high-risk" client should affect the nature, timing, and extent of audit procedures? Do you believe that Deloitte & Touche met these standards?

Internet Assignment

LO6 40. Using a data source such as the wsj.com, Factiva, or your local newspaper, find an article about a company relating to a fraud inquiry. You can also investigate some of the accounting frauds discussed in this chapter.

a. For the company you select, identify the pressure that led to the fraud and the opportunity present that allowed it to be committed. Speculate on the rationalization used by the fraudster to justify the fraud.

b. Describe the auditor's responsibility for detecting this fraud.

c. Identify procedures that the auditor might have used to detect this fraud.

6

Auditing the Acquisition and Expenditure Business Process

Learning Objectives

After studying this chapter, you should be able to:

1. Describe the acquisition and expenditure business process.
2. Explain the transactions in the business process.
3. Understand an applicable financial reporting framework (GAAP) for recording transactions in the business process.
4. Understand misstatements (errors and fraud) that could be expected in the acquisition and expenditure process.
5. Explain financial statement assertions for accounts in the business process.
6. Describe the methods the auditor uses to gather evidence for internal controls in the business process.
7. Understand the methods auditors use to gather substantive evidence using analytical procedures, substantive tests of transactions, and substantive tests of balances.
8. Describe auditing procedures for tangible assets—land, building, and equipment—and intangible assets.
9. Explain audit procedures for accrued liabilities.
10. Explain the disclosure requirements for accounts in the acquisition and expenditure business process.

Accounting and auditing standards relevant to this topic

For private companies

- **FASB Statement of Financial Accounting Concepts No. 5,** Recognition and Measurements in Financial Statements of Business Enterprises
- **FASB Statement of Financial Accounting Concepts No. 6,** Elements of Financial Statements
- **AU 110,** Responsibilities and Functions of the Independent Auditor
- **AU 316,** Consideration of Fraud in a Financial Statement Audit
- **AU Section 326,** Audit Evidence
- **AU Section 330,** External Confirmations
- **AU Section 342,** Auditing Accounting Estimates, Including Fair Value Accounting Estimates and Related Disclosures

- **Preface to Codification of Statements on Auditing Standards,** Overall Objectives of the Independent Auditor and the Conduct of an Audit in Accordance with Generally Accepted Auditing Standards

For public companies

- **FASB Statement of Financial Accounting Concepts No. 5,** Recognition and Measurements in Financial Statements of Business Enterprises
- **FASB Statement of Financial Accounting Concepts No. 6,** Elements of Financial Statements
- **AU 110,** Responsibilities and Functions of the Independent Auditor (Interim Standard Adopted by PCAOB)
- **AU 316,** Consideration of Fraud in a Financial Statement Audit (Interim Standard Adopted by PCAOB)
- **AU Section 330,** External Confirmations (Interim Standard Adopted by PCAOB)
- **AU Section 342,** Auditing Accounting Estimates, Including Fair Value Accounting Estimates and Related Disclosures (Interim Standard Adopted by PCAOB)
- **PCAOB Auditing Standard No. 3,** Audit Documentation
- **PCAOB Auditing Standard No. 15,** Audit Evidence

International standards

- **ISA 240,** The Auditor's Responsibility to Consider Fraud in an Audit of Financial Statements
- **ISA 500,** Audit Evidence
- **ISA 505,** External Confirmations
- **ISA 540,** Audit of Accounting Estimates
- **IAS 16,** Property, Plant and Equipment
- **IAS 38,** Intangible Assets
- **Framework for the Preparation and Presentation of Financial Statements,** International Financial Reporting Standards

Chapter Overview

This chapter describes auditing procedures that are used to review a specific class of transactions. In the acquisition and expenditure business process, the auditor considers transactions recorded when (1) inventory or supplies are purchased, (2) expenses are recorded, (3) land, building, equipment, and intangible assets are purchased or sold, (4) depreciation and amortization are recorded, and (5) accounts payable are paid. Accrued liability transactions related to this business process are also considered.

Gathering evidence to support the financial statement accounts in this business process is important to the audit process because of the significance of the inventory and expense accounts to the net income the company reports. Many financial statement errors investigated by the SEC involve manipulation of expenses because understating expenses increases net income, a positive result for company management. Bonuses to management often depend on growth in net income, which often leads to increases in earning per share, which tend to increase the price of the company's stock. Exhibit 6-1 summarizes the main steps in the audit process.

The Acquisition and Expenditure Business Process

LO1

Describe the acquisition and expenditure business process

The acquisition and expenditure business process involves income statement and balance sheet accounts. On the income statement, the acquisition and expenditure process includes all expense accounts including (1) cost of goods sold and (2) selling, general, and administrative expenses. On the balance sheet, the acquisition and expenditure

The Audit Process	Exhibit 6-1

Steps in the Audit Process	Discussed in this Section
Planning Phase	
Consider the Preconditions for an Audit and Accept or Reject the Audit Engagement	
Understand the Entity and Its Environment, Determine Materiality, and Assess the Risks of Material Misstatements	
Develop an Audit Strategy and an Audit Plan to Respond to the Assessed Risks	
Testing Phase	
Test Internal Controls? Yes No	
Perform Tests of Controls if "Yes"	√
Perform Substantive Tests of Transactions	√
Perform Substantive Tests of Balances	√
Assess the Likelihood of Material Misstatement	√
Decision Phase	
Review the Presentation and Disclosure Assertions	√
Evaluate the Evidence to Determine Whether the Financial Statements Are Prepared in Accordance with the Applicable Financial Reporting Framework	
Issue Audit Report	
Communicate with the Audit Committee	

process includes (1) purchases of inventory and supplies, (2) purchase returns and allowances, (3) accounts payable, (4) cash payments, and (5) changes in land, building, equipment, and intangible assets. The acquisition and expenditure process can include millions of transactions each year. As with all processes, the auditor is concerned with determining that the income statement transactions were recorded in accordance with the applicable financial reporting framework during the year (according to GAAP) and that the balances on the balance sheet are stated in accordance with the applicable financial reporting framework at year-end. See Exhibit 6-2 for the accounts included in the process.

As with all income statement accounts, the expense accounts begin the year with a zero balance, and then transactions for the entire year are recorded in the accounts. Normally, no credit entries are made to expense accounts or debit entries are made to revenue accounts. The totals in the revenue and expense accounts at year-end reflect all the transactions recorded during the year, which the auditor is responsible for gathering evidence to support. The auditor must determine whether the transactions recorded in these accounts during the year have been recorded in accordance with the applicable financial reporting framework.

Did You Know?

Rite Aid, at one time the nation's third largest drugstore chain, restated its earnings in 2000 by $1.6 billion. At the time, this was the largest revision of earnings in U.S. financial history.

The company engaged in several fraudulent accounting actions including reversing expense entries, recording fictitious credits from vendors for damaged and obsolete goods, recording revenue for drugs that customers never picked up, and failing to remove stolen inventory from its books. The CFO, Frank Bergonzi, ordered the accounting staff to prepare fictitious journal entries including crediting expense accounts for various expenses that had already been incurred and paid for. The result of these actions was to

Accounts in the Acquisition and Expenditure Process — Exhibit 6-2

+ Purchases or Inventory −	
Beginning Balance	
Inventory Purchased during the Year	Cost of Goods Sold
Ending Balance	

− Accounts Payable +	
	Beginning Balance
Payments on Account	Purchases and Expense items on Account
	Ending Balance

+ Expenses −	
Cost of Goods Sold	
Selling, General, and Administrative Expenses	
Depreciation Expense	
Ending Balance	

+ Land, Building, and Equipment −	
Beginning Balance	
Additions	Disposals
Ending Balance	

+ Purchase Returns & Allowances −	
	Purchase Returns
	Purchase Allowances
	Ending Balance

+ Intangible Assets − †	
Beginning Balance	
Additions	Disposals
Ending Balance	

+ Cash −	
Beginning Cash Balance	
Cash Received during the Year	*Cash paid out during the Year**
Ending Balance	

+ Accumulated Depreciation −	
	Beginning Balance
Accumulated Depreciation on Assets Sold	Accumulated Depreciation for the Year
	Ending Balance

+ Allowance Account for Decline in Value of Intangible Assets −	
	Beginning Balance
Additions	Disposals
	Decline in Value
	Ending Balance

* Cash payments are part of this process. Cash receipts were included in the revenue process.
† Intangible assets include goodwill, patents, trademarks, and copyrights.

overstate income in the quarter that the entries were recorded. The accounting staff was also ordered to make improper adjusting entries to reduce the cost of goods sold and accounts payable. These entries had no basis and were intended to manipulate income in the quarter in which they were recorded.

When an employee complained about the fictitious entries, the company gave her cash and a new car. A fired executive threatened to disclose the irregularities and was given a $6 million bonus to keep quiet. The civil and criminal indictment filed against the company stated that its executives lied extensively to the company's auditor, KPMG, LLP. Martin Grass, the former chief executive of Rite Aid, continued to manipulate company records after he resigned. He created letters authorizing severance arrangements worth several millions of dollars for a few executives and backdated them to a time when he was still CEO.

Seven executives have been convicted of fraud in the accounting fraud cases. Martin Grass was sentenced to eight years in prison for his role in the fraud.

Sources: Mark Maremont, "Rite Aid's Ex-CEO Sentenced to 8 Years for Accounting Fraud," *The Wall Street Journal,* May 28, 2004; Mark Maremont, "Rite Aid Judge Deals Stiffest Sentence So Far," *The Wall Street Journal,* May 27, 2004; Scott Kilman, "Federal Grand Jury Charges Executives in Rite Aid Probe," *The Wall Street Journal,* June 24, 2002; SEC Press Release 2002-92, June 21, 2002.

Why did the company prepare fictitious entries to reduce cost of goods sold and operating expenses? Did the auditors know about the fictitious entries?

The totals in the balance sheet accounts reflect only the amounts in the accounts on the last day of the year. They do not reflect all transactions recorded during the year but the *net* amount of the transactions recorded during the year. The balance sheet accounts have a beginning balance on the first day of the year, which reflects the ending (audited) balance from the prior year. During the year, increases and decreases in the balance sheet accounts are recorded in the accounts. Balance sheet accounts typically have debit and credit entries (both increases and decreases to the accounts). The balance at the end of the year reflects the balance in the account only as of the last day of the year. The auditor is responsible for determining only whether the ending balance in the balance sheet account is stated in accordance with the applicable financial reporting framework. The auditor is not responsible for reviewing all transactions recorded in the balance sheet account during the year.

For the income statement, the auditor gathers evidence to support the transactions recorded in the accounts for twelve months. For the balance sheet, the auditor gathers evidence to determine whether the account balance on one day of the year—the last day—is correct. The tests that an auditor uses to gather evidence relating to income statement transactions are called **substantive tests of transactions.** The tests an auditor uses to gather evidence relating to balance sheet transactions are called **substantive tests of balances.** They provide the auditor evidence about whether the account balance is correct (for balance sheet accounts) or whether the transactions recorded in the financial statements are correct (for income statement accounts). The auditor measures "correctness" by determining whether the transactions in the accounts have been recorded in accordance with the financial reporting framework.

Transactions Recorded in the Acquisition and Expenditure Process

LO2

Explain the transactions in the business process

The journal entries and the documents associated with these entries for the acquisition and expenditure process are in Exhibit 6-3. Asset accounts or expense accounts are increased when a liability is recorded. Cash is decreased when the liability is paid.

Documents in the Business Process

The auditor can find several documents useful for gathering evidence about the business process. These documents are discussed next.

Purchase requisition. A department uses this document to request goods or services. For example, the accounting department can complete a purchase requisition to purchase photocopy paper for the department.

Purchase order. Purchase orders are prepared by the purchasing department to initiate the purchase on the purchase requisition. A purchase order includes a description of the item to be purchased, its price, and the amount purchased, and a signature by a supervisor in the purchasing department authorizing the purchase.

Receiving document. The client prepares a receiving document when the goods ordered arrive. It is used to record the amount and type of goods received from the vendor. This document usually determines the date when the liability and corresponding expense or asset should be recognized according to the applicable financial reporting framework.

Vendor invoice. A document prepared by a supplier (vendor) that includes a description of the goods or services provided, the amount of goods sold, and the total

Journal Entries and Related Documents for the Acquisition and Expenditure Process	Exhibit 6-3

Journal Entry	**Documents**
Purchases Accounts Payable *(To record purchases of inventory on account for a periodic inventory system.)*	Purchase requisition, Purchase order, receiving document, vendor invoice, voucher
Inventory Accounts Payable *(To record purchases of inventory on account for a perpetual inventory system.)*	Purchase requisition, Purchase order, receiving document, vendor invoice, voucher
Accounts Payable Cash *(To record a payment on an accounts payable.)*	Voucher, cash disbursements journal
Accounts Payable or Cash Purchase returns and allowances *(To record a return or an adjustment in price for an item purchased.)*	Purchase journal, accounts payable subsidiary ledger, credit memo from vendor
Selling, General, and Administrative Expense Accounts Payable *(To record an expense on account.)*	Vendor invoice, voucher
Land, Building, and Equipment Accounts Payable *(To record land, building, or equipment purchased on account.)*	Land, building, and equipment subsidiary ledger, voucher
Depreciation Expense Accumulated Depreciation *(To record yearly depreciation expense.)*	Land, building, and equipment subsidiary ledger
Loss on Sale of Asset Cash Accumulated Depreciation Asset *(To record the sale of an asset at a loss.)*	Land, building, and equipment subsidiary ledger, cash receipts journal

Cash
Accumulated Depreciation
    Asset
    Gain on Sale of Asset
(To record the sale of an asset at a gain.)
	Land, building, and equipment subsidiary ledger, cash receipts journal

Intangible Asset (Patents, Trademarks, Copyrights) Cash or Liability *(To record the purchase of an intangible asset.)*	Intangible asset subsidiary ledger, cash payments journal

Goodwill
Assets Purchased
    Liabilities Purchased
    Cash or Stock
(To record the receipt of goodwill in a purchase transaction in which the price paid for the business is higher than its fair value.)
	Intangible asset subsidiary ledger, cash payments journal

Unrealized Loss on Decline in Fair Value of Reporting Unit Decline in Value of Reporting Unit *(To adjust the fair value of the reporting unit as a result of an impairment in value.)*	Adjusting journal entry report

amount owed including taxes and shipping costs. The vendor invoice lists the due date for the payment.

Voucher. The voucher is a document the client prepares to control the payment of the liability. A voucher request package typically includes the purchase requisition, purchase order, receiving report, vendor invoice, and voucher. An auditor reviews the documents filed in the voucher request packets when testing purchases and accounts payable. The liability is recorded based on the information in the voucher packet.

Purchase journal. This is a daily or monthly report including a list of purchase transactions for the time period.

Accounts payable subsidiary ledger. This is a detailed list of account payable balances by vendor. The total in this account should agree to the accounts payable balance in the general ledger and on the balance sheet.

Land, building, and equipment subsidiary ledger. This is a detailed list of land, building, equipment, and accumulated depreciation balances by asset. The total in this ledger should agree to the land, building, equipment, and accumulated depreciation account in the general ledger and on the balance sheet.

Intangible asset subsidiary ledger. This is a detailed list of intangible assets and decline in value adjustments as required according to the applicable financial reporting framework. The total in this ledger should agree to the intangible asset accounts in the general ledger and on the balance sheet.

Cash disbursements journal. This is a daily or monthly report including a list of cash disbursements for the time period.

Cash receipts journal. This is a daily or monthly report including a list of cash receipts for the time period.

Adjusting journal entry report. This report is a record of all adjusting journal entries made during a specific time period, organized by month-end, quarter-end, and year-end. This report is supported by documentation for the adjusting journal entries with the signature of the person initiating the entry.

Accounting Standards for Recording Transactions in the Acquisition and Expenditure Business Process

LO3

Understand the applicable financial reporting framework (GAAP) for recording transactions in the business process

Two financial reporting frameworks might be used by a company for preparing financial statements: (1) accounting standards for U.S. companies and (2) international accounting standards. We refer to the first set of standards as U.S. GAAP and the second set as International Financial Reporting Standards (IFRSs). Both frameworks provide similar rules for recognizing expenses and recording liabilities. The specific rules for each set of standards will be discussed next.

The accounting rules for recording transactions in the acquisition and expenditure business process are fairly easy to understand. According to the financial reporting framework used in the United States, FASB Concept Statement No. 5, *Recognition and Measurement in Financial Statements of Business Enterprises,* provides the basic rule for liability and expense recognition. According to this standard, an expense is recognized when the benefit of an asset has been reduced or when a liability has been incurred. The amount of the liability is based on the current exchange price at the date of recognition of the expense. Once a liability has been recognized, it continues to be measured at the amount initially recorded. Some expenses are matched to revenue (cost of goods sold). Many expenses are recognized during the period when cash is spent or the liability is incurred because the item is used up simultaneously with its acquisition (selling and administrative expenses). Other expenses are allocated to the income statement by a systematic method that allows the expense to be recognized when the asset provides a benefit (depreciation and insurance expense).

The international accounting standards provide rules for recording expense and liability in the *Framework for the Preparation of Financial Statements.* Liabilities are recognized when it is probable that an outflow of resources providing economic benefits will result from the settlement of a present obligation and the amount of the settlement can be measured reliably. Expenses are recognized when a decrease in future economic benefits related to a decrease in an asset or an increase in a liability has occurred and it can be measured reliably. In other words, expenses are recognized at the same time the company recognizes an increase in liabilities or a decrease in assets.

According to both frameworks, companies routinely incur liabilities to acquire the funds, goods, and services they need to operate. Borrowing money obligates the company to repay the loan. Buying assets on credit obligates a company to pay for them. Using the knowledge, time, and skill of employees obligates the company to pay for their use. A company incurs most liabilities in transactions by which it obtains the resources it needs to do business. The agreements associated with these transactions can be written or oral; they obligate the company to pay cash or provide goods or services in exchange for the benefits received. Applying these rules to the process to record expenses, the company should recognize an expense when it has consumed an economic benefit in the process of acquiring funds, goods, or services needed to operate a business. The amount of the expense recognized should equal the cash the firm expects to pay to reduce the liability to zero (excluding interest costs if applicable).

Possible Misstatements in the Acquisition and Expenditure Business Process

LO4

Understand misstatements (errors and fraud) that could be expected in the acquisition and expenditure process

Expenses and accounts payable are susceptible to both errors (unintentional misstatements) and fraud (intentional misstatements), so the auditor must design audit procedures to search for them in the acquisition and expenditures process.

Misstatements in this process can be overstatement or understatement. Clients can understate expenses and accounts payable due to cutoff problems. They can fail to recognize expenses at year-end although they received the benefit of them. Clients can overstatement a liability year-end by failing to record the cash payment to reduce it. **Understatement** misstatements are far more likely to occur in the acquisition and expenditures process than overstatement misstatements, so the auditor often looks for liabilities *that have not been recorded* in the acquisition and expenditures process. When misstatements occur (whether intentional or unintentional), expenses and accounts payable are frequently understated, misleading outsiders about the future cash flows when the liabilities are paid.

Did You Know?

Rent-Way, **the nation's second-largest company of rent-to-own stores,** reduced its earnings for 1999 and 2000 by $127 million. The fraud was discovered when Matthew Marini, the company's controller and chief accounting officer, went on vacation. During his absence, the new chief financial officer compared the inventory from the in-house inventory reports to the inventory on the balance sheet and questioned the discrepancy between the two numbers. Employees then provided information about journal entries made at the direction of Mr. Marini.

When the chief executive, William Morgenstern, asked him to explain the fraud, Mr. Marini indicated that the entries were made because of pressure to meet analyst forecasts. He insisted that he had merely "pushed the accounting rules" but had not violated them. To reduce expense, Mr. Marini had recorded large expenditures such as vehicle maintenance as assets. Several weeks before year-end, Rent-Way's accounting department stopped recording accounts payable. To reduce the expense associated with writing off missing or scrap inventory, the inventory was kept on the books even though it was no longer available for rent.

When Mr. Morgenstern met with Mr. Marini to discuss the fraudulent actions, Mr. Marini asked if he could keep his job. He was fired. His supervisor, Jeffrey Conway, the president and chief operating officer, was also asked to resign.

Sources: Queena Sook Kim, "Rent-Way Details Improper Bookkeeping, *The Wall Street Journal,* June 8, 2001.

Were Mr. Marini's actions merely "pushing the accounting rules"?

Examples of Expense or Accounts Payable Fraud   Exhibit 6-4

WorldCom *capitalized operating expenses* to increase income by $11 billion. The restatement is the largest restatement of earnings recorded in the United States.

Interpublic Groups, one of the world's largest advertising companies, restated earnings for five years after discovering that $68.5 million in expenses had not been properly recorded. One of its subsidiaries, McCann-Erickson, had failed to reconcile its intercompany accounts on a timely basis. It *failed to record* accounts payable at the end of the year.

Adelphia fraudulently excluded more than $2.3 billion in debt from the company's financial statements by shifting the debt to the books of its unconsolidated subsidiary. The financial statements issued by Adelphia gave the impression that the debt had been repaid. It *failed to record* long-term liabilities.

Rent-Way misstated expenses by $127 million. It recorded some large expenses as capital expenditures, stopped recording accounts payable for several weeks before year-end to reduce expenses, and kept obsolete inventory on the books rather than taking the expense for writing off the inventory. It *failed to record* accounts payable at the end of the year.

Rite Aid, a drug store chain, overstated its income for every quarter from 1997 to 1999. The total misstatement was $1.6 billion. The company recorded fictitious credits from vendors for damaged goods, falsified expense records, manipulated the accounts payable entries, reversed entries for expenses that had already been paid, reduced cost of goods sold and accounts payable, and failed to account fully for inventory shrinkage. It *failed to record* accounts payable at the end of the year.

UnitedHealth Group *failed to record fringe benefits* expense (compensation expense related to the stock option grant), overstating its earnings by $286 million by backdating the stock options it issued to executives in 2003–2005. UnitedHealth reported a "significant deficiency" in internal controls for the way it had administered and accounted for its stock option grants.

Sources: Young, S., "MCI to State Fraud was $11 Billion," *The Wall Street Journal,* March 12, 2004; O'Connell, V. "Interpublic Group Restates 5 Years of Its Earnings," *The Wall Street Journal,* August 14, 2002; *U.S. Securities and Exchange Commission,* Litigation Release No. 17627, July 24, 2002; Kim, Q. S., "Rent-Way Details Improper Bookkeeping," *The Wall Street Journal,* June 8, 2001; *U.S. Securities & Exchange Commission,* "SEC Announces Fraud Charges Against Former Rite Aid Senior Management," Press Release 2002-92, June 21, 2002; and Bandler, J. and C. Forelle, "UnitedHealth Cites 'Deficiency' in Option Grants," *The Wall Street Journal,* May 12, 2006.

The client can use a variety of methods to understate expenses and payables including these:

- Failure to record accounts payable at year-end
- Failure to record payroll expense or fringe benefits at year-end
- Failure to record accrued expenses at year-end
- Capitalization of expenses
- The recording of expense items at the wrong amount or in the wrong time period to understate expenses for the current year
- Failure to record long-term liabilities

Understatement of expenses and payables can be caused by the client's errors or fraudulent actions (intentional misstatement). The SEC has identified improper capitalization of expenses as assets to be the second most common problem it encounters in reviewing financial statement filings (revenue recognition is the most common problem). Examples of fraud reported by the SEC involving the acquisition and expenditure process are in Exhibit 6-4. All of these involve *fraudulent financial reporting.*

According to the data in the table, companies can commit expense or accounts payable frauds in several ways:

- *Failing to record* accounts payable at year-end, a failure to adhere to the applicable financial reporting framework.
- Failing to recognize liabilities and expenses that had incurred.

- *Capitalizing expenses by* taking expense items that would have reduced net income and moving them to the balance sheet as assets.
- Removing expenses from the income statement fails to match expenses to revenue as the applicable financial reporting framework requires.
- *Failing to record long-term liabilities* that the company was liable for on its balance sheet.

Did You Know?

The largest fraud in U.S. history occurred at WorldCom, a telecommunications company with 62,000 employees and 20 million customers based in Clinton, Mississippi. In 2002, WorldCom reported that earnings had been overstated by $11 billion in 2000 through 2002 because it had improperly recorded expenses as capital expenditures. WorldCom capitalized expenses by taking expenses from its income statement and recording them as assets on the balance sheet. The collapse of the company and the 2002 bankruptcy filing wiped out stock shares with a capitalization of $180 billion at their peak in 1999. In March 2005, Bernard Ebbers, former Chief Executive of WorldCom, was convicted of securities fraud, conspiracy, and making false filings to the securities regulators. He was sentenced to 25 years in prison and began his sentence in September of 2006.

Former AT&T Chief Executive, C. Michael Armstrong, reported that he was baffled at the results reported by WorldCom. AT&T couldn't figure out how WorldCom could lead the telecommunications industry in pricing and in producing strong profit margins. AT&T could not match the results reported by WorldCom. During this time period, stock analysts referred to AT&T stock as "sluggish" and its stock price fell. The company laid off employees and made business decisions based on the phony numbers reported by WorldCom. Mr. Armstrong did not know that WorldCom was fraudulently misstating earnings by recording operating expenses as capital expenditures (allowing the company to spread the expense out over many years). After the WorldCom earnings restatement, Mr. Armstrong learned that AT&T had outperformed WorldCom in many areas.

Sources: Dionne Searchy, "On Judgment Day, Assessing Ebbers's Impact," *The Wall Street Journal,* July 13, 2005; "Ex-WorldCom CEO Set to Start Prison Sentence," *The Wall Street Journal,* September 26, 2006; "Major Executive Trials," *The Wall Street Journal,* May 16, 2006.

How could the auditor identify fraud based on capitalizing assets?

An auditor can also find fraud in a company in the form of *misappropriation of assets* by (1) setting up accounts for fictitious vendors and processing payments to these vendors, (2) creating fictitious employees and misdirecting the payroll for these employees to their own accounts, and (3) purchasing inventory or supplies on the company account that employees use for their own personal benefit.

Did You Know?

Satyam is the fourth largest technology outsourcing company in India with many large U. S. clients, including Citigroup Inc., General Electric Co, Caterpillar Inc., and Coca-Cola Co. Company stock is listed on the Bombay Stock Exchange and the New York Stock Exchange. It reports that 53,000 employees work at its headquarters in Hyderabad.

In January 2009, *The Wall Street Journal* reported that Satyam had only 40,000 employees. Mr. Raju, the chairman of Satyam, had created 13,000 fictitious employees and had used the salaries to take money from the company. The cash was diverted to accounts belonging to Mr. Raju's brothers and mother and was used to buy thousands of acres of land around Hyderabad. The payment to the ghost employees came to about $4 million per month.

PricewaterhouseCoopers had audited the company. Two partners of the Indian arm of the accounting firm were arrested on charges of criminal conspiracy and cheating in connection with the fraud investigation.

Sources: Eric Bellman and Niraj Sheth, "Indian Prosecutors Allege Satyam Founder Siphoned Funds," *The Wall Street Journal,* January 23, 2009; Jackie Range, "Pricewaterhouse Partners Arrested in Satyam Probe," *The Wall Street Journal,* January 25, 2009.

Would this fraud have been easy for the auditors to identify?

How does the auditor find errors or fraud in the acquisition and expenditures process? The auditor should conduct the audit with an attitude of *professional skepticism.* This includes gathering evidence and planning the audit with a "questioning mind and being alert to conditions that can indicate possible misstatement due to fraud or error, and a critical assessment of audit evidence" (Overall Objectives of the Independent Auditor and the Conduct of an Audit in Accordance with Generally Accepted Auditing Standards). Auditing standards require members of the audit team in their planning stage to schedule a team meeting to discuss the potential for misstatement because of fraud in the acquisition and expenditure process, including the pressure on management to commit fraud, the opportunity for fraud to be perpetrated in the company, and the company's general environment or tone that could allow management to rationalize committing fraud. In planning the audit and assessing the risk for the acquisition and expenditures process, the auditor should consider the fraud risk factors identified in the auditing standards (AU316), using this information to assess the *risk of material misstatement for relevant assertions in significant accounts and disclosures* for the business process and to plan the level of substantive test work for the business process.

Did You Know?

Fleming, at one time the nation's largest supplier of goods to supermarkets and convenience stores, with 50 major distribution centers around the United States, improperly recorded transactions in 2001 and 2002 to increase earnings after experiencing financial difficulties.

The company negotiated side arrangements with its vendors for rebates and recorded the entire rebate as a reduction in expense even though the rebate was for future performance and should have been recognized in the future. Company executives negotiated large inventory purchases at the end of a quarter to generate rebates that offset expenses.

The SEC also charged suppliers who had cooperated in the side agreements. Dean Foods paid a $400,000 fine, and one of its executives paid $50,000. Kemps, a dairy supplier, paid a fine of $150,000, and two company executives paid $50,000 each. An executive at Frito Lay and another at Kraft Foods each paid $25,000. Several other companies and executives were fined for their involvement in the fraud. The SEC stated that Fleming would not have been able to perpetrate the fraud without the help of its suppliers.

The company is now out of business. Its successor, Core-Mark, is a distributor supplying goods to convenience stores.

Sources: Michael Schroeder, "Former Fleming Executives Charged with Securities Fraud," *The Wall Street Journal,* September 17, 2005; Judith Burns, "Claims Are Settled in Fleming Case about Accounting," *The Wall Street Journal,* September 15, 2004; SEC Accounting and Auditing Enforcement Release No. 2097, September 14, 2004.

Why did the auditors permit the company to record expense reductions early?

Management's Assertions for the Acquisition and Expenditure Business Process

LO5

Explain financial statement assertions for accounts in the business process

In the acquisition and expenditure business process, the auditor gathers evidence to evaluate management's assertions about the accounts in the process.

Management's Assertions

Existence or occurrence—for both classes of transactions and account balances
Completeness—for both classes of transactions and account balances
Valuation and allocation—for account balances
Rights and obligations—for account balances
Accuracy—for classes of transactions
Cutoff—for classes of transactions
Classification—for classes of transactions (AU 314 and ISA 315)

For the acquisition and expenditure process, management asserts that:

- Accounts payable *exist* at the balance sheet date and that the expense transactions recorded in the acquisition and expenditure process *occurred* during the year (existence and occurrence).
- *All* acquisition and expenditure transactions that should be presented in the financial statements are included (completeness).
- Accounts payable are *valued* correctly according to the applicable financial reporting framework rules at year-end (valuation) and that the company has the *obligation* to pay the accounts payable (rights and obligations).
- All expense accounts are *accurate,* that *cutoff* was done in accordance with the applicable financial reporting framework and that the expense accounts are properly *classified* (accuracy, cutoff and classification).

The auditor is required to gather audit evidence to support *relevant assertions for significant accounts* in the business process. The relevant assertions for any business process are linked to the **risk** in the accounting process. They are often associated with the misstatement expected in the process. Because the most likely misstatement in the acquisition and expenditure process is an understatement misstatement, **completeness** is often the relevant assertion for the process.

Did You Know?

The SEC charged Adelphia Communications (the sixth largest cable television provider in the United States) with fraudulently excluding billions of dollars of liabilities from its balance sheet by hiding them on the books of off-balance sheet affiliates. Between 1999 and 2001, Adelphia executives prepared financial statements excluding $2.3 billion in bank debt. Failure to record the debt violated GAAP requirements and led to a series of disclosures including the creation of sham transactions with fictitious documents to give the appearance that Adelphia had repaid the debt. The company issued misleading financial statements that gave the false impression in the footnotes that the liabilities listed on the balance sheet included all outstanding bank debt.

Adelphia agreed to a $715 million settlement with the U.S. Justice Department and the Securities and Exchange Commission. The $715 million settlement is the second largest recovery in an accounting fraud in SEC history, exceeded only by the $750 million WorldCom settlement.

Deloitte & Touche LLP, auditors for Adelphia, agreed to pay $50 million to settle charges related to the Adelphia audit. The SEC issued an order stating that Deloitte had engaged in "improper professional conduct and failed to detect the massive fraud perpetrated by Adelphia and members of the Rigas family."

Sources: Peter Grant and Deborah Solomon, "Adelphia to Pay $715 Million in 3-Way Settlement," *The Wall Street Journal,* June 26, 2005; Dionne Searchy and Li Yuan, "Adelphia's John Rigas Gets 15 Years," *The Wall Street Journal,* June 21, 2005; SEC Accounting and Auditing Enforcement Release No. 1599, July 24, 2004, SEC Press Release 2005-65, "Deloitte to Pay $50 Million to Settle."

Why did Deloitte & Touche fail to gather sufficient appropriate evidence to discover this misstatement?

Internal Control Testing

LO6

Describe the methods the auditor uses to gather evidence for internal controls in the business process

In regard to the acquisition and expenditure process, management should have designed internal controls to prevent or detect misstatements in financial statements. Management often uses internal controls in this process because of its large volume of transactions (when many transactions are processed, it is important to management to design controls to prevent or detect misstatements in the processing of the transactions). The auditor can choose to test these internal controls if he or she believes that they are effective in preventing or detecting misstatements in the financial statements. The decision to test internal control for a financial statement audit is always based on whether it is an efficient way to gather evidence for the business process. This means that sometimes management has designed internal controls but the auditor chooses not to test them because he believes that it is more efficient to use substantive testing to gather evidence for the business process.

Whether choosing to test or not to test internal controls, the auditor is required to obtain an understanding of internal control in this business process relevant to the audit (AU 314).

Although this book focuses primarily on manual control and leaves the discussion of IT controls to an information systems course, we consider a few of the IT controls related to this business process.

- Goods are received only for items with a valid purchase order.
- The accounting system matches information on the purchase order and the receiving report with the vendor invoice before the invoice is paid.
- The asset (supplies or inventory) or the expense is recognized based on the date on the receiving report.
- The IT system prepares exception reports for purchase orders for which the goods have not been received and receiving reports that have not been invoiced.
- The IT system restricts access to individuals authorized to input purchase orders, receiving reports, and vendor invoices.

Every control system developed by management is different. An auditor who decides to rely on internal control evidence will first document the internal control system using flowcharts and questionnaires. See Exhibit 6-5 for an example of an internal control questionnaire. In this questionnaire, questions answered "no" indicate control weaknesses. Questions answered "yes" indicate controls that potentially could be tested.

The auditing standards do not identify which controls *must* be tested in a business process, but an auditor often chooses to test internal controls for relevant assertions regarding significant accounts in the business process.[1] For the acquisition and expenditure process, the *significant accounts* can be (1) accounts payable or (2) expenses. The "decline in value account" used to recognize declines in the fair value of a reporting unit with goodwill can also be a significant account for some companies. Auditors often determine that the *relevant assertion* is **completeness** for both accounts payable and expenses. **Valuation** would be the relevant assertion for the Decline in Value allowance account. Depending on the industry or economic conditions, other accounts can be significant, and the auditor can consider other assertions to be relevant. Key controls for the acquisition and expenditures business process that management often uses to prevent or detect misstatements in the financial statements follow. These controls are organized by internal control procedure.

Internal Control Procedures

Segregation of duties
Authorization procedures
Documented transaction trails
Independent reconciliations
Physical controls that limit access to assets

The key control procedures for the acquisition and expenditure business process are as follows:

- Segregation of duties
  - The purchase requisition, purchase order, receiving reports, voucher requests, and cash payment functions are performed by different individuals.

[1] The PCAOB Auditing Standards are an exception to this statement. They do require the auditor to test internal controls for relevant assertions for significant accounts.

Internal Control Questionnaire—Acquisition and Expenditure Business Process	Exhibit 6-5

ENVIRONMENT

1. Are competitive bids received and reviewed for certain items?
2. Are all purchases made only on the basis of approved purchase requisitions?
3. Are purchase prices approved by a responsible purchasing officer?
4. Are all purchases routed through the purchasing department for approval?

EXISTENCE OR OCCURRENCE

5. Are the purchasing department, accounting department, receiving department, and shipping department independent of each other?
6. Are receiving reports prepared for each item received and copies transmitted to inventory custodians? To purchasing? To the accounting department?
7. Are purchases made for employees processed by the regular purchases procedures?
8. Are the quantity and quality of goods received determined at the time of receipt by receiving personnel independent of the purchasing department?
9. Are vendors' invoices matched against purchase orders and receiving reports before a liability is recorded?
10. Do managers compare actual expenses to budget?
11. Are vouchers cancelled with a PAID stamp when paid?
12. Are shipping documents authorized and prepared for goods returned to vendors?
13. Are invoices approved for payment by a responsible officer?

COMPLETENESS

14. Are the purchase order forms prenumbered and the numerical sequence checked for missing documents?
15. Are receiving reports prenumbered and the numerical sequence checked for missing documents?

16. Is the accounts payable department notified of goods returned to vendors?
17. Are vendors' invoices listed immediately on receipt?
18. Are unmatched receiving reports reviewed frequently and investigated for proper recording?
19. Is statistical analysis used to examine overall purchasing levels?
20. Are vendors' monthly statements reconciled with individual accounts payable?

RIGHTS AND OBLIGATIONS

21. Are purchase contracts authorized at the appropriate level?
22. Is accounting notified of terms of significant contracts?

VALUATION OR ALLOCATION

23. In the accounts payable department, are invoices checked against purchase orders and receiving reports for dates, quantities, prices, and terms?
24. Does the accounting department check invoices for mathematical accuracy?
25. Is the accounts payable listing balanced periodically with the general ledger control account?
26. Does the accounting manual give instructions to date purchase/payable entries on the date of their receipt?

PRESENTATION AND DISCLOSURE

27. Do the chart of accounts and the accounting manual give instructions for classifying debit entries when purchases are recorded?
28. Are disclosures reviewed by appropriate officers?
29. Are journal entries authorized at appropriate levels?
30. Is accounts payable reconciled to the general ledger every period?
31. Are monthly statements reviewed by senior officials?

- Authorization procedures
  - The purchasing department authorizes the purchase of an item based on the purchase requisition.
  - The accounting department authorizes the recording of the liability based on the receiving document, the purchase order, and the vendor's invoice.
  - The accounting department determines that the expenditure is consistent with the organization's mission and that the transaction will be recorded in the correct financial statement accounts before it is approved for payment.
- Documented transaction trails
  - The accounting department compares the amount and description on the purchase order to the amount and description on the receiving report and on the invoice before the invoice is approved for payment.
  - The accounting department compares the price on the purchase order to the price on the invoice before the invoice is approved for payment.
  - The accounting department mathematically verifies the vendor's invoice.

- Independent reconciliations
  - Supervisory personnel review reports of expenses and inventory purchases to determine that they appear reasonable.
- Physical Controls
  - When goods are received, they are counted and a receiving report is prepared.
  - Access to inventory and other items purchased is restricted.

The only controls the auditor can test are those that are documented. Audit procedures to test these controls are listed in the following table. For example, to test the authorization controls, the employee must have initialed or signed the form when the control was performed. Auditors perform tests of controls to determine whether the internal control procedures developed by management are **designed** effectively and whether the controls are **operating.** The auditor selects from a variety of **audit procedures** such as inquiry, observation, inspection, and reperformance of a control. If the controls are not designed appropriately or are not operating properly, the auditor is to design substantive tests to determine whether the internal control failures have led to misstatements in the financial statement accounts. The auditor uses sampling to test internal controls.

Internal Control Tests

Inquiries of employees
Inspection of relevant documentation
Observation of the application of the control
Reperformance of the control

Consider an internal control test that an auditor might perform in the acquisition and expenditure business process after documenting the internal control system and finding several controls relevant to the completeness and existence assertions for accounts payable.

- The auditor considers segregation of duties that are documented in the control system. If one person performs all duties, testing internal controls would not be useful. In this case, different people perform the five duties described related to (1) purchase requisitions, (2) purchase orders, (3) receiving reports, (4) voucher requests, and (5) cash payments. Because this is a large company, it appears to have a good segregation of duties.
  - Segregation of duties is tested by the auditor through *inquiry* and *observation.*
  - The auditor asks the client about the processing of transactions and perform a walk-through to gather information about the process used to record purchase transactions.
  - Next the auditor *observes* on one day or on several days the processing of transactions to see how employees actually perform this task. At the end of the observation, the auditor should be able to determine whether the individuals perform the job assigned to them or share the work with other employees.
- Then the auditor selects for review a *sample* of accounts payable transactions taken from all twelve months (because internal controls must be effective for the entire year). Half of the sample is selected from the monthly voucher requests and half from the monthly receiving reports. The audit firm's policy determines the exact number of accounts payable transactions to review. The auditor reviews all documents related to the purchase function (purchase requisition, purchase order, receiving report, voucher request, and cash payment). The voucher requests should be filed by date in the client's computer or paper files. The voucher request document has all the other documents attached to it. The receiving reports are filed by date in the client's files. For the sample selected from the receiving reports, the auditor makes the selection from the receiving report but finds the documents in the voucher request file because that is where they are filed.

- The *sample* selected from two sources allows the auditor to gather evidence related to two assertions: existence and completeness. Items selected from the monthly voucher request register give the auditor evidence about existence (the validity of the purchase is verified by the fact that the goods were received). Items selected from the monthly receiving report give the auditor evidence about completeness (liabilities were recognized for all items received). The first procedure is called *vouching,* the second procedure *tracing.* The difference in the two is the direction of the testing. The auditor cannot get evidence about completeness from vouching. Selection of a sample from the voucher request register is limited to only the items that were recorded. In such a situation, gathering evidence about the items not recorded would be impossible.
- For the items selected, the auditor *inspects the documentation* to determine whether the controls are present (the internal control test is performed). The control is either the initial or the signature of the person performing the control on the voucher request or the existence of the relevant document in the voucher request file. For the transactions selected, the auditor looks for the following controls:
  - Receiving documentation exists for all vouchers selected from the voucher register. Any documentation missing would be a control deviation.
  - Voucher requests exist for all purchases selected from the receiving reports. Any receiving report without a voucher request would be a control deviation.
  - The purchasing department authorized the purchase of the item and indicated approval by initialing the purchase order.
  - The accounting department authorized the recording of the liability after reviewing the purchase order, the receiving document, and the vendor's invoice. The accounting department compared the amount and description of the goods on the invoice to those on the receiving report. After making this comparison, the appropriate person in the accounting department initials the voucher request under "quantity and description agreed," indicating that the comparison was made.
  - The accounting department compares the price on the purchase order to the price on the invoice before approving the invoice for payment and initials are on the voucher request under "price agreed," indicating that this control was performed.
  - The accounting department has determined that the expenditure is consistent with the organization's mission and that the asset or expense debited is the correct financial statement account. The accounting clerk initials the voucher request under "mission ok" to indicate that this control was performed.
  - If a voucher request lacks any of the initials indicating the controls were performed, this would be a control deviation.
- For the items in the *sample,* the auditor could also perform a substantive test of transactions (a dual-purpose test). This test usually involves an internal control test where the auditor *reperforms the control* by doing the following:
  - Compare the invoice quantity and description to the receiving quantity and description to find out whether they agree. Compare the invoice price to the purchase order price to determine whether the company recognized the expense in accordance with the original agreement. Review the expense for consistency with the organization's mission and for being properly recognized in the financial statements.

After performing this internal control test, the auditor determines whether internal control is effective based on the number of deviations found in the internal controls tested. Firm guidelines, rather than auditing standards, determine the number of deviations that are acceptable to conclude that controls are working (only automated controls are effective 100% of the time). At the end of internal control testing, the auditor can conclude that (1) internal controls are effective in preventing or detecting misstatements for the assertion tested for the significant accounts in the business process at the assessed level of control risk specified by the auditor or (2) internal controls are not effective. The result indicating that the controls are effective allows the auditor to reduce the amount of substantive testing for the relevant assertion for the significant account. If the determination is that internal controls are not effective, the auditor gathers evidence for the relevant assertion in the significant account *using only substantive testing.*

Substantive Tests for the Acquisition and Expenditure Process

LO7

Understand the methods auditors use to gather substantive evidence using analytical procedures, substantive tests of transactions, and substantive tests of balances

The auditing standards have described several procedures the auditor could use to gather evidence to evaluate whether the financial statements are prepared according to the applicable financial reporting framework. These procedures are listed in the following table. Analytical procedures are discussed after it because they are usually performed as part of the planning process. The other audit procedures are found under the key substantive tests.

Substantive Audit Procedures
Analytical procedures
Inspection of records, documents or tangible assets
Observation
Inquiry
Confirmation
Recalculation
Reperformance

The auditor uses these procedures to gather evidence about the accounts in this business process. This evidence will determine whether the financial statement accounts are prepared in accordance with the applicable financial reporting framework.

Analytical Procedures

An auditor often uses several types of analytical procedures as evidence for whether the financial statement accounts are prepared in accordance with the applicable financial reporting framework including the following:

1. Compare the financial statement numbers for the current year to the previous year. This includes calculating the dollar amount of the change and the percentage change.
2. Calculate financial ratios for the current financial statements and compare them to ratios for the prior year financial statements.
3. Consider nonfinancial measures in the evaluation of changes from one year to the next, such as the number of vendor accounts in the current year with those of the prior year.

In the acquisition and expenditure business process, the auditor could choose to perform the following analytical procedures:

1. Compare accounts payable, accrued liabilities, cost of goods sold, and the balance in all expense accounts for the current year to those of the prior year. Investigate changes from the auditor's expectations that appear to be unreasonable.
2. Calculate the gross margin percentage for the current and prior years. Investigate any changes from the auditor's expectations that appear to be unreasonable.
3. Consider the number of vendor accounts for the current year and the prior year and the new vendors added or lost in each year.

Selected Financial Information for BCS — Exhibit 6-6

	Year 3	% Change	Year 2	% Change	Year 1
Accounts payable	$1,400,000	26% ↓	$1,900,000	12% ↑	$1,700,000
Accrued payroll expense	600,000	25 ↓	800,000	14 ↑	700,000
Accrued fringe benefits	200,000	0	200,000	0	200,000
Sales revenue	12,000,000	20 ↑	10,000,000	5 ↑	9,500,000
Cost of goods sold	$7,200,000	11 ↑	$6,500,000	5 ↑	$6,175,000
Gross margin	4,800,000	37 ↑	3,500,000	8 ↑	3,325,000
Gross margin percentage	40	14 ↑	35	0	35
Selling expense	1,100,000	38% ↑	800,000	60% ↑	500,000
General expense	800,000	13 ↓	920,000	3 ↓	950,000
Administrative expense	1,200,000	9 ↑	1,100,000	19 ↑	926,000
Number of vendor accounts	2,200	12% ↓	2,500	2% ↓	2,550
New vendors added	200		100		75

How does an auditor know whether the change is unreasonable? Companies do not dramatically change from year to year *without a reason* (planned expansion, bad cash flow, or poor economic conditions), so large increases or decreases in the accounts can be unreasonable. To make the decision about whether a change is unreasonable, the auditor must be knowledgeable about (1) the client's industry, (2) current economic conditions, and (3) the business under audit.

Refer to Exhibit 6-6 for selected financial information related to the acquisition and expenditure process for BCS for three years.

Year 3 is the current year, which is under audit. Accounts payable decreased by $500,000, a 26% decrease from year 2 to year 3. The number of vendor accounts decreased from 2,500 to 2,200, and the company added 200 new vendors, so it lost 500 vendors. Why did it lose vendors? Have they been slow in paying their bills? Is the accounts payable total lower than last year because some of the accounts payable at year-end were not recorded?

Accrued payroll expense decreased by $200,000, or 25%, from year 2 to year 3. The auditor could ask the client why this account decreased this year. Accrued fringe benefits have been constant for three years. The auditor could ask the client what is in this account and why the accrual at year-end has remained unchanged for three years. It is unlikely that accrued payroll expense would decrease and fringe benefit expense remain constant. These two expenses usually change in a consistent fashion. Accrued payroll and fringe benefit expense are based on the number of days of salary expense and fringe benefits owed at year-end. If salary expense decreases, fringe benefit expense also decreases because there are fewer days to accrue expenses.

Selling expense has increased by $300,000 in each of the past two years (a 38% increase from year 2 to year 3 and a 60% increase from year 1 to year 2). General expense has declined by $120,000 in the current year and by $30,000 in the prior year (13% and 3% decreases, respectively). The increase in administrative expense was $100,000 in the current year and $174,000 in the prior year (a 9% increase from year 2 to year 3 and a 19% increase from year 1 to year 2).

If the business and the economy have been relatively stable in the last three years, several changes here appear *unreasonable:* (1) the decline in accounts payable, (2) the decline in the accrued payroll with no change in fringe benefit expense, (3) the large increase in selling expense, (4) the decrease in general expense, and (5) the increase in administrative expense. The auditor would gather information from the client through *inquiry* and would then evaluate the client's explanations.

The auditor would also calculate the gross margin percentage. This is one of the easiest ways to evaluate cost of goods sold. The gross margin percentage ([sales revenue minus cost of goods sold] divided by sales revenue) for a company is a remarkably constant percentage. If the cost of purchasing the inventory increases, the client often increases the sales price because the client needs to maintain a certain gross margin to cover operating expenses. The gross margin percentage for the company was 35% in year 1 and 2 but increased to 40% in year 3. So, in years 1 and 2, the client kept 35 cents from each sales dollar to cover operating expense, but in year 3, kept 40 cents of each sales dollar for operating expense. How did the client manage to increase the gross margin without losing sales? Gross margin percentages do not usually change so dramatically unless the client has made a change in pricing policies (that the auditor would likely be aware of). The change in gross margin percentage from year 2 to year 3 can indicate a misstatement in cost of goods sold.

The auditor uses analytical procedures to focus attention on accounts that have changed from the prior year. Changes from one year to the next can have been caused by "real" events or can indicate misstatements in the financial statements. Because the financial statements from the prior year were audited, the auditor uses them as a base for identifying unusual changes in the current year.

Substantive Tests of Transactions

The auditor uses substantive tests of transactions to gather evidence for income statement accounts in a business process. In the acquisition and expenditure business process, the income statement accounts are Cost of Goods Sold, Selling expenses, General expenses, and Administrative expenses. There can be numerous accounts in each category of selling, general, and administrative expenses.

The auditor can perform substantive tests of transactions for these accounts as part of the audit of the internal controls by using dual-purpose tests. These tests allow the auditor to select one sample of transactions and perform internal control and substantive tests of transactions on it. If the client does not have internal controls or if the auditor decides not to rely on internal controls for this business process, the auditor could perform only a substantive test of details. In this case, the auditor would not look for the controls but would instead perform the comparisons that are important in determining that the transactions and the account balances were prepared in accordance with the applicable financial reporting framework.

The key substantive tests of transactions for the acquisition and expenditure business process are in the following numbered list. The audit ***procedure*** used to perform the test is identified in bolded, italicized print and the **assertion** tested by the audit test is at the end of the test (in blue print). Depending on the amount of evidence gathered using internal control tests, the auditor may perform *some or all* of these audit procedures.

The key substantive tests of transactions for the acquisition and expenditure business process are as follows:

1. ***Inspection.*** Select a *sample* of voucher requests for the year. Determine that the:
   a. Quantity ordered is equal to the quantity received and the quantity billed
   b. Price on the invoice is equal to the price on the purchase order
   c. Purchase is consistent with the organization's mission
   d. Transaction is recorded correctly in the financial statements
   e. Purchase order was approved by the appropriate level of management—**existence, accuracy, classification.**

2. *Inspection.* Select a *sample* of receiving reports for the year. Determine that the:
   a. Liability was recorded correctly in the accounts payable journal
   b. Quantity ordered is equal to the quantity received and the quantity billed
   c. Price on the invoice is equal to the one on the purchase order
   d. Purchase is consistent with the organization's mission
   e. Transaction was recorded correctly in the financial statements
   f. Purchase order was approved by the appropriate level of management—**completeness, accuracy, classification.**

The preceding two tests are similar to the dual-purpose tests from the internal control example. After completing the substantive tests of transactions, the auditor determines whether the income statement accounts in the acquisition and expenditure process were prepared in accordance with the applicable financial reporting framework. An auditor who has evidence that they are not proposes an audit adjustment to the accounts based on the evidence gathered.

Substantive Tests of Balances

The auditor uses substantive tests of balances to gather evidence for balance sheet accounts in the acquisition and expenditure process. These accounts are accounts payable and accrued liabilities.

A company's inventory purchase, incurrence of expense, or purchase of fixed assets creates an accounts payable liability. This expense or asset provides the company a benefit before year-end, but the liability owed for the benefit received has not been paid at year-end. Because the accounts payable is listed as a current liability on the balance sheet, it should represent the amount of **cash** the audit client will pay on the accounts payable the following year. The auditor's concern is whether the account balance represents the future cash flow from the account according to the applicable financial reporting framework.

A list of the key substantive tests of balances for the acquisition and expenditure business process follow. The audit *procedure* used to perform the test precedes the test title (identified in bold italic type), and the **assertion** (in blue type) related to the audit test is at the end. Unlike the revenue business process, accounts payable confirmations are not required for the acquisition and expenditure process but can be used to gather evidence regarding the existence and completeness of the accounts payable balance. Depending on the amount of evidence gathered using internal control tests and the risk of material misstatement for the process, the auditor may perform *some or all* of the audit procedures listed.

The key substantive tests of balances for the acquisition and expenditure process are as follows:

1. *Inspection.* Select a *sample* of accounts payable from the accounts payable subsidiary ledger at year-end. Vouch these amounts to the purchase order, receiving report, and invoice in the voucher file—**existence, rights and obligations.**
2. *Inspection, inquiry.* Perform a search for unrecorded liabilities—**cutoff, completeness.**

The first test is similar to the one performed for substantive tests of transactions; the only difference is the sample population. For tests of transactions, the auditor must sample from the entire year because the test of transactions is for an income statement account. For tests of balances, the auditor samples only from the year-end accounts payable balance because the substantive test of balances is used to evaluate whether the year-end balance in accounts payable was prepared in accordance with the applicable financial reporting framework. Selecting a sample from the accounts payable subsidiary ledger gives the auditor evidence only about existence. Because completeness is the most important assertion for the acquisition and expenditure process, the search for unrecorded liabilities is the most important test the auditor performs for this business process.

Search for Unrecorded Liabilities

Searching for unrecorded liabilities is an audit procedure performed *after* year-end to determine whether the client had recorded all liabilities *at* year-end. This procedure is based on the premise that a company can avoid recording all liabilities at year-end but will not avoid paying for them in the following year. This procedure provides evidence related to the completeness assertion. During the search, the auditor gathers evidence to determine whether the client has potential unrecorded liabilities at year-end.

The following list is a set of tests the auditor uses to find liabilities that have not been recorded by the client at year-end. As previously, the audit **procedure** used to perform the test is identified in bold italic type, and the **assertion** (in blue type) related to the audit test is at the end. During the search for unrecorded liabilities, the auditor should:

1. *Make inquiry.* Ask the client about its procedures for determining that all liabilities were recorded at year-end. Document the information received from the client—**completeness**.
2. *Inspect documents.* Review the unmatched receiving report file. For all items in this file received before year-end, the auditor should determine whether a liability was recorded at year-end. If not, an adjusting entry should be proposed—**completeness**.
3. *Inspect documents.* Review the unmatched vendor invoice file. Ask the client about the invoices in the file. Have the goods been received? Why did the vendor bill the client for the goods before they were shipped if they have not been received? Do any of these invoices represent liabilities owed at year-end—**completeness**.
4. *Inspect records.* Review the cash disbursements for a period after year-end (for example, review cash disbursements for January 1 through January 20 for a December 31 year-end). Vouch the cash disbursements to the receiving report and vendor invoice and determine whether the liability was recorded in the correct time period. Propose adjusting entries for any items that should have been recorded as liabilities at year-end but were not—**completeness**.

These procedures to identify unrecorded liabilities at year-end constitute the "search for unrecorded liabilities." The client could avoid recording the liability at year-end, but it is more difficult for the client to avoid paying the bill the following year. Vendors tend to cut off customers that do not pay their bills. Reviewing the bills paid after year-end is an effective way to identify liabilities that were unrecorded at year-end. Additional procedures to identify unrecorded liabilities can be performed depending on the risk of material misstatement for the acquisition and expenditure process.

Additional procedures include these:

- Confirm accounts payable balances. The auditor should include accounts payables with zero balances and small accounts payable balances in the sample because they are the most likely to be understated. Accounts payable confirmations are not required by the auditing standards and are not used as frequently as accounts receivable confirmations. Confirmations primarily provide evidence about existence, and completeness is the main risk for accounts payable.
- Review the open purchase file for evidence of purchase commitments. Purchase commitments can require footnote disclosure at year-end.

What the Auditor Knows at This Point in the Audit

The auditor at this point should have *sufficient appropriate* evidence to determine whether the accounts in the acquisition and expenditure process—Accounts Payable, Accrued Liabilities, Cost of Goods Sold, and selling, general, and administrative expense—are presented on the financial statements in accordance with the applicable financial reporting framework. An auditor who does not have enough evidence to make this decision gathers more evidence. If the accounts in the business process are prepared in accordance with the applicable financial reporting framework, the auditor would conclude that the accounts are prepared in accordance with the applicable financial reporting framework.

Based on the results of the audit work performed, relevant assertions for the significant accounts in the acquisition and expenditure process are prepared in accordance with the applicable financial reporting framework. ICS

An auditor who has proposed audit adjustments would modify the preceding statement to read:

*Based on the results of the audit work performed, relevant assertions for the significant accounts in the acquisition and expenditure process are prepared in accordance with the applicable financial reporting framework, **except for the adjustments noted.*** ICS

All evidence the auditor has gathered to make this decision is kept in the audit work papers in which the auditor has recorded the evidence gathered from internal control tests, analytical procedures, substantive tests of transactions, and substantive tests of balances, including the particular items tested and the conclusions from all evidence reviewed.

Auditing Changes in Land, Building, Equipment, and Intangible Assets Accounts

LO8

Describe auditing procedures for tangible assets—land, building, and equipment—and intangible assets

During a year, a company (1) purchases land, building, equipment, or intangible assets, (2) disposes of land, building, equipment, or intangible assets, (3) records depreciation on building and equipment, and (4) values intangible assets at year-end. Transactions related to these accounts are reviewed during the acquisition and expenditure business process.

Transactions involving land, building, equipment, and intangible assets are relatively large in dollar amount and made less frequently than purchase transactions. Because they represent large expenditures of money, the board of directors often authorizes the transactions.

The auditor gathers evidence about the land, building, equipment, and intangible asset accounts by reviewing *changes* in them *during the year* and reviewing the valuation adjustments for certain intangible assets at the *end of the year.* When testing is done, the auditor can review all asset additions and disposals or can take a sample of asset additions and disposals to review.

The auditor may perform *some or all* of the audit procedures in the following list based on the level of risk assessed for land, building, equipment, and intangible asset changes. Key substantive tests for changes in the land, building, equipment, accumulated depreciation, and intangible asset accounts in the acquisition and expenditure process follow. The audit ***procedure*** used to perform the test precedes the test title (identified in bold italic type), and the assertion (in blue type) related to the audit test is at the end.

1. ***Inspect records.*** Compare the beginning balance in each account to the prior year's audited balance—**completeness, accuracy**.

2. ***Inspect documents.*** Examine invoices supporting the dollar amount of the additions to land, building, equipment, and intangible assets. The cost of a new asset (according to U.S. accounting standards) is the price paid for it including the costs for shipping and preparing the asset for use (for example, installation costs or costs for

wiring a new piece of equipment). The cost of a new asset according to international accounting standards also includes the cost of disposing of the asset at the end of its useful life—**existence, accuracy, classification**.

3. ***Inspect tangible assets.*** Inspect the new tangible asset additions—**existence**.

4. ***Inspect documents.*** Examine sales documents relating to the assets sold. Vouch the cash received to the cash receipts journal—**cutoff, accuracy**.

5. ***Recalculation.*** Recalculate the gain or loss on the sale of assets; it is the difference between the cash received and the asset's book value (cost less accumulated depreciation)—**accuracy**.

6. ***Recalculation.*** Recalculate the ending balance in the accounts—**completeness, accuracy**.

7. ***Inquiry, recalculation.*** Recalculate depreciation expense. Consider the reasonableness of the asset's life and salvage value—**accuracy**.

8. ***Inquiry, inspect documents.*** Examine the valuation of the tangible assets at year-end. Companies using U.S. GAAP should value tangible assets at depreciated cost at year-end. Companies using international accounting should value tangible assets at depreciated cost or fair value. Similar valuation should be used for each class of assets (IAS 16).

9. ***Inquiry, inspect records.*** Examine the valuation of the intangible asset accounts at year-end according to the applicable financial reporting framework. Under U.S. GAAP, if the fair value of the reporting unit is less than the carrying value, a decline in value is recognized. A company using IFRS as the applicable financial reporting framework will value intangible assets at amortized cost unless an active market exists for the intangible asset. Then the company could choose to value the intangible asset at fair value.

See Exhibit 6-7 for an example of a fixed asset schedule prepared by the client. To audit this schedule, the auditor would review the changes including the additions, deletions, and depreciation in the accounts for the year.

Review Exhibit 6-8, the work paper in which the auditor has documented the evidence regarding changes in the land, building, equipment, and intangible asset accounts. Clearly, the auditor has followed the audit program discussed previously to review the additions and deletions in the land, building, and equipment account and has documented the conclusion at the end of the review.

Auditing Accrued Liabilities

LO9

Explain audit procedures for accrued liabilities

Accrued Liabilities

Accounts payable are recorded for items when the company receives an invoice based on receiving services or goods from a vendor. *Accrued liabilities* are recorded for transactions when the company incurs an expense but has not recorded the liability for it because it has received no invoice or goods. Typical liabilities recorded in the accrued liability account include *accrued interest, accrued taxes, accrued payroll and fringe benefits, and accrued warranty.*

To audit a company's accrued liabilities, the auditor reviews the *activity* in the accrued liability account for the year under audit. The auditor (1) compares the beginning balance of the account to the prior year's ending balance, (2) reviews the payments recorded during the year against the liabilities, and (3) determines whether the amounts accrued in the account at the end of the year are correct. An example using accrued interest expense follows.

Assume that the company has a ten-year loan at 12% interest with interest payments due on April 1 and October 1 each year. The loan's principal is $300,000 and will be repaid at the end of the loan.

Date of Purchase	Description	Asset Cost (in dollars)				Accumulated Depreciation (in dollars)			
		Beginning Balance	Additions	Disposals	Ending Balance	Beginning Balance	Additions	Disposals	Ending Balance
1/1/06	Land	2,500,000		500,000	2,000,000				
9/1/06	Office building	40,000,000			40,000,000	6,933,000	1,600,000		8,533,000
3/1/11	Warehouse		12,000,000		12,000,000		400,000		400,000
4/1/11	Printing machines	13,000,000		2,000,000	11,000,000	4,468,750	1,604,167	916,667	5,156,250
7/1/09	Assembly machines	6,000,000			6,000,000	1,062,500	750,000		1,812,500
5/1/09	Delivery trucks	500,000	75,000		575,000	116,667	102,500		219,167
12/15/09	Goodwill	10,000,000			10,000,000				
	Total	$72,000,000	$12,075,000	$2,500,000	$81,575,000	$12,580,917	$4,456,667	$916,667	$16,120,917

Buildings are depreciated over twenty-five years. Printing and assembly equipment are depreciated over eight years and trucks are depreciated for five years. The company uses straight-line depreciation with no salvage value and calculates monthly depreciation. The new warehouse was purchased on March 1, 2011. The new delivery truck was purchased on November 1, 2011. On March 1, 2011, the land was sold for $8,000,000. The printing machine was disposed of on December 1, 2011, for $100,000.

Land, Building, and Equipment *For the Year Ending December 31, 2011* **Exhibit 6-8**

Reference:	F-1
Prepared by:	ICS
Date:	Feb. 14, 2012
Reviewed by:	BRT
Date:	Feb. 30, 2012

BCS Company
Inspection, Recalculation of Changes in Land, Building, Equipment, and Goodwill
For the Year Ended December 31, 2011

		Asset Cost			
Date of purchase (MM/DD/YY)	Description	Beginning Balance (in dollars)	Additions (in dollars)	Disposals (in dollars)	Ending Balance (in dollars)
1/1/06	Land	2,500,000√		500,000 €	2,000,000 γ
9/1/06	Office building	40,000,000√			40,000,000 γ
3/1/11	Warehouse		12,000,000 ∞ # x		12,000,000 γ
4/1/11	Printing machines	13,000,000√		2,000,000 €	11,000,000 γ
7/1/09	Assembly machines	6,000,000√			6,000,000 γ
5/1/09	Delivery trucks	500,000√	75,000 ∞ #		575,000 γ
12/15/09	Goodwill	10,000,000√			10,000,000 γ β
	Total	$72,000,000	$12,075,000	$2,500,000	$81,575,000
		f	f	f	f

		Accumulated Depreciation			
Date of purchase (MM/DD/YY)	Description	Beginning Balance (in dollars)	Additions (in dollars)	Disposals (in dollars)	Ending Balance (in dollars)
1/1/06	Land				
9/1/06	Office building	6,933,000	1,600,000 s		8,533,000
3/1/11	Warehouse		400,000 x		400,000
4/1/11	Printing machines	4,468,750	1,604,167 s	916,667 €	5,156,250
7/1/09	Assembly machines	1,062,500	750,000 s		1,812,500
5/1/09	Delivery trucks	116 667	102,500 s		219,167
12/15/09	Goodwill				
	Total	$12,580,917	$4,456,667	$916,667	$16,120,917
		f	f	f	f

Tickmark symbols ↓

∞	Examined invoices to support the amount of the addition.
#	Inspected the asset additions. They exist.
€	Examined the sales documents related to the assets sold. Recalculated gain and loss. Vouched the cash to the cash receipts journal.
β	Determined that the valuation of goodwill at year-end is in accordance with the applicable financial reporting framework. The fair value of the reporting unit with goodwill has not declined in the current year.

Reference:	F-1
Prepared by:	ICS
Date:	Feb. 14, 2012
Reviewed by:	BRT
Date:	Feb. 30, 2012

BCS Company
Inspection, Recalculation of Changes in Land, Building, Equipment, and Goodwill For the Year Ended December 31, 2011

Tickmark symbols ↓

√	Compared the balance in the account to the prior year's audited balance.
γ	Recalculated the ending balance in the accounts.
s	Recalculated depreciation expense.
x	Warehouse was purchased on March 1 but was not ready for use until Nov. 1 because of needed repairs. Depreciation should be $80,000, not $400,000. Adjustment proposed below.
f	Footed

Conclusion: Based on the results of test work performed, land, building, equipment, and goodwill appear to exist, be complete, and to be correctly valued with the exception noted at Dec. 31, 2011. *ICS*

PROPOSED AUDIT ADJUSTMENT

Accumulated Depreciation.......	320,000	
Depreciation Expense.......		320,000

To record 2 months of depreciation on the warehouse rather than 10 months. The warehouse was not ready for use until Nov. 1, 2011.

Accrued interest has a $9,000 balance at the beginning of the year (reflecting three months of interest owed but not paid at the end of the prior year for October through December). The company pays $18,000 for interest on the loan on April 1 and again on October 1 (six months of interest). The balance in the account at the end of the year is $9,000. Journal entries follow.

4/1	Accrued Interest..........................	9,000	
	Interest Expense..........................	9,000	
	Cash..........................		18,000
10/1	Interest Expense......................	18,000	
	Cash..........................		18,000
12/31	Interest Expense......................	9,000	
	Accrued Interest..................		9,000

For this loan, the accrued interest account should reflect $9,000 due at the end of each year (three months of interest that will be paid on April 1 of the following year).

Because three months have passed since the last interest payment, the company has incurred a liability and an expense for the interest owed.

The auditor reviews the accrued liability accounts to determine whether their balances are prepared in accordance with the applicable financial reporting framework. Comparing last year's balance with the current year's balance by using analytical procedures can help the auditor identify liabilities that have not been recorded in the current year. As with all liability accounts, the auditor must determine whether the client has recorded *all* accrued liabilities at year-end in accordance with the applicable financial reporting framework.

Did You Know?

The former chief executive officer of UnitedHealth, William McGuire, resigned as a result of deficiencies in the company's administration and accounting for stock option grants. The company restated earnings for three years and reduced net income by $286 million. The SEC conducted an informal inquiry into the option practices of UnitedHealth.

Companies grant stock options to give managers an incentive to increase the company's stock price. An option represents the right to purchase a share of stock in the future at a particular price. An individual stands to gain only if the stock price increases. The SEC has investigated whether the options were backdated to give executives additional pay even if the stock price failed to increase.

William McGuire earned nearly $200 million from stock options from 2002–2005. At the end of 2005, he held stock options with another $1.8 billion of unrealized gains, about $1.6 billion that can be exercised any time.

In a filing with the SEC, United Health stated that it had found "significant deficiencies" in the way it had administered, accounted for, and disclosed stock option grants and that it could be required to restate its earnings to account for stock-based compensation expense. According to corporate governance experts, this disclosure raises questions about the independence of UnitedHealth directors and whether management is acting in the best interests of the shareholders. The board denied management the authority to issue stock options and will handle all future stock option grants.

Sources: James Bandler and Charles Forelle, "UnitedHealth Cites 'Deficiency' in Option Grants," *The Wall Street Journal,* May 12, 2006.

Did the auditors notice the company's failure to record accrued compensation expense related to these stock options?

Disclosure Requirements for the Acquisition and Expenditure Business Process

LO10

Explain the disclosure requirements for accounts in the acquisition and expenditure business process

The auditor gathers evidence in the acquisition and expenditure business process to evaluate management's assertions about the presentation and disclosure of the related accounts.

Management's Assertions

Occurrence and rights and obligation—disclosed events and transactions pertaining to the company have occurred

Completeness—all disclosures that should have been made have been made

Classification and understandability—financial information is appropriately presented and described; disclosures are clearly expressed

Accuracy and valuation—financial information and all other information is disclosed fairly and at appropriate amounts (AU 314 and ISA 315)

Management prepares the financial statements and the footnotes to the financial statements. When management hands the financial statements to the auditor, it asserts that the accounts in the acquisition and expenditure process are presented according to the applicable financial reporting framework and that all required disclosures regarding the accounts have been made. The disclosures related to the financial statements are usually made in one of two places: (1) the footnotes to the financial statements or (2) the Management's Discussion and Analysis section of the annual report.

Did You Know?

The former chief executive officer of Kmart, Charles C. Conway, and the former chief financial officer, John T. McDonald, were charged with preparing materially false and misleading disclosure about Kmart's liquidity in the Management Discussion and Analysis (MD&A) section of the 10-Q for the third quarter of 2001.

In the MD&A section, Kmart attributed its increase in inventory to "seasonal inventory fluctuations and actions taken to improve our overall in-stock position." This explanation was erroneous. In the summer of 2001, Kmart's chief operating officer, Mark Schwartz, made an $850 million inventory purchase to support the Blue Light Always program. When executives learned of the purchase, they decided to save cash by slowing down the payment of accounts payable. The project was known internally as Project Slow It Down. Kmart lied about the reason for the slowdown, blaming a software glitch for the slower payments. Of the $718 million increase in accounts payable in the third quarter of 2001, the company failed to disclose that at least $570 million was past due and had been deliberately withheld.

According to the SEC, Kmart management failed to "honestly inform investors that Kmart faced a liquidity crisis in the third quarter of 2001, how the company's own ill-advised action had caused the problem, and what steps management took to respond to it."

Kmart agreed to buy Sears, Roebuck, and Co in 2004, and both companies continue to operate under Sears Holding Corp.

Sources: Amy Merrick, "Kmart Ex-Officers Are Accused by SEC of Misleading Investors," *The Wall Street Journal,* August 24, 2005; "Text of SEC Statement on Charges Against Former Kmart Officials," *The Wall Street Journal,* August 23, 2005; Siobhan Hughes, "Former Kmart Executives Face SEC Fraud Allegations," *The Wall Street Journal,* August 23, 2005.

Where were the auditors in reviewing the financial disclosures made by management?

To evaluate the presentation and disclosure assertions made by management, the auditor should review the financial statements, footnote disclosures, and the disclosures made in the MD&A section to determine whether they are presented in accordance with the applicable financial reporting framework. The financial statement accounts and footnotes related to the acquisition and expenditure process for General Mills presented in Exhibit 6-9 are in bold type.

To evaluate the presentation and disclosure assertion made by management, the auditor should review management's financial statements and footnote disclosures to determine whether they are in accordance with the applicable financial reporting framework.

Activities relating to the acquisition and expenditures process are reflected in the cash flow from operations and the investing section of the statement of cash flows. Changes in accounts payable are reflected as increases or decreases in cash from operations, depending on the direction of the change. For General Mills, cash flow increased by $159.8 million in 2008 because accounts payable increased from $777.9 million to $937.3 million from 2007 to 2008. Purchases of land, building, and equipment are listed as uses of cash in the investing section. General Mills' cash decreased by $522 million in 2008 and $460.2 million in 2007 related to asset purchases. Proceeds from the sale of land, building, and equipment are listed as sources of cash in the statement of cash flows. General Mills' cash increased by $25.9 million in 2008 and by $13.8 million in 2007 related to sales of land, building, and equipment.

Acquisition and Expenditure Business Process Accounts and Disclosures for General Mills

Exhibit 6-9

CONSOLIDATED STATEMENTS OF INCOME
GENERAL MILLS, INC. AND SUBSIDIARIES

	Fiscal Year		
In Millions	2008	2007	2006
Net Sales	$13,652.1	$12,441.5	$11,711.3
Cost of sales	8,778.3	7,955.1	7,544.8
Selling, general, and administrative costs	2,625.0	2,389.3	2,177.7
Restructuring, impairment, and other exit costs	21.0	39.3	29.8
Operating Profit	$ 2,227.8	$ 2,057.8	$ 1,959.0

CONSOLIDATED BALANCE SHEETS
GENERAL MILLS, INC. AND SUBSIDIARIES

In Millions	May 25, 2008	May 28, 2007
Assets:		
Goodwill	$6,786.1	$6,836.4
Other intangible assets	3,777.2	3,694.0
	. . . .	. . . .
Total assets	19,041.6	18,183.6
Current liabilities:		
Accounts payable	937.3	777.9
Current portion of long-term debt	442.0	1,734.0
Notes payable	2,208.8	1,254.4
Other current liabilities	1,239.8	2,078.8
Deferred income taxes	28.4	00.0
Total current liabilities	$ 4,856.3	$ 5,845.1

CONSOLIDATED STATEMENTS OF CASH FLOWS
GENERAL MILLS, INC. AND SUBSIDIARIES

	Fiscal Year		
In Millions	2008	2007	2006
Cash Flows–Operating Activities			
Net earnings	$1,294.7	$1,143.9	$1,090.3
Adjustments to reconcile earnings to cash:			
Depreciation and amortization	459.2	417.8	423.9
After-tax earnings from joint ventures	(110.8)	(72.7)	(69.2)
Stock-based compensation	133.2	127.1	44.6
Deferred income taxes	98.1	26.0	25.9
Distributions of earnings from joint ventures	108.7	45.2	77.4
Tax benefit on exercises options	(55.7)	(73.1)	40.9

Pension and other benefits costs	(24.8)	(53.6)	(74.2)
Restructuring, impairment, and other exit costs	(1.7)	39.1	29.8
Changes in current assets, liabilities (except accounts payable)	(286.5)	44.1	168.9
Change in accounts payable	**159.8**	**105.0**	**15.0**
Other, net	(44.3)	2.4	70.2
Net cash provided by operating activities	1,729.9	1,751.2	1,843.5
Cash Flows–Investing Activities			
Purchases of land, buildings, and equipment	**(522.0)**	**(460.2)**	**(360.0)**
Acquisitions	0.6	(83.4)	(26.5)
Investments in Affiliates, net	64.6	(100.5)	0.3
Proceeds from disposal of land, buildings, and equipment	**25.9**	**13.8**	**11.3**
Proceeds from disposal of product lines	0.0	13.5	0.0
Other, net	(11.5)	19.7	4.9
Net cash used by investing activities	(442.4)	(597.1)	(370.0)

NOTES TO CONSOLIDATED FINANCIAL STATEMENTS
GENERAL MILLS, INC. AND SUBSIDIARIES

Note 2. Summary of Significant Accounting Policies

Land, Buildings, Equipment, and Depreciation. Land is recorded at historical cost. Buildings and equipment, including capitalized interest and internal engineering costs, are recorded at cost and depreciated over estimated useful lives, primarily using the straight-line method. Ordinary maintenance and repairs are charged to cost of sales. Buildings are usually depreciated over 40 to 50 years, and equipment, furniture, and software are usually depreciated over 3 to 15 years. Fully depreciated assets are retained in buildings and equipment until disposal. When an item is sold or retired, the accounts are relieved of its cost and related accumulated depreciation; the resulting gains and losses, if any, are recognized in earnings. As of May 2008, assets held for sale were insignificant.

Long-lived assets are reviewed for impairment whenever events or changes in circumstances indicate that the carrying amount of an asset (or asset group) may not be recoverable. An impairment loss would be recognized when estimated undiscounted future cash flows from the operation and disposition of the asset group are less than the carrying amount of the asset group. Asset groups have identifiable cash flows and are largely independent of other asset groups. Measurement of an impairment loss would be based on the excess of the carrying amount of the asset group over its fair value. Fair value is measured using a discounted cash flow model or independent appraisals, as appropriate.

Goodwill and Other Intangible Assets. Goodwill is not amortized and is tested for impairment annually and whenever events or changes in circumstances indicate that impairment may be occurred. Impairment testing is performed for each of our reporting units. We compare the carrying value of a reporting unit, including goodwill, to the fair value of the unit. Carrying value is based on the assets and liabilities associated with the operations of that reporting unit, which often requires allocation of shared or corporate items among reporting units. If the carrying amount of a reporting unit exceeds its fair value, we revalue all assets and liabilities of the reporting unit, excluding goodwill, to determine if the fair value of the net assets is greater than the net assets including goodwill. If the fair value of the net assets is less than the net assets including goodwill, impairment has occurred. Our estimates of fair value are determined based on a discounted cash flow model. Growth rates for sales and profits are determined using inputs from our annual long-range planning process. We also make estimates of discount rates, perpetuity growth assumptions, market comparables, and other factors.

We evaluate the useful lives of our other intangible assets, primarily intangible assets associated with the *Pillsbury, Totino's, Progresso, Green Giant, Old El Paso, Häagen-Dazs,* and *Uncle Tobys* brands, to determine if they are finite or indefinite-lived. We determine useful lives by considering future effects of obsolescence, demand, competition, other economic factors (such as the stability of the industry, known technological advances, legislative action that results in an uncertain or changing regulatory environment, and expected changes in distribution channels), the level of required maintenance expenditures, and the expected lives of other related groups of assets.

Our indefinite-lived intangible assets, primarily brands, also are tested for impairment annually, and whenever events or changes in circumstances indicate their carrying value may not be recoverable. We performed our fiscal 2008 assessment of our brand intangibles as of December 1, 2007. Our estimate of the fair value of the brands was based on a discounted cash flow model using inputs which included: projected revenues from our annual long-range plan; assumed royalty rates that could be payable if we did not own the brands; and a discount rate.

continued

Acquisition and Expenditure Business Process Accounts and Disclosures for General Mills   *concluded*

Note 6. Goodwill and Other Intangible Assets

The components of goodwill and other intangible assets are as follows:

In Millions	May 25, 2008	May 27, 2007
Goodwill	$ 6,786.1	$ 6,835.4
Other intangible assets:		
Brands	3,745.6	3,681.9
Intangible assets subject to amortization:		
Patents, trademarks, and other finite-lived Intangibles	44.0	19.2
Less accumulated amortization	(12.4)	(7.1)
Total goodwill and other intangible assets	$10,563.3	$10,529.4

Note 17. Supplemental Information

The components of certain Consolidated Balance Sheet accounts are as follows:

In Millions	May 25, 2008	May 27, 2007
Land, buildings, and equipment Land	$ 61.2	$ 60.7
Buildings	1,550.4	1,518.6
Equipment	4,216.4	3,991.7
Assets under capital lease	64.7	23.9
Capitalized software	234.8	225.1
Construction in progress	343.8	275.7
Total land, buildings, and equipment	6,471.3	6,095.7
Less accumulated depreciation	(3,363.2)	(3,081.8)
Total	$3108.1	$3,013.9

In Millions	May 25, 2008	May 27, 2007
Other current liabilities		
Accrued payroll	$ 364.1	$ 355.7
Accrued Interest	146.8	165.5
Accrued trade and consumer promotions	446.0	410.1
Accrued taxes	66.9	861.2
Derivatives payable	8.1	2.6
Accrued customer advances	17.3	6.8
Miscellaneous	190.6	276.9
Total	$1,239.8	$2,078.8

Chapter Takeaways

The acquisition and expenditure cycle is an important business process for the auditor. Incentives to misstate liabilities and expenses are great because the payoff is so high in terms of the impact on net income. The audit procedures in this process of testing internal controls and performing substantive tests should be performed with professional skepticism. The auditor should consider the risk that misstatements can occur in the recording of liabilities and expenses and gather sufficient appropriate evidence to determine that the accounts in the business process are prepared in accordance with the financial reporting framework at the end of the year.

This chapter presented these important facts:

- The transactions recorded in the acquisition and expenditure business process, the accounting rules related to these transactions, and the importance of this process to the financial statements.
- The susceptibility of the acquisition and expenditures process to fraud.
- The importance of *professional skepticism* in planning and performing audit procedures.
- The approach the auditor uses to gather evidence to support the assertion of *completeness,* including specific *internal control tests* performed in the process, and *substantive tests of balances* and *transactions* for the process.
- The importance of the completeness assertion for the acquisition and expenditure process because expenses and liabilities tend to be understated.
- The importance of internal controls in the acquisition and expenditure process because of the volume of transactions in the process and the significance of expenses to the overall financial statements.
- The important of the *disclosures* made by the client related to the transactions recorded in the business process.
- How to audit accrued liabilities and land, building, equipment, and intangible assets.

Be sure you understand these concepts before you go to the next chapter.

Review Questions

LO1 1. Describe the activities in the acquisition and expenditure business process. Write journal entries that would be used to record these transactions.

LO1 2. What is the most important account in this process? Describe the misstatement that is most likely to occur for this account.

LO2 3. List the main documents used in the acquisition and expenditure business process. Describe the purpose of each document and whether it is prepared by the firm or originates outside the firm.

LO3 4. Explain the accounting rules applicable to accounts in the expenditure and acquisitions process including:
   a. Liability
   b. Expense

LO4 5. Are understatement errors or overstatement errors more likely to occur in the expenditure and acquisition process? Explain why.

LO4 6. Identify the misstatements that are likely to occur in this process. Explain how the auditor considers the risk of fraud in it.

LO5 7. Describe management's assertions for the acquisition and expenditure process. Which assertion is the most important? Explain why this is so.

LO6   8. How does the auditor assess control risk for the acquisition and expenditure process? Is the auditor likely to test internal controls for this process? Explain your answer.

LO6   9. Describe the audit procedures used by the auditor to test internal controls.

LO6   10. Describe key internal controls for this process.

LO7   11. What substantive tests of transactions are typically performed for this process?

LO7   12. Describe the substantive tests of balances that are conducted for the acquisition and expenditure process. Identify the assertions associated with the tests.

LO7   13. Describe the search for unrecorded liabilities. Explain why this is an important test for this business process.

LO10   14. Explain how the accounts from this process have an impact on the financial statements. What are the presentation and disclosure issues associated with this process?

LO9   15. What are accrued liabilities? How does the auditor determine that the amount recorded in accrued liabilities is accurate?

LO8   16. Describe how property, plant, and equipment are audited.

Multiple Choice Questions from CPA Examinations

LO7   17. Which of the following comparisons would an auditor most likely make in evaluating an entity's costs and expenses?
   a. The current year's accounts receivable with the prior year's accounts receivable.
   b. The current year's payroll expense with the prior year's payroll expense.
   c. The budgeted current year's sales with the prior year's sales.
   d. The budgeted current year's warranty expense with the current year's contingent liabilities.

LO4   18. The auditor will most likely perform extensive tests for possible understatements of
   a. Revenues.
   b. Assets.
   c. Liabilities.
   d. Capital.

LO8   19. In testing plant and equipment balances, an auditor can inspect new additions listed on the analysis of plant and equipment. This procedure is designed to obtain evidence concerning management's assertion of

	Existence or Occurrence	Presentation and Disclosure
a.	Yes	Yes
b.	Yes	No
c.	No	Yes
d.	No	No

LO7   20. Which of the following procedures would an auditor most likely perform in searching for unrecorded liabilities?
   a. Trace a sample of accounts payable entries recorded just before year-end to the unmatched receiving report file.
   b. Compare a sample of purchase orders issued just after year-end with the year-end accounts payable trial balance.
   c. Vouch a sample of cash disbursements recorded just after year-end to receiving reports and vendor invoices.
   d. Scan the cash disbursements entries recorded just before year-end for indications of unusual transactions.

LO7   21. When using confirmations to provide evidence about the completeness assertion for accounts payable, the appropriate population most likely would be
   a. Vendors with whom the entity has previously done business.
   b. Amounts recorded in the accounts payable subsidiary ledger.
   c. Payees of checks drawn in the month after the year-end.
   d. Invoices filed in the entity's open invoice file.

LO7   22. Auditor confirmation of accounts payable balances at the balance sheet date can be unnecessary because
   a. This is a duplication of cutoff tests.
   b. Accounts payable balances at the balance sheet date cannot be paid before the audit is completed.
   c. Correspondence with the audit client's attorney will reveal all legal action by vendors for nonpayment.
   d. There is likely to be other reliable external evidence to support the balances.

LO7   23. Which of the following is a substantive test that an auditor most likely would perform to verify the existence and valuation of recorded accounts payable?
   a. Investigating the open purchase order file to ascertain that prenumbered purchase orders are used and accounted for.
   b. Receiving the client's mail, unopened, for a reasonable period of time after the year-end to search for unrecorded vendors' invoices.
   c. Vouching selected entries in the accounts payable subsidiary ledger to purchase orders and receiving reports.
   d. Confirming accounts payable balances with known suppliers who have zero balances.

LO5   24. In auditing accounts payable, an auditor's procedures most likely would focus primarily on management's assertions of
   a. Existence or occurrence.
   b. Presentation and disclosure.
   c. Completeness.
   d. Valuation or allocation.

LO7   25. To determine whether accounts payable are complete, an auditor performs a test to verify that all merchandise received is recorded. The population of documents for this test consists of all
   a. Payment vouchers.
   b. Receiving reports.
   c. Purchase requisitions.
   d. Vendors' invoices.

LO7   26. An auditor traced a sample of purchase orders and the related receiving reports to the purchases journal and the cash disbursements journal. The purpose of this substantive audit procedure most likely was to
   a. Identify unusually large purchases that should be investigated further.
   b. Verify that cash disbursements were for goods actually received.
   c. Determine that purchases were properly recorded.
   d. Test whether payments were for goods actually ordered.

Discussion Questions and Research Problems

LO6, LO7   27. **Internal control questionnaire.** The following questions are part of an internal control questionnaire for the acquisition and expenditure process. For each question:
   a. Describe the misstatement in the financial statements that could occur if the client answers "no."
   b. Explain how you would design a substantive test to evaluate the potential misstatement in the financial statements due to the missing control.

   c. If the client answers "yes" to the question, describe an internal control that it could use.

   d. Describe how you could test the internal control described in part (c).

Internal control questions:

1. Are all purchases made only on the basis of approved purchase requisitions?
2. Are the purchasing department, accounting department, receiving department, and shipping department independent of each other?
3. Do managers compare actual expenses to budget?
4. Are invoices approved for payment by a responsible officer?
5. Are unmatched receiving reports reviewed frequently and investigated for proper recording?
6. Does the accounting manual give instructions to date purchase/payable entries on the date of receipt of goods?

LO6, LO7   28. **Internal control tests.** An important control in the acquisition and expenditure process is the accounts payable clerk's comparison of the vendor invoices with the purchase orders and the receiving reports for dates, quantities, prices, and terms.

   a. Describe the misstatement in the financial statements that could occur if this control is not present.

   b. Explain how you would design a substantive test to evaluate the potential misstatement in the financial statements if the control is missing.

   c. Describe how you could test the internal control.

LO6, LO7   29. **Internal control questionnaire.** The following questions are part of an internal control questionnaire for the acquisition and expenditure process. The client has been asked to answer the questions for the acquisition and expenditure process:

   a. Are competitive bids received and reviewed for certain items?

   b. Are receiving reports prepared for each item received and copies transmitted to the inventory storerooms, the purchasing department, and the accounting department?

   c. Are vouchers cancelled with a PAID stamp when paid?

   d. Are purchase order forms and receiving report forms prenumbered and the numerical sequence checked for missing documents?

For each question:

(1) Describe the misstatement in the financial statements that could occur if the client answered the question "no."

(2) Explain how you would design a substantive test to evaluate the potential misstatement in the financial statements due to the missing control.

(3) If the client answers "yes" to the question, describe an internal control that the client could use.

(4) Describe how you could test the internal control described in part (3).

LO9   30. **Auditing warranty expense.** Massarra's Photos sells memory cards for digital cameras on the Internet, by catalog, and in numerous retail stores. The items are sold with a 90-day money-back guarantee. The customer can return any item within 90 days of purchase for replacement if it fails to work. At the end of each year, Massarra's records an accrual for warranty expense related to the potential claims at the end of the year. In your review of the warranty expense account, you note that sales for the last six months of year were $10,800,000. Sales for the fourth quarter totaled $6,400,000. The gross margin for this business is 45%.

   a. If 1% of sales are returned, what is your estimate of warranty expense at year-end?

   b. How would you determine whether management's estimate that 1% of all sales were returned is accurate?

   c. Propose an audit adjustment if the correct return rate is 1.25%.

LO7   31. **Auditing travel and entertainment expense.** The Wellness Center is a nonprofit residential treatment center for mentally disturbed teenagers. You have been assigned to review the travel and entertainment account for this client. During your review, you find expenses related to the following items:

- A receipt for $12,800 for yacht insurance.
- A bill from a hotel in Chicago for $800 for cigars purchased during a convention.
- A receipt for $8,000 for a helicopter tour in Hawaii taken during a corporate meeting.
- A bill for $4,000 for golf lessons for the spouses and children of managers who were attending a training session held in Florida.

a. Describe how you would audit expenses listed in the travel and entertainment account.

b. Prepare several questions that you would ask management in regard to these expenses.

c. Describe the internal controls that could be in place to prevent or detect misstatements in the expense accounts. What internal control could be effective for travel and entertainment expenses for nonprofit companies?

d. Is your decision regarding internal control or the nature of these expenses different for a public company? Explain your answer.

LO7   32. **Search for unrecorded liabilities.** Consider the audit procedure referred to as the "search for unrecorded liabilities."

a. How does the auditor perform it?

b. When does the auditor perform it?

c. What is its purpose?

d. Describe the assertions associated with the search for unrecorded liabilities. Explain why these assertions are important for the acquisition and expenditure process.

e. Identify the accounts that can be misstated if a search for unrecorded liabilities is not conducted.

f. If these accounts are misstated, how will outsiders be affected? Explain your answer.

LO7   33. **Expense account credit entries.** During your audit of several expense accounts in the acquisition and expenditure process, you notice several credit entries to them.

a. Identify several questions that you should ask of management regarding the credit entries.

b. Describe three possible scenarios to explain the credit entries in the expense accounts.

LO8   34. The fixed asset schedule for BCS Manufacturing at December 31, 2011, follows.

Date of Purchase	Description	Asset Cost (in dollars)				Accumulated Depreciation (in dollars)			
		Beginning Balance	Additions	Disposals	Ending Balance	Beginning Balance	Additions	Disposals	Ending Balance
1/1/92	Land	4,000,000		200,000	3,800,000				
4/1/93	Office building	35,000,000			35,000,000	21,874,998	1,600,000		23,474,998
9/1/93	Warehouse	8,000,000			8,000,000	4,888,888	266,667		5,155,555
1/1/94	Factory equipment	17,000,000			17,000,000	12,750,000	2,125,000		14,875,000
11/1/07	Delivery trucks	500,000	75,000		575,000	116,667	100,000		216,667
	Total	$64,500,000	$75,000	$200,000	$64,375,000	$39,630,553	$4,091,667		$43,722,220

Buildings are depreciated over thirty years. Factory equipment is depreciated over eight years, and trucks are depreciated for five years. The company uses straight-line depreciation with no salvage value and calculates monthly depreciation. The new delivery truck was purchased on November 1, 2011. On March 1, 2011, the land was sold for $8,000,000. The client recognized a gain of $7,800,000 on the sale of the land. You have been assigned to audit this schedule at year-end.

a. What is the balance for fixed assets shown on the balance sheet prepared by the client? In other words, what is the balance for which you are gathering evidence to support or correct?

b. Describe the audit procedures necessary to determine whether the ending balances are correct.

c. Perform the review needed to arrive at a decision regarding the balances. Do you think the client's calculations are accurate?

d. Evaluate the gain or loss recognized by the client for the asset disposals.

e. Propose the adjusting entry needed to correct the accounts.

f. What balance will be reported on the balance sheet if the proposed audit adjustments are recorded?

Real-World Auditing Problems

LO4, LO6   35. **Rite-Aid**

Review the description of the Rite-Aid accounting fraud described in the chapter.

a. Describe the audit procedures that could have discovered the misstatements and explain why these procedures might be effective.

b. Is it likely that internal controls would have been effective in preventing or detecting the fraud? Explain why.

LO4   36. **Rent-Way**

Refer to the information regarding the Rent-Way fraud in the chapter. Matthew Marini, its controller, described his accounting manipulations as merely "pushing the accounting rules." Do you think his description is accurate? Did outsiders receive information that was "free from bias" and designed to represent the "economic reality" of the transactions?

LO4, LO7   37. **WorldCom**

The WorldCom fraud described in the chapter involved a simple earnings manipulation through which the company capitalized expenses to increase net income. This transaction was recorded by a journal entry to debit capital assets and credit expenses.

a. Describe the substantive audit procedures that an auditor could use to determine whether financial statements are misstated by capitalizing expenses.

b. Identify analytical procedures that could have helped the auditor identify the risk of fraud at WorldCom.

LO4, LO7   38. **Fleming**

The Fleming fraud involved an expense manipulation designed to increase net income.

a. Describe a substantive audit procedure that an auditor could use to determine whether financial statements are misstated by early recording of purchase rebates.

b. Why do you think that the SEC held the suppliers responsible for perpetrating the fraud? Should companies be held responsible for the actions of its customers? Give reasons.

LO4, LO7   39. **Adelphia**

Refer to the facts described in the chapter relating to the fraud case involving Adelphia Communications.

a. What **assertion** did Adelphia violate? Explain how Adelphia prepared financial statements that violated this management assertion.

b. Describe how the auditor could design substantive audit procedures to determine whether the amount of debt reported on the financial statements is materially misstated.

c. How are outsiders harmed when debt is not recorded on the financial statements? In such a situation, does the information received by outsiders represent the "economic reality" of the transactions? Is the information outsiders received "unbiased"? Would you like to be an outsider making decisions based on inaccurate debt information? Explain your answer.

LO4, LO5, LO7   40. **UnitedHealth**

Consider the case of backdated stock options as reported in the chapter for UnitedHealth.

a. What happens to the financial statements when options are backdated and the company fails to record compensation expense? Do outsiders receive information that is materially misstated?

b. Describe two management assertions violated when a company fails to record compensation expense related to backdated stock options.

c. Describe a substantive audit procedure that an auditor could use to determine whether financial statements are misstated through backdating of stock options.

Internet Assignment

LO4   41. Go to the website for the SEC (www.sec.gov) and identify a company that has been cited for expense recognition problems. Describe the problem and identify the accounting principle that the company violated.

Auditing the Inventory Business Process

Learning Objectives

After studying this chapter, you should be able to:

1. Describe the inventory business process.
2. Explain the transactions in the inventory process.
3. Understand an applicable financial reporting framework (GAAP) for recording transactions in the inventory business process.
4. Describe misstatements (errors and fraud) that could occur in the inventory process.
5. Explain management's assertions for accounts in the inventory process.
6. Identify relevant assertions for the inventory process.
7. Describe the methods the auditor uses to gather evidence for internal controls in the inventory process.
8. Understand the substantive tests auditors use to gather evidence in the inventory process.
9. Explain the procedures for the physical inventory count.
10. Understand the importance of FIFO and LIFO pricing of inventory and the year-end valuation of inventory.
11. Describe the disclosure requirements for the inventory business process.

Auditing and accounting standards relevant to this topic

For private companies

- **FASB Statement of Financial Accounting Concepts No. 5,** Recognition and Measurements in Financial Statements of Business Enterprises.
- **FASB Statement of Financial Accounting Concepts No. 6,** Elements of Financial Statements.
- **AU 110,** Responsibilities and Functions of the Independent Auditor
- **AU 318,** Performing Audit Procedures in Response to Assessed Risks and Evaluating the Audit Evidence Obtained
- **AU Section 326,** Audit Evidence
- **AU 329,** Analytical Procedures
- **AU 331,** Audit Evidence—Specific Considerations for Selected Items
- **AU 339,** Audit Documentation
- **Preface to Codification of Statements on Auditing Standards,** Overall Objectives of the Independent Auditor and the Conduct of an Audit in Accordance with Generally Accepted Auditing Standards

For public companies

- **FASB Statement of Financial Accounting Concepts No. 5,** Recognition and Measurements in Financial Statements of Business Enterprises.
- **FASB Statement of Financial Accounting Concepts No. 6,** Elements of Financial Statements.
- **AU 110,** Responsibilities and Functions of the Independent Auditor (Interim Standards Adopted by PCAOB)
- **AU 329,** Analytical Procedures (Interim standard adopted by PCAOB)
- **AU 331,** Inventories (Interim standard adopted by PCAOB)
- **PCAOB Auditing Standard No. 3,** Audit Documentation
- **PCAOB Auditing Standard No. 15,** Audit Evidence

International standards

- **ISA 230,** Audit Documentation
- **ISA 500,** Audit Evidence
- **ISA 501,** Audit Evidence—Additional Considerations for Specific Items
- **ISA 520,** Analytical Procedures

Chapter Overview

This chapter discusses auditing procedures used to review a specific class of transactions. In the inventory process, the auditor considers transactions recorded at year-end including (1) counting inventory, (2) pricing inventory according to LIFO, FIFO, or average cost, and (3) valuing inventory according to the lower of cost or market rule. The audit of this business process primarily concerns the inventory *balance* at year-end. The *transactions* related to this business process are audited in other processes. Transactions related to the purchase of inventory are discussed in the acquisition and expenditure process. Transactions relevant to the sale of inventory are discussed in the revenue process. This chapter is part of the testing phase of the audit. Exhibit 7-1 summarizes the main steps in the audit process.

Gathering evidence to support the financial statement accounts in the inventory business process is important to the overall audit process. If the client has inventory, usually it is a highly significant account on the balance sheet. The accounting rules for inventory are more complex than those for many other accounts on the financial statements, and this complexity increases the risk of material misstatement associated with the account.

Overview of the Inventory Process

LO1

Describe the inventory business process

The inventory process involves both income statement and balance sheet accounts. On the income statement, the inventory process is related to *Cost of Goods Sold.* Adjustments to the ending inventory balance are always recorded against cost of goods sold. On the balance sheet, the inventory process includes an *inventory* and an *allowance account* for the LIFO adjustment to inventory if the company uses LIFO to determine the cost of its inventory. As with all business processes, the auditor is concerned with determining that the income statement transactions were recorded correctly during the year according to the applicable reporting framework (GAAP) and that the balances on the balance sheet are correct at year-end according to the applicable financial reporting framework. See Exhibit 7-2 for the accounts included in the process.

As with all income statement accounts, the expense accounts begin the year with a zero balance. Transactions for the entire year are recorded in the accounts. Normally, no credit entries are made to expense accounts or debit entries made to revenue accounts. The totals at the year-end in the revenue and expense accounts reflect **all** transactions

| The Audit Process | Exhibit 7-1 |

Steps in the Audit Process	Discussed in this Section
Planning Phase	
Consider the Preconditions for an Audit and Accept or Reject the Audit Engagement	
Understand the Entity and Its Environment, Determine Materiality, and Assess the Risks of Material Misstatements	
Develop an Audit Strategy and an Audit Plan to Respond to the Assessed Risks	
Testing Phase	
Test Internal Controls? Yes No	√
Perform Tests of Controls if "Yes"	√
Perform Substantive Tests of Transactions	√
Perform Substantive Tests of Balances	√
Assess the Likelihood of Material Misstatement	√
Decision Phase	
Review the Presentation and Disclosure Assertions	√
Evaluate the Evidence to Determine Whether the Financial Statements Are Prepared in Accordance with the Applicable Financial Reporting Framework	
Issue Audit Report	
Communicate with the Audit Committee	

recorded during the year, and this is the total that the auditor is responsible for gathering evidence to support. The auditor must determine whether the transactions recorded in these accounts during the year have been recorded in accordance with the applicable financial reporting framework.

The totals in the balance sheet accounts reflect only the amounts in the accounts on the last day of the year. They do not reflect all transactions recorded during the year but the *net* amount of the transactions recorded during it. The balance sheet accounts have a beginning balance on the first day of the year, which reflects the ending (audited) balance from the prior year. During the year, increases and decreases in the balance sheet accounts are recorded in the accounts. Balance sheet accounts typically have debit and credit entries (both increases and decreases to them). The balance at year-end reflects only the balance in the account as of the last day of the year. The auditor is responsible for determining only whether the ending balance in the balance sheet account is correct according to the applicable financial reporting framework (GAAP). The auditor is not responsible for reviewing all transactions recorded in the balance sheet account during the year.

Procedures for Recording Transactions in the Inventory Process

LO2

Explain the transactions in the inventory process

Refer to the journal entries used to record transactions in the inventory process in Exhibit 7-3. The appropriate journal entry for the transactions involving the LIFO reserve and market value adjustments is determined by the particular situation in the firm. If LIFO inventory is higher than FIFO inventory, Cost of Goods Sold is credited and the allowance account is debited. This would be an unusual situation, but it could occur in a year when the company reduces the quantity of inventory on hand. The loss

Accounts in the Inventory Business Process | Exhibit 7-2

+ Inventory −	
Beginning Balance	
Inventory purchased during the year	Cost of Goods Sold
Ending Balance	

+ Allowance to Reduce Inventory to LIFO −	
	Beginning Balance
Adjustment to reserve for the current year	Adjustment to reserve for the current year
	Ending Balance

+ Allowance to Reduce Inventory to Market Value −	
	Beginning Balance
Adjustment to reserve for the current year	Adjustment to reserve for the current year
	Ending Balance

+ Cost of Goods Sold −	
Cost of inventory items sold during the year	
Ending Balance	

account for a decline in market value of inventory could be debited rather than credited if it had increased from the previous year but was not higher than cost.

Documents in the Business Process

The auditor can find various documents useful for gathering evidence about the business process.

Purchase History Report

This is used to verify the purchase price of inventory; it provides amounts and prices of each inventory purchase.

Inventory Price File

The file is used for verifying the sales price for inventory items to determine the lower of cost or market valuation.

Inventory Count Tags

These are used during the physical count to record the inventory amounts.

Final Inventory List

This provides the detail to support the final inventory number reported on the balance sheet. It includes the final inventory amounts and cost assigned to each inventory item.

Adjusting Journal Entry Report

This document is a record of all adjusting journal entries made during a specific time period organized by month-end, quarter-end, and year-end. Documentation for the adjusting journal entries with the signature of the person initiating the entry supports this report.

Many inventory systems are automated today. Automated inventory systems can be used to maintain control over inventory both in terms of keeping track of production amounts and of maintaining correct inventory balances. IT technology related to inventory can be very useful in maintaining accurate accounting records for inventory balances, but like all IT applications, it is useful to the auditor only after he or she has determined that the internal controls for the technology have been effectively designed to prevent or detect misstatements of inventory.

Journal Entries and Related Documents for the Inventory Process

Exhibit 7-3

Journal Entries	Documents
Cost of Goods Sold	Final inventory listing
Inventory	Adjusting journal entry report
(To adjust book inventory to the physical count when book inventory is higher than the physical count.)	
Inventory	Final inventory listing
Cost of Goods Sold	Adjusting journal entry report
(To adjust book inventory to the physical count when book inventory is less than the physical count.)	
Cost of Goods Sold	Purchase history report
Allowance to reduce inventory to LIFO value	Inventory price file
(To reduce year-end inventory to LIFO cost, when LIFO cost is less than FIFO cost.)	Adjusting journal entry report
Allowance to reduce inventory to LIFO value	Purchase history report
Cost of Goods Sold	Inventory price file
(To adjust year-end inventory to LIFO cost, when LIFO cost is greater than FIFO cost.)	Adjusting journal entry report
Loss due to market decline of inventory	Purchase history report
Allowance to reduce inventory to market value	Inventory price file
(To reduce inventory to its market value.)	Adjusting journal entry report
Allowance to reduce inventory to market value	Purchase history report
Gain due to market recovery of inventory value	Inventory price file
(To record recovery of decline in market value of inventory.)	Adjusting journal entry report

Accounting Rules for Recording Transactions in the Inventory Business

LO3

Understand an applicable financial reporting framework (GAAP) for recording transactions in the inventory business process

Accounting Rules Applicable to the Inventory Process

Two financial reporting frameworks might be used by a company for preparing financial statements: (1) accounting standards for U.S. companies and (2) international accounting standards. We refer to the first set of standards as U.S. GAAP and the second set as International Financial Reporting Standards (IFRS). The international standards are written by the International Accounting Standards Board (IASB). The inventory rules for each set of standards will be discussed next.

For companies using U.S. GAAP as the financial reporting framework, the accounting rules for *recording transactions* in the inventory process and *valuing inventory* at year-end can be found in FASB concept statements and in the accounting standards. Concept Statement No. 5, *Recognition and Measurement in Financial Statements of Business Enterprises,* provides the basic rule for recording assets and recognizing changes in them. According to this standard, assets are recorded at the price paid on the date of recognition. Once an asset is recorded, it continues to be carried at the amount initially recognized until an event that changes the asset occurs (FASB No. 5, paragraph 88). One of the events that could change the asset value is a change in price. Inventory is **valued** at *lower of cost or market* at year-end. This accounting rule reflects a conservative approach to inventory valuation; it could more clearly be stated as "lower of the cost of inventory when purchased or the cost to replace the inventory item at year-end." If an inventory item cost $25 to purchase, sells for $42, and could now be purchased for $18, it should be valued at $18 at year-end.

Inventory is **recorded** at cost when purchased (cost includes all expenditures necessary to obtain the inventory) and **valued** at *lower* of original cost or the cost to replace the item at year-end. This valuation method is referred to as *lower of cost or market (LCM).*

According to IFRS, inventory is recorded at cost when purchased, the cost of inventory at the end of the year is determined using FIFO or average cost, and it is valued at lower of cost or market at the end of the year. International accounting standards do not permit a company to use LIFO to determine the cost of inventory at year-end.

Possible Misstatements in the Inventory Process

LO4

Describe misstatements (errors and fraud) that could occur in the inventory process

Inventory is susceptible to both errors and fraud, so the auditor must design audit procedures to search for errors (unintentional misstatements) and fraud (intentional misstatements) in the inventory process.

Misstatements in the inventory process can be overstatements or understatements. Clients can understate inventory (and overstate cost of goods sold) to reduce income tax expense. They can overstate inventory and understate cost of goods sold to increase net income. **Overstatement** misstatements are more likely to occur in the inventory process than understatement misstatements. When overstatement misstatements occur (whether they are intentional or unintentional), the cost of goods sold is understated, net income is overstated, and inventory is overstated. This misleads outsiders about the future cash flows when the inventory is sold.

Did You Know?

In 2007, the shareowners of Dell Inc. filed a class action lawsuit against the company. The lawsuit alleged that Dell had received "secret and illegal" kickbacks from Intel in exchange for Dell's commitment to using Intel chips in its computers. The suit alleges that the payments were received for not doing business with AMD. The payments received at the end of each quarter were used to reduce the cost of goods sold reported by Dell. The payments had a material impact on Dell's profit margins and allowed the company to report both a lower cost of goods sold and a higher net income than would have been possible without the kickbacks.

Each year Dell developed a computer model based on AMD chips. This model was used as a bargaining device to allow Dell to convince Intel to continue the policy of paying kickbacks. Each year Dell chose to use Intel chips in its computers when Intel agreed to pay a kickback for the use of its chips.

Source: Don Clark, Christopher Lawton, and John R. Wilke, "Dell's Woes Mount as Investors File Improper-Accounting Suit," *The Wall Street Journal,* February 2, 2007.

How could the auditor have discovered this misstatement?

Auditing standards require the auditor to assess the risk of material misstatement due to fraud relating to inventory and to plan the audit to control this risk.

The client can use a variety of methods to overstate inventory including:

- Inaccurate inventory counts
- Inaccurate inventory pricing
- Incorrect recognition of manufacturer rebates
- Failure to adjust inventory to lower of cost or market at year-end
- Incorrect LIFO reserve calculations
- Failure to write off obsolete inventory

How do auditors find errors or fraud in the inventory process? They should conduct the audit with an attitude of *professional skepticism.* This includes gathering evidence and planning the audit with a "questioning mind and being alert to conditions that can indicate possible misstatement due to fraud or error, and a critical assessment of audit evidence" (Overall Objectives of the Independent Auditor and the Conduct of an Audit in Accordance with Generally Accepted Auditing Standards). In planning the audit, team members are required to have a meeting to discuss the potential for misstatement due to fraud in the inventory process, including the pressure on management to commit fraud, the opportunity for fraud to be perpetrated in the company, and the general environment or tone in the company that can allow management to rationalize committing fraud.

In planning the audit and assessing risk for the inventory process, the auditor should consider the fraud risk factors identified in the auditing standards (AU316). The auditor should use this information to assess the *risk of material misstatement for relevant assertions in significant accounts and disclosures* for the business process and to plan the level of substantive test work for the business process.

Did You Know?

Ahold, the world's third largest supermarket group, was charged with filing false and misleading financial statements with the SEC because of its treatment of promotional allowances. This incorrect treatment allowed Ahold to overstate net sales by $41 billion for 2000–2002.

In 2002, when earnings were lower than anticipated and the prospect for bonuses appeared slim, managers of U.S. Foodservice, a division of Ahold, announced a new strategy to increase income and gain bonus payments. The company began ordering large amounts of food and paper products from manufacturing companies such as Sara Lee Corp., Kraft Foods Inc., Georgia-Pacific Corp., and Nestle SA. The manufacturers had agreed to pay large rebates ranging from 8% to 46% for the inventory purchases.

Rebates should be recorded as reductions in cost of goods sold and recognized when goods are sold. The rebates were booked immediately to increase 2002 earnings. However, the company did not sell the inventory in 2002, so the rebates on the unsold portion should have been recorded in the year of the sale. A year later, the company still had not sold the inventory and cut prices below cost to get rid of the excess purchases. This sales strategy allowed the company to meet earnings targets for 2002 but violated accounting principles and provided false and misleading filings with the SEC.

Sources: Anita Raghavan, "Ahold and SEC Settle with No Fine," *The Wall Street Journal,* October 14, 2004; Steve Stecklow, Anita Raghavan, and Deborah Ball, "How a Quest for Rebates Sent Ahold on an Odd Buying Spree," *The Wall Street Journal,* March 6, 2003.

How should the auditor discover this type of misstatement in the financial statements?

Management's Assertions for the Inventory Business Process

LO5

Explain management's assertions for accounts in the inventory process

In the inventory process, the auditor gathers evidence to evaluate management's assertions about the accounts in the process.

Management's Assertions

Existence or occurrence—for both classes of transactions and account balances
Completeness—for both classes of transactions and account balances
Valuation and allocation—for account balances
Rights and obligations—for account balances
Accuracy—for classes of transactions
Cutoff—for classes of transactions
Classification—for classes of transactions (AU 314 and ISA 315)

For the inventory process, management asserts that inventory exists at the balance sheet date and that the cost of goods sold transactions recorded in the inventory process occurred during the year (existence and occurrence). Management asserts that all inventory transactions that should be presented in the financial statements are included (completeness). Management also asserts that the company has the right to sell the inventory and collect the cash for its sale (rights and obligations) and that the ending inventory balance is valued correctly according to the applicable financial reporting framework rules at year-end (valuation). Finally, management asserts that cost of goods is accurate, that cutoff was done in accordance with the applicable financial reporting framework, and that cost of goods is properly classified (accuracy, cutoff, and classification).

Relevant Assertions for the Inventory Business Process

LO6

Identify relevant assertions for the inventory process

The auditor is required to gather audit evidence to support *relevant assertions for significant accounts* in the business process. The relevant assertions for any business process are linked to the **risk** in the accounting process. They are often associated with the misstatement expected in the process. Because the most likely misstatement in the inventory process is an overstatement, **existence** and **valuation** are often identified as relevant assertions for this process.

Did You Know?

Rent-Way, one of the largest rent-to-own stores in the United States, at one time owned more than 1,000 stores and did business in 42 states. It was founded in 1981 and became a public company in 1993. Rent-Way expanded in the years that followed its public offering, and management was often worried about meeting analysts' earnings expectations.

Jeffrey Conway, CFO, and Matthew Marini, controller, devised a fraudulent scheme to increase earnings and meet analyst forecasts. This scheme involved manipulating revenue and assets by making false and misleading entries in the financial records. Conway told Marini that they could both lose their jobs if the company failed to meet earnings targets. He told Marini to do whatever it took to meet these targets and not to tell Conway what he had done so Conway could maintain "plausible deniability" (he had no direct knowledge of the fraudulent actions).

Marini directed accounting staff to (1) make false entries in accounts to reduce expenses, (2) capitalize certain expenses, and (3) fail to record inventory shrinkage. A physical inventory showed actual inventory on hand worth $366,000; however, the general ledger reflected an inventory balance of $1,408,000. Marini failed to record the inventory shrinkage, overstated inventory, and understated expense.

Source: U.S. Securities and Exchange Commission, Litigation Release No. 18241, July 22, 2003, "SEC V. Rent-Way, Inc., et al., 03CIV 231E."

Were the auditors able to identify misstatements in the inventory account?

Internal Control Testing

LO7

Describe the methods the auditor uses to gather evidence for internal controls in the inventory process

In the inventory business process, the auditor can review internal controls that are part of the cost accounting system. The cost accounting system determines the cost of the inventory *manufactured* by the company. Auditing a cost accounting system requires the auditor to understand (1) how the cost accounting system tracks costs and (2) how the costs and amounts of inventory are reflected in the perpetual inventory files.

Inventory *costs* are assigned to the manufactured product as it moves through the manufacturing process. Accurate cost data for raw materials, work in process, and finished goods are obtained when direct material, direct labor, and overhead costs are added to the product as it moves through the manufacturing process. When testing the inventory records, the auditor must understand the internal controls in the cost accounting system including knowledge of how goods are transferred from raw materials to work in process and then to finished goods. The auditor must determine that controls are in place to assure that all costs are added and all physical goods are transferred. Depending on the controls in the cost accounting system, the auditor can choose to verify the direct material and the direct labor costs by reviewing purchase invoices for raw materials and payroll records for direct labor costs while performing substantive tests of details.

The *perpetual inventory files* reflect inventory at the beginning of the year and all additions and deletions to the inventory balance. The accuracy of this file determines whether the auditor can perform the physical examination of inventory before year-end. If the perpetual files are accurate, the auditor can test the physical inventory before the balance sheet date, perhaps in October or November for a client with a December year-end. If the perpetual files are not accurate, the auditor tests inventory at year-end. The internal controls that determine the accuracy of the perpetual inventory file were tested in the revenue process and the purchase and acquisition process because they involve the movement of inventory in and out of the perpetual inventory account. It is helpful for the auditor to be aware of the effectiveness of these controls because they will determine the accuracy of the year-end inventory balance—the balance that he or she is concerned about in this business process.

The transactions audited in the inventory process include determining the correct amount of inventory, pricing it according to accounting standards, and valuing the year-end inventory balance. The auditor considers only the ending balance of inventory in the inventory process, so internal controls relevant to transactions are not part of this process. To audit the inventory balances that are part of the inventory process, the auditor performs substantive tests of balances.

Substantive Tests for the Inventory Process

LO8

Understand the substantive tests auditors use to gather evidence in the inventory process

Typically, the auditor evaluates management's assertions regarding the financial statements using either substantive testing or a combination of substantive and internal control testing. In the inventory process, the auditor typically uses only substantive testing due to the nature of the accounts in the business process.

Auditing standards describe several procedures the auditor could use to gather evidence to evaluate whether the financial statements are prepared according to the applicable financial reporting framework. See the following table for a list of these procedures. We then discuss analytical procedures because they are usually performed as part of the planning process. The other audit procedures will be discussed later in the chapter.

Substantive Audit Procedures

Analytical procedures
Inspection of records, documents, or tangible assets
Observation
Inquiry
Confirmation
Recalculation
Reperformance

Let's consider how the auditor uses these procedures to gather evidence about the accounts in this business process. This evidence will tell her or him whether the financial statement accounts are prepared in accordance with the applicable financial reporting framework.

Analytical Procedures

Auditors often use analytical procedures to obtain evidence as to whether the financial statement accounts are prepared in accordance with the applicable financial reporting framework. Two types of analytical procedures are commonly used. In the first, auditors compare the financial statement numbers for the current year to the previous year. This comparison includes calculating the dollar amount as well as the percentage of change. In the second analytical procedure, auditors calculate financial ratios for the current financial statements and compare them to ratios for the prior year financial statements. When using analytical procedures, auditors often consider nonfinancial measures when evaluating changes from one year to the next. For example, auditors could consider the number of inventory product codes or the average cost of inventory per product code in the current year and the prior year.

In the inventory business process, auditors could perform the following analytical procedures:

1. *Compare inventory balances by category—raw material, work in process, and finished goods—for the current year with the prior year. Investigate any unexpected changes.* Sometimes auditor can expect changes in the inventory balance from one year to the next. For example, the company could have added a new product line or opened a new store. In different circumstances changes between the two years are not expected based on auditors' knowledge of the company. The auditors ask the client to explain unexpected changes and determine whether additional evidence is needed to verify the explanation.

2. *Compute gross margin for the current year and the prior year. Investigate any unexpected changes in the ratio.* The *gross margin* ratio is usually stable from year to year; if the cost of an item increases, the company increases its selling price. This happens because the company needs a certain percentage of each sales dollar to cover operating expenses. For example, if the cost of an item was $0.60 and the company sold the item for $1.00, the gross margin would be $0.40, or 40%. If the cost goes up to $0.65, the sales price will probably increase to $1.08 because the company needs 40% of each sales dollar to cover operating expenses. If the gross margin changes significantly from one year to the next, the company could have changed its pricing policy (decided it needed only 38% of each sales dollar to cover operating expenses) or have obtained the item at a lower cost (less than $0.60) and decided to keep the sales price the same so it would have more than 40% of each sales dollar for operating expenses.

3. *Compute inventory turnover. Compare the current year's turnover to that of the prior year. Investigate unexpected differences.* The inventory turnover ratio is calculated by dividing cost of goods sold by the average cost of inventory for the year. The turnover ratio tells auditors how many times inventory has come in and been sold during the year. For example, an inventory turnover ratio of 12 means that inventory has been purchased and sold every month (or that inventory is on hand on the average of 30 days before it is sold). Inventory turnover numbers that increase from the prior year mean the company is selling inventory faster. Inventory turnover numbers that decrease from the prior year mean that inventory is on hand longer than it had been in the prior year. Generally, companies want inventory turnover to increase rather than decrease because inventory that is on hand longer can become old, damaged, rendered obsolete, or be at greater risk of theft.

How does an auditor know whether the change is reasonable? Companies do not dramatically change from year to year *without a reason* (planned expansion, bad cash flow, or poor economic conditions), so large increases or decreases in the inventory accounts can be unreasonable. To make the decision about whether a change is unreasonable, the auditor needs to know (1) the client's industry, (2) current economic conditions, and (3) the business under audit.

Let's consider an example for the inventory process for BCS. See Exhibit 7-4 for selected financial information for the company for three years.

Year 3 is the current year that is under audit. Raw material inventory decreased by $500,000, or 56%, from year 2 to year 3. Work in progress inventory increased by $100,000, or 20%, from year 2 to year 3. Finished goods inventory decreased by $300,000, or 20% from year 2 to year 3. The auditor would be most interested in why finished goods inventory decreased because the changes in raw material inventory and work in process inventory could be easily explained by the production cycle of the plant (production can have been scheduled for early in year 2 so the raw materials were higher at this time to meet the needs of the planned production).

The auditor would also calculate the gross margin percentage. This is one of the easiest ways to identify potential misstatements in the inventory balance and cost of goods

Selected Financial Information for BCS   Exhibit 7-4

Item	Year 3	Percentage Change	Year 2	Percentage Change	Year 1
Raw material inventory	$ 400,000	56% ↓	$ 900,000	29% ↑	$ 700,000
Work in process inventory	600,000	20% ↑	500,000	29% ↓	700,000
Finished goods inventory	1,200,000	20% ↓	1,500,000	15% ↑	1,300,000
Allowance for LIFO reserve	75,000	25% ↓	100,000	5% ↑	95,000
Cost of goods sold	7,200,000	10% ↑	6,500,000	5% ↑	6,175,000
Sales revenue	12,000,000	20% ↑	10,000,000	5% ↑	9,500,000
Gross margin	4,800,000	37% ↑	3,500,000	5% ↑	3,325,000
Gross margin percentage	40%	14% ↑	35%	0%	35%
Average cost per finished goods item	10,000	11% ↑	9,000	6% ↑	8,500
Average sales price per finished goods item	15,385	11% ↑	13,846	6% ↑	13,077

sold. A company's gross margin (sales revenue minus cost of goods sold) is a remarkably stable percentage. The company's gross margin percentage (gross margin divided by sales revenue) was 35% in years 1 and 2 but increased to 40% in year 3. So in years 1 and 2, the client kept 35 cents from each sales dollar to cover operating expense; however, in year 3, the client kept 40 cents of each sales dollar for operating expense. How did the client manage to increase the gross margin without losing sales? Gross margin percentages do not usually change this dramatically unless the client has made a change in pricing policies (and the auditor would likely be aware of such a change). The change in gross margin percentage from year 2 to year 3 can indicate a misstatement in inventory and cost of goods sold.

The average *cost* per inventory item was $10,000 in year 3 and $9,000 in year 2, a 6% increase from the prior year in both year 2 and year 3. The average *sales price* per inventory item was $15,385 in year 3 and $13,846 in year 2, an 11% increase in each year. The percentage increase in either sales price or cost must be different in year 3 from that in year 2 if the gross margin percentage has gone from 35% to 40%. This also indicates a potential misstatement in inventory and cost of goods sold.

The inventory turnover for year 3 is 2.8 and for year 2 is 2.3. For year 3, this means that the company sold the inventory 2.8 times per year, or every 130 days. In year 2, it sold the inventory 2.3 times per year, or every 159 days. This is a fairly dramatic change in inventory turnover from year 2 to year 3. It is usually better to sell inventory more quickly, which is a good sign, but must be the result of a change in customer demand or in the company's manufacturing policy (produce closer to the time when inventory can be sold). It can also indicate a misstatement in ending inventory and cost of goods sold.

Auditors use analytical procedures to focus their attention on accounts that have changed from the prior year. Changes from one year to the next could have been caused by "real" events or could indicate misstatements in the financial statements. Because the financial statements from the prior year were audited, they are used to provide a base from which to identify unusual changes in the current year.

Substantive Tests of Balances

The auditor uses substantive tests of balances to gather evidence for balance sheet accounts in the inventory process. These accounts are inventory, allowance to reduce inventory to LIFO value, and the allowance to reduce inventory to market value.

See the following list for the key substantive tests of balances for the inventory business process. The audit **procedure** used to perform the test appears before the test (identified in bold, italic type), and the **assertion** tested by the audit test is at the end of the test (identified in blue type). Depending on the amount of evidence gathered using internal control tests, the auditor can perform *some or all* of these audit procedures.

The key substantive tests of balances for the inventory process follow:

1. ***Observation, Inspection.*** Select a sample of inventory items on the inventory listing at year-end. Perform test counts for the items selected—**existence, valuation.**

2. ***Observation, Inspection.*** Select a sample of inventory items from the warehouse shelves. Perform tests counts for the items selected—**completeness, valuation.**

3. ***Inspection, Reperformance.*** Select a sample of inventory items on the final inventory listing. Perform price tests to verify that the items are correctly priced at year-end—**valuations.**

4. ***Inspection, Reperformance.*** Review the lower-of-cost-or-market adjustment made by the client. Select a sample of inventory items and perform price tests to determine whether the lower-of-cost-or-market cost is correct—**valuation.**

5. ***Inspection, Reperformance.*** Review the LIFO adjustment if appropriate to determine whether it is reasonable. Select a sample of inventory items and perform price tests to determine whether the LIFO cost is correct—**valuation.**

Did You Know?

In its pro forma earnings reports in newspapers, 3Com reported an inventory write-down of more than $300 million in 2001 for obsolete and unneeded inventory. The write-down was reported as a nonrecurring loss. In this situation, investors assumed that they could ignore the write-down in assessing the company's performance and in predicting future earnings.

The following year, 3Com sold the inventory that had been written down and made a profit on the sale. The sale of the obsolete inventory was not described as a "nonrecurring" gain, and the company reported an improvement in earnings per share based on the profit earned on the sale of the inventory with no cost assigned to it after the write-down. The income earned on the sale of the obsolete inventory equaled half the increase in earnings per share.

Source: Robin Sidel, "3Com Inventory Gain Bares Faults of Pro-forma Results," *The Wall Street Journal,* July 19, 2002.

Are inventories that are written down often sold at a profit? What is the auditor's role in detecting this misstatement?

Physical Inventory Counting

LO9

Explain the procedures for the physical inventory count

If inventory is material to the financial statements, auditing standards require the auditor to obtain sufficient appropriate evidence regarding the existence and condition of inventory by (1) observing the physical inventory being counted and (2) performing audit procedures over the company's final inventory records to determine whether they accurately reflect the actual inventory count results. If the inventory is counted at a date other than year-end, the auditor should perform audit procedures to obtain evidence about whether changes in the inventory balance between the count date and year-end are recorded properly.

Counting physical inventory is important to the audit process. Most companies maintain inventory records using FIFO costing and perpetual inventory systems. The perpetual system records additions to inventory as it is manufactured or purchased and deletions from inventory as it is sold. They do not, however, record obsolete items, stolen items, shrinkage, or errors in recording inventory transactions. The only way to determine the correct balance in the inventory account at year-end is to count it. The company and the auditor have one chance each year to count inventory correctly. When the count has been completed, inventory moves around again (it is purchased and sold), and the correct count will be impossible to determine. The count process is important because:

The book inventory is adjusted to the physical count.

If attending the physical inventory counting is impracticable, the auditor must use alternative audit procedures to obtain sufficient appropriate evidence regarding the existence and condition of the inventory. If it is not possible for the auditor to do so, he or she should modify the audit opinion in accordance with the reporting standards.

The auditor does the following in preparation for attending the physical inventory count:

1. Identify the locations of the inventory and the amount at each location to plan to test.
2. Review the client's plans for taking the inventory, including the procedures for counting, controlling inventory tags or count sheets, identifying obsolete items during the count, controlling the movement of inventory during the count, and controlling shipping and receiving during the count.
3. Evaluate whether the involvement of specialists is needed during the count. Can the auditor recognize People's Republic of China No. 2 corn or 18 karat gold jewelry? Sometimes samples of inventory items are sent to a specialist for verification.
4. Tour the client's warehouse and manufacturing facility.
5. Select a sample of inventory transactions for entering and leaving the inventory process during the year. These transactions should include inventory entering the process from receiving reports, inventory requisitions that place raw material into the production process, and inventory leaving the account based on sales recorded with shipping documents. Trace the transactions to and from the perpetual inventory system.
6. If the client manufactures goods, review the overhead allocation reports and the cost of production reports to determine how it accumulated inventory costs.
7. Determine how the client intends to identify obsolete or slow-moving items during the count.

Did You Know?

Sonali, a small gold jewelry dealer in California, imported 22-karat gold to sell to jewelry stores in the United States. This 22-karat gold is a purer version than that normally sold in the United States. The jewelers refused to pay for the gold until they sold it, but Mr. Patangay, Sonali's owner, had to pay for the gold immediately upon purchasing it. To resolve this dilemma, Mr. Patangay created fictitious bank statements and sales documents to obtain loans from banks to cover the cost of the gold purchases. Based on the fictitious documents, he reported sales of $70 million per year to the bankers although sales had never been more than $1.5 million.

When the Ernst & Young auditors arrived to count the gold during the yearly audit, Mr. Patangay showed them gold-plated costume chains in 50-feet spools. He placed the gold chains into plastic bags and often included a cut piece of 22-karat gold in each bag. When the auditors requested a sample of gold to test to value the gold, Mr. Patangay suggested that they take the cut piece. Rather than cutting a piece of gold from the long chain, the auditors complied with his request.

The fraud was discovered when the bank received a call about Mr. Patangay. The bank sent its own auditors to the company, and they discovered the fraud. Mr. Patangay reported in *The Wall Street Journal* that the audit procedures used by the CPA firm had "big flaws that someone can take advantage of."

Source: Jeff D. Opdyke, "Fraud Perpetrator Points Finger at Auditors for Lax Standards," *The Wall Street Journal,* March 1, 2002.

Were the auditing procedures that the auditors used to verify the valuation of the gold jewelry adequate?

The auditor performs the following procedures during the physical inventory count:

1. Determines that inventory items on hand that are not owned by the client are identified.
2. Visits the shipping and receiving departments and obtains the last shipping number and receiving number used before the physical count. Inventory items are typically not received nor are shipments made during the physical count.
3. Observes the performance of the count procedures.
4. Determines that the inventory tags are properly controlled by being assigned to count teams and that all are returned.
5. Inspects the inventory.
6. Performs test counts. Some of the test counts should come from the floor and some test counts from the inventory listing. Compare the test counts to the client counts and resolve any differences immediately.
7. Observes that all inventory has been tagged and counted.

After the inventory has been counted, it must be priced. Let's consider the various methods that accounting standards allow a company for pricing inventory.

FIFO and LIFO Inventory Pricing and Inventory Reserves

LO10

Understand the importance of FIFO and LIFO pricing of inventory and the year-end valuation of inventory

Inventory Pricing and the LIFO Inventory Reserve

The inventory physical count gives the company inventory *amounts* that must be *priced* to determine the ending inventory balance reported on the balance sheet. The client determines the cost of inventory at year-end by using FIFO, LIFO, or average cost methods to calculate the cost (international accounting standards do not permit the use of LIFO for inventory pricing).

First, the client determines the cost of ending inventory using first-in, first-out (FIFO) to determine inventory cost at year-end regardless of whether it uses last-in, first-out (LIFO) or FIFO method. FIFO inventory pricing is calculated by using the purchase history file for each inventory item and pricing the amount of inventory counted at year-end based on the purchase prices paid for inventory during the year. The FIFO pricing method requires the auditor to assume that the items *sold* were priced according to that method. Therefore, the inventory remaining is priced according to the *last-in, still-there* method. For example, assume the client has the following purchase history for inventory item number 0015:

- February 5, purchased 100 units at $2.58 per unit
- April 28, purchased 138 units at $2.74 per unit
- July 9, purchased 145 units at $3.12 per unit
- November 21, purchased 185 units at $3.02 per unit

If the amount of inventory counted at year-end was 225 units, the FIFO pricing for the units would be $683.50 (185 units $\times$ $3.02 + 40 units $\times$ $3.12). Exhibit 7-5 illustrates the calculation of inventory cost at the year-end for this inventory item.

After the FIFO calculation, the client determines the LIFO cost for the inventory if it uses the LIFO method for determining inventory costs. This inventory pricing method assumes that the last items purchased were the first items *sold* (last-in, first-out). The LIFO inventory pricing method *prices inventory* using the *first-in, still there* method. The LIFO cost for the 225 units, assuming no inventory at hand at the beginning of the year, would be $600.50 (100 units $\times$ $2.58 + 125 units $\times$ $2.74). The difference between the FIFO cost and the LIFO cost is recorded in the LIFO reserve.

The LIFO reserve account is a permanent balance sheet account. Its ending balance is adjusted after considering its beginning balance. For example, if the LIFO reserve account had a balance of $41,000,000 at the end of 2011 and if the difference between

FIFO and LIFO Inventory Cost Example

Exhibit 7-5

Inventory Item 0015

Date of Purchase	Amount Purchased	Cost per Unit	Total Cost
February 5	100	2.58	258.00
April 28	138	2.74	378.12
July 9	145	3.12	452.40
November 21	185	3.02	558.70
Total units	568		1647.22
Total units sold	343		
Units in ending inventory	225		
Cost of ending inventory using FIFO costing method			
July 9	40	3.12	124.80
November 21	185	3.02	558.70
Ending inventory with FIFO	225		683.50
Cost of ending inventory using LIFO costing method			
February 5	100	2.58	258.00
April 28	125	2.74	342.50
Ending Inventory with LIFO	225		600.50
Difference between LIFO and FIFO ending inventory cost			83.00
FIFO inventory			683.50
Less allowance for LIFO reserve			(83.00)
LIFO inventory			$600.50

the LIFO inventory cost and the FIFO inventory cost was $45,000,000 at the end of 2012, the adjustment to the LIFO reserve would be $4,000,000.

+ Allowance for LIFO Reserve −	
41,000,000	Beginning balance
4,000,000	Yearly adjustment to allowance account
45,000,000	Ending balance

The client can use estimation methods to determine the LIFO reserve instead of pricing each inventory item. The auditor reviews the client's LIFO calculation by selecting a sample of inventory items from the year-end inventory listing and calculating the FIFO and LIFO amounts based on the information in the purchase file.

Lower-of-Cost-or-Market Adjustment for Inventory

Inventory is a current asset on the balance sheet. Current assets are expected to generate cash within one year. The amount of cash that should be generated by any current asset is equal to or greater than the asset's amount. Inventory is recorded at cost when it is purchased. At year-end, inventory must be *valued* at the lower-of-cost-or-market value. **Market value is determined not by what the inventory item can be sold for but by the cost of replacing it.** If 200 units of inventory with a cost of $3.10 can be purchased at a cost of $2.85 per unit at the year-end, the *value* of each at year-end must be recorded at $2.85. This accounting rule provides a conservative estimate of the cash flow expected from the current asset during the next year and ensures that the client does not list current assets at an amount more than the cash flow they will generate.

The client determines the lower-of-cost-or-market valuation needed for inventory at the end-of-the-year based on the current purchase prices of the inventory on hand. The auditor reviews this calculation and can select a sample of inventory items at year-end and determine the lower-of-cost-or-market value for those selected based on the cost information in the purchase file.

Did You Know?

American Tissue, one of the largest makers of paper products in the United States, overvalued its finished goods inventory in 2000 by $12.5 million by failing to write down its inventory to its market price. This caused the company to overstate its net income for the year by 100%. The company reported net income of $24.5 million when it was correctly $12 million. This overstatement was to conceal the presence of financial weaknesses in the business and to allow the company to continue to borrow money.

Source: SEC Litigation Release No. 18022, March 10, 2003.

Why did the auditor fail to test the lower-of-cost-or-market value of ending inventory?

The lower-of-cost-or-market allowance account is a permanent balance sheet account like the LIFO allowance account. The yearly adjustment to the LCM account considers its beginning balance. For example, if the LCM allowance account had a credit balance of $12,000,000 at the end of 2011 and the market value of the inventory was $15,000,000 less than the cost of the inventory at the end of 2012, the adjustment to the LCM reserve would be $3,000,000 (a credit to the Allowance to Reduce Inventory to Market Value account).

+ Allowance for LCM Valuation −	
12,000,000	Beginning balance
3,000,000	Yearly adjustment to allowance account
15,000,000	Ending balance

Exhibits 7-6 and 7-7 illustrate an audit program and audit procedures performed as substantive tests of balances for the inventory process.

The Auditor's Knowledge at This Point in the Audit

At this point in the audit, the auditor should have *sufficient appropriate* evidence to determine whether the accounts in the inventory process—inventory, cost of goods sold, allowance to reduce inventory to LIFO, and allowance to reduce inventory to market value—are presented on the financial statements in accordance with the applicable financial reporting framework. An auditor who does not have enough evidence to make this decision would gather additional evidence. If the accounts in the business process are prepared in accordance with the applicable financial reporting framework, the auditor would conclude that they were.

Based on the results of the audit work performed, relevant assertions for significant accounts in the inventory process are prepared in accordance with the applicable financial reporting framework. ICS

Audit Program for Substantive Testing of Inventory   Exhibit 7-6

Audit Procedures	W/P Ref	Completed by	Date
1. Select a sample of 15 inventory items on the year-end inventory listing.			
a. Perform test counts for the items selected.			
b. Compare the test counts to the client's counts; resolve all differences.			
2. Select a sample of 15 inventory items from the warehouse shelves.			
a. Perform test counts for the items selected.			
b. Compare the test counts to the client's counts; resolve all differences.			
3. Select a sample of 30 inventory items on the final inventory listing.			
a. Perform price tests to verify that the items are correctly priced at year-end according to FIFO.			
b. Perform price tests to verify that the items are correctly priced at year-end according to LIFO.			
c. Perform price tests to verify that the items are correctly priced at year-end according to lower of cost or market. To do this, verify the current cost to purchase the inventory item and determine that this cost is more than the FIFO cost for the item.			

An auditor who has proposed audit adjustments would modify the preceding statement to read:

Based on the results of the audit work performed, relevant assertions for significant accounts in the inventory process are prepared in accordance with the applicable financial reporting framework, **except for the adjustments noted.** ICS

All evidence the auditor has gathered to make this decision is kept in the audit work papers. In them, the auditor has recorded the evidence gathered from internal control tests, analytical procedures, substantive tests of transactions, and substantive tests of balances including the particular items tested and her or his conclusions from all evidence reviewed.

Presentation and Disclosure Requirements for the Inventory Business Process

LO11

Describe the disclosure requirements for the inventory business process

In the inventory business process, the auditor gathers evidence to evaluate management's assertions about the presentation and disclosure of the accounts in the business process.

Management's Assertions

Occurrence and rights and obligation—disclosed events and transactions have occurred and pertain to the company.

Completeness—all disclosures that should have been made have been made.

Classification and understandability—financial information is appropriately presented and described. Disclosures are clearly expressed.

Accuracy and valuation—financial information and all other information are disclosed fairly and at appropriate amounts (AU 314 and ISA 315).

Management prepares the financial statements and the footnotes to them. When management hands the financial statements to the auditor, it is asserting that the

Inventory	For the Year Ending December 31, 2012				Exhibit 7-7

Reference:	D-1	
Prepared by:	ICS	
Date:	Feb. 1, 2013	
Reviewed by:	BRJ	
Date:	Feb. 25, 2013	

BCS Company
Inventory Test Counts, Pricing, and Valuation
For the Year Ended December 31, 2012

Inventory Part number	Amount per Client		Amount per Auditor			
From inventory listing	$5625	√	$5625	F	L	M
s-320	7433	√	7433	F	L	M
e-100	586	√	586	F	L	M
f-891	948	E	950	F	L	M
y-299	2284	√	2284	F	L	M
s-616	9706	√	9706	F	L	M
t-377	2153	√	2153	F	L	M
a-455	1591	√	1591	F	L	M
c-367	9840	√	9840	F	L	M
d-411	8997	√	8997	F	L	M
w-815	8414	C	1202	F	L	M
r-566	4794	√	4794	F	L	M
i-233	1686	√	1686	F	L	M
p-455	6792	√	6792	F	L	M
x-835	3541	√	3541	F	L	M
v-499	1490	√	1490	F	L	M
From warehouse shelves						
n-188	7011	√	7011	F	L	M
b-425	3462	√	3462	F	L	M
k-914	4960	√	4960	F	L	M
l-106	9248	√	9248	F	L	M
d-404	7091	√	7091	F	L	M
s-471	0	S	325	F	L	M
y-485	2728	√	2728	F	L	M
o-382	2326	√	2326	F	L	M
y-185	3379	√	3379	F	L	M
j-368	3462	√	3462	F	L	M
g-639	968	√	968	F	L	M
f-034	6008	A	751	F	L	M
l-178	8465	√	8465	F	L	M
v-483	5425	√	5425	F	L	M
z-149	7195	√	7195	F	L	M
a-400	8314	√	8314	F	L	M

Reference:	D-1
Prepared by:	ICS
Date:	Feb. 1, 2013
Reviewed by:	BRJ
Date:	Feb. 25, 2013

BCS Company
Inventory Test Counts, Pricing, and Valuation
For the Year Ended December 31, 2012

Tickmark symbols ↓	
√	Agreed client count to auditor count without exception.
E	Auditor and client count do not agree. Auditor count is correct. Client adjusted.
C	Auditor and client count do not agree. Items are packed 7 per box. Client counted individual items. Auditor counted the number of cartons of 7 in the inventory. Items are recorded in inventory by carton of 7. Client adjusted its count to the auditor count.
S	Client forgot to count this inventory item. Client adjusted the count to the auditor's count after verifying it.
A	Auditor and client count do not agree. Items are packed 8 per box. Client counted individual items. Auditor counted inventory by the number of boxes of 8. Items are recorded in inventory by box of 8. Client adjusted their count to the auditor count.
F	Recalculated price of ending inventory quantity using FIFO pricing without exception.
L	Recalculated price of ending inventory quantity using LIFO pricing without exception.
M	Determined market value for inventory based on the last purchase price. All market values are higher than FIFO cost.

Conclusion:	Based on the results of test work performed, inventory appears to exist and be valued according to the applicable financial reporting framework at December 31, 2012. ICS

accounts in the inventory process are presented according to the applicable financial reporting framework and that all required disclosures regarding the accounts have been made. The disclosures related to the financial statements are usually made in one of two places (1) the footnotes to the financial statements or (2) in the Management's Discussion and Analysis (MD&A) section of the annual report.

To evaluate management's presentation and disclosure assertions, the auditor should review the financial statements, the footnote disclosures, and the disclosures made in the MD&A section to determine that they are presented in accordance with the applicable financial reporting framework. The financial statement accounts and footnotes related to the inventory process for General Mills are presented in Exhibit 7-8. In the financial statements, the accounts related to the inventory process are in bold type.

Activities relating to the inventory process are reflected in the cash flow from operations section of the Statement of Cash Flows. Changes in inventory are reflected as increases or decreases in cash from operations, depending on the direction of the change. For General Mills, Inc., cash flow decreased by $193.4 million in 2008 and $119 million in 2007 due to changes in the inventory account.

General Mills inventory is recorded at $1,366.8 million in 2008. Inventory represents 38% of the total current assets. General Mills sold inventory with a cost of $8,778.3 million during the year. About 70% of its inventory is valued at LIFO, the grain inventory is valued at market value (because it is a commodity), and the remaining inventory is valued at FIFO. The inventory that is valued at FIFO is held outside of the United States. International accounting standards do not permit LIFO valuation of inventory. Inventory is valued at lower-of-cost-or-market value.

Inventory Business Process Accounts and Disclosures for General Mills

Exhibit 7-8

CONSOLIDATED STATEMENTS OF INCOME
GENERAL MILLS, INC. AND SUBSIDIARIES

In Millions	Fiscal Year		
	2008	2007	2006
Net sales	$13,652.1	$12,441.5	$11,711.3
Cost of sales	**8,778.3**	**7,955.1**	**7,544.8**
Selling, general, and administrative costs	2,625.0	2,389.3	2,177.7
Restructuring, impairment, and other exit costs	21.0	39.3	29.8
Operating Profit	$ 2,227.8	$ 2,057.8	$ 1,959.0

CONSOLIDATED BALANCE SHEETS
GENERAL MILLS, INC. AND SUBSIDIARIES

In Millions	May 25, 2008	May 28, 2007
Current assets:		
Cash and cash equivalents	$ 661.0	$ 417.1
Receivables	1,081.6	952.9
Inventories	**1,366.8**	**1,173.4**
Prepaid expenses and other current assets	510.6	443.1
Deferred income taxes	-	67.2
Total current assets	$3,620.0	$3,053.7

CONSOLIDATED STATEMENTS OF CASH FLOWS
GENERAL MILLS, INC. AND SUBSIDIARIES

In Millions	Fiscal Year		
	2008	2007	2006
Cash Flows—Operating Activities			
Net earnings	1,294.7	1,143.9	1,090.3
Adjustments to reconcile earnings to cash:			
Depreciation and amortization	459.2	417.8	423.9
After-tax earnings from joint ventures	(110.8)	(72.7)	(69.2)
Stock-based compensation	133.2	127.1	44.6
Deferred income taxes	98.1	26.0	25.9
Distributions of earnings from joint ventures	108.7	45.2	77.4
Tax benefit on exercise options	(55.7)	(73.1)	40.9
Pension and other benefits costs	(24.8)	(53.6)	(74.2)
Restructuring, impairment, and other exit costs	(1.7)	39.1	29.8
Changes in current assets, liabilities (except inventory)	66.7	268.1	201.9
Change in inventory	**(193.4)**	**(119)**	**(18)**
Other, net	(44.3)	2.4	70.2
Net cash provided by operating activities	1,729.9	1,751.2	1,843.5

NOTES TO CONSOLIDATED FINANCIAL STATEMENTS
GENERAL MILLS, INC. AND SUBSIDIARIES

Note 2. Summary of Significant Accounting Policies

Inventories. All inventories in the United States other than grain and certain organic products are valued at the lower of cost, using the last-in, first-out (LIFO) methods, or market. Grain inventories and all related cash contracts and derivatives are valued at market with all net changes in value recorded in earnings currently. Inventories outside of the United States are valued at the lower of cost, using the first-in, first-out (FIFO) method, or market.

Shipping costs associated with the distribution of finished goods to our customers are recorded as cost of sales and are recognized when the related finished product is shipped to and accepted by the customer.

Note 17. Supplemental Information

The components of certain Consolidated Balance Sheet accounts are as follows:

In Millions	May 25, 2008	May 27, 2007
Inventories:		
Raw materials and packaging	$ 265.0	$ 242.1
Finished goods	1,012.4	898.0
Grain	215.2	111.4
Excess of FIFO or weighted cost over LIFO cost*	(125.8)	(78.1)
Total	$1,366.8	$1,173.4

* Inventories of $806.4 million as of May 25, 2008, and $805.9 million as of May 27, 2007, were valued at LIFO.

The balance in the LIFO reserve is $125.8 million at the end of fiscal year 2008. This means that the LIFO value of inventory is $125.8 million less than the FIFO value of inventory. The change in the LIFO reserve from 2007 to 2008 is $47.7 million. In fiscal 2008, cost of goods sold increased by $47.7 million reducing net income by $47.7 million due to the adjustment in the LIFO reserve account. LIFO inventory valuation is designed to allow the company to increase the cost of goods sold, decreasing net income and lowering the tax payment for the company.

Chapter Takeaways

The inventory process is very important to the auditor because of the complexities associated with counting, pricing, and valuing inventory according to the accounting standards. Incentives to misstate expenses are strong because the payoff is so high in terms of the impact on net income. The substantive audit procedures in this business process should be performed with professional skepticism. The auditor should consider the risk that misstatements can occur in the recording of inventory and cost of goods sold and gather sufficient evidence to determine that the accounts in the process are not materially misstated at year-end.

This chapter presented these important facts:

- The transactions recorded in the inventory process, the accounting rules related to these transactions, and the importance of this process to the financial statements.
- The susceptibility of the inventory process to fraud.
- The importance of *professional skepticism* in planning and performing audit procedures in the inventory process.
- The approach the auditor used to gather evidence to support the assertions of *existence and valuation* for *substantive tests of balances* for the process.

- Procedures for pricing and valuing inventory at year-end.
- The important of the *disclosures* made by the client related to the transactions recorded in the process.

Be sure you understand these concepts before you go to the next chapter.

Review Questions

LO1   1. Describe the activities in the inventory process. Write journal entries that would be used to record the transactions in the process.

LO2   2. What is the most important account in the inventory process? Describe the misstatement that is most likely with this account.

LO2   3. List the main documents used in the inventory process. Describe the purpose of each document and whether it is prepared by the company or originates outside it.

LO3   4. Explain the accounting rules applicable to inventory accounts at year-end.

LO4   5. Identify the misstatements that are likely to occur in this process. Explain how the auditor considers the risk of fraud in the process.

LO5   6. Describe management's assertions for the inventory process. Which assertion is the most important for this process? Explain why this is so.

LO7   7. How does the auditor assess control risk for the inventory process? Is the auditor likely to test internal controls for this process? Explain your answer.

LO8   8. What analytical procedures are typically done for the inventory process?

LO8   9. Describe the substantive tests of balances that are done for the inventory process. Identify the assertions associated with each test.

LO9   10. Describe the process used to count inventory. Once the inventory is counted, how does the client price it? How does the auditor test the inventory pricing?

LO10   11. Explain the process of valuing inventory at year-end.

LO11   12. Describe how the accounts from the inventory process impact the financial statements. What are the presentation and disclosure issues associated with this process?

Multiple Choice Questions from CPA Examinations

LO8   13. In a comparison of 2011 to 2012, Neir Co's inventory turnover ratio increased substantially even though sales and inventory accounts were essentially unchanged. Which of the following statements explains the increased inventory turnover ratio?
    a. Cost of goods sold decreased.
    b. Accounts receivable turnover increased.
    c. Total asset turnover increased.
    d. Gross profit percentage decreased.

LO8   14. During 2012, Rand Co. purchased $960,000 of inventory. The cost of goods sold for 2012 was $900,000, and the ending inventory at December 31, 2012, was $180,000. What was the inventory turnover for 2012?
    a. 6.4
    b. 6.0
    c. 5.3
    d. 5.0

LO4   15. Health Co's current ratio is 4:1. Which of the following transactions would normally increase its current ratio?
  a. Purchasing inventory on account.
  b. Selling inventory on account.
  c. Collecting an accounts receivable.
  d. Purchasing machinery for cash.

LO19   16. Jones Wholesalers stocks a changing variety of products. Which inventory costing method will be most likely to give Jones the lowest ending inventory when its product lines are subject to specific price increases?
  a. Specific identification.
  b. Weighted average.
  c. Dollar-value LIFO.
  d. FIFO periodic.

LO4   17. Dart Company's accounting records indicated the following information:

Inventory, 1/1/12	$ 500,000
Purchases during 2012	2,500,000
Sales during 2012	3,200,000

A physical inventory taken on December 31, 2012, resulted in an ending inventory of $575,000. Dart's gross profit on sales has remained constant at 25% in recent years. Dart suspects some inventory could have been taken by a new employee. At December 31, 2012, what is the estimated cost of missing inventory?
  a. $25,000.
  b. $100,000.
  c. $175,000.
  d. $225,000.

LO10   18. A company decided to change its inventory valuation method from FIFO to LIFO in a period of rising prices. What was the result of the change on ending inventory and net income in the year of the change?

	Ending inventory	Net income
a.	Increase	Increase
b.	Increase	Decrease
c.	Decrease	Decrease
d.	Decrease	Increase

LO10   19. Generally, which inventory costing method approximates most closely the current cost for each of the following?

	Cost of good sold	Ending inventory
a.	LIFO	FIFO
b.	LIFO	LIFO
c.	FIFO	FIFO
d.	FIFO	LIFO

LO3   20. Reporting inventory at the lower of cost or market is a departure from the accounting principle of
  a. Historical cost.
  b. Consistency.
  c. Conservatism.
  d. Full disclosure.

LO10   21. Which of the following statements are correct when a company applying the lower of cost or market method reports its inventory at replacement cost?
  I. The original cost is less than replacement cost.
  II. The net realizable value is greater than replacement cost.

  a. I only.
  b. II only.
  c. Both I and II.
  d. Neither I nor II.

LO3   22. How should unallocated fixed overhead costs be treated?
   a. Allocated to finished goods and cost of goods based on ending balances in the accounts.
   b. Allocated to raw materials, work in process, and finished goods, based on the ending balances in the accounts.
   c. Recognized as an expense in the period in which they are incurred.
   d. Allocated to work in process, finished goods, and cost of goods sold based on ending balances in the accounts.

Discussion Questions and Research Problems

LO7   23. **Internal control questionnaire.** The following questions are part of an internal control questionnaire for the inventory process. For each question:
   a. Describe the misstatement in the financial statements that could occur if the question if the client answered "no."
   b. Explain how you would design a substantive test to evaluate the potential misstatement in the financial statements due to the missing control.
   c. If the client answers "yes" to the question, describe an internal control that the client could use.
   d. Describe how you could test the internal control described in part (c).
   Answer the following internal control questions for the inventory process:
   (1) Does the receiving department prepare prenumbered receiving reports and account for the number periodically for all inventory received, showing the description and amount of materials?
   (2) Is all inventory stored under the control of a custodian in areas to which access is limited?
   (3) Is a detailed perpetual inventory master file maintained for raw materials inventory?
   (4) Are physical inventory counts made by someone other than storekeepers and those responsible for maintaining the perpetual inventory records?
   (5) Are standard cost records used for raw materials, direct labor, and manufacturing overhead?
   (6) Is there a stated policy with specific criteria for writing off obsolete or slow-moving goods?

LO10   24. **Pricing inventory according to FIFO and LIFO.** The book inventory at year-end is $10,258,329. After counting and pricing the inventory according to FIFO, the cost assigned to the inventory is $9,438,637. The cost of the inventory according to LIFO pricing is $8,571,284. Answer the following questions regarding the inventory.
   a. Describe three errors and three fraudulent actions that could have caused the discrepancy reported between the book inventory value and the FIFO inventory value according to the physical count.
   b. What audit evidence would you gather to determine whether the misstatements were caused by the specific errors and fraudulent actions that you suggested?
   c. Prepare the journal entry to record the adjustment to the book inventory needed assuming the client uses FIFO cost valuation.
   d. Assume that the company keeps its books based on FIFO inventory valuation and prepares a journal entry at the end of each year to adjust inventory to the LIFO valuation. Prepare the journal entry to record the adjustment to the book inventory needed to value the inventory using the LIFO valuation, assuming that the LIFO allowance account has a $200,000 credit balance before adjustment.
   e. How will the inventory appear on the company's financial statements? What disclosures related to inventory will the company prepare?

LO3, LO4   25. **Inventory calculations.** The inventory for BCS, Inc. at the beginning of the year was $158,752,000. During the year, the company purchased $5,731,600,300 of inventory. At the year-end, the value of inventory, after adjustment, was $102,003,250.

    a. What was cost of goods sold during the year?

    b. Calculate the inventory turnover ratio. Is this ratio good if the company sells computers? Explain your answer.

    c. If the inventory turnover ratio was higher last year, what misstatements in the financial statements could explain the difference in turnover ratios for the two years?

    d. If the inventory turnover ratio was lower last year, what misstatements in the financial statements could explain the difference in turnover ratios for the two years?

    e. If cost of goods sold is misstated, is net income correct? Is the value of inventory on the balance sheet correct? Which misstatement do the auditors worry about the most?

LO4   26. **Audit procedures.** As the partner in charge of the yearly audit of BCS, you are reviewing the audit work papers for inventory. Before you sign off on the audit, you need to determine that sufficient audit work was done to determine that inventory is not materially misstated. Inventory is a material account, and if the balances for it and cost of goods sold are materially misstated, the financial statements will be materially misstated.

    a. Describe the audit evidence the partner would expect to find in the work papers to determine whether inventory and cost of goods sold are materially misstated at year-end.

    b. How will the partner know that the risk of material misstatement for the inventory process was adequately addressed during the audit?

    c. What alternatives are available to the auditor if the audit evidence indicates that the account balance is materially misstated?

LO4   27. **Inventory returns.** Lynn's Photos sells memory cards for digital cameras on the Internet, by catalog, and in numerous retail stores. The items are sold with a 30-day money-back guarantee. A new model becomes available at least every six months, making the previous model more difficult to sell.

    a. Describe the risks associated with the audit of this inventory at year-end.

    b. What evidence should the auditor gather to determine whether the inventory is materially misstated at year-end?

LO9   28. **Physical inventory count.** Consider the audit procedure referred to as the "physical inventory count."

    a. How does the client perform this procedure? What are the auditor's responsibilities for it?

    b. When is it done?

    c. What is the purpose of the physical inventory count?

    d. Describe the assertions associated with the inventory count. Explain why they are important to the inventory process.

    e. Identify the accounts that can be misstated if a physical inventory count is not done.

    f. If these accounts are misstated, how will this affect outsiders? Explain your answer.

LO9   29. **Inventory adjustments.** During your audit of the inventory account, you notice several adjustments made to the inventory account at the year-end.

    a. Identify several questions that you should ask of management regarding the entries.

    b. Describe three possible scenarios to explain the entries that involve adjustments associated with error corrections.

    c. Describe three possible scenarios to explain the entries that involve fraudulent entries.

Real-World Auditing Problems

LO4, LO8   30. **Sonali**

Review the discussion of the Sonali accounting fraud described in the chapter.
a. Describe the audit procedures that could have discovered the misstatements and explain why they could be effective.
b. In your opinion, do the audit procedures used by CPA firms have "big flaws that someone can take advantage of"?

LO4   31. **Rent-Way**

Jeffrey Conway, the CFO of Rent-Way, told Matthew Marini, the controller, to do whatever he needed to meet analyst forecasts but not tell Conway about them so he could maintain "plausible deniability." In today's accounting environment, is it possible for a CFO to maintain "plausible deniability"? Explain your answer.

LO4   32. **Dell**

The Dell fraud described in the chapter involved an exclusive relationship with Intel that agreed to pay rebates on the purchase of computer chips in exchange for the right to sell computer chips to Dell.
a. What is the auditor's responsibility to disclose this relationship? Were outsiders harmed if they did not know about the arrangement?
b. Why did Dell shareholders file a class action suit against the company?
c. What is the auditor's responsibility when the audit client receives rebates from one of its suppliers? Explain your answer.

LO3, LO4   33. **Ahold**

Review the discussion of the Ahold/U.S. Foodservice accounting fraud described in the chapter.
a. Is it wrong for a company to receive rebates on inventory purchases? Explain your answer.
b. What did Ahold do to cause the SEC to charge it with filing false and misleading financial statements?
c. What evidence related to purchase rebates would the auditor gather? How would the auditor determine that Ahold had correctly accounted for the rebates on the financial statements?

LO4, LO5   34. **3Com**

Refer to the facts described in the chapter relating to the fraud case involving 3Com.
a. What financial statement **assertion** did 3Com violate? Explain how it violated this management assertion.
b. Describe how the auditor could design substantive audit procedures to examine "nonrecurring gains and losses."
c. How are outsiders harmed when companies prepare financial statements in the manner 3Com did? Does the information received by outsiders represent the "economic reality" of the transactions? Is the information received by outsiders "unbiased"?
d. Would you like to be an outsider making decisions based on inaccurate information? Explain your answer.

LO3, LO4   35. **American Tissue**

Consider the failure to apply the lower-of-cost-or-market valuation to year-end inventory as reported in the chapter for American Tissue.
a. What happens to the financial statements when inventory is overstated? Do outsiders receive information that is relevant and reliable?
b. What management assertion is violated when the company fails to record the adjustment to inventory?
c. Design a substantive audit procedure that an auditor could use to determine whether inventory is correctly valued at lower of cost of market at year-end.

Internet Assignment

LO3   36. Go to the SEC website (www.sec.gov) and identify a company that has been cited
             by the SEC for inventory problems. Describe the problem and identify the account-
             ing principle the company violated.

Chapter

8

Audit Sampling: Tests of Controls

Learning Objectives

After studying this chapter, you should be able to:

1. Describe what audit sampling is and its use for tests of controls.
2. Understand sampling risk and nonsampling risk.
3. Explain the difference between statistical and nonstatistical sampling.
4. Understand the use of sampling for gathering evidence regarding the effectiveness of internal controls, the use of dual-purpose tests, and the evaluation of sample errors.
5. Explain how the auditor develops an audit sampling plan to perform a test of controls.
6. Describe how sequential sampling could be used for tests of controls.
7. Explain how statistical sampling tables could be used to determine sample sizes for nonstatistical samples.
8. Describe an alternative method for calculating sample size based on the frequency of the control.

Auditing standards relevant to this topic

For private companies

- **AICPA Audit Guide,** *Audit Sampling*
- **AU 350,** Audit Sampling

For public companies

- **AICPA Audit Guide,** *Audit Sampling*
- **AU 350,** Audit Sampling (Interim standard adopted by PCAOB)
- **PCAOB Auditing Standard No. 5,** An Audit of Internal Control over Financial Reporting That is Integrated with an Audit of Financial Statements

International standards

- **ISA 530,** Audit Sampling and Other Means of Testing

Chapter Overview

Auditing standards require the auditor to gather evidence in one of three ways: (1) select all items in the population, (2) select specific items in the population, or (3) use audit sampling to select a sample of items in the population. The next two chapters discuss the third method, the use of audit sampling to gather evidence.

Why does the auditor sample? According to the auditing standards, the auditor is required to gather sufficient appropriate evidence to determine whether the financial statements are prepared in accordance with the applicable financial reporting framework. In the process of gathering evidence, the auditor uses sampling techniques because it is impossible to review 100% of the controls applied during the year. Because the auditor makes many audit decisions based on evidence gathered through sampling, the sampling methods used to provide evidence that is relevant and reliable to the audit process is important.

Audit sampling formerly was taught by having students learn about statistical methods to use in determining sample size and constructing confidence intervals around the sample estimate. Today the auditing standards and the Audit Guide, *Audit Sampling,* do not discuss mathematical formulas that are used in statistical sampling calculations. Knowledge of statistical sampling formulas that were once required to perform statistical sampling in auditing is no longer important because the formulas are written into the software accounting firms use to determine sample size, sample selection, and sample evaluation. Auditing standards assume that the auditor uses appropriate and reliable computer tables to perform the calculations needed for statistical sampling (AU 350). Today, the knowledge of statistical sampling calculations resides in the national offices of accounting firms where the decisions regarding sample size are made for the firm as a whole.

In this chapter, you will learn how to use sampling for tests of controls. A basic understanding of internal control sampling is important to the auditor because evidence about the effectiveness of internal controls is often gathered using sampling techniques. When testing internal control, the type of testing is often referred to as ***attribute sampling.*** In performing attribute testing, the auditor determines whether a characteristic of interest in the population (the internal control) is present by looking at a sample from the population. *The attribute of interest is the control.* Attribute testing is used to test the rate of deviation from a prescribed control (how often is the control missing). Attribute testing is not used when the auditor needs to quantify the dollar amount of the misstatement.

The next chapter discusses ***variables sampling*** using substantive tests of details (tests of transactions and tests of balances). Variables sampling techniques allow the auditor to determine the amount of misstatement in the financial statement account balance or class of transactions.

Audit Sampling for Tests of Internal Controls

LO1

Describe what audit sampling is and how it is used for tests of controls

Audit sampling is the selection and evaluation of a sample of items from a population so that the auditor expects the sample to be representative of the population. When a sample is representative, it is likely to provide a reasonable basis for making conclusions about the population. A representative sample results in conclusions that, subject to sampling risk, are similar to those that would be made if the same procedures were applied to the entire population (AU 350 and ISA 530). This chapter is part of the testing phase of the audit process. Exhibit 8-1 summarizes the main steps in the audit process.

When the auditor uses sampling to gather evidence he or she applies an audit procedure (confirmation, vouching, tracing, reviewing signatures, or reconciliations) to less than 100% of the population. The items selected for examination are referred to as the ***sample.*** All items in the account balance or the class of transactions are referred to as the ***population.*** *We use the evidence from the sample to arrive at a conclusion about the population.* For internal control testing, if we find control deviations in the sample, we assume those deviations would be found in the same proportion in the population.

To use the evidence from a sample to make a decision about the population, gathering a ***random*** sample is important. In a random sample, each item in the population has an equal chance of being selected. A random sample for tests of controls is a sample that is *representative* of the population. The characteristics of the population (in terms of control deviations) are captured in a random sample, allowing us to arrive at a decision concerning whether internal controls are effective in preventing or detecting misstatements in the financial statements.

The Audit Process	Exhibit 8-1

Steps in the Audit Process	Discussed in this Section
Planning Phase	
Consider the Preconditions for an Audit and Accept or Reject the Audit Engagement	
Understand the Entity and Its Environment, Determine Materiality, and Assess the Risks of Material Misstatements	
Develop an Audit Strategy and an Audit Plan to Respond to the Assessed Risks	
Testing Phase	√
Test Internal Controls? Yes No	√
Perform Tests of Controls if "Yes"	√
Perform Substantive Tests of Transactions	√
Perform Substantive Tests of Balances	√
Assess the Likelihood of Material Misstatement	√
Decision Phase	
Review the Presentation and Disclosure Assertions	
Evaluate the Evidence to Determine Whether the Financial Statements Are Prepared in Accordance with the Applicable Financial Reporting Framework	
Issue Audit Report	
Communicate with the Audit Committee	

Internal control tests are designed to provide information about the *effectiveness* of a control, which is deemed to be effective when it is present. If the auditor can observe evidence of the control, it has the ability to prevent or detect misstatements in the financial statements.

The basic question to be answered in an internal control test is whether the control works (can the auditor see evidence that it was applied)? Some accounting firms treat this as a "yes" or "no" question. The control is either working or it is not working. Other firms determine the **extent** of reliance possible for the control. When controls "work," the auditor reduces the amount of substantive testing. When controls do not "work," the auditor increases the amount of substantive testing beyond what would have been done if the control had been effective in preventing or detecting misstatements in the financial statements.

When thinking about control risk, the auditor can consider the *extent of reliance* that can be placed on internal controls or the *level of control risk* related to the control. The extent of reliance on internal controls (1 minus control risk) can be *high, medium,* or *low* corresponding to 30% control risk, 50% control risk, or 70% control risk, respectively. A control risk of 70% means that the auditor can rely on internal controls working to prevent or detect misstatements 30% of the time. In this case, 70% of the time, the control cannot be relied on to prevent or detect misstatements.

With internal control tests, the auditor asks:

Is the control working?	Yes	No
Or		
What is the risk of the control not working?	High	Control risk = 70%
	Medium	Control risk = 50%
	Low	Control risk = 30%

A control risk of 70% corresponds to a 30% reliance level.

A control risk of 50% corresponds to a 50% reliance level.

A control risk of 30% corresponds to a 70% reliance level.

When performing a test of internal controls, the only evidence the auditor finds concerns the control. The control could *not* be working, but the account balance or class of transactions can be correct because the transaction was recorded properly. The control can be working, but the account balance or class of transactions can still be incorrect because the individual performing the control indicates that the control has been performed (for example, by initials or stapling the correct forms together) although that person did not perform the procedure required by the control. For this reason, the auditor performs **dual-purpose** tests whenever possible to verify that the control activity was performed.

Internal control testing is *required* when the auditor plans to assess control risk below maximum for a relevant assertion in a significant account or class of transactions in an audit of the internal controls over financial statements (for public and private companies). Internal control testing is also *required* for audits of public companies for relevant assertions in significant accounts when the auditor issues an audit report on the effectiveness of internal controls over the financial reporting process.

Sampling and Nonsampling Risks

LO2

Understand sampling risk and nonsampling risk

Audit risk is the risk that material misstatements occur in the financial statements but the auditor does not detect them. Audit risk is typically set at approximately 5%. Therefore, 5% of the time material misstatements occur in the financial statements and are not detected by the auditor. Audit risk can be divided into two categories, sampling risk and nonsampling risk.

$$\text{Sampling risk} + \text{Nonsampling risk} = \text{Audit risk}$$

Sampling risk is the risk that the sample is not representative of the population. In this situation, the auditor's conclusion based on the sample can differ from the conclusion she or he would reach if the entire population was subject to the same audit procedure. *Sampling risk for tests of controls* includes the risk of (1) assessing control risk too high and (2) assessing control risk too low. Sampling risk can be calculated when the auditor uses statistical sampling. When nonstatistical sampling is used, the auditor estimates sampling risk by using professional judgment.

The *risk of assessing control risk too high* is an error that will affect the **efficiency** of the audit (the amount of time it takes to finish the audit). Assessing control risk higher than it really is causes the auditor to perform more substantive tests than necessary. This will affect the efficiency of the audit because doing so takes more time. The lack of efficiency will not affect the accuracy of the audit opinion issued.

The *risk of assessing control risk too low* is an error that will affect the **effectiveness** of the audit (arriving at the correct conclusion regarding whether the financial statements are materially misstated). When assessing control risk as being lower than it should have been, the auditor performs fewer substantive tests than otherwise had he or she assessed control risk correctly. This can result in an assumption that the financial statements are not materially misstated when they are.

The more serious error is the error related to the audit *effectiveness*. In this situation, the auditor could issue the wrong opinion. Wrong opinions generate more problems for an auditor than performing audit work that could not have been necessary. Auditors try to avoid making errors of effectiveness and design audit sampling procedures to avoid making them.

The auditor controls **sampling risk** in several ways. With statistical sampling, the auditor can quantify sampling risk, which allows him or her to keep it to an acceptable number. With nonstatistical sampling, sampling risk is controlled by (1) selecting appropriate sample sizes (sampling risk decreases as sample size increases), (2) taking a random sample so it is representative of the population, and (3) correctly evaluating sample results to consider sample risk.

Nonsampling risk includes all other aspects of audit risk not related to sampling. For example, nonsampling risk includes using the wrong audit procedures to gather evidence or interpreting evidence incorrectly. Nonsampling risk cannot be quantified by any sampling method. Auditors control it by planning and supervising employees.

Statistical and Nonstatistical Sampling

LO3

Explain the difference between statistical and nonstatistical sampling

Both statistical and nonstatistical sampling requires professional judgment for planning the sample, performing the procedures, and evaluating the evidence. The auditor can choose whether to use statistical or nonstatistical sampling methods according to the auditing standards (AU 350). The only evidence requirement is that the auditor "gather sufficient appropriate evidence" to determine whether the financial statements are materially misstated. The sufficiency of evidence is related to the audit sample's design and size.

Statistical sampling and nonstatistical sampling refer to (1) the *sample selection method* **and** (2) the way the auditor *evaluates the sample results*. **The audit procedures performed under either method are the same.** A statistical sample includes (1) a random selection of sample items and (2) the use of a statistical technique to evaluate the sample results including the measurement of sampling risk. If the sample does not have **both** of these characteristics, it is a nonstatistical sample. Today audit firms tend to use methods consistent with statistical sampling to select the items to sample but do not determine sampling risk or evaluate the sample results using statistical sampling theory. For this reason, much of the sampling done by accounting firms should be considered to be nonstatistical.

A *statistical sample* is a sample for which sampling risk can be calculated.

A *nonstatistical sample* is a sample for which sampling risk cannot be calculated.

Accounting firms today can use both statistical and nonstatistical sampling. Audit evidence can be gathered by either method, and audit firms are free to select the sampling method that works best for them. The sample sizes for nonstatistical sampling can be larger than those for statistical samples because sampling risk cannot be measured with nonstatistical sampling (and if it cannot be measured, the only way to lower sampling risk is to increase sample size). Nonstatistical samples can be a *less efficient* way to gather evidence but should not be viewed as a *less effective* way.

Statisticians in an accounting firm's head office often make sample size recommendations. The local office uses the decisions made by the statisticians by applying the guidelines from a *standard work sheet* to calculate sample sizes. This method ensures that the firm's auditors use similar approaches to calculating sample sizes. As a new auditor, you will determine sample sizes for audit procedures based on the firm's established *guidelines* that sometimes allow the auditor to choose from a range of sample sizes. An auditor who has a choice of sample size should consider the following factors in selecting the correct size:

- More testing will be required for manual controls than for automated controls because the manual ones are more prone to human error. IT (automated) controls that have been tested should continue to be reliable.
- The more frequently the control is performed, the more items are tested. More internal control tests are performed for controls that are performed daily than for those performed monthly.
- The more assurance the auditor receives from other audit procedures (for example, external confirmations, vouching, tracing), the less the control is tested.
- The more susceptible the control is to management override, the more the control is tested.

This chapter is designed to give you some background into the methods used by the head office in developing firm guidance on sampling. Consider that you recently joined an auditing firm. In determining sampling guidance, your firm begins with the procedures listed in the auditing standards (AU 350) and in the AICPA Audit Guide titled

Testing Internal Controls	Exhibit 8-2

To decide whether to test internal controls, the auditor should ask:

Based on my understanding of internal control, should control risk be assessed at less than maximum?

Yes

No

- The auditor has the choice to test or not test internal controls over the financial statements.
- For public companies, the auditor must answer "yes" to this question for relevant assertions for significant accounts for internal controls over the financial reporting process.

If "yes," the auditor designs and performs tests of controls to evaluate the controls' effectiveness in preventing or detecting misstatements in the financial statements.

With the evidence from the internal control tests, the auditor asks the following question:

Do the tests support the assessed level of control risk?

Yes

No

If "yes," the auditor designs substantive procedures based on the assessed level of control risk.

If no, the auditor adjusts the assessed level of control risk upward and designs substantive procedures based on the higher level of control risk.

If control risk is maximum for relevant assertions for significant accounts for public companies, the company has a significant deficiency or material weakness in its internal controls.

Audit Sampling. The AICPA Audit Guide provides sample sizes for statistical samples. The accounting firm uses these sample sizes to calculate sample sizes to provide instruction for both statistical and nonstatistical sample size calculations.

The most important things for you to understand about gathering audit evidence based on sampling procedures are (1) when to use a sample to gather evidence, (2) how to generate a random sample for your test, (3) how to perform the audit test, (4) how to evaluate the deviations found in your sample, and (5) how to use the sample results to arrive a conclusion about the population. We discuss these skills in this chapter and the following one.

One important thing to remember about sample sizes for internal control tests is that the size of the population usually has no effect on sample size for internal control tests. The only exception to this rule is a sample involving very small populations. For example, the sample size for a population of 1,000 is 90, for a population of 5,000 is 93, and for a population of 10,000 is also 93 (calculating a statistical sample size using a 5% risk of overreliance, a 1% expected population deviation rate, and a 5% tolerable rate). For this reason, sample size calculations typically assume a large population size of potential sampling units.

The Use of Sampling to Determine the Effectiveness of Internal Controls

LO4

Understand the use of sampling for gathering evidence regarding the effectiveness of internal controls, the use of dual-purpose tests, and how to evaluate sample errors

The auditor *can choose to* (1) rely on internal controls over financial statements or (2) perform a substantive audit for public and private company audits. Refer to Exhibit 8-2 for a guide describing how the auditor could make this decision. The auditor *must test* internal controls when evaluating internal controls over the financial reporting process for public companies. This testing must be done for relevant assertions for significant accounts for public company audits. Regardless of whether the auditor is testing internal controls over financial statements or over the financial reporting process, the purpose of an internal control test is to gather evidence about the control's operating effectiveness. The internal controls can be manually applied by the company's employees or IT controls by its computer systems. This chapter deals with testing manual controls; see Chapter 3 for testing IT controls.

An auditor who decides to test internal controls develops a sampling plan to test them See Exhibit 8-3 for an example of a sampling plan used to test controls. This plan corresponds to the documentation required by the auditing standards relating to tests of

Test of Controls Sampling Plan	Exhibit 8-3

Step 1 Describe the internal control being tested.	Step 6 Select the method for determining sample size.
Step 2 Determine the control objectives including the relevant assertion.	Step 7 Determine the method of sample selection.
Step 3 Define the population and the sampling unit.	Step 8 List the selected sample items.
Step 4 Define the deviation condition.	Step 9 Describe how the sampling procedure was performed.
Step 5 Determine the desired level of assurance, the tolerable deviation rate, and the expected population deviation rate.	Step 10 Evaluate the sample results and make a decision.

controls. We discuss the differences between performing internal control tests for financial statements and for the financial reporting process as they occur. Each step in the sampling plan is discussed in more detail in the section that follows.

Step 1. Describe the Internal Control Being Tested

Internal Control Procedures
Segregation of duties
Authorization procedures
Documented transaction trails
Independent reconciliations
Physical controls that limit access to assets

Of the five internal control procedures that a client could use to prevent or detect misstatements in the financial statements, sampling applies to only three of the procedures: (1) authorization procedures, (2) documented transaction trails, and (3) independent reconciliations.

In step 1 of the sampling plan for tests of controls, the auditor describes the procedure used by the client to prevent or detect misstatements in the financial statements. For example, monthly reconciliations can be performed to reconcile the cash balance on the financial statements to the bank balance on the bank statement. The auditor could review a sample of these monthly bank reconciliations.

Step 2. Determine the Control Objective

Internal control tests are performed to determine whether a control that has been identified is working. Usually the *test objective is to determine whether the control is present.* **For example,** a signature from management could be required on a purchase order to indicate approval for the item purchased. This signature provides evidence for the relevant assertions of accuracy, classification, and obligation.

The objective for a test of controls is to determine whether the required signature is on the purchase orders reviewed. The signature is the attribute condition and the auditor is testing the rate of occurrence of the attribute. The assertions associated with the testing are accuracy, classification, and obligation.

Step 3. Define the Population and the Sampling Unit for Test of Controls over *Financial Statements*

The *population* for internal control testing related to a financial statement audit *is usually all items in the class of transactions or account balance **for the year.***

A sampling unit can be a document, a journal entry, or a line item on an invoice. However the sampling unit is defined, each one represents one item in the population. The auditor must define the sampling unit to be consistent with the control being tested.

For example, if the control tested is the approval signature on a purchase order, each purchase order is a sampling unit. If the control tested is whether year-end adjusting entries are approved, each journal entry can be a sampling unit. The population to test the control for approval signatures on purchase orders would be a sample of all purchase orders processed during the year. The sampling unit would be the purchase order.

Step 3a. Define the Population for Test of Controls over the *Financial Reporting* Process

The population for an internal control test differs when its purpose is related to controls over the financial reporting process. In this case, the *population is usually all items in the class of transactions or account balances that the auditor believes are necessary to determine whether controls were effective at the **end of the year.*** According to the auditing standards, internal controls tested for the financial reporting process must be effective only at year-end. This differs from internal control testing for controls on financial statements, which must be effective for the entire year.

For example, if testing the control for a signature indicating approval on purchase orders was identified as a significant control for the financial reporting process, the population to test could be all purchase orders processed during the last 15 or 30 days of the year. If the control was identified as a significant control for the financial statements, the population to test would include all purchase orders for the year. The sampling unit would be the purchase orders.

Step 4. Define the Deviation Condition

A deviation occurs when there is no indication that the control has been performed. Defining the deviation conditions before testing begins is important so that the auditor has a clear understanding of the conditions necessary for the control to be working.

In the example in Step 3, a deviation condition would be a purchase order without the signature from management indicating approval. In this case, the attribute is missing.

Step 5. Determine the Sample's Tolerable Rate of Deviation, Expected Rate of Deviation, and Desired Level of Assurance

To determine the sample size for tests of controls, the auditor needs to estimate the following information based on his or her professional judgment:

- The tolerable rate of deviation for the population to be tested
- The expected rate of deviation for the population to be tested
- The desired level of assurance that the actual rate of deviation does not exceed the tolerable rate of deviation
- The number of sampling units in the population if the population for the test is very small, less than 500 (AU350)

These factors are discussed briefly next.

Tolerable Rate of Deviation

- The auditor sets the rate of deviation from prescribed internal control procedures related to the level of assurance the auditor expects to obtain.
- In practice, tolerable rates of deviation of 2–20% are often used. If the control risk is as low as 30%, the auditor would use a tolerable rate of deviation at the low end of the 2–20% range. Assessing control risk at high, or 70%, the auditor would use a tolerable rate of deviation at the high end of the 2–20% range. These decisions are based on the auditor's professional judgment.

Expected Rate of Deviation

- The rate of deviation expected in the population is based on the auditor's understanding of relevant controls or on the examination of a small number of items from the population.
- In practice, expected rates of deviation are estimated as 0.00% to 15.00%.

Desired Level of Assurance

- Based on the extent to which the auditor's risk assessment takes relevant controls into account
- In practice, the desired level of assurance is 95% or 90%
- Also used to calculate *the risk of overreliance,* stated as 5% or 10% (1 − Desired level of assurance).

The following table describes the effect of increases in the four factors on sample size. An increase in the tolerable rate of deviation results in a *decrease* in sample size. Increases in the expected rate of deviation and in the desired level of assurance result in an *increase* to the sample size. The size of the population usually has no effect on sample size.

As Factor Increases	Affect on Sample Size	Explanation
Extent to which auditor's risk assessment considers relevant controls	Sample size increases	The more assurance the auditor intends to obtain from the operating effectiveness of controls, the larger the sample size needs to be.
Tolerable rate of deviation	Sample size decreases	The lower the tolerable rate of deviation, the larger the sample size needs to be.
Expected rate of deviation	Sample size increases	The higher the expected rate of deviation, the larger the sample size needs to be so that the auditor can make an accurate estimate of the actual rate of deviation.
Desired level of assurance	Sample size increases	The higher the auditor's desired level of assurance that the results of the sample are representative of the population, the larger the sample size needs to be.
Population	Negligible	For large populations (>500), the size of the population has little or no effect on sample size.

Step 6. Determine the Method of Sample Size Determination

The method of determining the sample size can be statistical or nonstatistical. The size can be determined after the auditor has specified the tolerable rate of deviation, the expected rate of deviation, and the desired level of assurance for the sample. Often the auditor uses a sampling program designed by the firm's national office to determine sample size. The sampling program asks the auditor to input the tolerable rate of deviation, the expected rate of deviation, and the desired level of assurance for the sample into the program, and the sample size is calculated from this information.

Step 7. Determine the Method of Selecting the Sample

The auditor uses simple random sampling, systematic random sampling, or haphazard sampling to select the sample for a test of controls. Each method is discussed next. Random sampling and systematic random sampling can be used for statistical or nonstatistical sampling. Haphazard sampling can be used only for nonstatistical sampling.

Simple Random Sampling

The auditor uses random numbers to generate a simple random sample. To do this, the auditor generates random numbers from a random number table or a computer program and then selects the document number corresponding to the random numbers generated. Random sampling can be used only when the sampling units are prenumbered. When random-number sampling is used, each sampling unit in the population has an equal chance of being selected, so a sample selected with random numbers is a sample that is representative of the population. Random-number sampling can be used for statistical and nonstatistical sampling.

For example, the auditor could decide to review 30 purchase orders for the year to determine whether the approval signature is on them. The purchase orders are numbered from 10,306 to 14,921. To select a sample using random-number sampling, the auditor would generate 30 random numbers between 10,306 and 14,921 and then would review the purchase order numbers for the random numbers selected to determine whether the approval signature is on the form. If three signatures are missing in a sample of 30 (an actual deviation rate of 10%), the auditor would assume that 10% of the signatures would be missing in the entire population. The decision rules established by the firm would determine whether controls were working or not with three deviations.

Systematic Random Sampling

To use **systematic random sampling,** the auditor divides the number of units in the population by the number in the sample size to calculate a sampling interval and then generates a random number in the sampling interval. The random number is the first item chosen. The following items are found by taking the random number and adding the sampling interval. Systematic sampling can be used for statistical and nonstatistical sampling.

In the preceding example, assume the total population includes 4,616 purchase order numbers (14,921 − 10,306 plus 1 = 4,616) divided by a sample size of 30 equals a sampling interval of 153. The auditor generates a random number in the first sampling interval of 153, which would be between 10,306 and 10,459 (10,306 plus 153). Let's say this random number is 10,438. Purchase order number 10,438 is the first item in the sample. The second is determined by adding 10,438 and 153. So, the second item in the sample is 10,612. The third item is found by adding 10,612 and 153. The auditor moves through the sample in this fashion until 30 items have been selected.

Haphazard Sampling

The auditor can also use **haphazard sampling** in which the sample is selected without any conscious bias. Haphazard sampling must be used when items in the population are not prenumbered documents. A haphazard sample is not a careless sample but a description used to indicate that no random number method is used in the sample selection. Haphazard sampling can be used only for nonstatistical sampling.

For example, the purchase orders for the year can be kept in a file drawer either by date or alphabetically by vendor, but the purchase order is not a prenumbered form. In this case, the auditor opens the file drawer and haphazardly selects a sample of 30 documents, so each document has a chance of being selected. A selection of the first 30 documents would not be a haphazard sample and would not be representative of the population.

Step 8. List the Selected Sample Items

Auditing standards require the auditor to list the specific items sampled in the work papers or to describe the sampling method in such a way that another auditor could go back and pull the same sample.

Step 9. Describe How the Audit Procedure Was Performed

The auditor performs the audit procedure to determine whether the sample items contain deviations from the documented control. [**Note:** For an internal control test, the only factor of interest to the auditor is the *presence* of the control. So, if a supervisor is required to sign a purchase order indicating approval for the item requested, the only thing the auditor looks for is the signature.] A missing signature is a deviation. The auditor does not reperform the control to see whether the supervisor performed the control before signing the form *unless the auditor performs a dual-purpose test.*

The only possible evidence from an internal control test is the answer to the question: (1) is the control working, or (2) is the control working to the extent expected? "Yes" or "no" are the only possible answers to the question.

Internal control testing is typically performed while the interim fieldwork is being done. For example, the auditor can perform interim fieldwork in August for a client with a December year-end. In August, internal control testing is done for the first eight months of the year. When the auditor returns after year-end to perform year-end fieldwork procedures, internal control testing can be updated for the remaining four months of the year.

The auditor can also decide to stop internal control testing if the results from the items sampled indicate a higher rate of deviation than planned (actual deviation rate > tolerable rate). If the deviations in the sample already include more than would be acceptable according to the firm's guidelines, there is no reason to continue with the sampling plan. In this situation, the auditor increases control risk and performs more substantive audit procedures. This method of sampling, referred to as *sequential sampling,* is discussed in a later section of the chapter.

Step 9a. Describe the Performance of Audit Procedures with a Dual-Purpose Test

If the internal control test is a dual-purpose test, the auditor examines the item to determine whether it contains a deviation from the documented control, **and** *then the auditor reperforms the control.*

In the preceding example, the auditor would look for the signature of the supervisor on the purchase order. The signature is the internal control. It is either there or not. If it is not there, the purchase order is an internal control deviation. Remember that all internal control deviations do not necessarily mean that there is a misstatement in the financial statements.

Next the auditor reviews the purchase order to determine whether the supervisor should have signed it according to the company's rules regarding appropriate items to purchase. The auditor determines whether the purchase is consistent with the organization's mission and its expenditure policies. For example, when the supervisor approves a purchase order for yacht insurance for a hospital, this purchase is not consistent with the mission of the organization.

From a dual-purpose test, the auditor obtains the following evidence:

1. Is the control working?   Yes
                                                      No
2. Is the class of transactions recorded correctly? Yes
                                                      No

If not, what is the correct balance?

Step 10. Evaluate the Sample Results and Reach Conclusions

Whether the sample is statistical or nonstatistical, the auditor uses professional judgment to evaluate the sample results and to reach an overall conclusion. When reviewing the deviations, the auditor can determine that the missing controls have a common feature, for example, deviations came from one location or from one type of transaction. In this case, the auditor can decide to review all items in the population that have the common feature. Control deviations can also be intentional and indicate the possibility of fraud.

Auditing standards require the auditor to consider the qualitative aspects of the misstatements. These include the (1) nature and cause of the misstatement, such as whether it is caused by a misunderstanding of instructions or by carelessness and (2) the possible relationship of the misstatement to other parts of the audit. When the auditor discovers fraud, its possible implications are greater than when a control deviation due to an error is found.

The accounting firm often establishes guidelines for the number of deviations that can be found in a sample if internal controls are to be considered reliable. This is referred to as the ***tolerable deviation rate.*** The individual auditor typically follows this guidance in evaluating the sample results.

To evaluate the sample results, the auditor first calculates the actual deviation rate in the sample by dividing the number of deviations in the sample by the sample size. Five deviations in a sample of 100 items have a 5% actual deviation rate. If the sample represents the population, the population's deviation rate should also be 5%. Next the auditor compares the tolerable deviation rate to the actual deviation rate after adding an allowance for sampling risk to the actual deviation rate. If the auditor uses a statistical sampling program for the internal control test, it will calculate an allowance for sampling risk (also referred to as the *precision of the test*). When using nonstatistical sampling, the auditor uses judgment to determine the allowance for sampling risk. For example, when the actual deviation rate (without considering the allowance for sampling risk) exceeds the tolerable deviation rate, the auditor usually concludes that the allowance for sampling risk is unacceptably high and rejects the hypothesis that control risk is equal to the level tested. If the actual deviation rate (without adding the allowance for sampling risk) is near or equal to the tolerable deviation rate, the auditor must consider the risk that the result could be obtained even if the true deviation rate exceeds the tolerable rate for the population.

If the number of deviations found in the sample (the ***actual deviation rate plus the allowance for sampling risk***) is less than the ***tolerable deviation rate,*** the auditor relies on the effectiveness of internal controls to reduce the extent of substantive testing. If the actual deviation rate in the sample is higher than the tolerable deviation rate permitted by the audit firm's guidance, the auditor does not rely on the effectiveness of internal controls but increases his or her assessment of control risk, which will result in an increase in the amount of substantive testing done than had the internal controls had been effective in detecting or preventing misstatements in the financial statements.

For a test of controls, the auditor assumes that the sample deviation rate represents the population deviation rate. If the sample deviation rate is higher than the tolerable deviation rate, the auditor either assumes that controls are not working (and that control risk is 100%) or increases the control risk from the original assessment for the relevant assertion for the significant account. See the following for the conclusions that an auditor could reach after a test of controls.

Evaluating the Results of a Test of Controls

Is the control working?   Yes
    Results of the internal control test would indicate that
    Actual Control deviations + Allowance for sampling risk < Tolerable deviations
    In this case, the auditor would reduce the level of substantive testing
    based on her or his reliance on internal controls.

Is the control working?   No
    Results of the internal control test would indicate that
    Actual control deviations + Allowance for sampling risk > Tolerable deviations
    In this case, the auditor would increase the amount of substantive testing.
    Control risk would be 1.00, and the auditor would not rely on internal controls.*

OR

Is the control working to the extent expected?   Yes
    Results of the internal control test would indicate that
    Actual control deviations + Allowance for sampling risk < Tolerable deviations
    This means that the results of tests of controls support auditor's control risk assessment
    The auditor will rely on internal controls to reduce the amount of substantive
    testing done.
    Control risk could be 30% (low), 50% (medium), or 70% (high).

Is the control working to the extent expected?   No
>   Results of the internal control test would indicate that
>   Actual control deviations + Allowance for sampling risk > Tolerable deviations
>   This means that the results of tests of controls assessed by the auditor has not been supported. The auditor must increase control risk in this case and perform more substantive testing. Control risk could be 0.50 (medium), 0.70 (high), or 1.00 (maximum).†

---

*This model assumes that the decision about whether internal controls are working is a "yes" or no" decision. It is either working or it is not. The second model assumes that the auditor assesses the extent to which internal controls are working.

†Control risk could not be 0.30 (low) because if the auditor had assessed control risk to be 0.30 and actual control deviations were more than tolerable deviations, control risk would be increased to at least 0.50.

When determining that internal controls cannot be relied on (because the actual deviations plus the allowance for sample risk is more than the tolerable deviations), the auditor should also consider whether the presence of control deviations indicates a significant deficiency or a material weakness in internal control. Special reporting requirements apply to both significant deficiencies and material weaknesses. These issues were discussed in the internal control chapter.

When determining that the actual deviations in the sample (plus the allowance for sampling risk) are *less* than the tolerable deviations, the auditor assesses control risk at the level tested (0.30, 0.50, or 0.70) and *reduces* the amount of substantive testing. The auditor who determines that the actual deviations found in the sample are *more* than the tolerable deviations, does one of two things: (1) if the auditor tests internal controls to determine *whether* they can be relied on, he or she assesses control risk at 1.00 because the evidence indicates that they cannot be relied upon (the actual deviations are more than the tolerable deviations) or (2) if the auditor tests internal controls to determine the *extent* to which they can be relied on, he or she considers the number of actual deviations in the sample to see whether the test results support a higher level of control risk. In this case, he or she could assess control risk at 0.50 (medium), 0.70 (high), or 1.00 (maximum) based on the actual deviations in the sample compared to the tolerable deviations permitted for each control risk level.

The auditor does not *lower* control risk based on an internal control test because the test's only purpose is to determine whether the actual deviation rate exceeds the tolerable deviation rate. This is referred to as the *upper limit approach* (AICPA, *Audit Sampling Guide*). The only possible results from an internal control test are to confirm either that the control risk level assessed is supported by the evidence or that the control risk level should be increased to the level supported by the evidence from the test.

Audit Sampling Plan to Perform a Test of Controls

LO5

Explain how the auditor develops an audit sampling plan to perform a test of controls

Let's consider an audit sampling plan for a test of controls (Exhibit 8-4) and the completed working paper documenting this internal control test (Exhibit 8-5). Review the sampling plan in Exhibit 8-4 before continuing.

A review of the working paper in Exhibit 8-5 supports the fact that the auditor has documented five exceptions to the internal control test. In two cases, the purchase orders are missing. The other three purchase orders are missing the control. The substantive test of transactions found misstatements in the amount of $14,587. Travel and entertainment expense is overstated by $14,587, and payroll expense is understated by $14,587. The auditor first considers the reasons for the exception and then evaluates the sample results to arrive at a conclusion about the population. Let's consider the reasons for the exceptions first.

To understand why these exceptions occurred, the auditor should ask the client the following questions: (1) how could the two purchase orders be missing and (2) how many more purchase orders do you think are missing? The auditor also could question the missing signatures; however, it is reasonable to expect a manual control to have missing signatures. Based on the client's answers, the auditor determines risk for this control.

Internal Control Sampling Plan   *Management Approval on Purchase Orders*   Exhibit 8-4

STEP 1. DESCRIBE THE INTERNAL CONTROL BEING TESTED

The internal control tested is an *authorization procedure.* Management's signature is required on a purchase order to authorize the purchase.

STEP 2. DETERMINE THE TEST OBJECTIVE

The objective of the test is to determine that management's signature is on all purchase orders processed during the year. The relevant assertions are accuracy, classification (for income statement accounts), and obligation (for liability accounts).

*Explanation: The signature is the characteristic of interest. It is the **attribute** that the auditor tests. The auditor is interested in purchase orders that could be missing the attribute.*

STEP 3. DEFINE THE POPULATION AND THE SAMPLING UNIT

The population is all purchase orders processed during the year (from January 1 through December 31) numbered 10,306 to 14,921. Each purchase order is a sampling unit.

STEP 4. DEFINE THE DEVIATION CONDITION

A purchase order that does not have the signature of management is a deviation.

STEP 5. DETERMINE THE SAMPLE'S ACCEPTABLE RISK OF OVERRELIANCE, THE TOLERABLE DEVIATION RATE, AND THE EXPECTED POPULATION DEVIATION RATE

For this sample, the auditor determines that the acceptable risk of overreliance is 5%, the tolerable deviation rate is 15%, and the expected population deviation rate is 3.5%. These decisions are made based on professional judgment.

STEP 6. DETERMINE THE METHOD OF SAMPLE SIZE DETERMINATION

The sample is determined using the sampling software provided by the firm. The sample size based on the software is 40 with 2 deviations allowed. This size is based on the statistical sample size from Table A.1 of the AICPA *Audit Guide.* The auditor performs a nonstatistical sample.

STEP 7. DETERMINE THE METHOD OF SELECTING THE SAMPLE

The sample is selected by generating random numbers using a computer program.

Explanation: The sample could also be selected by using systematic sampling or haphazard sampling. All three methods are possible because the purchase orders are prenumbered and nonstatistical sampling is used. All methods give a representative sample of the population.

STEP 8. LIST THE SELECTED SAMPLE ITEMS

40 random numbers will be generated between 10,306 and 14,921. The auditor will list the numbers generated in the working papers.

STEP 9. DESCRIBE HOW THE AUDIT PROCEDURE WAS PERFORMED

The auditor reviews the purchase order to determine whether the signature is on it and whether the signature is from a manager. All purchase orders with signatures missing are treated as a control deviation. The auditor will also reperform the control as a substantive test of transactions (for a dual-purpose test). To gather evidence about whether the transaction was recorded in a manner consistent with company policy, the auditor reviews the purchase order to determine whether the supervisor should have signed it according to the company's rules. The auditor determines whether the purchase is consistent with the organization's rules and mission.

Explanation: The auditor believes that the purchase approval process is an important control for the company. This control is related to the accuracy, obligation, and classification assertions (relevant assertions) for accounts payable, a significant account. For this reason, the auditor will test internal controls and use the internal control sample to do a substantive test of transactions.

STEP 10. EVALUATE THE SAMPLE RESULTS AND REACH CONCLUSIONS

The auditor analyzes the exceptions found during the internal control test and the substantive test of transactions to determine the reason for the exception and whether additional testing is needed. If the exceptions indicate a pattern of misstatements, the auditor would investigate further to determine the total value of the misstatements in this significant account.

Because this test is a dual-purpose test, the auditor will get two types of evidence from the sample: (1) whether the control is working and (2) whether the transactions in the class of transactions have been recorded according to the applicable financial reporting framework?

In both cases, the auditor uses the evidence from the sample to make a decision about the population because a random sample is representative of the population.

Explanation: If the control is not working at the level expected, the auditor will find more deviations in the sample than are permitted according to the firm's guidance. In this case, the auditor increases control risk and performs more substantive tests. If the control is working at the level expected, the auditor will find fewer deviations in the sample than are permitted according to the firm's guidance. In this case, the auditor reduces the level of substantive testing.

For the substantive test of transactions, the auditor gathers evidence to determine whether the purchase transactions are recorded in accordance with the applicable financial reporting framework. If they are not, the auditor proposes audit adjustments to correct these accounts.

Dual-Purpose Test for Purchases *For the Year Ending December 31, 2011*   **Exhibit 8-5**

Reference:	F-5
Prepared by:	ICS
Date:	Jan. 14, 2012
Reviewed by:	BRT
Date:	Jan 30, 2012

BCS Company
Dual-Purpose Test, Internal Control and Substantive Test of Transactions for the Year Ended December 31, 2011

Purchase Order No.	r
13498	∞ x
13157	∞ x
11484	∞ x
11962	∞ x
11592	∞ y
14444	∞ x
11205	€
13418	∞ x
14782	∞ x
12434	∞ x
14181	∞ x
10626	∞ x
10856	# x
14204	∞ x
11809	∞ x
13754	∞ x
10767	∞ x
11838	∞ x
12617	# x
11323	∞ x
11059	∞ x
10717	∞ x
13096	∞ x
14745	# x
12410	∞ x
12247	∞ y
11313	∞ x
10543	€
12666	∞ x
13553	∞ x
12295	∞ x

Tickmark symbols

r	Generated 40 random numbers to select purchase order numbers in the range 10,306 to 14,921 using Excel randbetween function.
∞	Reviewed purchase order to determine that management's signature is on it. The signature indicates that the manager has approved the purchase and that the purchase is consistent with the organization's mission.
#	Purchase order does not have a signature.
€	Purchase order is missing. Client has no idea what has happened to it.
x	Reviewed the purchase order to determine whether it is consistent with the company's rules and mission. Purchase consistent without exception.
y	Purchase is not consistent with the company's mission. Payment is for personal item for manager. Purchase order 11592 is for $5,623 and purchase order 12247 is for $8,964. Both were recorded as travel and entertainment expense.

Conclusion: Actual control deviations are more than tolerable deviations, so control risk must be increased. Travel and entertainment expense is overstated by $14,587. ICS

The explanations for the exceptions found in the substantive test of transactions are more critical. They are fraudulent transactions. To determine the extent of misstatement in this class of transactions, the auditor would ask the client the following questions: (1) how many more transactions for personal items has a manager approved, (2) are other managers approving personal expenses, and (3) what is the dollar amount of misstatement associated with this fraud? The auditor would probably ask the client to investigate the extent of the fraud and report back to the auditor.

To evaluate the sample results, the auditor considers the internal control exceptions and the misstatements separately. For the internal control deviations, the auditor calculates the actual deviation rate based on those found in the sample. In this case, the auditor found five deviations in a sample of 40, so the actual deviation rate is 0.125. The auditor compares the actual deviation rate to the tolerable deviation rate established by the firm's guidelines. The tolerable deviation rate was 0.05 (2/40 = 0.05). In this case, the actual deviation rate is more than the tolerable rate. The auditor therefore rejects control risk at the planned level. In this case, the auditor either places no reliance on controls or sets control risk at a higher level than previously assessed depending on the firm's policy.

To evaluate the misstatement found in the substantive test of transactions, the auditor considers whether the misstatement is representative of a misstatement in the entire population. In this case, it is probable that it is not a representative misstatement. The client reviews all transactions related to this manager to determine the total amount of misstatement related to her or him. If no other managers are involved in this fraud, the total amount of the misstatement can be determined. The auditor could perform additional substantive tests to determine that the financial statement accounts associated with the purchase account are prepared in accordance with the applicable financial reporting framework.

The entry to record the misstatement identified by the auditor follows.

Payroll Expense	14,587	
Travel and Entertainment Expense		14,587
To correct a misstatement when a manager used company funds to pay personal expenses.		

This is a *known adjustment.* It is unlikely that the auditor found the only two purchase orders that the manager used to pay personal expenses, so when the investigation has been completed, there could be additional misstatements to record.

Therefore, from this dual-purpose test, the auditor gathers evidence from a sample that allows him or her to make the following decisions about the population:

1. Control risk for the accuracy, obligation, and classification assertions for purchase transactions is higher than expected. Additional substantive testing is needed. The internal control tested cannot be relied on to prevent or detect misstatements in the purchase transactions.

2. There are misstatements in the purchase transactions for the year. The auditor proposes audit adjustments to the client to correct these misstatements.

Audit Sampling Using Sequential Sampling

LO6

Describe how sequential sampling could be used for tests of controls

Audit samples for tests of controls can be designed using a fixed or sequential (*stop-or-go*) sampling plan. When using a fixed sampling plan, the auditor examines one sample of a specified sample size. All the examples considered in this chapter have fixed sampling plans. When using a sequential sampling plan, the auditor takes the sample in several steps with each step contingent on the results of the previous one. The auditor decides between the two sampling plans based on which plan she or he believes to be more efficient.

One of the limitations of a fixed sampling plan is that the sample either passes or fails at the conclusion of the testing. When finding unexpected deviations in the sample, the only thing the auditor can conclude is that the sample fails.

Sequential sampling is designed to give the auditor the alternative of expanding the sample. A sequential sampling plan usually consists of two to four groups of sampling units. The auditor determines the size of each group by specifying the risk of overreliance, the tolerable deviation rate, and the expected population deviation rate. The auditor uses either a computer program or sample size tables designed for sequential sampling.

After considering control deviations in the first group of sampling units, the auditor decides whether to (1) accept the assessed level of control risk as planned without examining additional units, (2) stop sampling because the tolerable rate of deviation cannot be achieved (actual deviations are more than tolerable deviations), or (3) examine additional sampling units because sufficient information to support the assessed level of control risk has not been found.

An example of a sequential sampling plan follows. This example is based on Table B.1 from the AICPA Audit Guide, *Audit Sampling.*

Group	Number of Sampling Units
1	50
2	51
3	51
4	51

This sampling plan is based on a 5% tolerable rate of deviation, a 10% level of reliance, and a 0.05% expected population deviation rate.

The auditor implements the sequential sampling plan in the following manner:

- If the auditor finds four deviations at any time during the testing, the testing stops and the assessed level of control risk is increased (or the auditor assumes that controls cannot be relied on to prevent or detect misstatements).
- If no deviations are found in the first group of 50, the auditor assumes that the sample supports the assessed control risk without examining additional sampling units.
- If 1, 2, or 3 deviations are found in the first group of 50, the auditor examines additional sampling units in the next group.
- The auditor continues to examine sampling units in the following groups until the sample results either support or do not support the assessed control risk.

Sequential sampling could be used to reduce sample size when the auditor believes the population has a low deviation rate. For example, the sample size for a fixed sample with the same parameters is 77. If the auditor does not find any deviations in the first group sampled using sequential sampling, she or he could look at 50 sampling units rather than 77. On the other hand, if the auditor finds a deviation in the first group, the sample size could increase to 203, many more than the fixed sample size of 77. The auditor uses professional judgment to determine the appropriate sampling plan for tests of controls.

Using a Statistical Sampling Table for Nonstatistical Sampling

LO7

Explain how statistical sampling tables could be used to determine sample sizes for nonstatistical samples

Although the auditor is not required to understand statistical sampling theory to calculate sample sizes for tests of controls, looking at some of the firm's statistical tables to develop sample size guidelines is helpful. Two tables are useful to the auditor:

- Statistical sample sizes for tests of controls—5% risk of overreliance
- Statistical sample sizes for tests of controls—10% risk of overreliance

See Exhibit 8-6 and Exhibit 8-7 for tables that give sample sizes and the number of deviations allowed when combining the three factors that determine sample size: the risk of overreliance, the expected deviation rate, and the tolerable deviation rate. Both tables assume large populations and stop at sampling sizes of more than 2,000. The tables are taken from Table A.1 and A.2 in the AICPA Audit Guide, *Audit Sampling.*

Statistical Samples Sizes for Tests of Controls—5 Percent Risk of Overreliance — Exhibit 8-6
(with number of expected errors in parentheses)

Expected Deviation Rate	Tolerable Deviation Rate										
	2%	3%	4%	5%	6%	7%	8%	9%	10%	15%	20%
0.00%	149 (0)	99 (0)	74 (0)	59 (0)	49 (0)	42 (0)	36 (0)	32 (0)	29 (0)	19 (0)	14 (0)
0.25	236 (1)	157 (1)	117 (1)	93 (1)	78 (1)	66 (1)	58 (1)	51 (1)	46 (1)	30 (1)	22 (1)
0.50	313 (2)	157 (1)	117 (1)	93 (1)	78 (1)	66 (1)	58 (1)	51 (1)	46 (1)	30 (1)	22 (1)
0.75	386 (3)	208 (2)	117 (1)	93 (1)	78 (1)	66 (1)	58 (1)	51 (1)	46 (1)	30 (1)	22 (1)
1.00	590 (6)	257 (3)	156 (2)	93 (1)	78 (1)	66 (1)	58 (1)	51 (1)	46 (1)	30 (1)	22 (1)
1.25	1,030 (13)	303 (4)	156 (2)	124 (2)	78 (1)	66 (1)	58 (1)	51 (1)	46 (1)	30 (1)	22 (1)
1.50		392 (6)	192 (3)	124 (2)	103 (2)	66 (2)	58 (1)	51 (1)	46 (1)	30 (1)	22 (1)
1.75		562 (10)	227 (4)	153 (3)	103 (2)	88 (2)	77 (2)	51 (1)	46 (1)	30 (1)	22 (1)
2.00		846 (17)	294 (6)	181 (4)	127 (3)	88 (2)	77 (2)	68 (2)	46 (1)	30 (1)	22 (1)
2.25		1,466 (33)	390 (9)	208 (5)	127 (3)	88 (2)	77 (2)	68 (2)	61 (2)	30 (1)	22 (1)
2.50			513 (13)	234 (6)	150 (4)	109 (3)	77 (2)	68 (2)	61 (2)	30 (1)	22 (1)
2.75			722 (20)	286 (8)	173 (5)	109 (3)	95 (3)	68 (2)	61 (2)	30 (1)	22 (1)
3.00			1,098 (33)	361 (11)	195 (6)	129 (4)	95 (3)	84 (3)	61 (2)	30 (1)	22 (1)
3.25			1,936 (63)	458 (15)	238 (8)	148 (5)	112 (4)	84 (3)	61 (2)	30 (1)	22 (1)
3.50				624 (22)	280 (10)	167 (6)	112 (4)	84 (3)	76 (3)	40 (2)	22 (1)
3.75				877 (33)	341 (13)	185 (7)	129 (5)	100 (4)	76 (3)	40 (2)	22 (1)
4.00				1,348 (54)	421 (17)	221 (9)	146 (6)	100 (4)	89 (4)	40 (2)	22 (1)
5.00					1,580 (79)	478 (24)	240 (12)	158 (8)	116 (6)	40 (2)	30 (2)
6.00						1,832 (110)	532 (32)	266 (16)	179 (11)	50 (3)	30 (2)
7.00								585 (41)	298 (21)	68 (5)	37 (3)
8.00									649 (52)	85 (7)	37 (3)
9.00										110 (10)	44 (4)
10.00										150 (15)	50 (5)
12.50										576 (72)	88 (11)
15.00											193 (29)
17.50											720 (126)

Statistical Samples Sizes for Tests of Controls: 10 Percent Risk of Overreliance (with number of expected errors in parentheses)

Exhibit 8-7

Expected Deviation Rate	Tolerable Deviation Rate										
	2%	3%	4%	5%	6%	7%	8%	9%	10%	15%	20%
0.00%	114 (0)	76 (0)	57 (0)	45 (0)	38 (0)	32 (0)	28 (0)	25 (0)	22 (0)	15 (0)	11 (0)
0.25	194 (1)	129 (1)	96 (1)	77 (1)	64 (1)	55 (1)	48 (1)	42 (1)	38 (1)	25 (1)	18 (1)
0.50	194 (1)	129 (1)	96 (1)	77 (1)	64 (1)	55 (1)	48 (1)	42 (1)	38 (1)	25 (1)	18 (1)
0.75	265 (2)	129 (1)	96 (1)	77 (1)	64 (1)	55 (1)	48 (1)	42 (1)	38 (1)	25 (1)	18 (1)
1.00	398 (4)	176 (2)	96 (1)	77 (1)	64 (1)	55 (1)	48 (1)	42 (1)	38 (1)	25 (1)	18 (1)
1.25	708 (9)	221 (3)	132 (2)	77 (1)	64 (1)	55 (1)	48 (1)	42 (1)	38 (1)	25 (1)	18 (1)
1.50	1,463 (22)	265 (4)	132 (2)	105 (2)	64 (1)	55 (1)	48 (1)	42 (1)	38 (1)	25 (1)	18 (1)
1.75		390 (7)	166 (3)	132 (3)	88 (2)	55 (1)	48 (1)	42 (1)	38 (1)	25 (1)	18 (1)
2.00		590 (12)	198 (4)	132 (3)	88 (2)	75 (2)	48 (1)	42 (1)	38 (1)	25 (1)	18 (1)
2.25		974 (22)	262 (6)	158 (4)	88 (2)	75 (2)	65 (2)	42 (1)	38 (1)	25 (1)	18 (1)
2.50			353 (9)	209 (6)	110 (3)	75 (2)	65 (2)	58 (2)	38 (1)	25 (1)	18 (1)
2.75			471 (13)	258 (8)	132 (4)	94 (3)	65 (2)	58 (2)	52 (2)	25 (1)	18 (1)
3.00			730 (22)	306 (10)	153 (5)	94 (3)	65 (2)	58 (2)	52 (2)	25 (1)	18 (1)
3.25			1,258 (41)	400 (14)	194 (7)	113 (4)	82 (3)	58 (2)	52 (2)	25 (1)	18 (1)
3.50				583 (22)	235 (9)	131 (5)	82 (3)	73 (3)	52 (2)	25 (1)	18 (1)
3.75				873 (35)	274 (11)	149 (6)	98 (4)	73 (3)	52 (2)	25 (1)	18 (1)
4.00					1,019 (51)	318 (16)	98 (4)	73 (3)	65 (3)	25 (1)	18 (1)
5.00						1,150 (69)	160 (8)	115 (6)	78 (4)	34 (2)	18 (1)
6.00							349 (21)	182 (11)	116 (7)	43 (3)	25 (2)
7.00							1,300 (91)	385 (27)	199 (14)	52 (4)	25 (2)
8.00								1,437 (115)	424 (34)	60 (5)	25 (2)
9.00									1,577 (142)	77 (7)	32 (3)
10.00										100 (10)	38 (4)
12.50										368 (46)	63 (8)
15.00											126 (19)
17.50											457 (80)

Internal Control Sample Sizes		Exhibit 8-8

Frequency of Control	Number in Population	Sample Size
Annual	1	100%
Quarterly	4	50
Monthly	12	20–50
Weekly	52	10–30
Daily	250	10–20
Many times per day	More than 250	40–60 items

As these tables in Exhibit 8-6 and Exhibit 8-7 indicate, sample size changes in the following ways:

- Decreases as the risk of overreliance increases from 5% to 10%
- Increases as the expected deviation rate increases
- Decreases as the tolerable deviation rate increases

The auditor can use the information from these tables to determine the correct sample size for a test of controls. When the risk of overreliance is 5%, the expected deviation rate is 2% and the tolerable deviation rate is 5%, the sample size is 181. In this sample, the auditor could find four deviations and still accept the assessed level of control risk. An auditor who finds more than four deviations would have to increase the assessed level of control risk (if the testing is based on the whether the auditor's assessed level of control risk is reliable) or if the auditor uses this test to determine whether internal controls are working, he or she would conclude that internal controls are not working and that control risk is 100%.

Varying each factor in the example (while holding the other factors constant) results in the effect of these three factors on the original sample size of 181:

- If the risk of overreliance is 10%, rather than 5%, the sample size is 132 and the auditor is allowed three deviations.
- If the expected deviation rate is 3% rather than 2%, the sample size is 361 with eleven deviations permitted.
- If the tolerable deviation rate is 7% rather than 5%, the sample size is 88 with two deviations allowed.

The auditor uses professional judgment to estimate the risk of overreliance, the expected deviation rate, and the tolerable deviation rate. The tolerable deviation rate can be related to the level of control risk the auditor believes to be present in the control. For example, the auditor could believe that control risk that is low (or 30%) could have a tolerable deviation rate of 2–5%. Control risk that is high (70%) could have a tolerable deviation rate of 10–20%. The particular tolerable deviation rate used by the auditor for high, medium, or low control risk is a matter of professional judgment, but controls with low risk should have lower tolerable deviation rates than controls with high risk.

Determining Sample Sizes Based on the Frequency of the Control

LO8

Describe an alternative method for calculating sample size based on the frequency of the control

Sometimes the auditor makes decisions about the sample size for a test of controls related to how *often* the control occurs. See Exhibit 8-8 for an example of a sample size work sheet related to the frequency of the control. It would be used when testing a manual internal control but not an IT control. The numbers in the work sheets are typically described as the minimum level of testing that would be acceptable under the firm's standards. Depending on the situation, the auditor can decide to increase the sample size. After finishing the testing, the auditor should have sufficient evidence to decide whether the control is operating effectively.

For example, if purchase orders are approved many times a day. the population is more than 250 purchase orders. According to this work sheet, the auditor would test 40–60 purchase orders for the year. These purchase orders would be randomly selected from the 12-month period. The decision to test 40 or 60 is based on the auditor's professional judgment. More can be tested if the auditor intends to examine the controls rather than reperform the control procedures.

Chapter Takeaways

Sampling is crucial to the audit process. The auditor relies on the information provided in the sample to arrive at a conclusion about the effectiveness of internal controls in the population. Sampling done incorrectly could lead the auditor to rely on internal controls when they are not effective, or the auditor can fail to rely on internal controls when they could have been effective to prevent or detect misstatements in the financial statements. Relying on internal controls when they are not effective is the more serious mistake because in that situation, the auditor reduces the level of substantive testing (believing that internal controls are effective) and can fail to gather sufficient appropriate evidence to support the audit report. In this situation, audit risk can be higher than the percentage set by the firm. Failing to rely on internal controls only causes the auditor to perform more substantive testing than had she or he correctly relied on internal controls. This is inefficient but should not result in an ineffective audit.

This chapter presented these important facts:

* The use of audit sampling to gather evidence related to internal controls
* The difference between sampling risk and nonsampling risk
* Differences between statistical and nonstatistical sampling
* The correct population for internal control testing for financial statements and internal control testing for financial reporting
* The audit steps necessary to perform a test of controls
* Sampling methods used to perform a random sample
* The use of dual-purpose tests in the audit process
* Methods used to evaluate internal control deviations
* Evidence obtained from an internal control audit
* Evidence obtained from a dual-purpose audit

Be sure that you understand these concepts before you go on to the next chapter.

Review Questions

LO1	1. Explain how sampling is used in the audit process.
LO2	2. What is sampling risk?
LO2	3. What is nonsampling risk?
LO2	4. How does the auditor control sampling risk and nonsampling risk?
LO3	5. How does statistical sampling differ from nonstatistical sampling? Explain how the auditor decides to use one method rather than the other.
LO4	6. Describe situations in which the auditor does not gather evidence by sampling.
LO5	7. What does the auditor know after testing internal controls? How is this evidence used?
LO5	8. In an internal control test, describe the test objective and the deviation condition.

LO5   9. What is the population for an internal control test of the financial statements? What is the population for an internal control test of the financial reporting process?

LO5   10. Describe the three methods that auditors use to select sample items. How does the auditor decide which method to use?

LO4   11. When performing an internal control test, what audit procedure does the auditor perform?

LO4   12. When does an auditor use dual-purpose testing? What evidence does a dual-purpose test provide the auditor?

LO5   13. How does the auditor evaluate the results from an internal control test? What conclusions could the auditor reach after conducting the test?

LO5   14. Define *tolerable deviation rate* and *actual deviation rate*. How are these terms used in an internal control test?

LO1   15. Explain how a sample differs from the population. What is the purpose of an audit sample?

LO6   16. Describe how to use sequential sampling to perform tests of controls.

Multiple Choice Questions from CPA Examinations

LO4   17. Which of the following is a step in an auditor's decision to assess control risk below the maximum?
   a. Apply analytical procedures to both financial data and nonfinancial information to detect conditions that could indicate weak controls.
   b. Perform tests of details of transactions and account balances to identify potential errors and fraud.
   c. Identify the controls that are likely to detect or prevent material misstatements.
   d. Document that the additional audit effort to perform tests of controls exceeded the potential reduction in substantive testing.

LO2   18. Samples to test controls are intended to provide the basis for an auditor to conclude whether
   a. The controls are operating effectively.
   b. The financial statements are materially misstated.
   c. The risk of incorrect acceptance is too high.
   d. Materiality for planning purposes is at a sufficiently low level.

LO1   19. An auditor uses the knowledge of internal control and the final assessed level of control risk primarily to determine the nature, timing, and extent of the
   a. Attribute tests.
   b. Compliance tests.
   c. Tests of controls.
   d. Substantive tests.

LO4   20. When numerous property and equipment transactions occur during the year, an auditor who plans to assess control risk at a low level usually performs
   a. Tests of controls and extensive tests of property and equipment balances at year-end.
   b. Analytical procedures for the current year's property and equipment transactions.
   c. Tests of controls and limited tests of the current year' property and equipment transactions.
   d. Analytical procedures for property and equipment balances at the end of the year.

LO1   21. Regardless of the assessed level of control risk, the auditor should perform some
   a. Tests of controls to determine the effectiveness of controls.
   b. Analytical procedures to verify the design of controls.
   c. Substantive tests to restrict detection risk for significant transaction classes.
   d. Dual-purpose tests to evaluate both the risk of monetary misstatement and preliminary control risk.

LO4   22. The risk of incorrect acceptance and the likelihood of assessing control risk too low relate to the
   a. Audit effectiveness.
   b. Audit efficiency.
   c. Preliminary estimates of materiality levels.
   d. Tolerable misstatement.

LO5   23. The likelihood of assessing control risk too high is the risk that the sample selected to test controls
   a. Does not support the auditor's planned assessed level of control risk when the true operating effectiveness of internal control justified such an assessment.
   b. Contains misstatements that could be material to the financial statements when aggregated with misstatements in other account balances or transaction classes.
   c. Contains proportionately fewer deviations from prescribed internal controls that exist in the balance or class as a whole.
   d. Does not support the tolerable misstatement for some or all of management's assertions.

LO5   24. As a result of sampling procedures applied as tests of controls, an auditor incorrectly assesses control risk lower than is appropriate. The most likely explanation for this situation is that
   a. The deviation rates of both the auditor's sample and the population exceed the tolerable rate.
   b. The deviation rates of both the auditor's sample and the population are less than the tolerable rate.
   c. The deviation rate in the auditor's sample is less than the tolerable rate, but the deviation rate in the population exceeds the tolerable rate.
   d. The deviation rate in the auditor's sample exceeds the tolerable rate, but the deviation rate in the population is less than the tolerable rate.

LO5   25. In addition to evaluating the frequency of deviations in tests of controls, an auditor should also consider certain qualitative aspects of the deviations. The auditor most likely would give broader consideration to the implications of a deviation if it was
   a. The only deviation discovered in the sample.
   b. Identical to a deviation discovered during the prior year's audit.
   c. Caused by an employee's misunderstanding of instructions.
   d. Initially concealed by a forged document.

LO1   26. Which of the following procedures most likely will provide an auditor evidence about whether an entity's controls are suitably designed to prevent or detect material misstatements?
   a. Reperforming the controls for a sample of transactions.
   b. Performing analytical procedures using data aggregated at a high level.
   c. Vouching a sample of transactions directly related to the controls.
   d. Observing the entity's personnel applying the controls.

Discussion Questions and Research Problems

LO5   27. **Testing internal controls.** ABC Company requires the amount and part number on the sales order and shipping document to be compared to the sales invoice before the invoice is mailed. An accounting clerk in billing performs the control and initials the company's copy of the invoice, indicating that the comparison has been made. The accounting clerk also verifies that the price on the sales order is equal to the price on the sales invoice. In the current year, 3,175 invoices have been processed. The invoice numbers are 200,326 to 203,500. The sales order, shipping document, and sales invoice are stapled together and filed by sales invoice number in several file drawers.
   a. You decide to test this control. Explain why you believe this control could be tested. What is the possible result from testing the control?
   b. What is the assertion related to the internal control?

   c. Prepare a sampling plan to test the control that has been performed many times daily. Additional evidence will be obtained regarding sales transactions from substantive tests.

   d. How will you select your sample? Do you have several choices in the method used to select the sample? Explain your answer.

   e. The accounting firm has determined that the number of tolerable deviations for this internal control test is two deviations. Explain how you will evaluate the results of your sample. State clearly the possible conclusions from your tests.

   f. Explain how you would modify this internal control test's audit procedures for a dual-purpose test. If a dual-purpose test is performed, what evidence will you obtain from it? Explain your answer.

   g. How will you control sampling risk and nonsampling risk in the test?

   h. Will you perform a statistical test or a nonstatistical test? Explain your answer.

LO5   28. **Testing internal controls.** Employees at Stuart Consulting Services prepare monthly time sheets allocating their work hours to various client projects. Time sheets are prepared online and sent to the supervisor for approval. The supervisor checks a box indicating approval of the hours and routes the time sheet to the payroll department to be processed. The payroll department checks to determine that all time sheets have supervisory approval (indicated by the check mark) before it makes the payment. Time sheets lacking the approval check should be returned to the supervisor.

   a. What is the purpose of supervisory approval for the time sheets? How could the financial statements be misstated if the time sheet is not approved?

   b. What is the assertion related to the internal control?

   c. Prepare a sampling plan to test the control. Assume the acceptable risk of over-reliance is 5%, the tolerable deviation rate is 15%, and the expected population deviation rate is 3.5%.

   d. Explain how your sampling plan would change if the internal control test was done as a test of internal controls over the financial reporting process.

   e. The accounting firm has determined that the number of tolerable deviations for the internal control test is zero deviations. Explain how you will evaluate the results of your sample. State clearly the possible conclusions from your tests.

   f. Can this internal control test be performed as a dual-purpose test? Explain your answer.

   g. How will you control sampling risk and nonsampling risk in the test?

   h. Will you perform a statistical test or nonstatistical test? Explain your answer. How will your sample differ if you perform a statistical test instead of a nonstatistical test?

   i. Explain why an accounting firm would prescribe sample sizes rather than permitting each individual auditor to determine it.

LO5   29. **Testing internal controls.** Tron Lumber prepares monthly reconciliations of the cash balance in its bank account with the cash balance on the books. An accounting clerk who does not deposit cash in the account or write checks makes this reconciliation and initials the monthly reconciliation, indicating that the balances agree and that any corrections needed have been made.

   a. Explain why this is an internal control that an auditor could test. Describe the potential misstatement in the financial statements that this control could prevent. What is the assertion related to this internal control?

   b. Prepare a sampling plan to test the control.

   c. The accounting firm has determined that the number of tolerable deviations for the internal control test is zero deviations. Explain how you will evaluate the results of your sample. State clearly the possible conclusions from your tests.

   d. Is it possible that the accounting clerk initials the reconciliation form without performing the reconciliation? Why would she or he do this and how would you know whether she or he has done the reconciliation?

   e. Can this internal control test be done as a dual-purpose test? Explain your answer.

f. How will you control sampling risk and nonsampling risk in the test?

g. Will you perform a statistical test or a nonstatistical test? Explain your answer. How will your sample differ if you perform a statistical test instead of a nonstatistical test?

LO5   30. **Internal control questionnaire.** The following questions are part of an internal control questionnaire for the long-term debt and owners' equity process. Answer the following internal control questions for the long-term debt and owners' equity process:

a. Did the board of directors authorize direct borrowings on notes payable?

b. Did the board of directors approve cash dividends?

c. Did senior officers review footnotes for long-term debt and owners' equity?

d. Did the board of directors approve stock options issued to management?

For each preceding question:

(1) Describe the misstatement in the financial statements that could occur if the client answered "no." What assertion in the financial statements is the misstatement related to?

(2) If the client answers "yes" to the question, describe an internal control that the client could use.

(3) Describe how you could test the internal control, including the population that you would test and the method you could use to select the sample.

LO5   31. **Internal control sampling.** You are responsible for developing and presenting training material on internal control sampling for staff auditors. After presenting it, you receive several questions from staff auditors. Explain how you would answer each question.

a. If population size has little impact on sample size for internal control testing, are there any advantages to using statistical sampling for internal control testing?

b. Is it always better to sample more items than fewer items?

c. How do I decide which internal controls to test? It seems like it would take a lot of time to test all controls.

d. How do I modify the sampling plan for an audit of internal controls over the financial reporting process instead of an audit of internal controls over the financial statement?

e. Can I skip internal control testing completely and simply perform substantive tests? It seems like internal control testing is a lot of work and may not be effective if the actual deviations are more than the tolerable deviations.

f. Can I do all internal control testing at year-end? I have a client who does no interim work.

LO5   32. **Controls over year-end adjusting entries.** During your audit of the inventory account, you notice several journal entries at the end of the year. Assume that the controller reviews all adjusting entries and initials the entry form indicating his or her review and approval.

a. You decide to test this control. Explain why you believe it should be tested. What is the possible result from testing the control?

b. What is the assertion related to the internal control?

c. Prepare a sampling plan to test the control. The test is performed at the end of the year.

d. How will you select your sample? Do you have several choices in the method used to select the sample? Explain your answer.

e. The accounting firm has determined that the number of tolerable deviations for this internal control tests is zero deviations. Explain how you will evaluate the results of your sample and state clearly the possible conclusions.

f. Explain how you would modify the audit procedures for a dual-purpose test. If a dual-purpose test is performed, what evidence will you receive from the test? Explain your answer.

g. How will you control sampling risk and nonsampling risk in the test?

h. Will you perform a statistical or nonstatistical test? Explain your answer.

Real-World Auditing Problems

LO5   33. **WorldCom**

The WorldCom fraud has been described in this book. A brief summary follows:

In 2005, Bernard Ebbers, the former chief executive of WorldCom, was convicted of conspiracy and securities fraud and sentenced to 25 years in prison for his role in directing the fraud. The fraud, which overstated revenue and understated expenses, eventually totaled $11 billion. It was done by recording operating expenses as capitalized assets. In effect, WorldCom removed expenses from its income statement and recorded them as assets on the balance sheet.

a. Suggest an internal control that would have been able to prevent or detect this misstatement. Describe how the control would work and how the auditor could test it.

b. If the auditor failed to detect deviations in the control, describe a substantive audit procedure that could have been effective in detecting the misstatement.

LO5   34. **Time Warner**

Time Warner inflated its revenue in 2000 and 2001 by entering into "round-trip" transactions with customers with which it had business relationships. Time Warner provided customers with funds to pay for online advertising. The customers entered into an agreement with Time Warner to purchase online advertising from it in an amount equal to the payment from Time Warner. Time Warner recognized revenue for the amounts received based on these "advertising agreements."

a. Is this type of misstatement difficult to prevent or detect by internal controls? Why? Explain your answer.

b. Describe a substantive test that the auditor might use to uncover misstatement involving round-trip transactions between the audit client and their customers.

LO5   35. **Tyco**

Former Tyco Chief Executive Dennis Kozlowski was sentenced to 25 years in prison for stealing hundreds of millions of dollars from the company. He took advantage of the company's prosperity to help himself to massive sums of money at the expense of shareholders. Business writers referred to his spending spree as the "brazen use of a public company as his personal cash machine."

Kozlowski borrowed money from the company and then forgave the loans. He granted stock options to himself and paid himself substantial bonuses. He spent company funds to purchase and decorate several personal residences including an apartment in New York City with a $6,000 shower curtain. He purchased an art collection worth $13.1 million, donated millions of dollars of Tyco funds to charity in his name, and spent $2 million on a 40th birthday party in Italy for his wife.

a. Suggest an internal control that would have been able to prevent or detect this misstatement. Describe how the control would work and how the auditor could test it.

b. Is this type of misstatement difficult to prevent or detect by internal controls? Why? Explain your answer.

LO5   36. **Qwest and Global Crossing**

The U.S. Congress investigated the telecommunications industry in 2002 because of its practice of recognizing revenue by swapping fiber-optic capacity. Companies such as Qwest and Global Crossing exchanged equal amounts of line capacity. Each company recognized revenue for the exchange and recorded the cost of providing the capacity as a capital expense. Witnesses before the House Energy Panel described the business environment in the telecom industry as a "pressure cooker." During this time, executives at the companies pushed their sales representative to meet the companies' quarterly earnings targets.

According to Patrick Joggerst, former head of sales at Global Crossing, "Not meeting the number was absolutely unacceptable." To meet the revenue targets, representatives from one company called their counterparts at the other company and worked out swap arrangements that helped the companies meet their sales targets. Robin Szwliga, Qwest's chief financial officer, testified that "there were well known consequences for not making the numbers but no clear consequences for cutting corners (Dennis Berman, "Three Telecom Companies Testify They Cut Side Deals with Qwest," *The Wall Street Journal,* September 25, 2002).

a. Is this type of misstatement difficult to prevent or detect by internal controls? Why? Explain your answer.

b. Is it likely that the auditors tested internal controls in the revenue process? Is it possible that the auditors found that control risk was low for the revenue process, even if these revenue misstatements were present in the financial statements?

LO5 37. **U.S. Foodservice**

Kevin Hall and Rosemary Meyer (KPMG partner and manager, respectively) were investigated by the SEC for improper professional conduct on the U.S. Foodservice (USF) audit.

Hall and Meyer found numerous examples showing that USF recognized revenue that it should not have. Although Hall and Meyer obtained and reviewed evidence documenting these improper transactions, they failed to act on the evidence. In some cases, the transactions were identified as audit exceptions requiring adjustment in the working papers, but the exceptions were subsequently covered up with liquid whiteout.

Hall and Meyer ignored red flags in the audit evidence. According to the SEC complaint, they "improperly and repeatedly relied on management representations to confirm previous management representations, even though these statements were contradicted by objective evidence."

USF is the nation's second largest distributor of food to restaurants, schools, hospitals, and hotels. For the years under investigation, a significant portion of its income was based on inflated manufacturer rebates. The company ordered huge amounts of food from major manufacturers including Sara Lee Corp., Kraft Food Inc., Georgia-Pacific Corp., and Nestlé SA. These manufacturers agreed to pay USF rebates on the purchases that ranged from 8.5% to 46%.

According to accounting rules, rebates should be recorded as reductions in inventory cost when the company pays for inventory. USF recorded the rebate amounts before the inventory was paid for and greatly inflated the dollar amount of the rebates. This allowed executives to meet earnings targets and earn bonuses. The amount of inventory ordered was much more than USF could sell. USF is owned by Ahold NV, a Dutch supermarket chain. Ahold is the world's third largest supermarket chain behind Walmart Stores, Inc. and Carrefour SA of France.

a. What financial statement **assertion** did USF violate? Explain how it violated this management assertion.

b. Suggest an internal control that would have been able to prevent or detect this misstatement. Describe how the control would work and how the auditor could test it.

Audit Sampling: Substantive Tests of Details

Learning Objectives

After studying this chapter, you should be able to:

1. Describe variables sampling and explain how it is used to gather evidence using substantive testing procedures.
2. Understand sampling risk and nonsampling risk for substantive testing.
3. Explain the difference between statistical and nonstatistical sampling in substantive testing.
4. Understand how the auditors use a sampling plan to conduct substantive tests of details.
5. Describe how the auditors use audit sampling to gather evidence related to material misstatements in account balances.
6. Explain how the auditors use audit sampling to gather evidence related to material misstatements in classes of transactions.

Auditing standards relevant to this topic

For private companies

- **AICPA Audit Guide,** *Audit Sampling*
- **AU 350,** Audit Sampling
- **AU 9350,** Interpretation: Applicability of Audit Sampling

For public companies

- **AICPA Audit Guide,** *Audit Sampling*
- **AU 350,** Audit Sampling (Interim standard adopted by PCAOB)
- **AU 9350,** Interpretation: Applicability of Audit Sampling
- **PCAOB Auditing Standard No. 5,** An Audit of Internal Control over Financial Reporting That Is Integrated with an Audit of Financial Statements

International standards

- **ISA 530,** Audit Sampling and Other Means of Testing

Chapter Overview

Sampling is important to the process of gathering evidence in the audit process. This chapter discusses how to gather evidence using sampling for substantive tests of balances and substantive tests of transactions. During the testing of account balances and classes of transactions, the sampling is often referred to as **variables** sampling. The evidence gathered from substantive testing is used to determine whether the account balances and classes of transactions in the financial statements are materially misstated which will determine the audit report issued for the financial statements.

The Use of Variables Sampling in Substantive Testing

LO1

Describe variables sampling and explain how it is used to gather evidence using substantive testing procedures

Variables sampling is the application of an audit procedure (confirmation, vouching, tracing) to less than 100% of an account balance (for the balance sheet) or a class of transactions (for the income statement) to determine whether the recorded amount is materially misstated. The items selected for examination are referred to as the **sample.** All the items in the account balance or the class of transactions are referred to as the **population.** *Auditors use evidence from the variables sample to arrive at a conclusion about the population.* If they find misstatements in the sample, they assume that misstatements similar to those in the sample would be found in the population. This chapter is part of the testing phase of the audit process. Exhibit 9-1 summarizes the main steps in the audit process.

Like internal control testing, the concept of a *random* sample is important to the sampling process. Because auditors sample to make a decision about the population, having a sample that *represents* the population is important for them. Auditors believe that the characteristics of the population are represented in a random sample. This fact allows auditors to make a decision about the population with evidence from a sample collected from it. The auditors use sampling for substantive tests of balances and substantive tests of transactions to determine whether the financial statements accounts associated with the account balance or class of transactions are materially misstated. Evidence obtained from substantive tests answers the question:

Is the account balance or class of transactions materially misstated?

Yes

No

If yes, the auditors perform additional tests to determine the material misstatement in the account balance or class of transactions.

If no, the auditors conclude that the relevant assertion for the account balance or class of transactions is not materially misstated.

Substantive tests of details can be performed manually or by using computer software to test the account balances or transactions recorded in the income statement accounts. This chapter covers tests that are performed manually. IT tests are discussed in Chapter 3.

Sampling and Nonsampling Risk

LO2

Understand sampling risk and nonsampling risk for substantive testing

Audit risk is the risk that material misstatements *occur* in the financial statements and are *not detected* by the auditors. The auditing standards require auditors to keep audit risk to an acceptably low level. Auditors often interpret this to be about 5%. Audit risk can be divided into two categories, sampling risk and nonsampling risk.

Sampling risk + Nonsampling risk = Audit risk

Sampling risk is the risk that the sample does not represent the population. In this situation, the conclusions that auditors reach about the sample do not represent the conclusions they would reach if they had reviewed all data. *Sampling risk for*

The Audit Process	Exhibit 9-1

Steps in the Audit Process	Discussed in this Section
Planning Phase	
Consider the Preconditions for an Audit and Accept or Reject the Audit Engagement	
Understand the Entity and Its Environment, Determine Materiality, and Assess the Risks of Material Misstatements	
Develop an Audit Strategy and an Audit Plan to Respond to the Assessed Risks	
Testing Phase	
Test Internal Controls? Yes No	
Perform Tests of Controls if "Yes"	
Perform Substantive Tests of Transactions	√
Perform Substantive Tests of Balances	√
Assess the Likelihood of Material Misstatement	√
Decision Phase	
Review the Presentation and Disclosure Assertions	
Evaluate the Evidence to Determine Whether the Financial Statements Are Prepared in Accordance with the Applicable Financial Reporting Framework	
Issue Audit Report	
Communicate with the Audit Committee	

substantive testing includes the risk of incorrectly accepting the account balance or class of transactions and the risk of incorrectly rejecting the account balance or class of transactions.

The *risk of incorrectly rejecting the account balance or class of transactions* is an error that affects the audit's **efficiency** (the amount of time it takes to finish it). Auditors who incorrectly reject the account balance or class of transactions as being materially misstated during a substantive test of transactions or test of balances must perform additional tests to determine the correct amount. This is inefficient because the auditors spend more time performing tests that are not needed because the account balance or class of transactions was not materially misstated.

The *risk of incorrectly accepting the account balance or class of transactions* is an error that affects the audit's **effectiveness** (arriving at the correct conclusion regarding whether the financial statements are materially misstated). Auditors who incorrectly accept the account balance or class of transactions as materially correct when it is not might determine that the financial statements are not materially misstated when they are because there are misstatements in the financial statements that are not known to the auditors.

The more serious error is that related to the audit's *effectiveness.* In this situation, the opinion issued by the auditors could be wrong. They try to avoid making errors of effectiveness and design audit sampling procedures to avoid these errors.

Auditors control sampling risk in several ways. With statistical sampling, auditors can quantify sampling risk, which allows them to keep it to an acceptably low number. With nonstatistical sampling, auditors estimate the amount of sampling risk based on professional judgment. Based on this estimate, they control sampling risk by selecting appropriate sample sizes (sampling risk decreases as sample size increases), taking a random sample so that the sample represents the population and correctly evaluating the sample's results to consider sample risk in the evaluation of the results.

Nonsampling risk includes all other aspects of audit risk that are not related to sampling. For example, nonsampling risk includes the use of inappropriate audit procedures to gather evidence or interpreting evidence incorrectly. Nonsampling risk cannot be quantified by either statistical or nonstatistical sampling. Auditors control for it by planning and supervising employees.

Statistical and Nonstatistical Sampling

LO3

Explain the difference between statistical and nonstatistical sampling in substantive testing

What does it mean to say that auditors use statistical or nonstatistical sampling? The audit procedures performed under either method are the same. The only things that change when the auditors move from statistical sampling to nonstatistical sampling are (1) the sample selection method and (2) the way the auditors evaluate the sample results. With statistical sampling, the auditors *must* use random-number or systematic sampling to *select* the sample. With nonstatistical sampling, the auditors *can* use random-number or systematic sampling and *can* use haphazard sampling. For a sample to be a statistical sample, the auditors must use the laws of probability to measure sampling risk and to evaluate the misstatements in the sample. In a statistical sample, auditors often calculate a confidence interval around the sample estimate. For example, based on a statistical sample, auditors might conclude that they are 95% confident that the true accounts receivable balance is between $9,000,000 and $9,500,000.

Both statistical and nonstatistical samples require professional judgment in *planning* the sample, *performing* the procedures, and *evaluating* the evidence. The auditors can sample using either statistical or nonstatistical sampling methods according to the auditing standards (AU 350 and ISA 530). Today many accounting firms use nonstatistical sampling. They use sample selection methods appropriate for statistical and nonstatistical sampling, but they rarely *evaluate* a sample based on statistical sampling. They follow the first requirement for a statistical sample (to use random number or systematic sampling methods to select the sample), but they do not follow the second requirement for a statistical sample (to use the laws of probability to measure sample risk). The sample size for a nonstatistical sampling is usually larger than for a statistical sample. Sample risk is estimated, rather than calculated, when the auditors use nonstatistical sampling, so they increase the sample size to address the lack of precision in determining the sample risk. Increasing sample size for a nonstatistical sample allows the auditors to keep sample risk to an acceptably low number even if they cannot calculate the exact amount of sample risk. Nonstatistical samples could be a *less efficient* way to gather evidence but should not be viewed as a *less effective* way to gather evidence.

Statisticians in an accounting firm's head office often make sample size recommendations. The local office often uses them by applying the guidelines from a standard work sheet to calculate sample size. This method ensures that auditors in a firm use similar approaches when calculating sample size. As a new auditor, you will determine sample sizes for audit procedures based on the *guidelines* established by your firm. Sometimes the guidelines will allow you to choose from a range of sample sizes. If you have a choice of sample size, you should consider the following factors in selecting the correct sample size. Similar to internal control testing, the number of items in the population will have almost no effect on sample size unless the population is small.

Factors that affect sample size include:

- The auditors' *desired level of assurance* (1.0—Risk of incorrect acceptance) that actual misstatement does not exceeded tolerable misstatement. The desired level of assurance is based on the auditors' assessment of the risk of material misstatement and the assurance obtained from other substantive procedures performed to obtain evidence for the same assertion. The sample size **increases** as the desired level of assurance increases.

- The *tolerable misstatement* is the amount of monetary misstatement in the account balance or class of transaction that is acceptable without causing the financial statements to be materially misstated. Tolerable misstatement is related to the client's

Sampling Plan for Substantive Tests	Exhibit 9-2

Step 1	Describe the objectives of the test, the accounts, and the assertions affected.	Step 6	Select the method for determining sample size.
Step 2	Define the population and the sampling unit.	Step 7	Determine the method of sample selection.
Step 3	Define *misstatement*.	Step 8	List the selected sample items.
Step 4	Determine the desired level of assurance, the estimated misstatement, and the tolerable misstatement.	Step 9	Describe how the sampling procedure was performed and list any misstatements identified in the sample.
Step 5	Determine the audit sampling technique used.	Step 10	Evaluate the sample results and reach a conclusion.

materiality level. Typically, a portion of total materiality is assigned to each account balance or class of transactions. This amount is often 50–75% of planning materiality. The sample size **increases** as the tolerable misstatement decreases.

- The *expected misstatement* is the amount of monetary misstatement that the auditors expect to find in the account balance or class of transactions. This expectation is based on professional judgment and is related to the results from the prior year's tests and current expectations for misstatement in the account balance or class of transactions. The sample size **increases** as the expected amount of misstatement increases.

- *Stratification* of the population affects sample size. Stratified samples **decrease** the sample size. Auditors stratify a sample when they divide the population into groups (often based on dollar value of the transaction). For example, the auditors might stratify external confirmations for accounts receivable by putting all customers with large balances in one stratum and all customers with small balances in another stratum. The auditors treat each stratum as a separate sample. Stratification results in a smaller sample size because it reduces the variability in the population.

Both statistical and nonstatistical sampling methods force auditors to assess these factors to determine the sample size for the audit test.

A Sampling Plan for Substantive Tests of Details

LO4

Understand how auditors use a sampling plan to conduct substantive tests of details

Auditors gather evidence about whether balance sheet and income statement accounts are materially misstated by performing substantive tests of details. When the auditors use sampling for substantive tests of details, they follow the sampling plan found in Exhibit 9-2. Each step in the plan is discussed in the following section.

Step 1. Describe the Objectives of the Test, the Accounts, and the Assertions Affected

The test objective for a substantive test is to determine whether the account balance or class of transactions is materially misstated.

For example, the auditors can use variables sampling to select accounts receivable balances to be confirmed at year-end. The *test objective* in this case is to determine whether the accounts receivable balance confirmed by the customer is equal to the client's accounts receivable balance. The *account tested* is accounts receivable and revenue and the *assertions* tested are existence and rights.

Step 2. Define the Population and the Sampling Unit

The population consists of all items in the account balance (for balance sheet accounts) or class of transactions (for income statement accounts.) Auditors use variables sampling to determine the reasonableness of the recorded amount in the population from the evidence in a sample of the population, so it is important to define the population correctly.

For example, for the accounts receivable confirmation procedure described in Step 1, the population is defined as the accounts receivable balance at year-end. If the auditors tested an income statement account, they will define the population as all transactions for the year in the class of transactions.

When planning a sample for substantive testing, auditors often identify items in a population that are individually significant and should be subject to 100% examination. The items that are individually significant are selected for examination, and those remaining become the population to be sampled.

For example, the auditors can determine ten accounts receivable balances are very large and that all ten of them should be confirmed. The auditors will select the *sample* of accounts receivable balances to confirm from the remaining population. The sample's population would be described as the accounts receivable balance at year-end minus the individually significant items.

Confirming 100% of the individually significant accounts reduces the variability in the sample and results in a smaller overall sample size than would be possible if all accounts had been considered together in the population. The sample is referred to as stratified when auditors sample at different rates for groups in the population.

A sampling unit could be a customer balance, one dollar, an individual transaction, or an individual entry in a transaction. However the sampling unit is defined, each represents one item in the population. The auditors must define the sampling unit consistent with the assertion being tested.

For example, the sampling unit for accounts receivable confirmations could be the customer's balances at year-end. Some substantive sampling methods use one dollar as the sampling unit. With this method, an accounts receivable balance of $830,000 at the end of the year would be composed of 830,000 sampling units, each unit equal to one dollar.

Step 3. Define *Misstatement*

A misstatement occurs when a customer confirms a balance that differs from the client's balance.

Step 4. Determine the Desired Level of Assurance, the Estimated Misstatement, and the Tolerable Misstatement

To determine the sample size for substantive tests of detail, the auditors need to estimate the following information based on their professional judgment:

- The tolerable misstatement for the population to be tested
- The estimated misstatement for the population to be tested
- The desired level of assurance that the tolerable misstatement is not exceeded by the actual misstatement (AU 350 and ISA 530).

These factors are discussed briefly in the following sections.

Tolerable Misstatement

- The maximum misstatement in the account balance or class of transactions that the auditors are willing to accept. Tolerable misstatement is the use of performance materiality for a particular sampling procedure. Tolerable misstatement can be the same amount or an amount lower than performance materiality. Tolerable misstatement can be lower than performance materiality when the sample population is less than the total population (which is always true in a sampling application).
- In a substantive test of details, the auditors' goal is to obtain an appropriate level of assurance that the tolerable misstatement they set is not exceeded by the actual misstatement in the population.
- In practice, tolerable misstatements are calculated as a percentage of the population ranging from 0.5% to 75%. Tolerable misstatement decisions are based on the professional judgment of the auditors.

The Effect of Changes in Factors on Sample Size		Exhibit 9-3
Change in Factor	**Effect on Sample Size**	**Factor Impact**
Assessment of inherent risk *increases*	Sample size *increases*	Desired level of assurance (risk of incorrect acceptance)
Assessment of control risk *increases*	Sample size *increases*	Desired level of assurance (risk of incorrect acceptance)
Assessment of risk related to other substantive procedures related to the same assertion *increases*	Sample size *increases*	Desired level of assurance (risk of incorrect acceptance)
Tolerable misstatement *increases*	Sample size *decreases*	Tolerable misstatement
Expected misstatement or the variance of the population *increases*	Sample size *increases*	Expected misstatement
Population *increases*	Change in sample size is *negligible*	Little or no effect on sample size for large populations

Expected Misstatement

- The auditors assess the amount of expected misstatement on the basis of professional judgment after considering factors such as the company's business risks, the results of prior year's substantive tests of details, the results of any related substantive tests, and the results of any test of related controls.
- As the expected misstatement approaches the tolerable misstatement, the auditors should use a larger sample size because more precise information about the misstatements is needed.
- Expected misstatement rates are listed as percentages of the tolerable misstatements (expected misstatement divided by tolerable misstatement). In practice, they range from 10% to 60%.

Desired Level of Assurance

- The desired level of assurance is based on the level of audit risk the auditors are willing to accept, the assessed risks of material misstatement (considering both inherent and control risk), and the detection risk for further audit procedures related to the same account and assertion, including tests of controls, analytical procedures, and substantive tests of details that don't involve sampling.
- In practice, the desired level of assurance ranges from 50% to 95%.
- Sometimes we use the complement of this term, *the risk of overreliance.* It ranges from 50% to 5% (1.0 − Desired level of assurance).

See Exhibit 9-3 for a description of the effect of changes in factors that affect sample size.

Step 5. Determine the Audit Sampling Technique Used

The auditors decide whether to use a statistical audit sampling technique or a nonstatistical sampling technique and the type of audit sampling technique to use. They can choose *monetary unit sampling* or *classical variables sampling* for substantive tests of details. Monetary unit sampling is most frequently used in substantive tests of details.

For example, auditors can choose nonstatistical monetary unit sampling as the technique to use for accounts receivable confirmations.

Nonstatistical Sample Size Calculation—No Misstatement Expected Substantive Test		Exhibit 9-4

Population		$2,350,000
Individually significant accounts	−	850,000
Population for sample	=	1,500,000
Tolerable misstatement (75% of materiality)		112,500
Confidence factor	/	3
Sampling interval	=	37,500
Population		1,500,000
Sampling interval	/	37,500
Sample size	=	40

Step 6. Select the Method for Determining Sample Size

The auditors select the method for determining sample size based on the guidelines established by their firm. See Exhibit 9-4 for an example of a worksheet for calculating the sample size for a nonstatistical sample. The sample sizes calculated using this work sheet are typically presented as the minimum level of testing that would be acceptable under firm standards. This nonstatistical sample size calculation is presented in the AICPA *Audit Sampling* Guide from theory underlying statistical sampling.

The auditors use professional judgment to determine the numbers that go into the calculation. For each test, the auditors must assess the (1) risk of incorrect acceptance, (2) expected misstatement, and (3) tolerable misstatement. They use a sampling table to determine the confidence factor based on these three measures. The confidence factors range from 1 to 3 and are based on how certain auditors want to be about the result. For example, when the expected misstatement is expected to be zero: (1) a confidence factor of 1 will give the auditors a confidence level of 63% and a risk of incorrect acceptance of 37%, (2) a confidence factor of 1.90 gives the auditors a confidence level of 85% and a risk of incorrect acceptance of 15% and (3) a confidence factor of 3 gives the auditors a confidence level of 95% and a risk of incorrect acceptance of 5%. The auditors adjust the sample size by determining the risk of incorrect acceptance and estimating the ratio of expected misstatements to tolerable misstatements. See Exhibit 9-5 for the confidence factors for the various levels of these assessments.

Let's look at an example to find how the auditors might calculate a sample size for a substantive test of details to confirm accounts receivable balances. The auditors determine that (1) the accounts receivable balance is $2,350,000 and that individually significant accounts total $850,000, (2) materiality is $150,000 and tolerable misstatement is $112,500, (3) the expected misstatement is zero, and (4) the risk of incorrect acceptance is 5% (the level of assurance is 95%). Review Exhibit 9-4 for the calculation of sample size of 40 for a nonstatistical sample.

If the auditors expected misstatements in the sample, the sample size condition would change. When misstatements are expected, the auditors calculate the ratio of expected misstatements to tolerable misstatements and select the confidence factor from the table corresponding to the ratio calculated and the risk of incorrect acceptance. In the previous example, if the auditors expect misstatements of $10,000 (rather than zero), the expected misstatement to tolerable misstatement ratio is 0.088 (10,000/112,500 = 0.088). Using a ratio of 0.10, the auditors would calculate a confidence factor of 3.68 at a 5% risk of incorrect acceptance. This would give the auditors a sampling interval of 30,570 (112,500/3.68 = 30,570) and a sample size of 50 (1,500,000/30,570 = 49.07). In sample

Confidence Factors for Monetary Unit Sampling   Exhibit 9-5

Ratio of Expected to Tolerable Misstatement	Risk of Incorrect Acceptance								
	5%	10%	15%	20%	25%	30%	35%	37%	50%
0.00	3.00	2.31	1.90	1.61	1.39	1.21	1.05	1.00	0.70
0.05	3.31	2.52	2.06	1.74	1.49	1.29	1.12	1.06	0.73
0.10	3.68	2.77	2.25	1.89	1.61	1.39	1.20	1.13	0.77
0.15	4.11	3.07	2.47	2.06	1.74	1.49	1.28	1.21	0.82
0.20	4.63	3.41	2.73	2.26	1.90	1.62	1.38	1.30	0.87
0.25	5.24	3.83	3.04	2.49	2.09	1.76	1.50	1.41	0.92
0.30	6.00	4.33	3.41	2.77	2.30	1.93	1.63	1.53	0.99
0.35	6.92	4.95	3.86	3.12	2.57	2.14	1.79	1.67	1.06
0.40	8.00	5.72	4.42	3.54	2.89	2.39	1.99	1.85	1.14
0.45	9.59	6.71	5.13	4.07	3.29	2.70	2.22	2.06	1.25
0.50	11.54	7.99	6.04	4.75	3.80	3.08	2.51	2.32	1.37
0.55	14.18	9.70	7.26	5.64	4.47	3.58	2.89	2.65	1.52
0.60	17.85	12.07	8.93	6.86	5.37	4.25	3.38	3.09	1.70

Source: AICPA Audit Guide, *Audit Sampling*, p. 125.

size calculations, the auditors always round to the larger sample size. Refer to Exhibit 9-6 for a summary of this calculation. In this case, the auditors will sample 50 rather than the 40 previously calculated when no misstatements were expected. As the ratio of expected misstatements to tolerable misstatements increases, the sample size increases. An increase in the ratio of expected misstatements to tolerable misstatements from zero to 0.088 results in an increase in the sample size from 40 to 50.

Step 7. Determine the Method of Selecting the Sample

The sampling methods for substantive samples are the same as those for internal control samples. Three methods could be used to select a variables sample: (1) simple random sampling, (2) systematic random sampling, and (3) haphazard sampling. Auditors often use systematic random sampling for substantive testing because it stratifies a sample. This allows the auditors to use a smaller sample size than would be possible with an unstratified sample. With a stratified sample, larger dollar amounts in the population are more likely to be selected for sampling.

With **simple random sampling,** the auditors generate random numbers from a random number table or a computer program and then select the dollar amount or document number that corresponds to the random numbers generated. Auditors use random sampling when the sampling units are prenumbered or when the cumulative balance of an account can be generated. When random-number sampling is used, each sampling unit in the population has an equal chance of being selected, so a sample selected with random numbers is a sample that is representative of the population.

For example, the auditors could decide to confirm 25 customer accounts at year-end in addition to the 10 significant items. The customer accounts are numbered from 3,000 to 3,400. To select a sample using random-number sampling, the auditors would generate 25 random numbers between 3,000 and 3,400. Random-number sampling can be used for statistical and nonstatistical variables sampling.

Systematic random sampling is a second way the auditors can select a sample. To use systematic random sampling, auditors divide the number of units or number of dollars in the population by the sample size to calculate a sampling interval. Then the auditors generate a random number in the sampling interval; it is the first item chosen. The following items are found by adding the random number to the sampling interval. In the **example** above where the auditor confirms 25 customer accounts, assume that the total

Nonstatistical Sample Size Calculation—Misstatement Expected Substantive Test		**Exhibit 9-6**

Population		$2,350,000
Individually significant accounts	–	850,000
Population for sample	=	1,500,000
Tolerable misstatement (75% of materiality)		112,500
Confidence factor	/	3.68
Sampling interval	=	30,570
Population		1,500,000
Sampling interval	/	30,570
Sample size	=	50

population includes 250 customers with account balances (after removing the 10 customers that are individually significant): 250 divided by a sample size of 25 equals a sampling interval of 10. The auditors generate a random number in the first sampling interval of 10. Let's say this random number is 3. Customer number 3,003 (3000 is the first customer number plus the random number of 3) is the first item in the sample; the second one is determined by adding 3 and 10. So, the second item in the sample is 3,013. The third item is found by adding 13 and 10, and the auditors move through the sample in this fashion until 25 items have been selected. Systematic sampling can be used for statistical and nonstatistical variables sampling.

When the auditors use systematic random sampling with an individual dollar as the sampling unit, we refer to this method of sampling as **monetary unit sampling (MUS).** It is a special form of systematic random sampling in which the sampling unit is $1 rather than a customer balance or a document number. Monetary unit sampling is also known as *probability proportionate to size (PPS)* sampling. See Sampling Plan 1 and Sampling Plan 2 later in the chapter. The former exhibits an example of a plan using monetary unit sampling with $1 as the sampling unit and sampling plan 2 shows a plan using systematic random sampling with invoice numbers as the sampling unit.

Haphazard sampling is the third method auditors can use to select a sample. When they use haphazard sampling, they select the sample without any conscious bias. A haphazard sample is not a careless sample but a description used to indicate that no random number method is used to select the sample. Haphazard sampling must be used when items in the population are not prenumbered documents. For example, the accounts receivable files can be kept in a file drawer. In this case, the auditors would open the file drawer and select a sample of 25 customer files from the drawer, selecting documents haphazardly from the entire drawer so that each document has a chance of being selected. Haphazard sampling can be used only for nonstatistical variables sampling.

Step 8. List the Sample Items

The auditors record a list of the sample items selected in the working papers.

Step 9. Describe How the Sampling Procedure Was Performed and List Any Misstatements Identified in the Sample

After the sample has been selected, the auditors perform the audit procedure described in the sampling plan.

For example, in the case of accounts receivable confirmations, the auditors mail confirmation letters to all customers with individually significant balances and to the

40 customers selected from the remaining population. Alternative procedures are performed for customers who fail to return the confirmation requests.

From the list of substantive audit procedures, you can see that sampling is appropriate for some of these procedures but not for others. Auditors could use sampling to inspect documents or assets, to confirm account balances, to recalculate amounts on documents, and to reperform documented control procedures. Sampling would not be used to *observe* the client performing procedures, make *inquiries* of the client, or to perform *analytical procedures*. The procedures cannot be performed based on a sampling basis.

Substantive Audit Procedures

Inspection of records or documents
Inspection of tangible assets
Observation
Inquiry
Confirmation
Recalculation
Reperformance
Analytical procedures

Step 10. Evaluate the Sample Results and Reach a Conclusion

Whether the sample is statistical or nonstatistical, auditors use professional judgment to evaluate the sample results. Based on the sample results, the auditors determine whether the account balance or class of transactions is materially misstated. If it is not, the auditors accept the account balance or class of transaction as being materially correct. If it is materially misstated, the auditors propose an audit adjustment so the account balance or class of transaction will not be materially misstated after the adjustment is recorded.

The auditors decide whether the misstatements found in the sample are material after extrapolating misstatements from the sample to the population. This gives them a likely misstatement in the population. The known misstatement and the likely misstatement are totaled to obtain the projected misstatements for the account balance or class of transactions. To calculate the likely misstatements from the known misstatements, the auditors select one of two acceptable methods.

The first method of extrapolating the misstatements found in the sample to the population is to divide the amount of the misstatement in the sample by the portion of total dollars in the sample. **For example,** the auditors could have sampled 20% of the population and found an overstatement error of $2,000. Their best estimate of the population error is $2,000/20 percent, or $10,000 (projected misstatement); $2,000 is the *known misstatement* in the population and $8,000 is the *likely misstatement* in the population.

Method 1

Population Size	Sample Size	Percentage Sampled	Misstatement in Sample	Projected Misstatement in Population	Known Misstatement	Likely Misstatement
100,000	20,000	20%	$2,000	$10,000	$2,000	$8,000

A second method of extrapolating misstatements found in the sample to the population is to calculate the average error in each sample item and project that error to the sample items in the population. **For example,** the auditors could have sampled 50 items and found $4,000 misstatement in them. The average difference between the recorded amount and the correct amount for each item in the sample is $4,000/50, or $80. If the population has 200 items, the auditors' best estimate of the population misstatement is

$16,000 (projected misstatement); $4,000 is the *known misstatement* in the population and $12,000 is the *likely misstatement* in the population.

Method 2

Population Size	Sample Size	Misstatement in Sample	Average Misstatement in the Sample	Projected Misstatement	Known Misstatement	Likely Misstatement
200	50	$4,000	$80	$16,000	$4,000	$12,000

If the auditors expect that the amount of misstatement relates to the item's size, they use the first approach. If they expect the amount of misstatement to be constant for all items in the population, they would use the second method.

To determine whether the account balance or class of transactions is materially misstated, the auditors determine the projected misstatement from the sample results and compare this amount to the tolerable misstatement allocated to the account balance or class of transactions (the percentage of materiality allocated to this account or transaction). The *projected misstatement* is the sum of the known misstatement and the likely misstatement. The *tolerable misstatement* is the amount determined by the auditors that the account balance or class of accounts can be misstated and still be considered to be "materially correct." If the projected misstatement is higher than the tolerable misstatement, the account balance or class of transactions is materially misstated. In this case, the auditors must gather additional evidence to determine the amount of the material misstatement. If the projected misstatement is less than the tolerable misstatement, then the auditors must "*give appropriate consideration to sampling risk*" in the determination of whether the projected misstatements plus sampling risk is higher than the tolerable misstatement. The relationships between projected misstatements, tolerable misstatements, sampling risk, and the decisions made by the auditors relative to projected and tolerable misstatement follow.

Projected misstatement = Known misstatement + Likely misstatement

If

Projected misstatement ≥ Tolerable misstatement

the account balance or class of transactions is materially misstated. Auditors must gather additional evidence to determine the amount of the misstatement.

If

Projected misstatement ≤ Tolerable misstatement

the auditors must consider the impact of sampling risk.

If

Projected misstatement + Sampling risk ≤ Tolerable misstatement,

the account balance or class of transactions is not materially misstated.

If

Projected misstatement + Sampling risk > Tolerable misstatement

the account balance or class of transactions is materially misstated. Auditors must gather additional evidence to determine the misstatement amount.

What does it mean to give "appropriate consideration to sampling risk" in the evaluation of the misstatements? The auditors know that the misstatements identified during the sampling procedure will not be equal to the misstatements that would be identified had the auditors tested 100% of the population. *Sampling risk is the difference between the sample results and the results the auditors would have obtained from looking at the entire population.* If the projected misstatement is close to the tolerable misstatement, the auditors must consider whether adding sampling risk to the projected misstatement would make the total higher than the tolerable misstatement. For example, if the tolerable misstatement was $50,000 and the projected misstatement was $45,000, the auditors would have to ask how likely it would be that the projected misstatement is higher than $50,000 after considering the effect of sampling risk on the projected misstatement. However, if the tolerable misstatement was $50,000 and the projected misstatement was $10,000, the auditors would not be very concerned about the effect of sampling risk on the projected misstatement. In this case, they would consider how likely it would be that the projected misstatement is higher than $50,000 after considering the effect of sampling risk on the projected misstatement of $10,000. For nonstatistical sampling, sampling risk must be determined by professional judgment. For statistical sampling, it can be quantified.

The auditors also add the projected misstatement in the account balance or class of transactions (after the client's adjustment) to **known** (misstatements identified in the sample) and **likely misstatements** (those projected in the population based on the misstatements found in the sample) in other account balances and classes of transactions to evaluate whether the financial statements as a whole are materially misstated. These adjustments are listed on the proposed audit adjustment schedule.

If the auditors stratified the population into two or more groups based on the size of the items in the population, they should project the misstatements for each group separately. If the auditors use systematic sampling, they should project the misstatement found in each sampling interval to the sampling interval rather than to the entire population.

The auditors also consider the misstatement nature and cause. These factors include whether the misstatement was caused by an error or by fraud; whether the misstatement was caused by carelessness or a lack of understanding; and the relationship of the misstatement to other phases of the audit. Misstatements caused by fraud and a lack of understanding of the instructions can cause the auditors to perform additional tests to determine whether remaining misstatements in the account balance or class of transactions exist.

The Use of Nonstatistical Sampling for Substantive Tests of Balances

LO5

Describe how auditors use audit sampling to gather evidence related to material misstatements in account balances

Now that we have an idea about how the auditors use audit sampling to gather evidence regarding material misstatements in account balances and classes of transactions, let's consider audit sampling plans to find how sampling can be used for two types of substantive tests of details: substantive tests of balances and substantive tests of transactions.

First let's consider an audit sampling plan for a nonstatistical substantive test of balances.

Sampling Plan 1

Step 1. Determine the Objectives of the Test, the Accounts, and the Assertions Affected

The objective of this test is to determine whether the year-end accounts receivable balance is materially misstated.

    Audit procedure: external confirmation

    Accounts: accounts receivable and sales revenue

    Assertions tested: existence and rights

Step 2. Define the Population and the Sampling Unit

The population is the accounts receivable balance of $52,600,000 at year-end. The sampling units are the individual dollars in the population. Each $1 represents a sampling unit.

The population is composed of ten individually significant accounts that total $5,400,000; 100% of them are confirmed rather than sampled. The remaining balance is subject to sampling procedures. (If the individually significant accounts are greater than the sampling interval, it is not necessary to pull them out of the sample. They will all be chosen during the selection process.)

Accounts receivable balance at year-end	$52,600,000
Individually significant accounts	$5,400,000
Accounts receivable subject to sampling	$47,200,000

Each of the 47,200,000 sampling units equals $1. For each dollar selected, the auditors confirm the customer's account balance. With monetary unit sampling, each individual dollar in the population has an equal chance of being selected.

Step 3. Define Misstatement

A misstatement occurs when an amount confirmed by the customer does not equal the accounts receivable balance on the balance sheet.

Step 4. Determine the Desired Level of Assurance, the Estimated Misstatement, and the Tolerable Misstatement

The desired level of assurance is 90% (10% risk of incorrect acceptance), the estimated misstatement is $86,250, and the tolerable misstatement is $862,500. The ratio of estimated misstatement to tolerable misstatement is 0.10.

Step 5. Determine the Audit Sampling Technique Used

Nonstatistical sampling is used. The auditors use $1 as the sampling unit.

Step 6. Select the Method for Determining Sample Size

The accounts receivable balance is $52,600,000, individually significant accounts total $5,400,000, the auditors' assessment of the ratio of expected misstatements to tolerable misstatements is 0.10, materiality is $1,150,000, and the risk of incorrect acceptance is 10%. Sample size is calculated as follows:

Population		$52,600,000
Individually significant accounts	−	5,400,000
Population for sample	=	47,200,000
Tolerable misstatement (75% of materiality)		862,500
Confidence factor (from Exhibit 9-5)	/	2.77
Sampling interval	=	311,371
Population		47,200,000
Sampling interval	/	311,371
Sample size	=	152

The auditors will send 162 confirmations, 152 selected by using monetary unit sampling (a form of systematic random sampling) from the population after removing the individually significant items and 10 confirmations for the individually significant items.

Step 7. Determine the Method of Sample Selection

The auditors use a cumulative dollar listing of the accounts receivable balance to select the samples for confirmation. Using systematic sampling, the auditors divide the population into equal groups of *dollars* and then select $1 value from each group. To begin, the auditors select a random number between 1 and the sampling interval, inclusive. This number is the *random start*. The first sample selected is the one that contains the dollar amount corresponding to the random start. The auditors add the sampling interval to the random start to get the second sample. They continue to add the sampling interval to the last sampling unit dollar to select the sample items.

In this case, the sample size is 152. The sampling interval is 47,200,000/152, or 311,371. A random number between zero and 311,371 is generated; in this case, it is 164,974. Using a *cumulative* list of accounts receivable balances, the first sample is the accounts receivable with dollar 164,974, the second sample is dollar 476,345, and the third sample is dollar 787,716. The auditors continue to add 311,371 to the last sampling unit dollar to select a sample of 152 units. All individually significant items are to be confirmed. The following is a portion of the table used to determine the customer balances sampled:

Customer Number	Account Balance	Cumulative Total	Sample Number
1	42,125	42,125	
2	11,084	53,209	
3	34,747	87,956	
4	80,621	168,577	1
5	12,543	181,120	
6	62,431	243,551	
7	125,905	369,456	
8	11,487	383,943	
9	78,891	462,834	
10	66,350	529,184	2
11	81,872	611,056	
12	42,126	654,182	
13	58,475	712,657	
14	27,476	740,133	
15	7,386	747,969	
16	48,412	796,381	3
:::	:::	:::	

Method: Generate a random start from 1 to 311,371. The random start is 164,974. Sample 1 (for customer 4) is the customer balance that contains the cumulative dollar value of $164,974. To find the second sample, the auditors add the sampling interval (311,371) to the first sample (164,974 + 311,371 = 476,345); customer 10 is the second sample selected. Sample 3 is obtained by adding 311,371 to sample 2 (476,345 + 311,371 = 787,716); it is customer 16. The auditors continue through the population to select 152 samples. One customer can be selected twice if its balance is large. If this happens, the audit procedure is applied only once to the sample. A customer balance higher than the sampling interval is always selected.

Step 8. List the Selected Sample Items

The auditors record the list of sample items selected in the working papers.

Step 9. Perform the Audit Procedure and Identify Misstatements

Positive confirmation letters are mailed to the customers. After two weeks, second requests are sent to all nonresponding customers. After three weeks, the auditors perform alternative procedures (check for subsequent payments, verify shipping with external shipping document) to determine the validity of the accounts receivable at year-end. The auditors investigate all differences between the amount confirmed and the accounts receivable balance.

Step 10. Evaluate the Sample Results and Reach a Conclusion

The following misstatements were found:

	Interval Size	Amount Sampled	Known Misstatements over/(under)	Likely Misstatement	Projected Misstatements
Individually significant accounts	$ 5,400,000	5,400,000	$234,000		$234,000
Sample of accounts	47,200,000				
Sample 1		311,371	80,621	42,387	$121,332	163,719
Sample 3		311,371	48,412	32,000	169,649	201,649
Sample 24		311,371	60,568	26,000	107,662	133,662
Total	$52,600,000			$334,387	$398,643	$733,030

Because the auditors used monetary unit sampling, the misstatements are projected to the population in each sampling interval in which they were found. The auditors found misstatements in three sampling intervals: all sampling intervals have 311,371 sampling units. The misstatement amount in the interval divided by the amount sampled in the interval is equal to the percentage of misstatement in the sample interval. This percentage is multiplied by the total number of dollars in the interval to find the projected misstatement, which is the amount the auditors were likely to find if they had tested all accounts in the interval. Because a portion of the misstatement is known, the auditors can calculate the likely misstatement in the interval by subtracting the known misstatement from the projected one. For interval 1, the total misstatement projected for the interval if the auditors had sampled all accounts in it is $163,719. Of this total, the auditors found $42,387 (the known misstatement). If the auditors had sampled the remaining accounts in the interval, they would have expected to find an additional $121,332 (the likely misstatement).

The amount of *known misstatements* in the accounts receivable balance is $334,387. The best estimate of misstatement *in the population* is $733,030 (the total of the known and likely misstatements). The auditors determined that estimating the misstatement in the population is best done by assuming that it is relative to the dollar value of the population rather than each individual unit. The *likely misstatement* is $398,643 (the projected misstatement in the sample minus the known misstatement). [**Note:** No "likely misstatement" is calculated for the individually significant items because they were not sampled; 100% was reviewed.]

The projected misstatement plus an allowance for sampling risk is compared to the tolerable misstatement for accounts receivable.

The materiality level for the client is $1,150,000. The auditors use 75% of materiality, which totals $862,500, as the tolerable misstatement level.

Projected misstatement + Sampling risk < Tolerable misstatement
$733,030 + Estimate of sampling risk < $862,500

The auditors decide to accept the account balance as materially correct if they determine that sampling risk is less than $129,470. The sampling program calculates the sampling risk for a statistical sample. When the auditors use nonstatistical sampling, they use professional judgment to determine the risk. For example, auditors using nonstatistical sampling would question the likelihood that the population is misstated by more than $862,500 given that the projected misstatement is $733,030. If they determine that this is not likely, they accept the account balance as being materially correct. If they determine that it is likely that the account balance is misstated by more than $862,500 when the projection of misstatements shows $733,030, they gather additional evidence to determine the misstatement amount. This can mean increasing the number of confirmations mailed or performing additional tests to determine whether the account balance is materially misstated.

The auditors add known and likely misstatements to the proposed audit adjustment schedule so they can consider these misstatements in combination with the others found to determine whether the financial statements *as a whole* are materially misstated.

The Use of Nonstatistical Sampling for Substantive Tests of Transactions

LO6

Explain how the auditors use audit sampling to gather evidence related to material misstatements in classes of transactions

Next let's consider an audit sampling plan for a nonstatistical substantive test of transactions for an income statement account.

Sampling Plan 2

Step 1. Describe the Objectives of the Test, the Accounts, and the Assertions Affected

The objective of this test is to determine whether sales revenue for the year is materially misstated.

>   Audit procedure: vouch sales invoice to shipping document
>
>   Account tested: sales revenue
>
>   Assertions tested: existence and accuracy

Step 2. Define the Population and the Sampling Unit

The population is sales revenue for the year, which totals $28,000,000.

The sampling unit is the individual sales invoice. The company processed 700 sales invoices prenumbered from zero to 700 during the year.

Step 3. Define Misstatement

Sales revenue is not supported by valid shipping documents.

Step 4. Determine the Desired Level of Assurance, the Estimated Misstatement, and the Tolerable Misstatement

The desired level of assurance is 85%, the risk of incorrect acceptance is 15%, and the ratio of the estimated misstatement to the tolerable misstatement is 0.05.

Step 5. Determine the Audit Sampling Technique Used

The auditors use nonstatistical sampling.

Step 6. Select the Method for Determining Sample Size

Sales revenue is $28,000,000. There are no individually significant items. The auditors' assessment of the ratio of expected misstatements to tolerable ones is 0.05, materiality is $1,200,000, and the risk of incorrect acceptance is 15% (all based on the professional judgment of the auditor). Sample size is calculated as follows:

Population		$28,000,000
Tolerable misstatement (75% of materiality)		900,000
Confidence factor	/	2.06
Sampling interval	=	436,893
Population		28,000,000
Sampling interval	/	436,893
Sample size	=	64

Step 7. Determine the Method of the Sample Selection

Random number sampling generates 64 random numbers between zero and 700. The sales invoice with the random number is selected. If an invoice selected is void, the next invoice number is selected.

Step 8. List the Selected Sample Items

The auditors record the list of sample items selected in the working papers.

Step 9. Describe How the Sampling Procedure was Performed and List any Misstatements Identified in the Sample

The items are selected from the sales invoice ledger for the year. The auditors will review the sales invoice document and shipping document for each item selected to determine that the shipping document supports the amount of revenue recorded. Exceptions are investigated.

Step 10. Evaluate the Sample Results

The following misstatements were found:

	Account Balance	Amount Sampled	Misstatements Over/(Under)	Known Misstatement	Likely Misstatement	Projected Misstatement
Sample of accounts	$28,000,000	$848,000	$35,000	$35,000	$1,131,667	$1,166,667

The amount of *known misstatements* in sales revenue is $35,000. The population's projected misstatement is $1,166,667 ($35,000/3%). The auditors sampled 3% of the population (848,000/28,000,000) and determined that estimating its misstatement is best done by assuming that the misstatements are relative to the dollar value of the population rather than each individual unit. The *likely misstatement* is $1,131,667 (projected misstatement in the population minus the known misstatement).

The auditors compare the projected and tolerable misstatements for sales revenue.

The materiality level for the client is $1,200,000. The auditors use 75% of materiality as the tolerable misstatement level, which is $900,000.

$$\text{Projected misstatement} > \text{Tolerable misstatement}$$
$$\$1,166,667 > \$900,000$$

Based on the sample results, the auditors decide that sales revenue is materially misstated. In this case, they could ask the client to investigate misstatements in the account and correct them, or they could increase the sample size and perform additional tests to identify the material misstatement amount. Any misstatements that the client does not correct are recorded as proposed audit adjustments.

Chapter Takeaways

Substantive tests of details are crucial to the audit process. Auditors rely on the evidence provided in the sample to determine whether the financial statements are materially misstated. If the evidence gathered by the auditors does not accurately reflect the misstatements found in the financial statements, the auditors could issue the wrong audit report. Many sampling decisions are guided by the audit firm's policy, but the auditors must understand factors that impact sampling decisions to correctly apply that policy.

This chapter presented these important facts:

- How variables sampling is used by the auditor to gather evidence
- The difference between sampling and nonsampling risk
- Differences between statistical and nonstatistical sampling
- How to determine the population for substantive testing
- The audit steps necessary to perform a substantive test of balances and a substantive test of transactions
- Sampling methods used to collect a random sample
- Methods used to calculate known and likely misstatements, tolerable misstatements, and projected misstatements

Be sure you understand these concepts before you go to the next chapter.

Review Questions

LO1   1. Describe variables sampling and how to use it to gather evidence in the audit process.

LO2   2. What are sampling risk and nonsampling risk for variables sampling?

LO3   3. What are the differences between performing a statistical substantive test and performing a nonstatistical substantive test?

LO4   4. List the steps in a sampling plan for performing substantive tests of balances and transactions.

LO4   5. What is the population for a substantive test of balances?

LO4   6. What sampling methods can the auditor use to select a sample for a substantive test?

LO4   7. How do the auditors determine sample size for a substantive test?

LO4   8. Identify the factors that impact sample size. Does the population size have an impact on the number of items sampled?

LO5, LO6   9. How do the auditors evaluate misstatements in a substantive test?

LO5, LO6   10. What evidence do substantive tests provide the auditors? How do they use it?

LO6   11. What is a proposed audit adjustment schedule? How do the auditors use it?

LO4   12. What are tolerable misstatements, known misstatements, projected misstatements, and likely misstatements? How are they used in substantive sampling?

Multiple Choice Questions from CPA Examinations

LO1   13. While performing a test of details during an audit, the auditors determined that the sample results supported the conclusion that the recorded account balance was materially misstated. This situation indicates the risk of
a. Incorrect rejection.
b. Incorrect acceptance.
c. Assessing control risk too low.
d. Assessing control risk too high.

LO4   14. When planning a sample for a substantive test of details, auditors should consider tolerable misstatement for the sample that should
a. Be related to the auditors' business risk.
b. Not be adjusted for qualitative factors.
c. Be related to preliminary judgments about materiality levels.
d. Not be changed during the audit process.

LO4   15. How would an increase in tolerable misstatement and an increase in assessed level of control risk affect the sample size in a substantive test of details?

	Increase in tolerable misstatement	Increase in assessed level of control risk
a.	Increase sample size	Increase sample size
b.	Increase sample size	Decrease sample size
c.	Decrease sample size	Increase sample size
d.	Decrease sample size	Decrease sample size

LO4   16. As lower acceptable levels of both audit risk and materiality are established, auditors should plan more work on individual accounts to
a. Find smaller misstatements.
b. Find larger misstatements.
c. Increase the tolerable misstatement in the accounts.
d. Decrease the risk of assessing control as being too low.

LO4   17. In conducting a substantive test of an account balance, auditors hypothesize that no material misstatement exists. The risk that sample results will support the hypothesis when a material misstatement actually does exist is the risk of

  a. Incorrect rejection.
  b. Alpha error.
  c. Incorrect acceptance.
  d. Type 1 error.

LO3   18. Using statistical sampling to assist in verifying the year-end accounts payable balance, and auditors has accumulated the following data:

	Number of accounts	Book balance	Balance determined by the auditors
Population	4,100	$5,000,000	?
Sample	200	$250,000	$300,000

Using the ratio estimation technique, the auditors' estimate of year-end accounts payable balance is
  a. $6,150,000.
  b. $6,000,000.
  c. $5,125,000.
  d. $5,050,000.

LO4   19. Which of the following sample planning factors would influence the sample size for a substantive test of details for a specific account?

	Expected amount of misstatements	Measure of tolerable misstatement
a.	No	No
b	Yes	Yes
c.	No	Yes
d.	Yes	No

LO2   20. Which of the following best illustrates the concept of sampling risk?
  a. A randomly chosen sample may not be representative of the population as a whole on the characteristics of interest.
  b. Auditors can select audit procedures that are not appropriate to achieve the specific objectives.
  c. Auditors could fail to recognize errors in the documents examined for the chosen sample.
  d. The documents related to the chosen sample could not be available for inspection.

LO1   21. An underlying feature of random-based selection of items is that each
  a. Stratum of the accounting population be given equal representation in the sample.
  b. Item in the accounting population be randomly ordered.
  c. Item in the accounting population should have an opportunity to be selected.
  d. Item must be systematically selected using replacement.

LO4   22. If certain forms are not consecutively numbered
  a. Selection of a random sample probably is not possible.
  b. Systematic sampling can be appropriate.
  c. Stratified sampling should be used.
  d. Random number tables cannot be used.

Discussion Questions and Research Problems

LO4   23. **Developing a sampling plan for a test of inventory valuation.** The auditors plan to perform a test of inventory pricing to verify that the client has correctly determined the lower-of-cost-or-market value of the inventory.
  a. What assertion are the auditors testing?
  b. Prepare a sampling plan to perform the test. The desired level of assurance is 90% (10% risk of incorrect acceptance). The ratio of estimated misstatement to tolerable misstatement is 0.05. The auditor uses 75% of materiality as the tolerable misstatement. The materiality level is $400,000, and the population is $4,800,000.

c. How will you select your sample? Do you have choices of the method to use to select the sample? Explain your answer.

d. Explain how you will evaluate the results of your sample. State clearly the possible conclusions from your tests.

e. If you reject the lower-of-price-or-market value of the inventory based on your test, what will you do?

LO4, LO5

24. **Developing a sampling plan for inventory test counts.** Auditors typically attend the client's year-end inventory count and make tests counts then to gather evidence regarding the ending inventory.

a. What assertion are the auditors testing for inventory?

b. Prepare a sampling plan to perform the test. The desired level of assurance is 95% (5% risk of incorrect acceptance). The ratio of estimated misstatement to tolerable misstatement is 0.15. The materiality level is $1,000,000, and the population is $14,800,000. The auditor assumes that tolerable misstatement is 75% of materiality.

c. How will you select your sample? Do you have choices in the method to use to select the sample? Explain your answer.

d. Explain how you will evaluate the results of your sample. State clearly the possible conclusions from your tests.

e. You have determined that ten inventory items have a large value. How will this change your sampling plan?

f. Assume that the ten items have an inventory value of $6,000,000. What is the new sample size? Will you count the ten items with high value? Explain your answer.

LO4, LO5

25. **Developing a sampling plan for accounts receivable confirmations.** The following schedule shows accounts receivable balances for the audit client at year-end. As a staff accountant, you have been assigned to select accounts receivable balances to confirm.

a. What assertion do auditors test when confirming account balances?

b. Prepare a sampling plan to perform the test. The desired level of assurance is 95% (5% risk of incorrect acceptance). The ratio of estimated misstatement to tolerable misstatement is 0.05. The materiality level is $25,000, and the population is $129,992. The auditor uses 75% of materiality as the tolerable misstatement.

c. Select a sample of accounts to confirm using systematic random sampling and the sample size that you calculated. Identify the accounts that you selected. Assume the random number generated for the first interval is 4002.

d. You find overstatement errors of $12,000 in your sample. How will you evaluate this misstatement?

e. Prepare the journal entries for the proposed audit adjustments you would make. Assume the misstatement is related to unrecorded credit memos for goods returned by the customer.

Herbal Medicine Stores

Accounts Receivable Listing as of December 31, 2011		
Customer	Year-End Balance	Cumulative Balance
Ang Siew Min	421.25	421.25
Beng Kok Med Hall	1108.00	1529.25
Ba Choo San	3474.70	5003.95
Chan Chin Chai Med Hall	4306.20	9310.15
Chang's Female Clinic	125.40	9435.55
Chia Ho Soon	244.15	9679.70

Chin Sook Fan	1212.75	10892.45
Choy Ear Clinic	561.30	11453.75
Eastern Acupuncture	6243.10	17696.85
Eng Siang Ear, Nose & Throat Clinic	450.00	18146.85
Foo King Chu Med Hall	1259.05	19405.90
Ghim Moh Med Specialists	1448.75	20854.65
Hui Min Chinese Physician	276.00	21130.65
Jie Ying Clinic	788.90	21919.55
King Kong Kong Med Store	350.00	22269.55
Koh Thiam Siew	8187.25	30456.80
Lai Kah Shing Clinic	4312.60	34769.40
Lim Siong Tye	847.50	35616.90
Lim Seah Clinic	2747.00	38363.90
Loh Chong Yick	783.65	39147.55
Lok Meng Free Clinic	4841.20	43988.75
Mee Na Tan Clinic	598.75	44587.50
Min Hin Med Hall	3874.00	48461.50
Moo Moo Kow	1908.45	50369.95
Nan Hwa Med Hall	5178.15	55548.10
New Man & Woman Acupuncture	139.60	55687.70
New World Herbalist Store	463.40	56151.10
Oh So Soon Clinic	8131.75	64282.85
Oh Seok Tin Clinic	1409.75	65692.60
Ong Thean Tin & Co	2753.00	68445.60
Pao Pao Med Hall	804.80	69250.40
Poh Heng Clinic	250.00	69500.40
Ren Her Med Store	1415.65	70916.05
Rimei Clinic & Health Food	3708.30	74624.35
Seng Seng Teck	4293.55	78917.90
Seow See See Clinic	706.70	79624.60
Serangoon Med Store	5488.80	85113.40
Shao Ren Med Hall	2363.60	87477.00
Sim Soo Good Clinic	646.65	88123.65
Singapore Acupuncture	847.50	88971.15
Sure Cure Clinic	7937.45	96908.60
Teck Min Clinic	249.00	97157.60
Teo Lian Hee	4763.60	101921.20
Thye Mong Med Hall	1648.35	103569.60
Tien Tien Lai Herbs	2979.00	106548.60
Tokyo Med Hall	835.50	107384.10
Wan Hin Med Hall	8685.80	116069.90
Win Yam Seng	767.70	116837.60
Woh Huat Med Hall	9146.65	125984.20
Xie Ming	3457.45	129441.70
Yung Sheng Herbs	549.95	129991.60
Total	**129,991.60**	

LO4, LO6

26. **Developing a sampling plan for fixed asset additions.** Tron Lumber had 20 additions to the fixed asset equipment account during the past year. Describe how you could perform a substantive test to audit these additions whose amounts are material.
    a. What assertion are you testing for this asset account?
    b. Prepare a sampling plan to perform the test. The desired level of assurance is 90% (10% risk of incorrect acceptance). The ratio of estimated misstatement to tolerable misstatement is 0.00. The materiality level is $10,800,000, and the population is $120,000,000. The auditor uses 75% of materiality as the tolerable misstatement.
    c. Explain how you will evaluate the results of your sample. State clearly the possible conclusions of your tests.
    d. If the additions are not audited by sampling, what other method could you use to gather substantive evidence? Explain your answer.

LO4, LO6

27. **Developing a sampling plan to audit investment securities.** Your audit client has a substantial portfolio of marketable securities that it holds at the end of the year. The detail for the marketable securities accounts follows. Your client purchased 100 securities as trading securities during the year and sold 75 of them. In the held-to-maturity category, it purchased one security at a cost of $1,000,000.

	Balance at 12/31/11	Balance at 12/31/12
Trading securities	$2,500,000	$3,400,000
Held-to-maturity securities	$5,000,000	$6,000,000

    a. Describe how you would use sampling to gather evidence regarding the purchases and sales in the trading and held-to-maturity security accounts. Would you use sampling to examine changes in both account types?
    b. Prepare a sampling plan to perform the test you have decided to do. The desired level of assurance is 90% (10% risk of incorrect acceptance). The ratio of estimated misstatement to tolerable misstatement is 0.00. The materiality level is $800,000. The client purchased 100 securities at a cost of $6,000,000 and sold 80 securities with an original cost of $5,100,000. The auditor uses 75% of materiality to determine tolerable misstatement.
    c. Explain how you will evaluate the results of your sample. State clearly the possible conclusions from your tests.

LO1

28. **Training material for substantive sampling.** You are responsible for developing training material for staff auditors on substantive sampling. After presenting it, staff auditors ask you several questions. Explain how you would answer them.
    a. Is it always better to sample more items than fewer items?
    b. When should I stratify a sample?
    c. How do I decide whether to perform substantive tests or to use analytical procedures? Analytical procedures are much easier than substantive testing.
    d. How do I convince the client that the likely misstatements are valid misstatements? For the known misstatements, I can show the client the documents to explain the misstatements. I can't do this for likely misstatements, so it is harder to convince the client that the misstatements are valid.
    e. Why do I put the misstatements I found on the proposed audit adjustment schedule if the tolerable misstatement is higher than the projected misstatement for the account I am auditing? Why can't I just ignore these misstatements?
    f. Can I do all the substantive testing at year-end? How long will it take?

LO4

29. **Auditing adjusting journal entries.** During your audit of the financial reporting process, you notice several adjusting journal entries recorded in the accounts at the end of each quarter and the end of the year. You decide to test them.

a. Prepare a sampling plan for the adjusting journal entries. The desired level of assurance is 90% (10% risk of incorrect acceptance). The ratio of estimated misstatement to tolerable misstatement is 0.00. Materiality is $1,000,000. The auditor uses 75% of materiality as tolerable misstatement. The adjusting entries total $4,800,000. There are 70 adjusting entries. 15 entries for each of the first three quarters and 25 entries at year end.

b. Explain how you will evaluate the results of your sample.

Real-World Auditing Problems

LO4   30. **OfficeMax**

The OfficeMax accounting fraud previously described in the book is summarized briefly here:

The third largest office supply store in the United States, OfficeMax restated earnings for the first three quarters of 2004 because of problems related to its employees' fabrication of vendor payments. They are widely used in the retail world as a marketing tool. Companies pay a fee and receive better shelf space or advertisements featuring their products. The company's employees generated false supporting documents for several million dollars in claims billed to a vendor. OfficeMax estimated that income was overstated by $4 to $6 million for the three quarters.

The nature of vendor payments makes them susceptible to fraud. When companies need to make quarterly revenue targets set by management or Wall Street analysts, they ask a supplier to give them a vendor allowance at that time for something they will buy in the future, thus allowing the company to meet its target revenue for the quarter. The company records vendor allowances as revenue at the end of the quarter although the inventory purchase will not be made until the following quarter, allowing the company to meet revenue targets for the quarter.[1]

a. Suggest a substantive test of either balances or transactions that could be effective in detecting the misstatement.

b. How would the auditors use sampling to perform the tests? What is the population for the test? How will the auditors evaluate the test's outcome? Explain your answer.

LO4   31. **Gemstar**

The SEC fined Gemstar–TV Guide International $10 million for overstating its revenue by $250 million from 1999 through 2002. Gemstar improperly recorded revenue for expired, disputed, or nonexistent contracts, accelerated the recognition of revenue under long-term agreements, used round-trip transactions to generate revenue for which Gemstar paid money to a third party that used the funds to buy advertising from Gemstar, and improperly reported advertising revenue based on nonmonetary and barter transactions.

KPMG LLP, Gemstar's auditors, was censured for engaging in "improper professional conduct" (Jonathan Weil, "KPMG Is Censured in Gemstar Matter," *The Wall Street Journal,* October 21, 2004) in connection with its audit work for Gemstar. The SEC stated that KPMG allowed Gemstar to record revenue in the absence of customer agreements. According to the SEC, KPMG relied on statements made by Gemstar's executives about its sales rather than gathering evidence to support these statements.[2]

What evidence should the auditors have gathered? Suggest a substantive test of balances or of transactions that could have been effective in detecting the misstatement.

[1] David Armstrong, "OfficeMax CEO Resigns; Results to Be Restated," *The Wall Street Journal,* February 15, 2005.

[2] Jonathan Weil, "KPMG Is Censured in Gemstar Matter," *The Wall Street Journal,* October 21, 2004; U.S. Securities and Exchange Commission, Press Release 2004–86, June 23, 2004.

LO4   32. **Just for Feet**

Deloitte and Touche LLP was censured in April 2005 for the failed audit of Just for Feet (JFF), a Birmingham, Alabama, shoe store. JFF issued fraudulent financial statements by recognizing fictitious revenue from its vendors and by failing to write off worthless inventory. The SEC noted that Deloitte's National Risk Management Program had identified JFF as a high-risk client but had failed to perform audit procedures required for this designation.[3]

Suggest a substantive test of balances or of transactions that could be effective in detecting the misstatement.?

LO4   33. **WPT Enterprises**

In July 2005, Deloitte & Touche LLP dropped WPT Enterprises as an audit client because the audit risk was too high for the Internet gambling client. WPT is a U.S. company offering online poker through its website.

The Federal Wire Act passed in 1961 prohibits Americans from placing bets over the telephone or the Internet. Because Internet gambling is illegal in the United States, most Internet gambling companies are incorporated outside the country. WBT must follow U.S. law as a company registered in the United States on the NASDAQ stock exchange. WBT's auditors must make sure that the company does not take bets from Americans.[4]

a. If your audit firm had accepted the audit engagement for this client, how would you ensure that the company complied with the U.S. prohibition against online gambling by American citizens?

b. Suggest a substantive test of balances or of transactions that could be effective in detecting the misstatement.

c. Is this a high-risk client in your opinion? How will you modify your audit procedures because of this risk?

LO4   34. **Merck-Medco**

Between 1999 and 2001, Merck-Medco recorded $12.4 billion of revenue that it will never collect. During this time, Merck included as part of revenue the copayments collected by pharmacies from patients even though it does not receive these funds. These copayments accounted for nearly 10 percent of Merck's total revenue during this time period.

The $12.4 billion represents the copayment, typically $10–$25 per prescription, paid directly to the pharmacies by customers using a prescription drug card from an insurance company. Merck reported expenses equal to $12.4 billion to offset the copayment revenue on the income statement. The net income that Merck reported was correct.[5]

Suggest a substantive test of balances or of transactions that could be effective in detecting the revenue misstatement.

---

[3] U.S. Securities and Exchange Commission 2005–66, "SEC Charges Deloitte & Touche and Two of Its Personnel for Failure in the Audit of Just for Feet," April 26, 2005.

[4] Seren Ng, "For Audit Firms, All Bets Are Off," *The Wall Street Journal,* July 21, 2005.

[5] Barbara Martinez, "Merck Books Co-Payments to Pharmacies As Revenue," *The Wall Street Journal,* June 21, 2002; and Barbara Martinez, "Merck Recorded $12.4 Billion in Revenue It Never Collected," *The Wall Street Journal,* July 8, 2002.

Chapter

10

Cash and Investment Business Processes

Learning Objectives

After studying this chapter, you should be able to:

1. Describe the cash and investment business processes.
2. Explain the transactions in the processes.
3. Understand generally accepted accounting principles (the applicable financial reporting framework) for recording investments, valuing investments at year-end, and recognizing gains and losses on investment sales.
4. Understand misstatements (errors and fraud) that could be expected in the cash and investment processes.
5. Explain financial statement assertions for accounts in the business processes.
6. Identify relevant assertions for significant accounts in the cash and investment business processes.
7. Describe the procedures that auditors use to gather evidence for internal controls in the process.
8. Understand the methods that auditors use to gather substantive evidence using substantive tests of transactions, analytical procedures, and substantive tests of balances.
9. Explain the disclosure requirements for accounts in the business processes.

Auditing and accounting standards relevant to these topics

For private companies

- **FASB Statement of Financial Accounting Concepts No. 5,** Recognition and Measurements in Financial Statements of Business Enterprises
- **FASB Statement of Financial Accounting Concepts No. 6,** Elements of Financial Statements
- **FASB Statements of Financial Accounting Standards No. 130,** Reporting Comprehensive Income
- **AU Section 312,** Materiality in Planning and Performing an Audit
- **AU Section 314,** Understanding the Entity and Its Environment and Assessing the Risks of Material Misstatements
- **AU 316,** Consideration of Fraud in a Financial Statement Audit
- **AU 318,** Performing Audit Procedures in Response to Assessed Risks and Evaluating the Audit Evidence Obtained
- **AU 326,** Audit Evidence

- **AU 329,** Analytical Procedures
- **AU Section 339,** Audit Documentation
- **AU Section 330,** External Confirmations
- **AU Section 332,** Audit Evidence—Specific Considerations for Selected Items
- **AU Section 342,** Auditing Accounting Estimates, Including Fair Value Estimates and Related Disclosures
- **Preface to Codification of Statements on Auditing Standards,** Overall Objectives of the Independent Auditor and the Conduct of an Audit in Accordance with Generally Accepted Auditing Standards

For public companies

- **FASB Statement of Financial Accounting Concepts No. 5,** Recognition and Measurements in Financial Statements of Business Enterprises
- **FASB Statement of Financial Accounting Concepts No. 6,** Elements of Financial Statements
- **FASB Statements of Financial Accounting Standards No. 130,** Reporting Comprehensive Income
- **AU 316,** Consideration of Fraud in a Financial Statement Audit (Interim standard adopted by PCAOB)
- **AU 329,** Analytical Procedures (Interim standard adopted by PCAOB)
- **AU Section 330,** The Confirmation Process (Interim standard adopted by PCAOB)
- **AU Section 332,** Auditing Derivative Instruments, Hedging Activities, and Investments in Securities
- **AU Section 342,** Auditing Accounting Estimates (Interim standard adopted by PCAOB)
- **PCAOB Auditing Standard No. 3,** Audit Documentation
- **PCAOB Auditing Standard No. 11,** Consideration of Materiality in Planning and Performing an Audit
- **PCAOB Auditing Standard No. 15,** Audit Evidence

International standards

- **ISA 240,** The Auditor's Responsibility to Consider Fraud in an Audit of Financial Statements
- **ISA 500,** Audit Evidence
- **ISA 505,** Audit of Accounting Estimates
- **ISA 545,** Auditing Fair Value Measurements and Disclosures
- **IAS 39,** Financial Instruments: Recognition and Measurement

Chapter Overview

This chapter describes auditing procedures that are used to review specific classes of transactions. In the investment process, the auditors consider transactions recorded when (1) investment securities are purchased, (2) investment securities are sold, (3) investment securities are valued at year-end, and (4) income is recognized from investment securities. The audit of the ending cash *balance* is also considered. The audit of cash *transactions* has been considered in the revenue and purchase business processes. This chapter describes activities that are part of the testing and decision phase of the audit process. Exhibit 10-1 summarizes the main steps in the audit process.

Gathering evidence to support the financial statement accounts in these business processes is important to the audit process because of the significance of the investment account to the assets reported on the balance sheet.

The Audit Process	Exhibit 10-1

Steps in the Audit Process	Discussed in this Section
Planning Phase	
Consider the Preconditions for an Audit and Accept or Reject the Audit Engagement	
Understand the Entity and Its Environment, Determine Materiality, and Assess the Risks of Material Misstatements	
Develop an Audit Strategy and an Audit Plan to Respond to the Assessed Risks	
Testing Phase	
Test Internal Controls? Yes No	√
Perform Tests of Controls if "Yes"	√
Perform Substantive Tests of Transactions	√
Perform Substantive Tests of Balances	√
Assess the Likelihood of Material Misstatement	√
Decision Phase	
Review the Presentation and Disclosure Assertions	√
Evaluate the Evidence to Determine Whether the Financial Statements Are Prepared in Accordance with the Applicable Financial Reporting Framework	
Issue Audit Report	
Communicate with the Audit Committee	

Describe the Cash and Investment Business Processes

LO1

Describe the cash and investment business processes

The cash and investment processes involve income statement and balance sheet accounts. On the income statement, the cash and investment processes include investment income from interest and dividends, unrealized gains and losses on trading securities, and gains and losses on the sale of investments. On the balance sheet, the cash and investment processes include the ending balance in the cash account, adjustments to other comprehensive income related to unrealized gains and losses on available-for-sale investment securities, and three categories of investments: investments held to maturity, trading securities, and available-for-sale investments. These investment accounts can be short or long-term assets. The cash and investment processes often include hundreds of transactions each year. As with all business processes, auditors are concerned with determining that the income statement and balance sheet accounts in the business process are recorded in accordance with the applicable financial reporting framework and that disclosure in the accounts associated with each business process is consistent with general accepted accounting standards. Activity in the accounts in each process is shown in Exhibit 10-2.

As with all income statement accounts, the gain and loss accounts and the income statement unrealized gain and loss accounts begin the year with a zero balance. Transactions for the year are recorded in the accounts. Year-end totals of the revenue and expense accounts reflect **all** transactions recorded during the year, and this is the total for which the auditors are responsible for gathering evidence to support. They must determine whether the transactions recorded in these accounts during the year are presented in accordance with the financial reporting framework.

The totals in the balance sheet accounts reflect only the amounts in the accounts on the last day of the year. They do not reflect all transactions recorded during the year but the *net* amount of the transactions recorded during the year. The balance sheet accounts

Accounts in the Cash and Investment Processes

Exhibit 10-2

+ Available-for-Sale Investments −	
Beginning Balance	
Investments purchased during the year	Investments sold during the year
Ending Balance	

+ Allowance for Available for Sale Investments −	
Beginning Balance	Beginning Balance
Increase to allowance	Decrease to allowance
Ending Balance	Ending Balance

+ Trading Securities −	
Beginning Balance	
Investments purchased during the year	Investments sold during the year
Ending Balance	

+ Allowance for Trading Securities −	
Beginning Balance	Beginning Balance
Increase to allowance	Decrease to allowance
Ending Balance	Ending Balance

+ Held-to-Maturity Investments −	
Beginning Balance	
Investments purchased during the year	Investments sold during the year
Ending Balance	

+ Premium or Discount on Held-to-Maturity Securities −	
Beginning Balance if premium	Beginning Balance if discount
Amortization of discount	Amortization of premium
Ending Balance if premium	Ending Balance if discount

− Gain / Loss on Sale +	
Loss on sale of securities	Gain on sale of securities
Ending Balance	Ending Balance

− Unrealized Gain / Loss on Trading Securities (income statement account) +	
Unrealized loss	Unrealized gain
Ending Balance	Ending Balance

− Unrealized Gain / Loss on Available-For-Sale Securities (owner's equity account) +	
Unrealized loss	Unrealized gain
Ending Balance	Ending Balance

+ Cash −	
Beginning Balance	
Increases to cash	Decreases to cash
Ending Balance*	

* The cash balance is part of this cycle. Cash receipts were included in the revenue process. Cash payments are part of the purchase and expenditure process.

have a beginning balance on the first day of the year, which reflects the ending (audited) balance from the prior year. During the year, increases and decreases in the balance sheet accounts are recorded in the individual accounts. Balance sheet accounts typically have debit and credit entries (both increases and decreases). The balance at year-end reflects only the balance in the account as of the last day of the year. The auditors are responsible only for determining whether the ending balance in the balance sheet account has been recorded in accordance with the applicable financial reporting framework. Auditors are not responsible for reviewing all transactions recorded in the balance sheet account during the year.

For the income statement, auditors gather evidence to support the transactions recorded in the accounts for 12 months. For the balance sheet, auditors gather evidence to determine whether the account balance on one day of the year, the last one of the year, is correct. The tests that auditors use to gather evidence relating to income statement transactions are called *substantive tests of transactions*. Auditors use tests to gather evidence relating to balance sheet transactions using *substantive tests of balances*. These

Journal Entries and Related Documents for the Cash and Investment Business Process

Exhibit 10-3

Journal Entries	Documents
Investment in Trading, Available-For-Sale, or Held-To-Maturity Securities Cash *(To record the purchase of investment securities.)*	Broker's advice, cash disbursement journal

Cash
    Investment in Trading, Available-For-Sale, or Held-To-Maturity Securities
    Realized Gain on Sale of Investment Securities
(To record the sale of investment securities at a gain.)
	Broker's advice, cash receipts journal

Cash Realized Loss on Sale of Investment Securities Investment in Trading, Available-For-Sale, or Held-To-Maturity Securities *(To record the sale of investment securities at a loss.)*	Broker's advice, cash receipts journal
Unrealized Holding Loss on Investment Securities Allowance for Decline in Valuation of Investment Securities *(To record an unrealized holding loss on an investment security. The unrealized loss account is an income statement account if the investment is a trading security but an owners' equity account if it is an available-for-sale security.)*	Adjusting journal entry report, market value report
Allowance for Increase in Valuation of Investment Securities Unrealized holding Gain on Investment Securities *(To record an unrealized holding gain on an investment security. The unrealized gain account is an income statement account if the investment is a trading security but an owner's equity account if it is an available-for-sale security.)*	Adjusting journal entry report, Market value report

tests provide evidence about whether the accounts in the cash and investment business processes are prepared in accordance with the applicable financial reporting framework. After gathering evidence using internal controls tests, substantive tests of transactions, substantive tests of balances, and analytical procedures, the auditors conclude whether the accounts in these business processes are prepared in accordance with the applicable financial reporting framework. If they are not, the auditors prepare adjusting journal entries to correct the accounts.

Transactions in the Cash and Investment Business Processes

LO2

Explain the transactions in the processes

Refer to Exhibit 10-3 for the journal entries used to record transactions in the cash and investment processes.

Documents in the Business Processes

Auditors could find several documents useful for gathering evidence about the business processes; some of them can be in electronic format.

Bank Statement

The company uses this document from the bank to verify cash disbursements and cash receipts during a month. Companies mailing checks rather than making electronic payments must perform a year-end bank reconciliation to determine the correct amount of cash that is on hand at year-end. In that case, a cutoff bank statement for a company with a December year end (a bank statement received in January, reporting the activity for the first ten days of January) is often used to determine the accuracy of adjustments on the year-end bank reconciliation.

Bank Transfer Schedule

The client prepares this schedule by showing the bank transfers made at year-end, typically for 10 days before and 10 days after year-end. Auditors use this schedule to determine the correct amount of cash at year-end and that the cash has been counted in one—not two—bank accounts.

Bank Reconciliation

A client using paper checks rather than electronic transfers to make and receive cash payments prepares a monthly reconciliation that is used to determine the correct cash balance at each month-end. The reconciliation is used to verify that checks written have cleared the bank in a timely fashion and that deposits made to the bank account have been recorded.

Standard Bank Confirmation

A confirmation is mailed to each bank in which the client has an account. The standard bank confirmation reports the cash balance at year-end in each account and indicates the amount of any loans outstanding or lines of credit at the bank currently available to the client.

Broker's Advice

The client receives this document (in electronic or paper form) from the broker to indicate the purchase or sales price of a security (stocks or bonds) when it is bought or sold. The broker's advice lists the number of shares sold or purchased, the price per share and the transaction fee.

Adjusting Journal Entry Report

This report is a record of all adjusting journal entries made during a specific time period, organized by month-end, quarter-end, and year-end. It is supported by documentation for the adjusting journal entries with the signature of the person initiating the entry.

Market Value at Year-End

The auditors verify the market valuation at year-end for the investments held at that time using the stock market information from *The Wall Street Journal* or another online source providing daily market prices for stocks.

Applicable Financial Reporting Frameworks for the Investment Process

LO3

Understand generally accepted accounting principles (the applicable financial reporting framework) for recording investments, valuing investments at year-end and recognizing gains and losses on investment sales

Two financial reporting frameworks might be used by a company for preparing financial statements: (1) accounting standards for U.S. companies and (2) international accounting standards. We refer to the first set of standards as U.S. GAAP and the second set as International Financial Reporting Standards (IFRS). The international accounting standards are written by the International Accounting Standards Board (IASB). The rules for investment securities will be discussed next.

FASB Concept Statement No. 5, *Recognition and Measurement in Financial Statements of Business Enterprises,* provides the basic rule for asset measurement and recognition of gains and losses according to U.S. GAAP. International accounting standards define asset recognition in a similar manner. According to the standards, an asset is recognized when the benefit of another asset has been reduced or when a liability has been incurred. The asset amount is based on the exchange price at the date the asset is

Accounting Standards for Investments			Exhibit 10-4

	Trading Securities	Available-for-Sale Securities	Held-to-Maturity Securities
Valuation at purchase	Cost	Cost	Cost
Valuation at year-end	Market value	Market value	Amortized cost
Effect of year-end valuation on financial statements (referred to as an *unrealized gain or loss*)	Increases or decreases net income	Increases or decreases owner's equity (part of other comprehensive income)	Increases net income as interest income is recognized
Effect of sale of security on the financial statements (referred to as a *realized gain or loss*)	Increases or decreases net income	Increases or decreases net income	Increases or decreases net income

recognized. Once an asset is recognized, it continues to be measured at the amount initially recorded unless an event occurs that changes its value.

One way that an asset value can change is through a change in price. Changes in the price are recognized if they are sufficiently relevant and reliable. Changes in price for trading securities and available-for-sale securities are recorded. Investments in trading securities and available-for-sale securities are valued at market price at year-end because the current market price is relevant and reliable. Held-to-maturity investments are not recorded at market value because their market value is not relevant or reliable. Held-to-maturity investments are valued at amortized cost (cost plus premium or cost minus discount) at year-end. By definition, a held-to-maturity investment is purchased as a long-term investment, so the market value at year-end is not a relevant or reliable price.

Unrealized holding gains and losses are recognized on trading securities at each year-end based on the difference between their purchase price and market value of the security. The security's carrying value can be more or less than its purchase price because the market value can increase or decrease. Unrealized holding gains and losses on trading securities are included on the company's income statement and have an impact on net income.

The available-for-sale investment account is also adjusted to market value at year-end, but the unrealized holding gain or loss entry for this type of security is an owners' equity account rather than an income statement account; thus, holding gains and losses on available-for-sale securities do not have an impact on net income. The unrealized holding gain or loss for an available-for-sale investment is a part of Other Comprehensive Income in the Owners' Equity section of the balance sheet.

Realized gains and losses are recognized on the sale of investments. The amount of the gain or loss is calculated as the difference between the investment's original cost and its sales price. This applies to trading and available-for-sale securities.

International accounting standards use the same categories for investment securities, and determine realized and unrealized gains and losses in the same manner as the U.S. accounting standards.

See Exhibit 10-4 for a summary of the rules for recording transactions related to investments according to the applicable financial reporting framework used in the United States and in countries that follow international accounting standards.

Possible Misstatements in the Cash and Investment Processes

LO4

Understand misstatements (errors and fraud) that could be expected in the cash and investment processes

The auditors' role in the audit of a business process is to determine whether the accounts in the process are prepared in accordance with the applicable financial reporting framework used by the company. The most efficient manner of doing this is for the auditors to consider misstatements that could occur and then to gather evidence to determine whether they actually have occurred. The auditors' understanding of what is likely to go wrong in a process is important so they can *plan* the audit and determine the *nature* of the evidence (whether to use internal control or substantive testing), the *timing* of the evidence collection (before year-end or at year-end), and the *extent* of the evidence to be gathered (the amount of testing needed). The higher the likelihood of misstatement in a business process, the more likely the auditors are to do more substantive testing at year-end than when the likelihood of misstatement is less.

When considering misstatements in a business process, auditors look for intentional and unintentional misstatements. The accounts in the cash and investment business processes are susceptible to both errors and fraud (overstatement or understatement). Clients could have understated cash, investments, or unrealized gains and losses on investment securities or overstated them. **Overstatement** misstatements are far more likely to occur in these processes than understatement misstatements because overstating cash and investments increases the value of total assets on the balance sheet and overstating gains increases net income. Misstatements that do occur (whether intentional or unintentional) frequently overstate assets, thus misleading outsiders about the future cash flows when the assets will be sold.

Overstatement misstatements are often caused by the client's fraudulent actions (intentional misstatement). **AU 316,** *Consideration of Fraud in a Financial Statement Audit* and **ISA 240,** *the Auditor's Responsibility to Consider Fraud in an Audit of Financial Statements,* requires auditors to assess the risk of material misstatement due to fraud and to plan the audit to control this risk.

The most common misstatements likely in these accounts involve overstating cash and misclassifying trading and available-for-sale securities. The client can use a variety of methods to overstate investment securities and cash:

- Misstating the amount of cash by manipulating the adjustments made to the year-end bank reconciliation. This applies only to companies not using electronic cash transfers.
- Manipulating the particular securities in the trading security and the available-for-sale accounts to overstate unrealized gains from holding securities and to increase income. This involves moving investments whose market value is more than the cost to the trading security account.

Companies want to report positive cash at year-end. More cash is usually better than less (within reasonable limits, of course). Although cash is fairly easy to audit, companies using checks to disburse cash could easily misstate it. In this case, the auditors determine the correct cash amount at year-end by using the confirmed balances from the banks and adjusting these amounts according to the checks outstanding and the deposits in transit. The client could manually make these adjustments, which are easy to misstate.

The unrealized gain and loss adjustment for trading securities impacts the income statement, but those for available-for-sale securities does not and is reported only in Other Comprehensive Income. Clients can transfer securities from one account to the other to change the amount of the unrealized gain or loss. Transferring an unrealized gain from an available-for-sale account to the trading securities account increases net income. Transferring an unrealized holding loss from the trading securities account to the available-for-sale account also increases net income. Companies can alter the amount of the *unrealized gain or loss* by moving securities from one account to the other to suit their purpose.

When assessing *inherent* risk for the cash and investment processes, auditors should consider the risk of these misstatements.

Did You Know?

Parmalat, an Italian company best known for its long-life milk, reported $4.73 billion in cash and marketable securities in a bank account that did not exist. The money was supposedly held in an account in the name of Bonlat, a wholly owned subsidiary of Parmalat registered in the Cayman Islands, at the Bank of America in New York City. However, neither the bank account nor the assets existed. The bank confirmation returned to the auditors in Italy had been forged by company management.

Executives at Parmalat have described the Bonlat Company as fraudulent; executives described it as a "virtual garbage can" to hide fraudulent transactions. Bonlat was created in 1998 with Grant Thornton's assistance to hide fraudulent transactions from the Deloitte auditors for Parmalat. By materially overstating company assets and understating company liabilities, Parmalat sold $100 million of unsecured debt to American investors, which later became worthless.

Sources: Alessandra Galloni and David Reilly, "Auditor Raised Parmalat Red Flag," *The Wall Street Journal,* March 29, 2004; SEC Litigation Release No. 18527, December 30, 2003.

> ***Is it hard for auditors to discover fraud when they receive fictitious external confirmations?***

How do auditors find errors or fraud in these business processes? They should conduct the audit with an attitude of professional skepticism. This includes gathering evidence and planning the audit with a "questioning mind and a critical assessment of audit evidence" (Overall Objectives of the Independent Auditor and the Conduct of an Audit in Accordance with Generally Accepted Auditing Standards). In planning the audit, members of the audit team should discuss the potential for misstatement due to fraud in the cash and investment processes, including the pressure on management to commit fraud, the opportunity for fraud perpetration, and the company's general environment or tone that could allow management to rationalize committing fraud.

In planning the audit and assessing risk for the cash and investment business processes, the auditors should consider the fraud risk factors listed in the auditing standards (AU316) and use this information to assess inherent risk for the processes and to plan the level of substantive testing needed.

Management's Assertions for the Cash and Investment Business Processes

LO5

Explain financial statement assertions for accounts in the business processes

In the cash and investment business processes, auditors gather evidence to evaluate management's assertions about the accounts.

Management's Assertions

Existence or occurrence—for both classes of transactions and account balances: Management asserts that cash and investments exist at the balance sheet date and that the investments' gain and loss transactions were recorded during the year.

Completeness—for both classes of transactions and account balances: Management asserts that cash and investments exist at the balance sheet date and that the investments' gain and loss transactions were recorded during the year.

Valuation and allocation—for account balances: Management also asserts that the investment accounts are valued correctly according to the rules of the applicable financial reporting framework at year-end.

Rights and obligations—for account balances: Management asserts that the company has the right to the assets of cash and investments.

Accuracy—for classes of transactions: Management asserts that all transactions related to the investment account have been accurately recorded.

Cutoff—for classes of transactions: Management asserts that cutoff for recording transactions was in accordance with the applicable financial reporting framework.

Classification—for classes of transactions: Management asserts that transactions related to the investment process have been properly classified.

Relevant Assertions for Significant Accounts in the Business Processes

LO6

Identify relevant assertions for significant accounts in the cash and investment business processes

Auditors are required to gather audit evidence to support relevant assertions for significant accounts for each business process. The relevant assertions are related to the ***risk*** and the likelihood of misstatement in the business process. Because the most likely misstatements in the cash and investment processes are overstatement errors, the most important assertion for the investment process is **valuation** and for the cash balance is **existence.** Auditors gather *evidence* to determine that cash *exists* and that investments are properly *valued* at year-end.

Internal Control Questionnaire—Investment Business Process

Exhibit 10-5

ENVIRONMENT

1. Does the board of directors authorize investment strategies?
2. Are investment strategies based on legitimate business goals?
3. Does company policy establish trading guidelines and limits?
4. Are derivatives used for legitimate company objectives?
5. Are brokerage relationships reviewed for potential conflicts of interest?

EXISTENCE OR OCCURRENCE

6. Are brokerage statements reconciled to the general ledger monthly?

COMPLETENESS

7. Are company traders monitored in their discussions with brokers?

RIGHTS AND OBLIGATIONS

8. Does the accounting department review all significant transactions?

VALUATION OR ALLOCATION

9. Are accounting personnel trained in standards for hedge accounting?
10. Are investment classifications based on legitimate management intentions?
11. Are changes in investments that are accounted for on the equity method monitored and recorded in the financial statements?

PRESENTATION AND DISCLOSURE

12. Does senior management review disclosures?
13. Are footnotes prepared to disclose clearly investment transactions?

Auditors gather evidence to evaluate management's assertions using either (1) internal control tests or (2) substantive tests of transactions or balances. Often the auditors use a combination of both types of tests. Let's consider internal control testing for the cash and investment business processes first.

Internal Control Testing

LO7

Describe the procedures that auditors use to gather evidence for internal controls in the process

In the cash and investment processes, management can design internal controls to prevent or detect misstatements in the financial statements depending on whether the volume of transactions justifies their use. The auditors can choose to test these internal controls if they believe that the controls are effective in preventing or detecting misstatements in the financial statements. The decision to test internal control for a financial statement audit is always based on whether it is an efficient way to gather evidence for the business process. This means that sometimes management has designed internal controls, but the auditors choose not to test them because they believe that using substantive testing to gather evidence for this process is more efficient.

Whether they choose to or not to test internal controls, the auditors are **required** to obtain an understanding of internal control *relevant* to the audit (AU 314).

Each control system developed by management is unique. Auditors who decide to rely on internal control evidence first document the internal control system using flowcharts and questionnaires. This documentation identifies controls that could have been designed to prevent or detect misstatements. Refer to Exhibit 10-5 for standard documentation using an internal control questionnaire. The questions that are answered "no" indicate control weaknesses. Questions answered "yes" indicate potential controls that could be tested. Because the ending balance of cash is the only portion of the Cash account that is included in this process, the internal control questionnaire covers only investments. The questionnaire for cash receipts is included in the revenue business process and that for cash disbursements is included in the expenditure business process.

Although we focus on manual controls in this book and leave the discussion of IT controls to an information systems course, let's consider a few of the IT controls that we could expect in the cash and investment business processes.

Cash

- An IT system restricts access to individuals authorized to adjust cash balances.
- An IT system restricts access to individuals authorized to input cash transfers between bank accounts.
- A bank transfer report is generated daily (weekly or monthly) and is reviewed by an individual one level above the level that made the transfer.

Investments

- Trading and available-for-sale investments must have a broker's advice number before being entered into the accounting system.
- Held-to-maturity investments must have a face value including the stated amount of the bond and the discount or premium on it.
- The accounting system matches information on the broker's advice with the purchase history of the investment security before processing a sale of investment securities.
- An IT system allows access only to individuals authorized to input investment purchases and investment sales.

Auditors usually test internal controls for relevant assertions for significant accounts. For the cash and investment business processes, the significant accounts are the cash balance for the cash process and the investment and investment valuation accounts for the investment process and the relevant assertions are existence (cash) and valuation (investments). Depending on the industry or economic conditions, other accounts can be identified as significant, and the auditors can consider other assertions to be relevant. Management often uses key controls for the cash and investment business processes to prevent or detect misstatements in the financial statements; see the following table. These controls are organized by internal control procedure.

What Are Internal Control Procedures?

Segregation of duties
Authorization procedures
Documented transaction trails
Independent reconciliations
Physical controls that limit access to assets

The key control procedures for investments are as follows:

1. Segregation of duties
   - The board of directors should authorize investment strategies.
   - Relationships with brokerage firms should be reviewed for potential conflicts of interest.
2. Authorization procedures
   - Company policy establishes guidelines and limits that are followed.
   - The accounting department reviews all significant transactions.
   - Investment purchases and sales are based on legitimate business goals.
   - If derivatives are used for investment purposes, they meet a legitimate company objective.
   - Investment classifications are based on legitimate management intentions and company investment policy.
   - Investment reclassifications should follow company policy and should be authorized.
   - Adjusting entries should be authorized at the appropriate level of management.
3. Documented transaction trails
   - Brokerage statements should be reconciled to the general ledger monthly.

- Communication between company traders and brokers should be monitored and reviewed.
- Brokers' advice documents should be maintained to provide evidence of trading activity.

4. Independent reconciliations
   - Supervisory personnel and the investment committee should review transactions made by the traders to determine that they are consistent with company guidelines.

5. Physical controls
   - A trust department outside the company should hold investment securities or they should be kept in a locked security box within the company. The company should restrict access to the securities and maintain an access log.

The key control procedures for the cash balance are as follows:

1. Segregation of duties
   - Companies that do not use electronic transfer procedures should separate the duties of the individuals issuing checks from those who make the monthly reconciliation of cash balances.

2. Independent reconciliations
   - Companies that do not use electronic cash receipt and disbursement procedures should assign bank reconciliations to an individual not involved in writing checks.
   - Someone not involved in transferring funds between accounts should review the year-end bank transfer schedule.

The only controls the auditors can test are those that are documented. Audit procedures to test these controls follow. For example, to test the authorization controls, an employee must have initialed or signed the form when the control was performed. Auditors perform tests of controls to determine whether the internal control procedures developed by management are **designed** and **operating** effectively. The auditors select from a variety of **audit procedures** such as inquiry, observation, inspection, and reperformance of a control. If the controls are not designed appropriately or not operating properly, the auditors need to design substantive tests to determine whether internal control failures have led to misstatements in the financial statement accounts.

Internal Control Tests

Make inquiries of employees
Inspect relevant documentation
Observe the control's application
Reperform the control

Substantive Tests for the Cash and Investment Business Processes

LO8

Understand the methods that auditors use to gather substantive evidence using analytical procedures, substantive tests of transactions, and substantive tests of balances

Auditing standards have described several procedures that auditors can use to gather evidence for use in evaluating whether the financial statements are prepared according to an applicable financial reporting framework; see the following table. Analytical procedures will be discussed following the table because they are usually performed as part of the planning process. The other audit procedures can be found under the key substantive tests section.

Analytical Procedures

Auditors often use two types of analytical procedures to obtain evidence as to whether the financial statement accounts are prepared in accordance with the applicable financial reporting framework. In the first analytical procedure, the auditors compare the financial statement numbers for the current year with those of the previous year. This comparison includes calculating the dollar amount and the percentage of change. In the second analytical procedure, the auditors calculate financial ratios for the current financial statements and compare them with ratios from the prior year's financial statements. When using analytical procedures, the auditors often consider nonfinancial measures in evaluating changes from one year to the next. For example, the auditors might consider (1) the number of investment securities purchased and sold in the current year and the prior year or (2) the average interest rate earned on held-to-maturity securities.

Substantive Audit Procedures

Perform analytical procedures

Inspect of records,
documents, or tangible assets

Observe

Make inquiries

Confirm

Recalculate

Reperform

In the cash and investment business processes, auditors can perform the following analytical procedures:

1. Compare the balances in the following accounts for the current year with those of the prior year: Cash, Investment in Trading, Available-for-Sale or Held-to-Maturity Securities, Allowance for Decline (Increase) in Valuation of Investment Securities, Realized Loss (Gain) on Sale of Investment Securities, Dividend Income, and Interest Income. Investigate changes from the auditors' expectations.

2. Calculate the rate of interest earned on the investment securities for the current and prior years. Investigate any changes from the auditors' expectations.

How does an auditor know whether the change is reasonable? Companies do not dramatically change from year to year *without a reason* (planned expansion, poor economic conditions), so large increases or decreases in the accounts could be unreasonable. To make the decision about whether a change is unreasonable, the auditors need to know (1) the client's industry, (2) the current economic conditions, and (3) the business under audit.

Let's consider an example for the cash and investment processes for BCS. See selected financial information for the company for three years in Exhibit 10-6.

Because the financial statements from the prior year were audited, they are used to provide a base to identify unusual changes in the current year. Year 3 is the current year, the year under audit. Trading securities increased by $1,500,000, a 60% increase from year 2 to year 3. Available-for-sale securities increased by $600,000, a 46% increase from year 2 to year 3. Held-to-maturity securities increased by $50,000, a 4% increase from year 2 to year 3. The Unrealized Gain (Loss) account for trading securities increased by $500,000, a 100% increase from year 2 to year 3. This account is an income statement account, so its change increased income by $500,000. The Unrealized Gain (Loss) account for available-for-sale securities decreased by $500,000, a 33% decrease from year 2 to year 3. This account is an owners' equity account, so the decrease in market value of the investments reported in it does not affect income. Interest income increased by $5,000, a 4% increase from year 2 to year 3. The average interest rate on held-to-maturity securities also increased from 9% in year 2 to 10% in year 3. Cash decreased by $1,000,000, a 33% decrease.

Based on this analytical review, the auditors would be interested in the fact that trading securities had a gain (that affects income) and available-for-sale securities had a loss (that does not affect income). The auditors' concern would be whether the securities in the trading account and the available-for-sale account are correctly classified. The company should plan to sell the securities in the trading account in the next year. Those in the available-for-sale account are available for sale, but the company must not currently plan to sell them in the next year.

The auditors would also ask about the increase in interest rate from 9% in year 2 to 10% in year 3. This interest rate is based on the interest income earned on the

BCS, Inc.—Selected Financial Information   Exhibit 10-6

	Year 3	Percentage Change	Year 2	Percentage Change	Year 1
Trading securities	$4,000,000	60% ↑	$2,500,000	7% ↓	$2,700,000
Available-for-sale securities	5,100,000	46 ↑	3,500,000	27 ↓	4,800,000
Held-to-maturity securities	1,250,000	4 ↑	1,200,000	17 ↓	1,450,000
Unrealized gain (loss) for trading securities	1,000,000	100 ↑	500,000	200 ↑	(500,000)
Unrealized gain (loss) for available-for-sale securities	(2,000,000)	33 ↓	(1,500,000)	150 ↓	(600,000)
Interest income	125,000	4 ↑	120,000	17 ↓	145,000
Average interest rate on held-to-maturity securities	10		9		8.5%
Cash	2,000,000	33 ↓	3,000,000	50 ↑	2,000,000
Current ratio	0.80	27 ↓	1.10	8 ↓	1.20

average held-to-maturity investment balance for each year. Held-to-maturity securities are usually held until they mature, and the time period for the bonds to reach maturity is often 10–20 years. So, the concern is how the company increased its interest rate on held-to-maturity securities without selling all of those in the investment account and purchasing new ones with higher interest rates?

The auditors would also calculate the current ratio (current assets divided by current liabilities), which has decreased from year 2 to year 3 and is presently below 1.00. A current ratio of 1.00 indicates that the company has enough liquid assets (cash or assets that will become cash in the next year) to cover the liabilities due in the next year. When the current ratio is below 1.00, the auditors should question the client as to how it expects to pay the liabilities due in the next year. A company could give many answers. It could have assets currently classified as long-term that can be sold for cash and used to pay the liabilities due next year. A low current ratio could also indicate that the company has cash flow problems. When a company does not have enough cash to pay its bills, the risk of material misstatement increases.

Auditors use analytical procedures to focus their attention on accounts that have changed from the prior year. Changes from one year to the next could have been caused by real events or could indicate misstatements in the financial statements.

Substantive Tests of Transactions

The auditors use substantive tests of transactions to test the recording of transactions during the year for the investment business process.

The key substantive tests of transactions for this process follow. The audit *procedure* used to perform the test is listed before the test (identified in bold italic type) and the assertion related to the audit test is listed at the end of the test (identified in bold blue type). Depending on the level of inherent risk for the process and tests performed as internal control tests and substantive tests of balances, the auditors can perform *some* or *all* of the audit procedures listed.

The key substantive tests of transactions for the investment process are as follows:

1. Select a sample of investments purchased during the year.
   a. *Inspection.* Inspect the documentation to support the purchase price. Determine that the investment was recorded at cost and correctly classified as a trading, held-to-maturity or available-for-sale investment—**existence, accuracy, classification.**
   b. *Inspection.* Trace payments for purchases of securities to bank statements—**existence, accuracy.**

    c. ***Inspection.*** Determine the existence of the security by reviewing documentation from the trustee, physically inspecting the security, or reviewing documentation from external sources indicating that the security was transferred to the client—**existence.**

    d. ***Inspection.*** Review minutes of the investment committee meetings to determine that purchases were authorized or in accordance with its guidelines—**existence, accuracy, classification.**

2. Select a sample of investments sold during the year.

    a. ***Inspection.*** Inspect the documentation to support the sales price. Determine that the cash received was recorded correctly and that the gain or loss recognized on the security was accurate—**existence, accuracy.**

    b. ***Inspection.*** Trace proceeds from the sales of securities to bank statements—**existence, accuracy.**

    c. ***Inspection.*** Review minutes of the investment committee meetings to determine that investment sales were authorized and made in accordance with committee guidelines—**existence, accuracy, classification.**

Substantive Tests of Balances

Auditors use substantive tests of balances to gather evidence for the balance sheet accounts in the cash and investment processes. The cash balance and the balance in the available-for-sale, trading, and held-to-maturity investment accounts are the primary balance sheet accounts tested in these processes. The Cash account is a current asset account; the investment accounts can be either current or long-term asset accounts, depending on the security's classification and the length of time it will be held.

The key substantive tests of balances for the cash and investment processes follow. The audit ***procedure*** used to perform the test is listed before the test (identified in bold italic type), and the **assertion** tested by the audit test appears at the end of the test (identified in bold blue type). Depending on the level of inherent risk for the processes and tests performed as internal control tests and substantive tests of transactions, the auditors could perform *some* or *all* of these audit procedures. External confirmations are often used for the cash and investment process to obtain verification from outside sources that the assets exist at year-end.

The key substantive tests of balances for the investment process are as follows:

1. ***Confirmation.*** Confirm the existence of the securities with the trustee or physically inspect the securities—**existence, rights and obligations.**

2. ***Inspection.*** Inspect documentation in paper or electronic form for activity after year-end—**existence, completeness.**

3. ***Analytical procedures.*** Perform analytical procedures, comparing current year balances to prior year balances—**completeness, valuation.**

4. ***Recalculation or analytical procedures.*** Test discount or premium amortization and accrued interest income either by recomputation or analytical procedures—**valuation.**

5. ***Recalculation or analytical procedures.*** Test interest income recognized during the year either by recomputation or analytical procedures—**completeness.**

6. ***Confirmation, Inspection or Reperformance.*** Select a sample of investments held at year-end. Identify the entity's method for determining fair market value at year-end and verify whether it is correct. **This is the most important audit procedure for investments**—**existence, valuation.**

7. ***Inspection.*** Determine that transfers between investment categories have been properly made according to company guidelines and are recorded in accordance with accounting standards—**valuation.**

The key substantive tests of balances for the cash balance are as follows:
For companies using electronic and nonelectronic means of transferring cash:

1. ***Confirmation.*** Confirm bank balances as of the balance sheet date using the standard bank confirmation form—**existence, rights and obligations.**

2. ***Inspection.*** Review the bank transfer schedule for transfers between bank accounts 10 days before and 10 days after year-end. Review the schedule to determine that the deposit and transfer sides of each transaction are recorded in the proper time period and that the time lag between the transfers appears reasonable—**existence.**

For companies using nonelectronic means of transferring cash:

3. ***Inspection or Confirmation.*** Arrange to have cutoff bank statements and canceled checks for 10–15 days following the balance sheet date sent directly to the auditors. If a cutoff bank statement is not available, arrange to receive the bank statement for the month following the year-end directly from the bank—**existence.**
4. ***Inspection.*** Obtain copies of the bank reconciliations prepared by the client as of the balance sheet date and trace the deposits in transit and the outstanding checks to the cutoff bank statement. Ascertain that the time lag is reasonable—**existence.**

Fair Value of Investment Securities

Investment securities include stocks, bonds, and derivative instruments. It can be easy or quite difficult for the auditors to determine the fair value of investment securities at year-end. For these investments, the auditors should (1) determine whether the applicable financial reporting framework specifies the method to be used to determine their fair value and (2) evaluate whether management's determination of fair value is consistent with the applicable financial reporting framework.

If quoted market prices are available for the investment securities, it is easy for the auditors to determine their fair value at year-end. Quoted market prices for investment securities listed on national exchanges or over-the-counter markets are available from financial publications, the exchanges, NASDAQ, or other pricing services. If quoted market prices are available, they provide sufficient evidence of the investment securities' fair value.

If quoted market prices are not available for investment securities, it is more difficult to determine their fair value. In this case, the company must *estimate* their fair value. Sometimes companies develop models that estimate fair value. Some companies use third-party sources to estimate fair value. The company or the third-party uses a *pricing model* or a *cash flow projection* for the estimate. Auditing standards require the auditors to review the procedures used to develop these estimates to determine whether they are consistent with the applicable financial reporting framework. To do this, the auditors must consider the assumptions that management used in selecting the valuation model and how it is used to generate estimates of fair value.

Standard Bank Confirmation

The client prepares the standard bank confirmation on a specific form (Exhibit 10-7). The auditors mail one to all banks in which the client maintains accounts, and the banks return it to the auditors. The client can list the cash balance as of year-end for the bank to confirm or can leave the balance blank for the bank to fill in. Often notes payable to the bank or credit lines with it are also confirmed on this form. Any collateral on debt should also be listed, allowing the auditors to obtain evidence relating to assets that are collateral for debt and could require disclosure. This confirmation is the most important procedure for the auditors because it allows them to verify from an independent source that the amount of cash listed by the company is valid (it exists).

Did You Know?

HealthSouth, the largest provider of outpatient surgery and diagnostic and rehabilitation services in the United States, overstated its earnings by at least $1.4 billion from 1999 to 2003 to meet Wall Street's expectations. The earnings overstatement was matched with an overstatement of assets and an understatement of liabilities including an overstatement of cash by $300 million in 2002. Ernst & Young, HealthSouth's auditors could not explain the misstatement. Outsiders question how cash can be misstated when it is so easy to audit with a confirmation from the bank.

Standard Bank Confirmation

Exhibit 10-7

STANDARD FORM TO CONFIRM ACCOUNT
BALANCE INFORMATION WITH FINANCIAL INSTITUTIONS

BCS Company

CUSTOMER NAME

Financial Institution's Name and Address

[

New World National Bank
Post Office Box 48
Fargo, ND 58001

[

]

We have provided to our accountants the following information as of the close of business on **December 31, 2011,** regarding our deposit and loan balances. Please confirm the accuracy of the information, noting any exceptions to the information provided. If the balances have been left blank, please complete this form by furnishing the balance in the appropriate space. Although we do not request nor expect you to conduct a comprehensive, detailed search of your records, should additional information about other deposit and loan accounts we may have with you comes to your attention during the process of completing this confirmation, please include such information below. Please use the enclosed

]

envelope to return the form directly to our accountants.

1. At the close of business on the date listed above, our records indicated the following deposit balance(s):

ACCOUNT NAME	ACCOUNT NO.	INTEREST RATE	BALANCE
Checking Account	*42888478*	*None*	
Payroll Account	*42888481*	*None*	

2. We were directly liable to the financial institute for loans at the close of business on the date listed above as follows:

ACCOUNT NO./ DESCRIPTION	BALANCE	DATE DUE	INTEREST RATE	DATE THROUGH WHICH INTEREST IS PAID	DESCRIPTION OF COLLATERAL
Line of credit	*52,000*	*Revolving*	*Prime + 2%*	*November 30, 2011*	*Inventory*
Note No. 311	*200,000*	*June 30, 2012*	*8%*	*September 30, 2011*	*None*

_____
(Customer's Authorized Signature)

_____
(Date)

This information presented by the customer is in agreement with our records. Although we have not conducted a comprehensive detailed search of our records, no other deposit or loan accounts have come to our attention except as noted above.

_____
(Financial Institution Authorized Signature)

_____
(Date)

_____
(Title)

EXCEPTIONS AND OR COMMENTS

Please return this form directly to our accountants:

Stuart & Cram, CPAs
2411 18th Street South
Fargo, ND 58002

Approved 1990 by American Bankers Association, American Institute of Certified Public Accountants, and Bank Administration Institute. Additional forms available from: AICPA-Order Department.

BCS, Inc. Bank Reconciliation

For the Year Ending December 31, 2011

Exhibit 10-8

Prepared by Client

Balance per bank statement			$508,411
Add			
Deposits in transit	December 29, 2011		37,837
	December 30, 2011		87,874
Deduct			
Outstanding checks			
4458	September 25, 2011	$3,762	
4523	November 19, 2011	2,733	
4631	December 27, 2011	5,981	
4632	December 27, 2011	6,322	
4633	December 28, 2011	4,311	
4635	December 29, 2011	3,699	
4636	December 30, 2011	4,764	
4637	December 31, 2011	227	
4638	December 31, 2011	329	
4640	December 31, 2011	3,267	
			−35,395
Adjusted bank balance			598,727

Weston Smith, HealthSouth's former CFO, said that efforts were made to prevent Ernst & Young from detecting the fraud. He described actions the company took to hinder the auditors' work: "You would push deadlines as tight as possible" to limit the time to review the information. At the same time, "tons of information would be given to auditors" in an attempt to overwhelm them.

Sources: Jonathan Weil, "Did Ernst Miss Key Fraud Risks at HealthSouth?" *The Wall Street Journal,* April 11, 2003; Securities and Exchange Commission, Accounting and Auditing Enforcement Release No. 1744, March 20, 2003; The Associated Press, "Ernst & Young Sues HealthSouth over Fraud," March 29, 2005.

Bank Reconciliation and Cutoff Statement

For audits of companies that have a nonelectronic cash transfer system (the client writes checks to transfer money to vendors and employees), the auditors often perform two additional procedures, the review of (1) a bank cutoff statement and (2) the year-end bank reconciliations. A cutoff bank statement (usually for the first half of the month following year-end) is used to verify the deposits in transit and the outstanding checks on the client-prepared year-end bank reconciliation. The auditors use this reconciliation to determine that the amount of cash listed by the client at year-end is correct. The client has confirmed *its* balance with the bank, but the client has adjusted this balance for deposits in transit and checks outstanding at year-end. The client can manually enter any amount in deposits in transit and outstanding checks to year-end adjustments. Auditors verify the accuracy of these adjustments by reviewing the cutoff bank statement. See an example of a year-end bank reconciliation in Exhibit 10-8.

Bank Transfer Schedule   Exhibit 10-9

Prepared by the Client

	Disbursing Account				Receiving Account		
Check Number	Bank	Amount	Date per Books	Date per Bank	Bank	Date per Books	Date per Bank
6842	Great Plains Bank	250,000	January 2, 2012	December 31, 2011	Minnesota Mutual	December 27, 2011	January 2, 2012
2088	First National Bank	400,000	December 29, 2011	January 3, 2012	Minnesota Mutual	December 29, 2011	January 3, 2012
3511	Minnesota Mutual	100,000	December 31, 2011	January 2, 2012	Great Plains Bank	December 31, 2011	January 3, 2012
4311	First National Bank	500,000	January 2, 2012	January 5, 2012	Great Plains Bank	January 4, 2012	January 5, 2012

Bank Transfer Schedule

The auditors review the bank transfer schedule to determine that the client counts cash in only one account at year-end. The transfer schedule lists all cash transfers from one client bank account to another for 5–10 days before and after year-end. See the bank transfer schedule in Exhibit 10-9. For example, $250,000 is in the Minnesota Mutual account at year-end, not in the Great Plains account. A client not using electronic transfer could misstate cash by listing this amount in both accounts at year-end and because a bank transfer can be added as a deposit in transit at year-end, the auditors would not have evidence that cash has been double counted without using the bank transfer schedule.

What the Auditors Know at This Point in the Audit

At this point in the audit, the auditors should have *sufficient appropriate* evidence to determine whether the accounts in the cash and investment processes are presented on the financial statements in accordance with the applicable financial reporting framework. If the auditors do not have enough evidence to make this decision, they would gather more evidence. If the accounts in the business processes are prepared in accordance with the applicable financial reporting framework, the auditors document their conclusion that this is so:

Based on the results of the audit work performed, relevant assertions for significant accounts in the cash and investment business processes are prepared in accordance with the applicable financial reporting framework. ICS

If they have proposed audit adjustments, the auditors would modify their conclusion to read:

*Based on the results of the audit work performed, relevant assertions for significant accounts in the cash and investment business processes are prepared in accordance with the applicable financial reporting framework **except for the adjustments noted**.* ICS

All evidence that the auditors have reviewed to make this decision is kept in the audit work papers. In them, the auditors record the evidence gathered from internal control tests, analytical procedures, substantive tests of transactions, and substantive tests of balances, including the particular items tested and their conclusions from all evidence reviewed.

Cash and Investment Process Accounts and Disclosures for General Mills	Exhibit 10-10

CONSOLIDATED BALANCE SHEETS (IN MILLIONS)
GENERAL MILLS, INC.

Fiscal Year Ended	May 25 2008	May 27, 2007
Assets		
Cash and cash equivalents	661	417
Prepaid expenses and other current assets	511	443
Other assets	1,750	1,587
Owners' Equity		
Accumulated other comprehensive income (loss)	176.7	(119.7)
Unrealized gain from securities	4.8	3.9

Disclosure Requirements for Accounts in the Cash and Investment Business Processes

LO9

Explain the disclosure requirements for accounts in the business processes

In the cash and investment business processes, auditors gather evidence to evaluate management's assertions about the presentation and disclosure of the accounts in the business processes.

Management's Assertions

Occurrence and rights and obligation—disclosed events and transactions have occurred and pertain to the company.

Completeness—all disclosures that should have been made have been made.

Classification and understandability— financial information is appropriately presented and described, and disclosures are clearly expressed.

Accuracy and valuation—financial and all other information is disclosed fairly and at appropriate amounts (AU 314 and ISA 315).

Management prepares the financial statements and the footnotes to them. When management hands the financial statements to the auditors, it asserts that the accounts in the business processes are presented according to the applicable financial reporting framework in the financial statements and that all required disclosures regarding the accounts have been made. The disclosures related to the financial statements are usually made in one of two places: (1) the footnotes to the financial statements or (2) in the Management's Discussion and Analysis (MD&A) section of the annual report.

To evaluate management's presentation and disclosure assertions, the auditors should review the financial statements and the disclosures in both the footnotes and the MD&A section to determine whether the assertions are presented in accordance with the applicable financial reporting framework. See Exhibit 10-10 for the financial statement accounts and footnotes related to the cash and investment processes for General Mills. In the financial statements, the accounts related to the business processes are in bold.

The General Mills balance sheet reports cash and cash equivalents (short-term investment with maturity of 3 months or less) at $661,000,000 in 2008 and $417,000,000 in 2007. The auditors verified that these amounts were not materially misstated by reviewing bank confirmations, the bank transfer schedule, and year-end bank reconciliations. The investments for General Mills are included in the balance sheet in the Prepaid Expenses and Other Current Assets category in short-term assets, and in the Other Assets category for long-term assets. The unrealized gain from available-for-sale securities at year-end is $4.8 million in 2008 and 3.9 million in 2007. The unrealized gains are reported on the balance sheet under Other Comprehensive Income. The auditors verified that these amounts were materially correct by confirmations with the trustee holding the investment securities and tests related to investment valuation at year-end.

Realized gains and losses on asset sales are included in the income statement, but General Mills does not provide information to determine their amounts at year-end. The financial statements also lack sufficient detail to determine the amount of unrealized gains and losses on trading securities on the income statement at year-end.

Chapter Takeaways

The cash and investment processes are important business processes for the auditors. Incentives to overstate assets are great because of their impact on the balance sheet. The audit procedures in this process of testing internal controls and performing substantive tests should be done with professional skepticism. The auditors should consider the risk that misstatements could occur in recording the assets and market valuations and therefore gather sufficient evidence to determine that the accounts in the process are prepared in accordance with the applicable financial reporting framework.

This chapter presented these important facts:

- The transactions recorded in the cash and investment processes, the accounting rules related to these transactions, and the importance of these processes to the financial statements.
- The susceptibility of the cash and investment processes to fraud.
- How auditors gather evidence to support management's assertions for account balances and classes of transactions using internal control and substantive tests.
- How the auditors evaluate the relevant assertions for the significant accounts in the business processes. Because cash and investments tend to be overstated on the financial statements, the most important assertion in these business processes is existence and valuation.

Be sure you understand these concepts before you go to the next chapter.

Review Questions

LO1	1. Describe the activities in the cash and investment business processes. Write journal entries to record the transactions in each process.
LO2	2. List the main documents used in these processes. Describe the purpose of each document and whether the firm or an outsider prepares it.
LO3	3. Explain the accounting rules applicable to investment accounts at year-end.
LO4	4. Are understatement errors or overstatement errors more likely to occur in the cash and investment processes? Explain why.
LO4	5. Identify the misstatements that are likely to occur in these processes. Explain how the auditors consider the risk of fraud in the processes.
LO5	6. Describe management's assertions for the cash and investment processes. Which are the most important for these processes? Explain why this is so.
LO7	7. How do the auditors assess control risk for the investment process?
LO7	8. Describe the audit procedures the auditors use to test internal controls.
LO7	9. Describe key internal controls for these processes.
LO8	10. What substantive tests of transactions are typically done for the investment process?
LO8	11. Describe the substantive tests of balances for the cash process. Identify the assertions associated with each test.

LO8   12. Describe the substantive tests of balances for the investment process. Identify the assertions associated with each test.

LO8   13. Describe the purpose of bank confirmations, bank reconciliations, and the bank transfer schedule. What evidence do the auditors gain from these documents?

LO9   14. Describe how the accounts from this business process impact the financial statements. What are the presentation and disclosure issues associated with these processes?

Multiple Choice Questions from CPA Examinations

LO8   15. The best evidence regarding year-end bank balances is documented in the
   a. Cutoff bank statement.
   b. Bank reconciliations.
   c. Interbank transfer schedule.
   d. Bank deposit lead schedule.

LO8   16. Which of the following sets of information does an auditor usually confirm on one form?
   a. Accounts payable and purchase commitments.
   b. Cash in bank and collateral for loans.
   c. Inventory on consignment and contingent liabilities.
   d. Accounts receivable and accrued interest receivable.

LO8   17. An auditor should test bank transfers for the last part of the audit period and first part of the subsequent period to detect whether
   a. The cash receipts journal was held open for a few days after year-end.
   b. The last checks recorded before year-end were actually mailed by year-end.
   c. Cash balances were overstated because cash was included in two accounts at year-end.
   d. Any unusual payment to or receipts from related parties occurred.

LO8   18. On receiving a client's bank cutoff statement, an auditor most likely will trace
   a. Prior-year checks listed in the cutoff statement to the year-end outstanding check list.
   b. Deposits in transit listed in the cutoff statement to the year-end bank reconciliation.
   c. Checks dated after year-end listed in the cutoff statement to the year-end outstanding check list.
   d. Deposits recorded in the cash receipts journal after year-end to the cutoff statement.

LO8   19. A client has a large and active investment portfolio that is kept in a bank safe-deposit box. If the auditor is unable to count the securities at the balance sheet date, the auditor most likely will
   a. Request the bank to confirm to the auditor the contents of the safe-deposit box at the balance sheet date.
   b. Examine supporting evidence for transactions occurring during the year.
   c. Count the securities at a subsequent date and confirm with the bank whether securities were added or removed since the balance sheet date.
   d. Request the client to have the bank seal the safe-deposit box until the auditor can count the securities at a subsequent date.

LO8   20. Which of the following is the most effective audit procedure for verification of dividends earned on investment in equity securities?
   a. Tracing deposited dividend checks to the cash receipts book.
   b. Reconciling amounts received with published dividend records.
   c. Comparing the amounts received with preceding year dividends received.
   d. Recomputing selected extensions and footings of dividend schedules and comparing totals to the general ledger.

LO8   21. A company makes a practice of investing excess short-term cash in trading securities that are traded regularly on national exchanges. A reliable test of the valuation of these securities is

a. Consideration of current market quotations.
b. Confirmation of securities held by the broker.
c. Recalculation of investment value using a valuation model.
d. Calculation of premium or discount amortization.

LO8   22. The auditor is most likely to verify the interest earned on bond investments by
a. Verifying the receipt and deposit of interest checks.
b. Confirming bond interest rate with the issuer of the bonds.
c. Recomputing the interest earned on the basis of face amount, interest rate, and period held.
d. Testing controls relevant to cash receipts.

LO3   23. Which of the following is not one of the auditor's primary objectives in an audit of trading securities?
a. To determine whether securities are authentic.
b. To determine whether securities are the property of the client.
c. To determine whether securities actually exist.
d. To determine whether securities are properly classified on the balance sheet.

LO8   24. In establishing the existence and ownership of an investment held by a corporation in the form of publicly traded stock, an auditor should inspect the securities or
a. Obtain written representations from management confirming that the securities are properly classified as trading securities.
b. Inspect the auditor's financial statements of the investee company.
c. Confirm the number of shares owned that are held by an independent custodian.
d. Determine that the investment is carried at the lower of cost of market.

Discussion Questions and Research Problems

LO7   25. **Internal control questionnaire.** The following questions are part of an internal control questionnaire for the investment process. For each question:
a. Describe the misstatement in the financial statements that could occur if the client answered "no" to the question.
b. Explain how you would design a substantive test to evaluate the potential misstatement in the financial statements due to the missing control.
c. If the client answers "yes" to the question, describe an internal control that the client could use.
d. Describe how you might test the internal control described in part (c).

Answer the following internal control questions for the investment process:

(1) Are brokerage statements reconciled to the general ledger monthly?
(2) Does the accounting department review all significant transactions?
(3) Are investment classifications based on legitimate management intentions?
(4) Does senior management review disclosures?
(5) Does the board of directors authorize investment strategies?

LO8   26. **Available-for-sale valuation at year-end.** The balance in the available-for-sale investment account at year-end is $10,400,600. After reviewing the confirmations from the trustee, the auditors determine that the cost assigned to the investment account is $9,438,637. The investments' market value is $8,200,350, and the balance in the allowance account from the prior year is a debit balance of $4,000,000. Answer the following questions regarding the investments.
a. Describe three errors and three fraudulent actions that could have caused the discrepancy reported between the book investment value and the confirmed value.
b. What audit evidence would you gather to determine whether the misstatements were caused by the specific errors and fraudulent actions that you suggested?
c. Prepare the journal entry to record the adjustment to the book investments needed.
d. Prepare the journal entry needed to correct the balance in the allowance account.
e. How will the investments appear on the financial statements of the company?

LO8

27. **Trading and held-to-maturity securities.** BCS, Inc. has trading and held-to-maturity securities on its books. It has bought and sold investments every month during the year. The ending balance in the accounts for the current year and the prior year follow.

	Balance at 12/31/11	Balance at 12/31/12
Trading securities	$2,500,000	$3,400,000
Held-to-maturity securities	$5,000,000	$6,000,000

a. Assume that $3,000,000 of trading securities and $4,000,000 of held-to-maturity securities were purchased during 2012. What is the cost of securities sold during 2012 in each category?

b. What is the amount of the loss or gain if investments with an original cost of $1,000,000 and a market value of $1,300,000 at 2011 year-end were sold for $900,000 on December 15, 2012?

c. If the market value of the trading securities was $4,000,000 at the end of 2011 and $2,000,000 at the end of 2012, what is the correct ending balance in the allowance account at the end of 2012?

d. Using the facts presented in part (c), what is the impact of recording the allowance account in 2012 on the financial statements?

e. Select the two most important assertions for the investment account, and describe one substantive test for each assertion that you might use to verify that the assertion is valid.

LO8

28. **Bank reconciliation.** Refer to the bank reconciliation for BCS, Inc. in the chapter. Answer the following questions about this document.

a. If this is the only cash account, what amount of cash should appear on the balance sheet for December 31, 2011?

b. How will the auditors determine whether the balance per the bank or the balance per the books is correct?

c. If the bank recorded the deposit for $37,837 on January 2, would you assume that the deposit had been listed correctly on the bank reconciliation?

d. If the bank recorded the second deposit for $87,874 on January 10, would you assume that the deposit had been recorded correctly on the bank reconciliation? What questions would you ask the client about this deposit?

e. What evidence would you use to verify that the outstanding checks were valid at year-end?

f. What would you assume if none of the outstanding checks had cleared the bank by January 15, 2012?

g. Is it likely that all checks will clear the bank by January 15, 2012? Explain your answer.

LO4, LO8

29. **Cash and investment work paper review.** As the partner in charge of the yearly audit for CWS, you are reviewing the audit work papers for the cash and investment accounts. Before you sign off on the audit, you need to determine that sufficient audit work was done to determine whether cash and investments are materially misstated at year-end. The balance in each account is a material amount, and if they are materially misstated, the financial statements will be materially misstated.

a. Describe the audit evidence the partner would expect to find in the work papers to evaluate whether cash and investments are materially misstated at year-end.

b. What alternatives are available to the partner if the audit evidence indicates that the account balance is materially misstated?

LO4, LO8

30. **Investment securities.** General Office Machines has investments in available-for-sale, trading, and held-to maturity securities. It buys and sells investments in each investment category each year.

a. Describe the risks associated with the audit of investment securities for General Office Machines at year-end.

b. What evidence should the auditors gather to determine that the investment balance is not materially misstated at year-end?

LO8   31. **Cash confirmations.** Consider the audit procedure referred to as "confirm cash balances at year-end."

a. How does the auditor perform this procedure? What are the auditors' responsibilities for this procedure?

b. When is the procedure performed?

c. What is the purpose of external bank confirmations?

d. Describe the assertions associated with a bank confirmation. Explain why they are important to the cash process.

e. Identify the accounts that may be misstated if cash confirmations are not done.

f. If these accounts are misstated, how will outsiders be affected? Explain your answer.

LO4   32. **Adjusting entries for cash and investments.** During your audit of the cash and investment accounts, you notice several adjusting entries in the accounts at year-end.

a. Identify several questions that you should ask management regarding the entries.

b. Describe three possible scenarios to explain the entries that involve adjustments associated with error corrections.

c. Describe three possible scenarios to explain the entries that involve fraudulent entries.

Real-World Auditing Problems

LO4   33. **Parmalat**

Review the discussion of the Parmalat fraud described in the chapter.

a. Describe the audit procedures that could have discovered the misstatements and explain why they could have been effective.

b. Why might a company set up a subsidiary to hide fraudulent transactions? Was it easier for fraud to occur and not be detected because this subsidiary was audited by a different auditor than the ones who signed the audit report? Explain your answer.

LO4   34. **HealthSouth**

Richard Schrushy, the CEO of HealthSouth, denied knowing about the fraud at his company. He says that executives working under him kept knowledge of the fraud from him.

a. Is this a possible explanation for his involvement in the HealthSouth fraud described in the chapter? If this is the case, how would he explain his certification of the financial statements indicating he was aware of the decisions the company made to prepare the financial statements?

b. When asked how the accounting fraud could have occurred while the firm audited the statements, Ernst & Young, HealthSouth's auditor, replied, "When individuals are determined to commit a crime, as the case with executives at HealthSouth, a financial audit may not detect that crime." Evaluate that statement made; is it a "good" excuse? What could have been its motivation to offer such an explanation?

c. Members of HealthSouth's board of directors, including a member of the audit committee, had significant business dealings with the company. What role could this factor have played in the fraud?

Internet Assignment

LO4   35. Consider the accounting problems described in the chapter for Parmlat or HealthSouth. Is the company still in business? If so, has it remained out of trouble since the incidents reported in the text?

11

Long-Term Debt and Owners' Equity Business Process

Learning Objectives

After studying this chapter, you should be able to:

1. Describe the long-term debt and owners' equity business process.
2. Explain the transactions in the business process.
3. Understand an applicable financial reporting frameworks (GAAP) for recording debt, capital stock, and retained earnings transactions.
4. Understand misstatements (errors and fraud) that could be expected in the long-term debt and owners' equity business process.
5. Explain financial statement assertions for accounts in the business process.
6. Identify relevant assertions for significant accounts for the long-term debt and owners' equity business process.
7. Describe the procedures auditors use to gather evidence for internal controls in the long-term debt and owners' equity process.
8. Understand the methods auditors use to gather substantive evidence in the long-term debt and owners' equity process using substantive tests of transactions and substantive tests of balances.
9. Explain the disclosure requirements for accounts in the business process.

Auditing and accounting standards relevant to this topic

For private companies

- **FASB Statement of Financial Accounting Concepts No. 5,** Recognition and Measurements in Financial Statements of Business Enterprises
- **FASB Statement of Financial Accounting Concepts No. 6,** Elements of Financial Statements
- **FASB Statement of Financial Accounting Concepts No. 7,** Using Cash Flow Information and Present Value in Accounting Measurements
- **FASB Statements of Financial Accounting Standards No. 130,** Reporting Comprehensive Income
- **AU Section 312,** Materiality in Planning and Performing an Audit
- **AU Section 314,** Understanding the Entity and Its Environment and Assessing the Risks of Material Misstatements
- **AU 316,** Consideration of Fraud in a Financial Statement Audit

- **AU 318,** Performing Audit Procedures in Response to Assessed Risks and Evaluating the Audit Evidence Obtained
- **AU 326,** Audit Evidence
- **AU 329,** Analytical Procedures
- **AU Section 339,** Audit Documentation
- **AU Section 330,** External Confirmations
- **Preface to Codification of Statements on Auditing Standards,** Overall Objectives of the Independent Auditor and the Conduct of an Audit in Accordance with Generally Accepted Auditing Standards

For public companies

- **FASB Statement of Financial Accounting Concepts No. 5,** Recognition and Measurements in Financial Statements of Business Enterprises
- **FASB Statement of Financial Accounting Concepts No. 6,** Elements of Financial Statements
- **FASB Statement of Financial Accounting Concepts No. 7,** Using Cash Flow Information and Present Value in Accounting Measurements
- **FASB Statements of Financial Accounting Standards No. 130,** Reporting Comprehensive Income
- **AU 316,** Consideration of Fraud in a Financial Statement Audit (Interim standard)
- **AU 329,** Analytical Procedures (Interim standard)
- **AU Section 330,** The Confirmation Process (Interim standard)
- **PCAOB Auditing Standard No. 3,** Audit Documentation
- **PCAOB Auditing Standard No. 5,** An Audit of Internal Control over Financial Reporting That Is Integrated with an Audit of Financial Statements
- **PCAOB Auditing Standard No. 8,** Audit Risk
- **PCAOB Auditing Standard No. 11,** Consideration of Materiality in Planning and Performing an Audit
- **PCAOB Auditing Standard No. 15,** Audit Evidence

International standards

- **ISA 230,** Audit Documentation
- **ISA 315,** Understanding the Entity and Its Environment and Assessing the Risks of Material Misstatement
- **ISA 330,** The Auditor's Procedures in Response to Assessed Risks
- **ISA 500,** Audit Evidence
- **ISA 505,** External Confirmations
- **ISA 520,** Analytical Procedures
- **ISA 545,** Auditing Fair Value Measurements and Disclosures
- **Framework for the Preparation and Presentation of Financial Statements,** International Financial Reporting Standards

Chapter Overview

This chapter discusses auditing procedures used to review a specific class of transactions. In the long-term debt and owners' equity business process, the auditors consider transactions recorded when (1) long-term debt or capital stock is issued, (2) interest expense is recorded, (3) dividends are paid, (4) payment is made on long-term debt, (5) repurchase of capital stock occurs, (6) retained earnings is adjusted, and (7) accumulated other comprehensive income is adjusted. Transactions in this process are part of the testing and decision phase of the audit process. Exhibit 11-1 summarizes the main steps in the audit process.

The Audit Process   Exhibit 11-1

Steps in the Audit Process	Discussed in this Section
Planning Phase	
Consider the Preconditions for an Audit and Accept or Reject the Audit Engagement	
Understand the Entity and Its Environment, Determine Materiality, and Assess the Risks of Material Misstatements	
Develop an Audit Strategy and an Audit Plan to Respond to the Assessed Risks	
Testing Phase	
Test Internal Controls? Yes No	√
Perform Tests of Controls if "Yes"	√
Perform Substantive Tests of Transactions	√
Perform Substantive Tests of Balances	√
Assess the Likelihood of Material Misstatement	√
Decision Phase	
Review the Presentation and Disclosure Assertions	√
Evaluate the Evidence to Determine Whether the Financial Statements Are Prepared in Accordance with the Applicable Financial Reporting Framework	
Issue Audit Report	
Communicate with the Audit Committee	

Gathering evidence to support the financial statement accounts in the long-term debt and owners' equity business process is important to the audit process because of the significance of the transactions in it. Long-term debt or stock could be issued only occasionally, but when it is, the transaction is highly significant. Transactions in this business process can also be complex. Capital lease transactions, transactions involving special-purpose entities, and related-party transactions are part of this process. Keeping debt off the books improves any company's appearance, so there are many incentives for companies to misstate long-term debt transactions.

The Long-Term Debt and Owners' Equity Business Process

LO1

Describe the long-term debt and owners' equity business process

The long-term debt and owners' equity business process involves income statement and balance sheet accounts. On the income statement, the long-term debt and owners' equity information includes interest expense accounts. On the balance sheet, the long-term debt and owners' equity information includes all long-term debt and owners' equity accounts. As with all business processes, the auditors' concern is to determine that the income statement transactions were recorded correctly during the year (according to the applicable financial reporting framework) and that the balances on the balance sheet have been prepared in accordance with the applicable financial reporting framework. See Exhibit 11-2 for the accounts included in the process.

Like all income statement accounts, expense accounts begin the year with a zero balance. Transactions for the entire year are recorded in the appropriate accounts. Normally, no credit entries are made to expenses accounts and no debit entries are made to revenue accounts. The totals at the year-end in the revenue and expense accounts reflect **all** transactions recorded during the year. Auditors are responsible for gathering evidence to support this total. The auditors must determine whether the transactions

Accounts in the Long-Term Debt and Owners' Equity Process	Exhibit 11-2

− Long-Term Debt +	
	Beginning Balance
Payments made during the year	New debt incurred during the year
	Ending Balance

+ Interest Expense −	
Interest expense for the year	
Ending Balance	

− Capital Stock +	
	Beginning Balance
Stock retired	Stock issued (par or stated value)
	Ending Balance

− Treasury Stock +	
Beginning Balance	
Purchases of stock during the year	Reissue of stock during the year
Ending Balance	

− Paid in Capital +	
	Beginning Balance
Stock retired	Stock issued (amount over par or stated value)
	Ending Balance

− Retained Earnings +	
	Beginning Balance
Net loss	Net income
Miscellaneous adjustments	Miscellaneous adjustments
Dividends declared	
	Ending Balance

− Accumulated Other Comprehensive Income +	
Beginning Balance	Beginning Balance
Foreign currency translation adjustments—loss	Foreign currency translation adjustments—gain
Unrealized loss from securities and hedge derivatives	Unrealized gains from securities and hedge derivatives
Pension net actuarial loss and prior service costs	Pension, net actuarial gains
Ending Balance	Ending Balance

recorded in these accounts during the year have been recorded in accordance with the applicable financial reporting framework.

The totals in the balance sheet accounts reflect only the amounts in the accounts on the last day of the year. They do not reflect all transactions recorded during the year; rather they reflect the *net* amount of the transactions recorded during the year. The balance sheet accounts have a beginning balance on the first day of the year, which reflects the ending (audited) balance from the prior year. During the year, increases and decreases in the balance sheet accounts are recorded in the accounts. Balance sheet accounts typically have debit and credit entries (both increases and decreases to the accounts). The balance at the year-end reflects only the balance in the account as of the last day of the year. Auditors are responsible for determining only whether the ending balance in the balance sheet account is correctly recorded according to the rules of the applicable financial reporting framework (GAAP). In this business process, auditors are likely to review all transactions in the accounts because each is likely to be significant in determining the ending balance.

For the income statement, auditors gather evidence to support the transactions recorded in the accounts for 12 months. For the balance sheet, auditors gather evidence to determine whether the account balance on one day of the year, the year-end, is correct. The tests that auditors use to gather evidence relating to income statement transactions are called **substantive tests of transactions.** Auditors use tests to gather evidence relating to balance sheet transactions that are called **substantive tests of balances.** These tests provide the auditors evidence about whether the account balance is correct (for balance sheet accounts) or whether the transactions recorded in the financial statements are correct (for income statement accounts) according to the rules of the applicable financial reporting framework.

Transactions in the Long-Term Debt and Owners' Equity Business Process

LO2

Explain the transactions in the business process

Refer to Exhibit 11-3 for the journal entries and the documents associated with entries for the long-term debt and owners' equity process. Asset accounts and expense accounts are increased when a company records a liability or issues stock. Cash is decreased when the liability or dividends are paid.

Documents in the Business Process

Auditors could find the following documents to be useful for gathering evidence about the business process.

Bond agreement. This agreement describes the legal contract between the company borrowing money and the company/individual lending it. The agreement specifies the interest rate, payment dates, maturity date, and stated bond value. Any debt covenants associated with the bond are described in the bond agreement.

Note payable agreement. This agreement describes the legal contract between the company borrowing the money and the bank loaning the money. The agreement specifies the interest rate, payment dates, maturity date, and principal amount of the loan. Any debt covenants associated with the note payable are described in the agreement.

Amortization table for long-term debt agreements. An amortization table provides a schedule of the interest expense and principal portion of each payment. The amortization table can be used to determine the interest expense for the year.

Stock register or stock certificate book. The stock register or stock certificate book provides information about individuals who own stock in the company, including their names and addresses and the number of shares each owns.

Adjusting journal entry report. This is a record of all adjusting journal entries made during a specific time period, organized by month-end, quarter-end, and year-end. This report is supported by documentation for the adjusting journal entries with the signature of the person initiating the entry.

Applicable Financial Reporting Frameworks for the Long-Term Debt and Owners' Equity Process

LO3

Understand applicable financial reporting frameworks (GAAP) for recording debt, capital stock, and retained earnings transactions

Because the auditor is responsible for determining that the accounts in the long-term debt and owners' equity business process are prepared according to the applicable financial reporting framework, he or she must review the accounting rules the client uses for recording transactions and balances in the business process at year-end.

Two financial reporting frameworks might be used by a company for preparing financial statements: (1) accounting standards for U.S. companies and (2) international accounting standards. We refer to the first set of standard as U.S. GAAP and the second set as International Financial Reporting Standards (IFRS). The international standards are written by the International Accounting Standards Board (IASB). The long-term debt and owners' equity rules for each set of standards will be discussed next.

| Journal Entries and Related Documents for the Long-Term Debt and Owners' Equity Process | Exhibit 11-3 |

Journal Entries	Documents
Cash Bonds Payable or Long-Term Notes Payable *To record the issuance of long-term debt.*	Bond agreement or note payable agreement, cash receipts journal

Cash
    Common Stock at Par or Stated Value
    Paid In Capital
(To record the issuance of stock.)
	Stock register, cash receipts journal

Bonds Payable or Long-Term Notes Payable Cash *(To record a payment on bonds payable or long-term debt.)*	Amortization table for bond or note payable, cash disbursements journal
Treasury Stock Cash *(To record the purchase of treasury stock.)*	Stock register, cash disbursement journal
Interest Expense Interest Payable *(To record the accrual of interest expense on long-term debt.)*	Amortization table for long-term debt agreement, adjusting journal entry report
Interest Payable Cash *(To record the payment of interest.)*	Amortization table for long-term debt agreement, cash disbursements journal
Retained Earnings Dividends Payable *(To record dividends when declared.)*	Stock register, adjusting journal entry report, board minutes
Dividends Payable Cash *(To record the payment of accrued dividends.)*	Cash disbursements journal
Unrealized Holding Gain on Available-for-Sale Securities Accumulated Other Comprehensive Income *(To close unrealized holding gain to accumulated other Comprehensive income at year-end; could be a gain on pension liability or foreign currency translation gain also.)*	Adjusting journal entry report, closing entries
Accumulated Other Comprehensive Loss Unrealized Holding Loss on Available-for-Sale Securities *(To close unrealized holding loss to accumulated other Comprehensive income at year-end; could be a loss on pension liability or foreign currency translation loss also.)*	Adjusting journal entry report, closing entries

FASB Concept Statement No. 5, *Recognition and Measurement in Financial Statements of Business Enterprises* provides the basic rule for liability and expense recognition for companies using U.S. GAAP as the reporting framework. According to it, long-term liabilities are reported at the present value of the future cash outflows that will satisfy the payment of the liability. Interest expense on the liability is recognized *as time passes* on its unpaid portion. After a liability has been recognized, it continues to be measured at the amount initially recorded unless its amount is reduced by payments on the principal balance of the liability.

According to FASB Concept Statement No. 6, *Elements of Financial Statements,* companies routinely incur liabilities to acquire the funds, goods, and services to operate or expand. Borrowing money obligates the company to repay the loan. Buying assets on credit obligates a company to pay for them. Using employees' knowledge, time, and skill obligates the company to pay for their use. A company incurs most liabilities in transactions when it obtains the resources it needs to do business. The agreements associated with these transactions, which can be written or oral, obligate the company to pay cash or to provide goods or services in exchange for the benefits received. When applying these rules to the process of recording interest expenses, companies should recognize an expense when they have consumed the economic resource in operating their business.

According to FASB Statement of Financial Accounting Standards No. 130, *Reporting Comprehensive Income,* companies are required to include an owners' equity account titled Accumulated Other Comprehensive Income on the balance sheet. This account reports gains and losses that result from certain of the company's transactions. Although the accounting standards do not require these items to be reported as part of net income, they do require that information related to the transactions be disclosed in owners' equity. These items include (1) foreign currency translation adjustments, (2) net losses not yet recognized as net periodic pension cost for pension liabilities, and (3) unrealized holding gains and losses on available-for-sale securities.

International accounting standards require companies to record long-term debt transactions and transactions involving owners' equity in the same manner as the U.S. accounting standards.

Possible Misstatements in the Long-Term Debt and Owners' Equity Business Process

LO4

Understand misstatements (errors and fraud) that could be expected in the long-term debt and owners' equity business process

Long-term liability and owners' equity transactions are susceptible to both errors and fraud, so auditors must design audit procedures to search for errors (unintentional misstatements) and fraud (intentional misstatements) in the long-term debt and owners' equity process.

Misstatements in this cycle can be overstatement or understatement misstatements. Clients can understate interest expense and interest payable when they fail to recognize expenses at year-end. Clients can overstatement a liability at the year-end by failing to record the cash payment to reduce the liability. **Understatement** misstatements are far more likely in the long-term debt and owners' equity process than are overstatement misstatements. When misstatements occur (whether intentional or unintentional), long-term liabilities are frequently understated. This misleads outsiders about the company's future cash flows to pay the liabilities and about its ability to add new debt to its financial statements.

Understatement misstatements are often caused by fraudulent actions (intentional misstatement) on the part of the client. **AU 316,** *Consideration of Fraud in a Financial Statement Audit,* requires auditors to assess the risk of material misstatement because of fraud and to plan the audit to control this risk.

The client can use a variety of methods to understate liabilities, interest expense, and long-term compensation expense associated with stock options including:

- Recording capital leases as operating leases to avoid recording the liability on the balance sheet.
- Designing off-balance sheet debt agreements with the sole purpose of keeping the debt off the books.
- Failing to disclose loan covenants on long-term debt agreements; these covenants can restrict dividend payments or limit the amount of additional debt taken on by the company.
- Failing to disclose special debt arrangements, such as transactions with special-purpose entities, in an attempt to keep these arrangements off the books.

- Failing to disclose related-party transactions. Debt associated with related-parties can carry a higher risk than debt associated with nonrelated parties.
- Failing to record interest expense.
- Changing the interest rate used to capitalize long-term liabilities to vary the amount of interest expense.
- Backdating stock options and failing to record compensation expense for the difference between the market price of the stock at the date of the grant and the price of the stock on the date of the backdating.

When assessing *inherent* risk for the long-term debt and owners' equity business process, auditors should consider the risk of these misstatements.

Did You Know?

In 2005, the SEC found that KPMG had permitted Xerox to misstate its income and thereby avoid a $3 billion gap between its actual earnings and the amount reported to the public. According to the SEC, KPMG failed to comply with generally accepted auditing practices and allowed Xerox to release fraudulent financial statements. In 1997–2000, KPMG issued a clean audit opinion stating that KPMG had applied generally accepted auditing standards to the audit, that Xerox's financial reporting was consistent with generally accepted accounting principles, and that the results it reported fairly presented the firm's financial position. During this time period, KPMG **knew** the financial statements issued by Xerox were materially misstated and **allowed** Xerox to issue fraudulent financial statements.

Xerox manipulated its revenue in several ways. It incorrectly recorded long-term lease contracts for copy machines it sold to recognize more of the revenue and profit in the early years of the contract than it actually realized. Xerox also used a one-time sale of accounts receivable to increase profits and used "cookie jar" reserves set aside for merger costs to meet earnings expectations.

Under U.S. GAAP, when companies make sales using a sales type lease, they should recognize revenue related to the value of the product immediately and should delay the recognition of revenue related to financing the lease, servicing the leased product, and providing supplies for it over the life of the lease. Before 1997, Xerox followed these rules. Beginning in 1997, however, it changed its accounting policies to allow financing and servicing revenue to be recorded as part of the equipment so that the company could recognize more revenue in the early years of the lease than it should have. Xerox did not disclose this change in the financial statements. The adjustments to record revenue for financing and service payments were often made by managers in the main office of Xerox in the United States.

Xerox paid a $10 million civil penalty to the SEC and restated its financial statements to reduce equipment revenue by $6.1 billion and pretax earnings by $1.9 billion in 1997–2000. KPMG paid a fine of $22.475 million, which included disgorgement of $9,800,000 that represented its audit fees from 1997–2000, interest on the payment, and a $10 million civil penalty. The SEC settlement agreement states that KPMG was aware of the fraudulent methods used by Xerox to overstate revenue and had allowed Xerox to use them.

During the time of the fraud, five KPMG partners were involved in the audits either as engagement partners, relationship partners, or concurring review partners. The SEC fined Joseph Boyle, the KPMG relationship partner assigned to the Xerox audit from 1997–2000, $100,000. According to the SEC complaint, the audit partner told Boyle that Xerox was engaged in improper accounting and that KPMG had an obligation to report these issues to the audit committee. Boyle ignored these warnings and allowed Xerox to make adjustments to its financial statements that permitted the company to issue financial statements that were materially misstated due to fraud. KPMG removed Ronald Safran, its lead engagement partner on the 1998 and 1999 audits, from the Xerox audit after he challenged some of the improper Xerox accounting methods. Xerox requested a new partner, and KPMG complied with this request.

At the time of the fraud, management at Xerox was paid more than $5 million in performance-based compensation and sold stock options at a gain of $30 million.

Sources: James Bandler, "Xerox Faces Criminal Inquiry Tied to Financial Restatement," *The Wall Street Journal,* September 24, 2002; SEC Litigation Release No. 19418, October 6, 2005; SEC Litigation Release No. 19191, April 19, 2005; and SEC Litigation Release No. 17954, January 29, 2003.

How do auditors find errors or fraud in this business process? They should conduct the audit with an attitude of professional skepticism. This includes gathering evidence and planning the audit with a "questioning mind and a critical assessment of audit evidence" (Overall Objectives of the Independent Auditor and the Conduct of an Audit in Accordance with Generally Accepted Auditing Standards). In planning the audit, members of the audit team should discuss the potential for misstatement because of fraud in the long-term debt and owners' equity process including the pressure on management to commit fraud, the opportunity for fraud to be perpetrated, and the general environment or tone in the company that could allow management to rationalize committing fraud.

In planning the audit and assessing risk for the long-term debt and owners' equity business process, auditors should consider the fraud risk factors listed in the auditing standards (AU316) and use this information to assess inherent risk for the process and to plan the level of substantive testing needed for it.

Management's Assertions for the Long-Term Debt and Owners' Equity Business Process

LO5

Explain financial statement assertions for accounts in the business process

In the long-term debt and owners' equity business process, auditors gather evidence to evaluate management's assertions for account balances and classes of transactions in the process. These assertions are listed in the table below.

Management's Assertions

Existence or occurrence—for both classes of transactions and account balances
Completeness—for both classes of transactions and account balances
Valuation and allocation—for account balances
Rights and obligations—for account balances
Accuracy—for classes of transactions
Cutoff—for classes of transactions
Classification—for classes of transactions (AU 314 and ISA 315)

For this business process, management asserts that long-term debt and owners' equity exist at the balance sheet date and that the transactions recorded in this process occurred during the year (existence and occurrence). Management asserts that all long-term debt and owners' equity transactions that should be presented in the financial statements are included (completeness). Management also asserts that the liability and owners' equity accounts are valued correctly according to the applicable financial reporting framework (GAAP or IFRS) at year-end (valuation) and that the company has an obligation to pay the liabilities (rights and obligations). Finally, management asserts that interest expense is accurate, that cutoff for recording debt obligations was made in accordance with the applicable financial reporting framework, and that interest expense for debt obligations or gains or losses associated with debt obligations are properly classified on the financial statements.

Relevant Assertions for Significant Accounts in the Business Process

LO6

Identify relevant assertions for significant accounts for the long-term debt and owners' equity business process

Auditors are required to gather audit evidence to support relevant assertions for significant accounts for each business process. The relevant assertions are related to the *risk* and the likelihood of misstatement in the business process. Because the most likely misstatement in the long-term debt and owners' equity business process is an understatement, **completeness** is often a relevant assertion. Auditors gather *evidence* to support the *completeness* of the accounts in this business process.

Did You Know?

In 2005, Deloitte & Touche paid a $50 million fine to the SEC in connection with the audit of Adelphia Communications Corporation. The SEC stated that Deloitte & Touche had failed to design its audit to detect the illegal acts at Adelphia. According to the SEC,

Deloitte & Touche had failed to identify material related-party transactions. Adelphia had understated its debt by $1.6 billion and overstated its owners' equity by $368 million by improperly combining related-party receivables and payables and netting them out. Adelphia also had failed to disclose the extent of its related-party transactions.

John Rigas founded Adelphia in 1952. He and his sons Timothy, Michael, and James were involved in running the company. Between 1999 and 2001, they issued fraudulent financial statements to exclude $2.3 billion in bank debt by deliberately moving those liabilities to the books of Adelphia's unconsolidated off-balance sheet affiliates. This failure violated generally accepted accounting principles and led to a series of fraudulent financial statements. Adelphia had created fictitious documents to show that it had paid off the debt when the firm had merely transferred it to the off-balance sheet affiliates. The company issued fictitious financial statements that gave the impression in the footnotes to the report that the liabilities listed on the balance sheet included all of the company's outstanding debt. Adelphia had also failed to disclose the Rigas family's use of company funds for personal items including the purchase of stock and timber rights in Pennsylvania. The family had also used company funds to construct a golf course, pay off personal loans and other family debts, and purchase luxury condominiums for family members in Colorado, Mexico, and New York City.

Adelphia, the sixth largest cable television provider in the United States, filed for bankruptcy protection in 2002. Time Warner and Comcast acquired the company in 2005. John Rigas was sentenced to 15 years in prison for fraud and conspiracy. His son, Timothy, was sentenced to 20 years in prison for his role in the fraud. Adelphia agreed to pay $715 million to settle cases brought by the U.S. Justice Department and the SEC.

Sources: SEC Litigation Release No. 17627, July 24, 2002; SEC Litigation Release No. 19202, April 26, 2005; SEC Press Release No. 2005-65, April 26, 2005; D. Searcey and L. Yuan, "Adelphia's John Rigas Gets 15 years," *The Wall Street Journal,* June 21, 2005; S. Hughes, "Deloitte Auditors Are Charged by SEC in Adelphia Case," *The Wall Street Journal,* October 1, 2005; P. Grant and D. Solomon, "Adelphia to Pay $715 Million in 3-Way Settlement," *The Wall Street Journal,* April 26, 2005.

As the story regarding the actions of Deloitte & Touche in the Adelphia audit exemplifies, the auditors should have assessed the risk of material misstatement to be high for the completeness assertion for long-term debt. The risk of material misstatement was high because Adelphia had numerous transactions with related parties. The financial statements for the related-party companies were not consolidated with those of Adelphia. This allowed Adelphia to remove debt from its financial statements and to place it on the financial statements of the unconsolidated companies. When auditors assess the risk of material misstatement to be high for the completeness assertion for long-term debt, they should gather sufficient appropriate evidence to determine that Adelphia had listed all debt for which it was responsible on the financial statements. Because the auditors failed to gather sufficient appropriate evidence, they decided that long-term debt was not materially misstated, when in fact, it was.

Auditors gather evidence to evaluate management's assertions using either (1) internal control tests or (2) substantive tests of transactions or balances. Often the auditors use a combination of both types of tests. Let's consider internal control testing for the long-term debt and owners' equity business process first.

Internal Control Testing

LO7

Describe the procedures auditors use to gather evidence for internal controls in the long-term debt and owners' equity process

In the long-term debt and owners' equity process, management can design internal controls to prevent or detect misstatements in financial statements. Management makes this decision based on whether the volume of transactions in this process justifies their use. If they believe that these internal controls are effective in preventing or detecting misstatements in the financial statements, auditors can choose to test them. This means that sometimes management has designed internal controls, but the auditors choose not to test them because they believe that the use of substantive testing to gather evidence for this process is efficient.

Whether they choose to test or not to test internal controls, auditors are ***required*** to obtain an understanding of internal control relevant to the audit (AU 314).

Internal Control Questionnaire—Long-Term Debt and Owners' Equity Process

Exhibit 11-4

ENVIRONMENT

1. Are notes payable records kept by someone who cannot sign notes or checks?
2. Are direct borrowings on notes payable authorized by the directors, the treasurer, or the chief financial officer?
3. Are two or more authorized signatures required on notes?
4. Are stock certificates kept in a secure location?

EXISTENCE OR OCCURRENCE

5. Are paid notes canceled, stamped "PAID," and filed?
6. Are the stock records maintained by a stock transfer agent outside the company?

COMPLETENESS

7. Is all borrowing authorization by the directors checked to determine whether all notes payable are recorded?
8. Does the board of directors authorize all issuances of stock?
9. Does the board of directors authorize all dividend payments?
10. Does the board of directors authorize stock options?

RIGHTS AND OBLIGATIONS

11. Are loan documents forwarded to accounting for review?

VALUATION OR ALLOCATION

12. Is the subsidiary ledger of notes payable periodically reconciled with the general ledger control accounts? Are interest payments and accruals monitored for due dates and financial statement dates?

PRESENTATION AND DISCLOSURE

13. Is sufficient information available in the accounts to enable financial statement preparers to classify current and long-term debt properly?
14. Do senior officers review footnotes?
15. Is sufficient information available in the financial statements and footnotes to allow financial statement users to evaluate prior period adjustments and other comprehensive income adjustments to owners' equity?
16. Is sufficient information available in the financial statements and footnotes to allow financial statement users to evaluate changes in capital stock and paid-in capital that occurred during the year?

Although we focus primarily on manual controls in this book and leave the discussion of IT controls to an information systems course, let's consider a few of the IT controls that we could expect to be used in this business process.

- Long-term debt is recorded when cash related to debt issues enters the accounting system.
- Increases in the Common Stock and in the Additional Paid-in Capital accounts are supported by increases in either cash or assets.
- Accrued interest entries must be supported by information about the principal, interest rate, and origination date of the debt.
- IT systems limit access to individuals authorized to input debt and stock transactions.

Every control system developed is different. If the auditors decide to rely on internal control evidence, they first document the system using flowcharts and questionnaires. This documentation allows them to identify controls that can be designed to prevent or detect misstatements in the financial statements. See Exhibit 11-4 for standard documentation using an internal control questionnaire. In this questionnaire, questions answered "no" indicate control weaknesses. Questions answered "yes" indicate potential controls that could be tested.

Auditors usually test internal controls for relevant assertions for significant accounts. For the long-term debt and owners' equity process, the significant account can be long-term debt and the relevant assertion is often completeness. Auditors are concerned that all long-term debt is *recognized* on the financial statements. Depending on the industry or economic conditions, other accounts can be identified as significant, and the auditors can consider other assertions to be relevant. Key controls for the long-term debt and owners' equity business process often used by management to prevent or detect misstatements in the financial statements follow. These controls are organized by the internal control procedures discussed in Chapter 3.

What Are Internal Control Procedures?

Segregation of duties
Authorization procedures
Documented transaction trails
Independent reconciliations
Physical controls that limit access to assets

The key control procedures for the long-term debt and owners' equity business process are as follows:

- Segregation of duties
  - Notes payable records are maintained by someone who cannot sign note payable documents.
- Authorization procedures
  - New long-term debt is authorized at the appropriate company level.
  - New issues of capital stock are authorized at the appropriate company level.
- Documented transaction trails
  - Notes paid are stamped PAID and filed for future reference.
  - Stock certificate records are maintained.
- Independent reconciliations
  - If a trustee does not maintain the stock certificate records, supervisory personnel review them to determine that their proper control has been maintained.
- Physical controls
  - If a stock certificate book is maintained within the company, access to the stock certificates is controlled and restricted.

The only controls the auditors can test are documented controls. Audit procedures to test these controls follow. For example, as a test of the authorization controls, the initials or signature of the employee who performed the control must be on the proper form. Auditors perform tests of controls to determine whether management-developed internal control procedures are **designed** and **operating** effectively. Auditors select from a variety of **audit procedures** such as inquiry, observation, inspection, and reperformance of a control. If the controls are not designed appropriately or operating properly, the auditors design substantive tests to determine whether the internal control failures have led to misstatements in the financial statement accounts.

Internal Control Tests

Make inquiries of employees
Inspect relevant documentation
Observe the application of the control
Reperform the control

Substantive Tests for the Long-Term Debt and Owners' Equity Business Process

LO8

Understand the methods auditors use to gather substantive evidence in the long-term debt and owners' equity process using substantive tests of transactions, and substantive tests of balances

Auditing standards describe several procedures the auditors could use to gather evidence to evaluate whether the financial statements are prepared in accordance with the applicable financial reporting framework. Analytical procedures are discussed next because they are usually performed during the planning process. The other audit procedures are discussed in the section describing the substantive tests of transactions and balances for this business process.

Substantive Audit Procedures

Perform analytical procedures
Inspect records, documents, or tangible assets
Observe
Make inquiries
Confirm
Recalculate
Reperform

Analytical Procedures

Auditors often use analytical procedures to obtain evidence as to whether the financial statement accounts are prepared in accordance with the applicable financial reporting framework. Two types using financial measures are commonly used. In the first, the auditors compare the financial statement numbers for the current year to those of the previous year. This comparison includes a calculation of the dollar amount and the percentage of change. Auditors perform the second analytical procedure by calculating financial ratios for the current financial statements and compare them to those for the prior year financial statements. When using analytical procedures, auditors often consider nonfinancial measures in evaluating changes from one year to the next. For example, the auditors could compare the average interest rate on long-term debt in the current year with that of the prior year as an analytical procedure for this business process.

In the long-term debt and owners' equity business process, the auditors could perform the following analytical procedures:

1. Compare the balances in the following accounts for the current year to the prior year: Long-Term Debt, Interest Expense, Capital Stock, Additional Paid-in Capital, and Retaining Earnings and investigate changes from expectations.

2. Calculate the debt-to-equity ratio for the current and prior year and investigate any changes from expectations.

How do auditors know whether the change is reasonable? Companies do not dramatically change from year to year *without a reason* (planned expansion, poor economic conditions), so large increases or decreases in the accounts can be unreasonable. For auditors to make the decision about whether a change is unreasonable, they need to understand (1) the client's industry, (2) current economic conditions, and (3) the business under audit.

Let's consider an example for the long-term debt and owners' equity process for BCS. Refer to selected financial information for the company for three years in Exhibit 11-5.

Because the financial statements from the prior year were audited, they are used to provide a base to identify unusual changes in the current year. Year 3 is the current year, the year under audit. Bonds payable increased by $1,500,000, a 60% increase from year 2 to year 3. Long-term debt decreased by $400,000, an 80% decrease from year 2 to year 3. Interest expense increased by $50,000, a 25% increase from year 2 to year 3. Capital stock remained unchanged. Retained earnings increased by $700,000, a 10% increase from year 2 to year 3. The auditors would be most interested in verifying the increase in bonds payable by reviewing the new bond agreement. The auditors would also question why interest expense increased by 25% when bonds payable increased by 60%. The average interest rate on bonds payable went from 8% in year 2 to 6.25% in year 3. It is possible that (1) $1,500,000 of bonds issued in year 3 have a very low interest rate, (2) the bonds were issued at the year-end so less than a year's interest expense has been recognized, or (3) the client has not recorded all interest expense on the new long-term debt. Inquiries with the client will tell the auditors which of the three alternatives is correct.

The auditors would also calculate the debt-to-equity ratio by dividing the sum of short-term and long-term liabilities by owners' equity. The debt-to-equity ratio increased this year, indicating that the company took on more debt. The auditors would ask the client about the reason for the increase in debt. Possible answers are cash flow problems because of industry pressure, declining sales, planned business expansion, or purchase

BCS, Inc.—Selected Financial Information
Exhibit 11-5

	Year 3	Percentage Change	Year 2	Percentage Change	Year 1
Bonds payable	$ 4,000,000	60% ↑	$ 2,500,000	7% ↓	$ 2,700,000
Long-Term notes payable	100,000	80 ↓	500,000	72 ↓	1,800,000
Interest expense	250,000	25 ↑	200,000	56 ↓	450,000
Capital stock and additional paid-in capital	15,000,000	0	15,000,000	0	15,000,000
Retained earnings	7,200,000	10 ↑	6,500,000	5 ↑	6,175,000
Debt-to-equity ratio	23%	28% ↑	18%	40% ↓	30%
Short-Term liabilities*	$ 1,000,000		$ 800,000		$ 1,800,000
Average interest rate on bonds payable	6.25%		8%		8%

*Short-term liabilities are not part of the long-term debt and owners' equity process, but the balance in short-term liabilities is needed to calculate the debt-to-equity ratio.

of another company. The answer as to why debt increased will give the auditors information to assess the risk of material misstatement in the financial statements.

Auditors use analytical procedures to focus their attention on accounts that have changed from the prior year. Changes from one year to the next can have been caused by real events or can indicate misstatements in the financial statements.

Substantive Tests of Transactions

The auditors use substantive tests of transactions to test the recording of transactions during the year for the long-term debt and owners' equity business process. Because these transactions are highly material, the auditors typically review all new transactions in the accounts.

The key substantive tests of transaction for the long-term debt and owners' equity process follow. The audit *procedure* used to perform the test is listed before the test (identified in bold italic type) and the **assertion** tested by the audit test is listed at the end of the test (identified in bold blue type). Depending on the level of inherent risk for the process and tests performed as internal control tests and substantive tests of balances, the auditors can perform *some* or *all* of the audit procedures listed.

The key substantive tests of transactions for the long-term debt and owners' equity process are as follows:

1. Obtain an analysis of notes payable, long-term debt, and lines of credit that originated during the year under audit.
   a. ***Inspection.*** For each new debt instrument determine the following: originating date, type, maturity value, face amount, interest rate, and timing and amount of payments to be made. Determine that the debt has been recorded properly—**existence, classification and accuracy.**
   b. ***Inspection.*** Trace the authorization of new debt to the minutes of meetings of the board of directors—**existence.**
   c. ***Inspection.*** Obtain copies of the debt instruments and note any restrictive covenants—**existence and classification.**
   d. ***Confirmation.*** Confirm outstanding balances, terms, conditions, and compliance with covenants with the grantor or trustee of the debt—**existence.**
   e. ***Inspection.*** Verify payments made on the debt and its interest expense recorded for the year—**accuracy.**
   f. ***Confirmation.*** Confirm and verify any new lines of credit for the company—**completeness.**

2. Obtain an analysis of the activity in the capital stock accounts including opening balances, closing balances, and all transactions recorded in them during the year. For the transactions recorded during the year:
   a. ***Inspection or confirmation*** (depending on whether an outside trustee or a company employee maintains the stock records). Account for all proceeds from stock issues—existence.
   b. ***Inspection.*** Trace authorization for stock options to the minutes of the board of directors meetings. Obtain a copy of stock option plans and verify that the options issued and exercised during the year are consistent with the plan—existence, completeness and accuracy.

Did You Know?

In 2003, Parmalat, an Italian company listed on the U.S. stock exchange, understated the long-term debt on its financial statements by at least $11.06 billion. At the same time, it overstated cash and marketable securities by at least $5.53 billion. The purpose of this understatement was to mislead investors about the value of stock and notes payable issued by the company.

The same year Parmalat marketed $100 million of notes payable to U.S. investors. The securities appeared to be issued by a company with less debt and a higher level of assets than was actually the case. Parmalat also told U.S. investors that it had used its excess cash balance to repurchase debt securities worth $4.06 billion. However, the company had not repurchased these securities and they remained outstanding. Parmalat removed the debt from the financial statements, stating that it did not have to record the debt because the company owned it. Outsiders could not understand why Parmalat did not simply cancel the debt, if it had been purchased, but of course, cancellation was impossible because the debt was still outstanding.

The SEC charged Parmalat with securities fraud, stating that from 1998 to 2002, Parmalat sold nearly $1.5 billion in notes and bonds to U.S. investors and "grossly and intentionally" misstated its financial statements during this time to misrepresent the risk associated with the notes and bonds.

The fraud perpetrated at Parmalat was simple. It forged documents on a scanner; ran the documents through a fax machine to make them look authentic; and forged signatures based on old documents and simply copied them on the new agreements. The financial accounts were inflated four times a year when the quarterly results were due. At times, the inflated results were unreasonable including the report that a unit of Parmalat sold enough milk to Cuba for each person to drink 55 gallons of milk a year.

From 1997 to 2003, Parmalat transferred at least $1.12 billion to the family's tourism business run by the daughter of Mr. Tanzi, the owner. More money is believed to have been transferred to Parmalat's soccer team, run by Tanzi's son Stefano. The Tanzi family company, La Coloniale SpA, owned 51% of Parmalat stock.

Parmalat filed for bankruptcy protection in December 2003. Grant Thornton and Deloitte & Touche, its auditors were fired. PricewaterhouseCoopers was hired to investigate the fraud and issued a report in January 2004 indicating that Parmalat had debt of $18 billion, $16 billion of which had not been reported before. The net income reported by Parmalat was five times the actual earnings.

The Parmalat fraud is the largest to occur in Europe. It surprised many people. Until 2003, Parmalat had received a clean audit opinion from its auditors, borrowed money from many international banks, and issued bonds with the assistance of investment bankers on Wall Street.

Sources: SEC Litigation Release No. 18803, July 28, 2004; SEC Litigation Release No 18527, December 30, 2003; H. Sender, D. Reilly, and M. Schroeder, "Parmalat Investors Missed Red Flags," *The Wall Street Journal,* January 7, 2004; A. Galloni, D. Reilly, and C. Mollenkamp, "Skimmed Off: Parmalat Inquiry Finds Basic Ruses at Heart of Scandal," *The Wall Street Journal,* December 31, 2003; A. Galloni, "Scope of Parmalat's Woes Emerges," *The Wall Street Journal,* January 27, 2004.

How could so many outsiders have missed the signs of Parmalat's deception?

Substantive Tests of Balances

Auditors use substantive tests of balances to gather evidence for the balance sheet accounts in the long-term debt and owners' equity process. All long-term debt and owners' equity accounts are balance sheet accounts tested in this process because of the accounts' significance.

The *long-term debt accounts* reflect obligations to repay money borrowed over a longer period of time than 1 year, usually for the purpose of financing a business expansion. The liability owed for the loan that has not been repaid at year-end remains the company's obligation. Because long-term debt is listed as a long-term liability on the balance sheet, it should represent the present value of the future cash flows needed to reduce the debt to zero. Auditors are concerned about whether the account balance accurately represents the future cash outflow required to pay off the debt.

The *capital stock accounts* (Capital Stock Par, Stated Value, or Paid-in Capital) reflect the interest of individuals who own stock in the company. The balance in the capital stock accounts at year-end should include the beginning balance in the account from last year's audited number plus new shares of stock sold during the year, minus shares of stock retired during the year. Shares of treasury stock do not reduce the capital stock accounts directly but remain in a treasury stock account unless the company retires the treasury stock.

Retained Earnings is an owners' equity account that reflects all net income (or net loss) that the company earned in the past and kept. Net income or net loss for each year is recorded in the Retained Earnings account. Dividends declared reduce the balance in this account. Companies are usually restricted from paying dividends if they have a negative retained earnings balance. The auditors determine that all dividend payments are consistent with the incorporation agreement of the firm. Several other miscellaneous adjustments can be found in Retained Earnings as the applicable financial reporting framework requires.

The key substantive tests of balances for the long-term debt and owners' equity process follow. The audit ***procedure*** used to perform the test is listed before the test (identified in bold italicized print), and the **assertion** related to the audit test is listed at the end of the test (identified in bold blue type). Depending on the level of inherent risk for the cycle and the internal control tests and substantive tests of transactions performed, the auditors can perform *some* or *all* audit procedures listed. Confirmations are often used to verify the outstanding balances of debt and common stock accounts at year-end and to determine that no violations of debt covenants exist.

The key substantive tests of balances for the long-term debt and owners' equity process are as follows:

1. Obtain a list of the ending balance of notes payable, long-term debt, and lines of credit.
   a. ***Confirmation.*** Confirm outstanding balances, terms, conditions, and compliance with covenants with the debt grantor or trustee—**existence and rights and obligations.**
   b. ***Inspection.*** Verify payments and interest expense on the debt for the year—**existence.**
   c. ***Inspection.*** Determine that long-term liabilities retired during the year have been removed from the books—**rights and obligations.**
   d. ***Confirmation.*** Confirm and verify any lines of credit with balances at year-end—**Completeness.**
2. Obtain a list of the ending balance in the capital stock accounts.
   a. ***Confirmation or Inspection.*** Verify the number of shares of stock outstanding by confirmation with the transfer agent or physically reviewing the stock certificate book—**existence.**
3. Obtain a schedule showing the ending balance in the Retained Earnings account and the Accumulated Other Comprehensive Income account.
   a. ***Inspection.*** Verify the beginning balance in both accounts—**completeness.**
   b. ***Inspection.*** Determine that net income or net loss was correctly recorded in the Retained Earnings account—**completeness and valuation.**
   c. ***Inspection.*** Verify that dividends declared were correctly recorded in the Retained Earnings account—**completeness and valuation.**

d. ***Inspection and Inquiry.*** Review any additional adjustments to the Retained Earnings account (other than income and dividends) to determine whether they were appropriately included according to the applicable financial reporting framework—**completeness and valuation.**

e. ***Inspection and Inquiry.*** Review any adjustments to Accumulated Other Comprehensive Income to determine whether they were appropriately included in Other Comprehensive Income according to the applicable financial reporting framework—**completeness and valuation.**

f. ***Recalculation.*** Verify the mathematical accuracy of both accounts' earnings—**completeness.**

What the Auditor Knows at This Point in the Audit

At this point in the audit, the auditors should have *sufficient appropriate* evidence to determine whether the accounts in the long-term debt and owners' equity process are presented on the financial statements in accordance with the applicable financial reporting framework. If they do not have enough evidence to make this decision, the auditors would gather more. If the accounts in the business process are prepared in accordance with generally accepted accounting principles, the auditors document their conclusions that this is so:

Based on the results of the audit work performed, relevant assertions for significant accounts in the long-term debt and owners' equity business process are prepared in accordance with the applicable financial reporting framework. ICS

If the auditors have proposed audit adjustments, they would modify their conclusion to read:

*Based on the results of the audit work performed, relevant assertions for significant accounts in the long-term debt and owners' equity business process are prepared in accordance with the applicable financial reporting framework **except for the adjustments noted**.* ICS

Auditors keep all evidence they have reviewed to make this decision in the audit work papers. In them, the auditors record the evidence gathered from internal control tests, analytical procedures, substantive tests of transactions, and substantive tests of balances, including the particular items tested and their conclusions from all evidence reviewed.

Disclosure Requirements for the Long-Term Debt and Owners' Equity Business Process

LO9

Explain the disclosure requirements for accounts in the business process

In the long-term debt and owners' equity business process, auditors gather evidence to evaluate management's assertions about the presentation and disclosure of the accounts in the business process.

Management's Assertions

Occurrence and rights and obligation—disclosed events and transactions have occurred and pertain to the company.

Completeness—all disclosures that should have been made have been made.

Classification and understandability—financial information is appropriately presented and described, and disclosures are clearly expressed.

Accuracy and valuation—financial and all other information is disclosed fairly and at appropriate amounts (AU 314 and ISA 315).

Management prepares the financial statements and the footnotes to the financial statements. When management hands the financial statements to the auditors, it asserts that the accounts in the business process are presented according to an applicable financial reporting framework and that all required disclosures regarding the accounts have been made. The disclosures related to the financial statements are usually made in one of two places: (1) the footnotes to the financial statements or (2) the Management's Discussion and Analysis (MD&A) section of the annual report.

Did You Know?

The corporate culture at Enron pushed everything to the extreme. Andrew Fastow, chief financial officer of the company, had a Lucite cube on his desk describing the company's values. One value was communication—Enron's version of it. According to the cube, when Enron said it was going to "rip your face off," it would "rip your face off."

The culture at Enron brought amazing growth. Kenneth Lay and Jeffrey Skilling had taken a conservative natural gas pipeline company and turned it into a global energy trader. Enron executives lived well. Investors and analysts described the company as one of the great success stories of the day; investors loved it. Analysts predicted continued growth. International banks were happy to finance Enron investments.

Special-purpose entities were not widely known until the Enron scandal. Enron used them to move assets that were not performing well off the company's balance sheets. Off-balance sheet partnerships were also used to create millions of dollars of reported income from assets removed from the balance sheet and to remove the debt associated with generating the income from the company's balance sheet. This allowed Enron to have the best of both worlds. The company could recognize revenue from transactions (for assets that were not on its books) and could avoid debt costs associated with generating the income (by keeping the debt off the balance sheet). Companies tend to look good when they can generate revenue without using any assets to do so. But Enron guaranteed the debt removed from the financial statements, and when the partnerships were unable to pay the debt, it came back to haunt Enron because it had to be put on the books before it could be paid.

On October 16, 2001, Enron released its quarterly earnings report. In it, the company stated recurring third quarter earnings of $0.43 per share. The company also reported non-recurring charges of $1.01 billion. The largest portion of the nonrecurring charge was due to the "early termination during the third-quarter of certain structured finance arrangements (R. Smith and J. R. Emshwiller, '24 Days': Behind Enron's Demise," *The Wall Street Journal,* August 8, 2003)." It was later determined that Andrew Fastow, chief financial officer of Enron, was the general partner in the partnerships holding the structured financing contracts, a position with a clear conflict of interest for Enron shareholders.

On November 8, 2001, Enron issued a press release announcing that it was writing off hundreds of millions of dollars of earnings and adding similar amounts of debt to its balance sheet. At the same time, it announced that the last four years of financial statements were no longer reliable.

By the time Enron filed for bankruptcy in December 2001, 6,000 employees had lost their jobs, and many of them had lost their entire retirement savings (invested in Enron stock). Almost $100 billion of shareholder value was destroyed as the Enron stock price fell to just pennies a share.

Sources: A. Raghavan, K. Kranhold, and A. Barrionuevo, "How Enron Bosses Created a Culture of Pushing Limits," *The Wall Street Journal,* August 26, 2002; R. Smith and J. R. Emshwiller, " '24 Days': Behind Enron's Demise," *The Wall Street Journal,* August 8, 2003; J. R. Emshwiller, "Lay's Last Months at Enron Probed," *The Wall Street Journal,* February 2, 2004; M. Pacelle, "Enron Report Give Details of Deals That Masked Debt," *The Wall Street Journal,* September 23, 2002.

To evaluate management's presentation and disclosure assertions, the auditors should review the financial statements, the footnote disclosures, and the disclosures in the MD&A section to determine that they are presented in accordance with the applicable financial reporting framework. See the financial statement accounts and footnotes related to the long-term debt and owners' equity process for General Mills in Exhibit 11-6. In the financial statements, the accounts related to the business process are in bold type.

General Mills reported net interest expense (interest income netted against interest expense) on its income statement of $427 million in 2007 and $399 million in 2006. According to footnote 17, interest expense was $397 million in 2007 and $367 million in 2006. This interest expense reflects the interest expense on long-term liabilities.

**Long-Term Debt and Owners' Equity Business Process
Accounts and Disclosures for General Mills**   **Exhibit 11-6**

CONSOLIDATED STATEMENTS OF EARNINGS
GENERAL MILLS, INC.

	Fiscal Year Ended		
In Millions	May 27, 2007	May 28, 2006	May 29, 2005
Operating profit	$2,058	$1,948	$1,900
Interest expense, net	427	399	455

CONSOLIDATED BALANCE SHEETS
GENERAL MILLS, INC.

In Millions	May 27, 2007	May 28, 2006
Long-term debt	**$3,218**	**$2,415**
Stockholders' equity:		
Common stock, 502 shares issued	**50**	**50**
Additional paid-in capital	**5,842**	**5,737**
Retained earnings	**5,745**	**5,107**
Common stock in treasury, at cost, shares of 162 in 2007 and 146 in 2006	**(6,198)**	**(5,163)**
Unearned compensation		**(84)**
Accumulated other comprehensive income (loss)	**(120)**	**125**
Total stockholders' equity	**$5,319**	**$5,772**

Footnote 8, Detail for Long-Term Debt
Summary on long-term debt is as follows:

In Millions	May 27, 2007	May 28, 2006
6% notes due February 15, 2012	$1,240	$1,240
Floating rate convertible senior notes due April 11, 2037	1,150	0
5,7% notes due February 15, 2017	1,000	0
Floating rate notes due January 22, 2010	500	0
3.875% notes due November 30, 2007	336	350
Medium-term notes, 4.8% to 9.1%, due 2006 to 2078 (b)	327	362
3.901% notes due November 30, 2007	135	135
Zero coupon notes, yield 11.1%, $261 due August 15, 2013	135	121
Debt of contract manufacturer consolidated under FIN 46R	37	0
8.2% ESOP loan guaranty, due June 30, 2007	1	4
5.125% notes due February 15, 2007	0	1,500
2.625% notes due October 24, 2006	0	500
Zero coupon convertible debentures yield 2.0%, $371 due October 28, 2022	0	268
Other	91	66
	4,952	4,546
Less amount due within one year	(1,734)	(2,131)
Total long-term debt	$3,218	$2,415

CONSOLIDATED STATEMENTS OF STOCKHOLDERS' EQUITY AND COMPREHENSIVE INCOME
GENERAL MILLS, INC.

	Fiscal Year Ended	
In Millions	May 27, 2007	May 28, 2006
Balance at the beginning of the year	5,772	5,676
Net income for year	**1,144**	**1,090**
Other comprehensive income, net of tax	**195**	**117**
Adoption of SFAS No. 158	**(440)**	
Stock compensation plans	**504**	**235**
Cash dividends declared	**(506)**	**(484)**
Shares purchased	**(1,385)**	**(892)**
Unearned compensation related to restricted stock awards	**(95)**	**(17)**
Earned compensation	**130**	**47**
Balance at year-end	5,319	5,772

CONSOLIDATED STATEMENTS OF CASH FLOWS
GENERAL MILLS, INC.

	Fiscal Year Ended	
In Millions	May 27, 2007	May 28, 2006
Net earnings	$ 1,144	$ 1,090
Cash flow provided by operating activities	1,765	1,848
Cash flow used by investing activities	(597)	(369)
Cash Flows—Financing Activities:		
Change in notes payable	**(280)**	**1,197**
Issuance of long-term debt	**2,650**	**0**
Payment of long-term debt	**(2,323)**	**(1,386)**
Common stock issued	**317**	**157**
Tax benefit on exercised option	**73**	**0**
Purchases of common stock for treasury	**(1,321)**	**(885)**
Dividends paid	**(506)**	**(485)**
Other, net	**(8)**	**(3)**
Cash flow used by financing activities	**(1,398)**	**(1,405)**
Increase (Decrease) in cash	(230)	74

On the balance sheet, General Mills reported long-term debt of $3,218,000,000 in 2007 and $2,415,000,000 in 2006. The details of long-term debt are provided in Footnote 8 in which General Mills notes that it had complied with all covenants associated with the debt agreements.

The stockholders' equity accounts of Common Stock, Additional Paid-in Capital, Retained Earnings, Common Stock in Treasury, Unearned Compensation, and Accumulated Comprehensive Income (Loss) are presented on the balance sheet. The changes in these accounts are reported in the Consolidated Statements of Stockholders' Equity and Comprehensive Income. This statement shows the beginning balance in stockholder's equity for each year. Net income was added to this balance ($1,144,000,000 in 2007 and $1,090,000,000 in 2006). Dividends declared were subtracted from the balance ($506,000,000 in 2007 and $484,000,000 in 2006). Treasury stock was also subtracted from the stockholders' equity balance. Treasury stock shares were purchased for $1,385,000,000 in 2007 and $892,000,000 in 2006. At the end of 2007, General Mills owned 162 million shares of the 502 million shares of its stock issued.

Because of General Mills' purchase of treasury stock, its Stockholders' Equity section differs from those of many other companies. General Mills has 502 million shares of common stock issued. The total amount in the Common Stock and Paid-in Capital accounts related to the 502 million shares was $5,892,000,000 in 2007. The value of treasury stock at the end of 2007 was ($6,198,000,000). Treasury stock represented 162 million shares of the 502 million shares of stock. General Mills owned 12% of its own stock. Treasury stock was subtracted from the common stock accounts, so without considering retained earnings, stockholder's equity for General Mills was ($306,000,000), an unusual number for a company because stockholders' equity typically is large and positive. The 502 million shares of stock had been issued several years before when the stock price was lower. When General Mills purchases its own stock, it must buy it in the market at the current market price. That is the reason that 162 million shares of treasury stock had a higher value than the 502 million shares when originally issued.

General Mills purchases treasury stock because it reissues some of it to management as compensation in the form of stock options. When the company purchases shares of its own stock, it reduces the dividend payment needed each year so it has determined that stock repurchase is a good use of the company's excess cash.

The auditors review other adjustments to the Stockholders' Equity account (other comprehensive income, adoption of SFAS No. 158, stock compensation plans, unearned compensation related to restricted stock awards, and earned compensation) to determine whether they are recorded in accordance with the applicable financial reporting framework.

Did You Know?

A stock option gives the holder the right to purchase shares of company stock at a future date, at a fixed price, usually the market price of the stock on the date of the grant. If the price of the stock rises, the executive can sell the stock for a profit. When stock options are backdated to a date when the stock price is lower, their value increases and the option holder could immediately cash it in and make money. This means that backdated stock options are "issued in the money." A stock option issued in the money has value immediately. The option holder could sell the stock for a profit. This removes one of the main roles of a stock option: to encourage the holder to manage the business in a fashion that increases the stock price so the option has value.

Backdating violates securities law when shareholders are told that stock option grants were issued at the market price on the date of the grant. If they were backdated, they were actually issued at a price lower than the market price on the date of the grant. In this case, the company should recognize compensation expense equal to the difference between the market price and the stock price effective on the date of the backdated option. Companies backdating stock option grants have failed to recognize this additional compensation expense in the past.

In 2008, Gregory Reyes, former CEO of Brocade Communications, was fined $15 million and sentenced to 21 months in prison for backdating stock options the company awarded him.

More than 140 companies have been investigated concerning the practice of backdating, and the Justice Department has conducted criminal investigations of several executives. Reyes is the first executive to be sentenced for improperly backdating stock options.

Sources: J. Scheck and S. Stecklow, "Brocade Ex-CEO Gets 21 Months in Prison," *The Wall Street Journal,* January 17, 2008; V. Fuhrmans and J. Bandler, "Ex-CEO Agrees to Give Back $620 Million," *The Wall Street Journal,* December 7, 2007.

Stock options are an important type of compensation for many companies. They are granted for two reasons: (1) to give executives compensation without the use of company cash and (2) to align management's needs with those of the company's owners for future growth. Executives with stock options benefit from them only if the company's stock price increases.

The auditors' role in reviewing stock options is to determine that they have been recorded in accordance with the applicable financial reporting framework. The accounting standards specify that when the stock's option price is equal to its market value on the date of the grant, the company is not required to record compensation expense for the difference between the option price and the market price (because this value is zero). However, when a company backdates stock options and selects a date (usually in the past quarter) when the stock is at its lowest price, the option price is lower than the market value of the stock and the accounting standards require the company to recognize compensation expense for the difference between the option price and the market price. The auditors verify that the company has followed the rules of the accounting standards by reviewing the grant dates for stock options and the market price of the options.

Activities relating to the long-term debt and owners' equity cycle are reflected in the cash flow from financing section of the statement of cash flows. Issuing new debt or stock increases cash from financing, and paying off long-term debt or purchasing treasury stock decreases it. When General Mills paid off notes payable the payment used cash in 2007 ($280 million), and the issue of new notes payable increased cash in 2006 ($1,197 million). The issuance of long-term debt increased cash in 2007 by $2,650 million. There was no issuance of long-term debt in 2006. Payments on long-term debt used cash of $2,323 million in 2007 and $1,386 in 2006. Issues of common stock in 2007 increased cash by $317 million and by $157 million in 2006. A tax benefit on an exercised option of $73 million increased cash in 2007, but there was no tax benefit in 2006. General Mill's purchase of treasury stock used $1,321 million in 2007 and $885 million in 2006. Dividends paid used cash in 2007 and 2006 ($506 million and $485 million, respectively).

Cash flow *used* by financing activities was $1,398 million in 2007 and $1,405 in 2006. Financing activities at General Mills used more cash than it generated. In 2007, cash flow from the company's operating activities provided $1,765 million in cash, investing activities used $597 million in cash, and financing activities used $1,398 in cash. The net decrease in cash for 2007 was $230 million. In 2006, the total of cash flow from operating activities was $1,090 million. That year, investing activities and financing activities used $369 million and $1,405 million in cash, respectively. The increase in cash for 2006 was $74 million.

One might ask where General Mills gets the cash that it spends? In 2007, the cash came from its daily operations and financing activities (issue of long-term debt). General Mills spends its cash to pay off debt, purchase treasury stock, pay dividends, and invest in new buildings and business partnerships. As to the amount the company paid its shareholders each year in dividends and that it keeps to reinvest in the company, in 2007, it paid 44% of earnings in the form of dividends, meaning that it reinvested 56% of its earnings in the business. Companies always balance paying dividends and parting with cash against keeping their shareholders happy. Shareholders with a short-term perspective would like a company to pay a high proportion of its earnings in the form of dividends; those with a long-term perspective can settle for a small payout in the form of dividends in the hope that money invested in the company will generate a higher stock price in the future.

Chapter Takeaways

The long-term debt and owners' equity business process is important for the auditors because of the significance of the transactions recorded in it. Incentives to misstate long-term liabilities are great because a company with debt finds it more difficult to borrow money than a company without debt. The audit procedures in this process of testing internal controls and performing substantive tests should be performed with professional skepticism. The auditors should consider the risk that misstatements can occur in recording liabilities and capital stock transactions and therefore gather sufficient evidence to determine that the accounts in the business process are not materially misstated at year-end.

This chapter presented these important facts:

- The transactions recorded in the long-term debt and owners' equity business process, the accounting rules related to these transactions, and the importance of this process to the financial statements.
- The susceptibility of the long-term debt and owners' equity process to fraud.
- How auditors gather evidence to support management's assertions of existence or occurrence, completeness, valuation and allocation, rights and obligations, accuracy, cutoff, and classification using internal control and substantive tests.
- How the auditors evaluate the relevant assertions for the significant accounts in the business process. Because long-term debt tends to be understated on the financial statements, the most important assertion in the long-term debt and owners' equity process is completeness.
- The importance of the client's *disclosures* related to the transactions recorded in the business process. Companies prefer not to disclose all of their liabilities, but doing so gives outside readers of the financial statements unreliable information.

Be sure you understand these concepts before you go to the next chapter.

Review Questions

LO1, LO2   1. Describe the activities in the long-term debt and owners' equity process. Write journal entries to record the transactions in the process.

LO6   2. What are the most important accounts in this process? Describe the misstatement that is most likely with them.

LO2   3. List the main documents used in this process. Describe the purpose of each and whether it is prepared by or outside the firm.

LO3   4. Explain the accounting rules applicable to long-term debt accounts.

LO4   5. Are understatement misstatements or overstatement misstatements more likely to occur in the long-term debt and owners' equity process? Explain why.

LO4   6. Explain how auditors consider the risk of fraud in this business process.

LO5   7. Describe management's assertions for the long-term debt and owners' equity process. Which assertions are the most important for it? Explain why this is so.

LO7   8. How do the auditors assess control risk for the long-term debt and owners' equity process? Are they likely to test internal controls for this process? Explain your answer.

LO7   9. Describe the audit procedures the auditors use to test internal controls.

LO7   10. Describe key internal controls for this process.

LO8   11. What substantive tests of transactions are typically performed for this business process?

LO8   12. Describe the substantive tests of balances that are used for the long-term debt and owners' equity process. Identify the assertions associated with them.

LO9   13. Describe how the accounts in this process impact the financial statements. What are the presentation and disclosure issues associated with it?

Multiple Choice Questions from CPA Examinations

LO8   14. An auditor's program to audit long-term debt should include steps that require
a. Examining bond trust indentures.
b. Inspecting the accounts payable subsidiary ledger.
c. Investigating credits to the bond interest income account.
d. Verifying the existence of the bondholders.

LO8 15. In gathering evidence to evaluate unrecorded long-term bonds payable, an auditor most likely will
    a. Perform analytical procedures on the bond premium and discount accounts.
    b. Examine documentation of assets purchased with bond proceeds for liens.
    c. Compare interest expense with the bond payable amount for reasonableness.
    d. Confirm the existence of individual bondholders at year-end.

LO5 16. During an audit of a company's equity accounts, the auditor determines whether restrictions have been imposed on retained earnings resulting from loans, agreements, or state law. This audit procedure most likely is intended to verify management's assertion of
    a. Existence or occurrence.
    b. Completeness.
    c. Valuation or allocation.
    d. Presentation and disclosure.

LO8 17. When a client's company does not maintain its own stock records, the auditor should obtain written confirmation from the transfer agent and registrar concerning
    a. Restrictions on the payment of dividends.
    b. The number of shares issued and outstanding.
    c. Guarantees of preferred stock liquidation value.
    d. The number of shares subject to agreements to repurchase.

LO8 18. An auditor usually obtains evidence of a company's equity transactions by reviewing its
    a. Minutes of board of directors meetings.
    b. Transfer agent's records.
    c. Canceled stock certificates.
    d. Treasury stock certificate book.

LO8 19. During the audit of a publicly held company, the auditor should obtain written confirmation regarding debenture transactions from the
    a. Debenture holders.
    b. Client's attorney.
    c. Internal auditors.
    d. Trustee.

LO6 20. Most likely, an auditor's purpose in reviewing the renewal of a note payable shortly after the balance sheet date is to obtain evidence concerning management's assertions about
    a. Existence or occurrence.
    b. Presentation and disclosure.
    c. Completeness.
    d. Valuation or allocation.

LO1 21. In the audit of a medium-sized manufacturing concern, which one of the following areas can be expected to require the least amount of audit time?
    a. Equity.
    b. Revenue.
    c. Assets.
    d. Liabilities.

LO8 22. An audit program for the retained earnings account should include a step that requires verification of the
    a. Fair value used to charge retained earnings to account for a two-for-one-split.
    b. Approval of the adjustment to the beginning balance as a result of a write-down of an account receivable.
    c. Authorization for both cash and stock dividends.
    d. Gain or loss resulting from disposition of treasury shares.

LO8 23. In performing tests concerning the granting of stock options, an auditor should
    a. Confirm the transaction with the Secretary of State in the state of incorporation.

    b. Verify the existence of option holders in the entity's payroll records or stock ledgers.

    c. Determine that sufficient treasury stock is available to cover any new stock issued.

    d. Trace the authorization for the transaction to a vote of the board of directors.

Discussion Questions and Research Problems

LO7

24. **Internal control questionnaire.** The following questions are part of an internal control questionnaire for the long-term debt and owners' equity process. For each question:

    a. Describe the misstatement in the financial statements that could occur if the client answered the question "no."

    b. Explain how you would design a substantive test to evaluate the potential misstatement in the financial statements because of the missing control.

    c. If the client answers "yes," describe an internal control that the client could use.

    d. Describe how you could test the internal control described in part (c).

    Answer the following internal control questions for the long-term debt and owners' equity process:

    (1) Did the board of directors authorize direct borrowings on notes payable?

    (2) Did the board of directors approve cash dividends?

    (3) Did senior officers review footnotes for long-term debt and owners' equity?

    (4) Did the board of directors authorize purchases of treasury stock?

    (5) Did the board of directors approve stock options issued to management?

LO8

25. **Bonds payable.** The balance in the Bonds Payable account at year-end is $200,000,000. After reviewing the confirmation from the trustee, the auditors determine that the correct balance is $225,000,000. Answer the following questions regarding the bonds payable.

    a. Describe two errors and two fraudulent actions that could have caused the discrepancy reported between the book value and the confirmed value.

    b. What audit evidence would you gather to determine whether the specific errors and fraudulent actions that you suggested caused the misstatements?

    c. How will the bonds payable appear on the company's financial statements? What disclosures related to bonds are needed?

LO6, LO8

26. **Auditing long-term debt.** Atlas Company has long-term debt on its books. It has issued new debt and made payments on the outstanding debt every year. The ending balance in the accounts for the current year and the prior year follow.

	Balance at 12/31/11	Balance at 12/31/12
Long-Term notes payable	$12,000,000	$11,400,000
Bonds payable	25,000,000	25,000,000
Discount on Bonds payable	4,300,000	4,000,000

    a. Assume that $3,000,000 of new long-term notes payable was issued in 2012. What is the amount of notes paid during the year? Show your calculations.

    b. Why has the balance in the Discount on Bonds Payable changed from 2011 to 2012, but the bonds' face value has not?

    c. The company's current ratio should be maintained at no less than 1.0 during the entire year according to the debt covenant on the new note payable. How will the auditors determine whether that condition has been met in 2012?

    d. The Bonds Payable account contains two debt covenants. The first covenant requires the company to cancel all management bonuses if the debt-to-equity ratio goes above 0.50. The second covenant permits the company to issue stock options only if net income increases by 20% per year. How will the auditors determine whether the company has met the debt covenants in 2012?

    e. Why have the bond holders included these particular debt covenants in their debt agreement? What do they hope to gain from the covenants?

    f. Describe assertions that could be important for the Long-Term Debt account, and describe one substantive test you could use to verify that the assertions are valid.

LO4, LO8   27. **Long-term debt and owners' equity work papers.** As the partner in charge of the yearly audit for Custom Manufacturing, you are reviewing the audit work papers for the Long-Term Debt and Owners' Equity accounts. Before you sign off on the audit, you need to determine that sufficient appropriate audit evidence was gathered to determine whether these two accounts are materially misstated at year-end. The balance in each account is material, and if either are materially misstated, the financial statements will be materially misstated.

    a. Describe the audit evidence you would expect to find in the work papers to determine whether Long-Term Debt and Owners' Equity accounts are materially misstated at year-end.

    b. How will you know that the risk of fraud was considered in the audit of this process?

    c. What alternatives are available to you if the audit evidence indicates that the account balance is materially misstated?

LO3, LO8   28. **Long-term debt.** JPS has notes payable and bonds payable in its long-term debt accounts. It makes payments on notes each year and issues new debt when it needs moneys to expand the business.

    a. Describe the risks associated with the audit of the long-term debt accounts for JPS at year-end.

    b. What evidence should the auditors gather to determine that the Long-Term Debt account balances are not materially misstated at year-end?

    c. How should the Long-Term Debt accounts be valued at year-end? How will the auditors determine that the accounts are properly valued at year-end?

LO4, LO8   29. **Confirmations for long-term debt.** Consider the audit procedure to confirm outstanding balances, terms, conditions, and compliance with covenants with the grantor or trustee of the debt at year-end.

    a. How does the auditor perform this procedure? What are the auditors' responsibilities for it?

    b. When is the procedure performed?

    c. What is the purpose of the external confirmation?

    d. Describe the assertions associated with the confirmation. Explain why they are important to the long-term debt process.

    e. Identify the accounts that could be misstated if confirmations are not performed.

    f. If these accounts are misstated, how will this effect outsiders? Explain your answer.

LO4   30. **Adjusting entries.** During your audit of the Long-Term Debt and Owners' Equity accounts, you notice several adjusting journal entries in them at year-end.

    a. Identify several questions that you should ask management regarding the entries.

    b. Describe two possible scenarios to explain the entries that involve adjustments associated with error corrections.

    c. Describe two possible scenarios that involve fraud to explain the entries.

Real-World Auditing Problems

LO4   31. **Xerox**

Review the discussion of the Xerox fraud described in the chapter.

a. Why would auditors consider performance-based compensation and stock options to be a risk factor in an audit?

b. Did KPMG consider these compensation methods to be risk factors in the Xerox audit?

LO4   32. **Adelphia**

John Rigas, founder of Adelphia Communications, said that he was sorry for the problems at his company, but he didn't think he deserved to be jailed. The judge rejected Rigas' argument, indicating that he had engaged in a blatant fraud by using shareholder money for his personal use.

a. The phrase, "feeding at the corporate trough" has been used to describe Rigas' actions at Adelphia. Explain what this phrase means. Is this a good thing? Discuss reasons for your opinion.

b. If you had owned stock at Adelphia, would you have been happy with Rigas' expenditures? Explain your answer.

c. What fraud risk factor is present in a family-run business? How do the auditors gather evidence to determine whether the financial statements are misstated in such businesses?

d. Explain how industry knowledge would be useful to auditors in a situation similar to that at Adelphia. What role did industry pressure play in the fraud?

LO4, LO8   33. **Parmalat**

Review the discussion of the Parmalat fraud in the chapter.

a. Why was the SEC upset about the missing debt on Parmalat's financial statements?

b. If you had owned stock in Parmalat, would you have been happy with the Tanzi family's expenditures? Explain your answer.

c. What fraud risk factor is present in a family-run business? How do the auditors gather evidence to determine whether the financial statements are misstated in this situation?

d. Parmalat was the largest audit client for Deloitte & Touche in Italy. What role could this have played in its audit of Parmalat?

e. Should Deloitte & Touche in the United States or Deloitte & Touche in Hong Kong be financially responsible for the failed audit at Deloitte & Touche in Italy? Explain your answer.

f. Consider the reputation of Deloitte & Touche. Did the actions of Deloitte & Touche in Italy hurt the company's reputation in the United States and Hong Kong? Explain your views and why they seem reasonable to you.

LO4   34. **Enron**

Enron engaged in a neat trick to improve its financial statements. It simply removed debt from them and transferred it to partnerships. The company remained liable for the debt, however, and when the partnerships failed to pay the debt, Enron became liable for it.

a. Why is it a problem for a company to keep debt off its balance sheet to make its financial statements look better? Who is harmed when this happened? Why would outsiders care?

b. What fraud risk factors were present in this company? How should the auditors gather information related to the fraud risk factors you identified?

c. As an auditor, when your client is engaged in a transaction that you do not understand, what should you do?

d. What role do you think the corporate culture at Enron played in the fraud?

e. Arthur Andersen lost its license to audit public companies as a result of its felony conviction related to the Enron audit (it was later overturned). Was the decision to take its license fair? If you had planned to issue stock for your company the year following the Enron fraud and the court decision on Arthur Andersen, would you have been willing to have Arthur Andersen audit the company?

f. Should the worldwide operation of an accounting firm suffer from the actions of one partner? Explain your answer.

LO3, LO4   35. **Brocade**

Review the discussion of the stock option fraud at Brocade Communications in the chapter.

a. According to the accounting standards, is backdating stock options wrong?

b. What is the auditors' concern when the company backdates stock options?

c. What assertions are important in auditing backdated stock options? What evidence should the auditors gather to determine that the client has correctly recorded backdated stock options?

d. Barnes and Noble often used backdating to issue stock options to senior managers. According to a report issued by the company, its managers believed that it was appropriate to select a date for the stock option grant if the date was reasonably close to the approval date. Is this correct? What does the company's statement indicate about its knowledge of accounting standards?

e. The SEC at one time investigated 140 companies for backdated stock options, so the practice appears to be quite common. Why did so many auditors apparently allow this fraudulent practice to continue?

Internet Assignment

LO4, LO9   36. Select a company and find its annual report for the current year. Answer the following questions about the company's long-term debt and owners' equity. Print out the balance sheet and footnotes you used to answer the questions.

a. What type of debt does the company have?

b. Did the company issue any new long-term debt this year?

c. Has the company used debt to generate cash or used it to pay off debt during the year?

d. Did the company issue stock?

e. Did the company issue stock options?

f. Does the company have treasury stock? If so, how much? How is it reported in the Owners' Equity section of the balance sheet?

g. Did the company pay dividends this year? If so, how much?

h. What have the retained earnings been over the life of the company?

i. What is the company's debt-to-equity ratio? What information does this ratio give you about the way the company generates cash?

12

Completing the Audit

Learning Objectives

After studying this chapter, you should be able to:

1. Explain the audit procedures for contingent liabilities and the importance of the attorney's letter regarding potential liabilities.
2. Describe the audit procedures for subsequent events and subsequently discovered facts.
3. Explain the audit procedures for dealing with related parties.
4. Describe auditors' responsibility for considering laws and regulations in the audit of financial statements.
5. Explain the auditors' responsibility for evaluating the going concern assumption for an audit client.
6. Identify the use of the representation letter in the audit.
7. Describe the review and documentation process for audit working papers.
8. Explain how auditors use audit evidence to determine whether the financial statements are materially misstated.
9. Describe how auditors evaluate the consistency of financial statements audits.
10. Explain how auditors review footnotes and other information associated with the financial statements.
11. Describe the end of fieldwork.

Auditing and accounting pronouncements relevant to this topic

For private companies

- **AU 312,** Evaluation of Misstatements Identified During an Audit
- **AU 314,** Understanding the Entity and Its Environment and Assessing the Risks of Material Misstatement
- **AU 317,** Consideration of Laws and Regulations in an Audit of Financial Statements
- **AU 318,** Performing Audit Procedures in Response to Assessed Risks and Evaluating the Audit Evidence Obtained
- **AU 329,** Analytical Procedures
- **AU 333,** Written Representations
- **AU 334,** Related Parties
- **AU 337,** Audit Evidence—Specific Considerations for Selected Items
- **AU 339,** Audit Documentation
- **AU 341,** Going Concern
- **AU 420,** Consistency of Financial Statements
- **AU 431,** Adequacy of Disclosure in Financial Statements
- **AU 550,** Other Information in Documents Containing Audited Financial Statements

- **AU 551,** Supplementary Information in Relation to the Financial Statements As a Whole
- **AU 558,** Required Supplementary Information
- **AU 560,** Subsequent Events and Subsequently Discovered Facts

For public companies

- **AU 317,** Illegal Acts by Clients (Interim standard)
- **AU 329,** Analytical Procedures (Interim standard)
- **AU 333,** Management Representations (Interim standard)
- **AU 334,** Related Parties (Interim standard)
- **AU 337,** Inquiry of a Client's Lawyer Concerning Litigation, Claims, and Assessments (Interim standard)
- **AU 341,** The Auditor's Consideration of an Entity's Ability to Continue as a Going Concern (Interim standard)
- **AU 550,** Other Information in Documents Containing Audited Financial Statements (Interim standard)
- **AU 551,** Reporting on Information Accompanying the Basic Financial Statements in Auditor-Submitted Documents (Interim standard)
- **AU 558,** Required Supplementary Information (Interim standard)
- **AU 560,** Subsequent Events (Interim standard)
- **PCAOB Auditing Standard No. 3,** Audit Documentation
- **PCAOB Auditing Standard No. 6,** Evaluating Consistency of Financial Statements
- **PCAOB Auditing Standard No. 14,** Evaluating Audit Results
- **PCAOB Auditing Standard No. 11,** Consideration of Materiality in Planning and Performing an Audit
- **PCAOB Auditing Standard No. 15,** Audit Evidence

International standards

- **ISA 230,** Audit Documentation
- **ISA 250,** Consideration of Laws and Regulations in an Audit of Financial Statements
- **ISA 260,** Communication of Audit Matters with Those Charged with Governance
- **ISA 320,** Materiality in Planning and Performing an Audit
- **ISA 450,** Evaluation of Misstatements Identified during the Audit
- **ISA 500,** Audit Evidence
- **ISA 550,** Related Parties
- **ISA 560,** Subsequent Events
- **ISA 570,** Going Concern
- **ISA 580,** Management Representations
- **ISA 720,** Other Information in Documents Containing Audited Financial Statements
- **IAS 10,** Events after the Reporting Period
- **IAS 37,** Provisions, Contingent Liabilities and Contingent Assets

Chapter Overview

This chapter discusses audit procedures that must be completed near the end of the audit before the audit opinion is issued. We refer to this period in the audit as the *end of fieldwork.* At the end of this time, an audit opinion is issued. The date on it is the last day of fieldwork. Transactions in this process are part of the decision phase of the audit process. Exhibit 12-1 summarizes the main steps in the audit process.

Near the end of the audit, auditors perform several audit procedures to gather evidence for evaluating (1) contingent liabilities, (2) subsequent events, (3) related-party

| The Audit Process | Exhibit 12-1 |

Steps in the Audit Process	Discussed in this Section
Planning Phase	
Consider the Preconditions for an Audit and Accept or Reject the Audit Engagement	
Understand the Entity and Its Environment, Determine Materiality, and Assess the Risks of Material Misstatements	
Develop an Audit Strategy and an Audit Plan to Respond to the Assessed Risks	
Testing Phase	
Test Internal Controls? Yes No	
Perform Tests of Controls if "Yes"	
Perform Substantive Tests of Transactions	
Perform Substantive Tests of Balances	
Assess the Likelihood of Material Misstatement	
Decision Phase	
Review the Presentation and Disclosure Assertions	√
Evaluate the Evidence to Determine Whether the Financial Statements Are Prepared in Accordance with the Applicable Financial Reporting Framework	√
Issue Audit Report	√
Communicate with the Audit Committee	√

transactions, (4) risk of material misstatement because of violations of laws and regulations, (5) going concern assessment, (6) management representation letter, (7) audit documentation, (8) proposed audit adjustment schedule, (9) other information in the financial statements, and (10) audit opinion to be issued. This chapter discusses these procedures necessary to gather evidence related to issues (1) through (9). Audit opinions are discussed in Chapter 13.

By the end of fieldwork, auditors should have gathered sufficient appropriate evidence to determine whether the financial statements are free of material misstatement, allowing the auditors to issue an opinion. It will state that the financial statements have been prepared in accordance with an "applicable financial reporting framework." In the United States, the applicable financial reporting framework used by clients is usually U.S. generally accepted accounting standards (often referred to as *GAAP*). A public audit client might also prepare financial statements according to international accounting standards, another "applicable financial reporting framework." At the end of fieldwork, auditors decide what audit opinion they should issue for the financial statements based on their assessment of whether the financial statements have been prepared in accordance with the applicable financial reporting framework that the client used. Does the audit evidence support a clean opinion, an opinion qualified because of material misstatements in the financial statements, a disclaimer of opinion because the auditors have been unable to gather enough evidence, or an adverse opinion because the evidence gathered indicates that the financial statements are materially misstated?

This stage of the audit requires auditors to make many professional judgments. The auditing standards provide guidance for the auditors relevant to the audit procedures performed at the end of the audit, but all decisions the auditors make require them to use professional judgment to assess the risk of material misstatement associated with the client decisions reviewed by the auditor at the end of the audit (going concern, contingent liabilities, subsequent events, for example). Let's begin the study of the audit procedures associated with "the end of the audit" with a discussion of the audit procedures for contingent liabilities.

Audit Procedures for Contingent Liabilities

LO1

Explain the audit procedures for contingent liabilities and the importance of the attorney's letter regarding potential liabilities

Contingent liabilities are those that could arise in the future based on an event that occurred during the current year. Because they relate to events in the current year, contingent liabilities could require disclosure or recognition in the year under audit. Contingent liabilities include (1) lawsuits requesting the company to pay damages for product liability or patent infringement, (2) product warranty claims, (3) guarantees of other parties' obligations, (4) liabilities for discounted notes receivable, and (5) income tax disputes. During the audit of contingent liabilities, auditors often use the opinion of an outside expert. Attorneys hired by the client to represent it against claims, litigation, and assessments provide auditors the evidence needed to determine whether the contingent liability should be recorded, disclosed, or ignored.

The auditing standards require auditors to design audit procedures and plan the audit to identify litigation, claims, and assessments involving the company that could increase the risk of material misstatement. Auditors do this by (1) asking management and others in the company, including the in-house legal counsel, about potential contingent liabilities, (2) reviewing minutes of meetings of those charged with governance and correspondence between the company and its external counsel, and (3) reviewing the expense accounts related to legal expense. In the evidence-gathering process, auditors seek to determine the existence of a condition indicating a contingent liability, the period in which the cause for the legal action occurred, the probability of an unfavorable outcome, and the amount of the potential loss. If during this process, auditors assess a risk of material misstatement because of a potential contingent liability, they should seek direct communication with the company's external legal counsel. The auditors do this by sending a letter of inquiry prepared by management requesting the company's legal counsel to communicate directly with them. If the auditors do not assess a risk of material misstatement related to a potential contingent liability, they are not required to contact the audit client's external counsel. For a copy of the request that auditors send to external counsel, see Exhibit 12-2.

The applicable financial reporting framework used by the client determines the correct accounting treatment for contingent liabilities. For companies using U.S. GAAP as the reporting framework, when a contingent liability exists, the likelihood for loss is evaluated as *probable, reasonably possible,* or *remote.* A probable loss is one that is likely to occur. A remote loss has a slight chance of occurring. A reasonably possible loss falls between probable and remote.

According to U.S. accounting standards, an estimated contingency loss should be recorded (by a charge to income and liabilities) if two conditions are met: the loss is *probable* and the amount of the loss can be *reasonably estimated.* Auditors often use the attorney's letter to determine both conditions.

If both conditions are not met, U.S. accounting standards require the *disclosure* of a loss contingency if it is *reasonably possible.* The disclosure of a loss contingency should include a description of it and an estimate, if possible, of the range of the loss amount or a statement that such an estimate is not possible.

For companies using international accounting standards, companies recognize loss provisions, but disclose contingent liabilities, unless the possibility of a loss is remote. The contingent liabilities that are disclosed are assessed continuously to determine whether the possibility of a loss is probable. If it becomes probable, a provision (a liability of uncertain timing or amount) is recognized in the financial statements for the period in which the change occurred. A provision is recorded when three conditions are met: (1) the company has an obligation as a result of a past event, (2) it is probably that a payment will be required to settle the obligation, and (3) a reliable estimate can be made of the amount of the obligation. When it is more likely than not (probable) that a

Attorney Letter	Exhibit 12-2

BCS, Inc.
400 Main Street
York, New York 20166

Stuart & Baesler Law Firm
250 First Avenue
New York, New York 42100

In connection with an audit of our financial statements at December 31, 2011, and for the year then ended, management of the Company has prepared, and furnished to our auditors Grant Alexander, 100 Tenth Street, New York, New York 20144, a description and evaluation of certain contingencies, including those set forth below involving matters with respect to which you have been engaged and to which you have devoted substantive attention on behalf of the Company in the form of legal consultation or representation. These contingencies are regarded by management of the Company as material for this purpose (management may indicate a materiality level if an understanding has been reached with the auditor). Your response should include matters that existed at December 31, 2011, and during the period from that date to the date of your response.

Pending or Threatened Litigation (excluding unasserted claims)

[Ordinarily the information would include the following: (1) the nature of the litigation, (2) the progress of the case to date, (3) how management is responding or intends to respond to the litigation (for example, to contest the case vigorously or to seek an out-of-court settlement), and (4) an evaluation of the likelihood of an unfavorable outcome and an estimate, if one can be made, of the amount or range of potential loss.] This letter will serve as our consent for you to furnish to our auditor all the information requested herein. Accordingly, please furnish to our auditors such explanation, if any, that you consider necessary to supplement the foregoing information, including an explanation of those matters as to which your views may differ from those stated and an identification of the omission of any pending or threatened litigation, claims, and assessments or a statement that the list of such matters is complete.

Unasserted Claims and Assessments (considered by management to be probable of assertion, and that, if asserted, would have at least a reasonable possibility of an unfavorable outcome).

[Ordinarily management's information would include (1) the nature of the matter, (2) how management intends to respond if the claim is asserted, and (3) an evaluation of the likelihood of an unfavorable outcome and an estimate, if one can be made, of the amount or range of potential loss.] Please furnish to our auditors such explanation, if any, that you consider necessary to supplement the foregoing information, including an explanation of those matters as to which your views may differ from those stated.

We understand that whenever, in the course of performing legal services for us with respect to a matter recognized to involve an unasserted possible claim or assessment that may call for financial statement disclosure, if you have formed a professional conclusion that we should disclose or consider disclosing concerning such possible claim or assessment, as a matter of professional responsibility to us, you will so advise us and will consult with us concerning the question of such disclosure and the applicable requirements of Financial Accounting Standards Board (FASB) *Accounting Standards Codification* (ASC) 450, *Contingencies.* Please specifically confirm to our auditors that our understanding is correct.

Please specifically identify the nature of and reasons for any limitation on your response.

[The auditor may request the client to inquire about additional matters, for example, unpaid or unbilled charges or specified information on certain contractually assumed obligations of the company, such as guarantees of indebtedness of others.]

Your response should be dated the end of fieldwork, March 1, 2012.

Very truly yours,

Michael Anderson
CEO, BCS, Inc.

present obligation exists at the end of the reporting period, the entity recognizes a provision. When it is more likely that no present obligation exist, the entity discloses a contingent liability, unless the possibility of payment is remote.

Auditors' primary responsibility regarding contingent liabilities and loss provisions is to determine that the client follows the rules of "the applicable financial reporting framework."

Contingent Liability Footnotes, Pfizer, Incorporated

December 31, 2008

Exhibit 12-3

FOOTNOTE 1D. CONTINGENCIES

We and certain of our subsidiaries are involved in various patent, product liability, consumer, commercial, securities, environment and tax litigations and claims, government investigations, and other legal proceedings that arise from time to time in the ordinary course of our business. Except for income tax contingencies, we record accruals for contingencies to the extent that we conclude their occurrence is probable and that the related liabilities are estimable and record anticipated recoveries under existing insurance contracts when assured of recovery. For tax matters, beginning in 2007 with the adoption of a new accounting standard, we record accruals for income tax contingencies to the extent that we conclude that a tax position is not sustainable under a "more-likely-than-not" standard and record our estimate of the potential tax benefits in one tax jurisdiction that could result from the payment of income taxes in another tax jurisdiction when we conclude that the potential recovery is more likely than not. We consider many factors in making these assessments. Because litigation and other contingencies are inherently unpredictable and excessive verdicts do occur, these assessments can involve a series of complex judgments about future events and can rely heavily on estimates and assumptions.

FOOTNOTE 4. CERTAIN CHARGES

A. Bextra and Certain Other Investigations

In January 2009, we entered into an agreement in principle with the U.S. Department of Justice to resolve previously reported investigations regarding allegations of past off-label promotional practices concerning Bextra as well as certain other open investigations. In connection with these actions, in the fourth quarter of 2008, we recorded a charge of $2.3 billion, pretax and after-tax, in *Other Deductions* and such amount is included in *Other Current Liabilities.**

B. Certain Product Litigation—Celebrex and Bextra

In October 2008, we reached agreements in principle to resolve pending U.S. consumer fraud purported class action cases and more than 90% of the known U.S. personal injury claims involving Celebrex and Bextra, and we reached agreements to resolve substantially all of the claims of state attorneys generally primarily relating to alleged Bextra promotional practices. In connection with these actions, in the third quarter of 2008, we recorded pretax charges of approximately:

- $745 million applicable to all known U.S. personal injury claims
- $89 million applicable to the pending U.S. consumer fraud purposed class action cases
- $60 million applicable to agreements to resolve civil claims brought by 33 states and the District of Columbia, primarily relating to alleged Bextra promotional practices. Under these agreements, we made a payment of $60 million to the states and have adopted compliance measures that complement policies and procedures previously established by us.

These litigation-related charges were recorded in *Other Deductions*. Virtually all of this amount is included in *Other Current Liabilities*. Although we believe that we have insurance coverage for a portion of the proposed personal injury settlements, no insurance recoveries have been recorded.

We believe that the charges of approximately $745 million will be sufficient to resolve all known U.S. personal injury claims, including those not being settled at this time. However, additional charges may have to be taken in the future in connection with certain pending claims and unknown claims relating to Celebrex and Bextra.

http://media.pfizer.com/files/annualreport/2008/financial/financial2008.pdf

* *Other Deductions* is an income statement account with a negative (debit) balance. *Other Current Liabilities* is a balance sheet account.

See an example of footnote disclosure for contingent liabilities for Pfizer Inc. (a drug company using U.S. GAAP) in Exhibit 12-3. Footnote 1d describes the company's policy for recording contingent liabilities and the accounting standard it follows in disclosing and recognizing them. Footnote 4 describes the expenses recorded in the financial statements related to contingent liabilities. The company clearly is both disclosing contingencies and recognizing expenses and liabilities associated with them. The auditor for Pfizer's has determined that the company's treatment of contingent liabilities is consistent with the financial reporting framework Pfizer used. The auditor based this determination on attorney letters from the law firms representing the company in these lawsuits and discussion with management regarding the estimation of future liability.

A company could have other *potential* liabilities in the form of commitments to lease holders, to suppliers of raw materials for purchasing a certain amount of a product at a stated price, or to consolidated or nonconsolidated subsidiaries in guaranteeing their debt. The liabilities associated with these commitments are not recorded in the financial statements but are disclosed in the footnotes to them. Their disclosure is important to outsiders doing business with the company because the cash flow for these obligations

Annual Report, Commitments and Contingencies Footnote, Dell Inc. *Fiscal Year Ended January 29, 2010*	Exhibit 12-4

NOTE 9—COMMITMENTS AND CONTINGENCIES

Lease Commitments

Dell leases property and equipment, manufacturing facilities, and office space under noncancelable leases. Certain of these leases obligates Dell to pay taxes, maintenance, and repair costs. At January 29, 2010, future minimum lease payments under these noncancelable leases were $112 million in fiscal 2011, $95 million in fiscal 2012, $60 million in fiscal 2013, $46 million in fiscal 2014, $37 million in fiscal 2015, and $90 million thereafter.

Rent expense under all leases totaled $93 million, $116 million, and $118 million for Fiscal 2010, 2009, and 2008, respectively.

Purchase Obligations

Dell has contractual obligations to purchase goods or services, which specify significant terms, including fixed or minimum quantities to be purchased; fixed, minimum, or variable price provisions; and the appropriate timing of the transaction. As of January 29, 2010, Dell had $313 million, $46 million, and $24 million in purchase obligations for fiscal 2011, 2012, and 2013, respectively.

Restricted Cash

Pursuant to an agreement between Dell Financial Services and CIT Group, Inc. (subsidiaries of Dell that finance receivables), Dell is required to maintain escrow cash accounts as recourse reserves for credit losses, performance fee deposits related to Dell's private label credit card, and deferred servicing revenue. Restricted cash of $147 million and $213 million is included in Other Current Assets on Dell's consolidated statements of financial position at January 29, 2010, and January 30, 2009, respectively.

Legal Matters

[The footnote continues with a description of Dell's contingent liabilities.]

has already been committed. See an example of a commitment footnote for Dell Inc. in Exhibit 12-4.

Audit Procedures for Subsequent Events and Subsequently Discovered Facts

LO2

Describe the audit procedures for subsequent events and subsequently discovered facts

Auditors are required to gather evidence for the financial statements for the year under audit. For a company with a December 31, 2011 year-end, the auditors gather evidence to determine that the financial statements for 2011 have been prepared in accordance with the applicable financial reporting framework. Normally, auditors' work does not extend into the following year. *However,* the auditing standards require the auditors to consider certain events that occur in the year following the audit, referred to as *subsequent events,* and to determine whether any of these events requires disclosure or adjustment in the financial statements under audit.[1]

Auditors are interested in two types of events. *Subsequent events* are events that occur between the date of the financial statements and the date of the auditors' report that require adjustment or disclosure in the financial statements. *Subsequently discovered facts* are facts that the auditors learn of after their report date that could have caused them to amend their report had they known of them (AU 561). The auditors' responsibility according to the auditing standards is to *search* for subsequent events, and to *respond* to subsequently discovered facts if they come to the auditors' attention.

The time frame for subsequent events, the report date, and the subsequently discovered facts for a company with a December 31, 2011, year-end, follows.

---

[1] International Accounting Standards refer to these types of events as "events after the reporting period". The rules for recognizing subsequent events are the same: (1) events after the reporting period that provide evidence of a condition that existed at the end of the reporting period are referred to as "adjusting events after the reporting period", and (2) those that provide information about an event that arose after the reporting period are referred to as "non-adjusting events after the reporting period".

Time Frame of Subsequent Events and Subsequently Discovered Facts

Year-end	End of fieldwork, report date	Report issued
December 31, 2011	February 25, 2012	March 8, 2012
Subsequent event	January 1, 2012 to February 25, 2012	
Subsequently discovered facts	February 25, 2012 to December 31, 2012	

For a December 31, 2011, year-end, the subsequent event time frame is from January 1, 2012, to the date of the audit report, February 25, 2012, in this example. The date of the audit report and of the end of fieldwork is the same.

The two types of subsequent events are type I and type II. Type I provides evidence concerning conditions that existed at year-end. For example, when a customer with an accounts receivable balance of $5,000,000 files for bankruptcy between the end of the year and the date of the audit report, a type I subsequent event has occurred. Such events are *recorded* in the financial statements, so the accounts receivable balance for the bankrupt customer should be written down to the amount the client expects to collect (probably zero for a bankrupt customer). For companies using international accounting standards these events would be known as "adjusting events after the reporting period."

Type II subsequent events concern evidence of conditions that arose after the date of the financial statements. These events should *not* be recognized in the financial statements but should be *disclosed* in the footnotes. Examples of type II subsequent events include the purchase of a new business, the loss of a plant or inventory as a result of fire or a flood, or the sale of a bond or capital stock issue during the subsequent event period. A Type II subsequent event would be known as "non-adjusting events after the reporting period".

The subsequent event period extends from the end of the year to the date of the audit opinion. This period could be as short as a few weeks or as long as three months. During this time, the auditors must perform a *search* for subsequent events that should involve the following audit procedures:

- Gain an understanding of the procedures used by management to ensure that subsequent events are identified.
- Inquire of management about whether any events have occurred after the date of the financial statements that could affect them (for example, significant changes in capital stock or long-term debt, unusual adjustments, or any new information about items recorded on the financial statements).
- Read the minutes of meetings of shareholders, directors, and management and inquire about matters discussed at such meetings for which minutes are not yet available.
- Read the interim financial statements.

The auditors have no obligation to continue to *search* for subsequent events, after the audit report date. However, if they learn of a subsequently discovered fact *before the report release date,* they should discuss the matter with management and determine whether the financial statements need to be changed. If management changes them, the auditors should perform the audit procedures necessary to verify the information and issue their report with a new date for the amended financial statements. If management does not change the financial statements but the auditors believe they need to be changed, the auditors should modify their audit opinion (express a qualified opinion or an adverse opinion) as required by the auditing standards.

Sometimes auditors choose to dual-date an audit opinion when subsequent events occur. This opinion contains two dates; the first, which is the end of fieldwork, applies to everything in the financial statements except for the subsequent event. The second date applies only to the subsequent event.

If the auditors learn of a subsequently discovered fact *after the report release date,* they should discuss it with management and determine whether the financial statements need to be amended. If management amends them, the auditors should perform the audit procedures necessary to verify the information and determine whether the audited financial statements have been made available to third parties. If they have been, the auditors must assess whether management has taken appropriate steps to ensure that anyone with the incorrect financial statements is informed that they are not correct. The auditors issue a new report with a new date for the amended financial statements. If the opinion on the amended financial statements differs from the opinion previously expressed, the auditors should include an additional paragraph that discloses the differences.

If management does not amend the financial statements and the auditors believe they need to be amended, the auditors should take action to prevent reliance on their report. To prevent future reliance on it, the auditors notify the client that their report must not be associated with the financial statements, notify the regulatory agencies that their report should no longer be relied upon, and notify each person known to the auditors to be relying on the financial statements that their report is no longer reliable.

Audit Procedures for Related Party Transactions

LO3

Explain the audit procedures for related party transactions

The accounting standards that establish the rules for recording transactions assume that those a company enters into are arm's-length transactions between a willing buyer and a willing seller who are acting independently of each other. In an *arm's-length transaction,* the buyer and seller are pursuing their own best interests (AU 334 and ISA 550). Transactions that are not made at arm's length are referred to as *related-party transactions.*

The Financial Accounting Standards Board (FASB) defines related parties as:

- Company affiliates
- Investments in other companies that are accounted for using the equity method of accounting for investment securities
- Trusts for the benefit of employees, such as pension and profit-sharing trusts that management supervises
- Principal owners of the company and their immediate family members
- Managers of the company and their immediate family members
- Other parties with which the company could deal if one party can control or significantly influence the other's management or operating policies
- Other parties that can significantly influence the management or operating policies of the transacting parties or that have an ownership interest in one of the transacting parties and can significantly influence those parties (AU 334).

Auditing standards have also identified transactions that could indicate the existence of related parties:

- Borrowing or lending at an interest-free rate or a rate of interest significantly above or below market rates
- Selling real estate at a price that differs significantly from its appraised value
- Exchanging property for similar property in a nonmonetary transaction
- Making loans with no scheduled terms concerning when or how the funds will be repaid (AU 334).

Because related parties are not independent of each other, accounting standards specify accounting and disclosure requirements for these relationships, transactions, and balances to allow financial statement users to understand the potential effects of related-party transactions on the statements. The auditors' concern regarding these transactions is whether they have been recorded as the applicable financial reporting framework requires. The auditors' responsibility for related-party relationships is (1) to obtain a sufficient understanding of them to determine whether fraud risk factors exist (because related parties can more easily commit fraud) and (2) to obtain sufficient appropriate audit evidence about whether their transactions have been appropriately identified, accounted for, and disclosed in the financial statements.

Auditors' Responsibility for Client Compliance with Laws and Regulations

LO4

Describe the auditors' responsibility for considering laws and regulations in the audit of financial statements

Every company is subject to laws and regulations, some of which directly impact the financial statements and others an indirect impact. Noncompliance with them could result in fines, litigation, or other consequences for the company that could have a material effect on the financial statements.

The responsibility for management is to ensure that the company complies with the laws and regulations affecting it and for the auditors is to identify material misstatements that could occur in the financial statements as the result of noncompliance.

How do the auditors identify misstatements in the financial statements because of noncompliance with laws and regulations? They gain an understanding of the company and the legal and regulatory environment in which it operates and how it complies with those that affect it. The auditors should obtain sufficient appropriate evidence for material amounts and disclosures determined by laws and regulations that have a *direct impact* on the financial statements. Examples of these laws and regulations include (1) specific reporting requirements for public companies (for example, SEC requirements in the U.S.), (2) industry-specific financial reporting issues (for example, laws related to regulated industries such as oil and gas and to nonprofit organizations), (3) accounting for transactions under government contracts, including the amount of revenue to be accrued, and (4) the accrual and recognition of income tax and pension expense. The auditors' responsibility to detect and report misstatements resulting from noncompliance that have a direct impact on the financial statements is the same as that for misstatements caused by errors or fraud: to gather sufficient appropriate audit evidence to determine whether the financial statements are materially misstated because of errors or fraud.

The auditors are also concerned about the client's compliance with laws and regulations that *indirectly impact the financial statements.* Because of an audit's inherent limitations, an unavoidable risk exists that some material misstatements could be undetected. This risk related to potential violations of laws and regulations increases because (1) many do not affect the financial statements, (2) noncompliance could involve conduct designed to conceal it, and (3) an action that constitutes noncompliance is a matter for a court of law to determine. For this reason, the *auditors are not responsible for preventing noncompliance and are not expected to detect noncompliance with all laws and regulations.*

Examples of laws and regulations have an *indirect* impact on the financial statements include (1) safety and health regulations, (2) food and drug administration rules, (3) environmental protection laws, and (4) equal employment legislation. For these laws and regulations, the auditors should perform audit procedures to identify instances of noncompliance that could have a material effect on the financial statements by (1) inquiring of management about the company's compliance with laws and regulations and (2) inspecting correspondence with relevant licensing or regulatory bodies. Noncompliance having an indirect impact on the financial statements often result in a fine, litigation costs, or other consequences for the entity. These costs must be provided for or disclosed in the financial statements.

If they determine that a company does not comply with the relevant laws and regulations, the auditors must report the noncompliance to management or those charged with governance. This could cause the auditors to modify their report by issuing a qualified, adverse, or disclaimer of opinion as appropriate. The auditors should also determine whether they have a responsibility, according to the regulations that apply to them as independent auditors, to report the suspected noncompliance to parties outside the company.

Audit Procedures for Going Concern Assessments

LO5

Explain the auditors' responsibility for evaluating the going concern assumption for an audit client

Financial statements are prepared with the assumption that the company will continue in business for a reasonable period of time in the future (not to exceed one year from the date of the financial statements). This assumption determines the valuation assigned to the balance sheet assets. The auditors' responsibility regarding the going concern assumption for each audit client is (1) to obtain sufficient appropriate evidence to evaluate the appropriateness of management's use of it in preparing and presenting the financial statements, (2) to conclude whether a material uncertainty about the client's ability to continue exists, and (3) to determine the implications of the evidence for the auditors' report. If this assumption is realistic, the auditors do not comment on it. If substantial doubt exists, the auditors comment on it, often in the audit opinion.

Auditors look at the following information to identify conditions that could indicate doubt that the company can continue as a going concern for a reasonable period of time:

- Net liability positions
- Fixed-term borrowings approaching maturity without realistic prospects of renewal or repayment
- Indications of creditors' withdrawal of support
- Negative operating cash flows
- Adverse financial ratios
- Substantial operating losses or significant deterioration in the value of assets used to generate cash flows
- Dividends in arrears or discontinued
- Inability to pay creditors on due dates
- Inability to comply with the terms of loan agreements
- Suppliers' change from credit to cash-on-delivery transactions
- Inability to obtain financing for new product development
- Management intention to liquidate the company
- Loss of key management without replacement
- Loss of a major market, key customer, franchise, license, or principal supplier
- Labor difficulties
- Shortages of important supplies
- Emergence of a highly successful competitor
- Noncompliance with capital or other statutory requirements
- Pending legal or regulatory proceedings against the entity that could result in claims that it is unable to pay
- Changes in law or regulation or government policy expected to adversely affect the company
- Occurrence of uninsured or underinsured catastrophes

In making the decision about whether a client will continue in business for a reasonable period of time, the auditors are not responsible for predicting future events. Companies that do not receive going concern opinions or disclosures could cease to exist within the one-year time period. This does not indicate auditors' inadequate performance; their opinions that do not refer to going concern problems should not be interpreted as assurance of the company's ability to continue as a going concern.

If the auditors decide that there is substantial doubt about a client's ability to continue as a going concern, they should consider management's plans for dealing with the situation. Based on the audit evidence obtained, the auditors must conclude whether a *material uncertainty* casts doubt on the company's ability to continue as a going concern. A material uncertainty exists when the size of the potential impact of the condition and the likelihood of occurrence are such that appropriate disclosure of the condition is necessary to prevent the financial statements from being misleading. The auditors often issue a modified report by adding an *emphasis of matter* paragraph explaining their uncertainty about the company's ability to continue as a going concern; when the auditors determine that a material uncertainty exists, they could also issue a qualified opinion or an adverse opinion. Modified reports are discussed in more detail in the next chapter.

Outsiders view any mention of a company's going concern problem as a serious issue. Stock prices typically fall, and companies with going concern opinions often close or file for bankruptcy. Auditors understand the seriousness of this decision and mention a going concern problem only when they believe the financial statements would be materially misleading without it.

Use of a Management Representation Letter as Evidence

LO6

Understand the use of the representation letter in the audit

Management makes many representations to the auditors during an audit. For example, management replies to the auditors' questions about subsequent events or possible contingent liabilities. At the end of the audit, the information management gave the auditors is formalized in a management representation letter. Its purpose is to clarify all information provided to the auditors during the audit. The letter states that management has answered all of the auditors' questions and has told the auditors everything they need to know to issue the audit report. See an example of a standard representation letter for an audit report date of March 1, 2012, in Exhibit 12-5. The auditors can add additional items to the letter if the company has issues regarding which they would like management's assurance that they have given the auditors complete information.

Auditors are required to obtain a representation letter from the client before issuing the audit report. It should be dated the last day of fieldwork and list all representations (statements) management made to the auditors during the audit.

The auditors give a draft of this representation letter to the client and ask him or her to prepare the letter on company letterhead. Management reviews the details of the letter, so it is aware of the representations it has made to the auditors when the appropriate individuals sign the letter.

The representation letter is dated the last day of fieldwork. The audit evidence should not be considered complete if a representation letter is not obtained. The auditors should disclaim an opinion on the financial statements if they conclude that sufficient doubt exists about management's integrity so that its written representations are not reliable or if management does not sign the written representation letter.

Audit Documentation Requirements

LO7

Describe the review and documentation process for audit working papers

As auditors gather evidence to determine whether the financial statements are prepared in accordance with the applicable financial reporting framework, they document the evidence in the working papers. If they find misstatements in the financial statements, the auditors prepare adjusting entries to correct them. The evidence includes information about who documented the evidence, who reviewed the evidence, and the date the work was done.

The auditors' supervisor reviews their audit evidence and conclusions. The manager on the engagement reviews most of the working papers. The partner reviews the working papers related to all significant findings and issues. Each piece of audit evidence is reviewed at least once, and evidence is often reviewed three times. The audit firm must be very careful to determine that "sufficient, appropriate" evidence has been gathered, giving the auditors a reasonable basis for their opinion.

The partner in charge of the engagement signs the audit opinion with the name of the audit firm and is responsible for the audit process.[2] Before this occurs in public company audits, a concurring partner who has not previously been involved with the audit reviews the work papers to evaluate the decisions the audit team made during the audit process. Both partners evaluate the work papers to determine whether the evidence supports the opinion issued. Their decision will be judged against the standard of due care. Did auditors gather the evidence other auditors would have gathered and evaluate the evidence as other auditors would? Let's consider the documentation requirements found in the auditing standards for public and private company audits.

---

[2] In some countries using international accounting standards for reporting, the audit partner signs his name and the name of the audit firm on the audit report.

Representation Letter, BCS Company Exhibit 12-5

March 1, 2012

To Stuart and Cram, LLP

This representation letter is provided in connection with your audits of BCS Company for the year ended December 31, 2011, for the purpose of expressing an opinion as to whether the financial statements are presented fairly, in all material respects, in accordance with accounting principles generally accepted in the United States (U.S. GAAP).

We confirm that, [to the best of our knowledge and belief, having made such inquiries as we considered necessary for the purpose of appropriately informing ourselves as of March 1, 2012]:

Financial Statements

- We have fulfilled our responsibilities, as set out in the terms of the audit engagement dated August 9, 2011, for the preparation of the financial statements in accordance with U.S. GAAP; in particular, the financial statements are fairly presented in accordance therein.
- Significant assumptions used by us in making accounting estimates, including those measured at fair value, are reasonable.
- Related-party relationships and transactions have been appropriately accounted for and disclosed in accordance with the requirements of U.S. GAAP.
- All events subsequent to the date of the financial statements and for which U.S. GAAP requires adjustment or disclosure have been adjusted or disclosed.
- The effects of uncorrected misstatements are immaterial, both individually and in the aggregate, to the financial statements as a whole. A list of the uncorrected misstatements is attached to the representation letter.
- [Any other matters that the auditors could consider appropriate.]

Information Provided

- We have provided you with:
  —Access to all information of which we are aware that is relevant to the preparation and fair presentation of the financial statements such as records, documentation, and other matters;
  —Minutes of the meetings of stockholders, directors, and committees of directors, or summaries of actions of recent meetings for which minutes have not yet been prepared;
  —Additional information that you have requested from us for the purpose of the audit; and
  —Unrestricted access to persons within the entity from whom you determined it necessary to obtain audit evidence.
- All transactions have been recorded in the accounting records and are reflected in the financial statements.
- We have disclosed to you the results of our assessment of the risk that the financial statements could be materially misstated as a result of fraud.
- We have disclosed to you all information in relation to fraud or suspected fraud that we are aware of and that affects the entity and involves:
  —Management;
  —Employees who have significant roles in internal control; or
  —Others where the fraud could have a material effect on the financial statements.
- We have disclosed to you all information in relation to allegations of fraud, or suspected fraud, affecting the entity's financial statements communicated by employees, former employees, analysts, regulators, or others.
- We have disclosed to you all known instances of noncompliance or suspected noncompliance with laws and regulations whose effects should be considered when preparing financial statements.
- There have been no communications from regulatory agencies concerning noncompliance with or deficiencies in financial reporting practices.
- We have disclosed to you the identity of the entity's related parties and all the related-party relationships and transactions of which we are aware (AU 333).

[Any other matters that the auditors could consider necessary.]

[Signature of] Chief Executive Officer

[Signature of] Chief Financial Officer

Audit Documentation for Public and Private Companies   Exhibit 12-6

	Documentation	
	Public Companies	**Private Companies**
Definition	Written record of the basis for the auditors' opinion; can be in paper or electronic or other media form	Same
Reviewers	Members of the audit team as well as a successor auditor and internal and external inspection teams	Same
Information required	A clear understanding of its purpose, source, and the conclusions reached	Same
Reference to auditing standards	Compliance with specific auditing standards should be documented, including, who performed the work, the date it was performed, the person who reviewed it, and the date of the review as well as allow an experienced auditor to understand the nature, timing, and extent of the audit procedures	Same
Item identification	Those items examined during sampling procedures and copies of significant contracts or agreements reviewed	Same
Significant elements	Identification of significant findings and issues, the action taken to address them, and the conclusions reached regarding them	Documentation of identification and resolution
Engagement completion	All significant findings and issues	No requirement
Document retention	7 years from the date of the audit report	5 years
Time Allowed for assembly	45 days after the date of the auditors' report	60 days
Addition(s)	Allowed but withdrawals not allowed	Same
Identification of departures from generally accepted auditing standards	Not required	Justification required

Audit Documentation for Public and Private Companies

PCAOB Auditing Standard No. 3, *Audit Documentation,* and AU 339, *Audit Documentation,* specify documentation standards for the working papers for public and private companies, respectively. Except for a few paragraphs, the standards for public and private companies have similar documentation requirements. The major documentation requirements of the standards are discussed in the section that follows. Exhibit 12-6 summarizes the documentation requirement and highlights differences between the PCAOB and the ASB standards.

- *Audit documentation* is defined as the written record of the basis for the auditors' conclusions (the audit report). The documentation can be in the form of paper, electronic, or other media.
- Members of the audit team performing the work review the audit documentation, which could also be reviewed by others including a successor auditor who reviews a predecessor auditor's audit documentation, internal and external inspection teams, auditors new to an engagement who review the prior year's documentation, and supervisory personnel who review documentation prepared by audit assistants on an engagement.
- Audit documentation should be prepared in sufficient detail to provide a clear understanding of its purpose, its source, and its related conclusions. The documentation should contain a clear link to the significant findings or issues in the audit.
- Audit documentation should demonstrate that the auditors complied with the auditing standards, support their conclusion concerning every relevant financial statement assertion, and demonstrate that the accounting records (in which the evidence

is gathered) agreed with the financial statements (on which the audit report is issued). The audit documentation must contain sufficient information to allow an *experienced auditor* to understand the nature, timing, extent, and result of audit procedures performed and to determine who performed the work, the date it was performed, the person who reviewed the work, and the date of the review.

- Audit documentation of audit procedures that involve inspection of records, confirmations, and walk-throughs should identify the specific items examined. Documentation of auditing procedures related to the inspection of significant contracts or agreements should include abstracts or copies of them.

- The auditors must document significant findings or issues, the action taken to address them, and the basis for the conclusions reached related to them that include the selection of accounting principles, accounting for complex transactions, accounting estimates, results of auditing procedures that require significant modification of the planned audit procedures, audit adjustments, disagreements among audit team members, circumstances that caused difficulty in applying audit procedures, significant changes in the assessed level of audit risk, and any issue that could result in modification of the audit report.

- The auditors must document all significant findings and issues in an *engagement completion document* that should include all significant findings or issues identified during the review of interim financial information (**required only for public company audits**).

- The auditors must retain audit documentation for 7 years following the date of the audit report (**5 years for private companies**).

- The complete and final set of audit documentation should be assembled 45 days after the date of the audit report (**60 days for private companies**).

- The auditors can add to the audit documentation after the time when the documentation is to be complete but cannot withdraw documentation from it. Added documentation must include the name of the person who prepared it, the date it was added, and the reason for adding it to the completed working papers.

- If the auditors deviate from generally accepted auditing standards, they must document their justification for doing so (**required only for private company audits**).

Use of Audit Evidence to Determine Whether the Financial Statements are Materially Misstated

LO8

Understand how auditors use audit evidence to determine whether the financial statements are materially misstated

As they gather evidence during the audit process, auditors evaluate whether the evidence supports the finding that the account balance or class of transactions is prepared in accordance with the applicable financial reporting framework. If auditors find misstatements in the account balance or class of transactions, they propose audit adjustments to correct the financial statements. At the end of the audit, the financial statements are reviewed to determine whether they have been prepared in accordance with the applicable financial reporting framework **subject to** the proposed audit adjustment schedule.

At the end of the audit, the auditors review the proposed audit adjustment schedule to determine the adjustments' impact on the balance sheet and the income statement in regard to **materiality.** Before the auditors issue a clean opinion, the evidence they gathered must support the conclusion that the financial statements are not **materially** misstated. This means that if they knew about the information on the proposed audit adjustment schedule, outsiders would ignore the misstatements if they were recorded in the financial statements and would not change their decision about the company.

Sometimes the impact of the adjustments in total has a material effect on the financial statements. Then the auditors must decide which adjustments to record to reduce the level of misstatement below the materiality level. At other times, the effect of an individual adjustment is material for a particular account but is not for the statements in total. This happens when an increase in one account is offset by a decrease in another

Proposed Audit Adjustments, BCS, Inc. *December 31, 2011* Exhibit 12-7

1. Sales Returns and Allowances. 5,000
    Accounts Receivable   5,000

To correct sales revenue and accounts receivable for credit memos issued but not recorded at year-end because of sales allowances given. Entry found as a result of accounts receivable confirmations. Sample totaled $94,000 of the $144,000 account receivable balance.

    Sales Returns and Allowances. 1,660
        Accounts Receivable   1,660

To record projected misstatements in the financial statements based on the results of the accounts receivable confirmation process: ([$5,000/94,000] × 144,000 =) 7,660 estimated total error in the population; 7,660 − 5,000 = 1,660 projected misstatement in the population not sampled.

2. Accounts Receivable 4,000
    Sales Revenue   4,000
    Cost of Goods Sold 1,800
    Inventory   1,800

To record shipments made at year-end, FOB shipping point because of cutoff testing. The gross margin for the company is 55%.

3. Cost of Goods Sold 12,600
    Inventory   12,600

To adjust the book inventory to the physical count at year-end.

4. Bad Debt Expense 2,500
    Allowance for
    Uncollectible Accounts   2,500

To increase the allowance for doubtful accounts based on a review of the prior year allowances, the actual write-offs for the current year, the client's credit policy, and an analysis of current economic conditions.

5. Depreciation Expense 8,000
    Accumulated
    Depreciation—Buildings   6,000
    Accumulated
    Depreciation—Equipment.   2,000

To record half a year's depreciation expense on an office building purchased during the year. The company uses the half-year-convention for recording depreciation.

6. General Expense 12,000
    Administrative Expense 8,000
    Accounts Payable   20,000

To record expenses based on accounts payable cutoff work. The $12,000 accrual represents supplies and utilities for bills due at the end of year but not paid. The $8,000 represents the final payment made after year-end to the Indonesian government to facilitate the construction of a factory in Jakarta, Indonesia.

7. Salaries Expense. 9,400
    Salaries Payable.   9,400

To record salaries expense for salaries due at year-end but not paid.

8. Interest Expense. 2,800
    Interest Payable   2,800

To records interest expense on long-term debt.

account, so the total effect is immaterial. Refer to Exhibit 12-7 and Exhibit 12-8 for examples of proposed audit adjustments and their impact on the financial statements. Let's consider the decisions made by the auditor based on this example.

Based on the audit evidence gathered, net income is overstated by $59,760 (revenue is overstated by $2,660, cost of goods sold is understated by $14,400, general expense is understated by $34,700, and administrative expenses is understated by $8,000). Total

Trial Balance, BCS, Inc.   *December 31, 2011*   Exhibit 12-8

Account	Unadjusted Trial Balance	Proposed Audit Adjustments	Impact on Balance Sheet	Impact on Income Statement	Adjusted Trial Balance
Cash	100,000 DR				100,000 DR
		5,000 CR (1)			
		1,660 CR (1)			
Accounts Receivable	144,000 DR	4,000 DR (2)	2,660 CR		141,340 DR
Allow for Doubtful Accounts	4,000 CR	2,500 CR (4)	2,500 CR		6,500 CR
		1,800 CR (2)			
Inventory	155,000 DR	12,600 CR (3)	14,400 CR		140,600 DR
Prepaid Expenses	59,000 DR				59,000 DR
Land	206,000 DR				206,000 DR
Building	219,000 DR				219,000 DR
Equipment	487,000 DR				487,000 DR
Accumulated Depreciation—Building	94,000 CR	6,000 CR (5)	6,000 CR		100,000 CR
Accumulated Depreciation—Equipment	184,000 CR	2,000 CR (5)	2,000 CR		186,000 CR
Accounts Payable	186,000 CR	20,000 CR (6)	20,000 CR		206,000 CR
Interest Payable		2,800 CR (8)	2,800 CR		2,800 CR
Salaries Payable		9,400 CR (7)	9,400 CR		9,400 CR
Notes Payable	177,000 CR				177,000 CR
Long-Term Debt	28,000 CR				28,000 CR
Common Stock	362,000 CR				362,000 CR
Retained Earnings	335,000 CR		59,760 DR		275,240 CR
Sales Revenue	1,575,000 CR	4,000 CR (2)		4,000 CR	1,579,000 CR
		5,000 DR (1)			
Sales Returns & Allowances	75,000 DR	1,660 DR (1)		6,660 DR	81,660 DR
		1,800 DR (2)			
Cost of Goods Sold	873,000 DR	12,600 DR (3)		14,400 DR	887,400 DR
Selling Expense	92,000 DR				92,000 DR
General Expense	85,000 DR	2,500 DR (4)			
		8,000 DR (5)			
		12,000 DR (6)			
		9,400 DR (7)			
		2,800 DR (8)		34,700 DR	119,700 DR
Administrative Expense	242,000 DR	8,000 DR (6)		8,000 DR	250,000 DR
Total DR	2,737,000 DR	67,760 DR			2,804,760 DR
Total CR	2,737,000 CR	67,760 CR			2,804,760 CR
Net Income	208,000			(59,760)	148,240
Total assets	1,088,000		27,560		1,060,440
Total liabilities & owners equity	1,088,000		(32,200) 59,760		1,060,440

Note: The numbers in parenthesis refer to the journal entries in Ex. 12–7

assets are overstated by $27,560. Total liabilities are understated by $32,200, and owners' equity is overstated by $59,760, the amount of the net income overstatement.

Are these misstatements material? According to the auditing standards, they are if this information would change an outside person's judgment. So, auditors ask whether knowing the following would have caused an outsider to change her or his investment or financing decision: net income was $148,240 rather than $208,000, assets were overstated by $27,560 (they were $1,060,440 rather than 1,088,000), and liabilities were understated by $32,200 (liabilities were $432,200 rather than $391,000). The auditors answer these questions by using quantitative materiality and evaluating the circumstances associated with the misstatement.

Let's say that materiality is $50,000. Then the misstatements are material, and the financial statements are materially misstated. The error in net income and owners' equity totals more than $50,000. So, the auditors should ask the client to reduce the misstatement in the financial statements to less than $50,000. This means that expenses (either cost of goods sold, general expense, or administrative expense) must be increased to decrease the error in net income and owners' equity to less than $50,000.

Once the auditors evaluate the quantitative materiality of the adjustments, they must determine whether any of the *circumstances* associated with the misstatements make them material. Auditing standards identify several circumstances that could cause quantitatively immaterial misstatements to be judged material:

- A misstatement that changes a loss into income
- The effect of the misstatement on compliance with loan covenants, contractual agreements, and regulatory provisions
- The existence of statutory or regulatory reporting requirements that could impact materiality levels
- A misstatement that in effect increases management's compensation
- A misstatement that involves fraud, illegal acts, violations of contracts, and conflicts of interest
- The effect of misclassifying income between operating and nonoperating income or recurring and nonrecurring items (AU 312).

Audit adjustment (6) in Exhibit 12-7 could be in the category of a material misstatement. A bribery payment of an *immaterial* amount could become a *material* transaction if a reasonable probability that the transaction could lead to a contingent liability or a loss of revenue exists. Bribery is illegal in the United States, and proving its occurrence can lead to a fine for the company.

When the final adjustments are recorded in the financial statements, auditing standards also require the auditors to use analytical procedures to determine whether the financial statements *as adjusted* appear reasonable. The standards require the use of analytical procedures (ratio calculations, comparing current year to prior year numbers) during the audit planning stage and the completion stage. During the planning stage, analytical procedures are selected to guide the evidence gathering. At the end of the audit, these procedures are used to determine whether the changes in the ratios or in the account balances between the current year and the prior year are reasonable based on the evidence gathered during the audit.

Evaluation of the Consistency of Financial Statements

LO9

Describe how the auditors evaluate the consistency of financial statements audits

Auditors of both private and public companies are required to evaluate the consistency of the financial statements. Auditing Standard No. 6 issued by the Public Company Accounting Oversight Board requires this of auditors of public companies and AU 333, *Consistency of Financial Statements,* requires it of auditors of private companies. What does "consistency of financial statements" mean?

Auditors issue an audit report that typically covers 2 years for the balance sheet and 3 years for the income statement, statement of changes in owners' equity, and the statement of cash flows. Standards for both public and private companies require the auditors to evaluate whether the financial statements for the years covered by the opinion have been prepared consistently in accordance with the applicable financial reporting framework.

Two factors could lead to inconsistent financial statements: (1) a change in accounting principle and (2) an adjustment to correct a misstatement in previously issued financial statements. If either of these events has occurred in the company under audit, the auditors should add an explanatory paragraph to the audit report, to explain the inconsistency in the financial statements. The explanatory paragraph is an *emphasis of matter* paragraph. The following is an emphasis of matter paragraph for a change in accounting principle resulting from the adoption of a new accounting pronouncement in 2008:

As discussed in Note X to the financial statements, in 2008, the entity adopted new accounting guidance FASB No. 157, *Fair Value Measurements.* Our opinion is not qualified with respect to this matter.

Notice that the auditors specifically comment in the audit opinion on the fact that the adoption of the new accounting standard did not result in a qualified opinion. The purpose of this paragraph is to call readers' attention to the fact that the financial statements presented in this annual report are not consistent from year to year because they were prepared using different accounting standards. In years when mandatory accounting standards go into effect, most annual reports contain an explanatory paragraph such as this.

Review of Footnotes and Other Financial Statement–Associated Information

LO10

Explain how auditors review footnotes and other information associated with the financial statements

Companies that issue an annual report including the financial statements and the footnotes to them often include additional information in it.

The auditors' responsibilities differ depending on the additional material in an annual report of which there are two categories: (1) that *required* by an accounting standard setter, which is audited, and (2) that *chosen* by the company, which is not audited, but reviewed by the auditors. Examples of information that the company chooses to include are (1) a report by management on operations, (2) financial summaries or highlights, (3) employment data, (4) planned capital expenditures, (5) financial ratios, (6) names of officers and directors, or (7) selected quarterly data. Financial summaries or highlights are often found in the Management's Discussion and Analysis (MD&A) section.

The General Mills Annual Report for 2007 consisted of the following with the number of pages in parentheses: product information with pictures, graphs, and tables to highlight company interests (24)[3]; Management's Discussion and Analysis of Financial Condition and Results of Operations (24); reports of management (3) and of the auditors (3), consolidated financial statements (5); and footnotes (28). Of this 87-page annual report, only 36 pages were audited; the auditors only reviewed the remaining 51 pages. All footnotes except footnote 18 reporting quarterly data for 2007 and 2006 were audited.

The following is a standard list of the footnotes to the consolidated financial statements found in most annual reports:

1. Basis of presentation and reclassifications
2. Summary of significant accounting policies
3. Acquisitions and divestitures
4. Restructuring, impairment, and other exit costs
5. Investments in joint ventures
6. Goodwill and other intangible assets
7. Financial instruments and risk management activities

---

[3] http://media.corporate-ir.net/media_files/irol/74/74271/GIS_AR07.pdf

8. Debt
9. Minority interests
10. Stockholders' equity
11. Stock plans
12. Earnings per share
13. Retirement and postemployment benefits
14. Income taxes
15. Leases and other commitments
16. Business segment and geographic information
17. Supplemental information
18. Quarterly data (unaudited)

In the past, users of the financial statements assumed that companies disclosed only what was required; they understood that gathering and reporting any type of information costs time and money, so companies disclosed only what was required, as did their competitors. Today the amount of disclosure made by businesses varies to a certain extent. Some companies disclose more than they are required because they want to set themselves apart from the criticism that financial statements do not provide outsiders sufficient company information. Sometimes annual reports exceed 150 pages as companies try to convince outsiders that the reports give them all vital information.

The *auditors' responsibility for the unaudited information* is to read the information and determine whether it is **consistent** with the information reported in the financial statements. This is what we mean when we say that auditors "review" as opposed to "audit" information. If it is not consistent, the auditors should ask the company to revise it.

Financial statements and footnotes report on past activity, but the unaudited material in an annual report often includes speculation about the company's future performance. In the MD&A section, which is one place in the annual report that includes speculative information, management reflects on past performance and suggests how well the company could do in the future. The auditors should read the speculation about future performance in the report and determine whether it is consistent with information in the financial statements. Management is probably more optimistic about the company than an outsider would be, so the auditors should review the speculatory comments to determine whether they are reasonable. Outsiders might not recognize the difference between the information content of the financial statements and the speculation about future performance, so the auditors' job is to determine whether the speculation is consistent with the audited financial statements.

End of Field Work

LO11

Describe the end of fieldwork

The last day of fieldwork on which the audit report is signed and the company releases its earnings to the public is important. The auditors' responsibility for evaluating the financial statements is complete unless they learn of a subsequent event.

The paperwork associated with an audit is important documentation for the auditors. The audit files belong to the auditors and should be maintained for at least 7 years (5 years for private companies). It is important that the documents show exactly what evidence was gathered, how the evidence was interpreted, and a resolution to all the misstatements found during the audit (either in terms of recording the adjustments or passing the adjustment as immaterial.) It is not sufficient for the auditors to have performed all required audit procedures, but it is necessary that documentation of the performance also be in the files.

The audit report is the only document that must be issued at the end of an audit. Auditors who sign a contract to do an audit agree to issue an opinion at the end of the process. They often issue a management letter as a service to the client at the close of the engagement although it is not required. A management letter includes suggestions to improve the effectiveness or efficiency of the client's operations and the internal control procedures. Some clients view the management letter as a service; others view it as a waste of time because the proposed efficiencies are too costly to implement.

Chapter Takeaways

The completion of the audit is important for the auditors. They have gathered evidence related to the company's subsequent events, related parties, compliance with laws and regulations, going concern assumption, and contingent liabilities. The auditors must review the proposed audit adjustment schedule, the footnote disclosure, and other information, obtain the signed management representation letter, and determine that the audit opinion they issue is consistent with the evidence gathered.

This chapter presented these important facts:

- Audit procedures for contingent liabilities
- The importance of the attorney's letter in evaluating contingent liabilities
- Audit procedures for compliance with laws and regulations and for evaluating the going concern assumption
- Audit procedures for subsequent events and auditors' continuing responsibility for the reliability of the financial statements
- The audit review process for working papers
- The disposition of proposed audit adjustments
- The importance of the management representation letter
- The review process for footnotes and other information in the annual report
- The importance of the end of fieldwork and the use of the management letter in the audit process

Be sure you understand these concepts before you go to the next chapter.

Review Questions

LO11	1. Describe the activities involved in completing the audit.
LO1	2. What are contingent liabilities? What audit procedures are used to gather evidence related to them?
LO2	3. Describe the two types of subsequent events. How is each type accounted for in the financial statements? Provide an example of each type of subsequent event.
LO3	4. Explain the audit procedures for related parties. Who are an audit client's related parties?
LO4	5. How do the auditors consider the laws and regulations related to an audit client during the audit process?
LO5	6. What is the going concern assumption? What is the auditors' responsibility related to it?
LO6	7. What is the representation letter? How is it used during the audit?
LO7	8. What are the documentation requirements for an audit? How are work papers reviewed at the end of the audit?
LO8	9. Describe the requirements of the auditing standards for determining whether the financial statements are materially misstated.
LO10	10. Describe the auditors' responsibility for reviewing the footnotes and other material found in the annual report.
LO11	11. How do the auditors know when the audit is over?

Multiple Choice Questions from CPA Examinations

LO1 12. A lawyer's response to an auditor's inquiry concerning litigation, claims, and assessments may be limited to matters that are considered individually or collectively material to the client's financial statements. Which parties should reach an understanding on the limits of materiality for this purpose?

  a. The auditor and the client's managements.
  b. The client's audit committee and the lawyer.
  c. The client's management and the lawyer.
  d. The lawyer and the auditor.

LO1 13. The primary reason an auditor requests letters of inquiry be sent to a client's attorney is to provide the auditor with

  a. The probable outcome of asserted claims and pending or threatened litigation.
  b. Corroboration of the information furnished by management about litigation, claims, and assessments.
  c. The attorney's opinions of the client's historical experiences in recent similar litigation.
  d. A description and evaluation of litigation, claims, and assessments that existed at the balance sheet date.

LO2 14. Which of the following procedures should an auditor ordinarily perform regarding subsequent events?

  a. Compare the latest available interim financial statements with the financial statements being audited.
  b. Send second requests to the client's customers who failed to respond to initial accounts receivable confirmation requests.
  c. Communicate material weaknesses in internal control to the client's audit committee.
  d. Review the cutoff bank statements for several months after the year-end.

LO2 15. Which of the following procedures would an auditor most likely perform to obtain evidence about the occurrence of subsequent events?

  a. Confirming a sample of material accounts receivable established after year-end.
  b. Comparing the financial statements being reported on with those of the prior period.
  c. Investigating personnel changes in the accounting department occurring after year-end.
  d. Inquiring as to whether any unusually adjustments were made after year-end.

LO2 16. After the date of the audit report, an auditor has no obligation to make continuing inquiries or perform other procedures concerning the audited financial statements, unless

  a. Information that existed at the report date and may affect the report comes to the auditor's attention.
  b. Management of the entity requests the auditor to reissue the auditor's report in a document submitted to a third party that contains information in addition to the basic financial statements.
  c. Information about an event that occurred after the end of field work comes to the auditor's attention.
  d. Final determinations or resolutions are made of contingencies that had been disclosed in the financial statements.

LO2 17. Which of the following events occurring after the issuance of the financial statements most likely would cause the auditor to make further inquiries about previously issued financial statements?

  a. An uninsured natural disaster occurs that may affect the entity's ability to continue as a going concern.
  b. A contingency is resolved that had been disclosed in the audited financial statements.

c. New information is discovered concerning undisclosed lease transactions of the audited period.

d. A subsidiary is sold that accounts for 25% of the entity's consolidated net income.

LO6 18. A purpose of a management representation letter is to reduce

a. Audit risk to an aggregate level of misstatement that could be considered material.

b. An auditor's responsibility to detect material misstatement that could be considered material.

c. The possibility of a misunderstanding concerning management's responsibility for the financial statements.

d. The scope of an auditor's procedures concerning related party transactions and subsequent events.

LO6 19. Which of the following matters would an auditor most likely include in a management representation letter?

a. Communications with the audit committee concerning weaknesses in internal control.

b. The completeness and availability of minutes of shareholders' and directors' meetings.

c. Plans to acquire or merge with other entities in the subsequent year.

d. Management's acknowledgement of its responsibility to report but not detect employee fraud.

LO6 20. For which of the following matters should an auditor obtain written management representations?

a. Management's cost-benefit justifications for not correcting internal control weaknesses.

b. Management's knowledge of future plans that may affect the price of the entity's stock.

c. Management's compliance with contractual agreements that may affect the financial statements.

d. Management's acknowledgement of its responsibility for employees' violations of laws.

LO6 21. To which of the following matters would materiality limits not apply in obtaining written management representations?

a. The availability of minutes of shareholders' and directors' meetings.

b. Losses from purchase commitments at prices in excess of market value.

c. The disclosure of compensating balance arrangements involving related parties.

d. Reductions of obsolete inventory to net realizable value.

Discussion Questions and Research Problems

LO2 22. **Subsequent events.** The following events occurred between the end of the year, December 31, 2012, and the date of the audit report, March 1, 2013. Assume that the impact of each of these events on the financial statements is material.

- A warehouse owned by the company you are auditing burned down on February 15, 2013. The warehouse contained 20% of its inventory.

- You learned that a new customer signed an agreement to purchase a substantial amount of inventory from your audit client in the future.

- An accounts receivable customer filed for bankruptcy on February 1, 2013. The account was previously considered to be collectible.

- The company signed an agreement to purchase another company on February 28, 2013.

- Gasoline is a major raw material purchased by your audit client. You learn that its price is expected to increase dramatically in the future.

a. Determine whether the events are type I or type II subsequent events.

b. Describe the appropriate accounting treatment for these events. Should they be recorded in the financial statements or disclosed in the footnotes?

c. What audit evidence would you gather to determine the impact of the events?

d. Does your responsibility as the auditor change if the events are immaterial? Explain your answer.

LO2   23. **Subsequent events after issuance of audit report.** Assume that the audit report for your client has been signed and distributed to outsiders. What is your responsibility related to new information that comes to your attention? Are you required to search for new information all year? Provide an example of a situation in which an auditor would have to disclose information to outsiders and one in which the auditor would have no responsibility to disclose information to outsiders.

LO1   24. **Audit of contingent liabilities.** During the audit of contingent liabilities, your audit client provides the following information regarding potential liabilities:

- Your client has agreed to guarantee a loan in the amount of $5,000,000 for a related party and will be liable to repay the loan if the related party cannot do so.

- You have filed a lawsuit against a competitor for unfair pricing policies. You expect to win the lawsuit and could get a settlement for $20,000,000.

- You have received a letter from the IRS indicating that it has audited the corporate tax returns of the company for 2010 and 2011. The IRS has indicated that an additional $10,000,000 in taxes and penalties is due. You plan to contest the audit findings.

- A client's employee has filed a lawsuit against the company alleging age discrimination. The client's attorney thinks it could lose the lawsuit based on the employee's claims.

a. How will you gather evidence to collaborate the information provided by the client regarding these potential liabilities?

b. Which of these items will be recorded in the financial statements?

c. Which of these items will be disclosed in the financial statements?

d. Are any of the items not relevant to the financial statements? Explain your answer.

LO1   25. **Contingent liabilities and subsequent event documentation.** Before you sign off on the audit, you need to determine that sufficient audit work has been done to determine whether contingent liabilities and subsequent events have been recorded in accordance with the applicable financial reporting framework at year-end.

a. Describe the audit evidence the partner would expect to find in the work papers to determine whether this information has been correctly recorded and disclosed in the financial statements.

b. What alternatives are available to the partner if the audit evidence indicates that disclosure is inadequate for these items?

LO10   26. **Footnote disclosure.** Your audit client believes that disclosing everything is the safest action to take today. Management believes that if the company tells outsiders everything it is required to tell them as well as additional information, they will not complain that they did not have sufficient information to make decisions about the company. Your client knows that there is a cost to gathering the information to disclose, but the company wants to distinguish itself from its competitors by offering very thorough disclosures. The client asks your advice about this approach.

a. What would you tell the client? What are the positive and negative outcomes from this approach?

b. Is more information always good? Would you recommend that the client follow this approach to financial statement disclosure?

LO6   27. **Client representation letter.** Consider the audit procedure to obtain a representation letter from the client at the end of the audit. The staff accountant on the engagement questions the necessity for this procedure, saying, "Isn't this procedure silly? I give the client a copy of the representation letter and ask them to type it on the company's letterhead. What good is this letter if I tell the client what to say? Couldn't they just say that they did what I told them to do and didn't really understand what they were signing?"

a. How would you answer this question?

b. How does the representation letter provide important audit evidence to the auditors? Why is it a required audit procedure?

LO10   28. **Footnote disclosure.** Your audit client will disclose information only that you force it to disclose.

a. What is the basic requirement for disclosure in an annual report?

b. The client believes that any events that do not affect the financial statements can be ignored in the footnotes. Is this correct? Explain your answer.

c. The client doesn't understand why you would ask them to disclose items that are uncertain. The company knows that you won't allow them to speculate in their financial statements, so they don't understand the reason for disclosing items based on speculation before the event actually occurs. Can you answer the client's question?

Real-World Auditing Problems

LO2   29. **IBM**

In its 2005 annual report, IBM disclosed the following subsequent events:

- On February 15, 2006, the company completed the acquisition of Micromuse for approximately $875 million. Micromuse is a publicly traded software company that provides network management software. The acquisition will be integrated into the company's software segment.

- On January 23, 2006, the company completed the sale of one of its real estate holdings in the United States for approximately $18 million. The company had previously recorded an impairment change because it had classified this property in the fourth quarter of 2005 as an asset held for sale for approximately $103 million and had recorded this asset in Other Income and as an expense in the consolidated statement of earnings.

- On January 31, 2006, the company announced that the board of directors had approved a quarterly dividend of $0.20 per common share payable March 10, 2006, to shareholders of record on February 10, 2006.

a. Are these type I or type II subsequent events? Explain your answer. The date of the audit report was February 28, 2006. IBM's year-end was December 31, 2005.

b. Why were these events disclosed in IBM's annual report?

c. How did the auditors gather evidence to verify the accuracy of these events?

LO2   30. **ThyssenKrupp**

ThyssenKrupp issued the following footnote in the interim financial statements for the first quarter ending December 31, 2007:

On the basis of the authorization granted by the Annual Stockholders' Meeting on January 18, 2008, the Executive Board of ThyssenKrupp AG resolved on January 31, 2008 to purchase up to around 15.8 million treasury shares before the authorization expires on July 17, 2009. This represents around 3% of the capital stock.

a. Is this a type I or type II subsequent event? Explain your answer.

b. Were the financial statements changed to reflect this decision?

c. Why was this information disclosed? Why would outsiders be concerned about the purchase of treasury stock?

LO1 31. **ThyssenKrupp**

ThyssenKrupp, in interim financial statements for the first quarter ending December 31, 2007 (a company with a year-end of September 30), disclosed a possible contingent liability related to payments received from the Italian government related to a special price for electricity purchase by the company's Italian division. The European Union has ruled the payments to be inadmissible and has asked Italy to recover the money paid to ThyssenKrupp under this arrangement. The company has filed a lawsuit regarding this decision, but it has not been resolved yet. According to the footnote, "If the outcome of the legal case is unfavorable, a material effect on the consolidated financial statements of ThyssenKrupp cannot be ruled out."

a. How would the auditors determine whether this contingent liability should be disclosed or recognized in the financial statements?

b. Because the contingent liability is disclosed, what must be true about it?

LO2 32. **TUI AG**

TUI AG issued the following subsequent event footnote in its 2006 annual report. Its auditors, PricewaterhouseCoopers, signed the report on March 5, 2007.

The integration of CP Ships into Hapag-Lloyd changed the primary economic environment of the companies operating in the shipping division to such an extent that the functional currency was changed from the euro to the U.S. dollar. The assessment of the functional currency was based on freight rates, cash inflow, and cost structures. As of January 1, 2007, the companies operating in the container shipping division will therefore prepare their financial statements in U.S. dollars.

a. What type of subsequent event is reported in this footnote? Explain your answer.

b. Why would outsiders be interested in the information provided by the footnote disclosure?

Internet Assignment

LO1, LO2 33. Select a company and search for contingent liabilities, commitments, and subsequent events in the annual reports.

a. Describe the nature of the contingent liabilities or commitments that you find. Are they disclosed or recorded in the financial statements?

b. Describe the subsequent event in the annual report. Is it type I or type II? How has it been handled in the financial statements?

Chapter

13

Audit Reports

Learning Objectives

After studying this chapter, you should be able to:

1. Explain the auditing standards for reporting.
2. Describe the process of forming an opinion and reporting on financial statements.
3. Explain when an *emphasis of matter* or *other matter* paragraph is and why they might be added to an unqualified audit report.
4. Describe modifications to the opinion in the independent auditors' report when (a) a qualified opinion, (b) a disclaimer of opinion, or (c) an adverse opinion is appropriate.
5. Identify auditors' reporting responsibilities and how they affect audit reports.
6. Describe auditors' responsibilities for reporting on financial statements prepared in accordance with a financial reporting framework generally accepted in another country.
7. Explain what auditor's report on internal control over financial reporting is.
8. Describe situations in which auditors modify the report on internal control over financial reporting.

Auditing standards relevant to this topic

For private companies

- **FASB Statement of Financial Accounting Concepts No. 5,** Recognition and Measurements in Financial Statements of Business Enterprises
- **AU 317,** Consideration of Laws and Regulations in an Audit of Financial Statements
- **AU 341,** The Auditor's Consideration of an Entity's Ability to Continue as a Going Concern
- **AU 380,** The Auditor's Communication With Those Charged With Governance
- **AU 411,** The Meaning of Present Fairly in Conformity with Generally Accepted Accounting Principles
- **AU 420,** Consistency of Financial Statements
- **AU 504,** Association with Financial Statement
- **AU 508,** Reports on Audited Financial Statements
- **AU 534,** Reporting on Financial Statements Prepared in Accordance with a Financial Reporting Framework Generally Accepted in Another Country
- **AU 543,** Audits of Group Financial Statements (Including the Work of Component Auditors)
- **AU 550,** Other Information in Documents Containing Audited Financial Statements
- **AU 551,** Supplementary Information in Relation to the Financial Statements as a Whole
- **AU 558,** Required Supplementary Information
- **AU 722,** Interim Financial Information

- **Preface to Codification of Statements on Auditing Standards,** Principles Governing an Audit Conducted in Accordance with Generally Accepted Auditing Standards

For public companies

- **FASB Statement of Financial Accounting Concepts No. 5,** Recognition and Measurements in Financial Statements of Business Enterprises
- **AU 317,** Illegal Acts by Clients (Interim standard)
- **AU 341,** The Auditor's Consideration of an Entity's Ability to Continue as a Going Concern (Interim standard)
- **AU 380,** Communication with Audit Committees (Interim standard)
- **AU 411,** The Meaning of Present Fairly in Conformity with Generally Accepted Accounting Principles (Interim standard)
- **AU 504,** Association with Financial Statement (Interim standard)
- **AU 508,** Reports on Audited Financial Statements (Interim standard)
- **AU 534,** Reporting on Financial Statements Prepared for Use in Other Countries (Interim standard)
- **AU 543,** Part of Audit Performed by Other Independent Auditors (Interim standard)
- **AU 550,** Other Information in Documents Containing Audited Financial Statements (Interim standard)
- **AU 551,** Reporting on Information Accompanying the Basic Financial Statements in Auditor-Submitted Documents (Interim standard)
- **AU 558,** Required Supplementary Information (Interim standard)
- **AU 722,** Interim Financial Information (Interim standard)
- **PCAOB Auditing Standard 1,** Reference in Auditors' Reports to the Standards of the Public Company Accounting Oversight Board
- **PCAOB Auditing Standard 4,** Reporting on Whether a Previously Reported Material Weakness Continues to Exist
- **PCAOB Auditing Standard 5,** An Audit of Internal Control over Financial Reporting that is Integrated with An Audit of Financial Statements
- **PCAOB Auditing Standard 6,** Evaluating Consistency of Financial Statements
- **PCAOB Auditing Standard 14,** Evaluating Audit Results

International standards

- **ISA 230,** Audit Documentation
- **ISA 250,** Consideration of Laws and Regulations in an Audit of Financial Statements
- **ISA 260,** Communication of Audit Matters with Those Charged with Governance
- **ISA 700,** The Independent Auditor's Report on a Complete Set of General Purpose Financial Statements
- **ISA 701,** Modifications to the Independent Auditor's Report
- **ISA 710,** Comparatives
- **ISA 720,** Other Information in Documents Containing Audited Financial Statements

Chapter Overview

This chapter describes the final stage of the audit: the issuing of the audit report. During this important time, auditors review the evidence collected and, *based on the evidence,* determine the audit opinion to issue. The vast majority of audit reports are clean, unmodified opinions. Even so, the process used by auditors to reach the decision to issue a clean opinion is important and complicated. Because they can issue a qualified opinion, a disclaimer of opinion, or an adverse opinion, auditors have leverage with the client to ensure that the financial statements contain no material misstatements. Clients want a clean opinion. Outsiders, including stockholders and lenders, react negatively to

The Audit Process   Exhibit 13-1

	Discussed in this Section
Steps in the Audit Process	
Planning Phase	
Consider the Preconditions for an Audit and Accept or Reject the Audit Engagement	
Understand the Entity and Its Environment, Determine Materiality, and Assess the Risks of Material Misstatements	
Develop an Audit Strategy and an Audit Plan to Respond to the Assessed Risks	
Testing Phase	
Test Internal Controls? Yes No	
Perform Tests of Controls if "Yes"	
Perform Substantive Tests of Transactions	
Perform Substantive Tests of Balances	
Assess the Likelihood of Material Misstatement	
Decision Phase	
Review the Presentation and Disclosure Assertions	
Evaluate the Evidence to Determine Whether the Financial Statements Are Prepared in Accordance with the Applicable Financial Reporting Framework	
Issue Audit Report	
Communicate with the Audit Committee	

a qualified opinion, disclaimer of opinion, and adverse opinion. It is in everyone's interest that the client correct material misstatements in the financial statements so the auditors can consider them to be prepared in accordance with the applicable financial reporting framework. This chapter discusses procedures that are part of the decision process of the audit. See Exhibit 13-1 for a description of the audit process.

This chapter discusses the various audit reports that auditors could issue and the situations in which each type of report would be appropriate. Auditing standards prescribe the audit report's specific wording, but auditors determine the particular report to be issued based on the evidence they gathered during the audit. When hiring auditors, the client contracts for an audit opinion to be issued but cannot specify the particular type of audit opinion that will be issued. The evidence and the professional judgment of the auditors determine the type.

The SEC requires audited financial statements for public companies to be filed with it 60 days after year-end. The audited financial statements for public companies in the U.S. include two reports. The first one states whether the financial statements have been prepared in accordance with the applicable financial reporting framework. If they have been prepared in this way, the financial statements receive a standard unmodified opinion. If the financial statements are materially misstated, they will receive a qualified opinion, disclaimer of opinion, or adverse opinion. The second report evaluates the effectiveness of internal control over the financial reporting process. This report can be a clean opinion, an adverse opinion, or a disclaimer of opinion.

Auditing Standards for Reporting

LO1

Explain the auditing standards for reporting

The auditing standards for reporting include (1) *Forming an Opinion and Reporting on Financial Statements,* (2) *Modifications to the Opinion in the Independent Auditor's Report,* and (3) *Emphasis of Matter Paragraphs and Other Matter Paragraphs in the Independent Auditor's Report.* The reporting standards require auditors to express in the form of a written report an opinion on the financial statements in accordance with their findings or to state that an opinion cannot be expressed. The opinion should state whether the financial statements are prepared, in all material respects, in accordance with the applicable financial reporting framework (the accounting standards used by the company). The reporting standards apply to audits of public and private companies, although the specific wording of the audit report for public and private companies could vary. Each of these standards is discussed in more detail in the following sections.

Formation of an Opinion and Reporting on Financial Statements

LO2

Describe the process of forming an opinion and reporting on financial statements

At the end of the audit, auditors form an opinion about whether the financial statements as a whole are prepared, in all material respects, in accordance with the applicable financial reporting framework. To form this opinion, auditors must conclude as to whether they have obtained *reasonable assurance* about whether the financial statements are *free from material misstatements,* whether because of error or fraud. Auditors must evaluate whether the financial statements meet the requirements of the applicable financial reporting framework in the following ways:

- Adequately disclose the significant accounting policies used
- Use accounting policies consistent with the applicable financial reporting framework
- Include reasonable accounting estimates made by management
- Present information that is relevant, reliable, comparable, and understandable
- Provide adequate disclosures
- Use appropriate terminology

Auditors must also consider:

- The overall presentation, structure, and content of the financial statements
- Whether the financial statements, including the footnotes, represent the underlying transactions in a manner that achieves fair presentation

Auditors should express an unmodified opinion when they conclude that the financial statements are prepared, in all material respects, in accordance with the applicable financial reporting framework. Auditors should modify their opinion if they conclude that (1) based on the evidence obtained, the financial statements are not free from material misstatement or (2) they are unable to obtain sufficient appropriate evidence to conclude that they are free from material misstatement.

An unmodified audit report (a clean opinion) is the most common audit opinion issued by auditors. The standard unmodified audit opinion contains four sections: an introduction, a description of management's responsibilities, a description of auditors' responsibilities, and an opinion paragraph. Refer to Exhibit 13-2 for an example of an unmodified audit report for a nonpublic company or a company not subject to the reporting requirements of PCAOB Standard No. 5 using U.S. accounting standards. Exhibit 13-3 is an example of an unmodified report for a company using international accounting standards. After years ending December 15, 2012, the audit report format will change, so some examples of audit reports for actual companies in this chapter will have slightly different wording. The audit report for a public company in the U.S. would be modified in the following fashion: (1) its title is to be Report of Independent Registered Public Accounting Firm; (2) the auditing standards referred to in the scope paragraph are to be the standards of the Public Company Accounting Oversight Board (United States); and (3) an *emphasis of matter* paragraph is to be added explaining the auditors' opinion on internal control over the financial reporting process.

The audit opinion is addressed to the board of directors and the shareholders, not to management. The board of directors hires the auditors, and the audit report is issued to them. In the title of the report, the auditors identify themselves as being independent of the company being audited (Independent Auditor's Report).

The first section of the report titled the Report on the Financial Statements is not necessary when the second subtitle Report on Other Auditing Requirements is not applicable. The second section describes *management's responsibilities.* Management is responsible for the preparation and fair presentation of the financial statements in

Independent Auditor's Report for an Unmodified Opinion

Exhibit 13-2

INDEPENDENT AUDITOR'S REPORT

To the Board of Directors and Shareholders of BCS Company

Report on the Financial Statements

We have audited the accompanying consolidated balance sheets of BCS Company and its subsidiaries as of December 31, 20X1 and 20X0, and the related consolidated statements of income, retained earnings, and cash flows for the years then ended.

Management's Responsibility for the Financial Statements   Management is responsible for the preparation and fair presentation of these consolidated financial statements in accordance with accounting principles generally accepted in the United States of America; this includes the design, implementation, and maintenance of internal control relevant to the preparation and fair presentation of consolidated financial statements that are free from material misstatement, whether due to fraud or error.

Auditor's Responsibility   Our responsibility is to express an opinion on these consolidated financial statements based on our audits. We conducted our audits in accordance with auditing standards generally accepted in the United States of America. Those standards require that we plan and perform the audit to obtain reasonable assurance about whether the consolidated financial statements are free of material misstatement.

An audit involves performing procedures to obtain audit evidence about the amounts and disclosures in the consolidated financial statements. The procedures selected depend on the auditor's judgment, including the assessment of the risks of material misstatement of the consolidated financial statements, whether due to fraud or error. In making those risk assessments, the auditor consider internal control relevant to the entity's preparation and fair presentation of the consolidated financial statements in order to design audit procedures that are appropriate in the circumstances, but not for the purpose of expressing an opinion on the effectiveness of the entity's internal control.* An audit also includes evaluating the appropriateness of accounting policies used and the reasonableness of significant accounting estimates made by management, as well as evaluating the overall presentation of the consolidated financial statements.

We believe that the audit evidence we have obtained is sufficient and appropriate to provide a basis for our audit opinion.

Opinion   In our opinion, the consolidated financial statements referred to above present fairly, in all material respects, the financial position of BCS Company and its subsidiaries as of December 31, 20X1 and 20X0, and the results of their operations and their cash flows for the years then ended in accordance with accounting principles generally accepted in the United States of America.

Report on Other Legal and Regulatory Requirements

[Form and content of this section of auditor's report will vary depending on the nature of the auditors' other reporting responsibilities.]

[Auditor's signature]

[Auditor's address]

[Date of the auditor's report]

* In circumstances in which the auditor has the responsibility to express an opinion on the effectiveness of internal control in conjunction with the audit of financial statements, this sentence would be worded as follows: "In making those risk assessments, the auditor considers internal control relevant to the entity's preparation and fair presentation of the financial statements in order to design audit procedures that are appropriate in the circumstances."

---

accordance with the applicable financial reporting framework. In the United States, this framework could be either accounting principles generally accepted in the United States or international financial reporting standards. Management's responsibilities include the design and implementation of internal controls relevant to the preparation of financial statements that are free of material misstatement.

The third section describes the auditors' *responsibilities.* Auditors are responsible for expressing an opinion on the financial statements. This section also describes the work done by auditors in the audit process, that is, they have conducted the audit based on either auditing standards accepted in the United States or auditing standards of the Public Company Accounting Oversight Board. Both sets of auditing standards require auditors to obtain **reasonable assurance** that the financial statements are **free of material misstatements.** To state that the financial statements are free of material misstatement means that the decision of outsiders would not change if they were to become aware of any misstatement that remains in the financial statements. This section also tells outsiders that the auditors considered the risk of material misstatement in the audit process, examined evidence on a test basis, considered the accounting principles used by the company, and evaluated the estimates made by management. This section establishes the level of assurance that outsiders could receive from the audit opinion (*reasonable* rather than *absolute* assurance).

Independent Auditor's Report for an Unmodified Opinion Exhibit 13-3
for Companies Using International Accounting Standards

INDEPENDENT AUDITOR'S REPORT

To the Board of Directors and Shareholders of BCS Company

Report on the Financial Statements
We have audited the accompanying financial statements of ABC Company, which comprise the balance sheet as at December 31, 20X1, and the income statement, statement of changes in equity and cash flow statement for the year then ended.

Management's Responsibility for the Financial Statements Management is responsible for the preparation and fair presentation of these financial statements in accordance with International Financial Reporting Standards, and for such internal control as management determines is necessary to enable the preparation of financial statements that are free from material misstatements, whether due to fraud or error.

Auditor's Responsibility Our responsibility is to express an opinion on these financial statements based on our audit. We conducted our audits in accordance with International Standards on Auditing. Those standards require that we comply with ethical requirements and plan and perform the audit to obtain reasonable assurance about whether the financial statements are free of material misstatement.

An audit involves performing procedures to obtain audit evidence about the amounts and disclosures in the financial statements. The procedures selected depend on the auditor's judgment, including the assessment of the risks of material misstatement of the financial statements, whether due to fraud or error. In making those risk assessments, the auditor considers internal control relevant to the entity's preparation and fair presentation of the financial statements in order to design audit procedures that are appropriate in the circumstances, but not for the purpose of expressing an opinion on the effectiveness of the entity's internal control. An audit also includes evaluating the appropriateness of accounting policies used and the reasonableness of accounting estimates made by management, as well as evaluating the overall presentation of the financial statements.

We believe that the audit evidence we have obtained is sufficient and appropriate to provide a basis for our audit opinion.

Opinion In our opinion, the financial statements present fairly, in all material respects, (or give a true and fair view of) the financial position of ABC Company as at December 31, 20X1, and (of) its financial performance and its cash flows for the year then ended in accordance with International Financial Reporting Standards.

Report on Other Legal and Regulatory Requirements
[Form and content of this section of auditor's report will vary depending on the nature of the auditors' other reporting responsibilities.]

[Auditor's signature]

[Date of the auditor's report]

[Auditor's address] (ISA 700)

The *Opinion* section states that the financial statements referred to in the introductory paragraph ***present fairly, in all material respects,*** the financial position (the balance sheet) of the company for the last two years and the results of their operations (the income statement) and their cash flows (the cash flow statement) for the years then ended.[1] The opinion paragraph also describes the applicable financial framework used in the preparation of the financial statements. In Exhibit 13-2, the financial statements are presented in accordance with accounting principles generally accepted in the United States of America.

Auditors use the subsection titled Report on Other Legal and Regulatory Requirements when they have an obligation to report on other matters that are supplementary to their responsibility to report on the financial statements. The form and content of this section varies based on the nature of the other reporting responsibilities. For example, for audits conducted under *government auditing standards,* auditors could be required to report on internal control over financial reporting and on compliance with laws, regulations, and provisions of contracts or grant agreements.

The auditor's report should include an original or printed signature by the partner in charge of the audit of the audit firm. The firm's address includes the city and state where auditors practice and the date of the annual report. This date should be no earlier than the date on which auditors have obtained sufficient appropriate evidence on which to base their opinion including evidence that the audit documentation has been reviewed; all statements

---

[1] In the past, companies in the United States have presented 2 years of balance sheet information and three years of income statement, cash flow, and owners' equity. This wording suggests that companies may begin to present only 2 years of income statement, cash flow, and owners' equity information.

that comprise the financial statements, including the footnotes, have been prepared; and management has asserted that it has taken responsibility for the financial statements.

Emphasis of Matter and Other Matter Paragraphs in the Independent Audit Report

LO3

Explain when an emphasis of matter or other matter paragraph is added to an unmodified audit report

Auditors use an *emphasis of matter* paragraph or an *other matter* paragraph when they want to draw the users' attention either to a matter that is appropriately presented or disclosed in the financial statements or any other matter that is relevant to users' understanding of the audit, auditors' responsibilities, or the auditor's report. An emphasis of matter paragraph is used when an issue has already been presented or disclosed in the financial statements. An other matter paragraph is used when auditors want to disclose any other issue that they believe is relevant to users' understanding of the audit. If the auditors expect to include an *emphasis of matter* or an *other matter* paragraph in their report, they should communicate with those responsible for governance regarding this expectation and the proposed wording of the paragraph.

Emphasis of matter paragraphs:

- Are found after the opinion paragraph in the auditor's report
- Use the Emphasis of Matter or another appropriate heading
- Include a clear reference to the matter emphasized and where the relevant disclosures that fully describe the matter can be found in the financial statements
- Indicate that auditors' opinion is not modified with respect to the matter emphasized

Other matter paragraphs:

- Should follow the opinion paragraph and any emphasis of matter paragraph(s) or appear elsewhere in the auditor's report if their content is relevant to the Other Reporting Responsibilities section
- Use the heading Other Matter or another appropriate heading
- Should be used when auditors consider communicating a matter they believe to be relevant to users' understanding of the audit, of the auditors' responsibility, or of the auditor's report other than those that are present or disclosed in the financial statements.

Circumstances in which an *emphasis of matter* paragraph could be necessary are:

- An uncertainty relating to the future outcome of exceptional litigation or regulatory action exists
- A new accounting standard that has a pervasive effect on the financial statements is applied early in advance of its effective date (when permitted)
- A major catastrophe has had, or continues to have, a significant effect on the entity's financial position
- Significant transactions with related parties exist
- Unusually important subsequent events occur

The inclusion of an *emphasis of matter* paragraph in the auditor's report does not affect their opinion. The auditing standards suggest that auditors should not engage in a widespread use of *emphasis of matter* paragraphs because doing so diminishes their effectiveness. Auditors are required to consider the amount of information disclosed in the emphasis of matter paragraph. To include more information in the emphasis of matter paragraph than is found in the financial statements could suggest that the matter has not been appropriately presented in the financial statements.

Circumstances in which an *other matter* paragraph could be necessary are:

1. The paragraph is necessary to users' understanding of the audit.
2. The paragraph is necessary to users' understanding of auditors' responsibilities or auditor's report.
3. The paragraph explains that the reporting applies to more than one set of financial statements.

Sometimes the auditors are unable to withdraw from the engagement although a management-imposed limitation prevents them from obtaining sufficient appropriate audit evidence. In this situation, the auditors could include an other matter paragraph to explain why it is not possible for them to withdraw from the engagement.

In the second circumstance, laws, regulations, or generally accepted practices could require or allow auditors to elaborate on matters to further explain their responsibilities in the audit. Other matter paragraphs used in this situation do *not* include circumstances in which the auditors have reporting responsibilities in addition to reporting on the financial statements.

In the third circumstance, an entity could prepare one set of financial statements in accordance with one applicable financial reporting framework and a second set in accordance with another framework such as accounting principles generally accepted in the United States or international financial reporting standards. If auditors have determined that the frameworks are acceptable in their respective situations, they can include an *other matter* paragraph in their report, referring to the fact that the entity has prepared another set of financial statements.

See Exhibit 13-4 for examples of an emphasis of matter and an other matter paragraph added to the audit report.

Report Modifications: Qualified Opinion, Disclaimer of Opinion, and Adverse Opinion

LO4

Describe modifications to the opinion in the independent auditor's report when (a) a qualified opinion, (b) a disclaimer of opinion, or (c) an adverse opinion is appropriate

Auditors can make three modifications to the opinion in the independent auditor's report issuing (1) a qualified opinion, (2) an adverse opinion, or (3) a disclaimer of opinion. Each of these options is discussed next.

Modifying the audit report is necessary when the auditors conclude that the financial statements are not free from material misstatements *or* when they are unable to obtain sufficient appropriate evidence to conclude that the financial statements are free from material misstatement. Auditors decide which of the modifications is appropriate based on (1) the *nature* of the matter causing the modification, that is, whether the financial statements are materially misstated or whether the auditors are unable to gather sufficient appropriate evidence and (2) the *pervasiveness* of the matter causing the modification to the financial statements.

A Qualified Audit Opinion

Auditors issue a qualified opinion in two cases: (1) they have sufficient appropriate audit evidence and conclude that the misstatements to the financial statements are material but not *pervasive* or (2) the auditors are unable to obtain sufficient appropriate evidence but conclude that the possible effects of the misstatement could be material but not pervasive. The effect of a misstatement is *pervasive* when (1) it is not confined to specific elements, accounts, or items of the financial statements, (2) if confined, it represents a substantial portion of the financial statements, or (3) in relation to disclosures, it is fundamental to users' understanding of the financial statements.

An Adverse Audit Opinion

Auditors issue an adverse opinion when they have sufficient appropriate evidence and conclude that the misstatements are *both* material and pervasive to the financial statements.

An *adverse* opinion states that the financial statements do not present fairly the financial position of the company or the results of operations or cash flows in conformity with the applicable financial reporting framework. When auditors issue an adverse audit report, they have sufficient evidence to determine that the financial statements are not free from material misstatements.

A Disclaimer of Opinion

Auditors issue a disclaimer of opinion when they are unable to obtain sufficient appropriate audit evidence on which to base an opinion and conclude that the possible misstatements could be *both* material and pervasive. Auditors issue a disclaimer of opinion

Independent Auditor's Report for an Unmodified Opinion with an *Emphasis of Matter* Paragraph and an *Other Matter* Paragraph	Exhibit 13-4

INDEPENDENT AUDITOR'S REPORT

To the Board of Directors and Shareholders of BCS Company

Report on the Financial Statements

We have audited the accompanying consolidated balance sheets of BCS Company and its subsidiaries, as of December 31, 20X1 and 20X0, and the related consolidated statements of income, retained earnings, and cash flows for the years then ended.

Management's Responsibility for the Financial Statements Management is responsible for the preparation and fair presentation of these consolidated financial statements in accordance with accounting principles generally accepted in the United States of America; this includes the design, implementation, and maintenance of internal control relevant to the preparation and fair presentation of consolidated financial statements that are free from material misstatement, whether due to fraud or error.

Auditor's Responsibility Our responsibility is to express an opinion on these consolidated financial statements based on our audits. We conducted our audits in accordance with auditing standards generally accepted in the United States of America. Those standards require that we plan and perform the audit to obtain reasonable assurance about whether the consolidated financial statements are free of material misstatement.

An audit involves performing procedures to obtain audit evidence about the amounts and disclosures in the consolidated financial statements. The procedures selected depend on auditor's judgment, including the assessment of the risks of material misstatement of the consolidated financial statements, whether due to fraud or error. In making those risk assessments, the auditor considers internal control relevant to the entity's preparation and fair presentation of the consolidated financial statements in order to design audit procedures that are appropriate in the circumstances, but not for the purpose of expressing an opinion on the effectiveness of the entity's internal control.* An audit also includes evaluating the appropriateness of accounting policies used and the reasonableness of significant accounting estimates made by management, as well as evaluating the overall presentation of the consolidated financial statements.

We believe that the audit evidence we have obtained is sufficient and appropriate to provide a basis for our audit opinion.

Opinion In our opinion, the consolidated financial statements referred to above present fairly, in all material respects, the financial position of BCS Company and its subsidiaries as of December 31, 20X1 and 20X0, and the results of their operations and their cash flows for the years then ended in accordance with accounting principles generally accepted in the United States of America.

Emphasis of Matter We draw attention to Note X to the financial statements, which describes the uncertainty[†] related to the outcome of the lawsuit filed against the company by XYZ Company. Our opinion is not qualified with respect to this matter.

Other Matter In our report dated March 1, 20X2, we expressed an opinion that the 20X1 financial statements did not fairly present the financial position, results of operations, and cash flows in accordance with accounting principles generally accepted in the United States of America because of two departures from such principles: (1) BCS Company carried its property, plant, and equipment at appraisal values, and provided for depreciation on the basis of such values, and (2) BCS Company did not provide for deferred income taxes with respect to differences between income for financial reporting purposes and taxable income. As described in Note X, the Company has changed its method of accounting for these items and restated its 20X1 financial statements to conform with accounting principles generally accepted in the United States of America. Accordingly, our present opinion on the 20X1 financial statements, as presented herein, is different from that expressed in our previous report.

Report on Other Legal and Regulatory Requirements

[Form and content of this section of the auditor's report will vary depending on the nature of the auditor's other reporting responsibilities.]

[Auditor's signature]

[Auditor's address]

[Date of the auditor's report]

* In circumstances in which the auditor has the responsibility to express an opinion on the effectiveness of internal control in conjunction with the audit of financial statements, this sentence would be worded as follows: "In making those risk assessments, the auditor considers internal control relevant to the entity's preparation and fair presentation of the financial statements in order to design audit procedures that are appropriate in the circumstances."

† In highlighting the uncertainty, the auditor uses the same terminology that is used in the note to the financial statements.

when they were unable to perform sufficient audit procedures to allow them to evaluate whether the financial statements are materially correct in conformity with the applicable financial reporting framework.

See Exhibit 13-5 for a summary of the various modified opinions and the appropriate situations for the auditors to issue each type.

Modified Opinions		Exhibit 13-5

	Auditor's Judgment as to the Pervasiveness of the Effects of the Misstatements or Lack of Evidence on the Financial Statements	
Nature of Matter Giving Rise to the Modification	**Material but Not Pervasive**	**Material and Pervasive**
Financial statements are materially misstated	Qualified opinion	Adverse opinion
Auditors unable to obtain sufficient appropriate evidence	Qualified opinion	Disclaimer of opinion

When modifying the opinion on the financial statements, auditors should include a paragraph in their report describing the matter that caused the modification. This paragraph should be placed immediately before the opinion paragraph and should have the heading Basis for Qualified Opinion, Basis for Adverse Opinion, or Basis for Disclaimer of Opinion, as appropriate.

A description of specific guidance provided in the auditing standards related to the information in the modified opinion follows:

- If there is a material misstatement in the financial statements that is related to a specific amount in the financial statements, the auditors should describe and quantify the financial effects of the misstatement in the basis for modification paragraph if at all possible. If it is not possible to quantify them, the auditors should state this is the basis for the modification paragraph.

- If the material misstatement relates to narrative disclosures, the auditors should explain how the disclosure is misstated in the basis for modification paragraph.

- If there is a material misstatement related to the omission of information required to be disclosed, the auditors should discuss the omission with those charged with governance and then describe the nature of the omitted information in the basis for modification paragraph and include the omitted information when it is practical to do so and when the auditors have obtained sufficient appropriate evidence about the omitted information.

- If the modification results because the auditors are unable to obtain sufficient appropriate evidence, they should include in the basis for modification paragraph the reason they were unable to obtain sufficient appropriate evidence.

- Even when auditors expresses an adverse opinion or a disclaimer of opinion, they should describe in the basis for modification paragraph any other matters of which they are aware that would have required a modification to the opinion. They should also include an *emphasis of matter* or *other matter* paragraph if they are aware of other matters that would have resulted in additional communications in their report that are not modifications to the auditors' opinion.

The auditing standards also specify disclosures needed in the opinion paragraph when auditors modify their opinion.

- A modification of the opinion paragraph should have the heading Qualified Opinion, Adverse Opinion, or Disclaimer of Opinion as appropriate.

- When they issue a qualified opinion because of a material misstatement, auditors should state in the opinion paragraph that, except for the effects of the matter described in the basis for modification paragraph, the financial statements are presented fairly, in all material respects, in accordance with the applicable financial reporting framework. When the modification is the result of the auditors' inability to obtain sufficient appropriate evidence, they should use the phrase "except for the possible effects of the matter(s) . . ." for the modified opinion.

- When they expresses an adverse opinion, auditors should state in the opinion paragraph that, in their opinion, the financial statements are not presented fairly in accordance with the applicable financial reporting framework because of the significance of the matter described in the basis for adverse opinion paragraph.
- When they disclaim an opinion because of the inability to obtain sufficient appropriate evidence, the auditors should state in the opinion paragraph that because of the significance of the matter described in the basis for disclaimer of opinion paragraph, they have not been able to obtain sufficient appropriate evidence to provide a basis for an audit opinion, and, accordingly, the auditors do not express an opinion on the financial statements.

Auditors also modify the paragraph describing their responsibility when they issue a modified opinion.

- When they issue a qualified or adverse opinion, auditors change the description of their responsibility to state that they believe that the audit evidence obtained is sufficient and appropriate to provide a basis for a modified opinion.
- When they disclaim an opinion because they are unable to obtain sufficient appropriate evidence, the auditors should amend the introductory paragraph of their report to state that they were engaged to audit the financial statements. The auditors should also amend the description of their responsibility and of the scope of the audit to state only the following: "Our responsibility is to express an opinion on the financial statements based on conducting the audit in accordance with generally accepted auditing standards. Because of the matter described in the Basis for Disclaimer of Opinion paragraph, however, we were not able to obtain sufficient appropriate audit evidence to provide a basis for an audit opinion."

When auditors expect to modify the opinion of an audit report, they should communicate with those charged with governance concerning the circumstances that led to the modification and its proposed wording.

See Exhibit 13-6, Exhibit 13-7, and Exhibit 13-8 for examples of modified opinions. The changes made from an unmodified report to a modified report are highlighted in blue. Exhibit 13-6 is an example of an opinion qualified because of a material misstatement in the financial statements. Exhibit 13-7 is an example of an adverse opinion because of a material misstatement in the financial statements. Exhibit 13-8 is an example of a disclaimer of opinion because of the auditors' inability to obtain evidence about a single element on the financial statements.

The Auditor's Reporting Responsibilities

LO5

Identify the auditors' reporting responsibilities and how they affect audit reports

This section focuses on several issues related to auditor's reporting responsibilities that have either not been previously discussed or that need additional information. These issues include:

- Determination of whether to refer to the work of a component auditor on the group financial statements in the auditor's report.
- Audit responsibility related to quarterly information included in the annual report.
- Restriction of the use of auditor's report.
- Communication with those charged with governance.

Each issue is discussed in one of the following sections.

Use of a Component Auditor's Work for a Group Audit Report

Auditors often issue an audit report on the consolidated financial statements for a group of reporting units. These units could be separate companies owned by the parent company or separate operating units of one company. Sometimes one audit firm audits the entire group of companies; in this case, the *group engagement* partner is responsible for the group

Independent Auditor's Report for a Modified Qualified Opinion Due to a Material Misstatement

Exhibit 13-6

INDEPENDENT AUDITOR'S REPORT

To the Board of Directors and Shareholders of BCS Company

Report on the Financial Statements
We have audited the accompanying consolidated balance sheets of BCS Company and its subsidiaries as of December 31, 20X1 and 20X0, and the related consolidated statements of income, retained earnings, and cash flows for the years then ended.

Management's Responsibility for the Financial Statements Management is responsible for the preparation and fair presentation of these consolidated financial statements in accordance with accounting principles generally accepted in the United States of America; this includes the design, implementation, and maintenance of internal control relevant to the preparation and fair presentation of consolidated financial statements that are free from material misstatement, whether due to fraud or error.

Auditor's Responsibility Our responsibility is to express an opinion on these consolidated financial statements based on our audits. We conducted our audits in accordance with auditing standards generally accepted in the United States of America. Those standards require that we plan and perform the audit to obtain reasonable assurance about whether the consolidated financial statements are free of material misstatement.

An audit involves performing procedures to obtain audit evidence about the amounts and disclosures in the consolidated financial statements. The procedures selected depend on the auditor's judgment, including the assessment of the risks of material misstatement of the consolidated financial statements, whether due to fraud or error. In making those risk assessments, the auditor considers internal control relevant to the entity's preparation and fair presentation of the consolidated financial statements in order to design audit procedures that are appropriate in the circumstances, but not for the purpose of expressing an opinion on the effectiveness of the entity's internal control.* An audit also includes evaluating the appropriateness of accounting policies used and the reasonableness of significant accounting estimates made by management, as well as evaluating the overall presentation of the consolidated financial statements.

We believe that the audit evidence we have obtained is sufficient and appropriate to provide a basis for our qualified audit opinion.

Basis for Qualified Opinion The company has stated inventories at cost in the accompanying balance sheets. Accounting principles generally accepted in the United States of America require inventories to be stated at the lower of cost or net realizable value. If the company stated inventories at the lower of cost or net realizable value, an amount of xxx and xxx would have been required to write the inventories down to their net realizable values of December 31, 20X1 and 20X0, respectively. Accordingly, cost of sales would have been increased by xxx and xxx, and net income, income taxes, and shareholders' equity would have been reduced by xxx, xxx, xxx, and xxx, xxx, xxx, as of December 31, 20X1 and 20X0, respectively.

Qualified Opinion In our opinion, except for the effects of the matter described in the Basis for Qualified Opinion paragraph, the consolidated financial statements referred to above present fairly, in all material respects, the financial position of BCS Company and its subsidiaries as of December 31, 20X1 and 20X0, and the results of their operations and their cash flows for the years then ended in accordance with accounting principles generally accepted in the United States of America.

Report on Other Legal and Regulatory Requirements
[Form and content of this section of the auditor's report will vary depending on the nature of the auditor's other reporting responsibilities.]

[Auditor's signature]

[Auditor's address]

[Date of the auditor's report]

* In circumstances in which the auditor has the responsibility to express an opinion on the effectiveness of internal control in conjunction with the audit of financial statements, this sentence would be worded as follows: "In making those risk assessments, the auditor considers internal control relevant to the entity's preparation and fair presentation of the financial statements in order to design audit procedures that are appropriate in the circumstances."

audit. At other times, several offices of one audit firm audit the entire company under audit. In other cases, separate audit firms could audit the various component companies in the group. A *component* is an entity or business activity for which component management prepares financial information that is included in the group financial statements. An auditor who works on the financial information of a component that will be used as audit evidence for the group audit is referred to as a *component auditor*. A component auditor can work for a network firm of the group engagement's partner's firm, a different office of the same firm, or a completely separate firm. A *group* is made up of all individual components whose financial information is included in the group financial statements.

Independent Auditor's Report for a Modified Adverse Opinion

Exhibit 13-7

INDEPENDENT AUDITOR'S REPORT

To the Board of Directors and Shareholders of BCS Company

Report on the Financial Statements

We have audited the accompanying consolidated balance sheets of BCS Company and its subsidiaries, as of December 31, 20X1 and 20X0, and the related consolidated statements of income, retained earnings, and cash flows for the years then ended.

Management's Responsibility for the Financial Statements   Management is responsible for the preparation and fair presentation of these consolidated financial statements in accordance with accounting principles generally accepted in the United States of America; this includes the design, implementation, and maintenance of internal control relevant to the preparation and fair presentation of consolidated financial statements that are free from material misstatement, whether due to fraud or error.

Auditor's Responsibility   Our responsibility is to express an opinion on these consolidated financial statements based on our audits. We conducted our audits in accordance with auditing standards generally accepted in the United States of America. Those standards require that we plan and perform the audit to obtain reasonable assurance about whether the consolidated financial statements are free of material misstatement.

An audit involves performing procedures to obtain audit evidence about the amounts and disclosures in the consolidated financial statements. The procedures selected depend on the auditor's judgment, including the assessment of the risks of material misstatement of the consolidated financial statements, whether due to fraud or error. In making those risk assessments, the auditor considers internal control relevant to the entity's preparation and fair presentation of the consolidated financial statements in order to design audit procedures that are appropriate in the circumstances, but not for the purpose of expressing an opinion on the effectiveness of the entity's internal control.* An audit also includes evaluating the appropriateness of accounting policies used and the reasonableness of significant accounting estimates made by management, as well as evaluating the overall presentation of the consolidated financial statements.

We believe that the audit evidence we have obtained is sufficient and appropriate to provide a basis for our adverse audit opinion.

Basis for Adverse Opinion   As described in Note X, the Company has not consolidated the financial statements of subsidiary XYZ Company it acquired during 20X1 because it has not yet been able to ascertain the fair values of certain of the subsidiary's material assets and liabilities at the acquisition date. This investment is, therefore, accounted for on a cost basis. Under accounting principles generally accepted in the United States of America, the subsidiary should have been consolidated because it is controlled by the Company. Had XYZ been consolidated, many elements in the accompanying financial statements would have been materially affected. The effects of the failure to consolidate on the financial statements have not been determined.

Adverse Opinion   In our opinion, because of the significance of the matter discussed in the Basis for Adverse Opinion paragraph, the consolidated financial statements referred to above do not present fairly, in all material respects, the financial position of BCS Company and its subsidiaries as of December 31, 20X1 and 20X0, and the results of their operations and their cash flows for the years then ended in accordance with accounting principles generally accepted in the United States of America.

Report on Other Legal and Regulatory Requirements

[Form and content of this section of the auditor's report will vary depending on the nature of the auditor's other reporting responsibilities.]

[Auditor's signature]

[Auditor's address]

[Date of the auditor's report]

* In circumstances in which the auditor has the responsibility to express an opinion on the effectiveness of internal control in conjunction with the audit of financial statements, this sentence would be worded as follows: "In making those risk assessments, the auditor considers internal control relevant to the entity's preparation and fair presentation of the financial statements in order to design audit procedures that are appropriate in the circumstances."

When issuing an audit report for a group audit, the group engagement partner who is responsible for the group audit report has two options concerning the component auditors' work. This partner must decide whether to assume the responsibility for their work, in which case the audit report does not mention their work, or if the partner does not assume responsibility for their work can refer to it. The group engagement partner cannot refer to work of component auditors unless they prepare the component's financial statements using the same financial reporting framework that the group financial statements used and the component auditors have performed their audit in accordance with generally accepted auditing standards and have issued an audit report that is not restricted as to use.

Chapter 13   *Audit Reports*   377

Independent Auditor's Report for a Modified Opinion Disclaimer of Opinion

Exhibit 13-8

INDEPENDENT AUDITOR'S REPORT
To the Board of Directors and Shareholders of BCS Company

Report on the Financial Statements
We have audited the accompanying consolidated balance sheets of BCS Company and its subsidiaries, as of December 31, 20X1 and 20X0, and the related consolidated statements of income, retained earnings, and cash flows for the years then ended.

Management's Responsibility for the Financial Statements   Management is responsible for the preparation and fair presentation of these consolidated financial statements in accordance with accounting principles generally accepted in the United States of America; this includes the design, implementation, and maintenance of internal control relevant to the preparation and fair presentation of consolidated financial statements that are free from material misstatement, whether due to fraud or error.

Auditor's Responsibility   Our responsibility is to express an opinion on these consolidated financial statements based on our audits. We conducted our audits in accordance with auditing standards generally accepted in the United States of America. Because of the matter described in the Basis for Disclaimer of Opinion paragraph, however, we were not able to obtain sufficient appropriate audit evidence to provide a basis for an audit opinion. ~~Those standards require that we plan and perform the audit to obtain reasonable assurance about whether the consolidated financial statements are free of material misstatement.~~

~~An audit involves performing procedures to obtain audit evidence about the amounts and disclosures in the consolidated financial statements. The procedures selected depend on the auditor's judgment, including the assessment of the risks of material misstatement of the consolidated financial statements, whether due to fraud or error. In making those risk assessments, the auditor considers internal control relevant to the entity's preparation and fair presentation of the consolidated financial statements in order to design audit procedures that are appropriate in the circumstances, but not for the purpose of expressing an opinion on the effectiveness of the entity's internal control.* An audit also includes evaluating the appropriateness of accounting policies used and the reasonableness of significant accounting estimates~~ ~~made by management, as well as evaluating the overall presentation of the consolidated financial statements.~~

~~We believe that the audit evidence we have obtained is sufficient and appropriate to provide a basis for our audit opinion.~~

Basis for Disclaimer of Opinion   The company's investment in XYZ Company, a joint venture, is carried at xxx on the company's balance sheet, which represents over 90 percent of the company's net assets as of December 31, 20X1. We were not allowed access to the management and the auditor of XYZ Company. As a result, we were unable to determine whether any adjustments were necessary relating to the company's proportional share of XYZ's assets that it controls jointly, its proportional share of XYZ's liabilities for which it is jointly responsible, its proportional share of XYZ's income and expenses for the year, and the elements making up the statements of retained earnings and cash flows.

Disclaimer of Opinion   Because of the significance of the matter described in the Basis for Disclaimer of Opinion paragraph, we have not been able to obtain sufficient appropriate audit evidence to provide a basis for an audit opinion. Accordingly, we do not express an opinion on these financial statements.

~~In our opinion, the consolidated financial statements referred to above present fairly, in all material respects, the financial position of BCS Company and its subsidiaries as of December 31, 20X1 and 20X0, and the results of their operations and their cash flows for the years then ended in accordance with accounting principles generally accepted in the United States of America.~~

Report on Other Legal and Regulatory Requirements
[Form and content of this section of the auditor's report will vary depending on the nature of the auditor's other reporting responsibilities.]

[Auditor's signature]

[Auditor's address]

[Date of the auditor's report]

~~* In circumstances when the auditor has the responsibility to express an opinion on the effectiveness of internal control in conjunction with the audit of financial statements, this sentence would be worded as follows: "In making those risk assessments, the auditor considers internal control relevant to the entity's preparation and fair presentation of the financial statements in order to design audit procedures that are appropriate in the circumstances."~~

See Exhibit 13-9 for changes in the audit report when the group engagement partner chooses to refer to component auditors' work. Reference in the audit report to a component auditor is not to be understood as a qualification of the opinion but as an indication of the divided responsibility between the auditors who conducted the audit of various components of the group. The group engagement partner discloses the magnitude of the portion of the financial statements audited by the component auditors by stating the percentages of total assets and total revenue they audited. Before choosing to refer to the work of a component auditor, the group engagement partner must obtain

| Independent Auditor's Report for an Unmodified Opinion When the Group Engagement Partner Refers to a Component Auditor's Work | Exhibit 13-9 |

INDEPENDENT AUDITOR'S REPORT

To the Board of Directors and Shareholders of BCS, Incorporated

Report on the Financial Statements
We have audited the accompanying consolidated balance sheets of BCS Company and its subsidiaries as of December 31, 20X1 and 20X0, and the related consolidated statements of income, retained earnings, and cash flows for the years then ended.

Management's Responsibility for the Financial Statements Management is responsible for the preparation and fair presentation of these consolidated financial statements in accordance with accounting principles generally accepted in the United States of America; this includes the design, implementation, and maintenance of internal control relevant to the preparation and fair presentation of consolidated financial statements that are free from material misstatement, whether due to fraud or error.

Auditor's Responsibility Our responsibility is to express an opinion on these consolidated financial statements based on our audits. We conducted our audits in accordance with auditing standards generally accepted in the United States of America. Those standards require that we plan and perform the audit to obtain reasonable assurance about whether the consolidated financial statements are free of material misstatement.

An audit involves performing procedures to obtain audit evidence about the amounts and disclosures in the consolidated financial statements. The procedures selected depend on the auditor's judgment, including the assessment of the risks of material misstatement of the consolidated financial statements, whether due to fraud or error. In making those risk assessments, the auditor considers internal control relevant to the entity's preparation and fair presentation of the consolidated financial statements in order to design audit procedures that are appropriate in the circumstances, but not for the purpose of expressing an opinion on the effectiveness of the entity's internal control.* An audit also includes evaluating the appropriateness of accounting policies used and the reasonableness of significant accounting estimates made by management, as well as evaluating the overall presentation of the consolidated financial statements.

We believe that the audit evidence we have obtained is sufficient and appropriate to provide a basis for our audit opinion.

We did not audit the financial statements of B Company, a wholly owned subsidiary, whose statements reflect total assets and revenues constituting 20 percent and 22 percent, respectively, of the related consolidated totals. Those statements were audited by other auditors whose report has been furnished to us, and our opinion, insofar as it relates to the amount included for B Company, is based solely on the report of the other auditors.

Opinion In our opinion, based on our audit and the report of the other auditors, the consolidated financial statements referred to above present fairly, in all material respects, the financial position of BCS Company and its subsidiaries as of December 31, 20X1 and 20X0, and the results of their operations and their cash flows for the years then ended in accordance with accounting principles generally accepted in the United States of America.

Report on Other Legal and Regulatory Requirements
[Form and content of this section of the auditor's report will vary depending on the nature of the auditors' other reporting responsibilities.]

[Auditor's signature]

[Auditor's address]

[Date of the auditor's report]

* In circumstances in which the auditor has the responsibility to express an opinion on the effectiveness of internal control in conjunction with the audit of financial statements, this sentence would be worded as follows: "In making those risk assessments, the auditor considers internal control relevant to the entity's preparation and fair presentation of the financial statements in order to design audit procedures that are appropriate in the circumstances."

an understanding of the component auditor by determining during the planning stage of the audit:

- Whether the component auditor understands and will comply with the ethical requirements relevant to the group audit and, in particular, whether the component auditor is independent.
- The component auditor's professional competence.
- The extent to which the group engagement partner will be able to be involved in the component auditor's work.
- Whether the group engagement team will be able to obtain information affecting the consolidation process from a component auditor.
- Whether the component auditor operates in a regulatory environment that actively oversees auditors.

If the group engagement partner determines that any of these requirements is not met, he or she should obtain sufficient appropriate evidence relating to the financial information of the component without using the component auditor's work.

Audit Responsibility for Quarterly Information in the Annual Report

The SEC in the United States requires public companies to submit quarterly information (Form 10-Q or Form 10QSB) that has been *reviewed* by auditors. The auditors are not required to issue an audit report based on this review, but the SEC report must state that auditors have reviewed the financial information.

The objective of the review is to provide auditors information to determine whether the quarterly reports are prepared in accordance with the applicable financial reporting framework. A review consists primarily of gathering information by performing analytical procedures and making inquiries of individuals responsible for accounting decisions. Companies often include the quarterly information as supplementary information in a footnote in the annual report. When this is done, the footnote is marked "unaudited."

Restriction of the Use of the Auditor's Report

All audit reports that we have discussed are classified as *general use*. This means that the reports are not restricted to view. Auditors' reports prepared in conformity with an applicable financial reporting framework are usually not restricted as to their use.

Auditors could be required or choose to restrict the use of an audit report. An audit report that is restricted as to use should contain an *other matter* paragraph. This paragraph should include a statement that the report is intended solely for the use of specified parties and identify those parties and that the report is not intended to be and should not be used by anyone other than the specified parties. Restricted-use audit reports are prepared for a particular purpose only. They often do not provide useful information to outsiders for any purpose other than the purpose for which they were prepared. For example, a report prepared by an auditor on the compliance of a university with federal guidelines for student loans is a restricted-use report. The report provides information on the university's compliance with these guidelines but does not provide information useful to outsiders.

Communication with Those Charged with Governance

Auditors are required to communicate certain matters related to the audit to those charged with governance in the company. The communication can occur after the auditors' report is issued and must be in writing for all public companies reporting to the SEC. The purpose of the communication is to give those charged with governance the information they need to meet their oversight responsibilities for the company's financial reporting process.

The following information should be communicated to those charged with governance:

- Auditors' responsibility under generally accepted auditing standards
- Significant accounting policies
- Management judgments and accounting estimates
- Audit adjustments
- Auditors' judgments about the quality of the entity's accounting principles
- Significant deficiencies and material weaknesses identified in internal controls over the financial statements (and over the financial reporting process for public companies)
- Other information in documents containing audited financial statements
- Disagreements with management
- Consultation with other accountants
- Major issues discussed with management prior to retention
- Difficulties encountered in performing the audit

If the auditors intend to use an *emphasis of matter* paragraph or an *other matter* paragraph or to issue a modified audit report, they must communicate that information to those charged with governance before issuing the audit report. This allows those charged with governance to provide the auditors additional information related to the matter causing the expected disclosure.

Reporting on Financial Reporting Frameworks Generally Accepted in Another Country

LO6

Describe the audit responsibilities for reporting on financial statements prepared in accordance with a financial reporting framework generally accepted in another country

Auditors have specific audit responsibilities when they issue an audit report on financial statements prepared in accordance with a financial reporting framework that is generally accepted in another country. These responsibilities apply only to audit reports issued on statements prepared in accordance with a financial reporting framework that the Council of the AICPA in the United States has *not* recognized. Frameworks recognized in the United States include those set by (1) the Financial Accounting Standards Board, (2) the Governmental Accounting Standards Board, (3) the Federal Accounting Standards Advisory Board, and (4) the International Accounting Standards Board (IASB). These special audit responsibilities also apply to financial statements prepared with a jurisdictional variation of international financial reporting standards (IFRSs) when the audited company's financial statements do not contain an explicit and unreserved statement in a note stating that the financial statements are in compliance with IFRSs as issued by the IASB. This type of situation could happen when a country voluntarily adopts IFRSs and calls them, for example, Singapore International Financial Reporting Standards. If the Singapore accounting standard board indicates that these standards are in compliance with the IFRSs as issued by the IASB, the special audit responsibilities do not apply. If the Singapore accounting standards board does not indicate that these standards comply with the IFRSs (because they do not or because they do not say that they comply), the specific auditing responsibilities apply.

When the specific auditing responsibilities apply, auditors must consider the following when accepting the engagement, planning and performing it, and forming an opinion and reporting on the financial statements:

Accepting the Audit Engagement

- The purpose for which the financial statements are prepared and whether the financial reporting framework used by the company is a fair presentation framework;
- The intended users of the financial statements; and
- The steps taken by management to determine that the financial reporting framework is acceptable in the circumstances.

Planning and Performing the Audit Engagement

- Auditors should comply with U.S. generally accepted auditing standards (except for the requirements related to the form and content of the audit report) when the financial statements are prepared for use *only* outside the United States.
- Auditors should understand the accounting standards used by the company.
- Auditors should understand and comply with the generally accepted auditing standards of the country in which the report will be issued.

Reporting—More Than Limited Use in the United States or Use Only Outside of the United States

- If the report is to have more than limited use in the United States, auditors should report using the U.S. form of report modified as appropriate (qualified or adverse) because of the departures from U.S. GAAP.
- If the report will be used only outside the United States, auditors should report using either the (1) U.S. style of report that reflects that the financial statements have been prepared in accordance with the accounting principles of another country or (2) the standard report form of the other country. When auditors use the standard report form of another country, they should comply with that country's reporting standards and identify the other country in the report (AU 534).

Report of Independent Registered Public Accounting Firm on the Consolidated Financial Statements and Related Financial Statement Schedule for General Mills

Exhibit 13-10

To The Board of Directors and Shareholders General Mills, Inc.

We have audited the accompanying consolidated balance sheets of General Mills, Inc. and subsidiaries as of May 27, 2007, and May 28, 2006, and the related consolidated statements of earnings, stockholder's equity and comprehensive income, and cash flows for each of the fiscal years in the three-year period ended May 27, 2007. In connection with our audits of the consolidated financial statements we also have audited the accompanying financial statement schedule. These consolidated financial statements and the financial statement schedule are the responsibility of the Company's management. Our responsibility is to express an opinion on these consolidated financial statements and financial statement schedule based on our audits.

We conducted our audits in accordance with the standards of the Public Company Accounting Oversight Board (United States). Those standards require that we plan and perform the audit to obtain reasonable assurance about whether the financial statements are free of material misstatement. An audit includes examining, on a test basis, evidence supporting the amounts and disclosures in the financial statements. An audit also includes assessing the accounting principles used and significant estimates made by management, as well as evaluating the overall financial statement presentation. We believe that our audits provide a reasonable basis for our opinion.

In our opinion, the consolidated financial statements referred to above present fairly, in all material respects, the financial position of General Mills, Inc. and subsidiaries as of May 27, 2007, and May 28, 2006, and the results of their operations and their cash flows for each of the fiscal years in the three-year period ended May 27, 2007, in conformity with U.S. generally accepted accounting principles. Also, in our opinion, the accompanying financial statement schedule, when considered in relation to the basic consolidated financial statements taken as a whole, presents fairly, in all material respects, the information set forth therein.

In fiscal 2007, as disclosed in Notes 1 and 2 to the consolidated financial statements, the Company changed its classification of shipping costs, changed its annual goodwill impairment assessment date to December 1, and adopted SFAS No. 123 (Revised), Share-Based Payment, and SFAS No. 158, Employers' Accounting for Defined Benefit Pension and Other Postretirement Benefit Plans an Amendment of FASB Statements No. 87, 88, 106 and 132(R).

We also have audited, in accordance with the standards of the Public Company Accounting Oversight Board (United States), the effectiveness of General Mills' internal control over financial reporting as of May 27, 2007, based on criteria established in Internal Control-Integrated Framework issued by the Committee of Sponsoring Organizations of the Treadway Commission (COSO), and our report dated July 26, 2007, expresses an unqualified opinion on management assessment of, and the effective operation of, internal control over financial reporting.

KPMG LLP
Minneapolis, Minnesota
July 26, 2007

The Auditor's Report on Internal Controls over Financial Reporting

LO7

Explain the auditor's report on internal control over financial reporting

Two standards issued by the PCAOB (Auditing Standard No. 4 and Auditing Standard No. 5) provide guidance related to financial reporting. They apply only to public companies. The audited financial statements include two reports that can be combined into one report. The first report states whether the financial statements are materially misstated. This is the report discussed previously in this chapter. The second report provides the auditor's opinion on the effectiveness of internal control over financial reporting. The annual report for General Mills for the year ending May 27, 2007, includes two separate reports issued by the auditor; see Exhibit 13-10 and Exhibit 13-11. In the annual report for Dell Computers for the year ending December 31, 2007, the two reports are combined; see Exhibit 13-12.

The report on the effectiveness of internal control over financial reporting must include the following elements:

- A title including the word *independent*
- A statement that management is responsible for maintaining effective internal control over financial reporting and for assessing the effectiveness of the internal control
- An identification of management's report on internal control

Report of Independent Registered Public Accounting Firm Regarding Internal Control over Financial Reporting	**Exhibit 13-11**

To The Board of Directors and Shareholders General Mills, Inc.

We have audited management's assessment, including the accompanying Management's Report on Internal Control over Financial Reporting, that General Mills, Inc. and subsidiaries maintained effective internal control over financial reporting as of May 27, 2007, based on criteria established in Internal Control-Integrated Framework issued by the Committee of Sponsoring Organizations of the Treadway Commission (COSO). General Mills' management is responsible for maintaining effective internal control over financial reporting and for its assessment of the effectiveness of internal control over financial reporting. Our responsibility is to express an opinion on management's assessment and an opinion on the effectiveness of the Company's internal control over financial reporting based on our audit.

We conducted our audits in accordance with the standards of the Public Company Accounting Oversight Board (United States). Those standards require that we plan and perform the audit to obtain reasonable assurance about whether effective internal control over financial reporting was maintained in all material respects. Our audit included obtaining an understanding of internal control over financial reporting, evaluating management's assessment, testing and evaluating the design and operating effectiveness of internal control, and performing such other procedures as we considered necessary in the circumstances. We believe that our audit provides a reasonable basis for our opinion.

A company's internal control over financial reporting is a process designed to provide reasonable assurance regarding the reliability of financial reporting and the preparation of financial statements for external purposes in accordance with generally accepted accounting principles. A company's internal control over financial reporting includes those policies and procedures that (1) pertain to the maintenance of records that, in reasonable detail, accurately and fairly reflect the transactions and dispositions of the assets of the

company; (2) provide reasonable assurance that transactions are recorded as necessary to permit preparation of financial statements in accordance with generally accepted accounting principles and that receipts and expenditures of the company are being made only in accordance with authorizations of management and directors of the company; and (3) provide reasonable assurance regarding prevention or timely detection of unauthorized acquisition, use, or disposition of the company's assets that could have a material effect on the financial statements.

Because of its inherent limitations, internal control over financial reporting may not prevent or detect misstatements. Also, projections of any evaluation of effectiveness to future periods are subject to the risk that controls may become inadequate because of changes in conditions, or that the degree of compliance with the policies or procedures may deteriorate. In our opinion, management's assessment that General Mills maintained effective internal control over financial reporting as of May 27, 2007, is fairly stated, in all material respects, based on criteria established in Internal Control-Integrated Framework issued by COSO. Also, in our opinion, General Mills maintained, in all material respects, effective internal control over financial reporting as of May 27, 2007, based on criteria established in Internal Control-Integrated Framework issued by COSO.

We also have audited, in accordance with the standards of the Public Company Accounting Oversight Board (United States), the consolidated balance sheets of General Mills, Inc. and subsidiaries as of May 27, 2007, and May 28, 2006, and the related consolidated statements of earnings, stockholders' equity and comprehensive income, and cash flows, for each of the fiscal years in the three-year period ended May 27, 2007, and our report dated July 26, 2007, expresses an unqualified opinion on those consolidated financial statements.

KPMG LLP
Minneapolis, Minnesota
July 26, 2007

- A statement that the auditors are responsible for expressing on opinion on the effectiveness of internal control over the financial reporting based on their audit
- A definition of internal control over financial reporting as stated in PCAOB Auditing Standard No. 5
- A statement that the audit was conducted in accordance with the standards of the Public Company Accounting Oversight Board (United States)
- A statement that the standards of the PCAOB require that auditors plan and perform the audit to obtain reasonable assurance about the effectiveness of internal controls over the financial reporting process
- A statement that an audit includes obtaining an understanding of internal control over financial reporting, assessing the risk that a material weakness exists, testing and evaluating the design and operating effectiveness of internal control based on the assessed risk, and performing other procedures that the auditors consider necessary;

Independent Auditor's Report on an Audit of the Financial Statements and an Audit of Internal Controls over the Financial Reporting Process

Exhibit 13-12

Combined Independent Auditors Report for Dell Computers

REPORT OF INDEPENDENT REGISTERED PUBLIC ACCOUNTING FIRM

To the Board of Directors and Shareholders of Dell Inc.

We have completed an integrated audit of Dell Inc. January 28, 2005, consolidated financial statements and of its internal control over financial reporting as of January 28, 2005, and audits of its January 30, 2004 and January 31, 2003, consolidated financial statements in accordance with the standards of the Public Company Accounting Oversight Board (United States). Our opinions, based on our audits, are presented below.

These financial statements and financial statement schedule are the responsibility of the company's management. Our responsibility is to express an opinion on these financial statements and financial statement schedule based on our audits.

In our opinion, the consolidated financial statements listed in the accompanying index present fairly, in all material respects, the financial position of Dell Inc. and its subsidiaries at January 28, 2005 and January 30, 2004, and the results of their operations and their cash flows for each of the three years in the period ended January 28, 2005, in conformity with accounting principles generally accepted in the United States of America. In addition, in our opinion, the financial statement schedule listed in the accompanying index presents fairly, in all material respects, the information set forth therein when read in conjunction with the related consolidated financial statements.

Also, in our opinion, management's assessment, included in Management's Report on Internal Control over Financial Reporting appearing under Item 9A, Controls and Procedures, that the company maintained effective internal control over financial reporting as of January 28, 2005, based on criteria established in *Internal Control–Integrated Framework* issued by the Committee of Sponsoring Organizations of the Treadway Commission (COSO), is fairly stated, in all material respects, based on those criteria. Furthermore, in our opinion, the company maintained, in all material respects, effective internal control over financial reporting as of January 28, 2005, based on criteria established in *Internal Control–Integrated Framework* issued by the COSO.

The company's management is responsible for maintaining effective internal control over financial reporting and for its assessment of the effectiveness of internal control over financial reporting. Our responsibility is to express opinions on management's assessment and on the effectiveness of the company's internal control over financial reporting based on our audit.

We conducted our audit of internal control over financial reporting in accordance with the standards of the Public Company Accounting Oversight Board (United States). Those standards require that we plan and perform the audit to obtain reasonable assurance about whether objective internal control over financial reporting was maintained in all material respects. An audit of internal control over financial reporting includes obtaining an understanding of internal control over financial reporting, evaluating management's assessment, testing and evaluating the design and operating effectiveness of internal control, and performing such other procedures as we consider necessary in the circumstances. We believe that our audit provides a reasonable basis for our opinions.

A company's internal control over financial reporting is a process designed to provide reasonable assurance regarding the reliability of financial reporting and the preparation of financial statements for external purposes in accordance with generally accepted accounting principles. A company's internal control over financial reporting includes those policies and procedures that (i) pertain to the maintenance of records that, in reasonable detail, accurately and fairly reflect the transactions and dispositions of the assets of the company; (ii) provide reasonable assurance that transactions are recorded as necessary to permit preparation of financial statements in accordance with generally accepted accounting principles, and that receipts and expenditures of the company are being made only in accordance with authorizations of management and directors of the company, and (iii) provide reasonable assurance regarding prevention or timely detection of unauthorized acquisition, use, or disposition of the company's assets that could have a material effect on the financial statements.

Because of its inherent limitations, internal control over financial reporting may not prevent or detect misstatements. Also, projections of any evaluation of effectiveness to future periods are subject to the risk that controls may become inadequate because of changes in conditions, or that the degree of compliance with the policies or procedures may deteriorate.

PRICEWATERHOUSECOOPERS LLP
Austin, Texas
March 3, 2005

- A statement that the auditors believe the audit provides a reasonable basis for their opinion
- A paragraph describing the inherent limitations of internal control
- The auditors' opinion on whether the company maintained effective internal control over financial reporting as of the specified date
- The signature of the auditors' firm

- The city and state, or city and country of the auditors
- The date of the report (AS 5.85)

If deficiencies in internal controls over financial reporting result in material weaknesses, the auditors must express an adverse opinion on the company's internal control over financial reporting unless the scope of the audit was restricted. Situations in which adverse opinions or disclaimer of opinions could be appropriate are discussed in the sections that follow. Refer to Exhibit 13-13 for the adverse opinion on internal controls over the financial reporting process for General Motors.

Following an audit report identifying a material weakness, auditors could be hired to complete a *voluntary* engagement to determine whether a material weakness has been corrected. Managers specify a date on which they believe that the material weakness was corrected. The auditors gather evidence and could issue an opinion on the existence of the material weakness as a result of this engagement. Auditing Standard No. 4 issued by the PCAOB provides guidelines for such an engagement. This type of audit report could be helpful for outsiders concerned about the impact of the material weakness on the company's financial statements in the time period before the next audit.

Modifications to the Auditor's Report on Internal Control over Financial Reporting

LO8

Describe situations in which the auditors modify the report on internal control over financial reporting

Auditors modify the standard report on internal controls over the financial reporting process in the following circumstances:

- Management's annual report on internal control is incomplete or improperly presented.
- The scope of the engagement is restricted.
- The auditors decide to refer to the report of other auditors for their own report.
- There is other information in management's annual report on internal control over financial reporting.
- Management's annual certification pursuant to Section 302 of the Sarbanes-Oxley Act is misstated. (AS 5.C1)

Each of these situations is discussed briefly in the following sections.

Management's Assessment of Internal Control Incomplete or Improperly Presented

If management's annual report on internal controls is incomplete or improperly presented, the auditors should modify their report to include an explanatory paragraph describing the reasons for determining that the report is incomplete or improperly presented. If the auditors determine that the disclosure relating to a material weakness is not fairly presented, they could express an adverse opinion on internal control over financial reporting.

When the auditors decide to express an adverse opinion on internal control over financial reporting because of a material weakness, their report must include the following:

- The definition of a material weakness.
- A statement that a material weakness has been identified and an identification of the material weakness that has been described in management's assessment. If management has failed to identify the material weakness, the audit report should include a description of the material weakness identified and its potential impact on the financial statements.

Scope Limitations

If the auditors are unable to apply the audit procedures necessary to determine the effectiveness of internal control over financial reporting, they should either withdraw from the engagement or disclaim an opinion. In a disclaimer of opinion, they state that they

Auditor's Report on Internal Control over Financial Reporting—Adverse Opinion, General Motors Report of Independent Registered Public Accounting Firm

Exhibit 13-13

General Motors December 31, 2008

REPORT OF INDEPENDENT REGISTERED PUBLIC ACCOUNTING FIRM

General Motors Corporation, Its Directors, and Stockholders:

We have audited General Motors Corporation and subsidiaries' (the Corporation) internal control over financial reporting as of December 31, 2008, based on criteria established in *Internal Control—Integrated Framework* issued by the Committee of Sponsoring Organizations of the Treadway Commission. The Corporation's management is responsible for maintaining effective internal control over financial reporting and for its assessment of the effectiveness of internal control over financial reporting included in Management's Report on Internal Control over Financial Reporting in Item 9A. Our responsibility is to express an opinion on the Corporation's internal control over financial reporting based on our audit.

We conducted our audit in accordance with the standards of the Public Company Accounting Oversight Board (United States). Those standards require that we plan and perform the audit to obtain reasonable assurance about whether effective internal control over financial reporting was maintained in all material respects. Our audit included obtaining an understanding of internal control over financial reporting, assessing the risk that a material weakness exists, testing and evaluating the design and operating effectiveness of internal control based on that risk, and performing such other procedures as we considered necessary in the circumstances. We believe that our audit provides a reasonable basis for our opinion.

A company's internal control over financial reporting is a process designed by, or under the supervision of, the company's principal executive and principal financial officers, or persons performing similar functions, and effected by the company's board of directors, management, and other personnel to provide reasonable assurance regarding the reliability of financial reporting and the preparation of financial statements for external purposes in accordance with generally accepted accounting principles. A company's internal control over financial reporting includes those policies and procedures that (1) pertain to the maintenance of records that, in reasonable detail, accurately and fairly reflect the transactions and dispositions of the assets of the company; (2) provide reasonable assurance that transactions are recorded as necessary to permit preparation of financial statements in accordance with generally accepted accounting principles, and that receipts and expenditures of the company are being made only in accordance with authorizations of management and directors of the company; and (3) provide reasonable assurance regarding prevention or timely detection of unauthorized acquisition, use, or disposition of the company's assets that could have a material effect on the financial statements. Because of the inherent limitations of internal control over financial reporting, including the possibility of collusion or improper management override of controls, material misstatements due to error or fraud may not be prevented or detected on a timely basis. Also, projections of any evaluation of the effectiveness of the internal control over financial reporting to future periods are subject to the risk that the controls may become inadequate because of changes in conditions, or that the degree of compliance with the policies or procedures may deteriorate.

A material weakness is a deficiency, or a combination of deficiencies, in internal control over financial reporting, such that there is a reasonable possibility that a material misstatement of the company's annual or interim financial statements will not be prevented or detected on a timely basis. A material weakness related to ineffective controls over the period-end financial reporting process has been identified and included in management's assessment. This material weakness was considered in determining the nature, timing, and extent of audit tests applied in our audit of the consolidated financial statements and the financial statement schedule listed in the Index at Item 15 as of and for the year ended December 31, 2008. This report does not affect our report on such financial statements and financial statement schedule.

In our opinion, because of the effect of the material weakness identified above on the achievement of the objectives of the control criteria, the Corporation has not maintained effective internal control over financial reporting as of December 31, 2008, based on the criteria established in *Internal Control—Integrated Framework* issued by the Committee of Sponsoring Organizations of the Treadway Commission.

We have also audited, in accordance with the standards of the Public Company Accounting Oversight Board (United States), the Consolidated Balance Sheets and the related Consolidated Statements of Operations, Cash Flows, and Stockholders' Equity (Deficit) of the Corporation as of and for the year ended December 31, 2008. Our audit also included the financial statement schedule listed in the Index at Item 15 as of and for the year ended December 31, 2008. Our report dated March 4, 2009, expressed an unqualified opinion on those financial statements and financial statement schedule and included (a) an explanatory paragraph expressing substantial doubt about the Corporation's ability to continue as a going concern; and (b) an explanatory paragraph relating to the adoption of Statement of Financial Accounting Standards No. 157, *Fair Value Measurements*.

/ s/ DELOITTE & TOUCHE LLP
DELOITTE & TOUCHE LLP
Detroit, Michigan
March 4, 2009

do not express an opinion on the effectiveness of internal control over financial reporting. In this situation, the auditors should state that the scope of the audit was not sufficient to warrant expressing an opinion; and in a separate paragraph, the auditors should explain the reasons for the disclaimer.

If the auditors plan to disclaim an opinion and the procedures they performed caused them to identify a material weakness, their report should include a definition of material weakness and a description of the particular material weakness the auditors have identified. The auditors should communicate in writing to management and the audit committee that they will be unable to complete the audit of internal control over financial reporting because of a scope limitation.

Auditors' Decision to Refer to the Report of Other Auditors in the Auditor's Report

Sometimes another auditor has audited the financial statements and internal controls over financial reporting of a subsidiary of the company. In this situation, auditors must determine whether they will act as the client's principal auditor, and this individual must be the principal auditor of internal control over financial reporting. If the auditors determine that they will assume responsibility for the financial statements as the principal auditor, they must also be the principal auditor for internal controls over the financial reporting process.

When acting as the principal auditor over financial reporting, the auditor must decide whether to refer to the other auditor in the report on internal controls over financial reporting. The rules for referring to another auditor in the report are the same for reporting on the financial statements or internal controls over financial reporting. If the auditor decides to take responsibility for the other auditor's work, no modification of the audit opinion is needed. However, a principal auditor who decides not to take responsibility for the work of the other auditor should modify the opinion to include a reference to the other auditor and indicate the division of responsibility between the principal auditor and the other auditor.

Occurrence of a Significant Subsequent since Year-End

Subsequent events that materially and adversely affect the effectiveness of internal control over financial reporting could occur between the date when this control is audited and the date of the auditor's report. Auditors must gather evidence about these subsequent events. If the auditors obtain knowledge about subsequent events that could have a material and adverse effect on internal control over the financial reporting process, they should issue an adverse opinion on the effectiveness of internal controls over financial reporting. If the auditors are unable to determine the impact of the subsequent event, they should issue a disclaimer of opinion on the effectiveness of internal controls over financial reporting. An explanatory paragraph should be added to the auditor's report to describe the event and its effects on internal controls over financial reporting.

Other Information Provided in Management's Report on Internal Control over Financial Reporting

Management's report could include information in addition to the assessment of the effectiveness of internal controls over financial reporting. The report could include disclosures about corrective actions the company has taken, it's plans to implement new controls, or a statement that the cost of correcting a material weakness is higher than its benefit. If management's report includes additional information, the auditors should disclaim such information by adding a paragraph to the auditor's report on internal controls over financial reporting. For example, if management questions the cost-benefit relationship of correcting a material weakness, the paragraph to disclaim the additional information could read:

We do not express an opinion or any other form of assurance on management's statement referring to the costs and related benefits of implementing new controls.

Certification Persuant to Section 302 of Sarbanes-Oxley General Mills, Inc.	**Exhibit 13-14**

CERTIFICATION PURSUANT TO SECTION 302 OF THE SARBANES-OXLEY ACT OF 2002

I, Donal L. Mulligan, certify that:

1. I have reviewed this annual report on Form 10-K of General Mills, Inc.;

2. Based on my knowledge, this report does not contain any untrue statement of a material fact or omit to state a material fact necessary to make the statements made, in light of the circumstances under which such statements were made, not misleading with respect to the period covered by this report;

3. Based on my knowledge, the financial statements, and other financial information included in this report, fairly present in all material respects the financial condition, results of operations and cash flows of the registrant as of, and for, the periods presented in this report;

4. The registrant's other certifying officer and I are responsible for establishing and maintaining disclosure controls and procedures (as defined in Exchange Act Rules 13a-15(e) and 15d-15(e)) and internal control over financial reporting (as defined in Exchange Act Rules 13a-15(f) and 15d-15(f)) for the registrant and have:

    (a) designed such disclosure controls and procedures, or caused such disclosure controls and procedures to be designed under our supervision, to ensure that material information relating to the registrant, including its consolidated subsidiaries, is made known to us by others within those entities, particularly during the period in which this report is being prepared;

    (b) designed such internal control over financial reporting, or caused such internal control over financial reporting to be designed under our supervision, to provide reasonable assurance regarding the reliability of financial reporting and the preparation of financial statements for external purposes in accordance with generally accepted accounting principles;

    (c) evaluated the effectiveness of the registrant's disclosure controls and procedures and presented in this report our conclusions about the effectiveness of the disclosure controls and procedures, as of the end of the period covered by this report based on such evaluation; and

    (d) disclosed in this report any change in the registrant's internal control over financial reporting that occurred during the registrant's most recent fiscal quarter (the registrant's fourth fiscal quarter in the case of an annual report) that has materially affected, or is reasonably likely to materially affect, the registrant's internal control over financial reporting; and

5. The registrant's other certifying officer and I have disclosed, based on our most recent evaluation of internal control over financial reporting, to the registrant's auditors and the audit committee of the registrant's board of directors (or persons performing the equivalent functions):

    (a) all significant deficiencies and material weaknesses in the design or operation of internal control over financial reporting which are reasonably likely to adversely affect the registrant's ability to record, process, summarize and report financial information; and

    (b) any fraud, whether or not material, that involves management or other employees who have a significant role in the registrant's internal control over financial reporting.

Date: July 9, 2010
/s/ Donal L. Mulligan
Donal L. Mulligan
Executive Vice President and
Chief Financial Officer

Source: http://www.sec.gov/Archives/edgar/data/40704/000095012310064517/c58945exv31w2.htm[7/22/2010 1:28:25 PM]

Management's Certification Pursuant to Section 302 of the Sarbanes-Oxley Act

If management's certification required by Section 302 of the Sarbanes-Oxley Act is misstated, the auditors should communicate this information to management and the audit committee as soon as possible. If they do not respond appropriately, the auditors should modify their report on the audit of internal control over financial reporting to include an explanatory paragraph to describe the reasons they believe that management's disclosures should be modified. This situation could occur if the auditors believe that client disclosure regarding modifications to internal controls over financial reporting that occurred in the fourth quarter was not adequate.

An example of the Section 302 Certification required by the Sarbanes-Oxley Act for General Mills is found in Exhibit 13-14.

Chapter Takeaways

Reporting standards are important for auditors. Although the majority of reports they issue are not modified, the fact that the auditors *can* issue modified reports provides the auditors alternatives when companies refuse to correct material misstatements in the financial statements or fail to make required financial statement disclosure. The requirements of the Public Company Oversight Board have increased the reporting responsibilities for auditors. Auditing standards provide examples of appropriate wording for audit reports; however, the auditors' professional judgment determines the correct report to issue given a specific client's particular circumstances.

This chapter presented these important facts:

- The auditing standards for reporting
- The content of the unmodified audit report and the circumstances when auditors use it
- The use of *emphasis of matter* paragraphs and *other matter* paragraphs in the audit report
- Circumstances when modified audit reports should be issued including qualified audit reports, disclaimer of opinion reports, and adverse opinion reports
- Auditors' reporting responsibilities in terms of (1) using another auditor's work, (2) using quarterly information in the annual report, (3) dating the auditor's report, (4) restricting the use of the auditor's report, and (5) communicating with those responsible for governance
- The content of auditor's report on internal control over financial reporting
- Situations in which the auditor's report on internal control over financial reporting is modified

Be sure you understand these concepts before you go to the next chapter.

Review Questions

LO1	1. Describe the auditing standard for reporting.
LO2	2. What is a standard unmodified audit report? When is it issued? What level of assurance does it provide users of financial statements?
LO3	3. How are explanatory paragraphs used in an audit report? Provide several examples that could be added to an audit report.
LO3	4. Is an audit report with an explanatory paragraph a clean opinion? Explain your answer.
LO4	5. When is a modified audit report issued? What level of assurance does it provide users of financial statements?
LO4	6. When is a disclaimer of opinion audit report used? What level of assurance does it provide users of financial statements?
LO4	7. When is an adverse audit report issued? What level of assurance does it provide users of financial statements?
LO5	8. Discuss auditors' various reporting responsibilities. Why are they important to the audit report?
LO7	9. What is the audit report on internal control over the financial reporting process? When is this report issued? What are auditors' responsibilities in preparing it?
LO8	10. What situations would cause auditors to modify the audit report on internal controls over the financial reporting process?
LO8	11. Describe the circumstances in which an auditor would issue an unqualified report on management's assessment of controls and an adverse report on internal controls over financial reporting.

Multiple Choice Questions from CPA Examinations

LO1   12. Which of the following best describes why an independent auditor is asked to express an opinion on the fair presentation of financial statements?
     a. Preparing financial statements that fairly present a company's financial position, results of operations, and cash flows without the expertise of an independent auditor is difficult.
     b. Management has the responsibility to seek available aid in the appraisal of the financial information shown in its financial statements.
     c. The opinion of an independent party is needed because a company may not be objective with respect to its own financial statements.
     d. Seeing that all shareholders receive an independent report on management's stewardship in managing the affairs of the business is a customary courtesy.

LO2   13. How are management's responsibilities and the auditor's responsibility represented in the standard auditor's report?

	Management's Responsibility	Auditor's Responsibility
a.	Explicitly	Explicitly
b.	Implicitly	Implicitly
c.	Implicitly	Explicitly
d.	Explicitly	Implicitly

LO2   14. The securities of Ralph Corporation are listed on a regional stock exchange registered with the Securities and Exchange Commission (SEC). Ralph's management engages a CPA to perform an independent audit of the company's financial statements. The primary objective of this audit is to provide assurance to the
     a. Regional stock exchange.
     b. Board of directors of Ralph Corporation.
     c. SEC.
     d. Investors in Ralph securities.

LO4   15. When the financial statements contain a departure from generally accepted accounting principles, the effect of which is material, the auditor should
     a. Qualify the opinion and explain the effect of the departure from GAAP in a separate paragraph.
     b. Qualify the opinion and describe the departure from GAAP within the opinion paragraph.
     c. Disclaim an opinion and explain the effect of the departure from GAAP in a separate paragraph.
     d. Disclaim an opinion and describe the departure from GAAP within the opinion paragraph.

LO2   16. The objective of the consistency standard is to provide assurance that
     a. There are no variations in the format and presentation of financial statements.
     b. Substantially different transactions and events are not accounted for on an identical basis.
     c. The auditor is consulted before material changes are made in the application of accounting principles.
     d. The comparability of financial statements between periods is not materially affected by changes in accounting principles without disclosure.

LO3   17. The following explanatory paragraph was included in the auditor's report to indicate a lack of consistency:

As discussed in note T to the financial statements, the company changed its method of computing depreciation in 2001.

How should the auditors report on this matter if they concurred with the change?

	Type of Opinion	Location of Explanatory Paragraph
a.	Unqualified	Before opinion paragraph
b.	Unqualified	After opinion paragraph
c.	Qualified	Before opinion paragraph
d.	Qualified	After opinion paragraph

LO4   18. When an auditor qualifies an opinion because of inadequate disclosure, the auditor should describe the nature of the omission in a separate explanatory paragraph and modify the

	Introductory Paragraph	Scope Paragraph	Opinion Paragraph
a.	Yes	No	No
b.	Yes	Yes	No
c.	No	Yes	Yes
d.	No	No	Yes

LO4   19. In which of the following situations will an auditor ordinarily choose between expressing a qualified opinion or an adverse opinion?
a. The auditor did not observe the entity's physical inventory and is unable to become satisfied as to its balance by other auditing procedures.
b. The financial statements fail to disclose information that is required by the financial reporting framework.
c. The auditor is asked to report only on the entity's balance sheet and not on the other basic financial statements.
d. Events disclosed in the financial statements cause the auditor to have substantial doubt about the entity's ability to continue as a going concern.

LO3   20. An auditor includes a separate paragraph in an otherwise unmodified report to emphasize that the entity being reported on had significant transactions with related parties. The inclusion of this separate paragraph
a. Is considered a qualification of the opinion.
b. Violates generally accepted auditing standards if this information is already disclosed in notes to the financial statements.
c. Necessitates a revision of the opinion paragraph to include the phrase, "with the foregoing explanation."
d. Is appropriate and would not negate the unqualified opinion.

LO4   21. An auditor may not express a qualified opinion when
a. A scope limitation prevents the auditor from completing an important audit procedure.
b. The auditor's report refers to the work of a specialist.
c. An accounting principle at variance with generally accepted accounting principles is used.
d. The auditor lacks independence with respect to the audited entity.

Discussion Questions and Research Problems

LO2, LO4   22. **Type of audit report to be issued.** Assume that auditors encounter the following situations during an audit. Describe what opinion they should issue in each case and any explanatory paragraphs or modifications to the standard report that could be necessary. If more than one opinion is possible, describe the two that could be used and how you would select the correct one.
a. The company has a $12 million loan due next year. It will not have the funds to repay the loan and could find refinancing it difficult.
b. The CEO of Ajax Company does not agree with accounting standards that require the use of fair market value for investment securities. The CEO uses only the cost basis to value securities.

    c. The company you are auditing has both capital and operating leases. A footnote describes the leases correctly, but they are not listed on the financial statements.

    d. Your client has been sued by a supplier for failure to comply with a service agreement. The attorney's letter suggested that the client would lose the lawsuit. Your client refuses to record the potential liability or disclose the lawsuit.

    e. Jones Industrial Products does not want to disclose its pension liability in a footnote. Management believes that the company's shareholders don't care about the potential liability related to the pension liability.

    f. The company refuses to sign the management representation letter.

LO4 23. **Audit report.** You are auditing a company with major production facilities outside the United States. The company has 50% of its inventory in a country with civil unrest. The firm is unable to confirm whether the inventory still exists, and you are unable to visit this country to verify that the inventory is still there. Inventory is 30% of the firm's assets.

    a. What audit opinion are you likely to issue in this situation?

    b. What would cause you to change your first opinion? Is the significance of inventory to the balance sheet important to your decision?

LO7 24. **Reporting responsibility for internal controls over the financial reporting process.** Explain auditors' reporting responsibility for internal controls over the financial reporting process. What types of audit reports can the auditors issue related to this process? What is the report's significance?

25. **Report modifications to the opinion on internal controls over the financial reporting process.** What causes auditors to modify a report on internal controls over financial reporting?

LO5 26. **Review versus audit.** What is the difference between reviewing financial information and auditing financial information? Is the difference important? What information is likely to be reviewed? What information will be audited? Are outsiders likely to understand the difference? What are the implications if outsiders do not understand the difference between information that is reviewed and information that is audited?

Real-World Auditing Problems

LO2, LO7 27. **Dell**

Review the annual report for Dell Computers in the chapter.

    a. What audit opinion did the auditor give Dell on the financial statements?

    b. What was the audit report on the effectiveness of internal control over financial reporting?

    c. Why is the same auditor required to issue reports on the financial statements and internal controls over financial reporting?

    d. What is the auditors' responsibility for the financial statements and for internal controls over financial reporting?

    e. What standard do the auditors use to determine whether the financial statements are materially misstated?

    f. What standard do the auditors use to evaluate the internal controls over financial reporting?

    g. Are these standards known to outside readers of the financial statements?

    h. What are the limitations of internal controls?

    i. What benefit should effective internal controls over the financial reporting process provide to outside readers of the financial statements?

    j. What should outside readers of the annual report conclude regarding the accuracy of the financial statements and the effectiveness of internal controls over financial reporting after reading the audit reports?

LO2, LO7

28. **General Mills**

Review the audit reports for General Mills found in the chapter.

a. How do the General Mills reports differ from those for Dell Computers?

b. What audit opinion did General Mills receive on the financial statements?

c. Describe the explanatory paragraphs in the General Mills report. Why are they included in the audit report?

d. What was the audit report on the effectiveness of internal control over financial reporting?

e. What is management's responsibility for the financial statements and for internal controls over financial reporting?

f. What standard do the auditors use to determine whether the financial statements are materially misstated?

g. What standard do the auditors use to evaluate the internal controls over financial reporting?

h. What are the limitations of internal controls?

i. What benefit should effective internal controls over the financial reporting process provide to outside readers of the financial statements?

j. What should outside readers of the annual report conclude regarding the accuracy of the financial statements and the effectiveness of internal controls over financial reporting after reading the audit reports?

Internet Assignment

LO2, LO7

29. Select a company and go to its website to find its current annual report. Review the independent auditor's report for the financial statements and for internal controls over financial reporting.

a. Describe the type of opinion issued for the financial statements. Did the report include an explanatory paragraph? If so, what type of paragraph is it? What additional information does the explanatory paragraph provide outside users of the financial statements?

b. Is the auditor's opinion on internal control issued as a separate opinion or as a combined opinion with the financial statement opinion? What is the auditor's opinion on the effectiveness of internal control over financial reporting?

c. Who is the auditor on the reports? How quickly was the audit opinion issued after year-end? Is anything unusual discussed in the opinion?

Chapter

14

The Auditing Profession

Learning Objectives

After studying this chapter, you should be able to:

1. Explain the certification procedures for the accounting profession.
2. Describe limitations in the current audit methodology.
3. Discuss the pressures on management and auditors that make auditing a difficult job.
4. Describe the auditor's responsibility when performing audits, attestation services, compilations, and reviews.
5. Discuss the AICPA Professional Code of Conduct.
6. Explain the International Code of Ethics for Professional Accountants.
7. Describe the legal liability associated with an audit engagement.

Auditing pronouncements relevant to this topic

For private companies

- AICPA Code of Professional Conduct

For public companies

- AICPA Code of Professional Conduct
- Sarbanes-Oxley Act of 2002

International standards

- Code of Ethics for Professional Accountants

Chapter Overview

Auditing is a profession. In the United States, to be a member of this profession, a candidate must pass the CPA exam and work under an experienced member of the profession for 1 or 2 years (depending on the particular state and whether the applicant has an undergraduate or an advanced degree). In other countries, members of the profession may have to pass licensing exams or obtain a degree from a university program in accounting. Members of the profession pay professional dues and meet yearly continuing education requirements to maintain their license to practice as auditors. The Code of Professional Conduct established by the American Institute of Certified Public Accountants (AICPA) sets the ethics standards for the accounting profession in the United States. International auditors follow the Code of Ethics for Professional Accountants written by the International Ethics Standards Board for Accountants (IESBA). Members of the profession agree to abide by the standards established by it. Failure to abide by these standards can lead to the forfeiture of membership.

The accounting profession offers exciting opportunities and great variety for the accountant. Working as a professional accountant presents significant challenges in the contemporary business environment of rapid change. Regulations change, and business transactions assume many forms. Clients are endlessly creative in their attempts to present financial statements that reflect positively on their performance. Both companies and auditors face tremendous pressure to prepare financial statements that make the company look good. Managers often lose bonuses, and accountants are sometimes fired when financial statements fail to meet management's expectations.

Although it is an exciting time to be an auditor, the profession also carries with it some risk. Third parties often sue auditors when companies fail. Because they perform personal services, much like a doctor, auditors sometimes struggle to protect themselves from personal liability in the lawsuits filed against them. They are often viewed as the party with deep pockets, so outsiders often blame them for the problems of a failed company.

Certification Procedures for the Accounting Profession

LO1

Explain the certification procedures for the accounting profession

How does an individual become certified to work as an independent accountant? The only way to obtain certification in the United States is to pass a uniform certification exam administered by the AICPA and meet the experience requirements of the state board of accountancy in which the accountant is licensed. State accounting regulations determine who can take the CPA examination, and these regulations set its provisional pass rules. Let's consider the elements of the AICPA Uniform CPA Examination.

The exam is composed of four parts: (1) auditing and attestation, (2) financial accounting and reporting, (3) regulation, and (4) business environment and concepts. The content of the auditing and attestation section is described in more detail following a description of the subject matter for the remaining three sections.

The exam's *financial accounting and reporting* section tests the candidates' knowledge and understanding of the financial reporting framework. This includes standards issued by the Financial Accounting Standards Board, the International Accounting Standards Board, the U.S. Securities and Exchange Commission, and the Governmental Accounting Standards Board. The *regulation* section examines the candidates' knowledge and understanding of ethics, professional and legal responsibilities, business law, and federal taxation. The *business environment and concepts* section pertains to the candidates' knowledge and skills necessary to demonstrate an understanding of the general business environment and business concepts. Topics in this section include knowledge of corporate governance and economic concepts essential to understanding the global business environment. Clearly, several of the topics included in the sections of the CPA examination have been discussed in this text (for example, ethical and professional responsibilities and SEC-issued standards).

Let's now consider the *auditing and attestation* section of the CPA exam. Effective January 1, 2011, candidates taking the auditing and attestation section of the CPA examination are expected to demonstrate an awareness of (1) the International Auditing and Assurance Standards Board (IAASB) and its role in establishing international standards on auditing (ISAs), (2) the differences between ISAs and U.S. auditing standards, and (3) the audit requirements under U.S. auditing standards that apply when audit procedures are performed on a U.S. company that supports an audit report based upon the auditing standards of another country. The exam's auditing section tests the person's awareness of (1) the International Ethics Standards Board for Accountants (IESBA) and its role in establishing requirements of the Code of Ethics for Professionals of the International Federation of Accountants (IFAC) and (2) the independence requirements that apply when audit procedures are performed on a U.S. company that supports an audit report based upon auditing standards of another country (ISAs).

In the auditing and attestation section of the CPA exam, candidates are expected to demonstrate knowledge and understanding of the professional standards and the skill to apply that knowledge to performing auditing tasks, some of which follow:

- Demonstrate an awareness and understanding of the process by which standards and professional requirements are established, including the role of standard-setting bodies in the United States and other bodies that have authority to develop international standards.
- Differentiate between audits, attestation and assurance services, compilations, and reviews.
- Differentiate between the professional standards for issuers and nonissuers.
- Identify situations that might be unethical or a violation of professional standards, conduct research and perform consultations regarding situations that might be unethical or a violation of professional standards as appropriate, and determine the appropriate action(s) to take.
- Recognize potentially unethical behavior of clients and determine its impact on the services performed.
- Demonstrate the importance of identifying and following requirements, rules, and standards established by the licensing board.
- Apply professional requirements in practice.
- Exercise due care in the performance of work.
- Demonstrate an appropriate level of professional skepticism in performing work.
- Maintain independence in mental attitude in all matters relating to the audit.
- Be able to research relevant professional literature.

Specific content parts of the auditing section of the exam and the percentage of questions related to them follow.

- Engagement Acceptance and Understanding the Assignment (12–16%)
- Understanding the Entity and Its Environment (including internal control) (16–20%)
- Performing Audit Procedures and Evaluating Evidence (16–20%)
- Evaluating Audit Findings, Communications, and Reporting (16–20%)
- Accounting and Review Services Engagements (12–16%)
- Professional Responsibilities (16–20%)

Limitations of Current Audit Methodology

LO2

Describe limitations in the current audit methodology

The audit methodology that accounting firms use currently is based on risk assessment and reliance on internal controls. Thirty years ago, the accounting profession conducted audits using more detailed transaction testing and placed less reliance on internal controls. Competition in the audit market is said to have caused the accounting firms to change their audit approach, relying more on internal controls and less on detailed transaction testing. The emphasis on internal control testing in the new audit standards issued by the PCAOB has even increased auditors' reliance on internal controls.

Several problems emerge when auditors rely on internal control evidence rather than engage in detailed testing when performing an audit. Internal controls are designed to prevent or detect misstatements. Companies often use internal controls for routine transactions but not for transactions that occur infrequently or are estimation transactions. Internal controls rarely apply to management activities or decisions. In this context, auditors who rely on internal control testing could neglect transactions that are not routine in performing audit procedures. In addition, management can often override internal controls, so fraudulent transactions it used to misstate financial statements could be difficult to discover if the auditors place too much reliance on internal controls.

Although its use has increased, auditors' knowledge of internal control systems has not increased in the last 30 years. Today auditors are required to understand internal control relevant to the audit, but auditors may not understand all the controls that a system, particularly an automated one, has. This lack of knowledge of automated systems could limit the auditors' ability to make good decisions regarding the effect of internal controls on the financial statements. Internal control systems are often complex. It is often difficult for one individual to understand all controls built into an internal control system. Other challenges exist as well. Internal control systems change every year. They are updated and modified, and controls that were present one year could have been removed the next year.

The most serious limitation of internal controls is that no causal relationship exists between good internal controls and good financial statements. Internal controls are rules that employees are supposed to follow, yet what people say they do and what they actually do are significantly different. For example, firms can establish good internal controls and employees can describe them to the auditor, but when auditors test the internal controls, they often find that they were not followed. An employee could say, "Yes, I am supposed to initial the voucher request indicating that I agreed the invoice amount to the amount on the receiving report and the purchase order." The auditor could then ask why the amount doesn't agree although the initials indicating agreement are on the voucher request—and the employee could have no explanation. There can be several explanations for such a discrepancy. It is easy for the employee to initial the form and forget to perform the control. It is also easy for the employee to perform the control but fail to initial the form, leaving the internal control (the initials) almost meaningless. The only internal controls the auditor can rely on are those performed by computers because they do not tire, are not interrupted when working, and perform repetitive tasks consistently.

At the extreme levels, a company with good internal controls (and low control risk) can have materially misstated financial statements. The internal control documentation could be present, but that does not mean that the control has been performed (the only way the auditor could tell this is to reperform the control for the items tested). At the other extreme, a company can have no internal controls (and a control risk of 100%) yet not have materially misstated financial statements. In this situation, the individuals recording the transactions recorded them accurately.

Whether you believe that the current audit methodology is good or bad, you will become quite familiar with internal control documentation and testing. The new legislation resulting from the passage of the Sarbanes-Oxley Act places great importance on internal control testing. For now, current audit methodology considers internal control testing to be an important tool of auditors. However, you should remember the inherent limitations of internal controls as described in the auditor's report on the effectiveness of internal controls.

Because of the inherent limitations of internal control over financial reporting, including the possibility of collusion or improper management override of controls, material misstatements due to error or fraud may not be prevented or detected on a timely basis. Also, projections of any evaluation of the effectiveness of the internal control over financial reporting to future periods are subject to the risk that the controls may become inadequate because of changes in conditions, or that the degree of compliance with the policies or procedures may deteriorate (PCAOB Statement No. 5).

Perform internal control testing as required by the standards, but use common sense and caution in forming conclusions about the accuracy of the financial statements based on internal control tests.

Pressure on Management and Auditors

LO3

Discuss the pressures on management and auditors that make auditing a difficult job

Management and the auditor face strong pressures that could make doing their job properly difficult. Both groups face strong pressures that could affect their performance and cost their jobs if they fail to perform well.

Management faces pressure from both within and outside the firm. Managers' bosses often pressure them to meet earnings or performance targets and reward them with cash bonuses or stock options for meeting these targets. Failure to meet the earnings target could result in the manager's firing or being rated poorly for failing to do the job. Outsiders who review a firm's performance usually expect it to show constant, increasing growth. The firm is expected to grow each year, often to show increasing amounts of growth. For example, growth of 5% one year should be followed by growth of 6 or 7% the next year. A company that grows each year at such an increasing rate is likely to be evaluated positively by the market. Given such expectations, outsiders (shareholders, lenders, stock analysts) pressure firms to report constant growth each year. Even if economic or industry conditions do not justify constant growth in a given year, management could try to twist the firm's earnings into the pattern that outsiders expect. Many methods used to manipulate earnings to show growth cause problems for the auditor.

Auditors also face pressure in performing their work. They are sometimes evaluated on whether they keep their clients happy. Clients who are unhappy with the audit could fire the audit firm, reducing the auditors' financial compensation. Auditors work closely with management, but they are hired by and report to the audit committee, the board of directors and shareholders. It could be difficult for auditors to resist pressure from management with whom they have a working relationship. In such circumstances, auditors could be inappropriately influenced by managers with whom they have worked most closely and fail to protect shareholders' interests.

Auditor Responsibility for Different Service Levels

LO4

Describe the auditor's responsibility when performing audits, attestation services, compilations, and reviews

A client could hire accountants to provide one or more of at least four levels of service (in addition to tax and various consulting services). Auditors could (1) perform an audit, (2) provide attest services, (3) perform a compilation, or (4) conduct a review. Each of these engagements is discussed briefly next. An audit requires the accountant to gather the most evidence and provides the highest level of assurance of the four types of engagements. A compilation requires no evidence and provides no assurance. In terms of the amount of evidence required and the level of assurance provided, the services are ranked from high to low or none as audit, attest, review, and compilation.

Audit

When accountants perform an audit, they follow the guidelines of the profession listed in the Statements on Auditing Standards, which are referred to as AU sections in this textbook. If the audit involves a public client, the auditors follow the guidelines of the profession issued by the Public Accounting and Oversight Board whose standards are referred to as AS standards in this textbook. We have discussed audits extensively throughout this textbook.

When accountants outside the United Stated perform an audit, they follow the guidelines of the International Auditing and Assurance Standards Board, which are referred to as ISA guidelines in this book. The auditing standards of the International Auditing and Assurance Standards Board and the AICPA Auditing Standards Board (the ISAs and the AUs) are converging into one set of standards, so most of the references to the auditing standards in this book are consistent both in and outside the United States.

Attest Services

When auditors perform attest engagements, they follow the guidelines of the profession listed in Statements on Standards for Attestation Engagements (SSAEs). These standards are referred to with AT paragraph numbers. Practitioners hired for an attestation engagement issue an examination, a review, or an agreed-upon procedures *report* (not an opinion). An attest engagement could be related to a number of issues such as historical or prospective performance, physical characteristics (for example, square footage of facilities), historical events (the price of a market basket of goods on a certain date), analyses (for example, break-even analysis), systems and processes (for example, internal control), and behavior (for example, compliance with laws and regulations, corporate governance).

Compilations and Reviews

Many nonpublic companies in the United States have their financial statements compiled or reviewed rather than audited. An audit is expensive, and only public companies in the United States are required by law to have one. When performing a compilation or a review, auditors follow the guidelines issued as Statements on Standards for Accounting and Review Services (SSARs), which are referenced with AR paragraph numbers. The difference between a review and a compilation is the level of assurance provided in the report prepared by the practitioner: A review provides limited assurance, but a compilation provides no assurance. The objective of a compilation engagement is to present information that is the representation of management in the form of financial statements but without expressing any assurance on the financial statements. The objective of a review engagement is to express limited assurance that no material modifications should be made to the financial statements in order for the statements to be in conformity with GAAP.

During a review engagement, practitioners perform limited procedures to review the financial statements. These could include analytical procedures and inquiries of management. During a compilation engagement, auditors perform no procedures to review the financial statements.

The practitioner issues a *report* (not an opinion) for both a compilation and a review. The specific wording of the report can be found in the auditing standards issued by the Auditing Standards Board.

AICPA Code of Professional Conduct

LO5

Discuss the AICPA Professional Code of Conduct

One of the hallmarks of a profession is that its members can be distinguished from nonprofessionals by the standards the professionals follow. One of the standards important to the accounting profession is the code of professional conduct. We refer to this as the "ethics code" for accountants. Failure to follow the principles and rules of the ethics code could result in the loss of the right to work as a professional accountant.

The AICPA code of professional conduct has two sections, one that describes the basic conceptual framework of the profession's rules and regulations, and the other that expresses the particular rules that govern the professional practice of the accountant. See a description of the concepts in Exhibit 14-1. For the particular rules that apply to professional practice, refer to Exhibit 14-2. For interpretations of the rules of conduct, see Exhibit 14-3. Most of these rules apply to every member of the profession, but some apply only to members in public practice.

The preamble to the professional code of conduct establishes the concept of professionalism embodied in the code:

These Principles of the Code of Professional Conduct of the American Institute of Certified Public Accountants express the profession's recognition of its responsibilities to the public, to clients, and to colleagues. They guide members in the performance of their professional responsibilities and express the basic tenets of ethical and professional conduct. The Principles call for an unswerving commitment to honorable behavior, even at the sacrifice of personal advantage (AICPA ET 51.02).

| The AICPA Principles of Professional Conduct | Exhibit 14-1 |

Principles

Article I—Responsibilities	In carrying out their responsibilities as professionals, members should exercise sensitive professional and moral judgments in all their activities.
Article II—The Public Interest	Members should accept the obligation to act in a way that will serve the public interest, honor the public trust, and demonstrate commitment to professionalism.
Article III—Integrity	To maintain and broaden public confidence, members should perform all professional responsibilities with the highest sense of integrity.
Article IV—Objectivity and Independence	A member should maintain objectivity and be free of conflicts of interest in discharging professional responsibilities. A member in public practice should be independent in fact and appearance when providing auditing and other attestation services.
Article V—Due Care	A member should observe the profession's technical and ethical standards, strive continually to improve competence and the quality of services, and discharge professional responsibility to the best of the member's ability.
Article VI—Scope and Nature of Services	A member in public practice should observe the Principles of the Code of Professional Conduct in determining the scope and nature of services to be provided.

The Principles

Six principles establish the basic conceptual framework for the professional code of conduct: responsibility, the public interest, integrity, objectivity and independence, due care, and the scope and nature of services performed by the accountant. Professionals are expected to exercise moral judgment in all activities. They are obligated to act in a way that serves the public interest, honors the trust of the public, and shows a commitment to the concept of professionalism. Accountants should perform their professional responsibilities with a high sense of integrity. When providing auditing services, professional accountants must be free of conflicts of interest and independent in *fact* and *appearance*. Accountants are expected to perform their jobs to the best of their ability. They are expected to use these principles to determine both the scope and nature of the services they perform. These principles are more specifically defined in the section of the professional code of conduct titled Rules and Interpretations of Rules.

The Rules

The current AICPA rules are divided into five sections, including a section reserved for future use. The rules include **Section 100**—Independence, Integrity, and Objectivity; **Section 200**—General Standards Accounting Principles; **Section 300**—Responsibilities to Clients; and **Section 500**—Other Responsibilities and Practices. **Section 400**—Responsibilities to Colleagues has been set aside for future additions. These sections are discussed briefly next.

Section 100-Independence, Integrity, and Objectivity

Section 100 is composed of two rules. Rule 101 addresses auditor independence in performing professional services. Rule 102 provides the requirements for objectivity and integrity in the performance of professional responsibilities. It also requires auditors to make their own judgment and to avoid subordinating their judgment to others.

Rule 101 is one of the most important rules in the professional code of conduct, and the AICPA has an extensive set of interpretations of it. If auditors are not independent in

| The AICPA Rules of Professional Conduct | Exhibit 14-2 |

Section 100— Independence, Integrity, and Objectivity	Rule 101— Independence	A member in public practice shall be independent in the performance of professional services as required by standards promulgated by bodies designated by Council.
	Rule 102— Integrity and Objectivity	In the performance of any professional service, a member shall maintain objectivity and integrity, shall be free of conflicts of interest, and shall not knowingly misrepresent facts or subordinate his or her judgment to others.
Section 200— General Standards— Accounting Principles	Rule 201— General Standards	A member shall comply with the following standards and with any interpretations thereof by bodies designated by Council. a. *Professional Competence.* Undertake only those professional services that the member or the member's firm can reasonably expect to be completed with professional competence. b. *Due Professional Care.* Exercise due professional care in the performance of professional services. c. *Planning and Supervision.* Adequately plan and supervise the performance of professional services. d. *Sufficient Relevant Data.* Obtain sufficient relevant data to afford a reasonable basis for conclusions or recommendations in relation to any professional services performed.
	Rule 202— Compliance with Standards	A member who performs auditing, review, compilation, management consulting, tax, or other professional services shall comply with standards promulgated by bodies designated by Council.
	Rule 203— Accounting Principles	A member shall not (1) express an opinion or state affirmatively that the financial statements or other financial data of any entity are presented in conformity with generally accepted accounting principles or (2) state that he or she is not aware of any material modifications that should be made to such statements or data in order for them to be in conformity with generally accepted accounting principles, if such statements or data contain any departure from an accounting principle promulgated by bodies designated by Council to establish such principles that has a material effect on the statements or data taken as a whole. If, however, the statements or data contain such a departure and the member can demonstrate that due to unusual circumstances the financial statements or data would otherwise have been misleading, the member can comply with the rule by describing the departure, its approximate effects, if practicable, and the reasons why compliance with the principle would result in a misleading statement.
Section 300— Responsibilities to Clients	Rule 301— Confidential Client Information	A member in public practice shall not disclose any confidential client information without the specific consent of the client. The rule shall not construed (1) to relieve a member of his or her professional obligations under rules 202 and 203, (2) to affect in any way the member's obligation to comply with a validly issued and enforceable subpoena or summons, or to prohibit a member's compliance with applicable laws and government regulations, (3) to prohibit review of a member's professional practice under AICPA or state CPA society or Board of Accountancy authorization, or (4) to preclude a member from initiating a complaint with, or responding to any inquiry made by, the professional ethics division or trial board of the Institute or a duly constituted investigative or disciplinary body of a state CPA society or Board of Accountancy.
	Rule 302— Contingent Fees	A member in public practice shall not 1. Perform for a contingent fee any professional services for, or receive such a fee from a client for whom the member or the member's firm performs, 　a. an audit or review of a financial statements; or 　b. a compilation of a financial statement when the member expects, or reasonably might expect, that a third party will use the financial statement and the member's compilation report does not disclose a lack of independence; or 　c. an examination of prospective financial information; or 2. Prepare an original or amended tax return or claim for a tax refund for a contingent fee for any client.

Section 400—Responsibilities to Colleagues	No current rulings.	
Section 500—Other Responsibilities and Practices	Rule 501—Acts Discreditable	A member shall not commit an act discreditable to the profession.
	Rule 502—Advertising and Other Forms of Solicitation	A member in public practice shall not seek to obtain clients by advertising or other forms of solicitation in a manner that is false, misleading, or deceptive. Solicitation by the use of coercion, over-reaching, or harassing conduct is prohibited.
	Rule 503—Commissions and Referral Fees	**1. *Prohibited commissions*** A member in public practice shall not for a commission recommend or refer to a client any product or service, or for a commission recommend or refer any product or service to be supplied by a client, or receive a commission, when the member or the member's firm also performs for that client a. an audit or review of a financial statements; or b. a compilation of a financial statement when the member expects, or reasonably might expect, that a third party will use the financial statement and the member's compilation report does not disclose a lack or independence; or c. an examination of prospective financial information. This prohibition applies during the period in which the member is engaged to perform any of the services listed above and the period covered by any historical financial statements involved in such listed services. **2. *Disclosure of permitted commissions*** A member in public practice who is not prohibited by this rule from performing services for or receiving a commission and who is paid or expects to be paid a commission shall disclose that fact to any person or entity to whom the member recommends or refers a product or service to which the commission relates. **3. *Referral fees*** Any member who accepts a referral fee for recommending or referring any service of a CPA to any person or entity or who pays a referral fee to obtain a client shall disclose such acceptance or payment to the client.
	Rule 505—Form of Organization and Name	A member may practice public accounting only in a form of organization permitted by law or regulation whose characteristics conform to resolutions of Council. A member shall not practice public accounting under a firm name that is misleading. Names of one of more past owners may be included in the firm name of a successor organization. A firm may not designate itself as "Members of the American Institute of Certified Public Accountants" unless all of its CPA owners are members of the Institute.

the performance of their job in public practice, they have nothing to offer outsiders. Outsiders could view auditors who lack independence as representing only the interests of management rather than considering the interests of outsiders. Accountants in public practice must be familiar with the requirements of this rule and the additional independence rules imposed by the PCAOB and the SEC.

According to Principle IV of the AICPA Code of Professional Conduct, Objectivity and Independence, auditors are required to be independent in *fact* and in *appearance*. Rule 101 and its interpretations provide guidance on determining whether auditors are independent in fact. If they conform to the rules in the professional code of conduct and the additional independence requirements imposed by the SEC and PCAOB for audits of public companies, auditors could be independent in fact. In addition, independence in appearance is judged by outside readers of the financial statements. To be independent in appearance, accountants should be judged from the

Interpretations for Rules of Conduct   Exhibit 14-3

Rule 101—Independence	• Interpretation of Rule 101 • Employment or association with attest clients • Performance of nonattest services • Honorary directorships and trusteeships of not-for-profit organizations • Loans from financial institution clients and related terminology • The effect of actual or threatened litigation on independence • Effect on independence of financial interests in nonclients having investor or investee relationships with a covered member's client • The effect on independence of relationships with entities included in the governmental financial statements • Modified application of Rule 101 for certain engagements to issue restricted-use reports under the Statements on Standards for Attestation Engagements • Independence and cooperative arrangements with clients • The effect of alternative practice structures on the applicability of independence rules • Financial relationships
Rule 102—Integrity and Objectivity	• Knowing misrepresentations in the preparation of financial statements or records • Conflicts of interest • Obligations of a member to his or her employer's external accountant • Subordination of judgment by a member • Applicability of Rule 102 to members performing educational services • Professional services involving client advocacy
Rule 201—General Standards	• Competence
Rule 202—Compliance with Standards	• None
Rule 203—Accounting Principles	• Departures from established accounting principles • Status of FASB and GASB interpretations • Responsibility of employees for the preparation of financial statements in conformity with GAAP
Rule 301—Confidential Client Information	• Confidential information and the purchase, sale, or merger of a practice
Rule 302—Contingent Fees	• Contingent fees in tax matters
Rule 501—Acts Discreditable	• Response to requests by clients and former clients for records • Discrimination and harassment in employment practices • Failure to follow standards and/or procedures or other requirements in governmental audits • Negligence in the preparation of financial statements or records • Failure to follow requirements of governmental bodies, commissions, or other regulatory agencies • Solicitation or disclosure of CPA examination questions and answers • Failure to file tax return or pay tax liability • Failure to follow requirements of governmental bodies, commissions, or other regulatory agencies on indemnification and limitation of liability provisions in connection with audit and other attest services.
Rule 502—Advertising and Other Forms of Solicitation	• False, misleading, or deceptive acts in advertising or solicitation • Engagements obtained through efforts of third parties
Rule 503—Commissions and Referral Fees	• None
Rule 505—Form of Organization and Name	• Application of Rules of Conduct to members who own a separate business • Application of Rule 505 to alternative practice structures

perspective of an outsider. One of the issues currently debated as a potential threat to independence in appearance is the auditor's role in providing management consulting services. Although they are currently allowed to provide many types of consulting services, audit committees of companies are often concerned that disclosure in the footnotes of management consulting fees paid to their auditor "appears" to impair the independence of the auditors. The audit committees of many companies choose to hire a second audit firm to perform consulting services rather than risk the perception of a loss of independence if the audit firm that does the company's audit performs consulting services.

For any engagement, the independence rules apply to all members of the engagement team and any partners who provide more than 10 hours of nonaudit services to the audit client. Interpretation 101-1 provides additional guidelines to determine auditor independence. According to this interpretation, *independence is impaired if the auditor has any direct or material indirect financial interest* in the client. A direct financial interest includes stock ownership or a loan to or from the client. An indirect interest will not impair independence if the amount involved is immaterial to the income and wealth of the accountant. An indirect financial interest occurs when an auditor has a financial interest in a company associated with the audit client. An auditor who invests in a mutual fund that owns shares of stock in the company being audited has an indirect financial interest in that company.

A loan to or from an audit client usually impairs independence. In some situations, however, a loan to or from an audit client does not impair independence. Some of these exceptions include car loans or leases collateralized by the car, loans fully collateralized by the cash surrender value of a life insurance policy, loans fully collateralized by cash deposits at the same financial institution, and credit cards and cash advances that reduce the outstanding amount to $10,000 or less by the due date. All loans that are excluded must be made under the normal lending procedures, terms, and conditions of the lending institution.

The independence rules apply to an accountant's immediate family (spouse and/or dependent). The accountant's spouse could work for the audit client as long as he or she was not employed in a position with significant influence over the client's financial or accounting policies.

Independence rules usually do not apply to an accountant's close relatives (parent, grandparents, siblings, or nondependent child) unless the close relative has a material interest in the client and the accountant is aware of the interest or the close relative can exercise significant influence over the client's financial or accounting policies.

Additional Independence Requirements Imposed by the Sarbanes-Oxley Act for Public Companies

The PCAOB adopted certain standards of the AICPA's Code of Professional Conduct on an interim basis in 2003 including Rule 101 and Rule 102 and the interpretations of both rules. The PCAOB has also issued several Ethics and Independence Rules including:

- Rule 3501   Definitions of Terms Employed in Section 3, Part 5 of the Rules
- Rule 3502   Responsibility Not to Knowingly or Recklessly Contribute to Violations
- Rule 3520   Auditor Independence
- Rule 3521   Contingent Fees
- Rule 3522   Tax Transactions
- Rule 3523   Tax Services for Persons in Financial Reporting Oversight Roles
- Rule 3524   Audit Committee Pre-approval of Certain Tax Services
- Rule 3525   Audit Committee Pre-approval of Non-audit Services Related to Internal Control over Financial Reporting
- Rule 3526   Communication with Audit Committees Concerning Independence

The Sarbanes-Oxley Act of 2002 also provides additional independence requirements that must be followed by accountants who audit public companies. These additional standards do not apply to audits of private companies.

Title II—Auditor Independence—of the Sarbanes-Oxley Act lists the following services that an auditor is prohibited from performing:

- Bookkeeping or other services related to the accounting records or financial statements of the audit client
- Financial information systems' design and implementation
- Appraisal or valuation services, fairness opinions, or contribution-in-kind reports
- Actuarial services
- Internal audit services
- Management or human resource services
- Broker or dealer, investment adviser, or investment banking services
- Legal and expert services unrelated to the audit
- Any other service that the PCAOB determines is not permissable

An accounting firm could engage in audit and nonaudit services only if the audit committee preapproves the activity.

Section 203 of the Sarbanes-Oxley Act requires that accounting firms rotate audit partners on the engagement for one client after 5 years. Section 204 requires the auditor to report to the audit committee all critical accounting policies and practices used; all alternative treatments of accounting information; and other material written communications between the client and the auditor, such as the management letter and the schedule of uncorrected audit adjustments. Section 206 discusses conflicts of interest between the accounting firm and the audit client. This section makes it unlawful for an accounting firm to perform an audit if the chief executive officer, controller, chief financial officer, chief accounting officer, or any person serving in an equivalent position in the company was employed by the accounting firm and participated in the audit during the one-year period preceding the start of the audit.

Section 200—General Standards Accounting Principles

Section 200 contains three rules. Rule 201 requires accountants to undertake only the professional services they are competent to perform, to perform those services with *due professional care* (an important standard to measure performance against), to plan and supervise adequately the professional services, and to gather sufficient evidence to support their conclusions.

Rule 202 requires accountants to follow the accounting standards. This rule is important because many of the accounting standards are rules only because the members agree to follow them. This rule requires accountants to follow accounting standards. If they fail to follow them, they have violated the professional code of conduct. Rule 202 gives the accounting standards the force of law for the profession.

Rule 203 of the standards states that accountants should not express an opinion stating the financial statements are in conformity with generally accepted accounting principles (GAAP) if the statements do not conform to these principles. There is an exception to this rule: Accountants are permitted to express an opinion on financial statements that are not in accordance with GAAP if they believe that the non-GAAP presentation is correct. Expressing an opinion on such statements would not violate Rule 203 of the Professional Code of Conduct. This rule does not apply to audits of public companies.

Section 300—Responsibilities to Clients

Section 300 comprises two rules that apply to accountants in public practice. Rule 301 prohibits an accountant from disclosing confidential client information to anyone without the client's consent. Rule 302 prohibits accountants from performing professional services or preparing tax returns for a contingent fee. A contingent fee varies based on the outcome of the service provided.

Section 500—Other Responsibilities and Practices

Section 500 is composed of four rules. Rule 501 specifies that an accountant should not commit an act discreditable to the profession. Some of the acts that are considered discreditable to the profession are the failure to file a tax return, negligence in the preparation of financial statements, and disclosure of CPA exam questions or answers. Rule 502 prohibits an accountant in public practice from engaging in false, misleading, or deceptive advertising.

Rule 503 addresses prohibited commissions, disclosure of permitted commissions, and referral fees. It prohibits members in public practice from recommending for a commission a product or service to a client for which they are also performing an audit or review of financial statements, a compilation of a financial statement, or an examination of prospective financial statement information. Members who are not prohibited from performing services for a client and who are paid a commission shall disclose that fact to the company to which they recommend the product or service. Any accountant who accepts a referral fee for recommending a service of a CPA to another person or company shall disclose the fee to the client. Rule 505 requires the accountant to practice public accounting in the form of organization permitted by law. Most states allow personal service firms to operate as partnerships or limited liability corporations. The name of the firm cannot be misleading. It could include the name of one or more past owners of the firm in the name of the new firm.

A firm cannot state that it is a "Member of the AICPA" unless all partners are members. This rule will cause problems for states that have not adopted the 150-hour rule (an AICPA requirement). A candidate taking the CPA exam without 150 hours will not be allowed to be a member of the AICPA.

IESBA Code of Ethics for Professional Accountants

LO6

Explain the International Code of Ethics for Professional Accountants

Accountants in the United States must be aware of the ethics code that applies in the international setting. The International Ethics Standards Board for Accountants (IESBA) has written the international code of ethics. It is a subcommittee of the International Federation of Accountants (IFAC). The International Code has three parts. Part A provides the fundamental principles of professional ethics for professional accountants and provides a conceptual framework that professional accountants should use in making decisions involving audit practice. Parts B and C describe how the conceptual framework applies in certain situations. Part B applies to professional accountants in public practice, and Part C applies to professional accountants in business. The fundamental principles described in Part A are discussed next. For a list of the content of Part B and Part C, see Exhibit 14-4.

Part A of the code of ethics for professional accountants requires the accountant to comply with the following principles:

- Integrity—to be straightforward and honest in all professional and business relationships
- Objectivity—not to allow bias, conflict of interest, or undue influence of others to override professional or business judgments
- Professional competence and due care—to maintain professional knowledge and skill at the level required to ensure that a client or employer receives competent professional services based on current developments in practice, legislation, and techniques and to act diligently and in accordance with applicable technical and professional standards
- Confidentiality—to respect the confidentiality of information acquired as a result of professional and business relationships
- Professional behavior—to comply with relevant laws and regulations and avoid any action that discredits the profession

IESBA Code of Ethics for Professional Accountants, International Federation of Accountants		**Exhibit 14-4**

Part A	General Application of the IESBA Code
Section 100	Introduction and Fundamental Principles
Section 110	Integrity
Section 120	Objectivity
Section 130	Professional Competence and Due Care
Section 140	Confidentiality
Section 150	Professional Behavior
Part B	Professional Accountants in Public Practice
Section 200	Introduction
Section 210	Professional Appointment
Section 220	Conflicts of Interest
Section 230	Second Opinions
Section 240	Fees and Other Types of Remuneration
Section 250	Marketing Professional Services
Section 260	Gifts and Hospitality
Section 270	Custody of Client Assets
Section 280	Objectivity—All Services
Section 290	Independence—Audit and Review Engagements
Section 291	Other Assurance Engagements
Interpretation 2005-1	Independence Requirements for Engagements that are not Financial Statement Audits
Part C	Professional Accountants in Business
Section 300	Introduction
Section 310	Potential Conflicts
Section 320	Preparation and Reporting of Information
Section 330	Acting with Sufficient Expertise
Section 340	Financial Interests
Section 350	Inducements

Source: www.ifac.org

Legal Liability Associated with an Audit Engagement

LO7

Describe the legal liability associated with an audit engagement

Auditors provide professional services to their clients. They can be sued in a court of law for their decisions by their client, regulators who believe they have violated the law, and by outsiders who rely on the financial statements and believe that they suffered harm because the financial statements were materially misstated. The auditor faces liability from four primary sources: (1) audit clients, (2) third-parties under common law, (3) civil action under the federal securities laws, and (4) criminal law. Each source of legal liability and auditors' defense against lawsuits filed from each source are discussed next. Individuals, groups of individuals, or regulatory bodies can file lawsuits in state or federal court. Damages awarded in a lawsuit could be financial in the form of fines or could take the form of punishment by prison sentences.

Legal Liability from Audit Clients

A legal contract establishes the relationship between a company and its auditors for the performance of an audit. Both parties are legally liable to meet the terms of the contract and can be sued for *breach of contract*. For example, the client could allege that the auditors were in breach of contract and because they were negligent in performing their duties, they failed to discover fraud or breached the confidentiality requirement. Auditors can use four defenses to defend themselves against client lawsuits: (1) lack of duty, (2) non-negligent performance, (3) contributory negligence, and (4) absence of causal connection. Auditors can use the "lack of duty" defense when they believe that they did not have a duty to perform the service. The best way to establish a lack of duty defense is to refer to the engagement letter and to indicate that the auditor performed the services specified in it.

Auditors could use the "non-negligent performance" defense when they believe that they have complied with the requirements of the auditing standards. In this case, the auditors state that they have gathered the evidence that another auditor would have gathered and interpreted it in a manner consistent with their interpretation. For this reason, the auditors should not be held legally liable for the performance failure that the client alleges.

A defense of "contributory negligence" alleges that because of the client's actions, the auditor was prevented from gathering the information necessary to make the correct decision. For example, the client who sets up post office boxes around the country and completes all accounts receivable confirmations verifying the balances for the fictitious accounts receivable could have contributed to the auditors' impression that the accounts receivable were collectible. A court of law would not hold auditors legally liable for failing to discover the fictitious accounts receivable.

Auditors who use an "absence of causal connection" defense contend that their actions in the audit did not cause the damage the client suffered. This defense argues that other conditions than the decisions made by the auditor caused the damage that the client suffered. Auditors could use this defense when they believe, for example, that general economic conditions led to the damage suffered by the client rather than the auditors' decisions.

Third-Party Liability under Common Law

Third parties include shareholders, lenders, customers, employees, and vendors. They claim legal liability because they *suffered harm* and their *reliance* on misleading financial statements was its cause. Common law liability is based on liability established from prior case law, not from violations of laws and regulations. The courts first interpreted legal liability under common law to third parties as a liability to individuals who were known users of the financial statements, but the courts have extended it to include *known* and *foreseeable* users. This increases auditors' potential liability to a larger group of third parties.

Auditors can use three of four defenses to defend against a legal liability claim by a third party: (1) lack of duty, (2) non-negligent performance, and (3) absence of causal connection. Contributory negligence is seldom used as a defense because third parties are generally not in a position to contribute to the negligence alleged in the misleading financial statements.

Civil Liability under the Federal Securities Laws

Auditors also face legal liability from violating federal securities laws. The Securities and Exchange Commission (SEC) often files these actions. The purpose of a civil lawsuit against the auditors is to recover monetary damages. Two federal securities laws provide a source of legal liability for auditors. The Securities Act of 1933 provides regulations for companies issuing new securities. Based on liability from this act, the only parties who can recover from auditors are purchasers of original securities. The Securities Act of 1934 regulates the requirements pertaining to the quarterly and annual submission of financial reports to the SEC. Every company with securities traded on one of the U.S. stock exchanges is required yearly to submit audited financial statements following the requirements of Form 10-K. Auditors are also legally liable for the quarterly information submitted to the SEC on Form 8-K.

Legal liability for auditors under the Securities Act of 1933 comes from the statement in the regulation specifying that any third party who purchases securities described in the registration agreement can sue the auditor for material misrepresentations or omissions of information in audited financial statements included with the registration statement. To hold the auditors liable for the misrepresentations, third parties must show only that the audited financial statements contained a material misrepresentation or omission; they are not required to show that the auditors were negligent or fraudulent in the audit. Auditors' defense under claims of misrepresentation brought under the Securities Act of 1933 is to show that an adequate audit was conducted or that the loss suffered by the third party was caused by factors other than the misleading financial statements.

Legal liability for auditors under the Securities Act of 1934 comes from the requirement that prohibits any fraudulent activities involving the sale or purchase of a security. This requirement has been interpreted to apply to auditors if they intentionally or recklessly misrepresent information given to third parties. The auditors' defense against claims for misrepresentation under the Securities Act of 1934 include (1) lack of duty, (2) non-negligent performance, and (3) absence of causal connection.

Did You Know?

In December 2009, the Securities and Exchange Commission charged Ernst & Young and six of its partners for their roles in an accounting fraud at Bally Total Fitness Holding Corporation. The SEC found that Ernst & Young knew or should have known about Bally's fraudulent financial accounting and disclosure. Ernst & Young issued unqualified audit opinions stating that Bally's 2001–2003 financial statements were presented in accordance with generally accepted accounting principles (the applicable financial reporting framework) and that the audits were conducted in accordance with generally accepted auditing standards. Those opinions were false and misleading.

According to the SEC, Bally fraudulently accounted for revenue, overstated its 2001 stockholders' equity by nearly $1.8 billion, or more than 340%. Bally also understated its 2002 and 2003 net loss by $92.4 million (9341%) and $90.8 million (845%), respectively.

Ernst & Young paid an $8.5 million fine to settle the SEC's charges. In addition to agreeing to pay the fine, Ernst & Young agreed to correct policies and practices relating to its violations and agreed to cease and desist from violating securities laws. All of the individual partners have settled the fines against them.

The SEC's order found that Ernst & Young had identified Bally as a risky audit because its managers were former Ernst & Young partners who had in the past "been aggressive in selecting accounting principles and determining estimates." Of more than 10,000 audit clients in North America, Ernst & Young had identified Bally as one of the 18 riskiest.

The SEC issued cease-and-desist orders against the Ernst & Young partners stating that they could not appear or practice as an accountant before the commission during a time period ranging from 9 months to 3 years.

The SEC also fined Bally's CFO and controller; the CFO was permanently barred from practicing before the SEC. It gave the controller a two-year suspension.

Sources: SEC Press Release 2009-271, "SEC Charges Ernst & Young and Six Partners for Roles in Accounting Violations at Bally Total Fitness," December 17, 2009; SEC Litigation Release No. 20470, February 28, 2008.

The SEC also has the power to sanction an auditor or an accounting firm, issue a cease and desist order against either, order the firm or individual to return all audit fees received during the period when the securities laws were violated (called *disgorgement of fees*), and order the firm or individual to engage a consultant to improve business practices to avoid future violations. The sanction power could be used to prevent an auditor or a firm from filing reports with the SEC or accepting new SEC clients for a period of 6 months or 1 year. When the SEC issues a cease-and-desist order, it orders the person or firm to avoid future violations similar to the ones currently reported. During the sanction period, the individual or firm is often required to participate in continuing professional education or to implement changes in practice that could prevent the problem from recurring. The SEC makes all of these remedies public, so they also serve as embarrassments to the sanctioned party.

Did You Know?

In 2004, Ernst & Young was suspended from accepting new SEC clients for 6 months. This suspension also included a cease-and-desist order from committing future independence violations, a disgorgement order (requiring Ernst & Young to return the audit fees billed to PeopleSoft for 1994–1999 totaling $1.7 million plus interest of $0.70 million), and a requirement to hire a consultant to advise the company on compliance with the independence requirement of the auditing standards.

The Securities and Exchange Commission charged Ernst & Young with securities violations for engaging in lucrative business deals with an audit client. Ernst & Young had entered into a marketing arrangement with PeopleSoft to sell and install its software. Under the agreement, Ernst & Young agreed to pay royalties to PeopleSoft of 15–30% for each software sale with a minimum guaranteed payment of $300,000. During the time of this agreement, Ernst & Young served as the auditor for PeopleSoft. According to the SEC, "an auditor can't be in business to jointly generate revenues with an audit client without impairing independence." Ernst & Young vigorously contested the charges, saying that its work for PeopleSoft "was entirely appropriate and permissible under the profession's rules. It did not affect our client, its shareholders, or the investing public, nor is the SEC claiming any error in our audits or our client's financial statements as a result of them."

Sources: SEC Initial Decision Release No. 249, Administrative Proceeding File No. 3-10933, April 16, 2004; Michael Schroeder and Scot J. Paltrow, "SEC Says Ernst & Young Violated Independence Rules in Past Audits," *The Wall Street Journal,* May 21, 2002.

The most important recent sanction was imposed in 2002 when Arthur Andersen was convicted of one felony count in connection with the flawed audit of Enron Corporation. This conviction required Arthur Andersen to surrender its accounting license and stop conducting public audits. Twenty-eight thousand employees had to find other jobs, and only a few employees remained. Although the U.S. Supreme Court overturned the conviction in 2005 due to a finding that the jury instructions were flawed, the firm's reputation had been destroyed.

Criminal Liability

The purpose of a lawsuit filed against auditors for criminal liability is to obtain monetary damages or prison terms for them. Auditors are subject to criminal liability under both federal and state laws. The Uniform Securities Act under state law provides requirements for securities similar to those of the SEC. Federal law including the Securities Acts of 1933 and 1934, the Federal Mail Fraud Statute, the Federal Conspiracy Statute, the Federal False Statement Statute, and the Sarbanes-Oxley Act, is likely to provide the source for criminal liability for auditors. All of these federal laws make defrauding another person by knowingly being involved in misstated financial statements illegal. The Sarbanes-Oxley Act also makes it a felony to alter, destroy, or create documents to obstruct a federal investigation, and an auditor could face both fines and jail time for altering or destroying documents. The auditor's defenses against claims for criminal liability include (1) lack of duty, (2) non-negligent performance, and (3) absence of causal connection.

Did You Know?

The investigations involving the collapse of Enron Corporation and the conviction of Arthur Andersen for one count of obstruction of justice led to several criminal charges with fines and jail time the result of jury decisions on the charges. The federal investigation by the Justice Department resulted in criminal charges against 30 individuals. Roughly half of them pleaded guilty to crimes and agreed to cooperate with prosecutors. Jeffrey Skilling, former president and chief executive of Enron, was sentenced to 24 years in prison for his role in the Enron scandal. Kenneth Lay, former Enron, chairman was found guilty of the charges against him but died before the length of his jail time was determined. His sentence was vacated because he died while his appeal was still pending. Andrew Fastow, former Enron chief financial officer, received a sentence of only 6 years in jail. Some business writers speculate that his sentence was lower than others because he cooperated with federal criminal authorities.

Sources: John Emshwiller, "Skilling Is Sentenced to 24 Years in Prison for Role in Enron Collapse," *The Wall Street Journal,* October 23, 2006; John Emshwiller, "Enron: The Tale of Two Sentencings," *The Wall Street Journal,* October 19, 2006.

Legal Liability for Management under the Sarbanes-Oxley Act

Both auditors and company management have legal liability for an audit. The liability associated with managers changed after the signing of the Sarbanes-Oxley Act. Let's consider some sections of the Sarbanes-Oxley Act and the impact they have on the legal liability of managers.

Section 302 of the Sarbanes-Oxley Act requires management to take responsibility for the financial reports. This section requires the company's principal executive officer and financial officer to certify in each annual or quarterly report filed with the SEC that (1) the officer has reviewed the report, (2) the report does not contain any untrue statements or omit facts that are necessary to understand the statements, (3) the financial statements fairly present the financial condition and results of operations of the company, (4) the signing officers are responsible for establishing and maintaining internal controls in the company, (5) the signing officers have disclosed to the auditor all significant deficiencies in the design or operation of internal controls and any fraud involving management or other employees, and (6) the signing officers have indicated in the report on internal control whether there were significant changes in internal controls before the date of their evaluation of controls (Sarbanes-Oxley Act, Sec. 302).

Business writers speculate that this section of Sarbanes-Oxley was designed to prevent excuses such as those given by Enron and WorldCom management during their trials. When asked about the misstatements in the financial statements, executives indicated that they had not been involved in the preparation of the financial statements and did not understand all of the items recorded in the statements; therefore, they could not be held liable for financial statement misstatements. This excuse was not effective during the Enron and WorldCom trials because the court believed that whether or not these individuals knew about the misstatement, they should have been aware of the information presented in the financial statements. Federal law was changed so this could no longer be a valid excuse.

Section 802 of the Sarbanes-Oxley Act, Criminal Penalties for Altering Documents, imposed the requirement that anyone knowingly altering, destroying, mutilating, concealing, or making a false entry in any record or document in federal investigations shall be fined, imprisoned for a period of not more than 20 years, or both. The felony conviction of Arthur Andersen was for obstruction of justice for altering or destroying audit evidence. Section 805 increased the federal sentencing guidelines for obstruction of justice and extensive criminal fraud, and Section 807 increased the criminal penalties for defrauding shareholders of public companies. All of the sections of Title 8 of the Sarbanes-Oxley Act increase the corporate and criminal liability for fraudulent reporting.

Title 9 of the Sarbanes-Oxley Act increases the criminal penalties for conspiracies to commit fraud, mail fraud, and wire fraud. Section 906 provides criminal penalties when the chief executive officer and the chief financial officer certify the quarterly or yearly financial reports knowing that they do not comply with Section 302 requirements. These officers could be fined $1 million or imprisoned for not more than 10 years (the fine increases to $5 million if the certification is done willfully and the time in prison is for not more than 20 years).

The dishonest auditor or manager has more to fear in the present environment for issuing materially misstated financial statements than previously. Of course, the incidence of audits involving lawsuits is still a small percentage of all audits (less than 1%), but the cost of these lawsuits is high in terms of professional reputation and fines levied against the parties.

Chapter Takeaways

The AICPA Professional Code of conduct provides important rules for auditors. The SEC, PCAOB, and the state boards of accounting also perform a regulatory function for the accounting profession. The current audit methodology that emphasizes internal control testing could have limitations because of the inherent limitations of internal controls. Auditors should be alert to transactions that are not processed as routine transactions.

This chapter presented these important facts:

- Certification requirements for accountants
- Limitations of current audit methodology
- Pressures on management and auditors
- The content of the AICPA Code of Professional Conduct and the International Code of Ethics for Professional Accountants
- Legal liability for accountants

Be sure you understand and can explain these concepts.

Review Questions

LO5	1.	Describe the AICPA Code of Professional Conduct.
LO5	2.	Explain the purpose of the principles of the AICPA Code of Professional Conduct.
LO5	3.	Describe the rule sections of this code of professional conduct including a description of each of the rules.
LO5	4.	Who enforces the code of professional conduct?
LO5	5.	What role does the PCAOB play in regulating the accounting profession?
LO5	6.	Describe the SEC's authority in the accounting regulatory environment.
LO1	7.	What role do state CPA societies serve in regulating the accounting profession?
LO2	8.	Describe several limitations of current audit methodology.
LO3	9.	What are pressures on management that could have an impact on the financial statements? How can these pressures affect an auditor's job?
LO3	10.	Does the auditor face pressure in the current audit environment? Explain your answer.
LO7	11.	Describe the legal liability the auditor faces when performing an audit.
LO7	12.	Explain how the Sarbanes-Oxley Act of 2002 has had a major impact on the accounting profession.

Multiple Choice Questions from CPA Examinations

LO5	13.	Which of the following statements best explains why the CPA profession has found it essential to promulgate ethical standards and to establish means for ensuring their observance?

    a. Vigorous enforcement of an established code of ethics is the best way to prevent unscrupulous acts.

    b. Ethical standards that emphasize excellence in performance over material rewards establish a reputation for competence and character.

c. A distinguishing mark of a profession is its acceptance of responsibility to the public.

d. A requirement for a profession is to establish ethical standards that stress primarily a responsibility to clients and colleagues.

LO5   14. The AICPA Code of Professional Conduct contains both general ethical principles that are designed to inspire the auditor and also a

a. List of violations that would cause the automatic suspension of a member's license.

b. Set of specific, mandatory rules describing minimum levels of conduct a member must maintain.

c. Description of a member's procedures for responding to an inquiry from a trial board.

d. List of specific acts discreditable to the profession.

LO5   15. An auditor strives to achieve independence in appearance to

a. Maintain public confidence in the profession.

b. Become independent in fact.

c. Comply with the generally accepted auditing standards of field work.

d. Maintain an unbiased mental attitude.

LO5   16. Which of the following most completely describes how independence has been defined by the CPA profession?

a. Performing an audit from the viewpoint of the public.

b. Avoiding the appearance of significant interests in the affairs of an audit client.

c. Possessing the ability to act with integrity and objectivity.

d. Accepting responsibility to act professionally and in accordance with a professional code of ethics.

LO5   17. The concept of materiality is least important to an auditor when considering the

a. Effects of a direct financial interest in the client upon the auditor's independence.

b. Decision whether to use positive or negative confirmations of accounts receivable.

c. Adequacy of disclosure of a client's illegal act.

d. Discovery of weaknesses in a client's internal control.

LO5   18. A CPA purchases stock in an audit client corporation and placed it in an educational trust for the CPA's minor child. The trust securities were not material to the CPA but were material to the child's personal net worth. Is the CPA's independence considered to be impaired with respect to the client?

a. Yes, because the stock is considered a direct financial interest and, consequently materiality is not a factor.

b. Yes, because the stock is considered an indirect financial interest that is material to the CPA's child.

c. No, because the CPA is not considered to have a direct financial interest in the client.

d. No, because the CPA is not considered to have a material indirect financial interest in the client.

LO5   19. Under the ethical standards of the profession, which of the following situations involving dependent members of an auditor's family is most likely to impair the independence of an individual participating in an audit engagement?

a. A parent's immaterial investment in a client.

b. A first cousin's loan from a client.

c. A spouse's employment with a client.

d. A sibling's loan to a director of a client.

LO5   20. The appearance of independence of a CPA, or that CPA's firm, is most likely to be impaired if the CPA

a. Provides appraisal, valuation, or actuarial services for an attest client.

b. Joins a trade association which is an attest client, and serves in a non-management capacity.

    c. Accepts a token gift from an attest client.

    d. Serves as an executor and trustee of the estate of an individual who owned the majority of the stock of a closely held client corporation.

LO5 21. In which of the following circumstances will a CPA who audits XM Corporation lack independence?

    a. The CPA is a director of, but does not control, YN Corporation, which has a loan from XM.

    b. The CPA and XM's president each owns 25% of FOB Corporation, a closely held company.

    c. The CPA has an automobile loan from XM, a financial institution. The loan is collateralized by the automobile.

    d. The CPA reduced XM's usual audit fee by 40% prior to the audit because XM's financial condition was unfavorable.

LO5 22. According to the profession's ethical standards, an auditor is considered independent in which of the following instances?

    a. The auditor's checking account, which is fully insured by a federal agency, is held at a client institution.

    b. The auditor is also an attorney who serves the client as its general counsel.

    c. A professional employee of the auditor is the treasurer of a charitable organization that is a client.

    d. The client owes the auditor fees for two consecutive audits.

Discussion Questions and Research Problems

LO5 23. **Independence requirements.** Based on the requirements of the AICPA Code of Professional Conduct, determine whether independence is impaired in the following situations.

    a. During the time of the audit, the auditor's spouse has a direct interest in the client.

    b. During the time of the audit, the auditor has a material indirect financial interest in the client.

    c. During the time of the audit, the auditor has a loan from the client.

    d. During the period of the professional engagement, the audit partner owns 8 percent of the client's stock.

    e. If the audit partner's spouse works in the sales department for one of the auditor's clients, is the partner's independence impaired?

    f. Is the CPA permitted to have credit card debt from an audit client?

    g. Is the CPA allowed to have a car loan from an audit client?

    h. Is a CPA permitted to accept an audit engagement for the mortgage company holding his or her home mortgage?

    i. You fail to file a state tax return in the current year. Have you violated the code of professional conduct by your action?

    j. Have you committed an act discreditable to the profession when you fail to pay payroll taxes for your housekeeper?

    k. You know that the financial statements for the client you are auditing are not materially correct, but you sign off on the audit opinion without requiring the client to make the corrections. Have you violated the code of professional conduct?

LO2 24. **Audit methodology.** A recent article in *The Wall Street Journal* reported a study[1] done by accounting researchers. They argued that over the last 20 years, auditors have changed their audit approaches and these changes make it less likely that auditors will discover misstatements by business executives. In the older style of

---

[1] Ken Brown, "Auditors' Methods Make it Hard to Catch Fraud by Executives," *The Wall Street Journal*, July 8, 2002.

auditing, the report argues, auditors looked at business transactions to determine whether they were recorded properly according to accounting rules. The new auditing methods, by contrast, focus on internal control. Relying on internal control documentation rather than reviewing transactions could catch misstatements by low-level employees, the researchers claimed, but corporate executives can circumvent internal control. This means that high-level misstatements are not easily discovered with contemporary audit procedures.

a. As you understand these audit techniques, what in each procedure could make it possible for auditors to detect misstatements that are generated by either low-level or high-level employees?

b. What aspect of the audit industry could be driving the decisions to concentrate on internal control documentation? Don't auditors want to discover misstatements that originate among high-level employees?

c. Can you identify problems in the business environment that could contribute to misstatements? How should the auditor respond to these problems?

LO5 25. **Confidential client information.** Anne Sorenson, an auditor for Stuart and Cram, is currently assigned to the audit of Amgen, Inc., a biotechnology company based in Thousand Oaks, California. The audit has gone well, but today Sorenson overheard a very exciting piece of information. Amgen has just completed a series of tests with mice related to the *ob* gene and leptin, the protein produced by the gene. During these tests, obese mice lost about 40% of their body weight after only a month of daily injections of leptin. With trials on humans ready to begin within a year, the promise of a cure for obesity seems hopeful. That evening, Sorenson talks to her parents over the phone. She is so excited about this finding that she tells her parents about the "potential" cure for obesity. After getting off the phone, she tells her roommate about her interesting day, when she realizes that she is divulging confidential client information. Her roommate, a stockbroker at Merrill Lynch, is excited about the information and wants to recommend that all her investment customers purchase Amgen stock before the information is public and the stock price goes up. Sorenson wonders about what she has just done.

a. Has Sorenson violated the Professional Code of Conduct? Explain your answer.

b. Would your evaluation of Sorenson's behavior change if her roommate was an artist who was uninterested in the stock market or if her parents did not act on the information to purchase Amgen stock? Why?

LO5 26. **Acts discreditable.** According to an article in a midwestern newspaper, stealing $2.3 million from the Dakota Credit Union was simple. Joe Kramer, who lost the money gambling, was the credit union's only full-time employee. Kramer said he began gambling to make the payments on a $50,000 loan to a friend because the friend was unable to repay it. In a one-year period, Kramer made fifteen trips to Las Vegas, gambling to cover the $50,000 loan. While waiting for sentencing on a federal charge of looting, Kramer was fired from the credit union 1 week before the state Credit Union Board declared the institution insolvent and closed its doors.

a. If Kramer is a licensed CPA, has he violated the AICPA Code of Professional Conduct?

b. Should Kramer be permitted to practice as a CPA when he is released from prison? Explain your answer.

LO5 27. **Lowballing audit fees.** When you prepare a bid for a new client, you always lowball the bid to get the client. You know that the fee is almost always adjusted at the end of the audit due to nonperformance on the part of the client, so you are not concerned that you will be unable to make a profit on the initial bid.

a. Does this practice of bidding low on the engagement fees to get the client violate the professional code of conduct? Explain your answer.

b. Why might an auditor determine an audit fee in this manner?

LO5 28. **Code of Professional Conduct.** A client contacts a public accountant about representing it regarding a hearing for a tax dispute with the IRS. In discussion with the client, the accountant stresses her extensive experience with the IRS. Because of this experience, she explains to the potential client that she will be able to influence the IRS to reduce the tax liability.

a. Has the accountant violated the professional code of conduct by referring to her influence with the IRS?

b. Describe the statements an accountant could make to the client in this situation.

LO5   29. **Code of Professional Conduct.** A former audit client calls and asks for a recommendation for someone to install a new accounting software package. You provide a referral for the service. Under what conditions can you charge a fee for the referral?

LO5   30. **Code of Professional Conduct and tax preparation.** An article in *The Wall Street Journal*[2] indicated that the big four audit firms earn approximately 20% of their total revenue from tax preparation. The article reported that big four accounting firms typically use temporary workers and part-time employees to prepare tax returns in the tax season, sometimes setting up separate "compliance centers" staffed by these employees and shipping returns to these central locations for processing. The temporary workers are paid as little as $10 per hour, but the clients are billed at the rate for big four employees, as much as $100 per hour or more. Most firms hide their use of temporary employees because they believe their clients are "indifferent" about who prepares their returns as long as a partner or manager of a big four firm signs it. The head of the tax division for one of the firms sees no reason to advise a client that a temporary employee filled out its tax return. "It doesn't seem relevant." This leads clients to believe they are receiving the services of accountants with "elite credentials" when they pay the premium fee charged by the big four accounting firms. A tax client of one of the firms, when informed of this practice, said that he is generally satisfied with the work the firm has done. He had known that the tax partner signing the return didn't actually prepare it. "But in all honesty, they should tell the clients" about mailing their return to temporary employees in other cities.

a. Does this practice violate the Code of Professional Conduct? Explain your answer.

b. Do you believe that all clients are indifferent about who prepares their returns as long as a big four manager or partner signs them?

c. Why do big four firms engage in this practice? Do they really believe that the client doesn't care?

Real-World Auditing Problems

LO5, LO7   31. **The Baptist Foundation**

Arthur Andersen LLP agreed to pay $217 million to settle a lawsuit over its audits for the Baptist Foundation of Arizona. At the time, this was the second largest settlement ever agreed to by a major accounting firm. The lawsuit alleged that Andersen accountants failed to detect fraudulent activity at the foundation. The lawsuit claimed that as a result, 11,000 people, most of them elderly investors, lost $570 million when the Baptist Foundation of Arizona filed for bankruptcy in 1999. The bankruptcy filing was one of the largest bankruptcy filings by a nonprofit organization.

The Baptist Foundation of Arizona was founded in 1948 to raise money to support Baptist causes and to pay a return for investors. It filed for bankruptcy in 1999 after many of the foundation's executives had been convicted of criminal charges or indicted for fraud.

The lawsuit against Arthur Andersen alleged that Andersen auditors failed to detect fraudulent activity at the Baptist Foundation including "hiding real-estate losses by transferring overvalued assets to shell companies in exchange for IOUs, and engaging in a Ponzi-like scheme of using new investor funds to make payments to previous investors." When the trial began, *The Wall Street Journal* stated,

---

[2] L. Berton, "You Paid Top Dollar: Who Did the Taxes?" *The Wall Street Journal,* April 13, 1995.

"For Andersen, the question probably isn't whether the firm is liable at all, but rather how much it should be required to pay."[3]

Dan Guy, an expert witness called to testify against Andersen over the foundation audits, said, "Arthur Anderson did not live up to the minimum requirements in the rules set for auditors." The lawsuit alleged that Arthur Andersen auditors did little to investigate allegations of fraud from whistle-blowers and because of this omission, they were complicit in concealing fraud from investors. During the trial, Mr. Guy testified that he had reviewed Andersen working papers as well as the depositions from the whistle-blowers and determined that the fraud at the Baptist Foundation was not impenetrable. With the information from the whistle-blowers, Andersen had an obligation to gather evidence to investigate the charges. Citing a 1997 conversation between Baptist Foundation accountant, Karen Paetz, and Ann McGath, the Andersen auditor, McGath acknowledged that the client told her that the Baptist Foundation was selling overvalued assets to a related-party company. According to Mr. Guy's testimony, such information would prompt a knowledgeable auditor to investigate further.

Additional evidence related to fraudulent activity that had been disclosed to the auditors was presented during the trial. Two chief financial officers of Texas Baptist Organization and a financial adviser from Mesa, Arizona, testified that they tried to alert Andersen to financial improprieties at the foundation and the likelihood that the foundation was broke.[4] Andersen had not responded to their calls.

Andersen placed the blame for the foundation's collapse on the company's executives, the foundation's law firm, and the state regulators who failed to investigate investor complaints in the early 1990s. According to statements by Andersen executives, "There is clear evidence that all members of the Baptist Foundation's senior management and [a] majority of the Board of Directors engaged in a conspiracy of silence to deny information about the Baptist Foundation's financial condition to the Arthur Andersen auditors."[5]

a. Explain how Arthur Andersen partners involved in the Baptist Foundation audit violated the principles section of the AICPA Code of Professional Conduct.

b. Identify specific code of conduct rules that Arthur Andersen partners violated based on the information provided.

LO5   32. **Ernst & Young**

Refer to the information on the Ernst & Young ethics code violation for its audit of PeopleSoft.

a. Evaluate the statement made by Ernst & Young that it did nothing wrong because no one was harmed. Is this an appropriate defense against a claim of lack of independence?

b. Can you develop a counterargument against Ernst & Young's position?

c. If the position taken by Ernst & Young seems to violate the independence rules, why did it take this position?

LO5   33. **Ernst & Young**

The Securities and Exchange Commission determined that Ernst & Young violated accounting rules in its audit of Cendant.[6] According to SEC records, Ernst & Young proposed a "value bank" that gave Cendant a reduction in audit fees in return for consulting work.

---

[3] Jonathan Weil, "Andersen Trial with Baptist Foundation Set to Begin," *The Wall Street Journal,* April 29, 2002.

[4] Anne Brady, "Andersen Was Lax in Auditing of Baptist Group, Witness Says," *The Wall Street Journal,* May 2, 2002.

[5] Jonathan Weil, "U.S. Will Argue," *The Wall Street Journal,* May 7, 2002.

[6] Michael Schroeder and Scot J. Paltrow, "SEC Says Ernst & Young Violated Independence Rules in Past Audits," *The Wall Street Journal,* May 21, 2002.

a. Does this arrangement violate the professional code of conduct? Explain the violation.

b. Why did Ernst & Young engage in this behavior if it violates the accounting rules?

LO5   34. **PricewaterhouseCoopers**

The SEC settled an independence case with PricewaterhouseCoopers (PWC) in July 2002.[7] The case found that from 1996 to 2001, PWC engaged in contingent fee arrangements with 14 public companies. In each instance, the client hired the audit firm's investment bankers to perform financial advisory services for a fee that was based on the success of the services. According to the SEC, this arrangement violated the AICPA Code of Professional Conduct. PWC agreed to pay the SEC $5 million and to provide independence training to all PWC professionals.

a. Identify the sections of the AICPA Professional Code of Conduct violated by the contingent fee arrangements.

b. Do you agree with the SEC finding?

c. Why did PWC engage in this behavior if it violates the code of professional conduct?

Internet Assignments

LO1, LO5   35. Review the website for the PCAOB or the AICPA.

a. Describe the type of information you found there.

b. Review the section on new developments and report on one professional issue that seems important to you.

LO1   36. Go to the website for the state board of accountancy for your state.

c. Describe the information found on the website.

d. On the website, can you find the report for violations of the professional code of conduct? Describe several actions reported on the website.

---

[7] "PricewaterhouseCoopers Settles SEC Auditor Independence Case," U.S. Securities and Exchange Commission, www.sec.gov/news/press/2002-105

Glossary

A

Acceptably low level of audit risk Audit risk is the risk that the auditor will issue an unqualified opinion when the financial statements are materially misstated; not defined by auditing standards; determined by the auditor's professional judgment. Typically, business writers believe that an acceptably low level of audit risk is about 5%.

Account balance The balance in the balance sheet accounts.

Accounting estimate An approximation of a monetary amount in the absence of a precise means of measurement.

Accounting records The records of initial accounting entries and supporting records, such as checks and records of electronic fund transfers; invoices; contracts; the general and subsidiary ledgers; journal entries; and other adjustments to the financial statements that are not reflected in journal entries; and records such as work sheets and spreadsheets supporting cost allocations, computations, reconciliations, and disclosures.

Analytical procedure Evaluation of financial information through analysis of plausible relationships among both financial and nonfinancial data.

Applicable financial reporting framework The financial reporting framework adopted by management in the preparation and presentation of the financial statements that is acceptable in regard to the nature of the company and the objective of the financial statements, or that is required by law or regulation. Also referred to as the accounting standards used to prepare the financial statements.

Appropriate audit evidence The measure of the quality of audit evidence whose appropriateness is its relevance and reliability in providing support for the conclusions on which the auditor's opinion is based.

Arm's-length transaction A transaction conducted on such terms and conditions between a willing buyer and a willing seller who are unrelated and are acting independently of each other and pursuing their own interests.

Assertions Representations by management that are embodied in the financial statements; used by the auditor to consider the different types of misstatements that could occur in the financial statements.

Attribute sampling The process by which an auditor makes a decision about a characteristic of interest (the internal control) in the population by reviewing a sample from the population. The attribute of interest is the control. Attribute sampling is used to test the rate of deviation from a prescribed control (how often it is missing) but is not used when the auditor needs to quantify the dollar amount of the misstatement.

Audit documentation The written record of the basis for the auditor's conclusions that provides support for the auditor's representations; includes records of the planning and performance of the work, procedures performed, evidence obtained, and conclusions reached by the auditor; can be referred to as *work papers* or *working papers* (PCAOB Audit Standard No. 3).

Audit evidence Information used by the auditor in arriving at the conclusions on which the auditor's opinion is based; includes both information contained in the accounting records underlying the financial statements and other information.

Auditing The process of reviewing the financial information prepared by the a company's management (the financial statements and the footnotes) to determine whether it conforms to a particular standard (the applicable financial reporting framework); assessment follows a set of standards (generally accepted auditing standards); person completing the assessment is not a company employee but works for an accounting firm that is associated with the company only by being hired to perform an audit (a firm that is independent from the company).

Audit risk The risk that the auditor could express an inappropriate audit opinion when the financial statements are materially misstated; a function of the risks of material misstatement and detection risk.

Audit sampling The selection and evaluation of a sample of items from a population of audit relevance such that the auditor expects the sample to be representative of the population.

Auditor Person conducting the audit, usually the engagement partner, other members of the engagement team, or the firm.

B

Big four audit firms The four largest auditing firms in the world. This list currently includes: PricewaterhouseCoopers, KPMG, Ernst & Young, and Deloitte & Touche.

C

Class of transactions The income statement accounts.

Comparative financial statements A complete set of financial statements for one or more prior periods included for comparison with the financial statements of the current period and covered by the auditor's opinion.

Compensating controls   Controls management uses to offset the risk in another procedure when management decides that it is not cost effective to implement particular control procedures.

Comprehensive income   The change in equity of a business enterprise during a period from transactions and other events and circumstances from nonowner sources (Concept Statement 6, FASB).

Contingent liability   An obligation that could occur in the future based on an event that occurred in the current year; can require disclosure or recognition in the year under audit.

Control risk   The risk that a misstatement that could occur in an assertion about a class of transactions, account balance, or disclosure that could be material and will not be prevented or detected and corrected on a timely basis by the company's internal control.

Corporate governance   The framework of rules and practices by which a board of directors ensures accountability, fairness, and transparency in the firm's relationship with its stakeholders, principally the shareholders, management, and the board of directors but also employees, customers, creditors, suppliers, regulators, and the community at large.

COSO   Committee of Sponsoring Organizations of the Treadway Commission, which created a recognized framework for documenting control systems.

D

Date of auditor's report   The date that the auditor puts on the audit report on the financial statements in accordance with the auditing standards.

Date of financial statements   The date at the end of the latest period covered by the financial statements.

Deficiency in internal control   Inadequacy in which the design or operation of a control does not allow management or employees to prevent or detect and correct misstatements on a timely basis.

Detection risk   The risk that the procedures performed by the auditor to reduce audit risk to an acceptably low level will not detect a misstatement that exists and that could be material.

Dual-purpose test   Examination in which the auditor reperforms an internal control procedure and a substantive audit procedure; provides the auditor evidence with which to evaluate whether a control is operating effectively and detect misstatements in the financial statements.

E

Emphasis of matter paragraph   A paragraph included in the auditor's report at the auditor's discretion that refers to a matter appropriately presented or disclosed in the financial statements.

Engagement partner   The partner in the firm who is responsible for the engagement and its performance and for the report that is issued on the firm's behalf.

Engagement team   All partners and staff performing the engagement and all individuals engaged by the firm who perform procedures on it.

Error   An unintentional misstatement in the financial statements.

Estimated misstatement   The amount of misstatement estimated by the auditor in the account balance or class of transactions on the basis of his or her professional judgment and after considering such factors as the company's business risks, the results of prior year's substantive tests of details, the results of any related substantive tests, and the results of any test of related controls.

Evidence   Information used by the auditor in arriving at the conclusions on which the auditor's opinion is based; includes information from the accounting records and from other sources both inside and outside the company.

External confirmation   Audit evidence obtained as a direct written response to the auditor from a third party in either paper, electronic, or other medium or through the auditor's direct access to information held by a third party.

F

Financial reporting framework   A set of criteria used to determine measurement, recognition, presentation, and disclosure of all material items appearing in the financial statements; includes accounting principles generally accepted in the United States of America (GAAP) and international financial reporting standards (IFRSs and IASs) issued by the International Standards Board (IASB).

Financial statement   A structured representation of historical financial information including footnotes intended to communicate the company's economic resources or obligations at a point in time or the changes therein for a period of time in accordance with a financial reporting framework.

Fraud   An intentional act by one or more individuals in a company involving the use of deception that results in misstatement in the financial statements; auditor's concern that it could cause a material misstatement in the financial statements.

Fraud risk factors   Events or conditions that indicate an incentive or pressure to perpetrate fraud, provide an opportunity to commit fraud, or indicate attitudes or rationalization to justify a fraudulent action.

Fraudulent financial reporting   A type of fraud that occurs when a company intentionally prepares materially misstated financial statements.

G

General-purpose financial statement   Financial statement prepared in accordance with a general purpose framework.

Going concern   The description of a company whose financial statements assume that the company will continue in business for a reasonable period of time in the future.

Going concern problem   The description of a company whose financial statements indicate that it may have a problem continuing in business for a reasonable period of time in the future.

Group audit   The audit that includes all components whose financial information is included in the group financial statements.

I

Inherent risk   The susceptibility of an assertion about a class of transactions, account balance, or disclosure to a misstatement that could be material before consideration of any related controls.

Internal control   A process initiated by those charged with governance designed to provide reasonable assurance about the achievement of the entity's objectives with regard to the reliability of financial reporting, effectiveness and efficiency of operations, and compliance with applicable laws and regulations.

Internal control over financial reporting   A process designed by the company's principal executive and principal financial officers, and implemented by the company's board of directors, management, and other personnel to provide reasonable assurance regarding the reliability of financial reporting and the preparation of financial statements for external purposes in accordance with the applicable financial reporting framework; includes those policies and procedures that (1) pertain to the maintenance of records that in reasonable detail accurately and fairly reflect the transactions and dispositions of the company's assets; (2) provide reasonable assurance that transactions are recorded as necessary to permit preparation of financial statements in accordance with an applicable financial reporting framework and that receipts and expenditures of the company are being made only in accordance with authorizations of management and directors of the company; and (3) provide reasonable assurance regarding prevention or timely detection of unauthorized acquisition, use, or disposition of the company's assets that could have a material effect on the financial statements (AS5.A5).

Internal control over the financial statements   The processes designed by management and others charged with governance to provide reasonable assurance that the company has met its responsibilities in three areas: (1) the reliability of financial reporting, (2) the effectiveness and efficiency of operations, and (3) compliance with laws and regulations.

Internal control tests   Examinations performed by the auditor to determine whether the company's internal controls prevent or detect misstatements in the financial statements; provide information as to whether the control is working (at the level expected) to prevent or detect misstatements in the financial statements.

K

Known misstatement   The amount of misstatement found by the auditor when reviewing the sample items.

L

Likely misstatement   The amount of misstatement estimated by the auditor based on the known misstatement and the percentage of the population sampled during the audit test.

M

Management   Individuals with responsibility to conduct the company's operations; for some companies includes some or all of those charged with governance.

Management bias   A lack of neutrality by management in the preparation and presentation of information.

Materiality   Misstatements that, based on the auditor's professional judgment, are considered to be material, individually or in the aggregate, if they could reasonably be expected to influence the decisions of users of the financial statements; must be judged considering the circumstances surrounding the misstatement and can be affected by the *size* or *nature* of the misstatement.

Material weakness   A deficiency in internal control causing a reasonable possibility that a material misstatement of the entity's financial statements will not be prevented or detected on a timely basis.

Misappropriation of assets   A type of fraud that occurs when a company's employees steal its assets (for example, cash or inventory) or cause the entity to pay for goods or services it did not receive.

Misstatement   The difference between the amount, classification, presentation, or disclosure of a reported financial statement item and the amount, classification, presentation, or disclosure required for the item to be in accordance with the applicable financial reporting framework; can result from error or fraud.

Modified opinion   A qualified opinion, an adverse opinion, or a disclaimer of opinion.

N

Negative confirmation request   A request that the confirming party respond directly to the auditor only if its information disagrees with that provided in the request.

Noncompliance   Acts of omission or commission by the company, either intentional or unintentional, which are contrary to the prevailing laws or regulations.

Nonsampling risk   The risk that the auditor will reach an erroneous conclusion for any reason other than sampling risk.

Nonstatistical sampling   An approach to sampling that does not have both characteristics of (1) random selection of the sample items and the (2) use of a statistical technique to evaluate sample risk. A nonstatistical sample usually has random selection of the sample items and the use of judgment, rather than a statistical technique, to evaluate sample risk.

O

Omitted audit procedure   A procedure considered necessary to be performed in the circumstances existing at the time of the audit of financial statements but was not performed.

Other matter paragraph   A paragraph included in the auditor's report that refers to a matter other than those presented or disclosed in the financial statements that, in the auditor's judgment, is relevant to users' understanding of the audit, the auditor's responsibilities, or the auditor's report.

P

Pervasive   A term used to describe the effect of a misstatement on the financial statements. If the misstatement is pervasive, it affects more than one or two accounts on the financial statements.

Population   The entire set of data from which a sample is selected and about which the auditor wishes to draw conclusions.

Positive confirmation request   A request that the confirming party respond directly to the auditor to provide the requested information or to indicate whether the party agrees or disagrees with the information in the request.

Preconditions for an audit   The preconditions for an audit that exist when management and those charged with governance (1) use an acceptable financial reporting framework in the preparation of the financial statements and (2) agree with the premise on which an audit is conducted.

Professional judgment   The application of relevant training, knowledge, and experience, within the context provided by auditing, accounting, and ethical standards in making informed decisions about the appropriate course of action in the circumstances of the audit engagement.

Professional skepticism   An attitude that includes a questioning mind, being alert to conditions that could indicate possible misstatement due to fraud or error, and being able to critically assess audit evidence.

Projected misstatement   The expected error in the population based on the sample results; the sum of the known misstatement and the likely misstatement.

Q

Quality control for an audit firm   Measures accounting firms take to ensure that their audits are conducted in accordance with generally accepted auditing standards; the objective of which is to obtain reasonable assurance that: (1) the firms comply with professional standards and applicable legal and regulatory requirements and (2) reports they issue are appropriate in the circumstances (Quality Control Standards, AICPA Professional Standards).

R

Random sample   The selection of an item in which each item in the population has an equal chance of being selected.

Reasonable assurance   A high level of assurance but one that does not provide absolute assurance.

Reasonable possibility   Condition in which the likelihood of a future event's occurrence is either reasonably possible (more than remote but less than likely) or probable (likely to occur).

Related party   The FASB designation of company affiliates related to investments accounted for using the equity method of accounting for investment securities; trusts for the benefit of employees such as pension and profit-sharing trusts managed by the company; principal owners of the company and their immediate families; management of the company and its immediate families; and other entities in which one member controls or can significantly influence the management or operating policies of the other, other parties that can significantly influence the management or operating policies of the other sometimes because it has an ownership interest in one of the transacting parties.

Relevant assertion   A financial statement declaration that has a reasonable possibility of containing a misstatement that would cause the financial statements to be materially misstated.

Report release date   The date on which the auditor grants the company permission to use the auditor's report in connection with its financial statements.

Representative sample   A random selection of items from the whole population about which conclusions will be made that, subject to the limitations of sampling risk, is similar to those that would be drawn if the same procedures were applied to the entire population.

Required supplemental information   Information that a designated accounting standard setter requires to accompany a company's basic financial statements.

Risk assessment procedure   Procedures performed during an audit to obtain an understanding of the entity and its environment including its internal control and to identify and assess the risks of material misstatement at the financial statement and assertion levels.

Risk of material misstatement   The risk consisting of two components—inherent and control— that the financial statements are materially misstated.

Roll forward   To obtain evidence about a control's effectiveness at an interim date but not to test it at year-end.

S

Sampling risk   The risk that the auditor's conclusion based on a sample could differ from auditor's conclusion if the entire population was subjected to the same audit procedure.

Sampling unit   The individual items constituting a population.

Service auditor   An auditor who reports on internal controls in a service organization.

Service organization   An organization that provides services to user companies relevant to financial reporting.

Significant deficiency   An inadequacy in internal control that is less severe than a material weakness yet important enough to merit attention by those charged with governance.

Significant risk   An identified risk of material misstatements that in the auditor's judgment requires special audit consideration.

Special-purpose financial statements   Financial statements prepared in accordance with a specified framework such as a cash basis, tax basis, regulatory basis, or contractual basis.

Statistical sampling   An approach to sampling that has the characteristic of random selection of the sample items and the use of a statistical technique to evaluate sample risk.

Stratification   The process of dividing a population into subpopulations, each of which is a group of sampling units intended to have similar characteristics. Stratification reduces the variance among the population items.

Subsequent events   Events occurring between the date of the financial statements and the date of the auditor's report that require adjustment or disclosure in the financial statements.

Subsequently discovered fact   Information that becomes known to the auditor after the date of the auditor's report that, had the auditor possessed at that date, could have caused the auditor to amend the report.

Substantive procedure   An audit procedure designed to detect misstatements at the assertion level including tests of detail (classes of transactions, account balances, and disclosures) and substantive analytical procedures.

Substantive tests of balances   Audit procedures performed to gather evidence of balance sheet accounts (assets, liabilities, and owners' equity) that determine whether the financial statement accounts present fairly the firm's financial condition in accordance with the applicable financial reporting framework.

Substantive tests of transactions   Audit procedures performed to gather evidence of income statement accounts (revenue and expense accounts) that determine whether the financial statement accounts present fairly the firm's financial condition in accordance with the applicable financial reporting framework.

Sufficiency of audit evidence   The measure of the quantity of audit evidence that is affected by the auditor's assessment of the risks of material misstatement and the quality of such audit evidence.

Summary financial statements   Statements that contain historical financial information derived from financial statements but contain less detail.

T

Test of controls   The audit procedure designed to evaluate the operating effectiveness of controls in preventing or detecting material misstatements at the assertion level.

Those charged with governance   The persons with responsibility for overseeing the strategic direction of the company and responsible for the obligations related to the entity's accountability.

Tolerable misstatement   The monetary amount the auditor sets in seeking to obtain an appropriate level of assurance that the actual misstatement amount of the population does not exceed tolerable misstatement; also referred to as *performance materiality.*

Tolerable rate of deviation   The ratio of departure from prescribed internal control procedures set by the auditor in seeking to obtain an appropriate level of assurance that the rate in the population does not exceed.

U

Uncorrected misstatement   The misstatement that the auditor has accumulated during the audit and that has not been corrected.

Unmodified opinion   The opinion expressed by the auditor upon concluding that the financial statements are prepared in all material respects in accordance with the applicable financial reporting framework.

V

Variables sampling   The application of an audit procedure (confirmation, vouching, tracing) to less than 100% (the sample) of an account balance (for the balance sheet) or a class of transactions (for the income statement) to determine whether the recorded amount is materially misstated; see *Population.*

W

Walk-through   An audit procedure during which the auditor documents the processing of a transaction from its initiation to its recording in the financial records or the preparation of the transaction's disclosure for the financial statements.

Index

Page numbers followed by n indicate footnotes.

A

absence of causal connection defense, 407
Academy Awards audit, 3–4
account balances, defined, 14
accounting cycle, defined, 13
accounting firms. *See also specific firms*
  "big four," 3
  quality controls, 41–42
  reputation of, 140
accounting regulatory bodies, 16–18
accounting standards. *See* auditing standards; *specific auditing or business processes*
accounts payable
  confirmation requests, 188
  fraud in, 176–178
  subsidiary ledgers, 174
accounts receivable
  allowance for uncollectible accounts, 109–111
  confirmation requests, 107–109, 110, 116–122
  sampling plan for testing, 272–276
  subsidiary ledgers, 92
accuracy assertion, 13, 293
ACL, 79
acquisition and expenditure process
  accounts in, 169–172, 180
  accrued liabilities, 190–194
  analytical procedures for, 184–186
  auditing/accounting standards for, 168–169, 174–175
  disclosure requirements, 194–198
  intangible asset accounts, 189–190
  internal control testing, 179–184
  land, building, equipment accounts, 189–190
  management assertions, 178–179, 194–195
  misstatements, 175–178
  overview, 169–172
  relevant assertions, 179
  substantive tests of balances, 172, 187
  substantive tests of transactions, 172, 186–187
  transactions recorded in, 172–174
  unrecorded liabilities, 188
Adelphia Communications, 40–41, 158–159, 176, 179, 318–319
adjusting events after the reporting period, 344n
adjusting journal entry reports
  acquisition and expenditure process, 174
  cash and investment processes, 290
  inventory process, 209

long-term debt and owners' equity process, 314
  revenue process, 92
adverse audit opinion, 371, 374, 376, 385
aged trial balance for accounts receivable, 92
Ahold, 95, 153, 212
AICPA. *See* American Institute of Certified Public Accountants
allocation assertion, 14, 293
allowance for uncollectible accounts, 109–111
American Institute of Certified Public Accountants (AICPA)
  auditing standards, 6–7, 14n, 21n, 397
  Audit Sampling, 237–238, 249, 267
  Code of Professional Conduct, 398–405
  materiality calculation worksheet, 30
  membership in, 405
  as regulatory body, 18
American Tissue, 221
amortization tables, 314
analytical procedures
  acquisition and expenditure process, 184–186
  as audit evidence, 12
  cash and investment processes, 297–298
  defined, 12
  in evidence gathering, 140–141
  inventory process, 214–216
  long-term debt and owners' equity process, 322–323
  revenue process, 103–105
  risk assessment process, 32–33
  sampling and, 270
annual report footnotes, 356–357, 379
AOL (America Online). *See* Time Warner
appropriate evidence. *See* sufficient appropriate evidence
arm's-length transactions, 346
Arthur Andersen, 5, 31–32, 148–149, 409–410
ASB, 6–7, 14n, 21n
asset misappropriation
  described, 149–152
  example, 157–158
  methods, 177
  risk factors, 156
asset recognition, 290
assets. *See* intangible assets; land, building, and equipment
assurance level
  in substantive tests, 263, 266
  in test of controls, 241
AT&T, 176, 177
attest services, 4, 397–398
attorney letters, 341, 342
attribute sampling, 234. *See also* audit sampling
audit adjustments, 352–355
audit and assurance services, 3

Audit Command Language (ACL), 79
audit committees, 65
audit evidence
    auditing/accounting standards for, 11–13, 138–139, 144
    audit procedures for, 140–142
    business processes in, 13–14
    defined, 11, 140
    documentation required, 146–149
    extent of, 146
    fraud risk and, 158–160
    management representation letter, 349, 350
    manager's assertions and, 142–143
    materiality and, 352–355
    nature of, 145
    reasons for, 139–140
    role in audit process, 140–142
    sufficient appropriate, 22, 55–56, 143–145
    timing of, 145–146
    types, 11–12
audit failures, 5
audit function, 3, 397
auditing
    description and importance, 1–3
    methodology limitations, 395–396
    purpose, 22
auditing profession
    auditing pronouncements for, 393
    audit methodology limitations, 395–396
    certification, 394–395
    characteristics, 3–4
    Code of Ethics (IESBA), 405–406
    Code of Professional Conduct (AICPA), 398–405
    legal liability, 406–410
    pressures in, 397
    service levels, 397–398
    standards, 6–13
auditing standards. *See also specific auditing or business processes*
    AICPA Auditing Standards Board (ASB), 6–7, 14n, 21n, 397
    AICPA rule 202, 404
    for audit function, 397
    on CPA exam, 394–395
    for evidence requirements, 11–12
    International Standards of Auditing (ISAs), 11, 394, 397
    Public Company Accounting Oversight Board (PCAOB), 7–11, 14n, 403
Auditing Standards Board (ASB), 6–7, 14n, 21n
audit opinions. *See* audit reports
auditor's responsibilities, in audit report, 368, 374
audit plan, 35–36, 37
audit procedure use
    contingent liabilities, 341–344
    going concern assessments, 347–349
    internal control testing, 56, 182–184
    related parties, 346

    subsequent events, 344–346
    subsequently discovered facts, 344–346
    substantive testing, 270
audit process phases, 23. *See also* planning phase; *specific tests*
audit reports
    AICPA rule, 203, 404
    auditing standards for, 364–365, 366–367, 380
    auditor's responsibilities, 368, 374–379
    audit risk reduction and, 36–41
    date of, 369
    described, 14–16
    emphasis of matter paragraph, 348, 356, 370–371, 372, 373
    examples of
        clean opinion, 15, 368, 369
        component auditor's work in, 378
        modified opinions, 375, 376, 377, 385
    foreign financial reporting frameworks and, 380
    forming opinion for, 367
    for internal controls over financial reporting audit
        reporting requirements, 70–75, 76, 381–384
        report modifications, 384–387
    for internal controls over financial statements audit, 60–61
    modified opinions, 371–374
    other matter paragraph, 370–371, 372, 373, 379
    restricted-use, 379
    unmodified (clean opinion), 367–370
audit risk
    "acceptably low level," 21n, 38–39
    defined, 22–23, 36, 236
    reducing, 36–41
    sampling vs. nonsampling, 236–237, 261–263
audit risk model, 38–41
audit sampling
    defined, 234
    for substantive tests
        auditing standards for, 260
        audit procedures and, 270
        overview, 261
        plan steps, 264–272
        results from, 270–272
        sample selection, 268–269
        sample size, 263, 267–268
        sampling risk in, 261–262
        statistical vs. nonstatistical, 263–264
        tests of balances plan, 272–276
        tests of transactions plan, 276–277
    for test of controls
        auditing standards for, 233
        deviation rates in, 240–241, 244, 252
        fixed vs. sequential plans, 248–249
        overview, 234–235
        plan development, 245–248
        plan example, 246

audit sampling—*Cont.*
   for test of controls—*Cont.*
      plan steps, 239–245
      results from, 243–245
      sample selection, 241–242
      sample size, 237, 241, 249–253
      sampling risk in, 236
      statistical vs. nonstatistical, 237–238
Audit Sampling (AICPA), 237–238, 249, 267
audit strategy, 35
authorization procedures
   as internal control activity, 51, 53, 181
   in internal control testing
      cash and investment processes, 295
      long-term debt and owners' equity process, 321
      revenue process, 100–101
      testing methods, 57
available-for-sale-securities, 291, 292

B

backdating stock options, 330
balance sheet accounts
   acquisition and expenditure process, 169–172
   business process model, 13
   cash and investment processes, 287–289
   long-term debt and owners' equity process, 312–313
   revenue process, 90
Bally Total Fitness Holding Corp., 408
bank confirmations, 290, 300–301
bank cutoff statement, 302–303
bank reconciliations, 290, 302–303
bank statements, 290
bank transfer schedules, 290, 303
BDO Seidman, LLP, 74, 75
"big four" accounting firms, 3
bond agreements, 314
breach of contract, 407
bribery, 355
Bristol-Myers, 88–89, 95
broker's advice, 290
buildings. *See* land, building, and equipment
business concepts, on CPA exam, 394
business processes, in evidence gathering, 13–14

C

CAATTs, 79
capital market systems, 2–3, 17
capital stock accounts, 325
cash
   disbursements journals, 174
   internal controls testing, 57–58
   IT controls for, 295
   prelisting of receipts, 92
   receipts journals, 174
cash and investment processes
   accounts in, 287–289, 295
   analytical procedures for, 297–298
   auditing/accounting standards for, 285–286, 290–291
   bank records for, 300–302
   disclosure requirements, 304–305
   fair value of investment securities, 300
   internal control testing, 294–296
   IT controls, 295
   management assertions, 293
   misstatements, 291–292
   overview, 287–289
   relevant assertions, 293–294, 295
   substantive tests of balances, 299–300
   substantive tests of transactions, 298–299
   transactions recorded in, 289–290
cease-and-desist orders, 408–409
centralized processing, 64
certification, of accountants, 394–395
channel stuffing, defined, 88
Citigroup, 53
civil liability, 407–409
classes of transactions, 13
classical variables sampling, 266
classification assertion, 13, 293
clean (unqualified) opinion, 15, 36, 367–370
client environment, understanding, 27–29
client relations
   legal liability and, 407
   principal-agent framework of, 2
   in quality control, 42
   securities violations and, 409
Coca-Cola Co., 112–113
Code of Professional Conduct (AICPA)
   principles, 398–399
   rule interpretations, 402
   rules, 399–405
collusion, 160
commissions and fees, 404–405
Committee of Sponsoring Organizations of the Treadway Commission (COSO), 52, 62–63
common law liability, 407
communication, by auditors, 379. *See also* audit reports
communication system, in internal control, 53, 54
compensating controls, 51–52
compilations, 398
completeness assertion
   acquisition and expenditure process, 179, 180, 187
   cash and investment processes, 293
   defined, 14
   long-term debt and owners' equity process, 318–319
completion phase
   auditing/accounting pronouncements for, 338–339
   contingent liabilities in, 341–344

end of fieldwork, 339, 357–358
  financial statements in
    consistency evaluation, 355–356
      footnotes, 356–357, 379
      materiality, 352–355
    going concern assessment, 347–349
    legal and regulatory compliance, 347
    management representation letter, 349, 350
    overview, 339–340
    related-party transactions, 346
    subsequent events, 344–346
    subsequently discovered facts, 344–346
    working papers, 349–352
component, defined, 375
component auditor, 375–379
computer-assisted audit tools and techniques (CAATTs), 79
Computer Associates, 95, 98
computer systems. *See* IT (information technology)
confidentiality, 404, 405
confirmation
  accounts payable, 188
  accounts receivable, 107–109, 110, 116, 122
  described, 106–107
  in evidence gathering, 142
  sampling and, 270
  standard bank, 290, 300–301
  working paper example, 147–148
consistency, of financial statements, 355–356
consulting services, 403
contingent fees, 404
contingent liabilities, 341–344
contributory negligence defense, 407
control activities, 53, 54. *See also specific activities*
control deficiencies, 70
control environment, 52, 54, 64
control risk, 38, 39, 235
cookie jar reserves, defined, 88
corporate governance process
  auditor's role in, 2, 5–6, 379
  on CPA exam, 394
  internal controls role in, 75–76
COSO, 52, 62–63
cost accounting systems, 213
cost of good sold, 186, 211
CPA examination, 18, 394–395
credit approval forms, 91
credit memos, 92
criminal liability, 409–410
cutoff assertion, 14, 293
cutoff tests, 107

D

Dean Foods, 178
decision phase, 23

deficiency in design, 70
deficiency in operation, 70
Dell Inc., 211, 344, 383
Deloitte & Touche
  Adelphia audit, 40–41, 158–159, 179, 318–319
  "big four" status, 3
  Just for Feet audit, 38–39
  Nortel Networks audit, 73
  Parmalat audit, 324
  WPT risk, 24
detection risk, 38, 39
deviation rates, in test of controls, 240–241, 244, 252
disclaimer of opinion, 371–372, 374, 377, 384–386
disclosure assertion, 14
disclosure requirements
  acquisition and expenditure process, 194–198
  cash and investment processes, 304–305
  inventory process, 222–226
  long-term debt and owners' equity process, 326–331
  loss contingency, 341
  revenue process, 112–115
discredits to profession, 405
disgorgement of fees, 408
documentary evidence
  acquisition and expenditure process, 172–174, 183
  cash and investment processes, 289–290
  inventory process, 209
  long-term debt and owners' equity process, 314
  revenue process, 91–92
documentation. *See* working papers
documented transaction trails
  as internal control activity, 51, 53
  in internal control testing
    acquisition and expenditure process, 181
    cash and investment processes, 295–296
    long-term debt and owners' equity process, 321
    revenue process, 101
    testing methods, 57–58
dual-purpose tests, 58–59, 236, 243, 247
due professional care, 12, 404, 405

E

earnings calls, 27
earnings management, 151
economic concepts, on CPA exam, 394
effectiveness of audit, 236, 262
efficiency of audit, 236, 262
emphasis of matter paragraph, 348, 356, 370–371, 372, 373
employees
  inquires of
    in internal control testing, 56, 57
    in planning process, 32
  internal control performance, 59
  IT department, 78

engagement completion document, 352
engagement letters, 24–26
engagement liability, 406–410
engagement performance, 42
Enron scandal, 5, 31–32, 148–149, 327, 409–410
enterprise risk management, 51, 62–63
Enterprise Risk Management—Integrated Framework
    (COSO), 52, 63
environmental protection laws, 347
equal employment legislation, 347
equipment. *See* land, building, and equipment
Ernst & Young
    Bally Total Fitness audit, 408
    "big four" status, 3
    HealthSouth audit, 300–302
    PeopleSoft and, 409
    sample reports by, 15, 73
    Sonali audit, 218
errors, defined, 149
estimated contingency loss, 341
ethics
    Code of Ethics (IESBA), 394, 405–406
    Code of Professional Conduct (AICPA), 398–405
    on CPA exam, 394–395
    in quality control, 41
eToys, 144
evidence gathering. *See* audit evidence
existence assertion
    cash and investment processes, 293
    defined, 14
    inspection and, 141
    in inventory process, 213
    revenue process, 98
expected deviation rate, 241, 252
expected misstatement, 264, 266
expenditure process. *See* acquisition and expenditure
    process
expenses, reducing, 4. *See also* acquisition and expenditure
    process
external confirmation. *See* confirmation

F

FASB, 17–18
Fastow, Andrew, 410
Federal Conspiracy Statute, 409
Federal False Statement Statute, 409
Federal Mail Fraud Statute, 409
federal securities law violations, 407–409
fees and commissions, 404–405
fieldwork, end of, 339, 357–358
FIFO inventory pricing, 219–220
Financial Accounting Standards Board (FASB), 17–18
financial reporting

fraudulent, 149–150, 152, 154–157
internal control over
    audit objective, 61
    auditor's assessment, 64–66
    defined, 61–62
    fraud risk in, 65
    management's assessment, 62–63
    management's written statements, 69–70
    reporting requirements, 70–75
    testing, 69, 240
    management responsibility for, 367–368, 410
    quarterly information, 379
financial statement audits. *See also specific auditing or
    business processes*
    client legal and regulatory compliance in, 347
    described, 2–3, 22–23
    reporting internal control deficiencies in, 60–61
    testing internal controls in, 54–59, 239–240
financial statements. *See also* misstatements
    amended, 345–346
    consistency evaluation, 355–356
    footnotes to, 356–357, 379
    internal controls on, 51–53
    management's assertions, 13–14, 33–34
    management's misstatements, 4–5
    SEC filing requirements, 366, 379
    unaudited information in, 357, 379
fixed sampling plans, 248–249
Fleming, 178
food and drug administration rules, 347
fraud
    acquisitions and expenditure process, 175–178
    cash and investment processes, 291–292
    defined, 149
    examples of, 154–158
    identifying, 150–152
    inventory process, 211–212
    long-term debt and owners' equity process, 316–318
    penalties for, 410
    reporting requirements, 160–161
    revenue process, 94–96
    risk factors, 155–156
    types, 149–150
fraud detection
    auditing/accounting standards for, 138–139
    auditor's responsibility for, 96–97
    roadblocks to, 160
fraud risk
    assessment of, 158–159
    audit team discussion of, 154
    control of, 160
    documentation of, 161
    factors in, 155–156
    in internal control over financial reporting audit, 65
    professional skepticism and, 152–153

fraud triangle, 150–152
frequency of control, 252–253
Frito Lay, 178

G

Gemstar-TV Guide International, 38
generally accepted auditing standards (GAAS), 6n, 7, 10
General Mills
    acquisition and expenditure example, 196–198
    annual report, 356
    audit reports, 381, 382
    cash and investment example, 304–305
    inventory process example, 224–226
    long-term debt and owners' equity example, 328–331
    materiality calculation example, 30–31
    revenue process example, 113–115
    Sarbanes-Oxley certification, 387
    understanding entity example, 27–28
General Motors, 385
Global Crossing, 152
going concern assessments, 347–349
Goodyear Tire & Rubber Co., 71, 72
government auditing standards, 369
government contract regulations, 347
gross margin percentages, 186, 215–216
gross margin ratios, 215
group audit reports, 374–379
group engagement partner, 374–379
growth, in revenue, 4
guarantees, as contingent liabilities, 341

H

haphazard sampling, 242, 269
health and safety regulations, 347
HealthSouth, 95, 300–302
Hecla Mining Company, 74, 75
held-to-maturity securities, 291
Hewlett-Packard Company, 15, 63, 73
human resources, of accounting firms, 42

I

IAASB, 11, 14n, 394, 397
IASB, 18
IESBA, 394, 405–406
IFAC, 11, 394, 405
IFRS. *See* International Financial Reporting Standards
income statement accounts
    acquisition and expenditure process, 169–172
    business process model, 13

cash and investment processes, 287–289
    long-term debt and owners' equity process, 312–313
    revenue process, 89–90
income tax, 341, 347
independence in appearance, 12, 401
independence in fact, 12, 401
independence rules
    AICPA, 399–403
    PCAOB, 403
    Sabanes-Oxley Act, 404
independent reconciliations
    as internal control activity, 51, 53, 182
    in internal control testing
        cash and investment processes, 296
        long-term debt and owners' equity process, 321
        revenue process, 101
        testing methods, 58
information system, in internal control, 53, 54. *See also* IT (information technology)
inherent risk, 38, 39
inquiry
    in evidence gathering, 141
    in internal control testing, 56, 182
    in planning process, 32
    sampling and, 270
inspection
    in evidence gathering, 141
    in internal control testing, 56, 57, 58, 102, 182
    in risk assessment process, 33
    sampling and, 270
intangible assets
    auditing changes in, 189–190
    subsidiary ledgers, 174
    working paper example, 192–193
integrated audits, 54, 61
integrity, in ethics codes, 399, 405
internal auditors, 58, 65
internal control
    in acquisition and expenditure process, 180–182
    auditing standards for, 50–51
    auditor's responsibilities for, 54
    auditor's understanding of, 29, 396
    computerized, 77–78, 99, 396
    in corporate governance process, 75–76
    decision to test, 238
    deviation rates, 240–241, 244, 252
    limitations of, 395–396
    over financial reporting
        audit objective, 61
        auditor's assessment, 64–69
        defined, 61–62
        entity level controls, 64–65
        fraud risk in, 65
        management's assessment, 62–63
        management's written statements, 69–70

internal control—*Cont.*
    over financial reporting—*Cont.*
        reporting requirements, 70–75, 381–384
        report modifications, 384–387
    over financial statements
        compensating controls, 51–52
        components, 52–54
        defined, 51
        management's use of, 51–53
        reporting requirements, 60–61
internal control questionnaires
    acquisition and expenditure process, 181
    investment process, 294
    long-term debt and owners' equity process, 320
    revenue process, 100
internal control testing. *See also* audit sampling
    acquisition and expenditure process, 179–184
    as audit evidence, 12
    auditor's responsibility for, 54
    cash and investment processes, 294–296
    conclusions from, 396
    control risk in, 235
    controls addressed in, 239
    defined, 12
    of financial reporting controls, 54, 69, 240
    of financial statement controls
        auditor's responsibility for, 55
        points to remember, 59
        sampling unit and population in, 239–240
        service organizations and, 55
        testing methods, 56–59
    inventory process, 213–214
    key question in, 235–236
    long-term debt and owners' equity process, 319–321
    methods, 56–59
    required, 236, 238
    revenue process, 99–103
International Accounting Standards Board (IASB), 18
International Auditing and Assurance Standards Board
        (IAASB), 11, 14n, 394, 397
International Ethics Standards Board for Accountants
        (IESBA), 394, 405–406
International Federation of Accountants (IFAC), 11, 394, 405
International Financial Reporting Standards (IFRS)
    acquisition and expenditure process, 174–175
    contingent liabilities, 341–342
    inventory process, 210–211
    long-term debt and owners' equity process, 314–315
    overview, 18
    revenue process, 92, 93
International Standards of Auditing (ISAs), 11, 394, 397
Interpublic Groups, 176
inventory count tags, 209
inventory list, final, 209
inventory price file, 209
inventory process
    accounts in, 209

analytical procedures for, 214–216
auditing/accounting standards for, 206–207, 210–211
disclosure requirements, 222–226
General Mills example, 224–226
internal control testing, 213–214
management assertions, 212–213, 222–224
market value in, 221
misstatements, 211–212
overview, 207–208
physical counts, 217–219
pricing in, 219–221
relevant assertions, 213
substantive tests of balances, 216–217
transactions recorded in, 208–210
turnover ratios, 215
valuation methods, 210–211, 219–221
investments. *See* cash and investment processes
ISAs, 11, 394, 397
IT (information technology)
    audit software, 79
    internal controls
        acquisition and expenditure process, 180
        cash and investment processes, 295
        clients' use of, 77–78, 99
        long-term debt and owners' equity process, 320

J

journal entries
    acquisition and expenditure process, 173
    cash and investment processes, 289
    inventory process, 210
    long-term debt and owners' equity process, 315
    revenue process, 91
Just for Feet, 38–39

K

Kemps, 178
Kmart, 70, 195
known misstatements, 270, 272
Kozlowski, Dennis, 62, 150
KPMG
    "big four" status, 3
    Gemstar audit, 38
    MedQuist audit, 63
    U.S. Foodservice audit, 153
    Xerox audit, 96, 317

L

lack of duty defense, 407
land, building, and equipment
    auditing changes in, 189–190
    fixed asset schedule example, 191

subsidiary ledgers, 174
  working paper example, 192–193
laws, client compliance with, 347
lawsuits, 341, 406–410
Lay, Kenneth, 327, 410
LCM, 211, 220–221
leadership, in quality control, 41
legal liability, 406–410
liabilities (financial)
  accrued, 190–194
  contingent, 341–344
  search for unrecorded, 188
LIFO inventory pricing, 219–220
likely misstatements, 148, 270, 272
litigation, 341, 406–410
long-term debt accounts, 325
long-term debt and owners' equity process
  accounts in, 312–313, 320
  analytical procedures for, 322–323
  auditing/accounting standards for, 310–311, 314–315
  disclosure requirements, 326–331
  internal control testing, 319–321
  management assertions, 318, 326–327
  misstatements, 316–318
  overview, 312–314
  relevant assertions, 318–319
  substantive tests of balances, 324–326
  substantive tests of transactions, 323–324
  transactions recorded in, 314–316
lower of cost or market (LCM), 211, 220–221
Lucent, 95

M

management
  inquires of, in planning process, 32
  in internal control
    over financial reporting, 62–63, 69–70, 384, 386–387
    over financial statements, 51–53
  legal liability, 410–411
  misstatement incentives, 4–5
  precondition agreements, 23
  pressures on, 397
management assertions
  acquisition and expenditure process, 178–179, 194–195
  cash and investment processes, 293
  described, 13–14
  in evidence gathering, 142–143
  inventory process, 212–213, 222–224
  long-term debt and owners' equity process, 318, 326–327
  in material misstatement risk assessment, 33–34
  revenue process, 98
management letters, 357–358

management override, 64, 160
management representation letter, 349, 350
management responsibilities, in audit report, 367–368
manufacturing process, 213
market value, of inventory, 221
materiality
  calculating, 30–31
  at end of audit, 352–355
  in planning process, 29–32
material misstatements. *See also* misstatements
  defined, 22, 29
  immaterial misstatements judged as, 355
  risk assessment, 27–34, 158–159
  risk assessment documentation, 161
  risk control, 160
  from substantive test sampling, 270–271
material uncertainty, 348
material weaknesses, 60, 70, 384
MedQuist, 63
Merck-Medco, 146
misstatements. *See also* fraud; material misstatements
  acquisition and expenditure process, 175–178
  cash and investment processes, 291–292
  in computerized systems, 78
  corrections of, 356
  defined, 33
  dual-purpose tests for, 58–59
  expected, 264, 266
  extrapolating from sample, 270
  inventory process, 211–212
  known, 270, 272
  legal or regulatory noncompliance and, 347
  likely, 148, 270, 272
  long-term debt and owners' equity process, 316–318
  management's incentives for, 4–5
  modified opinions and, 371–374
  pervasive, 371
  projected, 270, 271
  revenue process, 4, 88, 94–97
  sources of, 29–30
  tolerable, 31, 263–264, 265, 271
modified opinions, 371–375
monetary unit sampling (MUS), 266, 268, 269
monitoring
  in internal control, 53, 54
  in quality control, 42
MUS, 266, 268, 269

N

net income, increasing, 4, 211
non-adjusting events after the reporting period, 344n
nonissuers of stock, 6
non-negligent performance defense, 407
nonsampling risk, 236–237, 262–263

nonstatistical sampling, 237–238, 249–252
Nortel Networks Corp., 73
note payable agreements, 314
notes receivable, discounted, 341

O

objectivity, in ethics codes, 399, 405
observation
    in evidence gathering, 141
    in internal control testing, 56, 57, 182
    in risk assessment, 33
    sampling and, 270
occurrence assertion, 14, 293
OfficeMax, 34
opinions. *See* audit reports
opinion section, of audit report, 369
opportunity, in fraud, 151–152, 155, 156, 157, 158
other matter paragraph, 370–371, 372, 373, 379
overreliance risk, 241, 252
overstatements, 211, 292
owners' equity process. *See* long-term debt and owners'
        equity process

P

Parmalat, 292–293, 324
patent infringement, 341
PCAOB, 7–11, 14n, 403
PeopleSoft, 409
performance materiality, 31
period-end reporting process, 64–65
perpetual inventory files, 214
persuasive evidence, 145
pervasiveness of misstatements, 371
Pfizer Inc., 343
physical controls
    as internal control activity, 51, 53, 182
    in internal control testing
        cash and investment processes, 296
        long-term debt and owners' equity process, 321
        revenue process, 101
        testing methods, 58
planning phase
    auditing standards for, 21–22
    audit strategy and plan, 35–36, 37
    component auditors in, 378–379
    engagement letter, 24–26
    fraud detection and, 97, 178
    overview, 23
    preconditions, 23–27
    risk assessment, 27–34
population, defined, 234, 261

PPS sampling, 269
precision of test, 244
preconditions, for audit, 23–27
predecessor auditors, 24–26
prelisting of cash receipts, 92
presentation assertion, 14
present fairly in all material respects, 16
pressure, in fraud, 151, 155, 156, 157, 158
PricewaterhouseCoopers
    Academy Awards audit, 3–4
    "big four" status, 3
    Parmalat audit, 324
    sample reports by, 72
    Satyam audit, 177
Prince, Charles, 53
principal-agent relationships, 2
principal auditors, 386
private companies
    internal control testing, 56–58
    misstatements, 5
    working papers for, 351–352
probability proportionate to size (PPS) sampling, 269
probable loss, 341
product liability, 341
product warranty claims, 341
professional competence, 405
professional judgment, 145
professional skepticism
    acquisition and expenditure process audit, 178
    defined, 12
    fraud risk assessment, 152–153
    inventory process audit, 211
    revenue process audit, 97
projected misstatements, 270, 271
public companies
    auditing requirements, 54, 61
    independence rules for, 404
    internal controls over financial reporting, 61–62
    internal control testing, 56–58
    misstatements, 5
    working papers for, 351–352
Public Company Accounting Oversight Board (PCAOB),
        7–11, 14n, 403
purchase history report, 209
purchase journals, 174
purchase orders, 172, 183
purchase requisitions, 172

Q

qualified audit opinion, 371, 373, 375
quality control, 41–42
quarterly financial reporting, 379
Qwest Communications, 95, 97, 152

R

random samples, 234, 242, 261, 268–269

rationalization, in fraud, 152, 155, 156, 157, 158

realized gains and losses, 291

reasonable assurance, 12–13, 22, 368

reasonable possible loss, 341

recalculation, 142, 270

receiving documents, 172, 183

regulations

    client compliance with, 347

    on CPA exam, 394

related parties, defined, 346

related-party transactions, 346

relevant assertions

    acquisition and expenditure process, 179

    cash and investment processes, 293–294, 295

    defined, 29

    internal controls over financial reporting, 65–66

    inventory process, 213

    long-term debt and owner's equity process, 318–319

    revenue process, 98

relevant evidence, 143–144

reliable evidence, 143–144

reliance level, of internal controls, 235

remittance advice, 92

remote loss, 341

Rent-Way, 175, 176, 213

reperformance

    in evidence gathering, 142

    in internal control testing, 56, 58, 102, 183

    sampling and, 270

representation letter, 349, 350

results of operations, 64

retained earnings, 325

revenue process

    accounts in, 90

    accounts receivable confirmations, 107–109

    allowance for uncollectible accounts, 109–111

    analytical procedures for, 103–105

    auditing/accounting standards for, 87–88, 92–93

    disclosure requirements, 112–115

    internal control testing, 99–103

    management assertions, 98

    misstatements, 4, 88, 94–97

    overview, 88–90

    relevant assertions, 98

    substantive tests of balances, 106–107

    substantive tests of transactions, 105–106

    transactions recorded in, 91–92

revenue recognition, 92–93

reviews, 398

rights and obligations assertion, 14, 293

risk assessment

    in internal control

        of financial reporting, 64

        of financial statements, 52, 54

    material misstatement risk

        audit evidence and, 145–146

        designing procedures in, 32–33

        determining materiality, 29–32

        due to fraud, 158–159

        understanding entity, 27–29

        using information from, 33–34

risk reduction (audit risk), 36–41

Rite Aid, 170–172, 176

roll-forward procedure, 69

routine transactions, 152

rules of conduct (AICPA), 399–405

S

safety and health regulations, 347

sale orders, 91

sales invoices, 91–92

sales journals, 92

sales revenue sampling plan, 276–277

sales transactions

    analytical procedures for, 103–105

    substantive tests of, 105–106

sample, defined, 234, 261

sample population, defined, 234, 261

sampling. *See* audit sampling

sampling risk, 236–237, 261–263, 271–272

sanction power, of SEC, 408–409

Sarbanes-Oxley Act (SOX)

    criminal liability under, 409–411

    independence rules, 404

    internal controls regulation, 54, 61

    internal controls testing and, 396

    management certification under, 387

    PCAOB standards and, 7, 8

SAS, 6–7, 21n

Satyam, 177

scanning, 141

scope limitations, 72

SEC. *See* Securities and Exchange Commission

Securities Act of 1933, 16, 407–408, 409

Securities and Exchange Commission (SEC)

    financial statement filing requirements, 366, 379

    functions of, 16–17, 408–409

    powers of, 409–410

    revenue process guidelines, 92

Securities Exchange Act of 1934, 16, 407–408, 409

segregation of duties

    as internal control activity, 51, 53, 180

    in internal control testing

        acquisition and expenditure process, 180, 182

        cash and investment processes, 295, 296

segregation of duties—*Cont.*
    in internal control testing—*Cont.*
        long-term debt and owners' equity process, 321
        revenue process, 100
        testing methods, 57
    in IT department, 78
self-assessment programs, 65
sequential sampling plans, 248–249
service levels, 397–398
service organizations, 55
shipping documents, 91
significant accounts
    acquisition and expenditure process, 180
    cash and investment processes, 295
    determination factors, 65–66
    long-term debt and owners' equity process, 320
    revenue process, 98, 99
significant deficiencies, 60, 70
significant disclosures, 65–66
simple random sampling, 242, 268
Skilling, Jeffrey, 327, 409
Sonali, 218
SOX. *See* Sarbanes-Oxley Act
SSAEs, 397–398
staff accountants, 4
standards. *See* auditing standards
state boards of accountancy, 18
Statements on Auditing Standards (SAS), 6–7, 21n
Statements on Standards for Attestation Engagements
    (SSAEs), 397–398
statistical sampling, 237–238, 263–264
statistical sampling tables, 249–252
stock certificate books, 314
stock issuers, 54
stock options, 330–331
stock prices
    going concern problems and, 348–349
    misstatements and, 4–5
    valuation, 290, 300
stock registers, 314
stop-or-go sampling plan, 248–249
stratification of samples, 264, 268
subsequent events
    audit procedures for, 344–346
    confirmations and, 107
subsequently discovered facts, 344–346
substantive evidence. *See* substantive tests of balances;
    substantive tests of transactions
substantive tests of balances. *See also* audit sampling
    acquisition and expenditure process, 172, 187
    as audit evidence, 11
    cash and investment process, 299–300
    described, 12
    inventory process, 216–217
    long-term debt and owners' equity process, 324–326
    revenue process, 90, 106–107

substantive tests of transactions. *See also* audit sampling
    acquisition and expenditure process, 172, 186–187
    as audit evidence, 11
    cash and investment process, 298–299
    described, 12
    long-term debt and owners' equity process,
        323–324
    revenue process, 90, 105–106
sufficient appropriate evidence, 22, 55–56, 143–145,
        371–374. *See also* audit evidence
supervision, of engagement team, 36
Suprema Specialties, Inc., 93
swap transactions, 94
systematic random sampling, 242, 268–269

T

testing phase overview, 23. *See also specific tests*
test of controls. *See* internal control testing
third-party liability, 407
3Com, 217
Time Warner, 95, 96–97, 150, 154–157
tolerable deviation rate, 240, 244, 252
tolerable misstatement, 31, 263–264, 265, 271
tracing, 102, 183
trading securities, 291, 292
transaction recording
    acquisition and expenditure process, 172–174
    cash and investment processes, 289–290
    computerized, 77–78
    inventory process, 208–210
    long-term debt and owners' equity process, 314–316
    revenue process, 91–92
transaction trails. *See* documented transaction trails
transparent reporting system, 17
treasury stock, 325
Tyco, 62, 150, 157–158

U

understatements, 175–176, 316
Uniform Securities Act, 409
UnitedHealth Group, 176, 194
unmodified (clean) opinion, 15, 36, 367–370
unqualified (clean) opinion, 15, 36, 367–370
unrealized gains and losses, 291, 292
upper limit approach, 245
U.S. Federal Wire Act, 24
U.S. Foodservice, 153, 212
U.S. GAAP
    acquisition and expenditure process, 174
    contingent liabilities, 341
    inventory process, 210–211
    long-term debt and owners' equity process, 314–315
    revenue process rules, 92–93

V

valuation assertion
    acquisition and expenditure process, 180
    cash and investment processes, 293
    defined, 14
    inventory process, 213
    revenue process, 98
variables sampling, 234, 261. *See also* audit sampling
vendor allowances, 34, 70
vendor invoices, 172
vendor payments, 34
vouchers/voucher requests, 174, 183
vouching, 102, 143, 183

W

walk-throughs, 66
warranty claims, 341
working papers
    auditing standards for, 351–352
    defined, 32
    in evidence gathering, 146–149
    land, building, and equipment audit example, 192–193
    in planning process, 32, 35, 36
    public vs. private companies, 351–352
    in quality control system, 42
    retention guidelines, 147
    review of, 349
    risk assessment in, 161
WorldCom fraud, 144–145, 176, 177, 410
WPT, 24
write-off authorizations, 92

X

Xerox, 95, 96, 317

Auditor Decisions Made When Performing Internal Control Tests and Substantive Tests

To decide whether to test internal controls, the auditor should ask:

Based on my understanding of internal control, should control risk be assessed at less than maximum?

Yes
No

Explanation:

- The auditor has the choice to test or not test internal controls over the financial statements.
- For public companies, the auditor must answer "yes" to this question for relevant assertions for significant accounts for internal controls over the financial reporting process.
- If the auditor cannot answer "yes," the client has a significant deficiency or material weakness in its internal controls.

Answer:
If "yes," the auditor performs tests of controls to evaluate the controls' effectiveness in preventing or detecting misstatements in the financial statements.

With the evidence from the internal control tests, the auditor asks the following question:

Do the tests support the assessed level of control risk?

Yes
No

Answer:
If "yes," the auditor performs substantive procedures based on the assessed level of control risk. This reliance on controls will reduce the amount of substantive testing.
If "no," the auditor adjusts the assessed level of control risk upward and performs substantive procedures based on the higher level of control risk.

Evidence from a Substantive Test

Is the account balance or class of transactions materially misstated?

Yes
No

Explanation:

- If yes, the auditors perform additional tests to determine the material misstatement in the account balance or class of transactions
- If no, the auditors conclude that the account balance or class of transactions is not materially misstated